Multidimensional Contextual Practice

Diversity and Transcendence

Krishna L. Guadalupe

California State University, Sacramento, Editor
Division of Social Work

Doman Lum

California State University, Sacramento, Emeritus, Editor
Division of Social Work

THOMSON ™

BROOKS/COLE

Australia • Canada • Mexico • Singapore • Spain
United Kingdom • United States

THOMSON

BROOKS/COLE

Publisher/Executive Editor: *Lisa Gebo*
Assistant Editor: *Alma Dea Michelena*
Editorial Assistant: *Sheila Walsh*
Marketing Manager: *Caroline Concilla*
Marketing Assistant: *Mary Ho*
Advertising Project Manager: *Tami Strang*
Signing Representative: *Sierra Sears*
Project Manager, Editorial Production: *Jane Brundage*
Art Director: *Vernon Boes*
Print/Media Buyer: *Doreen Suruki*

Permissions Editor: *Kiely Sexton*
Production Service: *Sara Dovre Wudali, Buuji, Inc.*
Copy Editor: *Linda Ireland, Buuji, Inc.*
Illustrator: *Eunah Chang, Buuji, Inc.*
Cover Designer: *Irene Morris*
Cover Image: *Paul Nichols/Digital Vision*
Compositor: *Buuji, Inc.*
Printer: *Malloy Incorporated*

Printed in the United States of America
1 2 3 4 5 6 7 08 07 06 05 04

For more information about our products, contact us at:
Thomson Learning Academic Resource Center
1-800-423-0563

For permission to use material from this text
or product, submit a request online at
http://www.thomsonrights.com.

Any additional questions about permissions
can be submitted by email to
thomsonrights@thomson.com.

Library of Congress Control Number: 2004105077

ISBN 0-534-60624-5

Thomson Brooks/Cole
10 Davis Drive
Belmont, CA 94002
USA

Asia
Thomson Learning
5 Shenton Way #01-01
UIC Building
Singapore 068808

Australia/New Zealand
Thomson Learning
102 Dodds Street
Southbank, Victoria 3006
Australia

Canada
Nelson
1120 Birchmount Road
Toronto, Ontario M1K 5G4
Canada

Europe/Middle East/Africa
Thomson Learning
High Holborn House
50/51 Bedford Row
London WC1R 4LR
United Kingdom

Latin America
Thomson Learning
Seneca, 53
Colonia Polanco
11560 Mexico D.F.
Mexico

Spain/Portugal
Paraninfo
Calle Magallanes, 25
28015 Madrid, Spain

To our spouses and children

To Judy Guadalupe, for her passion to love and commitment to live in the wisdom of the present moment, our son Isaiah Luis for his brave heart and kind spirit, our son Elijah Luis for his magic and curiosity, and our daughter Rhia Lakshmi for her Goddess nature

To Joyce Lum, who has been a source of wisdom and love, and our children, Lori and her husband, Noel; Jonathan; Amy; and Matthew

Contents

CHAPTER 4

Practitioner's Professional Competence in Multidimensional Contextual Services 94

CHAPTER 13

White Ethnics   308
Debra L. Welkley

CHAPTER 16

Asian Pacific Islanders   388
Janlee Wong

PART 4 | **CONCLUSION** 431

CHAPTER 17

Conclusion 432

Foreword

I feel honored to have been asked to write the foreword to this fine and distinctive anthology coedited by Krishna L. Guadalupe and Doman Lum, *Multidimensional Contextual Practice: Diversity and Transcendence*. Perhaps it is appropriate for me to begin with the fact that Krishna Guadalupe is a former student of mine and a dear friend.

Let me tell you something about Krishna, whom I knew for many years as José. He arrived in the United States from Puerto Rico as a teenager, alone and without English language skills. By the time I met him, he was an undergraduate at The Richard Stockton College of New Jersey, where I teach Social Work, History, and Holocaust and Genocide Studies. Krishna enrolled in my group dynamics class, and we began to develop a close relationship. He was such a warm and enthusiastic young man! I recommended him to serve as my tutor in the basic skills/critical thinking courses I was teaching. I can say without equivocation that he was the very best tutor I worked with. Krishna has always had a great heart, an intuitive sense of humanity, and, to paraphrase his dear wife Judy, a spiritual connection with all living things. If you think I exaggerate, ask my son Max, now 20, who remembers Krishna as his first and most beloved babysitter. I recall Krishna showing up at one of Max's birthday parties, dressed as a clown, with guitar in hand, charming and dazzling his youthful audience.

Krishna has always been a pied piper with children, in part because he has never allowed the child within him to be crushed by false notions and expectations about adult behavior. He recognizes that matters of the brain can never trump matters of the heart, especially in his chosen field of human services. In that specific regard, this anthology reflects Krishna Guadalupe's philosophy of being.

In the Preface, Krishna discusses the "judgments and resentments" provoked by his name change, including the charge that it was a form of betrayal. I believe that Professor Guadalupe's experiences in this regard reinforced within him what drives this anthology: the notion that defining individuals through exclusive single dimensions such as ethnicity, gender, race, class, sexual orientation, and age is a disservice. As such, Guadalupe and Lum offer, instead, a multidimensional contextual practice perspective that seeks to "move beyond stereotypical approaches that have a tendency to marginalize people's experiences" (p. 2). In addition, they recognize that oppression and stereotyping occurs *within* as well as *between* groups—indeed, that "people have the potential to be the 'oppressor' within particular contexts and yet can also become vulnerable enough to be the 'oppressed' within other encounters" (p. 12).

Such an admirable and wise perspective resonates with my own experience as a historian and as a social worker who teaches students to always remember that a client is simultaneously a unique individual, a member of groups, and a human being and that isolating the historical injustices experienced by a particular group risks playing into what some have called a hierarchy of victimhood. I want my students to begin with the axiom that all peoples have histories, which include glory and shame, that all peoples have the capacity to regress toward intolerance, ethnocentrism, discrimination, and bigotry.

I know when I teach about experiences encountered by First Nations Peoples, many of my students struggle with the full force of the genocidal crimes committed by Europeans and Americans. It is important, for example, for them to understand that our history must always be framed by the coming together, involuntarily and violently, of three peoples from three continents: Europeans, Africans, and First Nations Peoples. But initial "successes" in the classroom can yield student despair at the singular injustices they now recognize. Just as many of them were excessive in their celebration of the American experience prior to entering my class, so now some see the United States as uniquely monstrous. In many ways, this is not much of an improvement on their previous state of ignorance. I think I have been consistent with Guadalupe and Lum's multidimensional *contextual* approach in suggesting to students that this terrible phenomenon of oppressors appropriating land and labor from victimized groups is, unfortunately, pervasive within global history. For example, when I traveled to Vietnam, my focus was on the ways in which they remained a "David" to our "Goliath." I felt some responsibility for what we as a nation had imposed on the peoples of Indochina during those terrible years of war. But in meeting with Vietnamese scholars, I discovered that their history includes a southward migration that imposed itself upon what we came to call Montagnards, the indigenous peoples of the Mekong Delta who were driven into the highlands to escape the conquering Vietnamese. And I came to recognize that the Vietnamese, in addition to being treated so badly by the United States, had the capacity to mistreat, in kind, their neighbors and, indeed, their own inhabitants. Each people's glory and shame.

When teaching my Social Work course on Ethnic and Minority Relations, I came upon an extraordinary essay that deepened my understanding of what Guadalupe and Lum posit. The author, the First Nations scholar Robert Allan Warrior, discussed his ambivalent feelings about the Exodus story. Warrior speaks of how strongly he was compelled by Martin Luther King's Exodus imagery of going to the mountaintop, seeing the Promised Land, crossing the river Jordan. He reported being stunned at the realization that Native Americans were in fact the Canaanites of the American experience and that, as such, the compelling biblical saga was tarnished by its impositions upon all the indigenous peoples of the world. As Warrior concluded, "I read the Exodus story with Canaanite eyes." (Robert Allan Warrior, "Canaanites, Cowboys, and Indians: Deliverance, Conquest, and Liberation Theology Today," in Rebecca T. Alpert, *Voices of the Religious Left: A Contemporary Sourcebook* [Philadelphia: Temple University Press, 2000]).

My friend Dan Bar-On, the Israeli psychologist who brings together Jews and Germans, Palestinians and Israelis, black and white South Africans, and Protestant and Catholic Irish, has taught me how difficult it is for victims to give up their desire for vengeance, their rage at the injustices they have experienced; how difficult it is for victimizers, and especially their accomplices, to come face to face with what they have wrought in causing human suffering.

In this America of ours, students need to struggle with what could be both costly and quite political; they need to understand the contradictory strands of heroism and knavery, and how many of our peoples have been both victimized and victimizers. The epicenter of instruction and practice must be the horror and the wonder, the pain and the humor of both selective memory and historical amnesia. In this regard, Guadalupe and Lum build on the Socratic wisdom of knowing oneself. The double helix of all peoples, the intertwining of their burdens and their inspirations, their hidden shames and forgotten accomplishments, makes it more likely that they will be able to recognize the same complexity—the multidimensionality and the contextuality—of others.

As teachers we struggle with students who hold back from authentically discussing issues of prejudice, who go silent or simply echo agreement. It is hard work to achieve honest discussions; all students enter with bruises. One must establish a trusting environment for such discussions to be fruitful. Trust does not exist at the beginning of a class; I tell students that the handshake is an apt metaphor for our relationship—I hold your hand, you hold mine—we trust one another, but I also prevent you from hitting me in case that is your hidden desire. And then we can begin to have an honest discourse.

Guadalupe and Lum and all of their contributors have established the basis for such an honest discourse. They urge practitioners "to be careful not to automatically categorize people due to their own preconceived ideas of what people may represent to them [and] allow the space for people-communities to define themselves" (p. 77). Multidimensional contextual practice assumes diversity within diversity.

Perhaps most impressively, all the authors within this anthology approach their subjects with enormous humility and modesty. Guadalupe and Lum emphasize "embracing a sense of 'not knowing'" (p. 106). They evoke "the wisdom of uncertainty" (p. 16). There is no better lesson for practitioners than the recognition that, first and foremost, they must *listen*, rather than predefine; they must encourage their clients to tell their stories in their own ways.

Multidimensional Contextual Practice urges human service providers to embrace a strengths perspective, which highlights the capacity of all individuals, families, groups, and communities to demonstrate resilience. Yes, there are truly victims, but we must always honor the extraordinary capacities of all oppressed peoples to transform victimhood into agency. When I teach my course on the 1960s, I always remind students that it is insufficient, distorting, and, indeed, insulting to view African Americans exclusively as victims. After all, our national musical heritage, which derives from African-American forms such as call-and-response, work songs, gospel, jazz, soul, rap, and the blues, is a demonstration of strength and resiliency. The blues, in particular, transform human pain, converting it into beauty, into art, into meaning, into transcendence. We only encourage client empowerment when we take into account this capacity for transcendence.

The authors offer another distinctive approach for practitioners in this anthology: the significance of language and the role of spirituality. They are to be commended for modeling sensitivity to the ways in which language can interfere with our recognition of human experience and to the ways in which our quest for meaning at what they call the magna-spiritual level is integral to human enrichment and transcendence.

Let me conclude by recommending this volume to all human services educators. The editors and their contributing authors have excelled in providing a distinctive and practical framework and a multiplicity of ways in which such a framework can be applied to diverse groups and special issues. I have to say that there is something quite wonderful about being asked to write a foreword to an anthology coedited by someone whom I have seen grow and mature into a productive scholar, a sensitive teacher, a caring friend, and a loving husband and father. There are few pleasures in life more satisfying. So, thank you, Krishna, and thank you, Doman, and thank you, Judy, and thank you, all of you who contributed to this exemplary anthology.

Paul Lyons
Professor of Social Work, Holocaust, and Genocide Studies
Associated Faculty in Historical Studies
The Richard Stockton College of New Jersey

Preface

The 21st century holds great promise for human service practitioners. Two of the major social science disciplines, psychology and social work, have recently published valuable texts in the field of human diversity. The field of counseling psychology has set the pace with two well-known texts that have spanned multiple editions: *Counseling Across Cultures,* 5th edition, edited by Paul B. Pedersen, Juris G. Draguns, Walter J. Lonner, and Joseph E. Trimble (Thousand Oaks, CA: Sage, 2002), and *Counseling the Culturally Diverse: Theory and Practice,* 4th edition, edited by Derald Wing Sue and David Sue (New York: Wiley, 2003). Social work has also responded with two recent texts on cultural competence: *Culturally Competent Practice: Skills, Interventions, and Evaluations,* edited by Rowena Fong and Sharlene Furuto (Boston: Allyn & Bacon, 2001), and *Culturally Competent Practice: A Framework for Understanding Diverse Groups and Justice Issues,* edited by Doman Lum (Pacific Grove, CA: Thomson Learning–Brooks/Cole, 2003). Each of these books emphasizes core themes related to cultural diversity and contains chapters on various ethnic and cultural groups. This book, *Multidimensional Contextual Practice: Diversity and Transcendence,* incorporates some of the themes addressed by the aforementioned texts, applying a different interpretation. It also brings forward new material and offers new directions.

As we observe ethnic and cultural groups in the United States, we are struck by the fact that in many parts of the country, a Black-White dichotomy still exists, particularly where there is a historical recognition of the guilt of slavery imposed on one group by another. Race relations in these areas consist of addressing Black and White community issues. Yet there are other ethnic groups (Latinos/as, Asian Americans, First Nations Peoples, etc.) who have been historically marginalized and are seeking recognition, dialogue, and power with the African-American and European-American communities. Hopefully we can transcend the traditional Black-White dichotomy and move toward a more inclusive composition of groups sharing discussion and decision making on an equal footing. This book addresses the nature of this multidimensional context. It also reframes the stereotypical categories of who is the oppressor and who is the oppressed.

One of the major purposes of this book is to address possible effects of stereotypes and stereotyping when learning and working within diversified communities of people. The content presented in this text holds the assumption that stereotypes have cognitive, emotional, behavioral, social, political, and cultural effects. This assumption has been supported by nationwide research conducted by one of these authors, in which educators considered to have expertise in the field of human diversity were surveyed and interviewed (Guadalupe, 2000). One hundred percent of the research participants agreed that stereotypes and stereotyping can, and often does, perpetuate systems of oppression. Thus, this text presents a multidimensional contextual framework aimed at encouraging ongoing explorations of strategies useful to reduce stereotypes during the process of social/health/human services provision. *While exploring the content addressed in this text, students enrolled in practice and diversity courses can be asked to engage in an ongoing dialogue regarding ways of strengthening their professional competence while exploring ways of moving beyond stereotypes.*

Writing this text has been both a rewarding and challenging experience, as the authors have had the opportunity to explore ways in which they themselves have perpetuated stereotypes or been affected by them. A significant event occurred in the life of one of the authors during the process of writing this text. Krishna L. Guadalupe was named José L. Guadalupe at birth. In 1988, an important teacher in his life gave him the name of Krishna. For years he had debated with himself whether or not to legally change his name from José L. Guadalupe to Krishna L. Guadalupe. In 2002, he reached a final decision, determining to legally change his name. Although family members and some of his close friends embraced his decision, some of his colleagues and other friends responded with judgments and resentments. During a conversation with a colleague and friend, it became obvious that some of the judgments and resentment were generated by fear of the unknown. Many questions were asked: "Why this change?" "What are you trying to prove?" "What are you now?" "Are you the same person I knew?" While for Krishna changing his name was symbolic of honoring change in his life, for some of his colleagues and friends it seemed to be symbolic of betrayal. The lesson learned through this experience is that although "being and becoming" seems to be a natural part of the human experience, perceptions often keep people locked in boxes.

We do not claim that the content in this book represents absolute "truth" or an "objective universal reality." We are simply sharing our current perceptions. There are many ways of knowing, interpreting, and being. Some of those are reflected in this text. You, as the reader, may find that some of these ideas resonate deeply with you, while others seem to be only vaguely documented, or you simply do not share the same perceptions. Languaging experiences of human diversity, commonalities, and controversies without perpetuation of stereotypes is a challenge in need of ongoing attention. In this text, we are making an attempt at giving this challenge the attention it deserves.

The editors hope that the content in this text raises more questions than it provides answers. Human beings are complex entities who are constantly changing. We must not let dogmatism limit our endless potential and possibilities. We encourage readers to question the assumptions presented throughout this text as well as to engage in self-reflections regarding their own paradigms. Together we can enter "the wisdom of uncertainty."

THE JOURNEY TOWARD THIS BOOK

Both editors of this book teach at California State University, Sacramento, Division of Social Work. Krishna L. Guadalupe brings to this project new understandings of human diversity, moving beyond stereotypes, and setting the stage for a discussion about multiple dimensions of the client and the contextual environments. Many of the ideas, concepts, and material presented in this book were initially explored in his doctorate studies and have been stretched out through further research and through educational and practice encounters. The nationwide dissertation research he completed in 1999, entitled "The Challenge: Developing of a Curriculum to Address Diversity Content without Perpetuating Stereotypes," generated innovative ideas that are presented in this text as "food for thought." Doman Lum supports the effort to link the multidimensional nature of person and environment with the contextual nature of discussing how to work with people. Both editors began discussing this book through a practice framework on various spheres of multiple dimensions and contexts and then dialogued about how chapters could flow from the framework. Dr. Guadalupe served as the primary author of framework chapters, while Dr. Lum critiqued that work and refined concepts and ideas. Both editors sought to write an inclusive book that would appeal to a broad range of human service practitioners in the human and social services including psychiatrists, psychologists, social workers, human service specialists, marriage and family counselors, and other related professionals.

In this text, the editors consider the importance of language and spirituality as two different and yet binding issues that interconnect groups of people. We have reached out to various faculty members and community leaders in our midst and across the country who are writing about various diverse populations. As the table of contents demonstrates, we have attempted to be as inclusive as possible. Yet, this text does not claim a totality of human diversity content. This text addresses both general population groups (women and men; gay/lesbian/bisexual/transgender people; people living with disabilities; and aging people) and a number of ethnic-specific communities of people (First Nations Peoples, White ethnics, African Americans, Latino/a Americans, and Asian Americans). We acknowledge that within and between these populations, commonalities, differences, and controversies exist.

Finally, we have summarized the essential issues of this book in a closing chapter that points the human services helping field toward *multidimensionality* and *contexts* as helpful themes in working with people. The reader is encouraged to make connections with the material in all these chapters, since it forms the texture of multidimensional contextual practice in the areas of diversity and transcendence.

SPECIAL ACKNOWLEDGMENTS

The editors of this book offer the following special acknowledgments to those who helped along the way:

- To each and every one of the contributors (in alphabetical order: Arlene Bowers Andrews, Chrystal C. Ramirez Barranti, Joyce Burris, Robin Wiggins Carter, Kathryn S. Collins, Judy A. Guadalupe, Susan L. Kirk, Myles Montgomery, Santos Torres, Jr., Deborah P. Valentine, Hilary N. Weaver, Debra L. Welkley, and, last but not least, Janlee Wong). The insights and thought-provoking ideas addressed by each of these contributors are what give life in individual and collective ways to the framework introduced in this text.
- To all the clients with whom we have interacted and worked throughout our professional careers, for their teachings while sharing their pain and resilience.

- To my (KLG's) brother in spirit, Santos Torres, Jr., for his constant encouragement, unconditional acceptance, friendship, support, and feedback.
- To Paul Lyons for being an influential role model in my (KLG's) life and for taking time from his event-filled schedule to read this manuscript and write the Foreword.
- To Debra L. Welkley for her support, availability, and contributions during the process of writing this text.
- To Blue Ray for her feedback, supportive editing, and wonderful heart.
- To Rowena Fong, professor of social work at the University of Texas, Austin, for her ideas on biculturalization of intervention, contextual social work practice, and cultural competence, which have been helpful concepts for my (DL's) reflection and writing.
- To Francis K. O. Yuen, professor of social work at California State University, Sacramento, who has been a source of inspiration for me (DL), for his commitment to the task of productive writing and for his constant help with ideas and technical assistance.
- To Howard J. Clinebell, Jr., professor emeritus of pastoral counseling at the Claremont School of Theology, who was my (DL's) teacher in counseling theory and practicum and a prime example of a writer who is still publishing as he reaches his eighties.
- To our diverse colleagues, staff, and students at California State University, Sacramento, where we both teach, research, write, and continue to grow personally as well as professionally.
- To human service practitioners, researchers, and educators all over the world who are attempting to learn, live, and work within a diversified world.
- To the reviewers of this manuscript for their responses to our chapters and for their fine suggestions for revision: Patricia Kolar, University of Pittsburgh; Kathleen Tangenberg, University of Iowa; Deana F. Morrow, University of North Carolina at Charlotte; and Beverly Greene, St. John's University

Special thanks are due to Lisa Gebo, executive editor for social work, counseling, and the human services, to her editorial assistant Sheila Walsh, to Alma Dea Michelena, assistant editor, and to the rest of the production staff at Thomson Learning–Brooks/Cole for their willingness to publish this book and for their encouragement and inquiry along the way. Special thanks and acknowledgment is given to Jane Brundage, Thomson Project Manager, for her leadership during the production of this text; to Sara Dovre Wudali, Buuji Inc., for her support and excellent work with the layout of this text; and a heartfelt thanks to Linda J. Ireland for her outstanding editorial work and feedback.

Above all, a special word of thanks and gratitude goes to our families who have seen us labor over the pages of this book:

- *From Krishna:* My partner, Judy, who teaches yoga as well as conducts workshops integrating meditation, movement, energy, and breath work, but most importantly, who lives with a strong devotion to spirit and divine imagination; my son Isaiah, who is currently in seventh grade and is filled with passion, kindness, determination, curiosity, and a brave heart; my son Elijah, who is presently in second grade and is filled with magic, a delightful spirit, and a marvelous way of being; and my daughter, Rhia, who is one year old and whose divine light has been an inspiration.

- *From Doman:* My wife, Joyce, who teaches first grade at Mary Tsukamoto Elementary School, Elk Grove, California School District; my daughter Lori, who is with the Pfizer Pharmaceutical Company in East Los Angeles, and her husband, Noel; my son Jonathan, who is an occupational therapist in the occupational therapy outpatient clinic at the University of Southern California–Los Angeles County Medical Center; my daughter Amy, who recently finished her master's of business administration at San Francisco State University; and my son Matthew, who is working for the Jet Propulsion Laboratory in Pasadena, California.

Our multidimensional and contextual tasks as friends, husbands, and fathers are a source of great joy, challenge, and ongoing growth.

OVERVIEW OF THE BOOK

The concept of human diversity has revolutionized what it means to be a person and has been key in the movement toward inclusion. Previous terms such as *ethnic minorities, multicultural,* and *people of color,* as well as the separate consideration of ethnic, women, and gay and lesbian people, were inadequate to describe the range and texture of people. Human diversity has opened the floodgates to consider simultaneously such diverse characteristics as age, class, skin color, culture, disability, ethnicity, family arrangement/structure, gender, marital status, national origin, religion, sex, sexual orientation, and so on.

Essential to the discussion of human diversity is the need for unifying application concepts that will translate the preceding categories into unifying ways of helping people across these many variables. Ethnic sensitivity, cultural awareness, cultural diversity, and recently cultural competence are working themes that have been applied during the last thirty years.

Recent concepts such as *multiple identities* and *intersectionality* have further moved the dialogue toward viewing the multidimensional nature of people and *contextual* aspects to highlight the importance of persons, events, and experiences in the *environmental situation*. In this text, the authors have sought to consolidate these themes into a helping approach, which we have called the **multidimensional contextual practice framework** or **a Framework for Human Diversity and Transcendence** (see diagram).

The multidimensional contextual perspective addressed in this text covers four major areas: (1) A Framework for Human Diversity and Transcendence; (2) Special Issues related to language and spirituality; (3) Diverse Groups, which consists of general population groups; and (4) Ethnic-Specific Communities of People. The Framework for Human Diversity and Transcendence is explained in detail in Chapters 2, 3, and 4. Then, in addressing specific issues related to language and spirituality, general population groups, and ethnic-specific communities of people, the

A Framework for Human Diversity and Transcendence

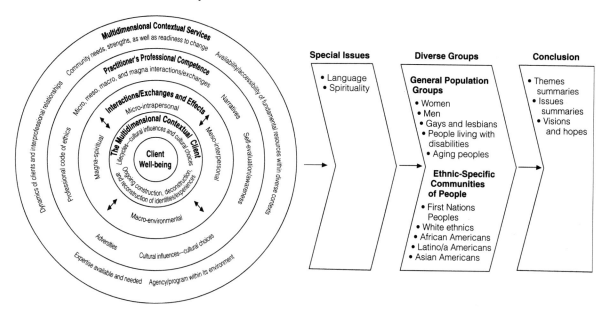

Special Issues
- Language
- Spirituality

Diverse Groups

General Population Groups
- Women
- Men
- Gays and lesbians
- People living with disabilities
- Aging peoples

Ethnic-Specific Communities of People
- First Nations Peoples
- White ethnics
- African Americans
- Latino/a Americans
- Asian Americans

Conclusion
- Themes summaries
- Issues summaries
- Visions and hopes

authors of Chapters 5 through 16 give life to the Framework for Human Diversity and Transcendence. The text ends with a conclusion chapter in which themes and issues addressed throughout the book are summarized and the future of multidimensional contextual practice is explored.

The Framework for Human Diversity and Transcendence consists of five distinct yet interdependent major areas: (1) client well-being; (2) the multidimensional contextual client; (3) interactions/exchanges and effects; (4) the practitioner's professional competence; and (5) multidimensional contextual services. In regard to the first area, the framework stresses the importance of considering the client well-being as a primary objective in the helping process. As the client well-being is prioritized, practitioners are encouraged to engage in an exploration of clients as multidimensional contextual entities (the second major area addressed by the framework). While doing so, practitioners are guided through an assessment of a possible relationship between cultural influences/cultural choices and how clients often undergo a process of construction, deconstruction, and reconstruction of identities and life experiences. The intention here is to assist practitioners in the process of avoiding marginalization and stereotypes of clients' meanings, interpretations, and experiences as well as in honoring the complexity of human diversity and commonalities.

The third major area the Framework for Human Diversity and Transcendence attends to is possible dynamics occurring in clients' experiences through interactions and exchanges between and within micro-intrapersonal, meso-interpersonal, macro-environmental, and magna-spiritual processes. Such exploration is intended to assist practitioners in the process of assessing internal/external strengths and challenges that enhance or injure client well-being. Again, the focus is to encourage practitioners to move beyond stereotypical paradigms and marginalization of clients' experiences through assessment of human commonalities, differences, and complexities.

The fourth area addressed by the Framework for Human Diversity and Transcendence focuses attention on the practitioner's professional competence, or lack thereof, and its effect in the helping process. While advocating for strengthening professional competence, the authors use the framework to explore areas such as possible effects of practitioners' life experiences while attempting to assist clients, as well as the importance of ongoing professional self-evaluation and self-awareness. Through self-reflection exercises practitioners are encouraged to explore their experiences with cultural influences and cultural choices, adversities, and resilience, among other areas.

Finally, through the Framework for Human Diversity and Transcendence, we examine the importance of promoting the development and maintenance of social/health/human services that are multidimensional and contextual by nature. Through reflective exercises, the framework is used to assist practitioners in the process of evaluating their placement of employment/professional practice. Areas explored include the paradigms affecting the cultures and subcultures of agency and program structures, objectives, methods for delivering services, effectiveness, professional environments, availability and accessibility of services, and client-worker relationships.

We hope that you will consider the multidimensional and contextual nature of working with people in terms of understanding the inclusive and complex nature of human identity, experiences, and ways in which settings and situations affect individuals, families, groups, and communities. A commitment to avoiding marginalizing people's experiences is considered central in the process of encouraging and promoting human empowerment. Let us join together in this effort.

Krishna L. Guadalupe, PhD, and Doman Lum, PhD, ThD
Division of Social Work
California State University, Sacramento

About the Contributors

Arlene Bowers Andrews is director and cofounder of the Institute for Families in Society in South Carolina, and a professor of social work. As a social worker and community psychologist, she specializes in public-private sector collaboration and family policy. Dr. Andrews is the author of *Victimization and Survivor Services,* coeditor of *The UN Convention on the Rights of the Child: Implementing the Right to an Adequate Standard of Living,* and author of several articles and book chapters regarding family violence prevention and community systems development. She recently authored the handbooks *Helping Families Survive and Thrive, Strong Neighborhoods and Strong Families,* and *Promoting Family Safety and Nurture.* Dr. Andrews was the founding executive director of several community programs for victims of domestic violence and child maltreatment. She was a founding board member of the Nurturing Center, the Alliance for South Carolina's Children, and the Columbia Mayor's Commission on Children and Youth. Professor Andrews serves as vice president of the Southern Regional Council, an organization devoted to justice and harmonious intergroup ethnic and race relations. She served for eight years as a gubernatorial appointee to the South Carolina Joint Legislative Committee on Children and Families and recently chaired South Carolina's Children's Services Study Committee, a legislative group charged with redesigning the state's services system. She has twenty-five years of experience in consulting with nonprofit community organizations regarding organizational development and evaluation. Her work has also included serving as a court-appointed expert witness, drafting legislation, monitoring child and family policy and program effectiveness, and participating in an international scholarly work group to monitor child well-being. She can be reached at aandrews@ss1.csd.sc.edu.

Chrystal C. Ramirez Barranti, MSW, PhD, is an assistant professor in the Division of Social Work at California State University, Sacramento. Dr. Barranti primarily teaches social work practice courses and is dedicated to encouraging and promoting the growth of her students as holistic practitioners. Additional interest areas include mental health, practice with elders, and Latino/a migrant farm-working individuals and families. She can be reached at cbarranti@csus.edu.

Joyce Burris, MSW, PhD, is a professor of social work at California State University, Sacramento. She wrote her dissertation on the topic of gerontological social work and has taught courses in Aging and Diversity. She currently teaches Human Behavior in a Social Environment, Death and Dying, and Advanced Policy at California State University, Sacramento in the Division of Social Work. She has conducted research in a variety of settings (i.e., on a NIMH grant with UC Medical Center, a study for the California Budget Project, participation in the evaluation of TANF for Sacramento County, CA), and she has written several chapters for edited books. She also works in the community with a local hospice unit. She can be reached at burrisj@csus.edu.

Robin Wiggins Carter, DPA, is a professor of social work at California State University, Sacramento and currently serves as department chair. She received her DPA from the University of Southern California. She has taught courses in Diversity, Social Work Practice, and Gerontological Social Work. She coedited (with Joseph Anderson) *Diversity Perspectives for Social Work Practice,* and she has contributed several chapters to books on practice with African Americans. She can be reached at carterr@csus.edu.

Kathryn S. Collins, MSW, PhD, is an assistant professor of social work at the University of Pittsburgh in Pittsburgh, Pennsylvania. Her primary research and clinical interests are in the areas of trauma symptomatology and community violence prevention interventions, women and children with neurological disabilities, and minority health and mental health initiatives. She is exploring the barriers that limit women and children in accessing appropriate mental health care. Currently, Dr. Collins is the principal investigator on a research project entitled Children's Attributions and Trauma Study (CATS), being conducted in the metropolitan Pittsburgh area. Dr. Collins teaches both Diversity and Practice courses in the Direct Practice concentration at the School of Social Work. She is a commissioner on the Council of Social Work Education, Commission on the Role and Status of Women. She can be reached at kscollins@rocketmail.com.

Judy A. Guadalupe's passion is to uncover the possibilities of being in harmony with all life and learning from and trusting the divine nature in children, the natural world, and all human beings. She does not profess to be perfectly competent at this, but she is enjoying the journey and always learning. She is trained and educated in counseling, energy medicine, and yoga. Her greatest teachers are her partner, Krishna, and their three children. She has a small practice in Sacramento called Inner Health, integrating yoga, counseling, and energy work to assist in bringing balance to body, mind, and soul for children and families. She also teaches pre- and postnatal yoga at the Sacramento Yoga Center. Judy may be reached at judypaz33@ hotmail.com.

Krishna L. Guadalupe is an associate professor at California State University, Sacramento in the Division of Social Work. He has held clinical, administrative, and program development positions in various contexts including family counseling agencies, drug and alcohol rehabilitation programs, and hospice settings. Workshops, seminars, and publication subjects include topics on human diversity, empowerment practice, spirituality, grief, loss and growth, youth violence, modern and postmodern schools of thought, and program evaluation. Krishna's community and research interests include: ongoing exploration into the mystery of the human spirit, human diversity and its complexities, and program evaluation. At a personal level, his primary goal is to continue an exploration into the heart of compassion. He can be reached at krishnag@csus.edu.

Susan L. Kirk is a licensed clinical social worker who specialized in child welfare practice for fifteen years. She is a lecturer at California State University, Sacramento and has interest in issues relating to the transgender, bisexual, lesbian, and gay communities. She is currently studying for a graduate degree in theological studies, hoping to explore how spirituality influences arenas traditionally left to social workers and human services providers. She can be reached at kirks@csus.edu.

Doman Lum is professor emeritus of social work at California State University, Sacramento. His previous books have been in the areas of culturally competent practice, process practice stages, social work practice and people of color, health care policy and social work, and suicidal crisis intervention. He has written chapters and articles on cultural diversity, spiritual diversity, Asian Americans, the American health care system, Chinese elderly, health maintenance organizations, lay counselors, the church and alcoholic prevention, and the mental health of children. He has been on the board of directors and the Commission on Accreditation for the Council on Social Work Education and was the 2000 recipient of the Distinguished Recent Contributions in Social Work Education award presented by the Council on Social Work Education. He was also selected as one of fifty social work educators and practitioners in the United States to be featured in *Celebrating Social Work Faces and Voices of the Formative*

Years in commemoration of the century founding of social work. Dr. Lum is also an ordained minister of the United Church of Christ, Northern California Conference. He can be reached at lumd@csus.edu.

Myles Montgomery is a teacher, social worker, and social activist. He currently lives and practices social work in Sacramento, California. His passion lies in writing on stereotypes, dynamics of language, and abuses against vulnerable populations. Myles is also an avid student of yoga and history. He may be reached at Myles_Montgomery@hotmail.com.

Santos Torres, Jr., is a professor and Graduate Program Director in the Division of Social Work at California State University, Sacramento. He holds a doctorate in Educational Psychology, Counseling, and Special Education, an MSW, and a BS degree in Sociology and Psychology. Santos has presented papers at the national conferences of the Council on Social Work Education, the American Counseling Association, the Roundtable on Cross-Cultural Psychology and Education, the Western Social Science Association, and the National Association for Ethnic Studies. Workshops, seminars, and publication topics include diversity, youth gangs, interviewing skills as a research tool, and school social work practice, programs, and policy. He can be reached at torres@csus.edu.

Deborah P. Valentine is currently a professor and director of the School of Social Work at Colorado State University. She teaches social work practice at the BSW, MSW, and PhD levels. Her areas of research interest include social work practice with children and families and people with developmental disabilities. She has facilitated a Faculty Development Institute at the Council on Social Work Education Annual Program Meeting entitled "The Scholarship of Teaching: Successful Transition to Social Work Educator" for the past ten years. Dr. Valentine has published numerous articles based on her research and has presented her work at national and international conferences. She has taught social work classes in Ecuador, Lithuania, and Korea. She began a three-year term as the editor-in-chief of the *Journal of Social Work Education* in May 2003. She can be reached at debvalentine@cahs.colostate.edu.

Hilary N. Weaver (Lakota) is an associate professor in the School of Social Work at the State University of New York in Buffalo. Her work focuses on cultural issues in the helping process, with a particular emphasis on First Nations Peoples. She is the author of more than thirty articles and chapters, a forthcoming book on cross-cultural social work, and two edited books on social work with First Nations Peoples. She serves on numerous boards and commissions and currently serves as president of the American Indian Alaska Native Social Work Educators' Association. She is in the process of developing a Diversity Resource Center to assist faculty in integrating diversity content in the social work curriculum. She can be reached at hweaver@acsu.buffalo.edu.

Debra L. Welkley completed her graduate work at Baylor University and has been teaching sociology courses for twelve years. For the past four years, she has been an adjunct faculty at California State University, Sacramento. She is also the program administrator of an area foster family agency. She has held a long-time interest in researching and exploring race relations in all contexts. She can be reached at dwelkley@attbi.com.

Janlee Wong is the executive director of the 12,000-member California Chapter of the National Association of Social Workers (NASW). Prior to working for NASW, Mr. Wong worked for the County of San Diego, the U.S. Office of Management and Budget, and the San Diego Union of Pan Asian Communities. Mr. Wong has worked in a number of multicultural communities including San Diego, Oakland, and San Francisco. He can be reached at naswca@naswca.org.

SEE ME

No, I am not the image printed in your mind,
for the mind is limited by its own perceptions and conditions.

No, I am not solely a reflection of a time in history,
for change is constant, transformative, and ultimately time is an illusion.

No, I am not exclusively a mirror of a culture, family system, a collective identity,
for to see me like that is like seeing the forest while failing to remember the
uniqueness and lifeness of each of the trees.

No, I am not my name, profession, human roles,
for those are boundaries through which we can begin communication.

No, I am not my pains, sorrows, glories, healings,
for these are only manifestations of my human experiences.

I am the emptiness which is whole.
I am the uncertainty which is certain.
I am the spaceless which is filled with possibilities.
Please, don't diminish my existence.

—*Krishna L. Guadalupe*

Practice Framework

We begin by introducing the multidimensional contextual practice framework. (See the diagram in the Preface, A Framework for Human Diversity and Transcendence). Chapters 1 to 4 explain the essential elements of the framework: client well-being; the multidimensional contextual client; interactions, exchanges, and effects; the practitioner's professional competence; and multidimensional contextual services.

At the core of the framework is the belief that the client's well-being needs to be honored and affirmed throughout the client-worker relationship. Furthermore, the client (i.e., a person, family, group, community, or a combination of these) is perceived as a multidimensional contextual entity who interacts with, makes exchanges within, and creates effects on diverse environments. We speak about the micro-intrapersonal, the meso-interpersonal, the macro-environmental, and the magna-spiritual levels. We offer guidelines for practitioners as well as social/health/human service agencies. In addition to this perception of the client, we provide ideas for strengthening the practitioner's professional competence and the nature of multidimensional contextual services, which have an impact on and are affected by clients.

As you read these chapters and participate in the exercises that apply these multidimensional contextual concepts, we hope that you will develop a more inclusive understanding of how to work with clients in your field.

Whatever authority I may have rests solely on knowing how little I know. —**Socrates**

1 | Beyond Stereotypes

Honoring Human Complexities

Multidimensional Contextual Practice recognizes that to approach the **client** (i.e., a person, family, small group of people, community, or a combination of these, seeking, needing, or receiving social/health/human services) through an exclusive single dimension such as ethnicity, gender, sexual orientation, or social class is a disservice. This text advocates for simultaneous consideration of multidimensional and contextual attributes (i.e., age, gender, sexual orientation, socioeconomic status, ethnicity, culture, physical and mental abilities and disabilities, religious and spiritual practices, personal and collective narratives, etc.)—the interplay, interdependence, and uniqueness of which reflect the complex being. *Multidimensional Contextual Practice* is based on the belief that intrapersonal, interpersonal, environmental, social, cultural, and spiritual factors simultaneously influence clients' lives and well-being. This book challenges readers to conceptualize and explore the multidimensional and contextual factors that influence and are influenced by the client's experiences. Based on research findings (Guadalupe, 2000), we believe that *Multidimensional Contextual Practice* provides human service practitioners with the opportunity to move beyond stereotypical approaches that have a tendency to marginalize people's experiences and helps them to embrace human diversity, commonalities, complexities, challenges, and strengths.

The **multidimensional** nature of practice, as presented in this text, identifies, explores, and fosters human diversity, commonalities, and adversities from a non-stereotypical perspective. For instance, the multidimensional component of the proposed practice approach encourages exploration of themes such as culture, human resilience, privilege, and oppressive forces. These experiences are multifaceted and are likely to take on different forms, meanings, and effects within particular contexts. A major assumption of multidimensionality is that people are more than what can be observed or measured. The mind is often limited to perceptions and conditions culti-vated through specific and contextual experiences. For instance, can we really say that we are our beliefs? Multidimensionality within this context stresses that while belief systems affect behaviors and perhaps the sense of self, they do not necessarily define the totality of one's identity or, for that matter, essence. This dynamic is reflected in the difference between cultural influences and cultural choices. While cul-tural influences may lead groups of people to develop specific belief and value sys-tems, a common language, and norms to guide interactions, cultural choices may illustrate people's inner knowing and outer determination to honor cultural influ-ences that are nurturing while attempting to change cultural influences that have been harmful to the human spirit (i.e., oppressive forces). Through the lens of multi-dimensionality, experiences such as the sense of self emerge from a simultaneous manifestation of multiple consciousness influenced by multiple encounters.

The multidimensional nature of practice stresses that people are not just bodies (biophysical experiences), nor are they just minds (cognitive and emotional processes). The interdependence of body, mind, and spirit within human experiences is recognized and explored through the lens of multidimensionality. People are influ-enced by the realm of the material world and the realm of spirit (though it is often challenging to conceptualize and find language in which to express the latter). Furthermore, as Saleebey (1994, 1996) emphasizes, what is considered "truth" within one culture is perhaps irrelevant within another. The intention of a multi-dimensional perspective is to move beyond monodimensional approaches that seem to neglect individual uniqueness in the name of the collective.

A pedagogical educational movement that has been gaining strength during the past three decades calls for simultaneous consideration of multidimensionality and contextualization when addressing human diversity, strengths, and challenges. Schriver (2001) discusses multiple diversities (individuals who have simultaneous memberships in multiple diverse groups) and the interrelatedness and interconnect-edness of human beings. Reed, Newman, Suarez, and Lewis (1997) talk about mul-tiple identities (social constructions based on gender, age, ethnic group, social class, and related ways of self-definition). Likewise, Spencer, Lewis, and Gutierrez (2000) raise the concept of multiple group memberships and identities. We venture to build on these ideas and put together a practical approach for social/health/human service practitioners.

The exploration of "multiple experiences" cannot ignore contextual exchanges that one entity may have with another or exchanges within and between a multiple set of entities. The **contextual** nature of *Multidimensional Contextual Practice* rec-ognizes the interplay between people and their environments, as well as between peo-ple and between environments. For instance, a community of men may experience privilege due to their gender identification, but discrimination due to their non-heterosexual orientation, mental or physical disabilities, or ethnic identification. These experiences often arise out of interactions and exchanges among and between people within environmental contexts.

A number of social science practitioners have broadened our knowledge of con-text. There has been a movement toward viewing context as the overarching theme that involves people and their environments as a part of the *sum total of the scope of understanding* the client and the situation. Context has inclusive meanings. Rose

(1990) speaks of context in terms of contextualization. For Rose this involves a focus on the client's own understanding of self-being. According to Rose, this allows a dialogue between the human service practitioner and the client to occur based on the client's interpretation of reality and the human service practitioner's assessment. (Note: The term **social/health/human service practitioner** as used here means one who practices professions under the umbrella of the health and human services field, offering services that address physical, mental, and social needs. The term *human service practitioner* applies to professionals who have completed, or are completing, educational degrees in professional disciplines such as psychiatry, psychology, social work, nursing, school counseling, marriage and family counseling, and pastoral counseling.) In this dialogue, clients can be encouraged to express, elaborate, and reflect upon their feelings and understanding about life. This reaching into the client's cultivated meaning and interpretation regarding life encounters and effects, as well as the client's contexts, is an important part of the contextual practice perspective. Kemp, Whittaker, and Tracy (2002) talk about person-environment practice and links between people's issues and the challenges and resources in daily life contexts. Among the dimensions of environment are the physical environment (natural and built), the social and interactional environment, the institutional and organizational environment, the cultural and sociopolitical environment, and the experienced environment (or any combination of these). There are also environmental strengths and resources.

We support the idea that simultaneous attention given to the multidimensional and contextual arenas can, and often does, encourage a focus on the interdependence of factors influencing clients' well-being and experiences. Two central concepts are used throughout this text: *context* (contextual, contextualization) and *dimension* (multidimensional, dimensionality, multidimensionality). **Context** is viewed as the point or mean of intersection creating transactions between two or more systems, entities, and experiences. The point of intersection is one of the elements that influences how relationships, settings, events, and environments are arranged or rearranged. **Dimension** is perceived as the magnitude or scope of an experience, system, or entity influenced by the interplay between and among two or more contexts, reflecting the interdependence of variables involved. Consideration of context and dimension while addressing human diversity and commonalities is critical in order for human services practitioners, educators, and agencies to minimize the possibility of marginalizing clients' experiences, strengths, and challenges.

The multidimensional contextual practice perspective presented in this text has been founded on and shaped by a number of social science theory concepts and the theological discussion of contextual ethics. The theoretical concepts of *multiple identities/experiences, critical consciousness, intersectionality,* and *positionality* are foundation points of reference that underscore the importance of past, present, and future configurations or connecting points that are contextual, yet multidimensional, in nature. The ultimate goal of this text is to assist practitioners and researchers, as well as other professionals, to move beyond stereotypical theoretical lenses and practice approaches when addressing the complexity of human diversity and commonalities.

The multidimensional contextual practice framework introduced in this text will serve as a guideline while readers explore the multiple and contextual sets of variables that influence individual and collective identities as well as human interactions and exchanges. Readers are advised not to take language for granted and are encouraged to question paradigms, even those reflected in this book. No absolute "truth" is presented through these words. Instead, readers are provided with an opportunity to continue the dialogue and enhance their commitment to action and change, seeking the promotion of social justice, world harmony, as well as individual, family, group, and community well-being.

SOCIAL CONCEPTS REVISITED

A starting point for understanding the meaning of multidimensional contextual practice is the re-examination of a number of concepts that have been used in the conceptualization of human society. In this section, we redefine such terms as *human diversity, transcendence, race, ethnicity, culture, ethnocentrism, marginalization, acculturation, assimilation,* and *privilege.* We also capitalize on ideas such as cultural influence, cultural choice, and the wisdom of uncertainty. The perspectives presented in this section should not be viewed as conclusive "truths," but rather as glimpses of understanding. Human diversity is a moving target that many have made a commitment to follow and explore, even with all its uncertainties and complexities. Human diversity is transformative, existing within a continuum of being and becoming. We hope that readers will compare their present notions with the ones presented in this text.

The United States has been a diversified society from the time it was established. An interesting social phenomenon can be observed in exploring human diversity historically: While some human diversity attributes become commonalities within some groups of people, these same characteristics also act as factors that differentiate individuals and communities. Living with similar physical and mental abilities or disabilities, speaking a common dialect, encountering a common history, or celebrating a similar sexual orientation are reflections of general commonalities that may unify groups of people. Thus, commonalities subsist within human differences and vice versa, neither being better than the other (Guadalupe & Freeman, 1999).

One of the ways of acknowledging the vast scope of attributes and complexities shaping **human diversity** is to view this entity as the points at which people differ. These points of difference include, but are not limited to, ethnicity, race, culture, nationality, geographic location, religious and spiritual practices, gender, sexual orientation, age, socioeconomic status, and physical and mental abilities and disabilities. In other words, human diversity can be recognized as variation reinforced by a multidimensional set of attributes. These attributes can reflect differences/uniqueness based on social experiences and conditions, rituals and customs, language and dialects, values and belief systems, and many other factors. Human diversity can be viewed as the interplay of domains (cognitive, physical, social, spiritual) that make one unique and distinctive. Human diversity—while including experiences generated through ethnic identity, race, gender, sexual orientation, socioeconomic status, physical and mental abilities or disabilities, and other attributes—transcends each of these individual points of reference, as reflected by variations among individuals considered to be members of the same specific group. Latinos/as, for example, may share an ethnicity and yet differ in terms of child-rearing practices, political orientations, and socioeconomic experiences, to mention only a few areas. Ethnicity can, and often does, serve as the glue that bridges inherited differences among Latinos/as. However, ethnicity cannot stand alone if the intention is to avoid marginalization of the experiences that make the whole of the person, family, group, or community. Human diversity is constantly *being* and *becoming*. Its totality goes beyond common thoughts and experiences.

As human beings we often encounter life experiences that transcend current human understanding. Resistance and fear of the unknown, lack of trust, and intellectual or mental dogmatism can, and often do, hold us back from experiencing endless possibilities. The multidimensional contextual practice framework presented throughout this text supports the notion that transcendence is not only possible, but also vital, if current undesirable human conditions (i.e., constructed oppressive forces such as sexism, heterosexism, racism, classism, etc.) are to be reduced or completely eliminated. **Transcendence** can be generally viewed as a process by which an individual, family, group, or community reaches higher understanding of nonordinary realities (i.e., understanding/ knowing that is not limited by logic and reasoning and that connects us to divine force or spirit). Transcendence acts as a catalyst to bridge the gap between the conditional mind limited by its paradigms and the realm of spirit—the gap between scientific thinking and esoteric knowing. It calls us to move beyond fears of the unknown. As someone once said, "Fear the fear, and do it anyway." Transcendence calls for a shift in consciousness through which the mind is seen as a tool for managing human experiences, and not as a master that is all-knowing.

Throughout human history people have documented the notion of a higher intelligence or power, or divine force, that connects us all. Transcendence has played a role in allowing this higher intelligence, power, or force to be experienced, and thus understood partially or completely through specific occurrences. The experience of transcendence is itself proof of the existence of nonordinary consciousness and realities that transcend the logical mind and its capacities. Transcendent experiences can emerge through religious and spiritual rituals such as prayer, meditation, chanting, vision quests, and yoga, all of which are intentional practices to invite transcendence and higher intelligence or consciousness. Spontaneous experiences of transcendent realities also have been reported on numerous occasions, however—for example, at the deathbed of a loved one, during an accident, or while simply walking and connecting with nature, climbing mountains, or performing various other physical activities. The experience of transcendence is not limited to people from specific groups in terms of ethnicity, gender, sexual orientation, age, socioeconomic background, or physical and mental abilities. Transcendent experiences exceed such categorizations.

Multiple meanings have historically been reflected when defining the terms *ethnic* and *ethnicity,* reflecting the nonstatic nature of language. As observed by Guzzetta (1995), the term *ethnic,* embedded in the concept of ethnicity, "originally derived from a Greek word for 'nation' and was used to distinguish particular national groups from other groups not identified by nation, such as Jews or Gypsies" (p. 2508). As observed by Guzzetta, interpretations of experiences such as time, place, and context, among other variables, have historically shaped the meaning of the terms *ethnic* and *ethnicity.* As with most terms used in discussing human diversity, no total consensus exists regarding the meaning of these manifestations.

Ultimately, the terms *ethnic* and *ethnicity* reflect the process of construction, deconstruction, and reconstruction of life experiences. The fundamental nature of these terms can be described as *elusive.* However, the term **ethnicity** is currently used when distinguishing one group of people from another as a result of ethnic affiliations, as recognized by ethnic categories such as Italian Americans, African Americans, Irish Americans, and Latino/a and Hispanic Americans, and so on. Thus, the term *ethnicity* seems to serve as a noun for the adjective identified as ethnic. The experience of ethnicity has historically reflected the notion of **collective individualism**—the "we" and "them," the "insider" and "outsider." The experience of ethnicity seems to carry within itself a constructed social identity based on an individual and collective sense of connectedness that is cultivated and perpetuated by a combination of factors. Such factors may be based on a unique set of cultural traits (common language or communication codes, values, beliefs, norms, etc.), biological ties (blood-related family systems), shared history (collective social encounters of a group of people), and a degree of solidarity that ascribes membership. Thus, ethnicity is often based on common customs, values, traditions, belief systems, and norms transcending physical appearances. As stressed by Guzzetta (1995), currently "populations specified as ethnic tend to fall into two broad categories: (1) ascribed and (2) optional. Ascribed ethnics are populations to whom the designation is applied from the outside; optional ethnics are people who choose to identify themselves" (p. 2508). Guzzetta's observation is supported by Helms's (1994) suggestions, which indicate that one must differentiate between ethnic classification (identity often established and promoted by external forces such as societal "dominate groups"; see the U.S. Bureau of the Census's ethnic categorization) and ethnic identity (self-defined). These authors add that while often no conflict is observed between ascribed and optional ethnic identities or ethnic classification and ethnic identity (i.e., these may be one and the same), that is not always the case. For instance, populations with **multiethnic identities** (i.e., groups of people born from parents who do not share the same ethnic affiliations) can, and often are forced to, struggle between ascribed and optional ethnic identities.

Similar to ethnicity, race is viewed here as a socially constructed category, the meanings and interpretations of which have historically changed and are likely to continue to vary with time, space, and context. Race can be perceived as a multifaceted experience, multidimensional and contextual by nature, and affected by cultural and social structures of power, dominance, and influence, as well as by interpretations of biological differences and designation. Race has often been conceptualized as biological characteristics (i.e., physical traits such as skin color and body shape, genetic codes and gene pools, etc.) that differentiate one group of people from another (Spickard, 1992). Pinderhughes (1994) observes that race takes on "ethnic meaning if [and when] specific ways of living have evolved for members of that biological group" (p. 264). The use of the term *Black* to refer to African Americans or *White* to refer to members from diverse European immigrant ethnic groups (Guzzetta, 1995) is an illustration of Pinderhughes's observation. Race, however, is not a fixed category, as the notion has often been perceived.

Race includes and yet transcends biology, as evidenced by how "racial distinctions" have been used throughout U.S. history to withhold or encourage the socioeconomic and political mobility of specific groups of people. For instance, when examining U.S. history, people with white skin and light physical attributes in general seem to have experienced a higher degree of social privilege than people with darker skin color. Spickard (1992) suggests that in the United States, the "dominant group" (traditionally defined as the group with the most control of and access to social opportunities, the means of production, and power to influence) has used race as an artificial way to divide people into Caucasian, Asian, Native American, African American, and other subgroups—a mechanism to promote dominance and social stratification. Spickard writes:

> From the point of view of the dominant group, racial distinctions are a necessary tool of dominance. They serve to separate the subordinate people as "Other." Putting simple, neat racial labels on dominated peoples—and creating negative myths about the moral qualities of those people—makes it easier for the dominators to ignore the individual humanity of their victims. It eases the guilt of oppression. (p. 19)

Yet Spickard recognizes that race itself is not positive or negative; it is simply how it is used (its meaning and interpretation) that creates a positive or negative effect. Spickard notes:

> From the point of view of subordinate people, race can be a positive tool, a source of belonging, mutual help, and self-esteem. Racial categories . . . identify a set of people with whom to share sense of identity and common experience. . . . It is to share a sense of peoplehood that helps locate individuals psychologically, and also provides the basis for common political action. Race, this socially constructed identity, can be a powerful tool, either for oppression or for group self-actualization. (p. 19)

As briefly illustrated through Spickard's (1992) observations, the interplay between the cultural and social structures of power, dominance, and influence, as well as the interpretations of biological differences and designations, cannot be ignored when exploring racial identities, forms of oppressions, and means for individual and group self-actualization.

Culture can generally be characterized as constructed ways of living or a totality of learned behaviors. These ways of living or behaviors are influenced by beliefs, values, symbols, boundaries, norms, and lifestyles that are arranged and modified through a collective process for meeting members' biopsychosocial and spiritual needs that serves as a means by which members can systematize their understanding of worldly experiences. Culture is based on co-creation of agreements that reveal roles and expectations for thinking, behaving, and being between those engaged through membership, whether influenced by biological ties, shared history, or social contracts. The experience of culture is subjective, contextual, transactional, and non-static by nature. It must not be explored in terms of conclusive reasoning if one is to remain receptive to the symbolic dynamics of interactions and its mystical evolution. The experience of culture is reflected by individuals who share, as well as those who do not share, an ethnic, gender, sexual orientation, or socioeconomic identity. In other words, culture occurs in multiple contexts. So, for example, while it may unify a group of ethnically diverse individuals due to their physical or mental disabilities, it also may promote distinction between groups of people based on economic, political, and social experiences. Thus, commonalities within the context of human diversity are reflected in the experience of culture, and vice versa.

As emphasized by Laird (1998), culture can be theorized in multiple ways, none of which is absolute. Culture may include the performative and improvisational (it provides space for behaving according to tradition or imagination); the fluid and emergent (it is contextual, constantly changing, and often unpredictable); intersection (it is multidimensional); the definitional and constitutive (it cannot be totally measured or generalized); and the political (it is influenced by people's experiences of inequality that lead to invisibility or marginalization). While identifying and exploring the multiple faces of culture, the *explicit* or *overt* aspects of culture (experiences that are often visible, such as dress codes, food habits, language, religiosity, etc.) and the *implicit* or *covert* cultural aspects (experiences that are often invisible or occur without much recognition, such as individual or collective perception of time, experiences with diverse cognitive and emotional processes, etc.) need to be equally honored (Banks & Banks, 1997). It is important to recognize that cultures and cultural patterns do not always promote encouragement and caring for members or for those perceived as outsiders. Oppressive forces such as sexism, racism, heterosexism and homophobia, classism, ableism, and ageism, to mention a few, are often promoted through the process of **culturalization.** (This is also known as cultural influences.)

As the United States continues to grow into an even more culturally and socially diverse society, the need to explore and promote human diversity content that is non-stereotypically based is strengthened. Content on cultural and social diversity within and between groups is vital in order to recognize the paradox and effects of **cultural influence** (conscious or unconscious systems of beliefs, values, and ways of thinking, believing, and behaving that are perpetuated through human encounters and reinforcements) and **cultural choice** (conscious identification and exploration of beliefs, values, and ways of thinking and behaving, followed by a determination to embrace these or to actively engage in conscious change). Educational curricula and literature can no longer afford to address diversity content and experiences in a generalized and fragmented fashion. Diversity content within the specific group being addressed can no longer be ignored, as the interplay between cultural influence and cultural choice constantly affects people's lives. Investigating commonalities, differences, and controversies within and between diverse populations with a keen awareness of individual and community uniqueness is the next evolutionary step in embracing, teaching, and working within the context of human diversity.

Human commonalities (the sharing of characteristics such as gender, sexual orientation, ethnicity, degree of physical or mental ability, socioeconomic conditions, etc., within and between groups of people) cannot be ignored when human diversity is addressed. By the same token, human diversity cannot be neglected in the name of human commonalities if we are to avoid underestimating the unique and unduplicated individual or community experiences, thereby causing people to become disempowered. There are many ways of knowing, thinking, believing, feeling, being, and behaving. Minimization of these experiences is likely to reinforce and perpetuate oppressive mechanisms (Guadalupe, 2000) such as those observed within the historical context of the United States.

At times in U.S. history, little attention has been paid to the implications of neglecting or minimizing human differences. The invasion and genocide of indigenous nations in the name of "new discovery," slavery and transportation of West Africans into the new world in the name of "new development," colonization of geographic locations and cultures in the name of "freedom," and a reluctant welfare state in the name of "democracy" are illustrations of the potentiality of living unconsciously, ignoring human differences/uniqueness, or consciously being in a state of ethnocentrism. **Ethnocentrism** refers to the psychological, cultural, and social state of mind that fosters belief in the superiority of one's own ethnicity, gender, sexual orientation, social and economic status, physical and mental abilities, culture, and nation, often coupled with oppressive actions toward individuals and communities considered to be different and inferior.

Marginalization (the exclusion of attributes and experiences that can help reveal a more comprehensive view of an individual, family, group, or community) and a degree of invisibility of human differences/uniqueness have been reflected in the guiding principles held, promoted, and supported by a number of historical and social movements (e.g., the Charity Organization Societies and the Settlement House Movement in the late 1800s). Such principles advocated for acculturation and assimilation of individuals and communities in the name of unity, opportunity, and progress. Historical themes such as distribution, control, and use of means of production, competition, and stereotypes remind us that neglect of human uniqueness has perpetuated social oppression and, consequently, disempowerment.

The beliefs held by a number of individuals have reinforced the tendency to think of human differences as something that needs to be controlled through processes such as acculturation or assimilation, while engaging in marginalization of these differences. Such individuals seem to lack trust in the human potentiality for achieving a collaborative understanding of interdependence and harmonious actions. The notion of sameness, different from that of shared commonalities, dismisses the experience of uniqueness and rejects a variety of ways of knowing, believing, feeling, thinking, acting, and being. There is a need to recognize, however, the *points at which people differ and connect through shared commonalities,* since they are contextual, transactional, tranformative, and multidimensional in nature. They do not subtract from, but add to, who we are and who we can become. This text challenges the ideas portrayed by assimilation and acculturation perspectives. These paradigms uphold a notion of sameness that is merely an illusion created to nurture our fears of what is unknown. Such paradigms reject human complexity.

Although the concepts are connected, the differences between *acculturation* and *assimilation* need to be emphasized. **Acculturation,** which may be forced or voluntary, is a conscious or unconscious process through which previously diverse individuals, families, groups, and communities blend together and act as if they have become one. As acculturation is cultivated and perpetuated, the original cultural values, norms, beliefs, and behaviors of the dominant group (the group in control of major decisive resources) are likely to be empowered and reflected in the end result of this process. Differences between group members are then minimized as the popular and most dominating culture is embraced. In this sense, acculturation and assimilation are the same. However, **assimilation** transcends acculturation, as it is based on a duality—the paradox between an individual's (or family's, group's, or community's) motivation and willingness to become a part of the popular culture and how well that individual (or family, group, or community) is welcomed and accepted by those in control of major decisive resources. Thus, a person, family, group, or community may be acculturated in terms of adapting the language, values, and norms of the dominant group, but not assimilated because of being rejected in other areas (i.e., not being seen as equal and therefore being exposed to oppressive forces such as economic deprivation, sexism, racism, homophobia, and classism, among others). Still, in the name of both acculturation and assimilation, the multidimensional contextual self is frequently perceived as nonexisting, and thus the individual, group, family, or community is often blamed for not "successfully" accomplishing tasks established within the status quo.

We question the notion that **oppression** (i.e., vicious use of power likely to create inequality, reduce access to valuable resources, and affect the well-being and optimal health of individuals, families, groups, and communities) is exclusively a "White" and "Black" issue and that the experience of privilege can be perceived only within the context and conflict of Black and White dynamics and interactions. Oppression does not exist only between diverse ethnic groups. Often it can be observed within group membership in its multiple forms: **sexism** (oppression based on gender differences), **racism** (oppression based on racial dissimilarities), **homophobia** (oppression based on sexual orientation), **heterosexism** (discrimination against individuals with a homosexual or bisexual identity by individuals or groups who consider themselves to be heterosexual), **ageism** (oppression based on age differences), **classism** (oppression based on diverse socioeconomic status), and other forms of discrimination, such as that based on physical and mental disabilities. (See Chapter 3 for more comprehensive descriptions.) For that matter, an exploration of oppression "between" groups of people while ignoring oppression "within" group membership seems to neglect the ultimate goal—the elimination of oppressive forces, whether these are reinforced by **supremacists** (individuals promoting a belief in the superiority of, and thus right of dominance of, one group of people over another, e.g., members of the Ku Klux Klan) or are promoted through systematic cultural, social, socioeconomic, and political structures.

Although diversity within group membership has been reflected historically, often it has been masked by the notion of collectivism. For instance, people sharing an ethic identity can, and often do, differ in terms of gender, sexual orientation, socioeconomic background, political orientation, and the kinds of "moral" dilemmas they experience. Sexism, homophobia, heterosexism, and classism, among other forms of oppressive forces, are alive and well within group membership. People may connect through an ethnic identity or common socioeconomic experiences and yet may differ in their perspectives regarding sexual orientation and gender expectations. In a video entitled "Black Is Black Ain't," producer and director Marlon Rigg (1995) exposed his viewers to commonalities, differences, and controversies experienced by African Americans. Rigg explores tensions among African Americans related to issues such as gender expectations, homosexuality, socioeconomic status, and traditions, among others. Rigg's model for exploring diversity within diversity is not only practical, but also vital. To deny oppression within group membership while attempting to confront oppression between groups is not only deceitful, but also neglectful if the ultimate goal is to stand up against injustice regardless of context, space, time, and perpetrator.

Traditionally, **privilege** has been defined, in terms of positive and negative outcomes, as a special advantage, immunity, or benefit granted by cultural, societal, economic, legal, and political norms, values, beliefs, and expectations. The multifaceted aspects of privilege are rarely discussed. For instance, privilege is contextual, as evidenced by socioeconomic conditions, gender, sexual orientation, and levels of mental and physical abilities within a particular ethnic group. Furthermore, the multidimensionality of privilege is hardly ever recognized within the literature. For that matter, neither is the privilege to be alive. Can we imagine being honored, respected, loved, and having access to opportunities simply because we exist?

Issues of privilege and oppressive dynamics of interactions need to be simultaneously considered as parts of our being. For instance, being White does not automatically make one an **oppressor** (a person, or group of people, who consciously or unconsciously harshly promotes and perpetuates oppressive hostile actions toward individuals, families, groups, or communities in an attempt to cultivate and maintain a degree of control and dominance) or a person with overprivilege, just as being non-White does not mechanically classify one as the **oppressed** (a person, or group of people, who is treated unjustly, is at a disadvantage, and has been dispirited). Oppression and privilege can be considered contextual and intersectional, as they are products of human interactions and exchanges. These experiences, which are not static but are constantly changing, can be revealed in multiple forms—including, among others, age, gender, sexual orientation, socioeconomic status, and physical or mental disabilities.

Because of their multidimensional and contextual capacities, people can be simultaneously dominant and targeted. In other words, *people have the potential to be the oppressor within particular contexts and yet be vulnerable enough to be the oppressed within other encounters.* For instance, a man may be dominant as a White man but targeted because of his sexual orientation or socioeconomic status. In his book *Being Peace,* Thich Nhat Hanh (1996) wrote the following poem, entitled "Please Call Me by My True Names":

Do not say that I'll depart tomorrow because even today I still arrive.
Look deeply: I arrive in every second to be a bud on a spring branch,
to be a tiny bird, with wings still fragile, learning to sing in my new nest,
to be a caterpillar in the heart of a flower, to be a jewel hiding itself in a stone.
I still arrive, in order to laugh and to cry, in order to fear and to hope.
The rhythm of my heart is the birth and death of all that are alive.
I am the mayfly metamorphosing on the surface of the river, and
I am the bird which, when spring comes, arrives in time to eat the mayfly.
I am the frog swimming happily in the clear pond, and
I am also the grass-snake who, approaching in silence, feeds itself on the frog.
I am the child in Uganda, all skin and bones, my legs as thin as bamboo sticks,
and I am the arms merchant, selling deadly weapons to Uganda.
I am the twelve-year-old girl, refugee on a small boat,
who throws herself into the ocean after being raped by a sea pirate, and
I am the pirate, my heart not yet capable of seeing and loving.
I am a member of the politburo, with plenty of power in my hands, and
I am the man who has to pay his "debt of blood" to my people,
dying slowly in a forced labor camp.
My joy is like spring, so warm it makes flowers bloom in all walks of life.
My pain is like a river of tears, so full it fills the four oceans.
Please call me by my true names, so I can hear all my cries and laughs at once,
so I can see that my joy and pain are one.
Please call me by my true names, so I can wake up, and
so the doors of my heart can be left open, the door of compassion. (pp. 63–64)

In this poem, Thich Nhat Hanh illustrates the complexity of that which we often call "self." We have the potentiality to be both the oppressor and the oppressed. We also have the possibility to become compassionate human beings as we recognize and eliminate the beliefs and pain that support oppressive behaviors while strengthening our capacities to do good. By moving beyond the boxes of "Black" and "White," we can open our potentiality to better understand the complexity of human diversity, challenges, and strengths. Individual and collective narratives can be used as methods for reducing the possibility of misunderstanding, marginalizing, stereotyping, and disempowering people.

PRACTICE CONCEPTS REVISITED

This section explores another set of terms often used in the social/health/ human service field. The definitions of terms presented in this chapter will be elaborated on throughout the book, but this introduction will create an initial baseline for understanding the perspectives of multidimensional contextual practice.

A **client** is a person, family, group, or community that is seeking, needing, or receiving social/health/human services. Those already receiving services can be identified as **active clients,** while those seeking or in need of services can be regarded as **potential clients.** The term **social/health/human services** is used to describe direct or indirect professional assistance geared to supporting clients in identifying, addressing, coping with, and transforming physical, cognitive, emotional, and social adversities that are interfering with the client's well-being. **Client well-being** refers to the attainment and maintenance of various domains of human functioning that promote optimal health, including, but not limited to, one's physical, cognitive, emotional, spiritual, social, and economic stability.

Stereotypes are generalized assumptions, beliefs, opinions, and images—positive or negative—held and perpetuated toward specific individuals, groups, families, and communities. Stereotypes disregard information available that contradicts or is more inclusive of variables influencing the identities or experiences of those being stereotyped. Human complexity is hidden through cultivation and perpetuation of stereotypes. O'Neil McMahon (1996) notes that "to stereotype means to attribute uniformly a set of characteristics to a group of people and to deny their individual differences" (p. 46). Stereotypes are a product or an end result of the practice of **stereotyping,** which is the process and methods that assist in the cultivation and prolongation of stereotypes.

Different kinds of stereotypes exist. Some stereotypes reinforce a notion of superiority or that which is desired, and some perpetuate a sense inferiority, stigma, or that which is rejected. Although "negative" stereotypes play a key role in reinforcing social issues such as hate crimes, discrimination, and oppression, "positive" stereotypes also can generate negative outcomes, especially when specific expectations are not met by individuals or groups of people (Laird, 1998). When stereotypes go unquestioned, they are likely to become uninterrupted baselines used to observe, interact with, judge, and evaluate others. Regardless of type, stereotypes have cognitive, emotional, behavioral, and social effects (Healey, 1997) and perpetuate marginalization of multiple attributes and invisibility of the aspects that make one unique, unduplicated, and whole.

Multiple forms of stereotypes (both "positive" and "negative") are reflected when exploring historical and current perspectives held toward Asian-American communities. Although diversified in multiple ways, Asian Americans often have been perceived as a common entity within U.S. mainstream culture. In the late 19th and early 20th centuries, large numbers of Asian Americans were generally considered inferior and thus were subjected to much individual and collective humiliation and discrimination. In the late 1980s and early 1990s, however, the term *model minority* emerged among those who attempted to distinguish these communities from others perceived as less desirable. The term *model minority* is supposed to reflect successes within Asian-American communities in terms of socioeconomic achievements, educational attainments, and skilled development. Authors such as Balgopal (1995) argue that although changes have occurred within Asian-American communities, the "successful image" held toward these groups is a myth. For instance, "factors such as longer hours of work and the reporting of household income, rather than the income of individual family members" (p. 233), often affect examinations of Asian Americans' economic achievements. A household income, for example, may be recorded as $45,000 a year, but the recording process may neglect the fact that this income was generated by three different individuals within a family of seven.

Stereotypes are often developed and maintained through a combination of factors including our selective interpretations of complex experiences, our custom of generalizing and categorizing, our appraisal of how the experiences we encounter relate to our lives, our emotional reactions to such experiences, and our memory of and attachment to that which we have learned and encountered. Thus, engaging in cognitive and social modification of stereotypes requires acquisition of mindful awareness, a conscious commitment to change, support from our surroundings, and practical tools to assist us in this continuous tranformative process.

Among other areas addressed in this text are environment, human adversities, individual and collective resilience, and professional competence. **Environment** represents the individual and collective physical, social, and mystical domains (and subdomains—the sum of the whole) affecting the evolutionary process of the human experience. Although environments are contextual by nature, they can simultaneously be viewed as multidimensional. Environments are in constant transactions with one another, demonstrating the interplay of human interdependence and relying on each other in order to survive.

An interesting phenomenon observed within environments is that as cultures and subcultures are constructed, the possibility exists for some people to benefit from the available resources more than others. Environments often do not seem to operate on mutual exchange (having an equal impact), as issues of ethnocentrism, privilege, inequality, control of means of production, and oppressive forces are often reinforced through values, belief systems, and manifestations of behavior. Thus, when addressing an environment, we must not ignore the issues of dominance influenced by the control of means (i.e., resources—power distribution, organization of formal and informal structures, and control of knowledge, among other factors). Both historically and currently within the United States, cultures and subcultures within a variety of environments have favored some groups of people over others, and thus many forms of human adversities have been constructed and perpetuated. In practice, we must be aware of these multidimensional and contextual environmental forces.

Human adversities are major factors that bring the client and practitioner to work together. These can be characterized as encounters filled with physical, cognitive, emotional, and social distresses (i.e., confrontation with oppressive forces such as sexism, racism, classism, homophobia and heterosexism, discrimination based on physical or mental abilities, internalization of oppressive forces, etc.) that put in danger the individual, family, group, or community well-being. In short, human adversities can be, and often are, life-threatening. A human adversity can be cultivated as a result of an event (e.g., being hospitalized after a brutal hate crime) and simultaneously as a continuous process of human interaction (e.g., perpetuation of stigmas regarding individuals considered to be members of a particular ethnic, gender, or sexual orientation group). The grief generated by human adversities as well as the healing process found within the power of vulnerability emphasize the importance of trusting beyond the walls that blind our limited understanding. These walls seem to be reinforced by dogmatic thinking, believing, and behaving.

To address human adversity without equally honoring human resilience would be a disservice to the field of social/health/human services. Within this context, **resilience** refers to the innate essence enacted in supportive relationships and resources that promote an ability to maintain, recover, or regain a level of control, intention, and direction before, during, or after an encounter with adversity. Resilience can also be affected by an outer privilege. An outer privilege increases the possibility for particular individuals, groups, or communities to gain access to environmental resources while reducing barriers for those being "honored." An interesting factor is that while some individuals or communities are considered privileged, others are not, which affects the dynamics of human interactions and exchanges. However true this may be in certain contexts, privilege in and of itself is not always blinded by stereotypes. Privilege can present itself in the most "unexpected" situations. For instance, an African-American woman who has experienced multigenerational poverty may, after receiving some family or social support, begin pursuing an education and obtain a degree in medicine. Doors to opportunities that were once closed may become open after her achievement, allowing her to experience some privileges that were not previously accessible to her.

Overall, glimpses of understanding regarding human resilience can be generated through the exploration of ways by which individuals, families, groups, and communities organize their inner and outer resources in order to address and transcend emotional, mental, physical, and social pain. For instance, former political prisoners such as Nelson Mandela in South Africa often relied on writing during their captivity as a way to maintain sanity and focus. Individuals such as Mahatma Gandhi in India have relied on spiritual reflections while promoting nonviolent political actions to confront political and cultural oppression. Furthermore, undocumented communities within the United States have, from time to time, relied on an underground economy.

An important phenomenon in addressing and working within the context of human diversity/uniqueness is professional competence. **Professional competence** refers to the ability to skillfully serve diverse individuals and communities within different contexts without engaging in stereotypical or immediately gratifying approaches that promote marginalization of important attributes or disempowerment of those being served. Professional competence often requires a balance between learned skills and cultivated values of respect regarding human diversity/

uniqueness, a degree of professional self-awareness and evaluation, confrontation of discriminative cognitive patterns and actions promoted in the name of professionalism, as well as a level of trust in the wisdom of uncertainty. (**Wisdom of uncertainty** refers to an inner knowing or innate intuitive power that reveals understanding of living experiences beyond conscious reasoning, yet it is often ignored in the name of empirical and scientific discoveries.) An individual with professional competence is able to assess, distinguish, and simultaneously embrace commonalities, differences, and controversies within and between diverse groups of people. Professional interventions, whether conducted at the micro-intrapersonal, meso-interpersonal, macro-environmental, or magna-spiritual level, or a combination of these, are not mechanically facilitated. They are planned and carried out with a degree of mindfulness. While cultivating professional competence, risk taking beyond professional comfort zones becomes vital in order for ongoing professional development to be broadened; yet, decisions involving risk must be evaluated as much as possible prior to their implementation in order to ensure client well-being.

In looking at history, we can see that no one person or community has had absolute answers to the issues and needs generated within the context of human diversity, interactions, and exchanges. In its totality and complexity, human diversity is vast and indefinable. We can only get glimpses of understanding as we cultivate competencies that enhance our interactions and dynamics within the context of human diversity. Thus, as readers, you are asked to carefully examine the content, exercises, and skills in this text with a healthy skepticism. We want you to question that which is unfamiliar or debatable, while engaging in critical analysis in the name of the human spirit. The following cannot be overemphasized: *The content in this text is directly influenced by the authors' personal, professional, and scholarly encounters.* Such content should not be minimized or neglected, as it is also an expression of human diversity. Take what you need and leave the rest, while remembering that in learning and evolving, we are often influenced by our own points of reference, which are subject to change. Take a deep breath now and then as you continue reading this book. The journey goes on in the next section, as we consider the theme of conscious change.

THE NEED FOR CONSCIOUS CHANGE

A review of the social science literature reveals that a significant number of authors have argued that the dominant model used in educational systems within the United States is based on Eurocentric paradigms (Boutte, 1999; Germain & Gitterman, 1996; Gilligan, 1982; McGoldrick, 1998; Schriver, 2001). Germain (1994), for instance, noted that content on human development is often addressed through progressive linear stages that neglect contextual individual or group experiences such as oppression. These traditional Western models reflect theoretical frameworks developed by individuals such as Freud, Piaget, Kohlberg, and Erikson. Germain (1994) stressed that stage-based theoretical frameworks ignore "human, cultural, and environmental diversity, and historical context . . ." (p. 97). She also emphasized that content that is by nature diversified is generally presented through exclusive paradigms. This neglect of models that reflect the life experiences of those being served through the educational system can, and often does, lead to the notion of "deviance," especially in regard to individuals (or communities) who, because they do not think and behave according to the dominant models of beliefs and behaviors, are not able to acculturate "successfully" into the dominant culture reflected through mainstream norms and paradigms. Such a notion of deviance can strengthen and perpetuate a system of oppression.

In her research, Fordham (1988) found that the use of exclusive paradigms transmits messages of rejection that have implications. Fordham's research findings (in her study of African Americans) illustrate that students who do not reflect, or are not represented by, the educational dominant model tend to become isolated and to develop what she called "racelessness identities." This experience seems to be generated by the need of those who are being marginalized and confronting cultural rejection to strive to become accepted by the dominant culture while making an effort to become successful in school. Fordham noticed that as educational programs neglect the many ways of knowing, believing, thinking, feeling, behaving, and being, large numbers of students are likely to feel excluded and ignored. Such marginalization is likely to result in **internalized oppression,** that is, the development and maintenance of self-defeating views affecting behavior as a result of feeling rejected during interaction with others (Fordham, 1988).

Sadker, Sadker, and Long (1997) stress that current educational curricula within the United States continues to discriminate against women, thus reflecting gender inequality. They identify six means (*linguistic bias, stereotyping, invisibility, imbalance, unreality,* and *fragmentation*) by which educational system contributes to the ongoing marginalization of the contributions women have made to the U.S. developmental process. The use of "masculine" terminologies (e.g., *mankind, caveman, forefathers,* etc.) to characterize and explore the societal contributions of men and women is an example of linguistic bias. The literature and curricula reflect biases of invisibility and imbalance in that only minimal, if any, attention is given to the specific ways in which women have historically affected U.S. sociopolitical and economic development. Sadker et al. argue that women's contributions are often underrepresented in the content of the literature, and that unrealistic bias is illustrated in the way that women's experiences are generalized and thus put into "boxes." An example of an unrealistic bias is the perception that women are, overall, passionate and sensitive; this perception may backfire when women act assertive. Such unrealistic biases rob individuals and communities of the opportunity to embrace complexity without then being penalized.

The observations that Sadker et al. (1997) make about fragmentation and invisibility are similar. Invisibility is based on the minimal attention given to the significant contributions of women throughout U.S. history (e.g., the roles and contributions of women during the Industrial Revolution, World Wars I and II, and the civil rights movement). Fragmentation, on the other hand, is evidenced when such contributions are identified but viewed as unique occurrences. Fragmentation of content is reflected within curricula when such content is highlighted within a particular segment of the curriculum rather than being infused throughout. Fragmentation often conveys the notion that the contributions are not major, but only rare incidents.

According to Gilligan (1982) and Taylor, Gilligan, and Sullivan (1995), fundamental differences exist between men and women. Gilligan, for instance, stresses that women's dominant values are highly influenced by a desire to intimately connect with others through caring and sensitive interactions, while men's values are frequently shaped by a desire for independence. Data generated by studies such as these cannot be ignored, as they provide glimpses of the possibility for understanding the general dynamics of interactions between women and men. Such studies, by the same token, cannot be generalized either, as context, social conditions, social expectations, cognitive patterns, and differences within groups of men and women, among other variables, are likely to affect the desires of specific men and women for intimate connections or independence. Much diversity exists within groups of women and men.

The means by which women's contributions to the U.S. sociopolitical and economic system have been marginalized (Sadker et al., 1997) can be used to describe similar experiences encountered by other populations. For instance, the social science literature, educational curricula, and the media often portray Latino communities as being made up of immigrants who are poor and unable to communicate proficiently in the English language (Chavez, 1991; Moore & Pachon, 1985). This image of Latino communities is based on unrealistic biases, fragmentation, and stereotypes; and it promotes the invisibility of contributions made by Latinos/as within U.S. sociopolitical and economic arenas. When educational literature and curricula use the means of marginalization identified by Sadker et al., students (potential future professionals) are deprived of valuable information that could enhance their professional competence.

As mentioned earlier, writers such as Germain (1994) have argued that European paradigms dominate the curricula on human development. Such paradigms (what we might call "imbalance biases" that promote standards) have generally dominated the way that **knowledge** (the range of information and understanding that is likely to be perceived in terms of truth, reality, and normality) and history are defined within curricula. For example, when exploring historical experiences such as the arrival of Christopher Columbus, multiple interpretations can be made. While one lens may reinforce that Christopher Columbus "discovered" the Americas, another can reveal that his arrival is not an illustration of "discovery," but rather *a reflection of invasions of many indigenousness nations* (Powell, Zehm, & Garcia, 1996). Marginalization promoted through linguistic bias, stereotyping, invisibility, imbalance, unreality, and fragmentation is likely to promote the notion that one ethnicity, culture, or nationality is superior to another, thereby reinforcing the oppressive pattern found in ethnocentrism.

The social science literature stresses that interdependence can be found between social and cultural experiences and individual and group identity development (Davis, 1993; Germain & Gitterman, 1996; Gilligan, 1982; Healey, 1997; Kelley, 1995; Pinderhughes, 1989, 1994; Schriver, 2001; Sue, 1981). According to Pinderhughes (1989), an individual, family, group, or community sense of self is affected by individual and collective social and cultural encounters. Ignoring this phenomenon, Pinderhughes noted, can lead to misunderstanding and, even worse, mistreatment of target groups of people (e.g., hate crimes). It should then be of no surprise to see findings, such as those presented by Fordham (1988), which emphasize that a number of African-American students, in order to attempt to adapt to a particular educational environment, tended to deny part of who they were in order to survive.

As illustrated in Figure 1.1, when misunderstanding becomes the center of human interaction, it can result in a sense of rejection. It is through this rejection that a person, family, group, or community may engage in a search for meaning with the inten-

Figure 1.1 | Possible Dynamics Affected by Misunderstanding

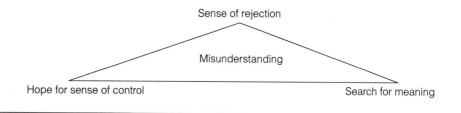

tion of finding a sense of control. Engaging in a search for meaning, however, does not automatically guarantee achievement of a sense of control or empowerment of self to confront possible adversity reinforced by misunderstanding or mistreatment. Another possibility is the internalization of the sense of rejection, leading to internalized oppression.

Figure 1.2 demonstrates how a sense of rejection leading to a search for meaning as an attempt to gain self-control does not necessarily mean automatic cultivation of skillful ways of coping. A sense of rejection may reinforce a process of self-fulfilling prophecy through which self-defeating patterns or rejection of self may emerge. Exclusiveness and the marginalization of attributes that help define one's experiences can transmit the message that the individual, family, group, or community does not hold the qualities needed to be considered within the construction and dynamics of conventional knowledge. This can generate, promote, and reinforce the possibility of internalized oppression (Boutte, 1999; Fordham, 1988). Unacknowledged differences and generalizations that neglect diversity within diversity set the standards for stereotypes, which often reinforce the cycle of individual and social oppression (Guadalupe, 2000). In sustaining paradigms that embrace some groups of people and reject others, the educational system and educational literature become part of the predicament, rather than being part of the solution (i.e., actively engaging in identification, exploration, and determination of methods that honor and strengthen the well-being of all those involved).

Figure 1.2 shows the internalization of a sense of rejection, which can be detrimental to both individual and collective social functioning and well-being. Human potential to withstand and bounce back from harmful intrapersonal, interpersonal, and environmental factors, however, cannot be underestimated. History has shown how individuals, families, groups, and communities have rebounded from life conditions that made them overwhelmingly vulnerable, including social, economic, political, and health challenges. It can be argued that human **essence** (an esoteric living entity, a transcendent force, that when activated connects us to higher intelligence and guides our endurance) allows individuals and communities to dismiss a sense of rejection and find a sense of direction that will promote the change necessary to strengthen well-being. This observation is illustrated in Figure 1.3.

A significant number of authors have argued that although social and cultural content has been incorporated into curricula promoted by diverse educational disciplines, this content has often been based on stereotypes (Carter et al., 1994; Cnaan,

Figure 1.2 | Possible Dynamics Affected by Misunderstanding

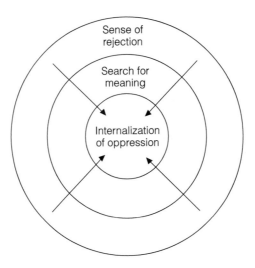

Figure 1.3 | Essence and Sense of Direction

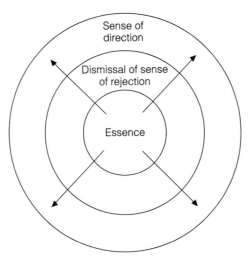

Goodfriend, & Newman, 1996; Guzzetta, 1995; Hooyman, 1994; Kropf, 1996; Morris, 1993; Newman, 1994; Soifer, 1991; Tice, 1990). Guzzetta (1995) noted that while many differences exist between individuals and groups categorized under the term "White ethnic groups" (i.e., diverse ethnic traditions, socioeconomic experiences, and sexual orientations, among others), the literature often fails to address diversity within and between these groups of people. Stereotypes are often promoted through lack of awareness. Guzzetta's observation is applicable to the way content regarding other diverse populations, such as African Americans, Latinos/as, First Nations Peoples, and Asian Americans, is generalized to the point that unique experiences are marginalized in the name of the collective (Boutte, 1999; Ramsey, 1979). Hooyman (1994) stresses that even though increased content on gender inequality can be observed when exploring curricula, stereotypes regarding gender have continued to be promoted. Furthermore, Tice (1990) indicates that when content regarding women is addressed in the curricula, content regarding experiences of women of color is frequently diminished. Kropf (1996) points out that although people affected by developmental disabilities are living longer, no significant effort has been made to increase understanding regarding these socially and culturally diversified populations. Stereotypical perspectives often go unquestioned.

The infusion of stereotypes affiliated with diverse individuals, families, groups, and communities can be observed throughout the multifaceted educational system in the United States. For instance, Boutte (1999) observes that one of the multiple ways in which the kindergarten through high school (K–12) educational curricula are infused with stereotypes is in the methods or themes selected for introducing student populations to ethnic or culturally specific holidays. Themes used to address holidays such as "Thanksgiving," Boutte argues, promote and perpetuate a false image regarding indigenous communities. "Thanksgiving" is presented as a celebration, a time of consolidation and partnership between Pilgrims and First Nations Peoples. This perpetuates a view of historical encounters through a superficial lens. Ramsey (1979) stresses that although a number of North Americans perceive "Thanksgiving" as a celebration, "many Native American groups [First Nations People] regard Thanksgiving as a day of mourning and observe it with fasting and vigils. For them, it is a symbol of the Europeans' first foothold on the North American continent and the demise of the Native way of life" (p. 26). Perhaps the issue is not the celebration of "Thanksgiving" (or should we say "Thanksliving"), since as human beings we have many things, people, and experiences to be thankful for. The issue, rather, is the images and marginalized interpretations of historical events used to justify the holiday.

Music focusing on ethnic groups as objects has also reinforced stereotypes. Ramsey (1979) pointed out that educational curricula within diverse contexts, especially in lower grades, often utilizes music as a mechanism to teach students about different subjects, including counting. When the objects for counting are associated with people and not things, which is the case with the song "Ten Little Indians," students seem to be consciously or unconsciously taught to devalue the richness of culture embraced by those representing the objects. As emphasized by Ramsey, "the inclusion of 'Indians' as objects to be counted implicitly equates this group of people with inanimate things or [savage] animals" (p. 28). Ramsey suggests that one way for people to directly experience the negative connotations carried by songs such as "Ten Little Indians" is to replace the ethnic identity used in the song with another more personal identity (e.g., "Ten Little Anglos/Whites," "Ten Little Blacks/African Americans," "Ten Little Hispanics/Latinos," etc.) and to evaluate possible reactions.

As this discussion has illustrated, lack of consideration of differences within and between groups of people and ignorance regarding the ways by which stereotypes are infused into educational curricula support a system of oppression (Boutte, 1999; Guadalupe, 2000; Healey, 1997; Pinderhughes, 1989, 1994). As long as stereotypes are perpetuated through literature, theoretical frameworks, and teaching strategies, the effort to promote human diversity and the well-being of individuals, families, groups, and communities is likely to continue to be fragmented. Boutte (1999), Germain (1994), Pinderhughes (1989, 1994), Ramsey (1979), and Sadker et al. (1997), among others, have identified various means that cultivate and perpetuate misunderstandings of differences, as well as possible implications. The time is ripe to advocate for conscious change.

Current social science literature has emphasized the importance of fostering an understanding and appreciation of human diversity/uniqueness in educational institutions, work settings, our personal lives, and within our society and world as a whole (Boutte, 1999; Cnaan, Goodfriend, & Newman, 1996; Commission on Accreditation, 1992; Cramer, 1995, 1997; Garcia & Van Soest, 1997; Gilligan, 1982; Healey, 1997; Pinderhughes, 1989). One rationale for supporting the philosophical view, often called **multiculturalism,** that is shaping an educational movement is the assumption that understanding and respecting differences can assist in reducing conflicts cultivated through variables such as marginalization, invisibility, and neglect of human diversity. Multiculturalism has been viewed in various ways, but each advocates for a common purpose—an integration of multicultural differences within educational and social settings. Boutte (1999) describes multiculturalism as a concept filled with assumptions favoring acceptance of human differences, an educational reform movement attempting to institutionalize the idea of and commitment to equal access to opportunities regardless of a person's or community's background or identity, and a process that is constantly evolving. The efforts made by the multicultural movement have strengthened people's personal and social capacities to embrace differences while challenging oppressive forces (i.e., racism, sexism, classism, ageism, homophobia, and anti-Semitism, to mention a few). Nevertheless, an exploration of the literature on human diversity reveals that the focus of multiculturalism is generally on "either/or" categories that often overlook the complexity of human differences. As a result, stereotypes continue to be generated, reinforced, and perpetuated—and the journey continues.

Although the multicultural movement has generally served as a stepping-stone in the struggle for equality, social justice, and the visibility of diverse ways of knowing, thinking, believing, feeling, behaving, and being, the movement has been limited by a number of factors, including the stereotypes that are perpetuated because of the lack of emphasis on the experience of diversity within diversity. For instance, a nationwide study of social work educators conducted by one of the authors of this text (Guadalupe, 2000) found that human diversity content has been traditionally addressed by social work curricula through a multicultural perspective, with only minimal or no attention given to the effects of stereotypes and stereotyping. As one research participant in the study stated, "I would have to say that the focus in my institution is to teach on diversity, but not necessarily with the purpose of reducing stereotypes. The focus is on getting the content to the students without acknowledging that we can err by stereotyping." Another participant wrote, "We talk and talk about specific groups as if there were no differences within the group membership. It is really frustrating that in the name of good intention . . ., we are prolonging suffering by prolonging stereotypes." Research participants in this study unanimously agreed that stereotypical lenses are likely to support and reinforce oppressiveness in the name of good intention.

The multicultural movement also has been restricted by what Andersen and Collins (2001) call "thinking comparatively." This is the process of learning about, and then comparing and contrasting, the experiences encountered by diverse groups of people in which the end result is often a ranking of experiences in terms of which group experiences the greatest degree of oppression and privilege—that is, "who is the most victimized" and "who has the most opportunities." Although such an approach has its strengths (i.e., it generates an understanding of how resources are often centralized and promotes the need to advocate for social egalitarianism), it also provides an artificial frame for understanding human diversity and its complexities (i.e., the context often promotes either/or categories while overlooking multidimensional linkages to the whole, and focuses on fragmented interventions to promote needed transformations). The "thinking comparatively" approach can, and often does, lead to what Martinez (2001) called the "Oppression Olympics"—a competition among diverse groups for the gold medal for being the most demoralized or victimized group. Rather than making comparisons of sufferings from a "less than" and "more than" perspective, however, an alternative is to learn about each other's unique experiences and to stand together in opposition to inequality and social injustice, regardless of which group is affected and to what extent.

Another factor that has held back the multicultural movement is the focus, sometimes unconscious and at other times conscious, on prioritizing one set of human diversity attributes (e.g., racial, ethnic, cultural) over another (e.g., gender, sexual orientation, mental and physical uniqueness). The issue is not separating diversity attributes for analytical purposes; rather, it involves the ignoring or minimization of the intersection of diversity variables affecting the well-being and optimal health of a person, family, group, or community. Minimizing or ignoring the intersection between these diverse variables within a contextual setting is likely to perpetuate the process of putting people and communities into boxes that deny their unique experiences and perpetuate blame regarding historical events over which they had no control. For instance, in his research, Gallagher (1995) noted that in the university context, many White students often feel like they are blamed or held accountable for discriminative actions, such as slavery, that were committed by, perhaps, their ancestors. He observed that, in general, White students feel that the multicultural curriculum is biased against them and often is not inclusive; their experiences are perhaps neglected. Atkin and Rich (2001) observed that stereotypes often become the instruments for scapegoating. They emphasized that Jewish North American women are often perceived as materialistic, self-centered, and wealthy. Such stereotypes, Atkin and Rich argue, set up Jewish women as scapegoats, perpetuate anti-Semitism, and promote historical oppression of Jews. As emphasized throughout this chapter, frequent prioritization of one set of diversity attributes over another is likely to reinforce marginalization of experiences as well as perpetuate stereotypical perspectives and strengthen the imbalance of biases.

Martinez (2001) stresses that Latino/a communities' experiences with racism in the United States are often ignored or minimized. Part of the reason for this dynamic is the stereotypical idea that racism is a White/Black issue. The White/Black paradigm is exclusive, often blind, and does not recognize the complexity of racial tension affecting multiple and diverse communities. According to Martinez, one way Latino/a experiences with racism are minimized is through the process of invisibility.

This is reflected in the one-dimensional view of Latino/a communities, regardless of the diversity within them. When Latinos/as are recognized, Martinez argues, it is often within the context of how they endanger the dominant position of other ethnic groups. Stereotypes held toward Latino/a communities, Martinez stresses, often deny their unique experiences.

A person's life is influenced by memberships that cut across diverse categories (e.g., a Latina woman may come from a poor socioeconomic background, have children, experience a physical disability, and consider herself to be bisexual). Prioritizing some diversity attributes over others, as is often done in the name of multiculturalism, has the tendency to minimize, neglect, and marginalize experiences that are part of the whole. This is what we call "blindness of the multiple experiences occurring in one body." The term *one body* includes both individual and collective consciousness as well as other multidimensional contextual factors that enhance or injure the life of a person, family, group, or community.

If we are to firmly confront and transform stereotypes in our educational, professional, and personal approaches to understanding, addressing, and working within the context of human diversity, we can no longer afford to be palliative. Stereotypes are cultivated and supported in the name of generalization. Stereotypes perpetuate images that are frequently exclusive of individual and collective uniqueness. [They are based on a view through a monolithic lens or a one-dimensional approach that often promotes invisibility and underrepresents the variables that affect groups of people, encourages imbalance in interpretations of experiences, and often portrays unrealistic expectations.] Multidimensional contextual practice is invaluable for embracing human complexities, confronting stereotypes, and guiding us to glimpses of understanding while engaging in professional interventions.

The term *multiculturalism* is actually misleading. It implies that human diversity is limited to the experience of culture. When human diversity is perceived as the point at which people differ—including, and at the same time transcending, the traditional emphasis on culture—the opportunity emerges for human complexities to be honored. While acknowledging that cultural influences often assist in shaping life experiences encountered within different human contexts, times, and spaces, we also must recognize that people frequently engage in choices that are not necessarily reflections of cultural influences (e.g., a woman who grew up Catholic but transforms her spiritual practice into Buddhism, or a man who overcomes experiences reinforced by a caste system). These choices may be driven by a need or **intuitive guidance** (an innate human quality that does not rely on conscious reasoning). Such newly embraced choices serve as baselines for creating even more experiences that then create new dynamics.

Exclusive focus on culture can minimize another type of experience that affects human interactions and dynamics: the **mystical experience** (i.e., the experience of relatedness and connectedness with animating spiritual forces that exceeds age, physical and mental abilities, gender, sexual orientation, socioeconomic status, and all other social, cultural, and spatial boundaries). For instance, the experience of ethnicity is an important component of people's cultural experiences, but when addressed within a universal context, this experience is not necessarily a holistic frame through which multidimensional human experiences can be understood. This is indirectly emphasized within the multicultural literature when the terms *culture* and *ethnicity* are used interchangeably. Multidimensional contextual practice provides the opportunity to address human diversity as inclusive of culture and ethnicity and yet expand beyond these boundaries. The complexity of human diversity beyond cultural and ethnic influences is illustrated by other attributes often found within individuals sharing a culture or an ethnic identity; age; gender; sexual orientation; religious and spiritual beliefs and experiences; regional, mental, and physical differences; diverse consciousness; and so on. This observation supports the need for being as inclusive as possible when addressing diversity attributes that support or injure the well-being and optimal health of a person, family, group, or community.

An interesting social phenomenon observed within the multicultural literature that has educational effects is the way language is used in defining diverse groups of people and addressing their experiences. **Language** is perceived as a constructed multidimensional and contextual agreement of uses, meanings, and interpretations of symbols, sounds, and experiences. While the multidimensional aspect of language is reflected by its abstract qualities (i.e., written and verbal terms, symbols, and experiences can be interpreted in multiple and distinctive ways), its individualistic and yet multiple contents are reflected by its contextual qualities (i.e., agreement of usage and meaning as well as interpretations of experiences can be, and often are, situational). Language is used to convey a message. For instance, the terms *White* and *People of Color* are constantly used within multicultural literature. They are used to categorize people in terms of skin color and physical characteristics, and to reveal a framework for addressing issues of social oppression and privilege that exist between individuals classified under these categories. These terms, however, often perpetuate the notion of monodimensionalism, as people are put into exclusive boxes that are supposed to represent who they are.

Another concern here is that *a relationship often exists between the power to define and the power to control.* As the literature continues to perpetuate terms conceptualized through research and scholarly activities, educational systems are likely to perpetuate them with limited consideration regarding the impact of generalization. Thus, students (future social/health/human service professionals) frequently become socialized with terminologies that are limited to a context of theories that may not always reflect the way that "everyday" people define themselves or perceive their experiences.

As emphasized earlier, oppression and privilege are constantly addressed in the literature in terms of the relationships occurring between Whites and non-Whites or People of Color. This process often minimizes or ignores oppression and privilege occurring within ethnic groups based on variables such as age, social class, gender, sexual orientation, and degree of physical and mental abilities. In other words, context is ignored when experiences such as privilege and oppression are not viewed within multidimensional settings. In order to be less fragmented when discussing and working within the context of human diversity, differences occurring in intragroup relationships must not go unnoticed. The "Band-Aid approach" to the cycle of human pain, suffering, and recovery is no longer useful.

The multidimensional contextual practice framework presented in this text advocates for the acknowledgment and embracing of human complexity while creating avenues for addressing human adversity within various contexts. It advocates for the exploration of commonalities, differences, and controversies within and between groups of people. Furthermore, it recognizes that understanding and interpretations of human diversity are often shaped by individual and collective stories (White, 1991; White & Epston, 1990). Thus, it simultaneously uses and integrates various approaches (both **emic,** which focus on cultural-specific factors, and **etic,** which focus on themes observed across cultures) as well as individual narrative when working with and addressing human diversity/uniqueness.

Because of the natural dynamics of change and the transformations that result directly from individual and social actions, understanding of human diversity cannot be seen as an "absolute truth." Understanding needs to be gleaned from contextual interpretations and experiences that assist us in understanding the process of co-creating meaning within a particular time and space. The multidimensional contextual practice framework introduced in this text honors and embraces the assumption that a paradox exists between **certainty** (knowledge that supports the notion that something is real; a fact beyond a doubt) and **uncertainty** (a state of being that reflects an understanding that things are subject to change, based not on concreteness or factual information but rather on indefinable sensations). The overall purpose of multidimensional contextual practice is to assist social/health/human service practitioners, educators, researchers, and community organizers, among others, in acknowledging and honoring the complexity of human diversity while moving beyond stereotypical approaches likely to injure people's lives in the name of good intention.

This chapter has illustrated the importance of developing nonstereotypically based approaches. As observed, although content on diversity has been increasingly included in educational curricula, avoiding stereotypes has not been a primary goal (Carter et al., 1994; Cnaan, Goodfriend, & Newman, 1996; Guadalupe, 2000; Hooyman, 1994; Kropf, 1996; Morris, 1993; Newman, 1994; Soifer, 1991; Tice, 1990). The lack of nonstereotypical approaches has significant implications for professional practice. If we are to avoid doing a disservice to diverse communities, the implications of our current approaches can no longer be ignored. The time for conscious change is here.

SUMMARY

This chapter introduced the concepts of multidimensionality and contextualization and discussed how the authors have joined them together in a multidimensional contextual practice framework that recognizes the concepts of multiple identities and diversity within diversity. The chapter also redefined and reinterpreted the meaning of various terms used in human diversity and human services literature. In subsequent chapters, the multidimensional contextual practice framework is explained in more detail. This framework operationalizes our conceptual base and offers practice principles. Its major themes are: client well-being; the multidimensional contextual client; micro, meso, macro, and magna levels; the practitioner's professional competence; and multidimensional contextual services.

References

Andersen, M. L., & Collins, P. H. (Eds.). (2001). *Race, class, and gender: An anthology* (4th ed.). Belmont, CA: Wadsworth/Thomson Learning.

Atkin, R., & Rich, A. (2001). "JAP"-slapping: The politics of scapegoating. In M. L. Andersen & P. H. Collins (Eds.), *Race, class, and gender: An anthology* (4th ed.). Belmont, CA: Wadsworth/Thomson Learning.

Balgopal, P. R. (1995). Asian Americans overview. In R. L. Edwards (Editor-in-Chief), *Encyclopedia of Social Work* (19th ed., pp. 231–237). Washington, DC: NASW Press.

Banks, J. A., & Banks, C. A. M. (1997). *Multicultural education: Issues and perspectives* (3rd ed.). Boston: Allyn & Bacon.

Boutte, G. (1999). *Multicultural education: Raising consciousness*. Belmont, CA: Wadsworth.

Carter, C., Coudrouglou, A., Figueira-McDonough, J., Lie, G. Y., MacEachron, A. E., Netting, F. E., Nichols-Casebolt, A., Nichols, A. W., & Risley-Curtiss, C. (1994). Integrating women's issues in the social work curriculum: A proposal. *Journal of Social Work Education, 30*(2), 200–216.

Chavez, L. (1991). *Out of the barrio: Toward a new politics of Hispanic assimilation*. New York: Basic Books.

Cnaan, R. A., Goodfriend, T., & Newman, E. (1996). Jewish ethnic needs in multicultural social work education. *Journal of Teaching in Social Work, 13*(1/2), 157–174.

Commission on Accreditation. (1992). *Handbook on accreditation standards and procedures*. Alexandria, VA: Council on Social Work Education.

Cramer, E. P. (1995). Feminist pedagogy and teaching social work practice with groups: A case study. *Journal of Teaching in Social Work, 11*(1/2), 193–215.

Cramer, E. P. (1997). Effect of an educational unit about lesbian identity development and disclosure in a social work methods course. *Journal of Social Work Education, 33*(3), 461–472.

Davis, L. V. (1993). Feminism and constructivism: Teaching social work practice with women. *Journal of Teaching in Social Work, 8*(1/2), 147–163.

Fordham, S. (1988). Racelessness as a factor in black students' school success: Pragmatic strategy or pyrrhic victory? *Harvard Educational Review, 58*(1), 54–84.

Gallagher, C. (1995). White reconstruction in the university. *Socialist Review, 24*(1–2), 165–187.

Garcia, B., & Swenson, C. (1992). Writing the stories of white racism. *Journal of Teaching in Social Work, 6*(2), 3–17.

Garcia, B., & Van Soest, D. (1997). Changing perception of diversity and oppression: MSW students discuss the effects of a required course. *Journal of Social Work Education, 33* (1), 119–129.

Germain, C. B. (1994). Human behavior and the social environment. In E. G. Reamer (Ed.), *The foundation of social work knowledge* (pp. 88–121). New York: Columbia University Press.

Germain, C. B., & Gitterman, A. (1996). *The life model of social work practice: Advances in theory and practice* (2nd ed.). New York: Columbia University Press.

Gilligan, C. (1982). *In a different voice: Psychological theory and women's development*. Cambridge: Harvard University Press.

Guadalupe, J. L. (2000). *The challenge: Development of a curriculum to address diversity content without perpetuating stereotypes*. Ann Arbor, MI: UMI Company.

Guadalupe, J. L., & Freeman, M. (1999, Fall). Common human needs in the context of diversity: Integrating schools of thought. *Journal of Cultural Diversity, 6*(3), 85–92.

Guzzetta, C. (1995). White ethnic groups. In R. L. Edwards (Editor-in-Chief), *Encyclopedia of Social Work* (19th ed., pp. 2508–2517). Washington, DC: NASW Press.

Hanh, T. N. (1996). *Being peace*. Berkeley: Parallax Press.

Healey, J. F. (1997). *Race, ethnicity, and gender in the United States: Inequality, group conflict, and power*. Thousand Oaks, CA: Pine Forge Press.

Helms, J. E. (1994). The conceptualization of racial identity and other racial constructs. In E. J. Trickett, R. J. Watts, & D. Birram (Eds.), *Human diversity: Perspective on people in contexts*. San Francisco: Jossey-Bass.

Hooyman, N. R. (1994). Diversity and populations at risk: Women. In E. G. Reamer (Ed.), *The foundation of social work knowledge* (pp. 309–345) New York: Columbia University Press.

Kelley, P. (1995). Integrating narrative approaches into clinical curricula: Addressing diversity through understanding. *Journal of Social Work Education, 31*(3), 347–357.

Kemp, S. P., Whittaker, J. K., & Tracy, E. M. (2002). Contextual social work practice. In M. O'Melia & K. K. Miley (Eds.), *Pathways to power: Readings in contextual social work practice* (pp. 15–34). Boston: Allyn & Bacon.

Kropf, N. P. (1996). Infusing content on older people with developmental disabilities into the curriculum. *Journal of Social Work Education, 32* (2), 215–226.

Laird, J. (1998). Theorizing culture: Narrative ideas and practice principles. In M. McGoldrick (Ed.), *Re-visioning family therapy: Race, culture, and gender in clinical practice* (pp. 20–36). New York: Guilford.

Martinez, E. (2001). Seeing more than Black & White: Latinos, racism, and the cultural divides. In M. L. Andersen & P. H. Collins (Eds.), *Race, class, and gender: An anthology* (4th ed.). Belmont, CA: Wadsworth/Thomson Learning.

McGoldrick, M. (Ed.). (1998). *Re-visioning family therapy: Race, culture, and gender in clinical practice.* New York: Guilford.

Moore, J. W., & Pachon, H. (1985). *Hispanics in the United States.* Englewood Cliffs, NJ: Prentice-Hall.

Morris, J. K. (1993). Interacting oppressions: Teaching social work content on women of color. *Journal of Social Work Education, 29*(1), 99–110.

Newman, B. S. (1994). Diversity and populations at risk: Gays and lesbians. In E. G. Reamer (Ed.), *The foundation of social work knowledge* (pp. 346–392). New York: Columbia University Press.

O'Neil McMahon, M. (1996). *The general method of social work practice: A generalist perspective* (3rd ed.). Needham Heights, MA: Allyn & Bacon.

Pinderhughes, E. (1989). *Understanding race, ethnicity, and power: The key to efficacy in clinical practice.* New York: The Free Press.

Pinderhughes, E. (1994). Diversity and population at risk: Ethnic minorities and people of color. In E. G. Reamer (Ed.), *The foundation of social work knowledge* (pp. 264–308). New York: Columbia University Press.

Powell, R. R., Zehm, S., & Garcia, J. (1996). *Field experience: Strategies for exploring diversity in schools.* Englewood Cliffs, NJ: Merrill.

Ramsey, P. (1979, September). Beyond ten little Indians and turkeys. *Young Children,* pp. 28–32, 49–50.

Reed, B. G., Newman, P. A., Suarez, Z. E., & Lewis, E. A. (1997). Interpersonal practice beyond diversity and toward social justice: The importance of critical consciousness. In C. D. Garvin & B. A. Seabury (Eds.), *Interpersonal practice in social work: Promoting competence and social justice* (pp. 44–77). Boston: Allyn & Bacon.

Rigg, Marlon (producer/director). (1995). "Black Is Black Ain't" (Video.)

Rose, S. M. (1990). Advocacy/empowerment: An approach to clinical practice for social work. *Journal of Sociology and Social Welfare, 17*(2), 41–52.

Sadker, M., Sadker, D., & Long, L. (1997). Gender and educational equality. In J. A. Banks & C. A. M. Banks (Eds.), *Multicultural education: Issues and perspectives* (3rd ed.). Boston: Allyn & Bacon.

Saleebey, D. (1994). Culture, theory and narrative: The intersection of meanings in practice. *Social Work, 39* (4), 351–359.

Saleebey, D. (1996). The strength perspective in social work practice: Extensions and cautions. *Social Work, 41* (3), 296–305.

Schriver, J. M. (2001). *Human behavior and the social environment: Shifting paradigms in essential knowledge for social work practice* (3rd ed.). Needham Heights, MA: Allyn & Bacon.

Soifer, S. (1991). Infusing content about Jews and about anti-Semitism into the curricula. *Journal of Social Work Education, 27*(2), 156–167.

Spencer, M., Lewis, E., & Gutierrez, L. (2000). Multicultural perspectives on direct practice in social work. In P. Allen-Meares & C. Garvin (Eds.), *The handbook of social work direct practice* (pp. 131–149). Thousand Oaks, CA: Sage.

Spickard, P. R. (1992). The illogic of American racial categories. In Maria P. P. Root (Ed.), *Racially mixed people in America.* Newbury Park, CA: Sage.

Sue, D. W. (1981). *Counseling the culturally different: Theory and practice.* New York: Willey-Interscience.

Taylor, J. M., Gilligan, C., & Sullivan, A. M. (1995). *Between voice and silence: Women and girls, race and relationships.* Cambridge: Harvard University Press.

Tice, K. (1990). Gender and social work education: Direction for the 1990s. *Journal of Social Work Education, 26* (2), 134–143.

White, M. (1991). Deconstruction and therapy. *Dulwich Centre Newsletter, 3,* 21–40.

White, M., & Epston, D. (1990). *Narrative means to therapeutic ends.* New York: Norton.

Zavella, P. (1994). Reflections on diversity among Chicanos. In S. Gregory & R. Sanjek (Eds.), *Race* (pp. 199–212). New Brunswick, NJ: Rutgers University Press.

No problem is solved by the same consciousness that created it. —**Albert Einstein**

2 | A Framework for Human Diversity and Transcendence

Countless professional frameworks have been designed as lenses for exploring, addressing, and advocating for thoughtful examination of human diversity, strengths, issues, and needs with the intention of strengthening professional competence (García & Van Soest, 1997; Green, 1999; Locke, 1992; Lum, 2003, 2004; Nakanishi & Rittner, 1992; Pinderhughes, 1979, 1989). Inductive and deductive reasoning has often shaped constructed **frameworks** (empirically and conceptually cultivated approaches designed to arrange paradigms, explain human dynamics and interactions, predict outcomes, guide practices, and evaluate professional assessments and interventions, or a combination of these). *Frameworks* are structures that systematically attempt to organize and arrange the essential parts of a perceived whole so that a person can understand the relationships of various components fitting together in a system. Frameworks, however, can never capture absolute "truth" or sustain unquestionable assumptions of possible perceived "realities." If we look hard enough, each framework reflects strengths and limitations. The multidimensional contextual practice framework presented in this section, also known as A Framework for Human Diversity and Transcendence, is no exception.

FRAMEWORK ORIENTATION

The theoretical orientations giving birth to the multidimensional contextual practice framework presented in this chapter examine what we might call *conventional realities/consciousness* and *transcendent realities/consciousness*. We use these terms to initiate a thought process through which readers can explore different views and interpretations of **reality** (that which is perceived as factual, truthful, accurate, and certain). The multidimensional contextual practice framework supports the notion that total objectivity is an illusion that attempts to promote **conventional realities/consciousness** (the idea that our lives are exclusively influenced by observable cause-and-effect patterns that can always be measured). The notion of total objectivity, as viewed by the multidimensional contextual practice framework, often seeks to control the great unknown reflected through our **transcendent realities/consciousness** (the endless nature of change that provides an opportunity to enter the wisdom of uncertainty). *Conventional realities/consciousness* is based on the idea of concreteness—knowledge, understanding, and expertise constructed to form a baseline of meanings and guidelines. Such concreteness can be useful for guiding **human interactions** (multiple forms through which people come together and relate) and **exchanges** (end results of dynamics emerging through human interactions; a process of give-and-take).

When we exclusively honor conventional realities/consciousness, we have a tendency to perceive such "concreteness" as conclusive evidence regarding the encounters affecting human experiences. In other words, we tend to view observable factors as the only forces shaping human occurrences. This aspect of conventional realities/consciousness is reflected by **conformism** (the act of unquestionably accepting and complying with dominant social and cultural beliefs, values, and norms, regardless of having had experiences that reflect gaps and incompleteness in such conventional realities/consciousness). Within the social/health/human service field, for instance, a leading notion that has traditionally been conveyed and sustained is that human experiences are routinely based on a process of scientific evolution and ongoing human socialization. Maintenance of this paradigm or belief system generally has been perpetuated through educational indoctrination that has minimized or ignored any link to possible spiritual inheritance affecting human experience. The idea that if something cannot be seen, measured, or proven, it does not exist (or is minimized) is symbolic of the characteristics of conventional realities/consciousness. These "realities" seem limited when compared to the vast mystical experiences that are yet to be understood by the human mind.

Transcendent realities/consciousness is based on an active investigation of the notion that people, things, and experiences are more than what they seem. Such transcendence reminds social/health/human service practitioners to both accept and, at the same time, move beyond their major conceptualized senses (i.e., the ability to see, hear, touch, feel, and taste), assumptions, and formed conventional realities/consciousness. Transcendent realities/consciousness is reflected in occurrences that exceed constructed human knowledge, understanding, and expertise—the so-called mystical spiritual experiences. **Mystical spiritual experiences** are encounters that are experienced beyond our senses (often activated through faith; meditation; prayer; spiritual beliefs, practices, and rituals; religious commitment; or any combination of these and other methods). Such encounters are often experienced from a place of inner knowing, from intuition—a sense beyond physical and mental boundaries. Although related to the "mysterious," the "great mystery," and the "Great Unknown," transcendent realities/consciousness is nonetheless often experienced with clarity and certainty beyond human senses and understanding. For instance, numerous stories of these encounters describe people simply knowing something spontaneously: a mother who knows her child is in danger moments before the child is in an accident across town; a person (perhaps a prophet) who accurately describes details of future events yet to come. The knowing is certain; the way of knowing is "mysterious." Such experiences are difficult to articulate through language and cannot be completely defined through mental approaches. These experiences form part of the great mystery—the transcendent realities/consciousness of human existence.

The multidimensional contextual practice framework presented in Figure 2.1 explores both conventional and transcendent realities/consciousness within the context of human diversity, commonalities, challenges, strengths, and complexity.

COMPONENTS OF THE FRAMEWORK

The relationship between multidimensional and contextual bases, the foundation of the Framework for Human Diversity and Transcendence, is one of **interdependence** through which bases influence, are linked to, and rely on one another for increasing effectiveness in purpose, operations, and transactions. These bases are surrounded by borders or edges that have both individual and collective functions. When explored individually, each border or edge has its own boundaries, which illustrates its contextual nature. The ingredients helping to identify and distinguish one border or edge from another are a whole, yet they are also interdependent with other ingredients to create a more holistic merger. Thus, as each border or edge intersects with another, and another, and another, multiple dimensions are formed, reflecting interactions and exchanges of a multidimensional nature. In other words, contextual bases comprise the multidimensional base, and vice versa.

As illustrated by Figure 2.2, the multidimensional and contextual bases are linked and commonly affect one another. No base is superior to another. The circles inside the bases underscore the primary principle of the Framework for Human Diversity and Transcendence: Interactions and exchanges created by the dynamics of individual and collective entities are interdependent, contextual, and yet simultaneously multidimensional. Individuals are able to function competently in specific and diverse contexts (e.g., school or work, family, neighborhood, community), yet they also possess multidimensional characteristics (e.g., ethnicity, gender, social class, etc.) that are affected by micro-intrapersonal, meso-interpersonal, macro-environmental, and magna-spiritual interactions and exchanges. (The term **magna** is used here to explain the great and encompassing nature of the spiritual. The word, which comes from the Latin word *magnus* meaning *great,* is used as an extension of the micro, meso, and macro dimensions traditionally focused on.) The intention of this framework is to promote a shift in paradigm from the dominant either/or categories (e.g., White versus non-White, powerlessness versus empowerment) that have predominated in the literature to an inclusive approach that recognizes multiple factors when addressing human diversity within and between groups of people.

FRAMEWORK PRACTICE PRINCIPLES

The multidimensional practice framework is supported by five major principles: (1) client well-being principle; (2) the multidimensional contextual client principle; (3) the micro, meso, macro, and magna principle; (4) the professional competence

Figure 2.1 | Multidimensional Contextual Practice: A Framework for Human Diversity and Transcendence

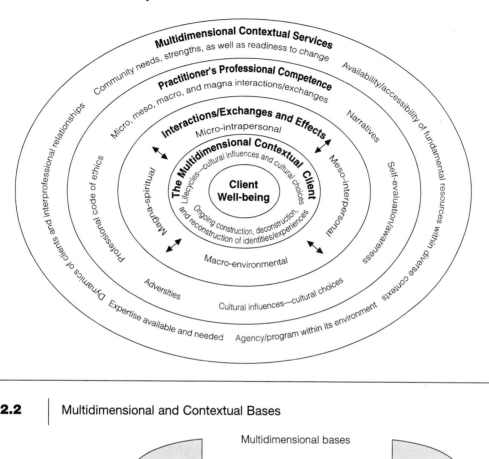

Figure 2.2 | Multidimensional and Contextual Bases

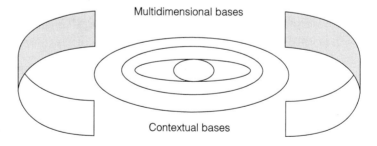

principle; and (5) the multidimensional contextual service principle. These principles are interrelated and interactive with each other. At the core of the Framework for Human Diversity and Transcendence is the concept of client well-being. This is the essential focus in how the authors of this text view and approach people. Using this orientation, we approach the multidimensional contextual client with recognition that the client, as an entity, is comprised of many parts that must be understood in relation to each other. We also speak about interactions and exchanges among and between micro-intrapersonal, meso-interpersonal, macro-environmental, and magna-spiritual dimensions—or multidimensionality. Finally, we are concerned about the social/health/human service practitioner's professional competence in mobilizing multidimensional contextual services on behalf of the client. The following sections explore these principles in more detail.

The Client Well-Being Principle

Client's well-being is perceived as the primary integrative theme, which focuses on the positive healthy functioning of the person, family, group, organization, and community.

As shown by the diagram in Figure 2.1, client well-being is placed in the center of the Framework for Human Diversity and Transcendence. In the diagram, the client is surrounded by a second circle that expands the principle of client well-being by viewing the client as a multidimensional contextual entity. Figure 2.1 illustrates the interactions and exchanges that occur between intrapersonal, interpersonal, environmental, and spiritual dimensions (third circle from the center), the importance of the practitioner's professional competence (fourth circle from the center), and the significance of multidimensional contextual services (largest circle in the diagram). An exploration of these dimensions can serve as a mechanism for identifying barriers that injure or promote clients' well-being.

Although an exploration of client well-being must take into account the areas just discussed, other related factors also significantly affect the well-being of the client. These include: **time** (individual and social perception of space as a continuum, with a past, present, and future; time is seen as either an interval between these or as cyclical, with no beginning or end); **human diversity, interactions and exchanges** (the point at which people differ, relate, and influence one another); **adversities** (encounters that create afflictions, difficulties, and crises, but which can be transformed into opportunities and growth); **client resilience** (the ability to respond to challenging situations); and **essence** (the fundamental and indispensable esoteric life-giving force that is constantly present and supports human endurance). The following text explores these notions of time, human diversity, adversity, client resilience, and essence in more detail, and demonstrates how each relates to client well-being.

While finding ways of strengthening client well-being, the multidimensional contextual practice framework explores, and makes every effort to understand, individual and collective interpretations of events occurring in **time as a continuum**. It embraces individual and collective narratives and life stories. It aims to identify how such interpretations affect the client in contextual and multidimensional surroundings. In considering individual and collective narratives, it separates *facts* (data, events, and experiences that are considered to be objectively verifiable) from stereotypical perceptions. For instance, racist, sexist, homophobic, and economic discriminative forces have been encountered by diverse groups of people throughout U.S. history, yet dominant paradigms and norms embraced in an era can provide individual and collective strength and resources, given a set of social, cultural, and economic conditions and movements promoting change.

Not all individuals, however, perceive time as a continuum (i.e., with a past, present, and future). As a continuum, time provides an opportunity to explore historical events affecting the present that might have possible future implications (e.g., the effect of slavery on current interactions within and between groups of people and possible effects in future generations). But as previously emphasized, there are many ways of knowing, thinking, believing, feeling, behaving, and being—and such variations also exist in the experience of time. In order to understand, reinforce, and strengthen client well-being, the social/health/human service practitioner needs to explore the client's perception of time.

The idea of **time as an interval** reminds practitioners that clients may perceive and respond to encounters from a point of reference influenced by one or more significant experiences that occurred in a particular period (e.g., historical and institutional experiences such as slavery or the Great Depression; personal debilitating events such as the death of a loved one or the emergence of a disability; etc). The concept of **time as cyclical** recognizes that some clients may perceive time as nonlinear (having no beginning or end). In this view, time is a circle that is open for multiple interpretations and exists only because of our need to create a structural baseline to guide our interactions. This notion of time is reflected in the medicine wheel, which has no beginning and no end—it is boundless, ageless, and eternal. In his book, *Many Lives, Many Masters,* Weiss (1988) discusses the idea that individuals live multiple lives (in our physical forms and through our spiritual boundless nature) simultaneously. He explores the notion of reincarnation, which emphasizes that after physical death, the **soul** (the immortal part of each person) reappears in another or different bodily form, making time endless.

Another goal of the multidimensional contextual practice framework is to explore the themes in the literature on human diversity in order to identify which of them injure, and which promote, client well-being. The following are some dominant themes we identified through a content analysis of the current literature:

- Dominant groups have been born as a result of experiences of privilege, control of means for survival, and physical, social, cultural, and other factors—or a combination of these, while subdominant groups have emerged as a result of a lack of, or only minimal, encounters with these elements (Healey, 1997; Jansson, 2001). This theme has been explored predominately through an examination of interactions and exchanges between different ethnic groups and when addressing relationships between women and men, but only fragmentally within group membership.

- The power held by dominant groups has, from time to time, become coercive, promoting various forms of injustice and the use of oppressive forces to protect and perpetuate the groups' own interests and visions (Freire, 1973; Germain & Gitterman, 1996; Jansson, 2001; Wambach & Van Soest, 1997). Again, this topic has been explored predominately through an examination of interactions and exchanges between different ethnic groups and when addressing relationships between women and men, but only fragmentally within group membership.

- Formal and informal movements have been formed or have re-emerged with the intention of promoting social justice or reinforcing the status quo (Banks & Banks, 1997; Jansson, 2001).
- Content on human diversity seems to consistently be explored through either/or and linear categories, in which diverse individuals, families, groups, and communities are often surveyed within the context of dominant paradigms (Andersen & Collins, 2001; Germain, 1994; Green, 1999; Schriver 2001). For instance, experiences of privilege, oppression, empowerment, and resilience are often viewed through a one-dimensional lens, where nondominant groups are compared to those perceived as dominant (e.g., Whites against non-Whites), thus fragmenting, minimizing, or omitting these experiences within group membership (Martinez, 2001).
- Stereotypes are perpetuated through overgeneralization of commonalities and differences within or between diverse groups of people to the point that such simplification tends to neglect uniqueness (Guadalupe, 2000).
- The idea of objectivity, when exploring human diversity, seems to promote the notion that the "inseparable" (i.e., a higher universal intelligence guiding or promoting human change) can be separated. This is reflected by the often-exclusive focus on contextual observable dynamics and conventional realities/consciousness, minimizing or ignoring transcendent realities/consciousness.
- When exploring human diversity, one may not neglect the many ways of knowing, feeling, believing, thinking, behaving, and being (Hartman, 1990, 1991, 1994; Laird, 1998; Pozatek, 1994; Saleebey, 1994).

Some of these themes from the current human diversity literature seem to encourage an ongoing, evolutionary development of understanding of human diversity, and of its dynamics and complexities, while others seem too rigid or detrimental to promote well-being. The multidimensional contextual practice framework, by identifying which themes may injure and which may promote clients' well-being, advocates for a paradigm shift. Instead of examining dominant and subdominant groups exclusively from a White and non-White paradigm, or men and women model, the multidimensional contextual practice framework encourages an exploration that includes the dynamics of oppression, privilege, empowerment, and resilience within group membership (diversity within diversity) as well. This idea has multiple purposes:

- Examining diversity within diversity to generate a more holistic understanding of the nature, complexity, and dynamics of privilege, internalized and socially/culturally expressed forms of oppression, ethnocentrism, and power, and the struggle to obtain means of survival by reflecting that there are multiple ways of knowing, responding, and being (Zavella, 1994)
- Examining coercive power and its effects within contextual and multidimensional dimensions of interactions and exchanges within and between groups of people
- Moving beyond traditional either/or and linear categories of surveying human diversity and its complexities in order to better understand multiple ways of knowing, believing, thinking, feeling, behaving, and being
- Minimizing the possibility for perpetuation of stereotypes through general categorization that neglects uniqueness

- Exploring human essence and resilience within and between individuals and groups of people

The Framework for Human Diversity and Transcendence presented in Figure 2.1 supports the principle that a one-dimensional or monodimensional approach to human diversity often becomes fragmented in its analysis. For instance, the White versus Black or non-White paradigm is one-dimensional. It organizes multiple and diverse groups of people into overwhelmingly large categories (Whites and non-Whites, Whites and People of Color, Whites and Blacks, dominant and subdominant) with the intention of analyzing group interactions and exchanges as well as developing intervention strategies. Either/or categories injure client well-being through stereotypes, stigmatizations, and marginalization of imperative attributes. Andersen and Collins (2001) write:

> White women, for example, may be disadvantaged because of gender, but privileged by race and perhaps (but not necessarily) by class. . . . For that matter, White Americans do not fit in "either/or" categories—either oppressor or oppressed. Isolating White Americans as if their experience stands alone ignores how White experience is intertwined with that of other groups. . . . Race, class, and gender are manifested differently, depending on their configuration with the others. . . . One might say Black men are privileged as men, [but] this [may] make[] no sense when their race and gender and class are taken into account. Otherwise, how can we possibly explain the particular disadvantages African American men experience as men—in the criminal justice system, in education, and in the labor market? For that matter, how can we explain the experience that Native American women experience as Native American women—disadvantaged by the unique experiences that they have based on race, class, and gender—none of which is isolated from the effects of the others? (p. 5)

With the ongoing significant changes taking place in world demographics, individuals often experience connections across group memberships—a phenomenon that is minimized or omitted by the White/Black or White/non-White approach. The Framework for Human Diversity and Transcendence aims to reduce the victimization of individuals, groups, families, and communities that has been promoted by views through stereotypical lenses in the name of good intention.

When attempting to move beyond stereotypical notions, we must be careful not to neglect commonalities within and between groups of people. For instance, although men from diverse White ethnic groups have experienced different degrees of social and cultural privilege in the U.S. socioeconomic political system, an examination of history reveals that all U.S. presidents have been "White European publically identified heterosexual males." This social fact does not seem to have occurred by accident. Although the U.S. Declaration of Independence stresses that "all men are created equal" (women are not recognized by this declaration), that statement seems to have been associated historically with a specific kind of man with certain qualifications. Some of the commonalities that all U.S. presidents have shared include:

- Establishment and perpetuation of a patriarchal system (a male-dominated societal model that reinforces an ongoing power struggle between and within the sexes)

- General glorification of "whiteness" or light skin color over dark skin color, strengthened and reinforced by dominant mainstream cultural norms
- General glorification of heterosexuality over any other sexual orientation, supported and perpetuated by dominant mainstream cultural norms, as well as power and control of social means in the hands of an elitist group

It is not surprising that from the time of slavery to current times, large numbers of men from non-White ethnic groups have engaged in social-political activism to voice their concerns regarding lack of equal legal treatment. Women, too, have voiced civil rights concerns through the women's movements in the 1800s and during the 1960s and 1970s. Legislation such as the Civil Rights Act, initially established in 1964, is a testament to some of the achievements of such social-political activists. The term **social-political activism** is seen as identification and exploration of, along with active determination to promote change in, all cognitive, cultural, political, and religious/spiritual beliefs and actions that injure people's well-being.

As emphasized within the literature on human diversity, *adversities* (encounters and procedures that create afflictions, difficulties, and crises that can often be transformed into opportunities and growth) are common denominators in the human experience. Pain, afflictions, grief, and loss seem to be inevitable (Guadalupe & Pagán, 1997; Walsh, 1998b). Furthermore, different types of adversities and encounters with adversity within diverse contexts shape the magnitude of pain, affliction, and other effects. Some adversities are natural ingredients of human existence (e.g., the natural death of a loved one and the stressors generated through change and new experiences, such as formation of a family, making new friends, giving birth to or adopting a child, moving to a new geographic location, etc.). Some adversities seem to be influenced by the mystical or involve the unexpected (e.g., the death of a loved one caused by a car accident or murder). Still other adversities are constructed through human interpretations, interactions, and exchanges (and may involve cultivated oppressive forces such as individual, institutional, and cultural discrimination based on age, sexual orientation, racial or ethnic background, socioeconomic status, religious and spiritual practices, gender, degree of physical and mental abilities, or a combination of these). The multidimensional contextual practice framework emphasizes that natural and mystical/unexpected adversities are, more often than not, inevitable, whereas constructed human adversities can be prevented or changed through assessment and intervention at the intrapersonal, interpersonal, environmental, and spiritual dimensions. Counseling and therapeutic services, educational community programs, social-political activism, as well as an active commitment to self-discovery and transformation are four strategies useful for promoting change.

Responses to adversities vary from person to person and from community to community, although common threads can be identified. Responses to adversities are influenced by multiple variables such as previous encounters and the results of them, supportive relationships, time, contexts, cultivated perceptions regarding the adversities, intention, sense of direction/control/empowerment, self-determination, persistence, and assertiveness. They also can be influenced by spiritual and religious practices, resilience and inner strengths, a sense of the collective, accessibility and availability of needed resources, and social action movements (Andrews, Guadalupe, & Bolden, 2003; Guadalupe & Bein, 2001; Saleebey, 2002; Walsh, 1998b). Our responses to adversities can strengthen or weaken our well-being. Multidimensional contextual practice supports the simultaneous exploration of mechanisms for preventing or directly confronting human adversities at the micro, meso, macro, and magna levels.

While exploring the nature of human adversity and strategies for alleviating and transforming human pain, the multidimensional contextual practice framework recognizes the importance and interconnectedness of *human resilience* and *essence*. These ingredients are vital to the process of human interactions and exchanges. *Resilience* is the manifestation of the innate essence enacted through supported relationships and availability of and accessibility to resources that promote an ability to maintain or regain a level of control, intention, and direction before, during, or after an encounter with adversity. *Essence* is the constantly present, fundamental and indispensable, esoteric life-giving force that supports human endurance. The multidimensional contextual practice framework is influenced by the belief that individuals, families, groups, and communities have basic physical, mental, cognitive, social, spiritual, and potentially esoteric life-giving forces that often strengthen their endurance. A metaphor to help us better understand this conceptualization of the relationship between essence and resilience is the following: Essence exists within the seed (the human being) and is activated through the care given by soil, water, and sun (supportive factors), manifesting the flower (resilience). The relationship between resilience and essence, then, can be understood as one of nature and nurture.

Many illustrations of individual and collective human resilience and essence can be found throughout history. Large numbers of First Nations Peoples have confronted colonialism (see Chapter 12) and still remained loyal to their principles of living. During the time of slavery, many slaves escaped to the North, seeking freedom. Likewise, people living with disabilities often have demonstrated the power of the human spirit through their ability to live life to its fullest regardless of what some may perceive as "limitations."

Resilience has been viewed as "an active process of endurance" (Walsh, 1998b, p. 4) that enables individuals, families, groups, and communities to withstand and recover from difficult individual and social challenges. We support Walsh's conceptualization, which emphasizes that resilience involves more than simply surviving harsh conditions, times, and experiences. Walsh stresses that "the qualities of resilience enable people to heal from painful wounds" (p. 4), and thus transcend a position of victimization blinded by dissolution, anger, guilt, or blame.

The Framework for Human Diversity and Transcendence supports an exploration of resilience as the manifestation of human essence when exploring adversities potentially affecting individual, family, group, and community well-being. As demonstrated by a number of empirical studies (Felsman & Vaillant, 1987; Garbarino, 1997; Garmezy, 1991; Wolin & Wolin, 1993), resilience has an impact on people's ability to confront and heal from adversities generated by social conditions such as poverty, oppressive forces, community violence, and substance abuse, as well as other challenging life encounters. Furthermore, resilience research has identified a variety of qualities inherent in resilient dispositions. The following resilient traits and dispositions have been identified as being likely to increase successful coping for those facing adversities: a well-built and solid sense of self-esteem, self-efficacy, and self-direction (Rutter, 1985); a feeling of confidence or faith that challenges confronted will be transformed; a sense of control and protective factors (Werner 1993); and an "optimistic bias" and persistent attitude (Murphy, 1987). Although these and other traits are important to consider, one must be careful not to engage in absolute thinking. Resilience cannot be forced. Instead, human service practitioners can facilitate the process through which people develop and strengthen their own endurance.

As stated previously, the multidimensional contextual practice framework makes client well-being the primary focus of professional assessment and intervention. When individuals, families, groups, and communities put their trust in our professional hands and cultivated "expertise," we must not betray their trust by neglecting our responsibilities, which include moving beyond stereotypical paradigms and approaches that are likely to injure our working relationship with clients.

Read and answer the questions related to client well-being in Reflection Exercise 2.1, which relates well-being to various dimensions of one's life. As you answer the questions, ask yourself how the exercise is heightening and enhancing your own sense of well-being, and how you can become more sensitive to the well-being of others.

The Multidimensional Contextual Client Principle

Individuals, families, groups, and communities are multi-dimensional contextual living entities which are constantly changing and interacting with each other so that we must reconstruct our understandings of situations in order to determine which entities influence a helping situation at any given time.

In Figure 2.1, the second circle from the center identifies experiences encountered through life cycles and dynamics, promoted by an intersectional flow of interactions between cultural influences and cultural choices. These experiences seem to promote an ongoing process of construction, deconstruction, and reconstruction of identities affecting life experiences. Perceptions of **self**—often influenced by nonstatic interactions and exchanges between the "I," or current identifications, and the "You," or perceptions of others—appear to be constantly changing, thus affecting mechanisms needed to support self-direction. In other words, what is needed to strengthen our sense of self and self-direction is likely to differ from context to context or from one experience to another. The process of construction, deconstruction, and reconstruction of identities affecting our life experiences and manifested throughout our life course seems to be cyclical, as reflected by Figure 2.3. Each of the circles is symbolic of a unique experience, and at the same time is influenced through interactions and exchanges occurring among and between one another.

The **construction of self-identity** and experiences is influenced by direct and indirect encounters with preexisting environments and occurrences in the process of becoming. For instance, children are born into preexisting family and cultural values, beliefs and norms, religious and spiritual principles, social conditions, and socioeconomic and political systems. Children's initial social perceptions of the "separated self," the "I" as opposed to the "us" or "oneness," seems to be influenced by encounters with the aforementioned occurrences. Changes, however, are constantly occurring within the multidimensional and contextual arenas of culture, religious and

2.1 | Reflection Exercise

Ask yourself the following questions. Once your responses have been generated, take a moment to reflect on the interdependence between dimensions of well-being identified in this diagram and review the principle of prioritizing individual and collective well-being.

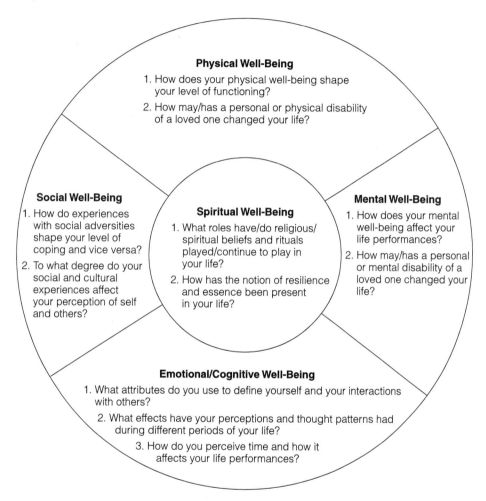

Physical Well-Being
1. How does your physical well-being shape your level of functioning?
2. How may/has a personal or physical disability of a loved one changed your life?

Social Well-Being
1. How do experiences with social adversities shape your level of coping and vice versa?
2. To what degree do your social and cultural experiences affect your perception of self and others?

Spiritual Well-Being
1. What roles have/do religious/spiritual beliefs and rituals played/continue to play in your life?
2. How has the notion of resilience and essence been present in your life?

Mental Well-Being
1. How does your mental well-being affect your life performances?
2. How may/has a personal or mental disability of a loved one changed your life?

Emotional/Cognitive Well-Being
1. What attributes do you use to define yourself and your interactions with others?
2. What effects have your perceptions and thought patterns had during different periods of your life?
3. How do you perceive time and how it affects your life performances?

spiritual experiences, and social, socioeconomic, and political systems. As children grow and engage in changes, social self-identification is likely to be expanded and transformed. The roles that are developed and embraced throughout the life course (e.g., student, worker, parent, partner, etc.) can and often do influence the emergence of **simultaneous multiple identities**. The idea of simultaneous multiple identities can be illustrated by the metaphor of a "house with multiple rooms." The house is symbolic of the overall mind/psyche frame, and the rooms represent multiple yet interdependent ways of perceiving self.

Figure 2.3 | Construction, Deconstruction, and Reconstruction of Perception of Self

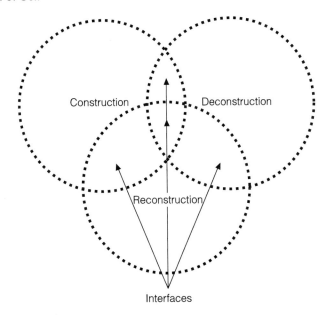

Interfaces

Deconstruction of self-identity and experiences occurs through a conscious critical examination or a nonintended process (an unplanned happening). This process can be affected by physical, mental, emotional, and spiritual experiences. The process of deconstruction of self-identity is likely to be activated through a crisis that brings awareness of a need for change or a cultivated awareness that current values, beliefs, cognitive patterns of relating to self or others, and behaviors are inconsistent or harmful within the context of unfolding experiences. Some of the experiences that are common during this process of the deconstruction of self-identity include: conscious and/or unconscious resistance to the newness presented by the unfolding encounters, fear of the unknown, behaviors reflecting immediate-gratification attitudes, and self-determination to mindfully face possible degrees of vulnerability and stressors. The process of deconstruction of self-identity and experiences can be illustrated simply by our life reviews. When we look back on our lives, we are likely to notice that the way we define ourselves has changed at various turning points. Thus, self-identity is subject to change throughout our life span.

Reconstruction of self-identity and experiences can arise from either a conscious determination to change or an unintentional process through which new ways of perceiving the self are cultivated and established. Through interactions between cultural influences and cultural choices occurring throughout the life course, individuals and communities encounter experiences and options; sometimes these are noticeable, while at other times they are uncertain. Such experiences and options stimulate the process for reconstruction of self-identity. In order for human service practitioners to support overall client well-being, they must understand the probable dynamics emerging through interactions and exchanges between construction, deconstruction, and reconstruction of self-identity. The dimensions of change presented by processes activated by the construction, deconstruction, and reconstruction of self-identity are a reminder to human service practitioners that client needs are likely to differ from context to context and from one experience to another.

Multiple factors affect the client as a multidimensional contextual entity. These include both individual (e.g., age, gender, physical and mental abilities) and collective (e.g., culture, political and economic system) factors (see Figure 2.4). Such factors are contextual and multidimensional by nature. Although some of these human attributes may be prioritized from one context to another, no single attribute accounts for a client's entire life experiences (Andersen & Collins, 2001; Laird, 1998). For instance, although ethnicity, gender, and sexual orientation often play major roles in clients' lives, these human characteristics cannot stand alone. Clients are simultaneously influenced by other equally important factors such as age, socioeconomic status, degree of physical and mental abilities, and spiritual and religious practices, to mention a few. Furthermore, client encounters with multiple human attributes influence client **multiple identities** (a variety of ways through which the "self" is perceived and defined). Examples of client multiple identities might be a First Nations middle-age woman from a middle-class economic background who practices Buddhism and identifies herself as a lesbian living with a physical disability, and a White man living with a mental disability who comes from a low socioeconomic background and identifies himself as a heterosexual.

The experience of multiple attributes allows us, as human beings, to perform competently in different contexts. In doing so, we engage in what has been called, in the educational setting, **code switching.** Our ability to participate in different communication procedures, behavioral patterns, and boundaries is an illustration of how we engage differently in our various relationships, depending on contexts, formal and informal norms, degrees of intimacy, and the type and function of each relationship. Code switching is also reflected through our capacity to communicate the same message to different people using distinctive communication styles, techniques, and languages. The multidimensional contextual practice framework aims at assisting social/health/human service practitioners to approach the client as being in simultaneous interactions and exchanges within surroundings that are both contextual (e.g., cycle of family members, friends, coworkers, etc.) and multidimensional (e.g., neighborhoods, communities, societies, socioeconomic and political systems, nationalities, the spiritual realm, etc.).

Individuals, families, groups, communities, and nations can share physical, regional, social, cultural, political, and spiritual commonalities, and yet no two ever experience these commonalities in the same way. China and Cuba are considered to be communist or socialist countries, and yet, because of differences in raw materials, social and cultural orientations, political movements, international relationships, and interpretations of paradigms, among other factors, each country has experienced communism or socialism differently. Just as one house often has multiple rooms, so may family members living under the same roof have different personalities, experiences, and interpretations.

Another assumption on which the Framework for Human Diversity and Transcendence is based is that the exploration of possible commonalities between clients should not be a justification for omitting an individualized assessment of

Figure 2.4   Factors Influencing Clients' Identities and Life Experiences

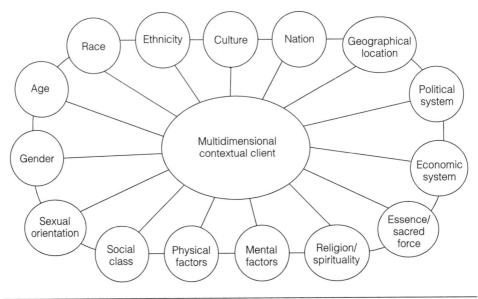

strengths and challenges encountered by clients. As mentioned earlier, stereotypes are likely to promote disempowerment. The Framework for Human Diversity and Transcendence, therefore, advocates for the reduction or, if possible, elimination of stereotypes through a focus on assessment that explores commonalities, uniqueness, and complexities among and between the clients being served. This principle is supported by the assumption that *an exclusive focus on collective or group commonalities while ignoring individual narrative and uniqueness is likely to promote and perpetuate oppression in the name of the collective.* Likewise, "ignoring collective experiences through exclusive focus on the individual narrative does not encourage a sense of community or personalization of social responsibility; that is, the collective consciousness needed to promote cooperative action to resist and modify oppressive forces such as sexism, racism, classism, ageism, and homophobia, among others" (Guadalupe, 2003, p. 27). See Reflection Exercise 2.2, which offers you an opportunity to think more about the ideas discussed in this section.

The Micro, Meso, Macro, and Magna Principle

Client well-being affects and is affected by micro-intrapersonal, meso-interpersonal, macro-environmental, and magna-spiritual interactions and exchanges, which need to be identified and mobilized in order to address interrelated issues.

In Figure 2.1, client well-being is placed in the heart of the diagram. The multidimensional contextual client is indicated by the second circle of the diagram, which is surrounded by a third circle illustrating the micro, meso, macro, and magna interac-

2.2 | **Reflection Exercise**

Take a moment to ask yourself the following questions, keeping in mind the notion that individuals, groups, families, and communities are multidimensional contextual entities that are constantly changing.

- What factors influence your current definition of self? Do you remember ever viewing yourself differently? If so, what influenced the change and what was the process like?

- Do you consider the factors that help define the ways you perceive yourself to be contextual, multidimensional, a combination of these, or none of the above? Explain.

- How is the notion of "code switching" reflected in your interactions with others? How has the experience of code switching been affected by factors that help define how you perceive yourself?

- Do you relate to the notion of "multiple identities"? If affirmative, explain how.

---

tions and exchanges that can affect and be affected by the client's formation, maintenance, and transformation of individual and collective identities and experiences. These interactions and exchanges are contextual and multidimensional by nature, and are interrelated. For instance, the multidimensional and contextual basis of *spirituality* is demonstrated in the variety of ways in which this experience has been defined. Joseph (1987), for example, defines **spirituality** as "the underlying dimension of consciousness which strives for meaning, union with the universe, and with all things; it extends to the experience of the transcendent or a power beyond us" (p. 14). Canda (1990) conceptualizes spirituality as "the gestalt of the total process of human life and development, encompassing biological, mental, social, and spiritual aspects. It is not reducible to any of these components; rather, it is wholeness of what it is to be human" (p. 13). Beckett and Johnson (1995) perceive spirituality as "the views and behaviors that express a sense of relatedness to something greater than the self; spirituality connotes transcendence or a level of awareness that exceeds ordinary physical and spatial boundaries" (p. 1393). Faiver, Ingersoll, O'Brien, and McNally (2001) wrote:

> Spirituality may be described as a deep sense of wholeness, connectedness, and openness to the infinite. . . . We believe spirituality is an innate human quality. Not only is it our vital life force, but at the same time it is also our experience of the vital life force. Although this life force is deeply part of us, it also transcends us. It is what connects us to other people, nature, and the source of life. The experience of spirituality is greater than ourselves and helps us transcend and embrace life situations. (p. 2)

Although each of these definitions of spirituality is unique, a common thread can be derived from them: Spirituality involves a supreme life force that embraces, and yet transcends, human experience. Spirituality is not based on dogma or indoctrinations. It can be individually or collectively embraced through a commitment to and active engagement in **mystical and religious rituals** (ongoing practices such as prayer, attending religious ceremonies, meditation, and the use of mantras) intended to connect or maintain a relationship with the "divine." We cannot emphasize enough that language is limited by its own boundaries. Thus, *the definitions and concepts regarding magna-spirituality do not speak of its totality, but provide only glimpses of understanding.*

Along with the magna-spiritual, we must also be aware of the macro-environmental, meso-interpersonal, and micro-intrapersonal interactions and exchanges. For instance, in terms of geographical environment, the United States forms part of one of the continents on the planet earth. The United States is currently composed of fifty states. Each state is made up of a number of cities, and each city consists of a number of communities and neighborhoods. Each of these units is organized by many environmental factors, including physical settings (e.g., constructed structures such as natural parks), economic and political atmospheres (e.g., living conditions, formal written policies, informal undocumented norms), and social surroundings (e.g., interactions with others and with operating systems). Although each dimension is comprehensive within itself, it is not independent from the others. The September 11, 2001, "terrorist attack," for example, served as a reminder that what we in the United States often call "foreign policy" is not so "foreign" after all.

The interpersonal pertains to dynamics generated through human relationships, interactions, and exchanges. Since "we take ourselves everywhere we go," our relationships at work, at school, and with our family systems, relatives, friends, organizations, and communities are likely to be directly or indirectly affected by one another. Just as every single cell in a body has within it the sum of the whole, and yet is part of a bigger arrangement, so a person—who can be considered a whole entity with body, mind, and spirit—is yet a component of larger arrangements: family, neighborhood, community, nation, and so on.

While identifying and exploring human diversity, strengths, and challenges, the Framework for Human Diversity and Transcendence does not view the relationship between spiritual, environmental, interpersonal, and intrapersonal factors through a progressive lens—that is, as a linear relationship. Instead, the framework views the dynamics created by interactions and exchanges involving these dimensions as transactional and ever-changing. As shown in Figure 2.5, these dimensions interface at various points. The Framework for Human Diversity and Transcendence encourages exploration of the interfaces between these dimensions and their effects on client well-being.

The **magna-spiritual interaction and exchange factors** relate to personal beliefs about a Higher Power, a Great Creator, a Higher Intelligence, the Divine Imagination, a Universal Force, or God (terms used in different contexts that reflect diverse interpretations of a supreme life force). The factors of magna-spirituality are reflected by the relationship that may exist between spirituality and religious practices. Although a relationship often exists between spirituality and religiosity, each of these entities has unique attributes (Guadalupe & Torres, 2001). Walsh (1998a) stresses that spirituality is generally composed of personal ingredients of **faith** (an intuitive trust in something or someone that sustains hope, but which is not necessarily based on logical proven evidence), while religiosity is, by and large, a collective interpretation of faith. According to Canda (1997), "religion involves the patterning of spiritual beliefs and practices into social institutions, with community support and traditions maintained over time" (p. 173). Religion can be viewed as a constructed "social phenomenon" shaped by factors such as **myths** (stories sustaining a collective belief system), **rites** (religious ceremonies), **culture** (collective beliefs, values, and norms), and a system of **symbols** (language, codes, regulations). Although religion can be a "social vehicle to nurture and express spirituality" (Faiver et al., 2001, p. 2), spirituality can be cherished independently from religious institutionalized ideologies.

Figure 2.5 | Micro, Meso, Macro, and Magna Interactions and Exchanges

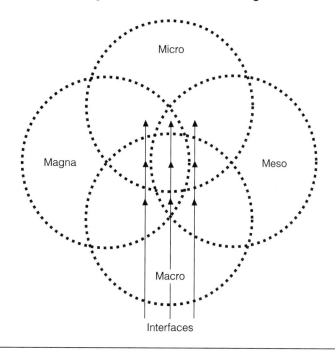

Magna-spiritual interaction and exchange factors may be experienced through participation in a particular church, synagogue, or mosque, which teaches spiritual and religious principles through texts such as the Bible, Torah, or Koran. Individual worshippers come together in gatherings and often influence each other in terms of their demonstrations of faith. Others may discover spirituality through nature and the universe, prayer, meditation, chanting, or an experience of a "higher power" or "transcending force." Spiritual practices are both individually and group based and may involve indigenous cultural beliefs and practices. In our own ways, we are often influenced by spiritual experiences, which can provide a more holistic framework, a deeper meaning.

Among the most noticeable **macro-environmental interaction and exchange factors** are the following: community, neighborhood, and hometown (residence); school and work (education and employment); goods and services (life-sustaining factors); social organizations and group experiences (social interaction); community building and renewal (community growth); and international relationships (world). These environmental interactions and exchanges are interrelated, and when seen within their interconnectedness, a multidimensional perspective can be cultivated. The loss of a job, for example, can have a detrimental effect on community growth trends if it means that the family is forced to move from their neighborhood community, that they are unable to afford basic services and groceries, and that the children must drop out of school.

The **meso-interpersonal interaction and exchange factors** revolve largely around family, friends, acquaintances, social groups, and persons in our school, work, church, and community spheres. Among the interpersonal factors are parent-child/sibling interaction (family bond), the husband-wife or partner relationship (spousal or intimate partnership), grandparents and relatives (extended family), significant others (friendships), employer-employee and business transactions (work relations), and religious congregation and spiritual counselor relationships (spiritual and religious resources). These primary relationships are often the focal point for personal concerns, joys, and challenges in our lives. The interpersonal context is the daily life narrative journey, which often affects how a person, family, group, or community feels and copes on the intrapersonal and environmental levels, and vice versa. Again, when the interdependence of these contexts is recognized, the multidimensional component can be embraced. For instance, a disturbance within the work relation context through loss of a job or ineffective communication with the employer is likely to affect the family bond due to possible stress levels caused by economic needs or lack of job satisfaction.

Among the **micro-intrapersonal interaction and exchange factors** are the following: age of the person (life span); perceptions, emotions, and thoughts (cognitive); gender and sexual orientation (generatic or sexual); social and economic status; self-identity (social, cultural, ethnic and racial, national, etc.); physical and mental abilities; spirituality and religious orientations; self-worth (selfhood); and resiliency/essence (relational/mystical). The attributes identified in these instances, as well as spiritual, environmental, and interpersonal factors, are not mutually exclusive. Attributes are likely to fit across categories, operate on a continuum, and be interconnected, as well as constantly changing in focus and importance. One or more interaction and exchange factors may be paramount and may dominate as a crucial factor for understanding the person; however, there may be rapid shifts as the person interacts in the helping process.

Reflection Exercise 2.3 will help you to apply the content addressed in this section. As you answer the questions in the exercise, think about how there are crossovers and interfaces in the micro-intrapersonal, meso-interpersonal, macro-environmental, and magna-spiritual dimensions.

The Professional Competence Principle

The social/health/human services practitioner's professional competence is strengthened through ongoing self-awareness and self-evaluation, assessment, a continuum of contact and intervention, as well as primary, secondary, and tertiary interconnections.

As reflected in Figure 2.1, practitioners are affected by micro-intrapersonal, meso-interpersonal, macro-environmental, and magna-spiritual multidimensional and contextual interactions and exchanges. In looking at professional competence, represented in Figure 2.1 by the fourth circle from the center, the practitioner's individual and collective evolutionary and contextual narrative, ongoing self-evaluation and awareness, cultural influences and cultural choices, experiences with adversities and effects, and professional code of ethics cannot be ignored.

2.3 | Reflection Exercise

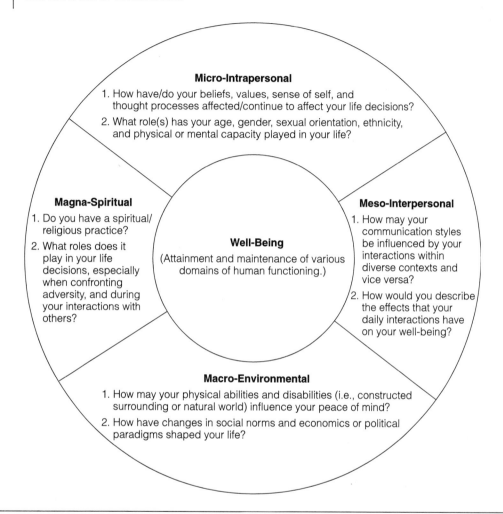

Micro-Intrapersonal
1. How have/do your beliefs, values, sense of self, and thought processes affected/continue to affect your life decisions?
2. What role(s) has your age, gender, sexual orientation, ethnicity, and physical or mental capacity played in your life?

Magna-Spiritual
1. Do you have a spiritual/religious practice?
2. What roles does it play in your life decisions, especially when confronting adversity, and during your interactions with others?

Well-Being
(Attainment and maintenance of various domains of human functioning.)

Meso-Interpersonal
1. How may your communication styles be influenced by your interactions within diverse contexts and vice versa?
2. How would you describe the effects that your daily interactions have on your well-being?

Macro-Environmental
1. How may your physical abilities and disabilities (i.e., constructed surrounding or natural world) influence your peace of mind?
2. How have changes in social norms and economics or political paradigms shaped your life?

The multidimensional contextual practice framework encourages human service practitioners to be directly involved (through both personal contact with diverse clients and relationships with diverse people) and indirectly exposed (through literature, documentaries, etc.) to diverse populations experiencing diverse encounters. The intention of this approach is to broaden individual and collective professional experiences, thus affecting the practitioner's individual and professional life narratives. The framework supports the assumption that it is easier to embrace stereotypical lenses if one is superficially exposed to the same groups of people within similar contexts. An interesting phenomenon about stereotypes is that if one looks hard enough for stereotypical experiences, one will find them, especially when one's professional and personal encounters are influenced by mechanical habits. Imagine a woman who has grown up in a perceived homogeneous community, influenced by the belief that what she has experienced, embraced, or encountered (including sexist, racist, and homophobic feelings) is the norm. Through her college experiences, her familiarity with "normality" may be only minimally challenged or not challenged at all, or perhaps perpetuated. How likely is it that such feelings will affect her behaviors during encounters with diverse populations, especially those toward whom she feels a sense of superiority? Imagine the possible scenarios that could arise in a practice setting. This example shows that in order to consistently acknowledge human diversity, we must constantly, in a conscious manner, acknowledge and move beyond our points of reference, thus providing ourselves with opportunities to either maintain or construct, deconstruct, and reconstruct our narratives through conscious awareness of multiple experiences. The process of construction, deconstruction, and reconstruction of self-identification previously discussed affects human service practitioners as well as clients. Direct conscious engagement in the helping process can make the difference between professional competency and incompetency.

The multidimensional contextual practice framework assumes that human service practitioners will use ongoing professional and personal self-evaluation as one mechanism for strengthening their work competency and self-awareness. **Self-awareness** refers to practitioners' cultivated understanding of how their paradigms, encounters, sense of "normality," and expertise may affect the process of client-worker interactions, exchanges, and success. **Self-evaluation** refers to practitioners' willingness to actively engage in mindful and conscious assessment, examination, review, and modification of their beliefs, assumptions, values, experiences, practices, and skills with the intention of increasing professional effectiveness. Self-awareness and self-evaluation can be perceived as cyclical experiences that are interdependent, as illustrated in Figure 2.6. Ongoing professional self-evaluation with the intention of strengthening self-awareness, and continual self-awareness with the purpose of increasing professional efficiency, therefore, seem to be vital. Such self-awareness and self-evaluation confront the possibility of conflicts that could be generated because of clients' unique experiences and practitioners' inaccurate assumptions influenced by elements such as practitioners' lack of familiarity with encounters clients have experienced, cognitive rigidity, and inflexibility. Self-awareness can be the practitioner's initial step in the process of analyzing and solving such conflicts, while constant self-evaluation can serve as a building block in the search for alternatives and in strengthening competency.

Possible **transference** (a conscious or unconscious process of projection of repressed emotions, desires, or expectations, reflected by either optimistic, encouraging, affirmative messages or harmful, distrustful, judgmental behavioral messages) cannot be ignored, especially within the practitioner's interactions and exchanges with diverse populations. Within a contextual and multidimensional process of human interactions, human service practitioners, like diverse clients, engage in constant dynamics that influence their cultivation of ways of knowing, believing, thinking, feeling, behaving, and being. Such dynamics are subject to **cultural influence** (conscious or unconscious systems of beliefs, values, ways of thinking, and behaving that are perpetuated and reinforced through human encounters) and **cultural choice** (conscious identification and exploration of beliefs, values, and ways of thinking and behaving, followed by a determination to embrace these or to actively engage in con-

Figure 2.6   Self-Awareness and Self-Evaluation Exchange

Self-awareness

Self-evaluation

scious change). In addition to self-awareness and self-evaluation, the Framework for Human Diversity and Transcendence encourages practitioners to also explore the dynamics of cultural influence and cultural choice within their lives and the possible effects these may have within their professional encounters. For instance, imagine how multigenerational family attitudes of prejudice related to ethnic, racial, or sexual orientation that were passed along to an individual who is now a human service practitioner are likely to be activated through the process of transference when he attempts to assist diverse clients about whom such perceptions are held. Exploration of cultural influences can, and often does, provide an opportunity to engage in a discovery of patterns that are no longer valuable, and to make a conscious decision to change (a cultural choice). Internalized, unexplored assumptions, beliefs systems, and prejudiced attitudes regarding diverse individuals and populations are likely to increase the possibility of misunderstanding clients' backgrounds, experiences, and needs, and thus injure one's professional capability to accurately serve the client (Pozatek, 1994).

As mentioned earlier, some forms of human adversities seem inevitable. Through their developmental, contextual, and multiple experiences, human service practitioners, like clients, have encountered adversities. By recognizing the effects of such adversities and their own dispositions toward resilience that assisted them in coping with and recovering from adversities, being aware of unresolved issues and unhealed wounds, and actively dealing with current emotions, behaviors, and experiences, human service practitioners can provide themselves with a constant reminder of the need for sensitivity during the provision of social/health/human services. Awareness of personal challenges and strengths in confronting one's own unhealed wounds, which block one's capacity to freely relate to others, can assist human service practitioners in their process of understanding the complexity of healing. It can also help them to see themselves as fallible, but with the potential to confront adversity. The professional and personal experiences of the authors of this text support the idea that self-awareness and self-evaluation are vital ingredients for human service practitioners when they work with others.

An anthropological principle emphasizes that learning about others activates learning about self, and vice versa. The multidimensional contextual practice framework supports this principle. As Bateson (1979) emphasized, "it takes two somethings to create a difference" (p. 68). Through the dynamics of the provision of services, a transactional process of give-and-take among those involved can emerge (Brill & Levine, 2002). Practitioners will be unable to give that which they do not have. Practicing self-acceptance, self-kindness, mindfulness, patience, and a commitment to self-healing can be crucial in multiple contexts.

Professional competence can be, and often is, strengthened by a **professional code of ethics** (guidelines that provide standards for professional practice and conduct). In addressing and working within the context of human diversity, multidimensional contextual practice advocates for ethical principles and values based on **social justice** (social-political activism to promote and sustain equality of access to resources, equal treatment, elimination of discriminatory and oppressive forces, etc.), **respect of both individual and collective dignity** (self-respect, sense of worth, etc.), **integrity** (truthfulness, honest relationships, etc.), **self-determination** (sense of control and self-direction, not injuring self or others, etc.), and **professional competence** (as previously defined). The Framework for Human Diversity and Transcendence encourages human service practitioners to honor each of these ethical principles, regardless of the capacity of the practice (e.g., direct individual interventions; group, family, and community organizing practices).

The multidimensional contextual practice framework provides practice guidelines to be considered during the helping process, both at the micro, meso, macro, and magna levels of intervention, and during the initial, intermediate, and termination phases of the professional process. The guidelines identified by the multidimensional contextual practice framework view the assessment and intervention dynamics as cyclical and transactional, as illustrated by the diagram in Figure 2.7. This diagram demonstrates how, ideally, the client's challenges and strengths are assessed throughout initial, intermediate, and termination contact. Although the helping process begins with a brief or extensive assessment and moves into an intervention after the development and implementation of a plan of action, it needs to return to a process of evaluation and assessment in order for other professional determinations to be made (e.g., modification of a plan of action, termination of service due to satisfied need).

Throughout the course of assessment and intervention, the practice guidelines provided by the multidimensional contextual practice framework can assist practitioners in embracing what has been called "practice wisdom" (Klein & Bloom, 1995). As used in this text, **practice wisdom** implies the integration of nonstereotypical knowledge and skills cultivated through practice, scientific methods and discoveries, intuitive experiences, professional self-evaluation, and clients' mutual participation in the helping process. Following is a description of four practice wisdom guidelines:

- *Mutual discovery.* This guideline involves initial and ongoing self-disclosure between client and practitioner; construction, preservation, or reconstruction of rapport; development, conservation, or re-establishment of a trustful and honest relationship; discovery of compatibilities or the lack thereof; and agreement to continue or terminate the relationship.
- *Mutual exploration and planning.* This guideline encourages identification, exploration, and review of clients' previous and current experiences with encounters; resources utilized and their effects; protective factors and resources; and environmental, interpersonal, and intrapersonal dynamics. This guideline underlines the opportunity for the client and practitioner to establish, renegotiate, or terminate a plan of action.

Figure 2.7 | Dynamics of Assessment and Intervention

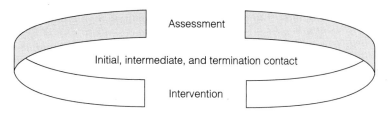

These guidelines are composed of changing multidimensional characteristics and contextual factors that must not be omitted during client-practitioner encounters. One of the major goals of the multidimensional contextual practice framework is to identify, understand, and honor multidimensional characteristics and contextual factors that can assist in facilitating successful client encounters in the helping process. Multidimensional contextual practice views the helping process as a series of client encounters with self, others, and the human service practitioner that is intended to strengthen and maintain ongoing well-being.

- *Mutual intervention.* The principle supporting this guideline is based on the notion that throughout the helping process, a give-and-take dynamic is constantly present. Clients can gain through the practitioner's competence, and the practitioner can gain through the opportunity presented by clients' uniqueness, experiences, needs, and wisdom. Self-care, patience, and a commitment to confront adversity are encouraged through this guideline. Through collaboration, meaningful self and situational change on the part of the client and the practitioner can emerge. Regeneration, empowerment, and transformation can be supported by self-evaluation.
- *Mutual evaluation.* This guideline honors the principle of ongoing assessment, discovery, modification, and growth. It focuses on the construction, deconstruction, and reconstruction of a plan of action for promoting and maintaining well-being, which includes care of self; use of supportive relationships, resources, and therapeutic methods; preservation of visions and hopes; and the possible exploration and implementation of strategies for engaging in social-political activism.

These guidelines are composed of changing multidimensional characteristics and contextual factors that must not be omitted during client-practitioner encounters. One of the major goals of the multidimensional contextual practice framework is to identify, understand, and honor multidimensional characteristics and contextual factors that can assist in facilitating successful client encounters in the helping process. Multidimensional contextual practice views the helping process as a series of client encounters with self, others, and the human service practitioner that is intended to strengthen and maintain ongoing well-being.

In order to strengthen the client-practitioner relationship and the effectiveness of services, the multidimensional contextual practice framework contains the themes of *primary/superficial assumptions, secondary interactional understandings,* and *tertiary transcendent wisdoms.* Although these are public health and mental health treatment terms, they are infused here with new meaning. The ultimate purpose of this practice framework is to provide human service practitioners with a lens for conceptualizing possible ways through which understanding of client dynamics emerge and how such understanding is likely to affect the intervention process. Understanding possible interactions and exchanges occurring among and between the primary/superficial, secondary, and tertiary dimensions of understanding is useful for human service practitioners when they are selecting and developing new strategies for conducting assessments and interventions without perpetuating stereotypes. As reflected in Figure 2.8, the relationship between primary/superficial, secondary, and tertiary dimensions is interdependent and made up of constant exchanges. Although this relationship is perceived as being one of interdependence, from time to time, one dimension may be prioritized over the others.

This practice framework can be used when engaging across levels of interventions (i.e., micro-intrapersonal, meso-interpersonal, macro-environmental, and magna-spiritual). Awareness of each dimension is important in individual, family, group, and community assessment and intervention. Although a single session used to assess or intervene must be considered to be an unduplicated sacred moment, the human service practitioner must not neglect the connectedness among sessions, whether they occur in the initial phase of interaction, during the ongoing working segment, or in the ending/transitional period.

The process of developing **primary/superficial assumptions** about clients seems to be naturally influenced by multiple dynamics including, but not limited to:

- The practitioner's previous direct and indirect experiences with individuals and communities that are believed to be a partial representation of clients being served
- Information and stereotypes perpetuated by the media, written documents, and educational systems
- The practitioner's experiences with cultural influences and cultural choices

Primary/superficial assumptions are often based on general conventional information composed of beliefs that are rarely tested. An illustration of primary/superficial assumptions is the traditional belief that boys are more destructive, competitive, and listen less well when compared to girls. Furthermore, boys are often perceived as being more "privileged." Gurian (1996) wrote, "If we care for our boys, our social progress depends on debunking the superficial stereotypes in which boys lead 'more privileged lives' [than girls]. . . . For every football star there are far more male drug addicts, teenage alcoholics, high school dropouts, and juvenile delinquents" (p. xviii). It is vital to develop a more accurate and nonstereotypical perspective for addressing individual and collective challenges and strengths encountered by both boys and girls. Another example of primary/superficial assumptions is the conventional notion that Latino/a children are taught not to look elderly people and other adults in the eyes when they are speaking. This stereotypical assumption does not hold true within all Latino/a family systems. A similar stereotypical paradigm that has been perpetuated through conventional information is that diverse Latino/a communities share more similarities than differences.

Primary/superficial assumptions cannot be taken for granted. If not enriched through other processes such as those generated through secondary interactional understandings and tertiary transcendent wisdoms, they can injure client-practitioner rapport building and trust development, and can prevent effective working relationships from developing. Primary/superficial assumptions are inevitable within the context of our current dominant paradigm based on either/or categories. Assumptions, however, can be identified, explored, and modified through professional self-

Figure 2.8 | Primary/Superficial, Secondary, and Tertiary Interactions and Exchanges

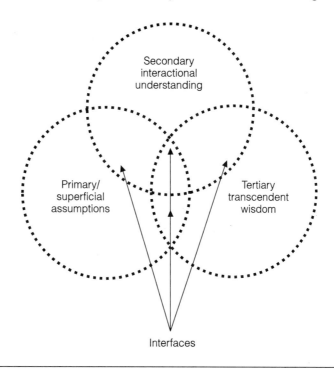

evaluation and individualization of services. Primary/superficial assumptions need to always be in question.

Secondary interactional understandings, as perceived within the multidimensional contextual practice framework, are based on individualized awareness that is intentionally cultivated through unduplicated client-practitioner interactions. These understandings emerge, and often are strengthened, through the course of the helping process as the client and practitioner become more familiar with each other. Information shared by the client through discussion of individual and collective life narratives is what helps human service practitioners cultivate secondary interactional understandings.

Secondary interactional understandings are the practitioner's cultivated awareness regarding clients' unique and unduplicated perceptions, challenges, and strengths. Such understandings are generated and honored through clients' **self-disclosure** (i.e., verbal and nonverbal expressions of meanings and interpretations regarding experiences, strengths, challenges, and hopes) and practitioners' **receptive listening skills** (i.e., the ability to move beyond conditions likely to disrupt a client-centered focus). Recognizing and honoring **intersectionality** (the space/point at which a practitioner and client interact, exchange, and connect, which may include connections that transcend intellectual stimulation) is vital while cultivating secondary interactional understandings. The space of intersectionality is not necessarily bonded to a social or physical environment, or even to an understanding by the human mind, but rather is symbolically viewed within the context of an inner connection made possible through unconditional acceptance.

Although a client's meanings, interpretations, challenges, and strengths may be similar to those reflected by another person, they need to be treated as unique. One of the ideas behind secondary interactional understandings is the prevention of a mechanical point of reference that may be sustained by practitioners who exclusively perform from primary/superficial assumptions. The principle of secondary interactional understandings honors the process of cultivating understanding regarding diversity within diversity (e.g., a community of women may connect through gender similarities, but differentiate due to diversity in sexual orientation, ethnic background, and degree of physical and mental abilities).

Tertiary transcendent wisdoms, in some ways, are similar to secondary interactional understandings. This principle supports the idea that individual uniqueness cannot be neglected. Understanding generated by tertiary transcendent wisdoms does not necessarily depend on the client's self-disclosure and sharing of individual and collective interpretations of experiences, challenges, and strengths. Tertiary transcendent wisdoms are based, rather, on glimpses of understanding regarding transcendent realities/consciousness and **transpersonal means** (higher intelligences that exceed human personal ego-bound self-identity and perceptions of others based on our limited senses of sight, touch, feeling, hearing, and taste) that affect, and can interfere with, human interactions. Such glimpses of understanding assist human service practitioners in appreciating client uniqueness beyond that which can be observed and support the notion of individualized assessment and intervention.

Tertiary transcendent wisdoms are mirrored by intuitive assessment and intervention procedures (not necessarily based on scientifically established data, rationally perceived processes, or a constructed framework, although the end result may reflect effectiveness). Intuitive procedures may or may not be supported by conventional realities/consciousness or consciously learned knowledge. Tertiary transcendent wisdoms can be perceived as one of the great mysteries. How do we explain the "gut feelings" that often shape professional assessment and intervention? How do we explain the experience of hospice patients who become completely cured from terminal cancer without drastic medical treatment? Was it because of love, the client's faith and answered prayers, a practitioner's kindness and unconditional acceptance, or some combination of these factors? Was it a **miracle** (an experience unable to be explained by conventional realities/consciousness and knowledge)?

Tertiary transcendent wisdoms can be partially understood by exploring exchanges manifested through the multifaceted relationship between **body** (physical organism), **matter** (material substance), **mind** (psyche), and **spirit** (innate animating force that often serves to guide us through human interactions and dynamics and that serves as a means for connecting the material and nonmaterial worlds). Tertiary transcendent wisdoms encourage human service practitioners to be open to endless possibilities in terms of spiritual realms when working within the context of human diversity/uniqueness. They remind practitioners to explore and not to neglect notions supported by principles of transpersonal theories. These theories hold that the "self" is inseparable from what appears to be outside it; the self is an entity that is fundamentally one with all. The understanding brought by tertiary transcendent wisdoms evolves out of, and yet transcends, conventional realities/consciousness.

In assessing clients' strengths, challenges, and hopes, practitioners can benefit from glimpses and increased understanding of the dynamics generated by primary/superficial assumptions, secondary interactional understandings, and tertiary transcendent wisdoms. Practitioners can begin to develop understanding of these dynamics by exploring their own perceptions regarding the three dimensions and possible effects within the context and purpose of the helping process. Figure 2.9 identifies three intervention objectives: interventions for maintenance of clients' well-being, interventions for prevention of forces and experiences that are likely to affect client well-being, and interventions for changing forces and experiences affecting client well-being. Begin your own exploration by asking yourself the following questions:

- To what degree do I agree or disagree with the material presented here regarding primary/superficial assumptions, secondary interactional understandings, and tertiary transcendent wisdoms?
- What would I add to or eliminate from this content in order to strengthen the helping process while attempting to reach one (or a combination) of the intervention objectives identified in Figure 2.9?

Practitioners can continue to explore their perceptions and understanding by examining the roles that conventional realities/consciousness and transcendent realities/consciousness play in clients' day-to-day experiences. A connection exists between body or matter, mind, and spirit (Millman, 1995). The discussion regarding primary/superficial assumptions, secondary interactional understandings, and tertiary transcendent wisdoms has only touched the surface.

Reflection Exercise 2.4 was developed to assist readers in evaluating their sense of their own professional competence as practitioners. Some of the content presented in this text may contain new ideas to be absorbed. Therefore, we invite you to take some time to go deeper into the content by engaging in Reflection Exercise 2.4. You may choose to do the exercise individually or with a partner.

Figure 2.9 | Interventions for Maintenance of Client Well-Being

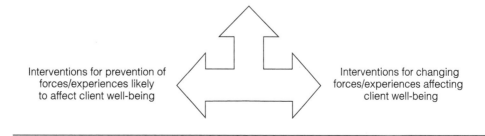

Interventions for prevention of forces/experiences likely to affect client well-being

Interventions for changing forces/experiences affecting client well-being

2.4 Reflection Exercise

Take a moment to ask yourself the following questions. Once your responses have been generated, reflect back to the principle regarding the importance of professional competence when working within the context of human diversity.

- What is your perspective regarding professional self-evaluation/awareness and its relationship to professional competence?
- How are the notions of cultural influences and cultural choices reflected in your life experiences?

- What are some of the benefits and dangers in describing the process of assessment and intervention as cyclical?
- Within what contexts do you feel that the "mutual discovery," "mutual exploration and planning," "mutual intervention," and "mutual evaluation" guidelines may be useful? Within what contexts might they be ineffective?
- What strengths and limitations may be attributed to the "primary/superficial assumptions," "secondary interactional understandings," and "tertiary transcendent wisdoms" interface perspective?

The Multidimensional Contextual Service Principle

Multidimensional contextual services promote, strengthen, and reinforce individual and collective well-being. Multidimensional contextual services rely on community and resource understanding, relevant agency programs, professional expertise, and client-professional and interprofessional relationships, among other factors. Services take into consideration multiple factors affecting client well-being while remaining client-centered and community-specific.

As illustrated by Figure 2.1, a multidimensional contextual emphasis is vital in providing professional services. When providing services at the micro (i.e., individual, family, and group) level, practitioners must not ignore macro implications (i.e., community or societal effects) and possible needs for change if client well-being is to be sustained. Neglecting macro community factors when intervening at the micro level is a reflection of fragmented services. It is like putting a Band-Aid on an injury that needs to be repaired with surgery. Therefore, the multidimensional contextual practice framework emphasizes that consideration must be given to factors such as the following:

- *Community needs, strengths, and readiness to change.* This is mirrored by basic physical, mental, cognitive, social, cultural, and spiritual necessities that are vital for attainment or sustainability of well-being, as well as internal and external resources that enhance the potentiality and capacity to satisfy needs through willingness and commitment to embrace a process of change.
- *Availability and accessibility of fundamental resources within diverse contexts.* This is reflected by supportive means (economic revenues, encouraging relationships, etc.) that are obtainable and offered through diverse systems (employment, family, friendships, social action groups, etc).

- *Agency/program within its environment.* This includes, but is not limited to, factors such as organizational life cycles and practice orientations; social, political, and cultural movements; relationships with other organizations/programs; internal and external political, economic, social, and cultural systems affecting funding sources; agency/program's comprehension and ability to advocate for social, economic, political, and societal changes; agency/program's capability to manage funding and to develop and maintain effective services; type and capability of services being offered; agency/program's ability to evaluate, redesign, and promote programs based on individual, family, group, and community needs; agency/program's ability and willingness to recruit and maintain competent staff; and agency/program's ability and willingness to establish and maintain a clear mission, goals, objectives, and methods for achieving its purpose.

- *Professional expertise, both available and needed.* This is illustrated by human service practitioners' formal and informal educational experiences, practice orientations, diverse backgrounds, demonstrated experiences, knowledge, and skills, as well as the relevance and usefulness of professional expertise when addressing challenges presented by the individuals, families, groups, and communities being served.

- *Dynamics of client-professional and interprofessional relationships.* This is mirrored by factors such as frameworks affecting practice, effects of diverse communication styles, the interplay between professional and personal codes of ethics, practitioner's commitment to ongoing professional and personal growth, and interactions and exchanges affecting rapport building between client and practitioner and between practitioners themselves. It is also mirrored by the establishment of supportive relationships based on trust and honesty, as well as an ability to co-create effective networking agreements and procedures leading to the overall purpose of competently serving the client.

These factors are constantly changing and are affected by multidimensional and contextual micro, meso, macro, and magna interactions and exchanges. The multidimensional contextual practice framework encourages careful exploration of all of these factors, as well as recognition and understanding of the linkages between them. These elements are not mutually exclusive.

Often agencies and programs get caught in the middle of individual and cultural or societal promotion of oppressive forces. This often leads to **institutionalization of multiple oppressive means** (i.e., institutionalized racism, sexism, homophobia, discrimination based on degree of mental and physical abilities or disabilities, diverse political orientations, etc.). The multidimensional contextual practice framework advocates for an awareness of the possibility of such institutionalized dynamics and encourages practitioners to become actively involved in the process of change.

Provision of services is crucial in promoting client well-being and serving the needs of the multidimensional contextual client. The range of services, however, ought to address micro-intrapersonal, meso-interpersonal, macro-environmental, and magna-spiritual needs. Practitioner and agency professional competence are essential in the planning, design, provision, and implementation of services. Read the case scenario presented in Reflection Exercise 2.5 and answer the questions in that exercise with this perspective in mind.

2.5 | Reflection Exercise

Take a moment to engage in the following exercise. Once your responses have been generated, reflect back to the principle that individual and collective well-being can be promoted, strengthened, and reinforced through a multidimensional contextual perspective of services.

You are employed as a practitioner at a drug and alcohol rehabilitation outpatient program. In the program, client rehabilitation needs have been frequently addressed through group interventions. Individual services have been significantly decreased over the past two years because of a significant increase in workers' caseloads and a belief that clients have similar biopsychosocial needs as affected by chemical dependency. The decrease in individual services has affected understanding of possible unique challenges and strengths encountered by individual clients. A significant number of clients have requested individual sessions during the past two years, but such requests generally have not been satisfied.

You recognize that the number of cases assigned to individual practitioners is extremely high. You have also observed that an hour and a half group intervention service is not sufficient to effectively serve clients, as reflected by constant client relapses. As your concern increases, you decide to speak to other practitioners and administrative staff. You have noticed already that some of your coworkers share your observations, some disagree, and others remain neutral. Through ongoing interaction with other practitioners and administrative staff, a number of factors and dynamics become clearer:

- Diverse practitioners and staff backgrounds influence theoretical and practice orientations.
- Conflictive professional relationships are often affected by rigidity in thinking patterns and resistance to change.
- Internal and external political, economic, and social systems affect funding sources and the program's capacity for maintaining diverse forms of services.
- The program's mission, purpose, objectives, and methods for achieving goals are unclear.
- The program lacks ongoing evaluation regarding client/community needs and experiences.
- The community demands change.

1. How may you assess further implications of the needs/issues identified?
2. What internal and external systems might you take into consideration when attempting to promote additional understanding of the needs/issues being presented?
3. What assets will you need in order to support your assessment?
4. If it is discovered that change is vital in order to strengthen the services being provided, what goals and objectives will you establish?
5. What systems might be helpful in influencing change?
6. What resources may be vital for evaluating risks, accomplishing goals, and establishing a potentially successful process?

SUMMARY

The multidimensional contextual practice framework, also known as A Framework for Human Diversity and Transcendence, makes every effort to focus on multiple "realities" encountered by clients as well as factors affecting practitioners' professional competence within the context of multidimensional contextual services. The notion of multidimensionality goes beyond the person and the environment. As emphasized in this chapter, multidimensionality also includes the magna or spiritual, often reflected by the wisdom/power of uncertainty. It encompasses all that a client brings to the helping relationship from a chronological time, an ontological being, and an identity essence perspective. From a chronological time perspective, the client brings ethnic, gender, social class, and cultural entities, to mention a few. From an ontological being perspective, the client develops an inner sense of self that influences personality and behavior. From an identity essence perspective, the client brings an inherent wisdom, a self that gradually evolves a sense of personhood, which is expressed by outward appearance, personal and public tastes, and value choices. These dimensions, however, interact with various settings or backdrops and affect how clients respond and interact within a particular environment, experience, time, and space. Ultimately, the multidimensional contextual practice framework provides an opportunity for addressing basic human commonalities, differences, and complexities without perpetuating stereotypical paradigms that have affected professional practice within the social/health/human service field.

References

Andersen, M. L., & Collins, P. H. (Eds.). (2001). *Race, class, and gender: An anthology* (4th ed.). Belmont, CA: Wadsworth/Thomson Learning.

Andrews, A. B., Guadalupe, J. L., & Bolden, E. (2003). Faith, hope, and mutual support: Path to empowerment as perceived by women in poverty. *Journal of Social Work Research and Evaluation, 4*(1), 5–18.

Banks, J. A., & Banks, C. A. M. (1997). *Multicultural education: Issues and perspectives* (3rd ed.). Boston: Allyn & Bacon.

Bateson, G. (1979). *Mind and nature: A necessary unity.* New York: Dutton.

Beckett, J. O., & Johnson, H. C. (1995). Human development. In R. L. Edwards (Ed.), *Encyclopedia of social work* (19th ed., Vol. 2, pp. 1385–1405). Washington, DC: NASW Press.

Brill, N. I., & Levine, J. (2002). *Working with people: The helping process* (7th ed.). Boston: Allyn & Bacon.

Canda, E. R. (1990). Afterword: Spirituality re-examined. *Spirituality and Social Work Communicator, 1*(1), 13–14.

Canda, E. R. (1997). Does religion and spirituality have a significant place in the core HBSE curriculum? Yes. In M. Bloom & W. C. Klein (Eds.), *Controversial issues in human behavior in the social environment* (pp. 172–177, 183–184). Boston: Allyn & Bacon.

Faiver, C., Ingersoll, R. E., O'Brien, E., & McNally, C. (2001). *Explorations in counseling and spirituality: Philosophical, practical, and personal reflections.* Belmont, CA: Wadsworth/Thomson Learning.

Felsman, J. K., & Vaillant, G. (1987). Resilient children as adults: A 40-year study. In E. J. Anthony & B. Cohler (Eds.), *The invulnerable child.* New York: Guilford.

Freire, P. (1973). *Pedagogy of the oppressed.* New York: Seabury.

Garbarino, J. (1997). *Raising children in a socially toxic environment.* San Francisco: Jossey-Bass.

Garcia, B., & Van Soest, D. (1997). Changing perception of diversity and oppression: MSW students discuss the effects of a required course. *Journal of Social Work Education, 33*(1), 119–129.

Garmezy, N. (1991). Resiliency and vulnerability to adverse development outcomes associated with poverty. *American Behavioral Scientist, 34,* 416–430.

Germain, C. B. (1994). Human behavior and the social environment. In E. G. Reamer (Ed.), *The foundation of social work knowledge* (pp. 88–121) New York: Columbia University Press.

Germain, C. B., & Gitterman, A. (1996). *The life model of social work practice: Advances in theory and practice* (2nd ed.). New York: Columbia University Press.

Green, J. W. (1999). *Cultural awareness in the human services: A multi-ethnic approach* (3rd ed.). Needham Heights, MA: Allyn & Bacon.

Guadalupe, J. L. (2000). *The challenge: Development of a curriculum to address diversity content without perpetuating stereotypes.* Ann Arbor, MI: UMI Company.

Guadalupe, K. L. (2003). Empowerment perspective. In J. Anderson & R. W. Cater (Eds.), *Diversity perspectives for social work practice.* Boston: Allyn & Bacon.

Guadalupe, J. L., & Bein, A. (2001). Violence and youth: What can we learn? *International Journal of Adolescence and Youth: Special Issue on Youth and Violence, 10*(1/2), 157–176.

Guadalupe, J. L., & Pagán, M. T. (1997). *Vida consciente muerte divina: Una experiencia individual y colectiva* [Conscious life divine death: An individual and collective experience]. Hato Rey, PR: Publicaciones Puertorriqueñas.

Guadalupe, J. L., & Torres, S., Jr. (2001). Puerto Rican healing practices: The spiritual, the religious, the human. In W. DuBray (Ed.), *Spirituality and healing: A multicultural perspective.* San Jose, CA: Writers Club Press.

Gurian, M. (1996). *The wonder of boys: What parents, mentors, and educators can do to shape boys into exceptional men.* New York: Jeremy P. Tarcher/Putnam.

Hartman, A. (1990). Many ways of knowing. *Social Work, 35*(1), 3–4.

Hartman, A. (1991). Words create worlds. *Social Work, 36*(4), 275–276.

Hartman, A. (1994). Social work practice. In E. G. Reamer (Ed.), *The foundation of social work knowledge* (pp. 14–50). New York: Columbia University Press.

Healey, J. F. (1997). *Race, ethnicity, and gender in the United States: Inequality, group conflict, and power.* Thousand Oaks, CA: Pine Forge Press.

Jansson, B. S. (2001). *The reluctant welfare state: American social welfare policies—past present, and future* (4th ed.). Pacific Grove, CA: Brooks/Cole–Thomson Learning.

Joseph, M. V. (1987). The religious and spiritual aspects of clinical practice: A neglected dimension of social work. *Social Thought, 13*(1), 12–23.

Klein, W., & Bloom, M. (1995). Practice wisdom. *Social Work, 40*(6), 799–807.

Laird, J. (1998). Theorizing culture: Narrative ideas and practice principles. In M. McGoldrick (Ed.), *Re-visioning family therapy: Race, culture, and gender in clinical practice* (pp. 20–36). New York: Guilford.

Locke, D. (1992). *Increasing multicultural understanding: A comprehensive model.* Newbury Park, CA: Sage.

Lum, D. (Ed.). (2003). *Culturally competent practice: A framework for understanding diverse groups and justice issues* (2nd ed.). Pacific Grove, CA: Brooks/Cole.

Lum, D. (2004). *Social work practice and people of color: A process-stage approach* (4th ed.). Pacific Grove, CA: Brooks/Cole.

Martinez, E. (2001). Seeing more than Black and White: Latinos, racism, and the cultural divides. In M. L. Andersen & P. H. Collins (Eds.), *Race, class, and gender: An anthology* (4th ed.). Belmont, CA: Wadsworth/Thomson Learning.

Millman, D. (1995). *The laws of spirit: Simple, powerful truths for making life work.* Tiburon, CA: HJ Kramer Inc.

Murphy, L. (1987). Further reflections on resilience. In E. J. Anthony & B. Cohler (Eds.), *The invulnerable child.* New York: Guilford.

Nakanishi, M., & Rittner, B. (1992). The inclusionary cultural model. *Journal of Social Work Education, 28*(1), 27–35.

Pinderhughes, E. B. (1979). Teaching empathy in cross-cultural social work. *Social Work, 24*(4), 312–316.

Pinderhughes, E. (1989). *Understanding race, ethnicity, and power: The key to efficacy in clinical practice.* New York: The Free Press.

Pozatek, E. (1994). The problem of certainty: Clinical social work in the postmodern era. *Social Work, 39*(4), 396–403.

Rutter, M. (1985). Resilience in the face of adversity: Protective factors and resistance to psychiatric disorder. *British Journal of Psychiatry, 147,* 598–611.

Saleebey, D. (1994). Culture, theory and narrative: The intersection of meanings in practice. *Social Work, 39*(4), 351–359.

Saleebey, D. (2002). *The strengths perspectives in social work practice* (3rd ed.). Boston: Allyn & Bacon.

Schriver, J. M. (2001). *Human behavior and the social environment: Shifting paradigms in essential knowledge for social work practice* (3rd ed.). Needham Heights, MA: Allyn & Bacon.

Walsh, F. (1998a). Beliefs, spirituality, and transcendence: Keys to family resilience. In M. McGoldrick (Ed.), *Re-visioning family therapy: Race, culture, and gender in clinical practice* (pp. 62–75). New York: Guilford.

Walsh, F. (1998b). *Strengthening family resilience.* New York: Guilford.

Wambach, K., & Van Soest, D. (1997). Oppression. In R. L. Edwards (Editor-in-Chief), *Encyclopedia of social work: Supplement* (19th ed., pp. 243–252). Washington, DC: NASW Press.

Weiss, B. L. (1988). *Many lives, many masters.* New York: Simon & Schuster.

Werner, E. E. (1993). Risk, resilience, and recovery: Perspective from the Kauai longitudinal study. *Development and Psychopathology, 5,* 503–515.

Wolin, S., & Wolin, S. (1993). *The resilient self: How survivors of troubled families rise above adversity.* New York: Villard.

Zavella, P. (1994). Reflections on diversity among Chicanos. In S. Gregory & R. Sanjek (Eds.), *Race* (pp. 199–212). New Brunswick, NJ: Rutgers University Press.

I am what you see and yet what
I am transcends into the unknown
and invisible. —**Krishna L. Guadalupe**

3 | Well-Being and the Multidimensional Contextual Client

Chapter 1 revisits and reinterprets a number of human diversity and practice concepts, while Chapter 2 presents the multidimensional contextual practice framework with five principles. This chapter details the framework, starting with a number of practice principles related to the well-being of the multidimensional contextual client. By starting with well-being when working with clients—whether individuals, families, groups, or communities—we focus on wholeness and healthy functioning. Rather than viewing the client as problem-oriented, multidimensional contextual practice affirms the client as a living entity. Social/health/human service practitioners are encouraged to begin by finding the well-being of the client.

Existential therapy starts with a well-being orientation. Maslow (1962) speaks of health or the process of well-being as "the presence within the human being of a tendency toward, or need for growing in a direction that can be summarized in general as self-actualization, or psychological health. . . . [T]he human being is so constructed that he [or she] presses toward fuller and fuller being and this means pressing toward what most people would call good values, toward serenity, kindness, courage, honesty, love, unselfishness, and goodness" (p. 147). This self-actualization striving of one's being toward qualities of wholeness has an internal and external constructed reality. It moves inward toward contacting the being of the person, and it moves outward to reach beyond the micro to the meso, macro, and magna elements.

Tillich (1952) describes the power of being as courage over the forces of non-being: "Courage needs the power of being, a power transcending the non-being which is experienced in the anxiety of fate and death, which is present in the anxiety of emptiness and meaninglessness, which is effective in the anxiety of guilt and condemnation. The courage which takes this threefold anxiety into itself must be rooted in a power of being that is greater than the power of oneself and the power of one's world" (p. 155). In other words, being seems to have a transcendent power to rise above and to cope with the ordinary and present circumstances. Yet, being also must cope with the dynamics of non-being, which in the end strengthen being.

We could view oppression as a major expression of non-being. That is, within our current human times, living in harmonious relationships with self and others seems to be agitated by patterns of oppressive forces such as ageism, sexism, homophobia/heterosexism, racism, classism, discrimination based on physical or mental disabilities, as well as linguistic, social, cultural, and geographical imperialism, among others. **Oppressive forces** are perceived as means cultivated and reinforced either intentionally or unintentionally and used to promote and sustain intrapersonal-interpersonal-environmental systems of dominance and subordination. These ultimately injure cognitive, emotional, mental, physical, behavioral, social, and spiritual well-being. An interesting phenomenon of oppressive forces is that these can be strengthened or weakened by intrapersonal and interpersonal (i.e., individual, institutional, cultural, social, environmental, etc.) patterns. In other words, while some cognitive, emotional, behavioral, social, and cultural dynamics (i.e., cultivation, maintenance, and perpetuation of stereotypes and stereotyping) seem to promote and reinforce oppressive forces, others (i.e., awareness of possible effects generated through stereotypes and stereotyping as well as a commitment to nonstereotypical approaches) appear to help with the transformation of these (Guadalupe, 2000). Contributing to the reduction and ultimately the elimination of oppressive forces needs to be an integral component of the overarching goals of practitioners, keeping in mind the interplay between the aforementioned factors.

In recent years, the discussion regarding human diversity has shifted to a focus on strength and resilience. This updates the existential paradigms and infuses the former themes with new dimensions. Strength and resilience are qualities that reflect what has been called **utopia** (i.e., a world through which human beings connect through commonalities and mindfully acknowledge, embrace, and strengthen human relationships through a commitment to explore the complexities of differences without perpetuating stereotypes and judgments from ethnocentric practices). This notion seems to be beneficial in visualizing and taking steps toward its creation.

Integral to our discussion of well-being is the need to embrace what is comparable and different. These are facets of diversity, which are essential to our understanding of well-being. Awareness of basic human commonalities as well as multiple attributes that make individuals, families, groups, and communities unique seems to be fundamental in visualizing the endless possibilities toward the creation of a society or world in which all members can learn to value differences as a strength. Some critics may perceive this statement as an unrealistic dream, as overly idealistic. History, however, has shown that people such as Cesar Chavez, Mahatma Gandhi, Martin Luther King, Jr., Audre Lorde, Rosa Parks, and Mother Teresa, among many other social-political activists, have committed themselves to this possibility, and the results have been remarkable. Practitioners have ethical and professional responsibilities to the people and communities they serve. Exploring cognitive, emotional, behavioral, cultural, and social effects of stereotypes and stereotyping, as well as ways through which we can move beyond the superior/inferior ethnocentric patterns of thinking, strengthened through stereotypes, provides a spirited baseline.

Related to practice principles of well-being is the contextual nature of understanding the client. Recognizing and honoring multidimensional and contextual experiences possibly reinforcing or injuring client well-being seems to be vital in order for practitioners to better serve the people and communities to whom services are being provided. The contextual setting surrounding the client is an important area of practice because the context influences the client, and the client responds to and also influences the context.

This chapter focuses on the exploration of four practice principles related to well-being and context: (1) basic human needs and commonalities; (2) multidimensional and contextual attributes and variables influencing human identities, diverse experiences, and well-being; (3) oppressive forces within the context of human diversity and vice versa; and (4) human resilience—strengths and endurance. Although identified here separately for exploration purposes, we recognize that these areas overlap due to their interdependence. These principles are starting points and need to be considered as a collective when working with individuals, families, groups, and communities.

BASIC HUMAN NEEDS AND COMMONALITIES

Practice principles related to basic human needs and commonalities relate to a number of themes. Maslow (1962) formulated a hierarchy of needs that are related to each other in terms of development and priority. The five interrelated needs are: basic physiological needs, personal safety needs, belongingness and love needs, esteem needs (self-esteem and the esteem of others), and self-actualization needs. It is important to identify and examine these and other basic needs throughout the helping relationship. From our perspective, needs are not problems. **Needs** represent wants, desires, and demands shaped by human interactions, exchanges, and conditions. Unmet needs should be taken into consideration and explored when addressing human diversity/uniqueness, strengths, and challenges. As Hepworth, Rooney, and Larsen (2002) observe: "Determining unmet needs, then, is the first step in identifying resources that must be tapped or developed. If resources are available but clients have been unable to avail themselves of the resources, it is important to determine the barriers to resource utilization" (p. 204).

While identifying unmet needs experienced by individuals, families, groups, and communities, the practitioner can rely on the client's own exploration of individual and collective narratives, as well as on an ongoing examination of societal dynamics assembled by human interactions, exchanges, and conditions. Practitioners are encouraged to consciously make an attempt to move beyond their own possible preconceived ideas about those being served and to allow the active listener within to come alive. While exploring unmet basic human needs, the following questions can be useful:

a. What are basic human needs?
b. Whose values and beliefs are influencing the conceptualization of basic human needs? What are the implications generated by such influences?

c. How may basic human needs be experienced differently by diverse groups of people?

d. What commonalities are reflected as basic human needs are experienced by diverse populations?

e. What effects may unmet needs have in the process of achieving and maintaining mental, emotional, and physical health and well-being?

f. What resources are available, accessible, or need to be created to promote mental, emotional, and physical health and well-being?

g. What social dynamics and conditions need to be changed?

h. How do I (personally and professionally) perpetuate unnecessary individual, institutional, and environmental conditions that enable people's inabilities to fully satisfy their basic human needs?

i. To what degree is my commitment to necessary change reflected in my personal and professional actions?

j. What do I do with this new awareness?

An understanding of the meaning of human diversity implies the notion of similarities (commonalities) and differences (uniquenesses). Lum (2003) states:

> *Diversity* focuses on the differences that make a person distinct and unique from another person [a family from another family, a group from another group, a community from another community, etc.]. It offers an opportunity for a person [family, group, community, etc.] to name these distinctions and invites another person [family, group, community, etc.] to discover those particular qualities about that particular individual [family, group, community, etc]. . . . Yet diversity recognizes that there are commonalities between persons that bind people together as part of our common humanity. There may be common and uncommon experiences, needs, and beliefs that cause bonding and distinctiveness. Human diversity calls for discovery, learning, and understanding of each other. (p. 36)

A focus on human diversity without simultaneously recognizing human commonalities, and vice versa, can lead to *fragmentation,* or disintegration of a larger whole. As emphasized in earlier writings, "the danger is not in separating portions from the whole in order to examine ideas and/or experiences within a specific context; but, instead, in the processes that evolve and perpetuate omission of attributes perceived as less important" (Guadalupe & Freeman, 1999, p. 88).

A review of the literature on human diversity demonstrates that content is often addressed in terms of human differences or universal common bonds. When an attempt is made to tackle both of these interdependent entities, one is frequently emphasized more than the other, often perpetuating the notion that one is more important. By the same token, special attention is not usually given to the tendency that exists for generating and perpetuating stereotypes through exploration of human differences and commonalities. Through reflections on the multidimensional contextual nature of common human attributes discussed here, the reader is reminded to move beyond stereotypical categorizations that tend to neglect diversity within diversity.

In the mid-1900s, Towle (1945) pioneered work on human needs and commonalities. She emphasized the importance of understanding and honoring common human needs and commonalities in order for government officials and community members to advocate for the development of social policies that were more inclusive when servicing diverse populations. According to Towle, regardless of cultural and social differences, people experience common needs and similarities in their relationships with self and others, in their health, and in their emotional-cognitive well-being. For instance, Towle stressed that individuals and communities frequently encounter common life experiences such as fear of the unknown, adaptation to change, and impulses toward bettering their lives. According to Towle, every individual, family, and community has **physiological needs** (i.e., needs for food, optimal health, sense of physical safety), **cognitive needs** (i.e., a sense of identity and worth, of direction and control, of belonging and emotional safety), as well as **social needs** (i.e., needs for employment, recreation, social networks, a sense of social safety). We would like to add another dimension, **spiritual needs** (i.e., the need to participate in and/or create meaning out of esoteric, uncertain, and transcendent experiences). While satisfaction of the aforementioned needs, according to Towle, is likely to enhance individual, family, group, and community living experiences, lack of satisfaction is likely to injure daily functioning, human potential, and well-being.

Towle (1945) reminds the reader not to neglect the importance of contexts, economic conditions, political dynamics, and historical times when exploring basic human needs and commonalities. According to Towle, individuals, families, groups, and communities may, for different reasons, experience some human needs more intensely within specific contexts or life cycles, or even throughout their life spans. We would add that *because basic human needs are experienced differently by different people, they need to be explored within the context of human diversity, and vice versa, in order for individuals, families, groups, and communities not to be marginalized.* For example, while a large number of families experience lack of physical, emotional, cognitive, and social safety because of encounters with family violence, attributes such as sexual orientation and socioeconomic background may affect the type of services provided to specific family systems. Economically stable middle-class Latino/a communities may experience financial disturbances and loss of employment generated by a crisis in the domestic or world economy, but not all individuals within those communities will face racial or sexual discrimination during their search for new jobs. Differentiating the particular context of needs is important in understanding the unique characteristics of the need situation.

An additional factor examined by Towle (1945) is fear of the unknown. Towle stressed that this fear is not uncommon within the human experience. Fear of the unknown is reinforced by different life encounters, influencing different responses. Fear of the unknown may be reinforced by a sense of uncertainty generated as a result of directly experiencing an unexpected physical, emotional, or social crisis. Such fear also may be internalized after constant messages of distrust are reflected in, and perpetuated by, the social environment. Although fear of the unknown may be present, some communities take radical risks with the intention of creating more favorable living conditions, others take a more conservative approach, some become isolated or withdrawn, and some exhibit a combination of these approaches. The forces behind each position cannot be totally defined, but the interplay of "certainty" and "uncertainty" cannot be ignored.

In general, we agree with Towle's (1945) conceptualization of basic human needs and commonalities. We also advocate, however, for an awareness of the multidimensional and contextual nature and complexity of basic human needs and commonalities in order to move beyond the tendency to engage in stereotypical thinking. *Physical, cognitive-emotional, social, and spiritual needs are not linear. They seem to operate transactionally, with none being of more or less importance than the others as they overlap and interconnect.* Furthermore, people do not experience basic human needs at only one time or in only one way. As Towle stressed, people experience some basic human needs more intensely at different times and within different contexts. Thus, **contexts** (space as well as social, economic, and political circumstances within which needs are manifested), **historical times** (chronological periods), and **individual times** (individualized interpretations of and meanings given to experiences and their effects), as well as variables such as **individual and societal dynamics and resources,** all seem to play a role in the way basic human needs are experienced.

The same seems to apply to human commonalities. People do not encounter all human commonalities at the same time, in the same way, or within the same environment. For instance, the *physical needs* of some individuals may be more severe than those of others—such as a person diagnosed with fourth stage cancer versus a person whose cancer is in remission. By the same token, *cognitive needs* can be, and often are, intensified by health challenges, patterns of violence, mental health issues, poverty, oppressive forces, and the unexpected deaths of loved ones. Oppressive forces such as heterosexism/homophobia, social stratification, sexism, racism, ageism, and ableism often complicate people's abilities to fulfill their *social needs*. Furthermore, while some groups of people may satisfy their *spiritual needs* through collective spiritual rituals (e.g., group meditation, chanting, sweat lodge ceremonies, etc.), others may choose to address such needs through individualized spiritual practices (e.g., a **vision quest** in which a person undergoes a period of fasting in isolation from others in order to connect with the Great Creator/Spirit and gain deeper insight into her or his life purpose and self-improvement). Overall, to omit diverse human experiences while exploring basic human commonalities, or vice versa, seems to be a disservice to people and communities being assisted by social/health/human service practitioners.

The following scenario about a family illustrates how people interpret experiences differently and exemplifies human commonalities and differences:

> Maria is 45 years old. She has been divorced for five years and has two children: Tony, 27, and Andrea, 25. Tony and Andrea are both married with children and are very supportive of Maria's life decisions. Maria and her ex-husband Steve have continued to be good friends and to encourage one another since their divorce. Maria, who initiated their divorce, identifies herself as a lesbian, working-class, spiritual White woman who is not willing to conform to societal and family expectations. Maria's sister, Marta, 47 years of age, is often critical of Maria. Marta condemns Maria "for not providing her children and grandchildren with a positive image of womanhood." Marta bases her views on "Christian values" learned during childhood. Raised by the same biological parents (Isabel, 65, and Paul, 70), both Maria and Marta were taught that homosexuality is a "sin" and "immoral" behavior. According to Isabel and Paul, once married, divorce is not an option regardless of any circumstances. While Marta feels ashamed and guilty about being divorced for ten years as a result of domestic violence, Maria refers to her divorce as a feeling of "liberation, an opportunity to re-evaluate life experiences." Maria continues to embrace and honor a "Christian orientation" filled with spiritual principles intro-

duced to her by her parents, but her interpretations differ from those of her sister and her biological parents. Maria has re-educated herself and her children about homosexuality issues and has become an advocate for social and political acceptance of homosexuality. Marta, on the other hand, continues to believe that homosexuality is a "sin."

This narrative is based on a true-life story, though the names have been changed for confidentiality purposes. We hope that this brief illustration of family dynamics will help readers increase their capacity for recognizing diversity within the context of commonalities, and vice versa. Context, historical time, and individual time cannot be ignored if our goal is to attain understanding of unique and collective experiences, such as those encountered by the family in this vignette. Although the two women were raised by the same biological parents, who enforced a particular code regarding what is "moral" and what is "sinful," they generated diverse interpretations of the experience. This process could have been reinforced by a variety of factors, including the diverse contexts in which Marta and Maria interacted, their unique experiences (e.g., support or lack of support through relationships outside the family), genetic differences, and constructed individual interpretations. Once again, differences exist within the context of human commonalities, and vice versa.

Like Towle (1945), writers such as Fromm (1955), Maslow (1970), and Brill and Levine (2002) have identified common physical, emotional, intellectual, social, and spiritual needs and commonalities in humans. In his writings, for instance, Fromm stressed that all human beings have *the need to engage in meaningful relationships* in which a sense of love and appreciation has been cultivated and nourished. Meaningful relationships include relationships with self, significant others, and living environments. Fromm emphasized that an individual, family, group, or community's identity is influenced by experiences of past, present, and future visions. Thus, the need to revisit the past often emerges as a means for promoting a current sense of connectedness and for examining conflictive experiences affecting the present; the need to review the present becomes vital in the process of assessing future goals and possible setbacks. Recognizing the past when working with individuals, families, groups, and communities, Fromm would likely emphasize, is extremely important so that norms, rituals, customs, values, and beliefs that have been influential do not go unnoticed.

Fromm (1955) pointed out that human beings have *the need to develop individual and collective identities* that serve as vehicles to create meaning that guides relations with self, others, and the living surroundings. Fromm reminded readers that identities are constantly changing as life challenges, experiences, and human potential are developed and strengthened. Fromm advocated for the creation of a society where priority is given to human beings over profits, where basic human needs are not difficult to satisfy, and where people have equal access to opportunities that strengthen human potential, well-being, and growth—the constant process of "being and becoming." Fromm's inclusion of social, economic, and political issues, while identifying basic human needs and commonalities, has been vital in promoting the importance of people uniting and engaging in social change that challenges the status quo based on discrimination and injustice.

While Towle (1945) and Fromm (1955) seem to have written about basic human needs and commonalities with a primary intention to advocate for macro community and societal changes, Brill and Levine (2002) focused on basic human needs and commonalities from the perspective of how helping practitioners can better serve clients within therapeutically based micro contexts. In their writings, Brill and Levine encourage human service practitioners *to recognize their own basic human needs* while attempting to understand what they referred to as *"the human condition"* when working with diverse populations. While recognizing the basic biopsycho-social-spiritual needs and human commonalities mentioned by Towle and Fromm, Brill and Levine's writings tend to focus on *cognitive and learning needs.*

Brill and Levine (2002) stress that human beings have, and continue to undergo, a *lifelong search for the meaning of self in relationship to others and their surroundings.* According to these authors, people, at one point or another in their lives, ask themselves the following questions:

- What kind of creature am I?
- Where do I come from, and where do I go?
- How can I understand and control myself, my own behavior, my relationships with others, my life, and my future? (p. 19)

Like Fromm (1955), Brill and Levine emphasize that *the need for self-understanding in relationship to others and living environments* is universal. This need is related to people's desire to create meaningful relationships. According to Brill and Levine, each individual begins to learn attitudes and behaviors as the need to respond to circumstances and experiences emerges from birth and continues throughout life. They stress that through repetition, depending on the type of reinforcement received from significant others and surroundings, the individual often learns to distinguish "right" from "wrong." We would add that *right* and *wrong* responses seem to be contextual by nature. What an individual or group of people may consider the right response, in a particular context, can be perceived as inappropriate by another individual or group within a different context—or, for that matter, within the same context. Furthermore, the perception of what makes responses right or wrong changes as individuals, families, groups, and communities experience what Fromm (1955) called the ongoing process of "being and becoming." Thus, "right" and "wrong" responses do not seem to be universal.

According to Brill and Levine (2002), *cultures* developed by family interactions and dynamics, peer groups, schools, social institutions, and so on *set guidelines through which attitudes and behaviors are judged.* Cultures, they stress, "define significant roles and set up expectations of the behaviors that accompany them" (p. 22). While recognizing that cultures influence people's values, beliefs, boundaries, and behaviors, Brill and Levine also acknowledge that diversity among those being influenced by cultural guidelines must not go unnoticed. Brill and Levine stress that when "role definitions become rigid, they tend to be counterproductive, because both individuals and social groups are constantly in the process of change and adaptation to the differences that are part of life" (p. 22). In other words, rigidity promoted through cultural norms seems to ignore a fundamental and universal principle: Change is constant and inevitable.

Brill and Levine (2002) emphasize that universally people have a tendency to use coping mechanisms such as denial, projection, regression, and fantasy at different times in their lives. They write that the "selection of the particular mechanism used is strongly influenced by the culture and setting as, for example, a family that supports the use of humor to deal with painful feelings" (p. 23). Coping mechanisms such as denial, projection, regression, and fantasy, according to Brill and Levine, cannot be automatically judged as inappropriate or ineffective, as "they can be an effective part of the process of dealing with the demands of living. They can also be ineffective when used rigidly or unrealistically" (p. 23).

We agree with Brill and Levine (2002) that throughout their life spans, *human beings often develop coping mechanisms that are used to confront old or new life demands.* Brill and Levine seem to limit these coping mechanisms, however, to cognitive and emotionally based responses generated to cope with life circumstances and experiences. According to them, coping mechanisms include cognitive-emotional responses to life demands. Coping mechanisms, however, are also reinforced by esoteric and mystical exchanges between communities of people and the **Great Unknown** (mystical-spiritual source/s that transcend human limitations). Spiritual practices (prayers, meditation, fasting, etc.) often provide a medium for the esoteric and mystical exchanges between individuals/communities of people and the Great Unknown (Guadalupe & Torres, 2001). The cognitive is only one of what seems to be multiple sources influencing responses to life encounters.

The coping mechanisms identified by Brill and Levine (2002) can generally be described as defense mechanisms used by individuals, families, groups, and communities to temporarily alleviate the impact of a particular life experience. Coping mechanisms, however, are not simply used to alleviate pain or life stressors; they can and often do promote change. For instance, journal writing and meditation practices can be used to assist individuals, families, groups, and communities in ongoing self-reflection, both as coping mechanisms and with the intention of promoting necessary changes in demanding living situations. Physical exercise routines are often used not only as a coping mechanism, but also to improve or support a positive sense of self and to strengthen the physical body. Coping mechanisms often become life patterns. This is evident in a community of people who, after feeling betrayed on a number of occasions by diverse professional service providers, have developed a tendency to question before accepting or rejecting professional assistance.

In reflecting on the writings of Towle (1945), Fromm (1955), and Brill and Levine (2002), we acknowledge that basic human needs and commonalities are vast and endless. They go beyond those reflected in this discussion; only glimpses of understanding have been mirrored here. Though the list could go on and on, in the helping process, the range of common needs between clients and practitioners can be summarized through the following principles:

- Identification, acknowledgment, and understanding of symbolic interactionism (Goffman, 1959, 1967) within human diversity and human commonality contexts (Symbolic interactionism refers to multiple cognitive/communication/behavioral patterns, rituals, signs, boundaries, codes, meanings, and interpretations, as well as any combination of these, used by individuals, families, groups, and communities during processes of interactions and exchanges.)
- Sensitive practice (i.e., skillful responsiveness to clients' strengths and challenges as well as practitioners' capacities and restrictions)
- Well-intended and consciously based assessments and plans of action that are inclusive of multidimensional contextual factors affecting client well-being

- Identification, advocacy, and the development of needed resources to better serve clients
- Ongoing, consciously thought-out individual and collective stimulators to trigger human potential and growth in all areas of the self and collective (physically, intellectually, emotionally, socially, spiritually, etc.)
- Acknowledgment and celebration of individual uniqueness and interdependence with others; recognition of individualized interpretations of the experience of culture, cultural influences, and cultural choices (culture within culture); and the ongoing process of "being and becoming" (Fromm, 1955)
- Honoring the client as a multidimensional contextual entity
- Recognition and embracement of individual and collective human resilience
- The need not to deny, marginalize, or attempt to disempower others through fear of the unknown, stereotypes, and ignorance
- The need to at least acknowledge that human experiences are full of mysteries to be lived; that **divine interventions** (interventions that are not founded on human-based theories but rather are affiliated with the mystery of the Great Unknown) often play a role in addressing human-based encounters; that the so-called human senses are perhaps limited to specific performances; and that **human intuition** (the act of knowing that is not based on human reasoning, logic, or rationale) can serve as a medium between what is considered conventional consciousness (commonly accepted human perceptions limited to that which can be touched, heard, tasted, felt, seen, and measured) and transcendent consciousness (individual and collective awareness that transcends ordinary consciousness in the experience of glimpses of the Great Unknown)

This list of principles is not to be considered linear (i.e., with some being superior to others) or, for that matter, absolute. Rather, this list is a reflection of these authors' work in progress. Satisfaction of optimal well-being requires acknowledging and honoring basic human needs and commonalities, reinforcing human potential and strengths, as well as making social resources available and accessible. Among other factors affecting optimal individual and collective well-being is the degree to which we understand multiple socially constructed human identities, the attributes influencing these, and diverse living experiences (including encounters with oppressive living forces). As human service practitioners, not only must we make an effort to address basic human needs and to affirm commonalities, but we also must identify, honor, and take into consideration the multiple dimensions of persons.

MULTIPLE IDENTITIES AND DIVERSE EXPERIENCES

As stressed earlier, attributes influencing human identities and diverse experiences also affect individual and collective well-being. Although glimpses of understanding are constantly being cultivated through human interactions and exchanges, as well as transactions occurring between conventional and transcendent realities/consciousness, *thinking that any human being has total understanding of the vast and endless attributes injuring or ensuring well-being is naive.* Any comprehension can be strengthened, however, by examining glimpses of understanding through nonstatic eyes in order to honor the expansion of interpretations formed and modified by initial understanding. This can be called **keeping an open heart,** recognizing that the mind is a *tool* used to partially understand human encounters, and not a *master* of the experience identified as *life*. As evidenced by the literature on human diversity, glimpses of understanding have led to the construction of multiple conceptualizations, reflecting the *many ways of knowing.*

It is important to make an effort to recognize the multiple identities often cultivated through a person's, family's, group's, or community's diversity. While examining the notion of **human identities** (or ways through which individuals, families, groups, and communities deliberately or unconsciously perceive themselves from one context to another), numerous multidimensional contextual variables seem to link together, cultivating the *multiple-self* (which includes both individual and collective multiple identities, or the multidimensional contextual self). Among the vast number of variables influencing the unique or collective multiple-self, some are based on socially-culturally constructed meanings generated through human interactions, exchanges, and dynamics; some are materialized by individual interpretations of human experiences; and yet others appear to be influenced by encounters with the Great Unknown (magna).

Figure 3.1 conceptualizes a number of factors that seem to contribute to the cultivation of multiple identities possibly experienced by individuals, families, groups, and communities. The **multiple-self** is comprised of individual and collective dimensions: the uniqueness of the person, and the collective contributions of significant oth-

Figure 3.1 | A Sample of Multiple Variables Affecting the Cultivation of the Multiple-Self

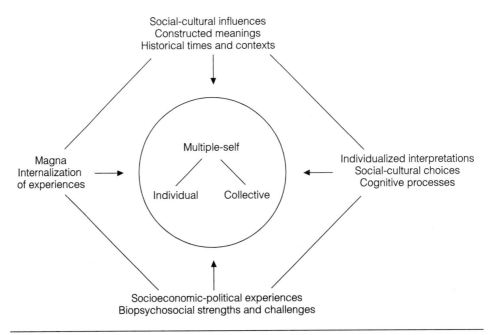

ers such as families, friends, communities, societies, as well as the Great Unknown. A number of influential interactions occur between the multiple-self and related entities, such as social-cultural influences—constructed meanings, historical time and contexts, individualized interpretations, social-cultural choices, cognitive processes, socioeconomic-political experiences, biopsychosocial strengths and challenges, the internalization of human experiences, and the experience of the magna (Great Unknown). Honoring the multiple-self is reflected through receptivity toward human complexities as well as the wisdom of uncertainty; it is the recognition that the nature and purpose of the multiple-self is constantly changing and that certainty is limited.

The idea of multiple-self is confined to the human experience, since it is based on human meanings, interpretations, and encounters. It is not uncommon for individuals, families, groups, and communities to refer to themselves or others according to attributes such as race, ethnicity, gender, sexual orientation, social class, degrees of physical or mental abilities, religious-spiritual orientation, or any combination of these common socially constructed identities. Furthermore, it is not unusual for social experiences such as racism, sexism, classism, ageism, ableism, homophobia/heterosexism, anti-Semitism, and other discriminatory-oppressive forces to affect the ways through which people define themselves or others, especially if such experiences have been internalized. Individual, family, group, and community marginalization reinforced through notions of "normal" and "deviant" often perpetuates the notion of better or worse than, more or less important. This is what we refer to as the **ethnocentric lens.** When the notion of deviant, worse than, or less important is internalized and stigmatization is perceived as "truth," individuals, families, groups, and communities can experience a sense of self-rejection. Self-identification may then be influenced by a sense of feeling inferior when compared to the status quo.

A simple yet profound way of honoring the multidimensional contextual self, beyond the status quo sense of "normality" and "appropriateness," is to recognize what we call the *unique interdependent triangle*. As Figure 3.2 shows, interdependent relationships seem to exist between the experience of "YOU/HE/SHE/THEY," "I," and "US/WE." The experiences of YOU/HE/SHE/THEY, I, and US/WE are filled with individual interpretations influenced by unique encounters within a framework of time, content, processes, and contexts. These experiences are also influenced by the notion of "the other" (e.g., YOU/HE/SHE/THEY as separate from the I or US/WE, and vice versa). And yet, the I is included within the YOU/HE/SHE/THEY/US/WE.

Figure 3.2   Unique Interdependent Triangle

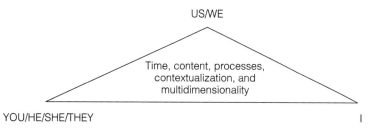

Although interdependence exists between these dimensions of the multidimensional and contextual self, the uniqueness of each dimension is reflected by specific attributes. No two persons are the same, even though they may share common experiences and basic needs (i.e., the US, WE, THEY), since the individual multiple encounters that they experience will lead to the cultivation of unique multiple identities (i.e., the I within the WE, US, THEY). For example, while two Filipino women who are living with physical disabilities may share many experiences and needs, one may identify herself as a working-class woman with children, who is involved in a homosexual relationship and practicing Catholicism, while the other may identify herself as being middle-class, with no children, involved in a heterosexual relationship, and practicing Buddhism. In other words, a person, family, group, or community's multidimensional and contextual self is unique, and yet interdependent with a bigger whole.

The social/health/human service practitioner can utilize the following questions while tuning into clients' individual and collective experiences. Individual and collective encounters are seen as frameworks from which the multidimensional and contextual self and multiple identities are generated. **Rapport building** (a process by which trust is cultivated, enabling risk taking and strengthening the working relationship between the client and human service practitioner) is vital if the intention is to create an environment where clients can explore their strengths and challenges through professional supportive services. Rapport building can be enhanced through a recognition of dynamics emerging in new relationships (Shulman, 1999) and an exploration of one's own perceptions, which include a degree of understanding regarding:

- What possible effects do human diversities and commonalities have within dynamics generated throughout a professional relationship?
- How does a lack of acknowledgment regarding previous experiences (individually or collectively encountered by the client and the human service practitioner) play a role in injuring or enhancing the development of a professional partnership between the client and the human service practitioner?
- What strategies are available and accessible to assess and work with individuals, families, groups, and communities while honoring multidimensional and contextual selves and multiple identities and avoiding marginalization and stereotypical lenses?
- To what degree may the exploration of one's own multidimensional contextual self and multiple identities facilitate the process of acknowledging and honoring such encounters in others?
- What supportive systems and services are available in the community or within the specific agency or program to enhance ongoing professional growth for human service practitioners?

Constructed human identities, meanings, and interpretations play a significant role in human interactions and exchanges. For instance, individual and collective identities based on ethnic dimensions have historically shaped experiences within U.S. society. In her work, Solomon (1976) expressed how historically "black communities have been subjected to negative valuations [and stigmatization] from the larger society. . . ." (p. 12). Subjection to negative valuations (and stigmatization), according to Solomon, has generated different effects within Black communities. While some Black communities have been able to develop a strong sense of ethnic identity that serves as a "cushion or protective barrier against negative valuations" (p. 21), others have accepted "these valuations as 'right' or at least inevitable and therefore make no effort to exert power at all. . . . The powerlessness that they exhibit can be considered power absence rather than power failure" (p. 21). As observed by Solomon, individual and collective identities are relational to a sense of power and control. Thus, recognizing who defines whom is vital. Those who do the defining often experience a sense of control and power, as evidenced by general definitions influencing formal and informal social policies in the United States that have been used to pass judgment, determine a sense of "correctness" and "normality," as well as to rationalize punishment. For instance, in the South, slavery was supported by legislation that subjected Blacks/African Americans to inhuman physical and psychological treatment. As slaves, Black men, women, and children could be chained, sold or traded, humiliated, beaten, exploited, and tortured. Although the system of slavery was legally abolished in 1865 through the bloody Civil War (with Abraham Lincoln's primary goal being to save the Union), it was replaced by another oppressive, legally organized order: the Jim Crow laws, also known as "separate but equal." History has shown that the experience of "separate but equal" really meant separation of resources based on people's skin color, with resources for people with dark skin or those who were categorized as such being inferior to those available to Whites.

We must emphasize that experiences such as ethnicity, gender, sexual orientation, social class, and encounters with oppressive forces do not automatically become identities. These experiences can be points of reference that do not necessarily determine one's perception of self in relationship to others. A geographical location, for instance, may be perceived by an outside group of people as a "ghetto" because of the socioeconomic conditions of those living in it, while groups of people living in it may refer to the location as a nurturing and resourceful community. Individuals may choose to identify themselves in terms of nationalities rather than the multiple ethnicities that they may represent. For that matter, individuals may determine to identify themselves as multiethnic rather than by any single ethnic identification. Furthermore, some strive to let go of any attachment to ancestral histories in an attempt to cultivate new identities or to live mindfully one moment at a time. While an outsider may judge this as lack of awareness or lack of responsibility toward the collective, the person or community taking this approach may perceive it as a conscious choice or determination to move beyond grouping. Human service practitioners need to be careful not to automatically categorize people based on their own preconceived ideas of what people may represent. One's face does not necessarily represent one's gender (as is the case with transsexuals) or one's ethnicity (as is the case in multiethnic communities). Although gender, ethnic, cultural, sexual orientation, religious-spiritual, and social class identifications are often "relational and comparative—with reference to an other" (Erickson, 1997, p. 45), in order to avoid stereotypical practices, human service practitioners must question their own assumptions and allow space for people and communities to define themselves.

While exploring the experience referred to as multiple-self or multiple identities, it is important to acknowledge and honor interactions and intersections of human attributes such as sex, age, gender, sexual orientation, race-ethnicity, socioeconomic-political experiences, degrees of physical and mental abilities, cultivated culture, time context, and religious-spiritual practices, among others, and it becomes *essential to examine and recognize the diversity within and between the multiple group memberships* that are often developed in relation to these attributes. Individuals, families, groups, and communities participate in and develop a sense of belonging to more than one group category. For instance, people may share a sexual orientation identification and yet differ in terms of ethnic, gender, or socioeconomic encounters—or vice versa. As emphasized throughout this discussion, the multiple-self seems to be influenced by a simultaneous interplay among and between multiple human attributes and variables. The identity of an individual, family, group, or community is not exclusively determined by the experience of ethnicity in isolation from the experience of gender, sexual orientation, socioeconomic encounters, degree of physical and mental abilities, and so on. The multiple-self is like a single home with multiple rooms: Just as each room is a dimension/extension of the whole, no single attribute or variable can account for the totality of one's multiple-self.

Variation of encounters with attributes such as those mentioned previously tends to reinforce multicultural experiences, reflected by beliefs, values, attitudes, norms, and behaviors that are contextual and multidimensional by nature. For instance, Erickson (1997) stresses that

> It is not possible for individuals to grow up in a complex modern society without acquiring differing subsets of culture-differing software packages that are tools that can be used in differing kinds of human activities; tools that in part enable and frame the activities in which they are used. From the nuclear family, through early and later schooling, through peer networks, and through life at work, we encounter, learn, and, to some extent help create differing microcultures and subcultures. Just as everyone learns differing variants and styles of the various languages we speak so that everybody is multilingual (even those of us who only speak English), so everybody is multicultural. (p. 34)

Erickson's emphasis reminds us that cultures do not live in total isolation, nor do individuals, families, groups, or communities of people. A common denominator within and between groups of people seems to be the experiences of multiple identities often shaped by individual and collective experiences.

Due to social-cultural experiences, time and context, and individual interpretations of meaning and choices presented, among other variables, people are likely to experience different degrees of identification with the various attributes and variables mentioned earlier. For instance, within a specific context and historical time, an individual may experience a strong sense of sexual orientation identification resulting from a need for group solidarity while experiencing an almost nonexistent ethnic identity. Furthermore, the multiple-self opens the doors to conflictive experiences, thus reflecting human complexity. As stated by Banks (1997), "A woman who has a strong Catholic identification but is also a feminist might find it difficult to reconcile her beliefs about equality for women with some positions of the Catholic church, such as its prohibiting women from becoming ordained priests" (p. 14). Ignorance of the process of construction, deconstruction, and reconstruction of identities, as discussed in Chapter 2, can injure professional competence within the context of human diversity/uniqueness.

Experiences such as race, ethnicity, gender, sexual orientation, social class, and degrees of physical and mental abilities have become means by which individuals, families, groups, and communities tend to identify themselves. Transformation of experiences into identities can be accredited to multiple factors and processes, including intrapersonal and interpersonal forces pressing for a sense of belonging and collectiveness, as well as other needs that may arrive during the life span through the interplay of cultural influences and cultural choices, encounters with the wisdom of uncertainty, and so on. The meanings given to such socially-culturally constructed identities, furthermore, often undergo processes of co-creation between people-communities and their environments in order to create a baseline for interactions and exchanges.

The term *co-creation* must not be confused with the concept of mutual exchange. While the concept of **mutual exchange** seems to promote the notion that people and communities experience equal social and cultural power in the process of prolonging or changing socially-culturally constructed norms, meaning, and conditions, the idea behind the term **co-creation** emphasizes that although social and cultural power is not equally distributed, participation occurs at different levels, for different reasons, and is a compilation of different efforts. Participation to promote or change a status quo, for instance, may come from a conscious effort that is made after people or communities have evaluated their choices presented by internalization of disempowering forces that can lead to isolation and withdrawal from direct participation, by promotion of indirect input, or by ignorance likely to influence a decision without evaluating possible outcomes. To dismiss the interchange that occurs between cultural influences and cultural choices (the process of co-creation, the magna), as well as other intrapersonal and interpersonal forces influencing the construction, deconstruction, and reconstruction of the multiple-self, is to marginalize people's and communities' experiences.

It is important to honor the multiple-self and multiple identities that often emerge when working with individuals, families, groups, and communities. Careful attention needs to be given to the tendency to promote stereotypical perspectives in the name of good intention. Although the multiple-self is often influenced by encounters with attributes such as race, ethnicity, gender, sexual orientation, social class, degrees of physical or mental abilities, and religious-spiritual orientation, it is not exclusively confined to these experiences. For instance, experiences such as parenthood, sisterhood, and brotherhood, among other types of relationships, as well as people's professional occupations and types of formal or informal education, also seem to play a significant role in the way people define themselves in conjunction with, or regardless of, racial, gender, sexual orientation, or ethnic identifications. Furthermore, multiple identities are not exclusively based on observable and measurable experiences. The multiple-self is not simply a product generated from a process of interactions and intersections among and between human attributes and variables; it is the process itself, and it is constantly changing. *Ultimately, the nature of identity is infinite and nonconclusive.*

The diagram in Figure 3.3 was introduced in Chapter 2 during the exploration of the client as a multidimensional contextual entity. Take a moment to examine the degree to which attributes identified in this diagram may be influencing your perception of self. Use the following questions as guidelines:

- How do I generally tend to describe myself?
- Which of the attributes identified in the diagram do I relate to the most, possibly generating my self-identity?

Figure 3.3 | Factors Influencing Clients' Identities and Life Experiences

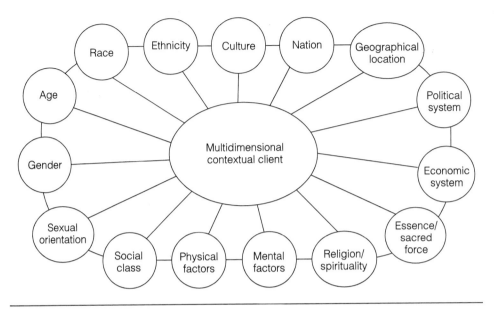

- What combination of these attributes best reflects the multiple ME?
- To what degree does my self-identity change from one context to another (e.g., when I am with my family, significant other, and friends; when I am in my place of employment, at school, traveling in another country, etc.)?
- What effects have my gender and sexual orientation had on my self-identity?
- What effects do my nationality and geographic living location have on the way I view myself?
- What effects do my mental and physical abilities or disabilities have on the way that I view myself?
- What roles do the socioeconomic and political systems that I experience play in the way that I perceive myself?
- What role does religion or spiritual convictions (or the lack thereof) play in the way I relate to myself?
- Who is this "I" that I am attempting to describe?

OPPRESSIVE FORCES WITHIN THE CONTEXT OF HUMAN DIVERSITY

Not only is it important to consider well-being and multiple identities within the context of human diversity, but it is also important to consider what Tillich (1952), an existential theologian, calls non-being. We want to recast the concept of non-being in terms of oppression, which is relevant to understandings of socioeconomic status, ethnicity, culture, gender, and sexual orientation. As emphasized earlier, **oppressive**

forces are means that are cultivated and reinforced, either intentionally or unintentionally, and used to promote and sustain intrapersonal-interpersonal-environmental systems of dominance and subordination, ultimately injuring cognitive, emotional, mental, physical, behavioral, social, and spiritual well-being. Oppressive forces can be strengthened and perpetuated or reduced and eliminated by individual persons, social institutions, and established cultural and social norms, or a combination of these. Examples of oppressive forces are:

- **Sexism** or oppression based on stereotypical gender roles and expectations through which the notion that one of the sexes is superior to the other is reinforced and perpetuated by unequal access to social opportunities and resources, as well as exposure to physical, psychological, and social exploitation
- **Racism** or oppression based on a conviction that people can be separated into innately different biological or hereditary populations, in which one group of people is believed to be superior in regard to mental and social capacities when compared to another, carrying on the idea of right to dominance of the superior group, reinforced and perpetuated through unequal access to social opportunities, resources, and privilege, as well as exposure to physical, psychological, and social exploitation of the group perceived as inferior
- **Homophobia** or oppression based on variations of sexual orientation demonstrated by personal or societal mistreatment of homosexuals (gays, lesbians, bisexuals, transsexuals, etc.) and the institutionalization of heterosexual social privilege that reinforces and perpetuates unequal access to social opportunities and resources, as well as exposure to physical, psychological, and social exploitation
- **Ageism** or oppression based on age differences
- **Classism** or oppression based on diverse socioeconomic status—social class stratification, socioeconomic and political domination, and economic deprivation— as well as ruling values and belief systems
- **Discrimination based on physical or mental abilities and disabilities**
- **Discrimination based on religious-spiritual practices**

Other forms of oppressive forces are forced **geographical colonialism,** exemplified by dispossession of land; **cultural imperialism,** mirrored by dehumanization, invasion, and demolition of diverse cultural heritages, meanings, and practices; **linguistic imperialism,** illustrated by the power to linguistically define, manipulate, and control individuals, families, groups, and communities; **empirical imperialism,** displayed by the generalization of the notion of "normal versus abnormal" that is created, reinforced, and perpetuated through scientific empirical research; and so on.

Although individually unique, oppressive forces often do not operate in isolation from one another. The interdependence among and between oppressive forces can be exemplified by groups of people experiencing multiple oppression resulting from variables such as gender, sexual orientation, ethnicity, and socioeconomic status. Gutierrez (1990) emphasizes that women who are categorized as "women of color," or non-White, often experience "double jeopardy." Because of their gender and ethnic or racial identities, Gutierrez stresses, women of color often encounter sexism and racism. If the same women are lesbian or bisexual, another strike is added. We would add that a similar observation can be made when exploring multidimensional and contextual experiences encountered by "White" women. This group of people does not necessarily escape a combination of oppressive forces such as sexism, classism, homophobia, and ageism. The "double (or triple, etc.) jeopardy" reinforces individual and collective multiple struggles, and groups of people are forced to engage in multiple tasks in order to survive multiple oppressions. Although "women of color" and "white women" may encounter multiple oppressive forces, exploration of such experiences cannot neglect the fact that these experiences are reinforced by unique factors and cannot be perceived as the same. Categorizing women as a collective, while neglecting intergroup and between-group uniqueness, can be oppressive within itself.

Oppressive forces can be supported and reinforced by a single person, a family, a group of people, a community, or a nation at large (i.e., popular or dominating cultural norms). While some forms of oppressive forces are visible and explicit (e.g., blatant racism, homophobia, sexism, or anti-Semitism), others have a degree of invisibility and can be considered implicit (e.g., covert racism, as when an apartment is suddenly unavailable or jobs are suddenly filled when individuals representing a particular ethnicity apply) (Yamato, 2001). Oppressive forces, individually as well as collectively, are multidimensional and contextual by nature. For instance, the social class differential, one of the fundamental variables reinforcing classism, is more than diversity based on possession of economic and materialistic resources. In a writing entitled *Tired of Playing Monopoly?*, Langston (2001) emphasizes that class transcends financial resources. Class, according to Langston, is also culture. She writes:

> Class is more than just the amount of money you have; it's also the presence of economic security. For the working class and poor, working and eating are matters of survival, not taste. However, while one's class status can be defined in important ways in terms of monetary income, class is also a whole lot more—specifically class is also culture. As a result of the class you are born into and raised in, class is your understanding of the world and where you fit in; it's composed of ideas, behaviors, attitudes, values, and language; class is how you think, feel, act, look, dress, talk, move, walk; class is what stores you shop at, restaurants you eat in; class is the school you attend, the education you attain; class is the very jobs you will work at throughout your adult life. Class even [often] determines when we marry and become mothers. Working-class women [frequently] become mothers long before middle-class women receive their bachelor's degrees. We experience class at every level of our lives; class is who our friends are, where we live and work, even what kind of car we drive, if we own one, and what kind of health care we receive, if any. Have I left anything out? In other words, class is socially constructed and all-encompassing. When we experience classism, it will be because of our lack of money (i.e., choices and power in this society) and because of the way we talk, think, act, move—because of our culture. (pp. 126–127)

Langston's perspective reflects the complexity of social class as well as its multi-dimensional and contextual nature.

Langston (2001) also stresses that classism is not a socially constructed phenomenon existing exclusively between "The Haves in Abundance," "The Haves Little," and "The Haves Not." This claim is supported by both the historical struggles and the discriminatory actions observed within the upper middle classes, middle classes, and working classes, especially when one explores social class in relationship to ethnicity, gender, and sexual orientation, to mention only a few diversity attributes. Due to racist, sexist, and homophobic values, beliefs, and attitudes, classism has been supported and perpetuated within and between social class classifications. Thus, it is not uncommon to observe individuals or groups of people who have been oppressed because of their ethnic identification and stigmatization engaging in oppressive actions against another group due to other differences, such as sexual orientation. This can be called the **paradox between being oppressed and oppressing.**

The multidimensional and contextual magnitudes of oppressive forces can also be observed in the multifaceted and unique faces of racist expressions. Yamato (2001) has observed four ways through which racism is demonstrated: (1) aware/blatant racism; (2) aware/covert racism; (3) unaware/unintentional racism; and (4) unaware/self-righteous racism. While aware/blatant racism is mirrored by outright racist language, beliefs, behaviors, and social-cultural norms, aware/covert racism is demonstrated through conscious yet masked discriminative actions (e.g., the jobs or apartments that are no longer available when an individual, family, or group representing a particular ethnic group applies for them). Unaware/unintentional as well as unaware/self-righteous manifestations of racism are reflections of the internalization of racist beliefs, values, norms, and attitudes not being consciously recognized. According to Yamato, unaware/unintentional racism is mirrored by the lack of awareness exhibited by people, families, groups, or communities regarding their own social-cultural privilege; rather than dealing "with ending racism, they sit and ponder their guilt. . . . Meanwhile, racism picks up momentum and keeps on keepin' on" (pp. 91–92). Yamato provides an example of unaware/self-righteous racism in groups of "good Whites" (as contrasted to "bad Whites") who are "often so busy telling people of color what the issues in the Black, Asian, Indian [First Nations Peoples], Latino/a communities should be that they don't have time to deal with their errant sisters and brothers in the white communities. Which means that people of color are still left to deal with what the 'good whites' don't want to . . . racism" (p. 92). Yamato's observations regarding diverse forms of racist demonstrations are also illustrated when exploring homophobic and gender issues, as well as other forms of oppression within and between groups of people.

Multidimensional and contextual magnitudes of oppressive forces can, and often are, manifested in multiple forms, including individually, institutionally, environmentally, culturally, and socially. Oppressive forces are often reinforced through language patterns, beliefs, values, and behaviors held by a person or group of people. These can be systematically institutionalized into the structures and arrangements of social systems (e.g., the family, educational programs, the political system), as well as being infused into the process of socialization-culturalization. Oppressive forces are often supported and reinforced through **models of dominance** (cognitive, emotional, behavioral, social, political, legal, and cultural ruling patterns). These patterns carry on the notion of "normality," "desirable" ambitions, as well as "appropriate" ways of thinking, believing, and behaving, reinforced by a society's status quo and handed down to diverse communities of people for internalization. Within the U.S. historical context and current dynamics, a number of models of dominance are visible, including:

- The importance of white skin color and its historical association to opportunities (both individual and social privilege)
- The notion of power, control, and dominance given to "masculine" qualities over "feminine" characteristics in their constructed social expectations
- The conviction that herosexuality is the "absolute normality" and "moral" sexual orientation, as reflected by most social policies and homosexuals' struggle for equal treatment
- The notion that being or looking "chronologically young" is somehow better than becoming "elderly," as reflected by products of beauty advertised in the media and the common inclination toward "I can't tell you my age"
- The notion that all people can become economically and socially successful and self-sufficient if they only work hard, which minimizes experiences of unequal access to quality education and other social resources, as well as discriminatory social and cultural practices

Models of dominance often minimize human diversity in their process of reinforcing a false sense of collectiveness or commonalities, and thus human oppression seems inevitable when such models are in operation. Models of dominance perpetuate a notion of "normative" to be honored by diverse populations. It seems impossible to escape oppressive forces in a socioeconomic-political system in which daily human relationships are, to one degree or another, shaped by models of dominance.

We ask the reader to take a moment to reflect on the following question: Would you be able to honestly take all your clothes off, be naked in front of a mirror, take a look at your physical body, and make absolutely no judgment about any of its parts? Do you know of anyone who can honestly do this? For years one of the authors of this text (KLG) has raised this question in diversity courses, and so far not one person has been able to honestly answer yes to these questions. This is sad, but not surprising, since the media in the United States constantly bombards people with images of the "perfect" body. As someone once said, "as long as some people are oppressed, nobody is free." Thus, confrontation with the intention to promote personal and societal change becomes inevitable if oppressive forces are to ultimately be eliminated. The endless possibility of change and reconstruction should never be taken for granted. It is never too late to join the journey!

Andersen and Collins (2001) used a "matrix of domination" approach to explore oppressive forces. Their model "posit[s] multiple, interlocking levels of domination that stem from the societal configuration of race, class, and gender relations. . . . [T]his structural pattern affects individual consciousness, group interaction, and group access to institutional power and privilege" (p. 4). The matrix of domination developed by Andersen and Collins explores effects that oppressive forces have at intrapersonal, interpersonal, and macro capacities. Andersen and Collins stress that due to historical institutional racism, sexism, and homophobia, among other oppressive forces, some institutions have met the needs of some people while neglecting the needs of others. This reflects the institutionalization of oppression fostering economic deprivation and reduction of access to social resources. While exploring oppressive forces within the context of human diversity, and vice versa, significant wounds that have been historically cultivated can be observed. Two of the most visible wounds have been the dehumanization of people's lives and the breakdown of trust and safe-felt connections within and between groups of people. Oppressive forces have hurt the human spirit and injured individual and collective well-being. Cultivation and internalization of unnecessary fears, defensiveness, confusion, resentments, and anger-hatred toward self and others have been reflected throughout history as oppressive forces have played a significant role in relationships within and between groups of people.

The internalization of oppressive forces plays a role in the development of a sense of **disempowerment,** injuring natural human tendencies to effect change and individualized human capacity to exercise some control over self-direction, as well as promoting self-blame, persistent self-invalidation, and cultivation of a sense of a better-or-less-than lens mirrored by ethnocentric perspectives. Internalization of oppressive forces is often manifested externally as reflected by both the **institutionalization** and **culturalization** of oppressive forces, and vice versa (Yamato, 2001). While institutionalization of oppressive forces creates a system in which resources are controlled and unequally distributed, culturalization of oppressive forces establishes the social norms to foster such dynamics (Wambach & Van Soest, 1997). Institutionalization and culturalization of oppressive forces reinforce differential social power and accessibility to resources. These forces are coupled with the explosive power exemplified in the United States by the most powerfully resourceful groups (i.e., those who hold and control the means of production), who also impose on society their norms, beliefs, values, customs, language, and so on, often through dehumanizing social policies that are internalized by those with less resources. Institutionalization and culturalization of oppressive forces cultivate competition for cheap labor, creating the space for simultaneous exploitation and stigmatization of **poor communities** (communities with little or no financial or other resources, working in exchange for financial or other resources in order to keep up with daily life demands). Exploitation of communities also occurs to those who are perceived as being in the middle of the ladder (the middle classes), since they often work urgently at upholding their material goods and financial achievements. Competition for labor often fosters a notion of superiority-inferiority based on economic resources. The competition for resources, power differentials, and ethnocentric perspectives all create a sense of "better than" and foster social stratification (Healey, 1997). **Social stratification** refers to a system or arrangement where socioeconomic mobility is relatively predetermined by discrepancies in ways that diverse groups of people are treated.

Although most human diversity literature has had the tendency to historically document the wounds experienced between "White ethnic groups" and "non-White ethnic groups," the human pain and suffering cultivated through oppressive force includes and yet moves beyond these group categorizations. Oppressive forces are reflected within *group membership.* For instance, while much was accomplished by the ideals of equal opportunity and social justice supporting the 1960s–1970s civil rights movement, many of its heterosexual supporters rejected gay men, lesbian women, and bisexuals because of differences in sexual orientation. A similar dynamic operated in the 1960s–1970s reemergence of the women's movement where large numbers of White women, who called themselves feminists, on a quest for social justice could not move beyond their racist attitudes, values, and beliefs, and thus treated non-White women accordingly. Regardless of family arrangements (opposite-sex or same-sex family configurations, blended family systems, communal family structures, etc.), families often seem to struggle with socially constructed gender expectations and roles of dominance and subordination.

Oppressive forces also have been reflected within what are commonly considered White ethnic groups. As observed by Takaki (2001), "during the nineteenth century, the Irish, like the Chinese, were victims of British colonialism. . . . Representing a Catholic group seeking to settle in a fiercely Protestant society, the Irish immigrants were targets of American nativist hostility. They were also what historian Lawrence J. McCaffrey called 'the pioneers of the American urban ghetto,' 'previewing' experiences that would later be shared by the Italians, Poles, and other groups from southern and Eastern Europe" (p. 57). Ferber (2001), in a writing entitled *What White Supremacists Taught a Jewish Scholar about Identity,* documents how her research on White supremacy reveals a correlation between White supremacy, anti-Semitism, and racism. Ferber writes:

> White supremacists see Jews as threats to racial purity, the villains responsible for desegregation, integration, the civil-rights movement, the women's movement, and affirmative action—each depicted as eventually leading white women into the beds of black men. Jews are believed to be in control everywhere, staging a multipronged attack against the white race. . . . Contemporary white supremacists define Jews as non-white: 'not a religion, they are an Asiatic race, locked in a mortal conflict with Aryan man,' according to The New Order. In fact, throughout white-supremacist tracts, Jews are described not merely as a separate race, but as an impure race, the product of mongrelization. (pp. 115–116)

The individualized and collective history of Irish, Italian, Pole, and Jewish communities within the United States illustrates the importance of considering context, chronological times, socioeconomic-political conditions and demands, as well as interpretations of meanings, when exploring oppressive forces. These *histories* individually and collectively reflect how experiences such as race are socially constructed and constantly changing. For instance, as emphasized by Ferber (2001), as a collective, the Jewish community has been perceived within the U.S. mainstream culture as a White ethnic group, whereas according to the White-supremacist movement, the Jewish community is an impure race threatening White identity. Ferber wrote, "For White supremacists, the central goal is to naturalize racial identity and hierarchy, to establish boundaries" (p. 118). Ferber's observations make it easier to recognize that racial classifications are socially constructed and often tied to social power. As observed, internalization, institutionalization, and culturalization of oppressive forces affect all of us within context.

Within the U.S. context, race has often been perceived in terms of "White versus Black" or "White versus non-White." Some groups of people have been categorized as the oppressor (i.e., White communities, especially men with socioeconomic-political power), while others have been referred to as the oppressed (i.e., non-White communities). However, the dynamics generated by oppressive forces—who implements them and benefits from them—are more complicated than the simplistic idea of "White versus non-White." This observation is not intended to minimize historical facts illustrated by groups of people who have shared a number of attributes from the models of dominance discussed earlier, which often seem to outdistance some of the social obstacles presented to other groups. As mentioned previously, for instance, U.S. presidents have shared some common denominators (i.e., being White, male, and publicly pronounced heterosexual). However, each individual, family, group, and community has the potential to be *the oppressor* within specific contexts and yet become submissive enough within other contexts to be *the oppressed.* This is not to say that people experience oppressive forces the same way. To pretend that people experience oppressive forces the same way is to ignore human diversity and complexities. Rather, acknowledgment of people's capacity to be oppressors and their potential to be the oppressed reflects the multidimensional and contextual aspects of oppressive forces.

Although historically oppressive forces have been mostly documented in terms of White "domination" and non-White "subordination," this perspective is fragmented when we look at a larger whole, and thus tends to marginalize oppressive experiences encountered within group membership. As noted, an individual or community may be the oppressor within one context and the oppressed within another, regardless of race, ethnicity, sexual orientation, socioeconomic status, and so on. Authors such as Aponte (1995) have emphasized that a distinction "should be made between oppression that has occurred due to ethnic and racial differences versus oppression due to gender, sexual orientation, disability, and religious differences . . ." (p. 47). We would add another dimension: oppression that is multifaceted. Such distinctions can be helpful in identifying and examining the multidimensional and contextual aspects of oppressive forces affecting individual and collective well-being while attempting to explore strategies for promoting change. Separate exploration and analysis is valuable; however, connecting it to the collective whole cannot be neglected if profound changes are to be achieved.

Social/health/human service practitioners are strongly encouraged not to neglect people's encounters with oppressive forces during the process of providing professional services. Furthermore, from a multidimensional contextual perspective, generalization of experiences that neglects differences is not encouraged. One way in which clients' encounters with oppressive forces can be recognized and honored is by simply engaging in **reflective listening practices.** These are practices by which the practitioner encourages clients to share their life encounters, meanings, interpretations, and effects, and especially how these relate to current challenges. Reflective listening practices can be coupled with **paraphrasing** (i.e., the process of restating clients' verbal statements to encourage clients to listen to themselves while the human service practitioner continues to search for elaboration or clarification of messages being presented). The practitioner is asked to start where the client is and to treat each individual, family, group, and community as a potential source of internal and external change. **Closed-ended questions** (i.e., questions restricting response to a few words or limited content) and **open-ended inquiries** (i.e., questions inviting expanded expressions and clarification or elaboration of content being discussed) can be used as baselines for assessing clients' narratives, strengths, and challenges. (Note: For detailed content on intervention skills, refer to books such as D. H. Hepworth, R. H. Rooney, and J. A. Larsen's *Direct Social Work Practice: Theory and Skills,* 6th edition (2002), and B. F. Okun, J. Fried, and M. L. Okun's *Understanding Diversity: A Learning-as-Practice Primer* (1999), both from Brooks/Cole Publishing Company, Pacific Grove, CA.)

To encourage the reader to further explore the content of this chapter, we have constructed the following vignette. Examine this vignette carefully, and address the questions that follow:

> Since September 11, 2001, stigma and public distrust toward immigrants has been strengthened, as evidenced by legislation proposals, policy implementations, and the hate crimes that have occurred in a significant number of communities. Such stigma and distrust have reinforced cognitive, emotional, behavioral, social, and political stressors, especially for immigrants of Middle-Eastern origin. Imagine that the community you are serving through your place of employment is a community composed largely of individuals, families, and groups from the Middle East.

- What attributes may these individuals, families, and groups have in common?
- How may these individuals, families, and groups differ from one another?
- What forms of oppressive forces might be reflected in the experiences encountered by this community of people?
- What cognitive, emotional, behavioral, and social effects might be created by the oppressive forces within this community?
- What strategies would you consider for promoting social mobilization (i.e., to encourage awareness regarding differences and commonalities, as well as the effects of stigmatization, marginalization, and distrust)?

HUMAN RESILIENCE: STRENGTHENING ENDURANCE

Human diversity is not exclusively about pain caused by constructed oppressive forces or natural forms of adversities (e.g., death of a loved one). Human diversity is also about learning through differences and commonalities; it is about celebrating the potential that exists when embracing the human spirit; it is about cheering for people's potential and ability to construct, deconstruct, and reconstruct experiences—often to lift themselves above challenges reinforced by vulnerable life conditions; and it is about honoring human resilience, strengthening individual and collective hopes, as well as cultivating new visions. When exploring human diversity, we must not neglect the ability of individuals, families, groups, and communities to overcome adversities as well as their potential for cultivating equilibrium-fostering well-being.

Individual and collective **resilience** (an innate essence enacted in supportive relationships and resources that promotes an ability to maintain, recover, or regain a level of control, intention, and direction before, during, or after an encounter with adversity) has been reflected throughout history. An example of individualized resilience can be found in the life of Sojourner Truth (1797–1883). She was born as a slave under the name of Isabella Baumfree, escaped to New York and lived as an outlaw, and changed her name to Sojourner Truth, reflecting her intentions to travel and reveal the truth about slavery and the treatment of slaves. Ms. Truth had a mission, and she pursued it despite the physical and psychological punishment she often encountered. After slavery was legally abolished, Sojourner Truth continued to campaign against the individual and social inequality and injustice experienced by African-American men and women. Sojourner Truth's resilience was illustrated through her self-efficacy, sense of self-direction, faith that slavery could be abolished, and persistent attitude.

Another example of individual resilience is mirrored by the life of Frederick Douglass. Frederick Douglass (1817–1895) grew up as a slave during the early 1800s, secretly taught himself to read and write despite possible emotional and physical abuse if caught, escaped to New York when he was 21 years old, and became one of the most influential persons in the fight for the abolition of slavery. Mr. Douglass's resilience was reflected by the determination he showed while achieving a number of accomplishments that were unprecedented for a Black man: He went from slavery to establishing the *North Star* newspaper in 1847, assisting and influencing President Abraham Lincoln in allowing Black soldiers into the Union Army, to becoming America's minister to Haiti in 1889. Resilience has also been illustrated in the lives of individuals such as Nelson Mandela (South Africa), Mahatma Gandhi (India), Julia de Burgos (Caribbean), and so on. As emphasized in Chapter 2, resilience is a process of inner power, fostered by protective factors, that enables individuals, families, groups, and communities to withstand and recover from life challenges, as well as strengthening their endurance (Walsh, 1998b). As might be expected from our discussion so far, diverse people within different contexts, encountering diverse experiences, exemplify resilience differently.

Resilience is not exclusively experienced and demonstrated individually, but can be found within and between groups of people as well. History has shown how First Nations Peoples have been harmfully affected as collective subcommunities by colonialism, and yet socioeconomic-political activism has been cultivated, reinforced, and encouraged by persistence and a belief that strength is found in collaboration. Relational resilience has been mirrored in other collective socioeconomic-political activism as well, including the labor movement, the poverty movement, the civil rights movement, the women's movement, and the gay/lesbian/bisexual/transgender movement. Relational resilience has been evidenced by bonds built within and between groups of people to serve as a means of organizing or arranging resources with the intention of satisfying members' biopsychosocial and/or spiritual needs. Advocacy and establishment of social policies and laws aimed at protecting people's rights (e.g., the Civil Rights Act) also provide evidence of results achieved through relational resilience. Relational resilience is cultivated through a shared support intended to reduce or change social-cultural conditions that injure collective well-being. Community links and nourishment serve as fuel and protective factors when groups of people are confronting diverse life challenges. Community connections, thus, foster relational resources (Walsh, 1998b).

Individualized and relational resilience also seem to be reinforced through protective factors. Kinship care, spiritual rituals and practices, and grassroots movements, to mention a few, have often served as fundamental resources for strengthening the human spirit. Furthermore, as indicated by Walsh (1998a), "being able to give meaning to a precarious situation makes it easier to bear. It can also be transforming, bringing clarity and new vision to life. . . . [R]esilience is forged by coming to terms with experience and integrating that understanding with new challenges" (p. 67). Meaning, however, is not enough. It must be accompanied by an optimistic orientation promoting hope, perseverance, commitment, courage, and confidence. *While a positive outlook, lifting up the human spirit when coping with life stressors and crises, reflects hope, perseverance mirrors the strong-willed, encouraging, continuous attempts to confront adversities regardless of the number of unsuccessful attempts. Moreover, while courage enables risk taking, confidence embraces trust, and commitment encourages action.* Practitioners would benefit from recognizing the supportive relationships that help to cultivate and strengthen hope, perseverance, courage, commitment, and confidence. Thus, relationships with clients must not be mechanical; they must be considered sacred in order for human commonalities, basic needs, differences, oppressive forces, and individualized as well as relational manifestations of resilience not be marginalized.

Finally, according to Greene and Livingston (2002), interventions incorporating resilience have at least twenty-one characteristics, which can be grouped according to the following system levels:

- Micro level: helping clients access their own resources, motivating and engaging clients by focusing on strengths, building personal capacity, enhancing client self-awareness, and tapping innate individual abilities
- Meso level: stabilizing and normalizing the situation, identifying the possible, tapping intrinsic worth, illuminating opportunities, working to clarify meaning and purpose of events, facilitating problem-solving abilities, and offering group support
- Macro level: providing for basic needs (e.g., safety, food, water, electricity); attending to diversity and respecting ethnicity, gender, race, sexual orientation, and so on; challenging oppressive situations and seeking equity; combating negative environmental messages; tapping into wellness programs; dealing with institutional belief systems; working with social supports, mentors, peers, clergy, and teachers; and identifying community stakeholders, building on community assets, engaging in community action and renewal strategies, and enhancing community power (p. 81)

We would like to add another system level to those identified by Greene and Livingston:

- Magna level: challenging the notions of "true objectivity," "correctness," "normality," and "absolutes"; embracing complexities and the wisdom of uncertainty; relying on intuition; and transcending conventional consciousness/realities

While exploring individual, family, group, and community resilience, the practitioner is encouraged to survey the role of language (e.g., the way a client defines resilience may be different from the practitioner's conceptualization). Again, using reflective listening practices can be useful while exploring clients' meanings, interpretations, and effects. A multidimensional and contextual focus (i.e., recognizing the interplay between micro, meso, macro, and magna factors) can enhance the process of identifying and embracing intrapersonal, interpersonal, environmental, and spiritual sources needed to promote and strengthen individual and relational resilience.

The following case study was constructed by one of the authors of this text (KLG) and Dr. Arlene Bowers Andrews (Professor/Director of the Institute for

Families in Society, University of South Carolina, in Columbia, SC). It presents an individual, Michael, encountering experiences within different contexts and with different intensities. As you read the case study and explore Michael's transactions, assess his strengths and develop a possible plan of action.

CASE STUDY

Michael is a 26-year-old man who lives alone in an apartment. Michael has two children (Elijah, 7, and Isaiah, 5). Ever since he and Madeline (the biological mother of Elijah and Isaiah) broke up, Michael has stopped spending much time with his kids. Michael loves his children, however, and feels that he has not been a good role model for them. While in his relationship with Madeline, Michael was unfaithful and often verbally abusive. Currently, Michael and Madeline often engage in arguments when he goes to visit his kids. Michael is not comfortable with his behavior. He emphasizes that if he knew how to change it, he would do so. Michael lost his construction job. As a result of lack of funding, the company for which he worked laid off a number of employees. Michael's car has broken down and he cannot fix it because of a lack of funds. Michael has been looking for a job in the classified ads. The jobs that he feels he is qualified for are hard to get to on public transportation. Michael lives in a poor neighborhood. Some of his friends like to get together at the bar on the weekends and often disregard Michael's experiences. He does not feel that he can talk to them and be heard. Others like to spend most of their time with their spouses or significant others and children. Michael is often invited to their homes, but he rejects these invitations because he feels that he would be invading their privacy. Michael has encountered a lack of support from the religious community. Most of the religious leaders distrust Michael because of his previous encounters with the law. Michael has been charged with two robberies and attempted murder, which he says was self-defense. Michael's parents and siblings, as well as some friends, have provided him with emotional support. Michael seems optimistic that his situation will change.

Reflection on Case
- What would you consider to be indicators of Michael's individual strengths and resilience?
- What factors reflect relational resilience?
- How could Michael's resilience be strengthened while his challenges are addressed?
- What steps would you take to construct a plan of action for continuing to assess Michael's encounters while promoting necessary changes?

SUMMARY

This chapter has covered a number of key beginning principles of working with the client from a multidimensional contextual practice perspective. We encourage practitioners to start with a positive sense of client well-being, to uncover and discover the multiple identities and experiences of the client, to understand the external and internal nature of oppressive forces, and to mobilize resilience as a strength. In the following chapter, we build on these themes, focusing on services and the practitioner.

Discussion Questions

1. What is your perspective regarding basic human needs?
2. How may human commonalities be used to reduce the effects of oppressive forces?
3. To what degree do you relate to the notion of multiple-self or multiple identities? What would you add to, and what would you eliminate from, this paradigm? How may this perspective be useful in reducing stereotypical thinking and increasing client well-being?
4. To what degree do you agree or disagree with the notion that multiple levels of realities/consciousness (i.e., both conventional and transcendent realities/consciousness) exist? In what ways may multiple levels of consciousness be important or unimportant when addressing strengths and challenges within human diversity?
5. To what degree do you agree or disagree with the notion that multiple models of dominance exist, reinforce, and perpetuate oppressive forces within the United States? What cultural and social dynamics do you think can be used to strengthen or weaken models of dominance affecting human interactions and exchanges?
6. Do you believe that human resilience can lead to the creation of an egalitarian society? How can you contribute to this process?

References

Andersen, M. L., & Collins, P. H. (Eds.). (2001). *Race, class, and gender: Anthology* (4th ed.). Belmont, CA: Wadsworth/Thomson Learning.

Aponte, C. I. (1995). Cultural diversity course model: Cultural competence for content and process. *Arete, 20*(1), pp. 46–55.

Banks, J. A. (1997). Multicultural education: Characteristics and goal. In J. A. Banks & C. A. M. Bank (Eds.), *Multicultural education: Issues and perspectives* (3rd ed., pp. 3–31). Needham Heights, MA: Allyn & Bacon.

Brill, N. I., & Levine, J. (2002). *Working with people: The helping process* (7th ed.). Boston: Allyn & Bacon.

Erickson, F. (1997). Culture in society and in educational practices. In J. A. Banks & C. A. M. Bank (Eds.), *Multicultural education: Issues and perspectives* (3rd ed., pp. 32–60). Needham Heights, MA: Allyn & Bacon.

Ferber, A. L. (2001). What White supremacists taught a Jewish scholar about identity. In M. L. Andersen & P. H. Collins (Eds.), *Race, class, and gender: An anthology* (4th ed., pp. 115–118). Belmont, CA: Wadsworth/Thomson Learning.

Fromm, E. (1955). *The sane society.* New York: Rinehart & Company, Inc.

Goffman, E. (1959). *The presentation of self in everyday life.* Garden City, NY: Doubleday.

Goffman, E. (1967). *Interaction rituals: Essays on face-to-face behavior.* New York: Pantheon Books.

Greene, R. R., & Livingston, N. C. (2002). A social construct. In R. R. Greene (Ed.), *Resiliency: An integrated approach to practice, policy, and research* (pp. 63–93). Washington, DC: NASW Press.

Guadalupe, J. L. (2000). *The challenge: Development of a curriculum to address diversity content without perpetuating stereotypes.* Ann Arbor, MI: UMI Company.

Guadalupe, J. L., & Freeman, M. (1999, Fall). Common human needs in the context of diversity: Integrating schools of thought. *Journal of Cultural Diversity, 6*(3), 85–92.

Guadalupe, J. L., & Torres, S., Jr. (2001). Puerto Rican healing practices: The spiritual, the religious, the human. In W. DuBray (Ed.), *Spirituality and healing: A multicultural perspective.* San Jose, CA: Writers Club Press.

Gutierrez, L. M. (1990). Working with women of color: An empowerment perspective. *Social Work, 35*(2), 149–153.

Healey, J. F. (1997). *Race, ethnicity, and gender in the United States: Inequality, group conflict, and power.* Thousand Oaks, CA: Pine Forge Press.

Hepworth, D. H., Rooney, R. H., & Larsen, J. A. (2002). *Direct social work practice: Theory and skills* (6th ed). Pacific Grove, CA: Brooks/Cole–Thomson Learning.

Langston, D. (2001). Tired of playing monopoly? In M. L. Andersen & P. H. Collins (Eds.), *Race, class, and gender: An anthology* (4th ed., pp. 125–134). Belmont, CA: Wadsworth/Thomson Learning.

Lum, D. (Ed.). (2003). *Culturally competent practice: A framework for understanding diverse groups and justice issues* (2nd ed.). Pacific Grove, CA: Brooks/Cole.

Maslow, A. H. (1962). *Toward a psychology of being.* Princeton, NJ: D. Van Nostrand Company.

Maslow, A. H. (1970). *Motivation and personality* (2nd ed.). New York: Harper & Row.

Okun, B. F., Fried, J., & Okun, M. L. (1999). *Understanding diversity: A learning-as-practice primer.* Pacific Grove, CA: Brooks/Cole.

Shulman, L. (1999). *The skills of helping individuals, families, groups, and communities* (4th ed.). Itasca, IL: F. E. Peacock.

Solomon, B. (1976). *Black empowerment: Social work in oppressed communities.* New York: Columbia University Press.

Takaki, R. T. (2001). A different mirror. In M. L. Andersen & P. H. Collins (Eds.), *Race, class, and gender: An anthology* (4th ed., pp. 52–65). Belmont, CA: Wadsworth/Thomson Learning.

Tillich, P. (1952). *The courage to be.* New Haven, CN: Yale University Press.

Towle, C. (1945). *Common human needs.* Silver Spring, MD: NASW Press.

Walsh, F. (1998a). Beliefs, spirituality, and transcendence: Keys to family resilience. In M. McGoldrick (Ed.), *Re-visioning family therapy: Race, culture, and gender in clinical practice* (pp. 62–75). New York: Guilford.

Walsh, F. (1998b). *Strengthening family resilience.* New York: Guilford.

Wambach, K., & Van Soest, D. (1997). Oppression. In R. L. Edwards (Editor-in-Chief), *Encyclopedia of social work: Supplement* (19th ed., pp. 243–252). Washington, DC: NASW Press.

Yamato, G. (2001). Something about the subject makes it hard to name. In M. L. Andersen & P. H. Collins (Eds.), *Race, class, and gender: An anthology* (4th ed., pp. 90–94). Belmont, CA: Wadsworth/Thomson Learning.

*You must be the change you wish to
see in the world.* —**Mahatma Gandhi**

4 | Practitioner's Professional Competence in Multidimensional Contextual Services

In Chapters 1 and 2, we discussed the meaning of multidimensional contextual practice and explained its various layers. In Chapter 3, we elaborated on the concept of client well-being as it relates to micro, meso, macro, and magna perspectives and offered direct service practice principles. We now concentrate on the social/health/human services practitioner and agency services as we complete our discussion of the elements of the multidimensional contextual practice framework.

The practitioner's professional competence has been established historically as an important element in the cultural competence movement. The topics of educational and training perspectives (APA, 1980; Manoleas, 1994; Sue, Arredondo, & McDavis, 1992), professional issues related to macro-cultural competence (Ponterotto, Casas, Suzuki, & Alexander, 1995; Pope-Davis & Coleman, 1997), and agency services related to multicultural concerns (Cox & Ephross, 1998; Iglehart & Becerra, 1995) have been raised during the preceding decade. Now, in this chapter, we seek to identify issues and concerns related to the practitioner's competence and agency services regarding client-professional relationships such as conventional and transcendent realities/consciousness; the lights and shadows of services; self-awareness; systemic effects on professional competence; codes of ethics; and practice principles related to professional competence and agency services.

Goffman (1959, 1967) has emphasized that people often engage in conscious and unconscious patterns of interactions using constructed symbols, codes, beliefs, behaviors, and roles while attempting to communicate, challenge encountered life situations, and accomplish specific personal or professional goals. In regard to client-professional relationships, Goffman stressed (and we agree) that a variety of constructed professional roles are used to separate the helper from those receiving help. In such roles, influential power is often placed in the hands of the helper/professional to define the magnitude of the needs of those requesting or receiving services and to determine whether or not they "should be" institutionalized. Through repetitive processes of interactions between those considered as having needs and those considered as helpers, codes, symbols, beliefs, values, and behaviors seem to be constructed, perpetuated, and institutionalized as "objective" norms. This sense of "objectification," Goffman stressed, often becomes a rigid mean guiding professional interactions and client-worker relationships. We would add that the notion of "objectivity" is reinforced by a view of separation instigated and supported by conventional knowledge sustaining conventional consciousness. The **conventional realities/consciousness** (commonly accepted human perceptions limited to that which can be touched, heard, tasted, felt, seen, and measured) reinforced by the "objectification" process often rejects the possibility of **transcendent realities/consciousness** (individual and collective awareness that transcends conventional consciousness in the experience of glimpses of the Great Unknown, as described in the previous chapter).

In the name of good intention, a process of domination by helpers and submission of those receiving services is likely to occur whenever rigidity and inflexibility of "objective" norms sustain the helping process. The process of domination and submission can become more intensified when the vulnerability of those receiving help has shadowed their potential, sense of direction, and empowerment and the helper becomes blinded by mechanical professional procedures considered to be reinforced by so-called "objective" norms and rules. Practitioners are encouraged to keep in mind that **dogmatism** (cultivation and perpetuation of a set of thinking and believing patterns pronounced as absolute truth) can injure ongoing understanding and interactions within the context of human diversity. Practitioners choosing to use **positivist methods** (scientific strategies carrying on the notion that all "reality" can be observed and measured) for generating **knowledge** (constructed information believed to be important) are encouraged to be cautious with the application of "empirical" findings. The cultivation of **facts** (experiences perceived as "real," "truthful," and "essential") is often contextual and relevant to specific time and space. Generalization, although often convenient and useful within a given context, is simplistic in its inclusion, especially when compared to human complexity and its indefinable extension. Generalization tends to marginalize significant human attributes perceived as "less" important. As emphasized earlier, empirical imperialism displays the notion of "normal versus abnormal." Such a notion has implications within the context of human diversity.

The study facilitated by Lewis (1968) on Puerto Rican urban families living and experiencing poverty in the United States and Puerto Rico illustrates a classic example of empirical imperialism creating stereotypical senses of "realities." Using culture of poverty theory as a theoretical framework, Lewis attempted to explore reasons why Puerto Rican families in poverty seem to be poorer as a collective than families in any other Latino community. Lewis wanted to generate findings that would explain multigenerational poverty observed in the families selected in his sample with the intention of creating a general baseline for understanding poverty among Puerto Rican families. While generally focusing on personal characteristics of men and women experiencing poverty (e.g., degree of personal inspiration, attitudes and

beliefs regarding the future, etc.), Lewis seems to have minimized cultural and societal forms of oppressive forces interfering with the economic mobility of those being
researched, as well as the possible internalization of oppressive messages. His generalizations that Puerto Rican families encountering poverty experience indifferent
thoughts toward the future, lack inspiration, and hold pessimistic attitudes toward
life are contrary to observations made by the authors of this book, one of whom
(KLG) personally experienced poverty within a Puerto Rican urban family while
growing up. Within the context of this author's family experiences, education was
perceived as the ticket out of poverty. Sacrifices were made by the author's single
mother and other parents within this poor community to encourage children's education with the intention of terminating the cycle of poverty. Although all the efforts
were not "successful" in terms of all the children within this poor community growing up and experiencing a different socioeconomic status as adults, the attempts
reflected an optimistic attitude toward life, inspirations, and an unquestionable belief
in future opportunities.

An interesting aspect about generalizations that tend to neglect diversity within
diversity, as reflected by the general ideas that have emerged and been reinforced
through empirical work such as Lewis's (1968) research, is that these often engender
and enable stereotypes to be transformed into paradigms believed to reflect "normal"
dynamics occurring within a particular group. As stereotypes are perpetuated
through documents, interactions, and "educational" experiences, the assumptions
that these stereotypes establish are often institutionalized as "objective" written and
verbal norms. As emphasized earlier, language is a powerful tool in that it helps to
create, reinforce, and modify the world in which we live. As Foucault (1980) stresses,
language influences social processes. Although sometimes conscious and at other
times unconscious, language—whether written, verbal, or nonverbal—has and carries
with it intentionality. Its intention, however, does not constantly benefit all human
beings equally. As observed by Foucault, the language, meaning, and interpretations
of people holding social, economic, and political control of communal resources and
decision-making processes often tend to dominate social processes. The language and
constructed knowledge of populations who are in control of means of production,
Foucault points out, are often accepted as "truth," and the experiences of communities of people with lesser or no control of means of production are marginalized.

Time, context, and specific circumstances, among other variables, are often neglected by the notion of total "objectivity" established in the name of professional
effectiveness. Can practitioners honestly say that their subjective experiences do not,
in one way or another, influence professional decisions within the context of service
provision? Who should be perceived as the "true" expert with valuable information—the practitioner observing the client's experience, or the client who is encountering it? Practitioners need to be open to the endless and diversified experiences as
well as the possibilities emerging during the helping process in order to appropriately
and effectively serve those requesting or receiving services. Awareness of the dynamics of power, control, and manipulation that may emerge during the process of co-
creation of experiences, mirrored in the helping process, is a vital commitment to
mutual partnership and collaboration. Practitioners can benefit from exploring how
constructed social orders often become normalized and perceived as absolute "objec-

tive realities" (Foucault, 1980). To disregard the inseparable (i.e., to separate the observed from the observer) is to deny the subjective components of the perceptions, interpretations, meanings, and approaches that often affect professional interactions and the development of paradigms.

As discussed in this chapter, a degree of "relational objectification" is likely to emerge through constructed collective agreements (e.g., killing and eating a cow is socially and legally accepted within the United States, whereas killing and eating a dog is not). However, constructed collective agreements are contextual by nature and may not be generalized in ways that neglect diversity within (e.g., in other parts of the world, cows are considered sacred but dogs can be eaten). The multidimensional contextual perspective presented throughout this text is to be used as a friendly guideline to provoke thinking within and beyond the conventional boxes of knowledge. It serves as a medium for reminding the reader that the notion of total objectivity is an illusion—an oversight of the "lights" and "shadows" of services affecting professional competence. It is a setup for disappointment. This chapter addresses two major areas: (1) professional competence (an exploration of the interplay of lights and shadows of services), and (2) an exploration of multidimensional contextual services through an analysis of assessment, service development and delivery, as well as an evaluation of outcomes without the perpetuation of stereotypes.

PROFESSIONAL COMPETENCE: THE INTERPLAY OF LIGHTS AND SHADOWS OF SERVICES

We recognize that the notion of *absolute* professional competence is an illusion, and belief in it is likely to lead to disappointment. Social/health/human service practitioners will make mistakes throughout their professional careers while serving diverse communities of people. However, a degree of professional competency in human diversity (i.e., an ability to serve diverse individuals and communities within different contexts, without engaging in stereotypical or immediate-gratification approaches that promote marginalization of important attributes or the disempowerment of those being served) is vital if client well-being is a goal. As mentioned earlier, professional competence often requires a balance between learned skills, cultivated values of respect regarding human diversity, professional self-awareness/evaluation, confrontation of discriminative cognitive and emotional patterns and actions promoted in the name of professionalism, and a level of trust in the wisdom of uncertainty. In order for practitioners not to become mechanical in their professional assessments and interventions, they need a degree of awareness regarding their strengths, areas in need of improvement, clients' potentialities, basic human needs, resources, and adversities encountered by those being served. Mindful planning and delivery of professional support and resources, conducted at the micro-intrapersonal, meso-interpersonal, macro-environmental, and magna-spiritual levels, can be strengthened by an exploration of the "lights" and "shadows" of services.

The intention behind the conceptualization of lights and shadows of services is to encourage practitioners in the process of identifying, exploring, strengthening, and modifying personal-professional patterns of interactions as well as experiences that reinforce or injure the process of serving others in the name of professionalism. Practitioners are not immune to human pain generated through natural or constructed human adversities. Human service practitioners, like clients, are individuals with the potential to overcome adversities through the nurturing of personal and relational resilience. As is the case with clients, human service practitioners have many ways of knowing, feeling, thinking, behaving, and being, and these cannot be ignored if the individualization of ongoing professional development is to be fostered. Yet, due to the nature of the "helper" role and the need to be resourceful, we encourage human service practitioners to also engage in processes intending to strengthen professional competence. By this time, it should not be surprising to the reader that the authors of this text have some ideas (and biases) about what some of those processes need to be.

Cultivation and Maintenance of a Degree of Self-Awareness

The client-practitioner relationship can be strengthened by the practitioner's cultivation and maintenance of a degree of awareness regarding personal wounds, as well as a commitment to engage in ongoing processes of healing. The practitioner's ongoing professional self-evaluation and self-awareness, leading to necessary change, are viewed as critical if professional competence is a goal. Adversities generating emotional-cognitive pain seem to be universal, although contextually individualized. As stressed earlier, practitioners are not excluded from human pain. Furthermore, human pain can give rise to multiple responses including a conscious commitment to promote change or an unconscious engagement in emotional-cognitive-behavioral patterns instigating additional pain in one's self and others. Exploration of our emotional-cognitive wounds, produced through human encounters and exchanges, can create baselines that remind us to be sensitive when assisting others in their processes for achieving optimal health and well-being. Self-reflection can be a vehicle for identifying emotional, cognitive, and behavioral ways in which we may participate in promoting unnecessary pain. The goal can be to continuously engage in self-reflection with the intention of awakening to possible cognitive-behavioral patterns that harmfully affect our professional encounters and to explore possible options to engage in necessary transformation. Recognizing that professional competence and awareness are moving targets can be useful in understanding the importance of ongoing professional self-evaluation and growth. Human beings, conditions, and dynamics are frequently changing. Thus, working with people requires a degree of awareness of one's strengths and a constant commitment to work on both personal and professional areas that need improvement.

The concept of "lights" of service is symbolic of a degree of awareness encouraging practitioners not to use professional encounters to satisfy the ego or to medicate undealt-with cognitive-emotional wounds. Rather, it supports practitioners' participation in an ongoing process of transformation while consciously, carefully, respectfully, and competently servicing others. The lights of service are reflected by practitioners' willingness to recognize and work on their own discriminative views and stereotypical paradigms affecting professional encounters. They also are illustrated by a commitment to ongoing professional self-reflection that encourages mindfully planned professional actions. The concept of lights of service does not emphasize reaching "enlightenment" or perfection prior to serving others, but, rather, is a demonstration of integrity that endorses using professional honesty to guide interventions based on the promotion of client well-being rather than professional hidden agendas.

We would like to stress that honoring and embracing the lights of service does not necessarily imply having "absolute" awareness of emotional, cognitive, and behavioral patterns and surroundings. This can be the ideal, however, and anyone's achievement of such a challenging task would certainly be a call for celebration. Honoring the lights of service means recognizing ourselves as works in progress and requires an ongoing commitment and recommitment to be present as much as possible and to act in accordance with the best of our capacities at any given time. It is an intention set to explore motives influencing our desires and skills that are needed for serving others. It is using the mind as a tool for promoting necessary change (i.e., personal healing of wounds) that is helpful in competently serving others, and not as a master enslaving us with emotional, cognitive, and behavioral patterns (effects of internalized racism, sexism, classism, ageism, homophobia, etc.) that are destructive by nature. Honoring the lights of service involves creating a balance between the many ways of knowing, including both conventional and transcendent consciousness based on scientific paradigms and intuition (or, should we say, the wisdom of uncertainty). It is not an exclusive mental exercise of rationalization, but an opportunity to discover or uncover the potentiality that exists within each of us to promote or injure our own and others' optimal health and well-being. Mahatma Gandhi once stated, "Action without contemplation is blind." In other words, ongoing professional self-reflection, with the intention of consciously cultivating awareness as an initial ingredient to establishing and carrying on a commitment to engage in necessary change, is a component of the lights of service. Self-reflection is vital while engaging in conscious nonstereotypical practice.

The idea of "shadows" of service is represented by the notion of "wounded healers." **Wounded healers** are practitioners who, themselves, are in need of recovering and healing from cognitive-emotional wounds generated through life experiences, yet they do not seem to be aware of these wounds, or are aware of them but unwilling to confront them. Unawareness or unwillingness to take care of "unfinished business" increases the possibility of services being shadowed by the practitioner's own personal wounds. For instance, inflexible professional behavioral patterns resulting from personal wounds, generating an unbendable need for control, are likely to unfavorably affect client-helper rapport and interactions within diverse contexts of services (i.e., micro, meso, macro, magna). A subconscious need for absolute power and control, stimulated by feelings of inadequacy, can injure the process of encouraging clients to experience their uncertainties, resources, and strengths needed to promote necessary change. As emphasized within another context, "shadows of services are reflections of hidden masks buried in personal narratives" (Guadalupe, 2003, p. 33). It can be argued that we all have shadows that affect our interactions with others. Thus, recognition of the shadows of service and a commitment to make necessary changes are vital in order for professional competence to be strengthened.

The social/health/human service practitioner's need to be needed, resulting from undealt-with experiences of loss and fear of abandonment, is likely to play a role in determining when the practitioner decides that a person, family, group, or community receiving services is ready for termination. How often, when individuals, families, groups, or communities refuse or terminate service, does one hear statements such as, "They are just in denial" or "They are resistant to change." Through professional experiences, we have observed that these comments are often made with minimum to no assessment of clients' reasons for refusing or terminating services, reflecting the shadows of service in those making these statements. Practitioners can benefit from the idea that "true empowerment" of clients means working oneself out of a job. The idea is to facilitate and trust clients' potential for change without taking ownership of clients' fruitful experiences, recognizing that our values and ideas of "success" may be very different from those held by clients.

While a constant need for a sense of power and control over those receiving services as well as an obsession with servicing others (used as a means to avoid cultivating awareness and confronting individualized pain) are some of what the metaphor of shadows of service addresses, a commitment to ongoing professional self-evaluation encouraging transformation of destructive cognitive, emotional, and behavioral patterns is an attribute reflected by the lights of service (Straub, 2000). It is common within the helping process to attempt to take full credit for constructive changes observed in the lives of those being served—to want to say, "Look at how great I am." The need to be recognized and to put oneself on a pedestal over those requesting assistance signifies a lack of humility and seems to be symbolic of **ego autostimulation,** a process that reinforces the shadows of service. Recognizing the power that exists in vulnerability and developing a sense of impeccability seem to be vital while unmasking the shadows of service. Becoming impeccable with our words and actions is generally process-oriented. It requires a willingness to engage in self-reflection as well as "honesty, humility, and trust in one's own [internal and external] power in the face of vulnerability . . ." (Guadalupe, 2003, p. 33). Ruiz (1997) in his book *The Four Agreements,* emphasizes that when one is impeccable, one assumes responsibility for one's actions. Accountability is influenced by a degree of awareness regarding variables influencing one's actions.

Micro, Meso, Macro, and Magna Effects on Professional Competence

As emphasized previously, shadows of service are buried in personal narratives. As seems to be the case with lights of services, shadows of service can be reinforced and perpetuated through encounters with cultural influences and experiences of conscious personal and professional choices. These choices generally reflect the interplay and effects of micro, meso, macro, and magna factors. A practitioner's micro experiences or intrapersonal emotional-cognitive patterns perpetuating dynamics shaped by constructed belief, value, and attitude systems are interconnected to meso or interpersonal interactions and exchanges occurring within single or multiple environments. Ongoing interplay between micro and meso factors (i.e., intrapersonal and interpersonal components of practitioners' human encounters) plays a significant role in the co-creation of experiences that may or may not reinforce professional competence.

Cultivation and modification of cognitive perceptions and behavioral patterns seem to be influenced by interactions and exchanges occurring within and between micro and meso experiences. As the reader may have noticed, a person's developmental processes are significantly influenced by childhood experiences within the contexts of immediate environments (i.e., families, friends, neighborhoods). Yet micro and meso interactions and exchanges cannot be seen in isolation from macro or environmental transactions and magna or spiritual orientations encouraging or injuring professional competence. Macro transactions, partially illustrated through the effects that socioeconomic and political conditions have on practitioners in both a personal and professional capacity, can and often do influence the extent of professional competence. How can practitioners serve holistically if resources are not available or accessible to those requesting or receiving services? How is professional competence limited if practitioners carry on in the belief that their job is to focus exclusively on encouraging clients to change their experiences by changing their perceptions without advocating for the development and maintenance of social and macro resources?

Like micro, meso, and macro transactions within and between multidimensional contextual arrangements, magna experiences influencing human service practitioners' personal and professional orientations, decision-making capacities, and behavioral patterns cannot be marginalized. Magna experiences are abstract and subjective by nature. Therefore, practitioners may not perceive them as being less or more important when compared to the interplay between micro, meso, and macro factors. It is important to recognize that what one person may perceive as an oppressive encounter instigating unnecessary human pain, another may call a spiritual experience carrying on a purpose. This point can be illustrated by the promotion of the system of slavery existing in the United States and supported by "Christian values" prior to 1865, historical legal segregation of churches and ritualistic spiritual practices, historical social services sustained by "Christian morals" coupled with social Darwinism orientations (e.g., Charity Organizations Societies in the 1800s), and interpretations of biblical messages to devalue or value homosexual life experiences. The events occurring on September 11, 2001, when a group of individuals took control of four airplanes and crashed them (two into the World Trade Centers in New York City, one into the Pentagon in Washington, DC, and yet another in a small town in Pennsylvania), causing massive human deaths, are another example supporting this observation. Those who perpetuated the act were said to have done so from the perspective that it was God's will, while others saw it as an act of violence and creation of unnecessary human pain, and others interpreted these events as a spiritual catalyst reflecting a need for changes in world politics. As has been emphasized throughout this text, micro, meso, macro, and magna factors affect all aspects of human life, including professional competence, meanings, and interpretations.

Codes of Ethics and Professional Competence

Professional competence can be encouraged or injured by codes of ethics. Interdependent multiple forms of codes of ethics often influence professional practice, including personal, interpersonal, and interprofessional structural codes of ethics. **Personal codes of ethics** can briefly be described as individualized orientations or points of reference formed, maintained, or changed through the life span serving as baselines for beliefs, values, attitudes, and norms guiding a person's decision-making processes and perceived appropriate choices underlined by a principle of "right" or "wrong" behavior. Personal codes of ethics can be reflected through the dynamics of choices made by individuals. Cultivation of a set of **interpersonal codes of ethics** is similar to the process of cultivating personal codes of ethics, with the exception that it involves a shared collective agreement between a group of people. Beliefs, values, and norms shared and practiced as a collective by a family system or group of people are illustrations of interpersonal codes of ethics. Sharing cultural or subcultural principles and values held by a community or subcommunity also reflects the notion of interpersonal codes of ethics. **Interprofessional structural codes of ethics** are constructed guidelines for engaging in and directing professional practices. Such guidelines are often based on theoretical orientations, principles, values, and the mission of the particular professional discipline (e.g., social work, sociology, psychology, political science, education). Furthermore, such guidelines often advocate for specific standards of conduct and courses of action believed to be vital in achieving overall professional purposes.

An interesting phenomenon that can be observed when exploring the development of codes of ethics is that these are often influenced by conscious and unconscious exchanges among and between groups of people occurring within both single and multiple environments. For instance, interprofessional structural codes of ethics are often constructed as a result of transactions between clients and professionals, as well as among professionals themselves. These exchanges can also be described as the interplay between cultural influences and cultural choices in which beliefs, values, attitudes, and norms are constructed through unconscious and conscious patterns of interactions and exchanges cultivating dominant paradigms. As is the case with professional competence, interactions and exchanges influencing the development or modification of codes of ethics cannot be explored in isolation from micro, meso, macro, and magna factors if a more comprehensive understanding of their effects and implications is a primary goal.

Codes of ethics that reinforce a notion of "professional superiority" over those requesting or receiving services are oppressive by nature, support the shadows of service, and are in need of modification if client well-being is to be at the center of services. It is important to examine who is perceived to be the "expert" (client or worker) within a set of codes of ethics as part of an initial attempt to explore the dynamics of power and control within the helping process. After all, who knows better about challenges than those encountering them? Codes of ethics honoring the lights of service endorse collaborative partnerships in which clients' optimal health and well-being are prioritized over a need for *ego autostimulation*. Furthermore, codes of ethics honoring the lights of service encourage clients' influential participation in identifying and exploring their own strengths, challenges, and options available to promote necessary change. Such codes of ethics are likely to voice a need for a degree of awareness regarding symbolic interactionism (exemplified by the complexity of meanings, boundaries, as well as formal and informal effects of human interactions and exchanges) as an attempt to support conscious actions against interpersonal, institutional, cultural, and social oppressions perpetuated in the name of so-called objective norms and mechanical professional procedures. While interpersonal oppression within the context of the helping process can be illustrated by professional behaviors that marginalize clients' experiences, institutional, cultural, and social forms of oppression can be reflected by inflexible and discriminative formal and informal policies developed in the name of "objectivity." For instance, the fact that numerous educational systems predominantly use stage-based theoretical frameworks to educate diversified communities of students (often future practitioners) is an institutionalized form of oppression perpetuated through the overall culture of education.

Codes of ethics based on dogmatic paradigms are likely to disregard the many ways of knowing, feeling, thinking, behaving, and being while attempting to preserve a compilation of thinking and believing patterns put forth as conclusive resolutions. These types of codes of ethics are likely to injure professional competence within the context of human diversity. Codes of ethics embracing the notion of lights of service within the context of human diversity seem to be more likely to encourage recognition of multiple realities constructed through subjective experiences, meanings, and interpretations. These types of codes of ethics are likely to honor the complexity of human dynamics through recognition of nonstereotypical theoretical frameworks and practice approaches that are inclusive of diversity within diversity.

As emphasized within another context, "an exploration of one's own narrative is [believed to be] a prerequisite to conscious practice at any level and within any context [including the micro, meso, macro, and magna]. Cultivating understanding and acceptance of one's own wounds and shadows [influenced by both natural and constructed adversities] creates a place where reinforcement of the 'Light' of service can be embraced" (Guadalupe, 2003, p. 33). An exploration of one's own narrative also requires an examination of cultural influences and cultural choices, as well as professional codes of ethics being developed, maintained, and perpetuated through individual and collective professional practices. The following text examines core practice principles that can be useful for initiating and strengthening this ongoing process.

PRACTICE PRINCIPLES: STRENGTHENING PROFESSIONAL COMPETENCE

Recognition and Exploration of Lights and Shadows of Service

A commitment to honesty seems vital in the process of recognizing and exploring what has been conceptualized in this chapter as the lights and shadows of services. Self-honesty is reflected by a willingness to explore, and active devotion to continuous exploration of, one's strengths and restrictions experienced throughout one's personal life and professional career. As emphasized before, we take ourselves everywhere we go, and that includes work! Thus, interdependence exists between the personal and professional, and the notion of total "objectivity" is misleading and often hurtful. **Self-honesty** can be viewed as the process of taking a sincere look at our life experiences and the effects that these experiences may have had in the development, maintenance, and modification of life orientations, values, beliefs, and attitudes influencing both personal and professional decisions, as well as behaviors from one context to another.

Tuning into the lights and shadows of services often requires a degree of patience and vulnerability, as cultivated professional images and masks are revealed through this process. While some people are likely to embrace the power that can emerge from vulnerable experiences (e.g., recognition of human pain that may have been reinforced through professional images), others may hold back as they begin to recognize the uncertainty and possible cognitive-emotional pain that this process may bring forth. Consciously ignoring or unconsciously rejecting the lights and shadows of services may allow for temporary cognitive-emotional relief of personal and professional distresses; however, lack of recognition and exploration of lights and shadows of services also may rob human service practitioners of the opportunity to honor their highest potential to change hurtful cognitive, behavioral, and social patterns. Furthermore, ignoring the lights and shadows of services can hinder the possibility for professional services to be habitually influenced by a generosity that transcends prerequisites rather than being based on judgments reinforced through professional conditions.

Although we believe that as human beings we all have the potential to change cognitive, behavioral, and social patterns affecting individual and collective well-being, an assessment of readiness cannot be ignored. Time and context are also perceived as extremely significant. Read the following practice activities, which were constructed to promote recognition and exploration of the lights and shadows of services, and if and when you feel prepared to engage in these exercises, set aside some undisturbed time to do so (one to two hours per activity) in order to fully embrace these process-oriented self-evaluation courses of action, triggers, and possible emotional responses.

Recognition and Exploration of Constructed Theories of Self

As a person, how would you currently describe yourself (e.g., personality, life orientations, communication patterns, self-identity)? To what degree does this description differ from or is reflected in your professional encounters? To what degree does your current description of self differ from ways that you viewed yourself in the past? If your perceptions have changed, what do you think promoted such changes? Which of your beliefs, values, and behavioral patterns do you find strengthening or weakening your encounters with others? While responding to these questions, take the following themes into consideration:

a.   Identity formation (social, cultural, ethnicity, gender, sexual orientation, socio-economic, nationality, religion, age, etc.), maintenance, and change over time
b.   Family, societal, and cultural influences and your cultural choices, as well as the meaning of identity and its effects (e.g., sense of ethnocentrism)
c.   Roles that gender and sexual orientation have played in your human interactions, and the acceptance or rejection of others (e.g., emergence of feelings of superiority, inferiority, or neutrality)
d.   Effects of living with mental or physical abilities and disabilities (e.g., how have these experiences affected your sense of self and your relationships with others?)
e.   Effects of socioeconomic background and religious and spiritual practices and convictions
f.   Relatedness to issues of social and cultural privilege and experiences of social and cultural oppression (e.g., perspectives regarding affirmative action, social stratification, distribution of social resources, social competition for resources, etc.)

g. Perspectives regarding personal and social power, authority, collaboration, and "wealthy" and "unwealthy" clients

h. Observed effects of personal experiences on professional orientation, decisions, and behavioral patterns, and vice versa (e.g., conflict or reconciliation between interpersonal codes of ethics and interprofessional structural codes of ethics)

Through recognition and exploration of the constructed theories of self that they hold, human service practitioners can obtain glimpses of understanding of some of the attributes reinforcing the lights and shadows of professional services, and can use this understanding in the process of planning other strategies for strengthening professional growth. A process of grief, loss, and growth is likely to accompany this activity as practitioners explore identity formation, maintenance, and change, as well as their effects in professional encounters. To alleviate discomfort at the end of this activity, we suggest using *meditative or calm music.*

Another tool that practitioners can use is to develop a *gratitude list* in which they identify personal experiences that have clearly helped strengthen their professional development. Furthermore, they can construct a *collage* reflecting their visualization of future goals. By completing this activity on an optimistic note, practitioners are likely to increase their own willingness to continuously engage in other similar activities.

Value Recognition and Exploration

Identify and prioritize at least ten (10) of your personal values (e.g., integrity, faith in God, importance of material goods, etc.). When do you remember these values initially becoming important to you? How have these values been strengthened or weakened over time? To what degree are these values reflected within the community in which you live? To what degree are they embraced by other members of your family? How and to what degree do these values influence you as a human service practitioner? While responding to these questions, reflect on the following themes:

a. Effect of values on your basic philosophy of life, behavior, and relationships with other individuals

b. Ways you may perceive and behave toward individuals, families, groups, and communities that do not share your values

c. Strengths and constraints of value systems

d. The extremes to which you might go to protect and maintain these values

Reflections on Communication Perspective

How would you define "effective" communication (including both verbal and nonverbal messages)? To what degree is your definition inclusive or exclusive of diverse communication styles reflected within the context of human diversity? What are some of your major expectations when communicating with other people? How might you know when others are receiving your messages, and vice versa (i.e., how might you know when you have effectively understood the messages being transmitted by others)? Consider the following themes while responding to these questions:

    a. What barriers have you experienced when communicating with people with whom you *share* social or cultural commonalities?

    b. What barriers have you experienced when communicating with people with whom you *do not share* social or cultural commonalities?

    c. How have you managed these barriers?

    d. What are some of your most common responses when you perceive that those with whom you are attempting to communicate are unable to receive your messages, and when you are unable to receive theirs?

    e. How might you continue to strengthen your communication patterns?

Additional Ways of Strengthening Professional Competence

In addition to the three activities provided in the previous text, practitioners also can work on strengthening their professional competence through a commitment to being "impeccable" with their word. According to Ruiz (1997), being impeccable with one's word consists of being accountable for one's actions. It is being honest and avoiding making false promises. It is not putting oneself or others down, but recognizing the potentiality to create necessary changes that exist in each moment. It is not getting stuck in the forces of fear, but transcending them through the recognition of love and human resilience. Like any other skill, being or becoming impeccable with one's word requires practice and active devotion.

Furthermore, practitioners can strengthen their professional competence by embracing a sense of "not knowing." A tendency exists to make assumptions about most or all of our human experiences. Statements that reflect types of assumptions that are not necessarily helpful in promoting a deeper exploration of the experience being presented include: "I know how you feel"; "I know about men"; "Women are that way"; and "Latino people are family-oriented." Ruiz (1997) emphasizes that assumptions are often unquestioningly converted into perceived "truths" that ultimately lead to misunderstandings, challenges in our communications, and unnecessary human suffering. Ruiz gives an example: "making assumptions in our relationships is really asking for problems. Often we make the assumption that our partners know what we think and that we don't have to say what we want. We assume they are going to do what we want, because they know us so well" (p. 66). Such assumptions often lead to feelings of hurt, anger, and disappointment, especially when the expectations carried by the assumptions are not fulfilled. Committing oneself to examining one's assumptions through asking questions can be useful in embracing a sense of "not knowing." Ultimately a sense of "not knowing" is likely to assist human service practitioners in identifying and honoring multiple ways of knowing, thinking, behaving, being, and becoming.

The balance between self-reflection and social action can create a strong foundation for professional activism at any capacity (micro, meso, macro, or magna). It is well understood that the process of recognizing lights and shadows of services is a complex one. Several activities will not be enough to complete the process. Thus, practitioners are encouraged to be eclectic in their approaches and to continuously work on their professional development. Allowing oneself periodic times of silent meditation, allowing oneself to witness the thoughts running through one's mind and the sensations felt throughout one's body, can be useful in bringing oneself back to the present moment. As emphasized within another context:

> Meditation need not be used as a drug to numb people to experience, but rather as a tool to mindfully reawaken them to explore alternatives and actions to promote necessary change. . . . Other practices such as journal writing, poetry, and listening to heart inspiring music can be useful in unfolding and transforming our own 'unfinished business.' As energy-draining cognitive, emotional, or behavioral patterns are released, space is created for cultivating individual and collective compassion [the generosity of the heart that is not restrained by the human intellect]. Intellectual knowledge of human diversity, [strengths,] issues, and needs does not automatically translate into action that is compassionate and promote change for the better. (Guadalupe, 2003, pp. 33–34)

The need for conscious commitment to challenging and modifying cognitive, emotional, behavioral, cultural, and social patterns that injure interactions and exchanges within the context of human commonalities and diversity cannot be overemphasized.

Cultivation of an Eclectic Approach

Merging strengths from diverse schools of thought, theoretical frameworks, and practice orientations can reinforce the cultivation of an eclectic approach to practice. For instance, in their article entitled "Common Human Needs in the Context of Diversity: Integrating Schools of Thought," Guadalupe and Freeman (1999) argue that "in spite of their individual limitations, modern and postmodern schools of thought have specific strengths that when integrated can provide a mean for embracing common human needs and similarities within the context of diversity" (p. 3). Modern schools of thought (i.e., cognitive-behavioral theories, Erikson's psychosocial theory, ego psychologies) are generally influenced by a belief that individuals, regardless of gender, sexual orientation, age, ethnicity, culture, socioeconomic background, and so on, share common human needs (sense of safety, belonging, love, etc.). On the other hand, postmodern schools of thought (constructivism and social constructionism, epistemology, ethnographic approaches, etc.), by and large, stress the uniqueness of human differences, as the notions of "reality" and "truth" are viewed as socially constructed, subjective, and contextual by nature. An integration of the strengths deriving from these paradigms can assist human service practitioners while exploring human commonalities within the context of human differences and vice versa. Neither is superior to the other. An eclectic approach to practice, as illustrated here, can reduce professional dogmatism, which is hurtful within the process of serving others in the name of professionalism (Guadalupe & Freeman, 1999).

While in the process of attempting to become eclectic in one's approach, it is vital for the human service practitioner to explore and identify possible strengths and restrictions observed in theoretical frameworks and practice orientation models. Practitioners can begin their exploration by learning about the theoretical frameworks and practice orientation models identified in Table 4.1. The content within most of these theoretical frameworks and practice orientation models does overlap, making it difficult to cluster them in mutually exclusive categories. In the table, we have attempted, instead, to group them in terms of major focuses.

Table 4.1 | Theoretical Frameworks and Practice Orientations

Focus of Theoretical Framework	Examples
Intrapersonal processes	• Freud's psychoanalytic theory • Erikson's psychosocial theory • Piaget's cognitive theory • Ego psychology
Pathologies rather than individual and group strengths	• The medical model • Biological theories • Social problem models • Culture of poverty theory • Social Darwinism
Assumption of a single reality, universal laws, and objectivity	• Logical positivism • Melting pot model
Issues of acculturation, biculturalism, and integration of cultures	• Cultural pluralism models • Acculturation and assimilation theories
Person-in-environment, transactions among different size systems, and the interface where change can occur	• Ecological approaches (e.g., life model by Germain and Gitterman) • System theory • Dual perspective • Multidimensional contextual practice framework
Human interaction through the lens of inequality, oppression, and power and privilege differences, as illustrated by dominant and nondominant groups	• Feminist theories • Conflict theory • Marxist perspectives • Empowerment approaches • Critical theory
Individual, group, and community potential and ability to change	• Strength perspective • Resilience
Eclecticism	• Generalist practice models • Focus on themes rather than specific traits
Cultural specificity	• Afrocentric • Ethnic-sensitive models • Cultural variant perspectives
Postmodern approaches	• Constructivism and social constructionism • Narrative models • Ethnographic approaches
Human behavior in terms of social and cultural influences as well as interpersonal relationships	• Cognitive-behavioral theories • Social-behavioral theories • Identity development theories • Attribution theories
Consideration of spiritual factors	• Transpersonal theories

Focus of Theoretical Framework	Examples
Individual and group identity development	• Transculturality • White identity models • Minority development models
Issues of acculturation, biculturalism, and integration	• Acculturation theories • Standpoint theory
Individual and group communication and exchanges	• Communication theory • Symbolic interactionism • Conflict theory • Contact theory • Social exchange theory

While exploring the strengths and restrictions of theoretical framework and practice orientation models, we find the following questions to be useful:

Is the theory consistent in respecting and supporting human diversity? Does the theoretical framework uphold faith in the human spirit and its potential for transcending adversities? Is the theoretical framework reliable in simultaneously considering the multidimensional set of variables interchangeably affecting the well-being of diverse individuals, families, small groups, and communities? Is the theory practice-oriented? In other words, does the theory incorporate a practice model(s) that assists in the process of strengthening professional competence while guiding professional engagement, assessment, planning, intervention, as well as evaluation? Answering the aforementioned questions optimistically does not imply that the theoretical framework/practice orientation models would not have limitations. Instead, it provides a baseline from which to begin. For example, empowerment theory and practice has had its restrictions. However, the contributions made to the health/social services have transcended its limitations. As a constantly evolving theoretical framework with various practice models, the empowerment approach has, in its basic beliefs, honored, encouraged, valued, and incorporated human diversity principles while advocating for social justice, individual and community well-being, as well as the development of an egalitarian society. (Guadalupe, 2003, pp. 23–24)

The practitioner is also encouraged to explore whether or not theoretical frameworks or practice orientation models are shaped by inflexible dogmatic principles. What biases are reflected in the language used to portray the assumptions held by the specific theoretical framework or practice orientation model? Who is considered to be the expert (i.e., client or worker), and what are the possible implications?

The multidimensional contextual practice framework recommends the practice orientation model identified in Figure 4.1. This model suggests consideration of intrapersonal, interpersonal, social-cultural, as well as spiritual factors affecting well-being and the functioning of individuals, families, groups, and communities. This model proposes a baseline from which practitioners can begin their assessments and considerations for possible interventions in different capacities (i.e., micro, meso,

Figure 4.1 | Multidimensional Contextual Professional Assessments and Interventions

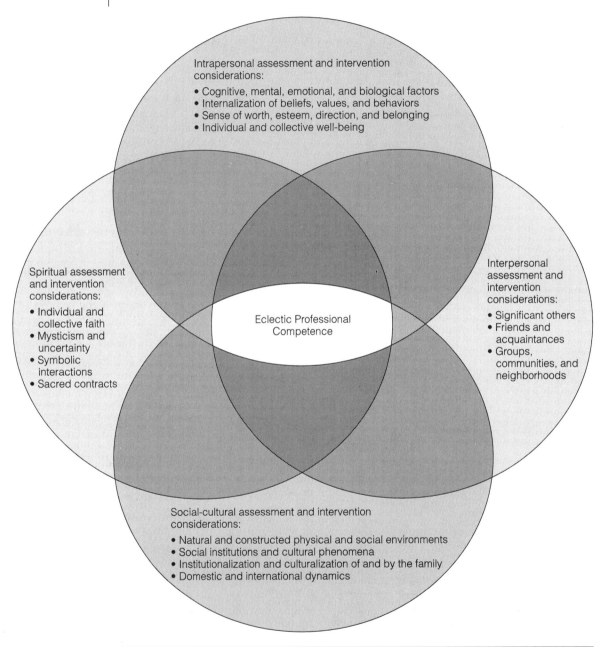

Intrapersonal assessment and intervention considerations:
- Cognitive, mental, emotional, and biological factors
- Internalization of beliefs, values, and behaviors
- Sense of worth, esteem, direction, and belonging
- Individual and collective well-being

Spiritual assessment and intervention considerations:
- Individual and collective faith
- Mysticism and uncertainty
- Symbolic interactions
- Sacred contracts

Eclectic Professional Competence

Interpersonal assessment and intervention considerations:
- Significant others
- Friends and acquaintances
- Groups, communities, and neighborhoods

Social-cultural assessment and intervention considerations:
- Natural and constructed physical and social environments
- Social institutions and cultural phenomena
- Institutionalization and culturalization of and by the family
- Domestic and international dynamics

macro, magna). We recommend that while practitioners use this practice orientation model, they simultaneously continue to concentrate on merging strengths derived from diverse schools of thought and theoretical frameworks, such as those previously mentioned.

MULTIDIMENSIONAL CONTEXTUAL SERVICES

Numerous models have been developed to guide professional practices within the context of diverse populations (Boutte, 1999; Dean, 1993; García & Van Soest, 1997; Gilligan, 1982; Gutierrez, 1990; Keefe & Padilla, 1987; Locke, 1992; Lum, 2003, 2004; Nakanishi & Rittner, 1992; Pinderhughes, 1989; Saleebey, 1994, 2002; Solomon, 1976; Sue, 1981). As a common theme, models have often been based on theoretical principles, assumptions, and practice strategies with the intention of effectively and accurately understanding, developing, and delivering services to diverse individuals, families, groups, and communities. As illustrated previously, the multidimensional contextual practice framework presented in this text is not excluded from this observation. The multidimensional contextual practice framework, however, is eclectic in its approach and claims no absolute "truth" or "reality." Rather, the multidimensional contextual practice framework encourages assessment, intervention, and services that move beyond stereotypical paradigms and approaches that tend to marginalize experiences encountered by individuals, families, groups, and communities.

The multidimensional contextual practice framework reminds readers and its supporters that social/health/human service practitioners need to open themselves to the wisdom of uncertainty that can be, and often is, reflected in so-called esoteric or mystical experiences—the birth and evolution of the unexpected. Using Saleebey's (1994) words, "To do so may require a shift in our understanding of the nature of reality and our stance toward what is 'true'" (p. 351). This shift in understanding can assist us in the process of recognizing and honoring the connectedness between contextual experiences and multidimensional contextual dynamics. A shift in understanding can assist us in moving beyond the marginalization of encounters that seem to be "less important," which is reflected through stereotyping and which overlooks diversity within diversity.

Reflections of Multidimensional Contextual Practice in Other Writings

Multidimensional contextual practice derives from principles, ethics, and skills supported by numerous theoretical frameworks, including so-called postmodern theories such as narrative and ethnographic perspectives, constructivism and social constructionism, postmodern feminism, empowerment-strengths perspectives, and phenomenological thoughts. Multidimensional contextual practice is not a new perspective, as it has been mirrored contextually by ideas and practices of numerous researchers, writers, practitioners, and schools of thought. For instance, a major architectural design trend that relies on multidimensional contextual practice is the Chinese practice of feng shui. **Feng shui** is the study of movements of energy and how it travels in patterns, affecting every aspect of our lives. Quantum physics confirms that all physical matter, no matter how solid it may feel, is energy vibrating in diverse forms with different capacities and purposes reflecting contextual and multiple dimensions. All around us, including realms that we cannot see (i.e., the space between thoughts, the air we breathe), energy exists. Feng shui is interested in visible as well as invisible experiences. It emphasizes that these general dimensions affect human functioning and well-being. The amount of natural light flooding in through the windows, the color of the walls, the types of chairs, the types of pictures and ornaments, the music one listens to, as well as the presence or absence of living plants, among other factors, have an effect on our physical, emotional, cognitive, and spiritual well-being. Furthermore, according to feng shui, the energy vibrating within various places makes us feel differently. Imagine, for example, walking into a room after a fierce argument has taken place there. You are likely to feel the tension; in fact, you might say that you could 'cut the atmosphere with a knife' because of the tension in the space. Likewise, scientific equipment has now been developed to measure the smallest movement of energy. The lie detector can register the most imperceptible fluctuation in vibrations of energy movement in the body. The places in which we live carry evidence and symbols of our past experiences and thoughts and dreams. If we want to change and improve the quality and direction of our lives, we need to understand how, or at least acknowledge that, everything around us interconnects.

Multidimensional contextual practice is an attempt at being inclusive of unique, common, and different experiences encountered by human beings within numerous sets of contexts. Multidimensional contextual practice reminds readers that while some experiences are visible and can be observed, other experiences are invisible and cannot be measured. It further advocates for the recognition that the experience of context is not exclusively about physical locations, geography, or social-environmental configurations. Context is inclusive of invisible dynamics affecting cultivation of cultures and subcultures, traditions and customs, and socioeconomic political systems reflected in so-called history. Context is often explained as locality to describe the physical nature of it. Contexts, however, are modifiable, changeable, and fluid in nature. Context has a broader meaning of surrounding, including, and yet transcending, institutional environments. Some contexts, for instance, are incomprehensible to the human mind. Glimpses of their totality are revealed and reflected by the interface where spiritual reawakening takes place—the context and space between thoughts.

Murphy and Dillon (1998) articulate an interesting understanding of the context of behavior. By context, they mean "when, with whom, and under what circumstances the target behavior occurs" (p. 183). Murphy and Dillon point out that context is important for understanding clients' life experiences and stories. They emphasize that the immediate context (what we might refer to as a combination of micro and meso contexts) involves the client's personal circumstances where there are happenings pertaining to current living arrangements, family and social relationships, economic status, personal history, health, and the particulars of daily life. However, the immediate context is often embedded in a larger system context (which is included in what we refer to as the multidimensional aspects of practice), where economic, social, political, and religious forces and institutions affect global relationships and developments. Murphy and Dillon further advocate for consideration of direct and indirect contexts affecting clients' behaviors, functions, and well-being in order for effectiveness of professional services to be strengthened.

Inclusiveness and Fragmentation

Fragmentation is often reflected in written and verbal discussions of contexts and their attributes. Fragmentation is not the actual issue: it is often useful in promoting a tentative analysis related to specific dynamics occurring within a specific context. A challenge often materializes when, through fragmentation, other contexts and variables that are directly or indirectly influencing interactions and exchanges within the context being analyzed are neglected. The right hand, right foot, right eye, or left side of the brain are unique characteristics of a bigger whole called the human body. Feminist theories hold that the personal is political, for that matter. Neglecting macro issues when addressing so-called micro individual experiences, or vice versa, often leads to assessment that is marginalized and, consequently, to interventions that are likely to be exclusive. A similar case can be made when the magna is neglected while addressing micro, meso, and macro encounters through the vehicle identified as the human body. For instance, in his book *The New Revelation: A Conversation with God,* Walsch (2002) points out that what has been identified as political, economic, and military challenges is rooted in beliefs that are perpetuated by specific interpretations of writings found in holy books such as the Bible, the Bhagavad-Gita, the Book of Mormon, the Veda, and others. Walsch stresses that the "spiritual arrogance" generated through human arguments and interpretations of "sacred scriptures" has cultivated and perpetuated much human suffering, as reflected by the following fallacies:

a. Human beings are separate from each other.
b. There is not enough of what human beings need to be happy.
c. To get the stuff of which there is not enough, human beings must compete with each other.
d. Some human beings are better than other human beings.
e. It is appropriate for human beings to resolve differences created by all the other fallacies by killing each other. (pp. 37–38)

Multidimensional contextual practice encourages practitioners to engage in multidimensional contextual services that are inclusive of micro, meso, macro, and magna factors. To do otherwise seems neglectful. As previously emphasized, human beings are multilayered, with the capacity to interact simultaneously within different contexts; and they possess the potential to affect and the vulnerability to be affected by multiple biopsychosocial-spiritual systems (i.e., micro, meso, macro, magna), which are multidimensional and contextual by nature. No individual context holds a monopoly of absolute "truth" or "reality" when exploring diverse human experiences. Therefore, a multidimensional contextual perspective (i.e., simultaneous exploration and consideration of unique and numerous contexts) becomes vital in gaining additional insight into human diversity, strengths, and challenges.

Although evidence exists regarding many ways of knowing, being, and becoming, we have observed—through an extensive literature review and professional practice experiences—that human services are often shaped by paradigms that favor a sense of certainty over a degree of uncertainty and professional approaches that are considered measurable. As a result, human services often become limited to these paradigms, which affects assessments and interventions within the context of human diversity. Professional practices based on multidimensionality (i.e., simultaneous exploration and consideration of the visible and invisible, the certain and uncertain, conventional knowledge/consciousness and transcendent knowledge/consciousness) seem to be rare. This situation is perpetuated through written documents often used to guide human services. For example, Compton and Galaway (1994) have been traditionally concerned about the physical context between the client and the worker. They stress, "The context or setting for the interview will often be that of an agency offering defined services to applicants bringing specified problems, but it may also be the applicant's home or the offices of other agencies. The context, of course, provides a limit to the communications and becomes a basis for the elimination of extraneous material that is not related to the particular context" (p. 310). We encourage practitioners to be cautious if and when attempting to eliminate material that seems "irrelevant" to the specific context of assessment and intervention. As emphasized in previous writings, individuals' lives, along with professional interactions and exchanges, seem to have relational links to socioeconomic and political dynamics (Foucault, 1980). Practitioners may consciously choose to strengthen their services by not falling into professional patterns in which assessments and interventions become Band-Aids covering biopsychosocial-spiritual conditions that, in actuality, may be in need of "surgery-aid."

A social movement has emerged within the past forty to fifty years promoting the importance of exploring interactions, exchanges, and dynamics of people, families, groups, and communities within contexts (Germain & Gitterman, 1996). One of the major objectives of this movement has been the cultivation of approaches that are inclusive of time, space, individual, and collective cultural/social/economic/political conditions affecting the functioning and well-being of a person, family, group, or community. This social movement has encouraged the construction of what Schriver (2001) calls "alternative paradigms," which are further described as worldviews that challenge dominant notions of "normality" and "functionality"—concepts that are often exclusive of vast human diversity. It has challenged the notion that human biopsychosocial-spiritual development and processes occur exclusively through progressive and linear steps, and has encouraged a paradigm shift that includes moving beyond stage-based theories, such as those reflected by Piaget's cognitive framework and Sigmund Freud's psychoanalytic approach. Stage-based theories have been criticized for generally ignoring cultural and environmental differences as well as historical contexts and exceptional human transactions and uniquenesses (Germain, 1994). Practitioners, researchers, and scholars are encouraged to consider transactions occurring simultaneously at contextual and multidimensional capacities, with the intention of being more inclusive of numerous factors influencing and affecting human diversity, strengths, and challenges.

One of the main goals of multidimensional contextual practice is *to encourage understanding and identification of multidimensional characteristics as well as contextual factors in order to strengthen the facilitation of processes while serving others.* Another major purpose of multidimensional contextual practice is *to promote the notion that understanding is not always rational, certain, absolute, or objective— it is a moving target. Thus, constant exploration of that "which is" and trust in the wisdom of uncertainty is vital.* The practice principles presented in the following section were developed with the intention of reaching these objectives. Practitioners are facilitators in the sense of being present to make the growth process of those we serve professionally less difficult by assuming the role of a conduit. We encourage practitioners to consider and explore the following practice principles in the process of embracing multidimensional contextual services.

PRACTICE PRINCIPLES: EMBRACING MULTIDIMENSIONAL CONTEXTUAL SERVICES

Questioning Assumptions: Agency and Program Competence

The multidimensional contextual practice framework advocates for constant exploration of agency and program competence, or the ability to serve individuals, families, groups, and communities skillfully without perpetuating stereotypes or prioritizing self-interest over the needs of those being served. (Note that the terms *agency* and *program* are used here interchangeably to identify services that have been formally developed, institutionalized, and promoted through diverse forms of action with the purpose of addressing intrapersonal, interpersonal, environmental, and religious/spiritual challenges. Agencies and programs operate under specific orientations, value and belief systems, and norms and regulations that are often reflected in both formal and informal protocols.) Furthermore, the multidimensional contextual practice framework encourages programs to periodically perform needs assessments in order to keep ongoing strengths and challenges of the clientele being served at the heart of the services being offered by the particular agency. Needs assessments are useful for helping agencies question assumptions held toward the community of clients being served. A **needs assessment** can be viewed as a process in which evaluative-oriented strategies (preferably a combination of quantitative and qualitative methods) are used periodically to identify community strengths, challenges, needs, conditions, and resources that would be valuable in meeting identified difficulties encountered by the clientele being served. Needs assessments are also used to foster the process of planning, designing, establishing, and delivering needed services. The multidimensional contextual practice framework views needs assessments as interdependent continuum processes, not as isolated events.

Needs assessments are vital in giving a voice to the client (i.e., individuals, families, groups, communities, or a combination of these entities receiving professional services). Through the facilitation of needs assessments, clients' understanding of experiences and readiness for taking specific courses of action are identified and explored. An agency's capability to meet identified demands is also evaluated through the process of a needs assessment. In other words, a needs assessment has at least a dual purpose: identification of client challenges, needs, strengths, and readiness to engage in changes within diverse contexts, and evaluation of the program's competence to serve the target clientele. Needs assessments are key components in evaluating the effectiveness of previous services; strengthening or promoting changes in services being delivered; advocating for the planning, design, establishment, and promotion of new services; identifying funding sources; and linking needs with appropriate resources. Overall, needs assessments serve as a significant function in the process of consciousness-raising with the intention of promoting necessary change intended to strengthen client well-being.

While conducting a needs assessment, practitioners are encouraged to take into consideration multiple factors, including socioeconomic and political dynamics occurring within the geographic location being assessed, as well as nationally and globally. Although the focus may be kept at the local capacity of the specific geographic area being assessed, national and global socioeconomic and political issues cannot go unnoticed, as these are likely to directly or indirectly affect the local geographic community. A simple way to keep oneself informed is by reading printed documents that are published by both mainstream and alternative newspapers. Listening and documenting individual and collective narratives of active and potential clients is also fundamental in this process. Visiting and meeting with government officials as well as community leaders is, moreover, indispensable. Furthermore, when conducting a needs assessment, the purposes and functions of other programs and agencies established within the geographic area directly being assessed need to be explored. Reading brochures published by such agencies, scheduling meetings with the agencies' administrators and staff, and asking identified community leaders about these programs can help to initiate this learning process. The practitioner must keep in mind that needs assessments are built on action plans: They are conducted with the objective of learning and becoming informed in order to skillfully plan, design, implement, and modify services that are specific to communities.

Needs assessments are limited if agencies focus exclusively on external communities and neglect to simultaneously examine the culture (values, orientation paradigms, norms, patterns of interactions, etc.) created within the agency itself. The multidimensional contextual practice framework, therefore, advocates for a simultaneous evaluation of the agency's theoretical frameworks and practice models shaping provision of services while conducting community needs assessments. In order to foster their capacity to deliver appropriate services, programs need to be aware of issues, challenges, and strengths encountered by clients being served, resources available and accessible within the larger community, as well as their own restrictions and potentials when attempting to meet identified demands. Assessments can be useful to assist agencies in identifying possible discrepancies between expertise available and needed, availability and accessibility of appropriate and needed resources, along with variations between clients' responses to services and professionals' perceptions and feelings toward clients. The strengths and restrictions of the agency within its socioeconomic, political, and spiritual/mystic environments cannot be neglected. Like professional competence, agency competence is a moving target. Thus, agencies' cultivation of competencies needs to be perceived as never-ending.

The multidimensional contextual practice framework does not emphasize that all programs have to simultaneously provide direct services at the micro, meso, macro, and magna dimensions. Rather, it stresses that regardless of the dimensions at which services are being provided, intrapersonal, interpersonal, environmental, and spiritual encounters must not be neglected and need to constantly be assessed. Direct assessment and consideration of intrapersonal, interpersonal, environmental, and spiritual encounters affecting agency dynamics, within the context of the community of people being served, can allow the program to be more holistic in its approaches. We suggest that the following activities be considered when assessing agency competence, when conducting a community's needs assessment, and while promoting multidimensional contextual services recommended within the context of human commonalities and differences/uniqueness.

Needs Assessment Perspective—Questions to Be Answered

    a.   What major beliefs does your agency have about needs assessments?

    b.   On a scale of 1 to 10, in which 1 symbolizes lowest prioritization and 10 highest prioritization, how would you evaluate the prioritization that your agency holds regarding facilitation of needs assessments?

    c.   What implications have such degrees of prioritization had in the **planning** (i.e., creation of a new vision or determination to strengthen the established one), **design** (i.e., development or structuring of goals, objectives, and methods used to achieve or strengthen vision, as well as the monitoring of progress and evaluation of accomplishments), establishment, and delivery of new services?

    d.   While developing and facilitating a needs assessment, how much attention does your agency give to **community collaboration** (i.e., active participation of those being assessed and served) and **partnership** (i.e., collective initiative between perceived clients and professional/agency geared toward reaching a common goal)?

    e.   If needs assessments are not used periodically to evaluate the effectiveness of services being delivered and to evaluate changes in the populations being served, how are decisions regarding prioritization and ways of strengthening services made?

    f.   What baseline is used to promote services and to acquire additional funding?

    g.   How is diversity within diversity recognized or ignored during the process of serving those identified as clients?

    h.   How much consideration would your agency give to local, national, and global socioeconomic and political issues when conducting a needs assessment?

    i.   How much consideration would your agency give to the purpose and function of other programs operating within the geographic location of clients being assessed?

Considerations during Needs Assessments

This section identifies possible processes to be considered during the development and facilitation of a needs assessment. We suggest beginning with a clear and comprehensive idea of the *purposes* of the assessment. Needs assessments have multiple purposes, including informative, planning, focus and organizational, and evaluative purposes. Informative purposes are established to become familiarized with strengths, challenges, conditions, and resources encountered by the target clientele. The goal of planning purposes is to identify ways of strengthening established services or developing new ones. Focus and organizational purposes assist agencies in identifying ongoing changes encountered by the clientele being served, monitoring progress in the achievement of objectives established (as reflected in the services being offered), and making decisions to adjust and strengthen services while in operation. Evaluative purposes are reflected in the overall assessment of accomplishments, both as a process and the final outcome. Needs assessments often operate under a combination of these purposes.

While planning and conducting needs assessments, the theoretical framework influencing this process cannot be ignored. The following questions can be useful in evaluating this framework:

a. Do the principles guiding the theoretical framework focus on deficits over strengths?
b. Are theoretical principles based on pragmatic paradigms?
c. Does the theoretical framework recognize human resilience within contexts of adversities?
d. Is the theoretical framework inclusive in its promotion of assessments and courses of action?
e. To what degree does the theoretical framework advocate for assessment and intervention at the micro, meso, macro, and magna capacities?
f. Is the specific theoretical framework diversity-oriented?
g. What are the preconceived assumptions held by the theoretical framework regarding the clientele being served?
h. Do assumptions sustaining the theoretical framework perpetuate stereotypical approaches over an exploration of diversity within diversity?
i. Does the theoretical framework advocate for exploration of common human needs?

Other themes to be considered when conducting needs assessments are the following:

- *Structure of the plan of action:* Strategies to be used for conducting assessments, collecting data, and analyzing findings, as well as the roles and responsibilities of professionals involved at different levels of the needs assessment; timing of assessment and time management; methods used for increasing community collaboration and partnership; ethical dilemmas; consideration of setbacks and possible alternatives
- *Compatibility between needs assessment and agency objectives:* Reflection of the agency mission and vision in the structure of a developed plan of action; congruence between professional skills and assignment of tasks; relationship between agency orientation and performance
- *Benefit-risk assessment:* Consideration of whether expected rewards, possibly generated through the needs assessment, will surpass the expected risks of participant/community harm; whether the end will justify the means; how the risk of misinterpreting the findings can be minimized; and what methods are being used for addressing professional biases, prejudices, and self-interest
- *Content, context, and process:* Clientele being assessed (i.e., individuals, families, groups, or a variety of communities); geographic location; socioeconomic and political conditions; cultures and subcultures (i.e., beliefs, values, and norms); community composition, norms, values, traditions, and rituals; community structure (open or closed system) and boundaries; community narrative and history, including power, influence, and leadership; diversity and controversies within the community (both separation and collaboration); community internal and external stressors; community's own awareness of issues and needs; readiness or resistance to engaging in necessary change; community strengths and resiliency, as well

as restrictions; availability and accessibility of resources, and any gaps between available resources and those needed; possible role and impact of the media and other community programs; target for community change (direct or indirect involvement)

It cannot be overemphasized that while conducting needs assessments, the skills to listen and elicit information, as well as a degree of professional self-awareness, are vital. *Patience also plays a significant role in this process.* Immediate-gratification efforts can lead to more harm than good. Thus, needs assessments are to be carefully planned before being implemented.

Interplay between Needs Assessment and Program Evaluation

Needs assessments of clients being served are one way of strengthening agency competence or skillfulness when servicing diverse communities of clients. Agencies, however, also need to engage in periodic internal program evaluation. Rossi, Freeman, and Lipsey (1999) define program evaluation as "the use of social research procedures to systematically investigate the effectiveness of social intervention programs that is adapted to their political and organizational environments and designed to inform social action in ways that improve social conditions" (p. 2). As an initial step in engaging in program evaluation, agencies are encouraged to explore the following question: What theoretical frameworks or practice orientation principles have been guiding the program's **mission** (i.e., reason for existing), **vision** (i.e., the inspiring ultimate goal/baseline that sustains the planning process, the development of objectives, as well as the selection of assessment and intervention modalities), **objectives** (i.e., aims and tasks developed and promoted in order to strengthen attainment of ultimate goals), and **methods** (i.e., activities and strategies used to deliver and evaluate effectiveness of service)?

While engaging in program evaluation, agencies are encouraged to explore possible discrepancies and consistencies among the program's mission, vision, objectives, methods used to deliver and evaluate effectiveness of services, and client strengths and challenges (see Figure 4.2). Client strengths and challenges need to be considered a baseline from which program/service development is initiated in order for client-oriented services to be strengthened. Thus, interdependence exists between in-house program evaluation and community assessment. Although awareness of discrepancies and consistencies between the variables identified in Figure 4.2 does not, by itself, guarantee change, it is important in shaping follow-up decisions.

Program evaluation provides an opportunity to explore theoretical and practice paradigms influencing services. We recommend that while examining the impact of theoretical frameworks and practice orientation principles, agencies also explore explicit and implicit **organizational cultures and subcultures** (i.e., formal and informal policies and codes, such as language used, channels of communication, relationship patterns among professionals, and rituals, values, norms, and ethics directing organizational behaviors). Furthermore, the **organizational design, structure, and subcomponents** must not go unnoticed (i.e., management—set of systems or processes designed, established, and implemented to accomplish the agency's mission or overarching purpose; authority, dimensions of power, hierarchy, positions, status,

Figure 4.2 | Discrepancies and Consistencies

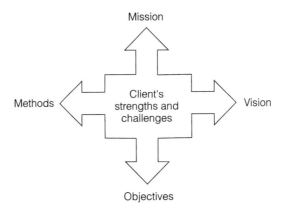

roles, leadership, expectations, boundaries, and supervision; support and encouragement; and decision making). During facilitation of a program evaluation, consideration also needs to be given to **organizational function and degrees of competence** (interplay between types of services provided, community challenges and strengths, as well as resources available within the contexts of organizational environments, program potentiality, etc.). An overall exploration of **organizational life span and cycles** (changes over time, type and capacity of services, development of new mission/focus, etc.) is vital while assessing an agency's growth and restrictions (i.e., socioeconomic and political challenges). While considering these program evaluation components, the following questions can be useful:

a. What are the guiding principles, mission, and vision of the program?
b. What is the history of the program?
c. Has the agency engaged in previous program evaluations? If so, what were the results of those assessments?
d. What is the structure of the program? Who is responsible for what?
e. What is the composition of the staff, and what are their qualifications?
f. What strategies are used to promote staff professional development?
g. What are the interprofessional dynamics, relationships, and communication patterns?
h. What are the objectives and functions of supervision procedures, and how effective are they?
i. What protocols have been established by the program?
j. Who is the population being served? What assumptions do staff hold regarding the population being served?
k. What services are provided by the program? Are the services community-specific?
l. How has the program addressed previous community changes?
m. To what degree is the mission reflected in the goals, objectives, and services of the program?

n. What is the agency perspective regarding multidimensional contextual services?
o. Do services reflect a stereotypical or mechanical perspective?
p. How are services delivered? How accessible are services to the target population?
q. What strategies are used to evaluate effectiveness of services and program achievements?
r. How reliable and valid are the strategies used to evaluate effectiveness of services?
s. On a scale of 1 to 10, with 1 being the least receptive and 10 being the most receptive, how would you evaluate the program's degree of receptivity toward change? The program's use of professional intuition? The program's sense of trust in what may appear uncertain?
t. How are services documented? What is the level of reliability and validity of the documentation?
u. How effective are the instruments used to document services in terms of collecting valuable information?
v. To what degree is the clientele encouraged to become involved in the evaluation of services?
w. Who are the funding sources? What conditions have they established for the program or organization? How have these conditions influenced the establishment and delivery of services? Are there deviations between funding conditions and clients' need for services? How skillfully does the agency manage financial fundings?
x. To what degree is the organization in compliance with requirements instituted by funding sources?
y. What external and internal stressors affect the performance of the program/organization? What stressors affect the program's supporters?
z. What other resources are available and accessible to the program?

(Adapted and modified from Guadalupe & Torres, 2001.)

Strengthening Nonstereotypically Based Services

Agencies can address diverse populations being served within different contexts and capacities in multiple ways. The multidimensional contextual practice framework encourages agencies to identify, develop, implement, and promote nonstereotypically based services within the context of human commonalities and differences. Like practitioners, agencies are also encouraged to question assumptions held toward individuals, families, groups, and communities being served. The activities identified previously can be useful in this process. The commitment to nonstereotypically based multidimensional contextual services needs to be reflected in the way that agencies' missions and visions are written as well as in the establishment of service objectives and service-delivery and evaluation methods. Theoretical frameworks and practice orientation principles also need to reflect such a commitment. In training program staff to honor nonstereotypically based approaches, the multidimensional contextual practice framework recommends inclusion of content (see Table 4.2), teaching and learning related themes (see Table 4.3), as well as approaches summarized in Table 4.4.

Table 4.2   Content Related Themes

- **Identifications and explorations of differences, commonalities, and controversies within and between groups of people** seem central to addressing human diversity without perpetuating stereotypes. For instance, content that addresses diversity (i.e., geographic, socioeconomic, gender, sexual orientation, age, religious differences) within groups of people who share an ethnic identity is as important as content that looks at differences and commonalities between ethnic groups. A focus on person-in-environment can strengthen content on human diversity and commonalities.

- Content on human diversity and commonalities can be strengthened through consideration of experiences such as **multiethnic identities and experiences, encounters with oppressive forces, privilege, influences of social powers, along with individualized and relational resilience affecting the developmental processes, functioning, and well-being of individuals, families, groups, and communities.**

- **Individual and collective historical experiences (cultural heritage, socioeconomic and political treatment, etc.) encountered by communities of people due to diverse mental or physical abilities and disabilities and racial-ethnic/gender/sexual orientation identities,** among others, cannot be ignored when addressing diversity content in nonstereotypical ways. Diversity within diversity or content that identifies multiple interpretations of the same events is vital. The collective is not more important than the individual and vice versa. Individual and collective narratives are equally important. People growing and living in the "same" family system are likely to perceive encountered experiences differently.

- Limiting diversity content to "cross-cultural" differences does not seem to be an inclusive approach when addressing human uniqueness. A large number of cross-cultural approaches have also promoted the notion that *culture* and *ethnicity* are one and the same, as evidenced by the fact that these terms are often used interchangeably. **Content on human diversity can be enriched through the recognition of differences and any interdependence between the experiences of culture and ethnicity.** As explored in the previous chapters, cultures transcend ethnicities, as evidenced by cultures and subcultures established between ethnic groups in contexts such as churches, schools, and interethnic relationships, to mention a few.

- The concepts identified as **"diverse group" and "oppressed group"** need further clarification in order for staff to understand uniqueness and possible correlation between these areas. Human diversity transcends experiences of oppression, as evidenced by illustrations of resilience and potentiality to create a world beyond imagination. Furthermore, oppression has historically and is currently evidenced within and between groups of people (e.g., the overall oppression of women within and between diverse ethnic groups). Content regarding human potentiality as well as content regarding ways in which oppressive forces are manifested within and between groups of people is vital.

- The implications of **positive and negative stereotypes** need to be addressed when teaching and learning about human diversity. Exploration in this area can generate discussion likely to cultivate the opportunity to promote necessary changes. Questioning built assumptions through presentation of content is indispensable.

The templates presented in Tables 4.2 and 4.3 and Table 4.4 can be useful when consciously attempting to assist agencies in the initial design, implementation, and promotion of services that are nonstereotypically oriented. Stereotypes and stereotyping, however, are pervasive and subtle. Changes will require an ongoing commit-

Table 4.3 | Teaching and Learning Related Themes

- Content on **complexities regarding human diversity** needs to be infused throughout agency mission, vision, documentation forms, objectives, as well as methods used to assess and intervene. Diversity content addressed through a historical as well as current emphasis reflecting commonalities, differences, and controversies within and between groups of people can be useful in reducing stereotypical perspectives.

- Human diversity has many faces. Assumptions supported through theoretical frameworks need to be questioned, promoting an opportunity for staff to **move away from traditional practice methods that explore human diversity through stereotypically based lenses (e.g., "This is how the Latino/a community is"; "African Americans are religious"; "Men cannot be trusted")**. Practice models introduce to staff the need to be comprehensive and inclusive of differences among communities of people who simultaneously share commonalities. **Human diversity has many faces** (differences based on socioeconomic status, sexual orientation, gender, culture/ethnicity/race, mental and physical abilities, age, spiritual practices/orientations, etc.). **When addressing human diversity content, its complexity must not be ignored** in order to reduce the possibility of stereotyping.

- Theoretical frameworks that address diversity content from **a person-in-environment perspective, focusing primarily on transactions, time, and contexts** (i.e., the life model, dual perspective, ecosystem approaches) along with eclectic and flexible practice approaches (e.g., multidimensional contextual practice) are useful for addressing diversity content while seeking to stop stereotyping.

- **Addressing diversity content through a focus on common themes** (e.g., strengths and restrictions observed in populations historically encountering oppressive experiences, common biopsychosocial needs faced by individuals encountering poverty) is considered an important strategy to avoid neglecting collective human experiences. Human commonalities are encouraged to be explored within the context of human diversity, and not from a progressive or linear theoretical framework built under the assumption of a single "objective" reality.

- **Strategies that promote professional self-evaluation and awareness** (e.g., journal writing, self-reflection exercises, staff's direct involvement within diverse communities) are useful for teaching about culturally and socially diverse populations without perpetuating stereotypes.

- Diversity content must **not exclusively be addressed from an oppressive/group conflict perspective**. An emphasis on individual/group/family/community strengths, resilience, and potentiality is needed and must be equally valued.

- **Consider micro, meso, macro, and magna factors while teaching and learning about human diversity.** These factors need to be considered as being equally important, with none of them being superior to the others.

ment to the mindful evaluation of intrapersonal and interpersonal human dynamics with the intention of cultivating strategies helpful in promoting transformation. A focus on *belief development and perpetuation* can assist the social/health/human service practitioner (and agency/program) in exploring possibilities to promote change. As we emphasize throughout this text, stereotypes often harm human interactions and exchanges. A shift in consciousness is not only needed, but is also

Table 4.4 | Specific Approaches: An Attempt at Reducing Stereotypically Based Practices

Approaches	Examples
A combination of strategies and teaching activities, keeping emphasis on staff's collective learning experiences	• Audio-video tapes that address diversity within diversity content (e.g., "Black Is—Black Ain't," "The Way Home") • Guest speakers and panel presentations with diverse perspectives regarding the topic being discussed and clientele being served • Role-playing and/or case studies to illustrate diversity and commonalities among potential and active clientele • Development and assignment of tasks intended to encourage staff involvement with diverse communities
Strategies that promote professional self-evaluation and awareness, keeping emphasis on staff's individualized experiences	• Encouraging staff to develop a genogram of their own family systems to experience the possible effects of using such a tool with clients being served • Encouraging staff to keep a confidential learning log in which they can reflect their assumptions and effects during the process of working within the context of human diversity and commonalities • Using supervision sessions that encourage staff to explore variables (personal cultural-ethnic experiences, belief and value systems, etc.) affecting ideas and perspectives held toward clients being served (For specific professional self-evaluation activities, see *Culturally Competent Practice: A Framework for Understanding Diverse Groups and Justice Issues,* Doman Lum, 2003)
Exploration of similarities, differences, and controversies among and between groups of people being served	• Exploration of individual and group construction, deconstruction, and reconstruction of identities through the use of storytelling and the sharing of narratives • Examination of discrepancies and consistencies between cultural influences and cultural choices
Addressing content on human diversity and commonalities through a focus on themes	• Interpersonal relationships • Communication patterns • Common human needs • Collective encounters with adversities • Relational resilience
Practice activities that focus on person-in-environment	• Ethnographic interviewing • Narrative approaches • Constructivist principles • Ecosystem guidance
Eclectic approaches when facilitating assessments and promoting interventions	• Examining the strengths of strategies derived from different schools of thought, theoretical frameworks, and practice orientation models with the intention of developing and employing an inclusive approach

vital in the process of increasing human connectedness based on interactions and exchanges that move beyond stereotypes and the marginalization of human uniqueness.

An agency's commitment to promoting nonstereotypically based services needs to move beyond the development of "isolated" events (e.g., one or two workshops a year regarding how to work with the group of the week, such as "the African-American community" or "the Latino/a community"). A commitment to nonstereo-typically based services needs to be reflected in the agency's ongoing processes while developing and putting into practice written policies, in the administration's consideration and honoring of diversity within its professional body, and in the agency's community actions. Equally important are the ways in which clients are treated. As reflected by Figure 4.3, the partnership created by the program, the human service practitioner, and the client needs to be client-oriented. This requires individualization of client assessment as well as a plan of action that moves beyond stereotypical perceptions. Each client needs to be approached as a unique and unduplicated entity (the newness of each experience) who may or may not share much commonality with the community of people believed to be "represented" by the client being served.

As agencies construct service baselines that promote multidimensional contextual services, encouraging consideration of individual and collective experiences encountered by both current and potential clients, agency administrators and human service practitioners/staff need to strengthen their awareness regarding possible institutional oppression. Within this context, **institutional oppression** refers to formal or informal systematic procedures promoting injustice and dehumanization toward any groups of people attempting to be served. Agencies need to remain aware of possible culturalization of oppressive forces such as racism, sexism, classism, heterosexism, ageism, ableism, and ethnocentrism cultivated in the process of agency policy development, decision making, and use of practice-oriented assessment and intervention

Figure 4.3 | Individualized Partnership

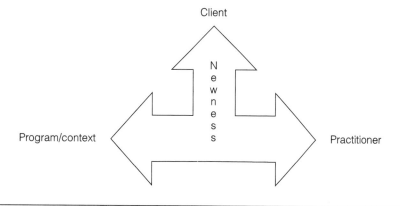

strategies. Periodic program evaluation and community needs assessment can assist the agency in the process of cultivating and maintaining this awareness. Actions, however, speak louder than words. Thus, a commitment to promote necessary change needs to be action based.

SUMMARY

This chapter has addressed the social/health/human service practitioner's professional competence and activities that can be used to strengthen it. Furthermore, the chapter has examined some strategies believed to be useful in initially promoting multidimensional contextual services. Readers are reminded that the possibilities and strategies available for strengthening professional competence and multidimensional contextual services are endless. Those presented in this chapter reflect mere glimpses of understanding when compared to the vastness of possibilities.

References

American Psychological Association (APA), Educational and Training Committee of Division 17. (1980, September). *Cross-cultural competencies: A position paper.* Paper presented at the annual meeting of the American Psychological Association, Montreal, Canada.

Boutte, G. (1999). *Multicultural education: Raising consciousness.* Belmont, CA: Wadsworth.

Compton, B. R., & Galaway, B. (1994). *Social work processes.* Pacific Grove, CA: Brooks/Cole.

Cox, C. B., & Ephross, O. H. (1998). *Ethnicity and social work practice.* New York: Oxford University Press.

Dean, R. G. (1993). Teaching a constructivist approach to clinical practice. *Journal of Teaching in Social Work, 8*(1/2), 55–75.

Foucault, M. (1980). *Power/knowledge: Selected interviews and other writings.* New York: Pantheon.

García, B., & Van Soest, D. (1997). Changing perception of diversity and oppression: MSW students discuss the effects of a required course. *Journal of Social Work Education, 33*(1), 119–129.

Germain, C. B. (1994). Human behavior and the social environment. In E. G. Reamer (Ed.), *The foundation of social work knowledge* (pp. 88–121). New York: Columbia University Press.

Germain, C. B., & Gitterman, A. (1996). *The life model of social work practice: Advances in theory and practice* (2nd ed.). New York: Columbia University Press.

Gilligan, C. (1982). *In a different voice: Psychological theory and women's development.* Cambridge: Harvard University Press.

Goffman, E. (1959). *The presentation of self in everyday life.* Garden City, NY: Doubleday.

Goffman, E. (1967). *Interaction rituals: Essays on face-to-face behavior.* New York: Pantheon.

Guadalupe, K. L. (2003). Empowerment perspective. In J. Anderson & R. W. Carter (Eds.), *Diversity perspectives for social work practice.* Boston: Allyn & Bacon.

Guadalupe, J. L., & Freeman, M. (1999, Fall). Common human needs in the context of diversity: Integrating schools of thought. *Journal of Cultural Diversity, 6*(3), 85–92.

Guadalupe, K. L., & Torres, S., Jr. (2001, June). *Final report: Community housing opportunities corporation's resident services program evaluation* (Davis, CA).

Gutierrez, L. M. (1990). Working with women of color: An empowerment perspective. *Social Work, 35*(2), 149–153.

Iglehart, A. P., & Becerra, R. M. (1995). *Social services and the ethnic community.* Boston: Allyn & Bacon.

Keefe, S. E., & Padilla, A. M. (1987). *Chicano ethnicity.* Albuquerque, NM: University of New Mexico Press.

Lewis, O. (1968). *La vida.* New York: Vintage.

Locke, D. (1992). *Increasing multicultural understanding: A comprehensive model.* Newbury Park, CA: Sage.

Lum, D. (2003). (Ed.). *Culturally competent practice: A framework for understanding diverse groups and justice issues* (2nd ed.). Pacific Grove, CA: Brooks/Cole.

Lum, D. (2004). *Social work practice and people of color: A process-stage approach* (5th ed.). Pacific Grove, CA: Brooks/Cole.

Manoleas, P. (1994). An outcome approach to assessing the cultural competence of MSW students. *Journal of Multicultural Social Work, 3,* 43–57.

Murphy, B. C., & Dillon, C. (1998). *Interviewing in action: Process and practice.* Pacific Grove, CA: Brooks/Cole.

Nakanishi, M., & Rittner, B. (1992). The inclusionary cultural model. *Journal of Social Work Education, 28*(1), 27–35.

Pinderhughes, E. (1989). *Understanding race, ethnicity, and power: The key to efficacy in clinical practice.* New York: Free Press.

Ponterotto, J. G., Casas, J. M., Suzuki, L. A., & Alexander, C. M. (Eds.). (1995). *Handbook of multicultural counseling.* Thousand Oaks, CA: Sage.

Pope-Davis, D. B., & Coleman, H. L. K. (Eds.). (1997). *Multicultural counseling competencies: Assessment, education and training, and supervision.* Thousand Oaks, CA: Sage.

Rossi, P., Freeman, H., & Lipsey, M. (1999). *Evaluation: A systematic approach* (6th ed.). Thousand Oaks, CA: Sage.

Ruiz, D. M. (1997). *The four agreements.* San Rafael, CA: Amber-Allen.

Saleebey, D. (1994). Culture, theory and narrative: The intersection of meanings in practice. *Social Work, 39*(4), 351–359.

Saleebey, D. (2002). *The strengths perspectives in social work practice* (3rd ed.).Boston: Allyn & Bacon.

Schriver, J. M. (2001). *Human behavior and the social environment: Shifting paradigms in essential knowledge for social work practice* (3rd ed.). Needham Heights, MA: Allyn & Bacon.

Solomon, B. (1976). *Black empowerment: Social work in oppressed communities.* New York: Columbia University Press.

Straub, G. (2000). *The rhythm of compassion: Caring for self, connecting with society.* Boston: Tuttle.

Sue, D. W. (1981). *Counseling the culturally different: Theory and practice.* New York: Willey-Interscience.

Sue, D. W., Arredondo, P., & McDavis, R. J. (1992). Multicultural counseling competencies and standards: A call to the profession. *Journal of Counseling and Development, 70,* 477–486.

Walsch, N. D. (2002). *The new revelation: A conversation with God.* New York: Atria.

Special Issues

We continue with a chapter on language and a chapter on spirituality, which are related to the preceding framework. Language is based on constructed human agreement of use of symbols for communicating values, culture, ideas, thinking patterns, beliefs, change, behaviors, as well as historical and current contexts. Spirituality is generally perceived as the expression of meaning in life and existence for people who are a part of the universe. Both are transcending and unifying connections that meet needs of individuals, families, groups, and communities; sections of countries and the countries themselves; as well as the world as a bigger whole. The two chapters that follow are elaborations on the Framework for Human Diversity and Transcendence discussed in Part 1 of this text. Historically, content on language and spirituality has been generally neglected or minimized within the social/health/human services field. In recent texts, however, more attention has been given to the roles that language and spirituality play in human interactions and exchanges. We would like to continue stressing the importance of these experiences. Language and spirituality are widespread experiences within and between groups of people. Neglecting or minimizing these experiences is a disservice to clients being served.

In a society such as ours, but basically in any society, there are manifold relationships of power which permeate, characterize, and constitute the social body, and these relationships of power cannot themselves be established, consolidated nor implemented without the production, accumulation, circulation and functioning of a discourse. —**Michel Foucault**

5 | Language and Multidimensional Contextual Practice

MYLES MONTGOMERY

Language used each day contains profound power: It shapes thoughts, ideas, and perceptions that affect interactions with the self and others (i.e., internalization of meanings and interpretations). When language is used to narrowly identify individuals, families, groups, and communities by singular attributes, characteristics, or qualities, stereotypes are created and perpetuated. Essentially, stereotypes reduce the wide and limitless spectrum of human experiences to an infinitesimal perspective. When stereotypes are promoted, reiterated, and repeated, they can and often do construct notions of truth that normalize inequality for some and maintain privilege for others. The multidimensional contextual perspective regards the use of language as an important factor in the expansion or contraction of understanding among individuals, families, groups, and communities within different contexts, including the micro, meso, macro, and magna levels; thus, it is through language that ideas, which allow or prevent connection with others, are constructed. Language is an essential component of the process of construction, deconstruction, and reconstruction of human experiences.

This chapter is divided into five distinct yet interrelated sections. The first section examines the ways that constructed notions of truth through language affect the social construction of human identities and experiences, while the second section explores some of the ways that stereotypical notions of truth are proliferated through education and the social media (i.e., curricula, advertisements, television programming, and movie productions). The third segment presents a critical framework that examines the use of language for social/health/human service practitioners and reviews the ways that language may be used as a vehicle for change at the micro, meso, macro, and magna levels. The fourth subdivision elaborates on perspectives of language through the implementation of multidimensional contextual practice. The final section features practical application exercises to help the reader practice the principles discussed throughout the chapter.

SOCIAL SYMBOLISM OF LANGUAGE, IDENTITIES, AND EXPERIENCES

Symbolic interaction theorists posit that human identity "involves shared significant symbols (or shared meanings) that emerge in the process of interaction with others" and that self-conceptions "develop through the process of interaction and are shaped, in part, by the views and attitudes that others hold about us" (Robbins, Chatterjee, & Canda, 2001, pp. 267–269). The process of construction, deconstruction, and reconstruction of identities affects and is affected by human interactions, exchanges, and experiences. From this perspective, the influence of symbols in human interactions should not be minimized, but closely explored and analyzed. Although the term *symbol* may invite many broad and general definitions, in this chapter it indicates one of the most prevalent symbols among human interactions: language.

As indicated by Guadalupe and Lum in Chapter 1 of this text, **language** may be understood "as a constructed multidimensional and contextual agreement of uses, meanings, and interpretations of symbols, sounds, and experiences. While the multidimensional aspect of language is reflected by its abstract qualities (i.e., written and verbal terms, symbols, and experiences can be interpreted in multiple and distinctive ways), its individualistic and yet multiple contents are reflected by its contextual qualities (i.e., agreement of usage and meaning as well as interpretations of experiences can be, and often are, situational)" (p. 25). According to Moore (2001), language, as a symbol, conducts thinking by affecting the construction of thoughts: "language not only *expresses* ideas and concepts but actually *shapes* thought" (p. 322). Strings of thought that are preserved as **knowledge,** which is based on and transmitted through the medium of language, originate from "the meanings people attribute to their experiences" (Pinderhughes, 1994, p. 276). Therefore, a symbiotic relationship appears to exist between the formation of knowledge and the social influence through the symbol of language.

Also integral to this discussion is the term *culture.* According to Saleebey (1994), **culture** "is the means by which we receive, organize, rationalize, and understand our particular experiences in the world" (p. 352). From this perspective, knowledge is based on meaning derived through social interactions and predicated on language in a given culture. We utilize cultural knowledge to continually create, destroy, and rebuild notions about ourselves, which seem to influence our interactions and exchanges with self and others. The multidimensional contextual framework understands individual self-identity as a series of constructions, deconstructions, and reconstructions, based on fluid and changing bodies of knowledge over the course of a lifetime. The role that language plays in this process is crucial in that it molds, fashions, and adjusts cognitive processes and behavioral responses.

Knowledge constructed and disseminated within the context of a social environment may lead some to accept it as a notion of truth. Notions of truth, taken as absolutes, may arise through the socially accepted meaning of specific words. To illustrate this point, Moore (2001) writes a brief paragraph in which he uncovers the direct denotations of common terms:

> Some may blackly (angrily) accuse me of trying to blacken (defame) the English language, to give it a black eye (a mark of shame) by writing such black words (hostile). . . . But attempts to blackjack (to compel by threat) me will have a Chinaman's chance of success, for I am not a yellow-bellied Indian-giver of words, who will whitewash (cover up or gloss over vices or crimes) a black lie (harmful, inexcusable). (p. 323)

Although Moore seems to exhaustively concentrate on the contrast between variations of the adjectives "black" and "white," his observations contain larger implications—chiefly, that language affects human understanding in that it forms, shapes, and perpetuates meaning. When meaning becomes socially accepted, it promotes notions of what is believed to be true between and within individuals, families, groups, and communities.

The power of language seems to spring from its ability to create, organize, and promote notions of what is considered to be truth. As a result, uncritical use of language can support notions of truth that are unintended or undesirable. The effects of stereotypical perspectives reflect this. For instance, Elrich (1994), a teacher of a diverse sixth-grade class in Baltimore, noted that after he showed a brief film, the consensus of his class was that they thought something bad was going to happen whenever an African-American boy entered the scene (even if nothing bad actually occurred). Elrich reported that, regardless of ethnicity or gender, the majority of his students held this belief. It seems that the meaning of the term *black,* as constructed in the context of this class, carried a negative connotation and affected the class's notion about what they considered to be true of individuals with whom they identified that term. From this reasoning, is it also possible that any African-American students in this class, who constructed a notion of their self-identities with this term, could experience feelings of marginalization, low self-esteem, and low self-expectations?

As illustrated in the previous example, stereotypical language consolidates understanding of individuals and larger groups into one fixed notion. Allowing such fixed notions to control our thinking process promotes an automatic and prejudiced ideation of others. On the other hand, the multidimensional contextual perspective seeks to promote awareness and mindfulness of the connotations associated with terms used to describe individuals, families, groups, and communities—words such as *Hispanic, White, Black, Asian, gay, disabled, minority, woman, man,* and *poor*—as the first step in recognizing the influence of language in the creation and perpetuation of stereotypes. As a result, this perspective advocates for an understanding of others through a scope without limits rather than a myopic lens. The critical framework, presented in the third section of this chapter, provides some ideas to assist in this process.

EDUCATION AND SOCIAL MEDIA

The use of language in the contexts of education and the social media (i.e., curricula, advertisements, television programming, and motion pictures) is significant to an understanding of stereotypes for two important reasons, among others. First, schools and social media transmit information to large cross-sections of diverse communities on a daily basis. Second, these two sources of information appear to be perceived as credible by many and, as a result, influence perceptions of truth. Control and use of these mediums, therefore, seem to carry an important implication: Constructions of knowledge and truth about individuals, families, groups, and communities are portrayed through each of these mediums. When language is used in either medium to construct stereotypical notions of truth, the message is relayed to millions. This process often promotes disparities on emotional, social, economic, and political levels. For example, from a political perspective, large-scale transmissions of stereotypical perspectives seem to influence notions about what constitutes a "family," immigration policies, and affirmative action laws. Therefore, it seems possible that education, both formal and informal, may promote or challenge stereotypical perspectives.

Learning and Education

How we learn to perceive self and others seems largely dependent on the formal and informal education we receive. Formal education includes lessons we are taught from learning institutions, such as classes at private and public colleges and universities, K–12 educational systems, as well as preschools. Informal education, on the other hand, comprises lessons learned from our peers, from our parents, from our colleagues, from our informal daily interactions with others, and so on. The composite of what we learn from our formal and informal education is frequently used to construct our notions of what we perceive to be true. Moreover, the language used throughout our education often guides, shapes, and shifts these perceptions over time. The language used inside and outside of classrooms can potentially construct, deconstruct, or reconstruct stereotypical notions of truth. For instance, the educational system in the United States has done poorly in educating general communities about strengths and challenges experienced by transgender, bisexual, lesbian, and gay (TBLG) individuals. Thus, many misunderstandings and stereotypes about these groups of people exist. Hate crimes are only one example of the consequences. Lessons learned in a formal setting may reinforce or dispute stereotypical perspectives learned in an informal setting, and vice versa. However, as informal education is often less predictable than formal education, this section deals primarily with the latter while acknowledging the influence of the former.

Examples of the power of language in formal educational settings are available in a number of contexts. For instance, because of its ability to influence such a great number of students, use of language at college campuses continues to be a contentious issue. Hartman (1991) discusses the Speech Protection Act of 1991—a bill introduced to Congress that challenged the "growing number of college behavior codes that have been developing in response to the upsurge of racial and sexual tensions and harassments on college campuses" (p. 275). The creation of this bill appears to underscore the use of language as a political issue: "the lines have been sharply drawn: the right to freedom of speech versus the right not to be denigrated, threatened, or harassed" (Hartman, 1991, p. 275). Rather than arguing one side over another, perhaps it is more useful to reflect on the reasons why this issue is raised, especially in regard to curricula.

The impact of the internalization of meaning received through the content of class curricula may strongly influence constructed notions of truth that people have about themselves and others. For example, a great deal of discussion currently surrounds classes taught on diversity in human populations for social/health/human service practitioners. If taught in a way that generalizes traits, characteristics, attributes, or qualities for members of a specific culture, ethnicity, religion, gender, sexual orientation, or socioeconomic status, such classes portray members of these categories as homogenous and, consequently, neglect the diversity that exists in all individuals, families, groups, and communities (Pinderhughes, 1994). By contrast, the multidimensional contextual approach prefers the notion that people have identities that are constructed from multiple categories, and they are not served well through understandings that reduce them to one. As a result, the language used in such curricula (or any curriculum for that matter) should be viewed with a critical perspective. Appropriate questions for any educational setting could be:

- Who controls the curriculum that I am learning?
- To what degree do I understand, relate to, and agree or disagree with the meanings and interpretations identified and promoted through the curriculum being endorsed?
- To what extent is the language used through the endorsed curriculum inclusive or exclusive of many ways of knowing, thinking, and being?
- What are the overall objectives of the curriculum that I am being exposed to?
- How does what I am learning affect the way I perceive experiences, others, and myself?
- Why has this curriculum been selected over others available?
- Who is evaluating the curriculum, and how is its effectiveness being measured?

Each of these questions examines education from a critical perspective and recognizes language as a gateway to constructed notions about truth. The next section offers a critical framework that may be used to further analyze language.

A CRITICAL FRAMEWORK: THE DYNAMICS OF LANGUAGE AND CHANGE ON THE MAGNA, MACRO, MESO, AND MICRO LEVELS

If language can be used to frame ideas in ways that are narrow and restricted, then it seems equally plausible that language may be used to widen the scope of ideas as well. The following critical framework contains four areas of inquiry—*expectations, responsibilities, conflicts,* and *alternatives*—that may be used to analyze the use of conventional (and often loaded) terms. The first three steps of the framework deconstruct the term being analyzed, while the fourth step invites a re-creation of understanding. This section then applies this critical framework to the process of facilitating change in understanding and language on the magna, macro, meso, and micro levels of human interaction.

Critical Framework

The first area of inquiry in this framework, **expectations,** invites consideration about what a term seems to expect with regard to whomever it is applied. Corresponding questions for this step are:

- What does this term seem to expect one to believe?
- Does the answer to this question change according to various contexts such as one's ethnic background, age, gender, sexual orientation, socioeconomic status, or religion?
- How does the meaning of the particular term construct notions of truth?

After examining the expectations, the next area of inquiry involves grasping a sense of what **responsibilities** appear to come with the term. For this area, it is important to consider any differences that exist between the responsibilities for the party using the term and those of the party labeled by the term. In other words:

- What actions need to accompany the belief system contained in the term for both of these parties?
- Do the expected behaviors vary among diverse individuals, families, groups, and communities?

The third area of inquiry ponders potential **conflicts** that may arise as a result of the expectations and subsequent responsibilities of a specific term. More precisely:

- Are there negative repercussions for individuals, families, groups, and communities who do not meet the expectations or carry out the responsibilities suggested by the term?
- What are some of the consequences that might occur as a result of deviance from the expectations?
- Is there an escalating level of risk for such individuals, families, groups, or communities?

The point here is not to make moral judgments about behavior (labeling it right or wrong) but to simply imagine reactions that have occurred or could occur as a result of behaving in a way that is not congruent with the information discovered in the first two areas of inquiry.

Finally, **alternatives** that construct different meanings for the term are considered. This step involves rethinking the term to create more opportunities for understanding. Refashioning meaning, in this way, can lead to ways of conceiving of a term that will lower the potential for conflict and, thus, mitigate the risk of marginalization. The key here is not to provoke polemics about the meaning of particular words but, instead, to invite a wider range of meaning for terms that appear to be taken for granted in their usage.

Magna

While exploring magna-spirituality, it becomes essential to recognize that many ways of knowing, experiencing, and being exist. Spirituality has a unique and individualistic component that cannot be neglected in the name of the collective, since such neglect increases the possibility for marginalization of some people's experience. Multidimensional contextual practice, therefore, advocates for practitioners to individualize their assessments and interventions when working with clients. Rather than anticipating that clients will follow the practitioner's meaning and interpretation of magna-spirituality, the practitioner is encouraged to ask questions and listen attentively with an open mind.

Through the use of skills such as active listening, clarification questions, and paraphrasing, practitioners are encouraged to work together with clients to form a plan of action that reflects the clients' experiences. In doing so, practitioners act professionally, sensitively, contextually, and responsibly, avoiding misconceptions and conflicts. Practitioners need to keep in mind that their primary role is to be of service to clients.

Macro

Words on a macro level should be scrutinized for their content and meaning through a variety of contexts in order to avoid a stereotyped usage. Failing to do so may perpetuate ideas and, consequently, policies that promote exclusivity. Words can, and frequently do, affect the way that human beings understand themselves on a broad scale. From this context, it is possible to apply the critical framework. For example, the September 11, 2001, attacks on the World Trade Center and the Pentagon seem to have created an understanding of what it means to be *patriotic* in the United States. In regard to *expectations,* this word seems to emphasize support for decisions and policies made by the leadership of the U.S. government. *Responsibilities* for this expectation appear to include approval of these policy decisions in words, thoughts, and actions. Actions, in this context, include continued (or increased) consumerism. *Conflicts,* in this scenario, seem to begin with *unpatriotic* thoughts and behaviors. *Unpatriotic* may indicate dissension regarding the decisions and policies of the U.S. government. From this perspective, *unpatriotic* may indicate actions or beliefs that deviate from the best interests of persons living in the country. However, according to Moore (2002), this term may be expanded to include some of the actions taken by the government itself. For example, Moore cites some of the recent policies, drafted in response to the attacks (i.e., those that curb civil liberties and discourage opposition to the government's actions), that run contrary to ideas specified by the Constitution and, therefore, also may be considered *unpatriotic.* Perhaps this kind of vigilance—watching out for the protection of personal liberties and compliance with the Constitution—can be considered a kind of *patriotism.* Consequently, this *alternative* understanding enlarges the scope of the denotations of the term *patriotic* (and its derivative, *unpatriotic*) and constructs meanings that are more inclusive than exclusive.

For another example, the term *immigration* has received a great deal of attention since September 11, 2001. *Webster's Universal Collegiate Dictionary* (1997) defines this term as follows: "to come to a country of which one is not a native" (p. 407). Although the denotation of this word seems quite simplistic on the surface, it seems to take on greater meaning when viewed against a larger historical context. Since the attacks on the Pentagon and the World Trade Center, the term has appeared more frequently in the political arena and has been met with a skepticism that has altered national policies. For instance, U.S. Attorney General John Ashcroft responded swiftly to the attacks by increasing the time of legal detention from 24 to 48 hours, and making it indefinite for "extraordinary" circumstances (Miller, 2001). The attacks also prompted Congress to consider a reduction in the overall admissions of immigrants allowed into the United States and an increase in the number of guards at each border (Miller, 2001). From this context, the term has become highly politicized as *expectations* for this term are redefined. The prevailing belief system seems to be alarmist in nature and cautious in action; and therefore, immigrants seem to be increasingly *responsible* for justifying their presence inside the borders of the United States. *Conflicts* result when members of immigrant communities cannot provide reasons for their presence that are satisfactory to immigration authorities (under the new legislation) or when they appear to be involved (whether this is substantiated or not) with the attackers of the Pentagon and World Trade Center. An *alternative* understanding of the term is derived from a question that returns to the term's original meaning: How many cultures that presently occupy the mainland territory of the United States are actually native to it? By this definition, nearly every group that occupies the continent is a non-native group. Without this kind of questioning about and consideration of contexts, words may lapse into a widely accepted mold that promotes stereotypical notions.

Once again, shifts in the contexts of language can produce changes in the way that perceptions of the words are constructed. For the examples used in this section, the understanding of terms may change with the expansion of their meaning, illustrating how the perceptions of a term's meaning seem to affect interactions among those using it. This process can potentially affect the formation of thoughts and, ultimately, policies. Without critical examination of terms, narrow denotations may be accepted as notions of truth. On the other hand, reframing a term in a variety of contexts can promote change in thoughts, which can lead to individual and collective change.

Meso

The meso level of human interaction has a great deal to do with interactions among groups and families, neighborhoods and cohorts. As such, the language used on this level also has a great deal to do with these interactions. Labels that describe a particular group can minimize or expand the ideas that others have about that group and can also affect what that group believes about itself. Critical analysis of words and labels can produce changes in thoughts and behaviors among and between groups.

Words that describe groups and families on a meso level can obscure or accentuate the richness that exists in the context of various cultures. The term *American Indian* provides an example for discussion. According to Champagne (1997), the term *American Indian* can be deceptive:

> Most ethnic groups are restricted to fit the definition of a people with a shared history or culture or major historical experience. If we are restricted to the latter definition, then American Indians also are an ethnic group. . . . American Indians, however, do not see themselves sharing either culture or history with most other American Indian communities, but rather see themselves largely within tribal historical and cultural context. American Indians view history from the viewpoint and cultural orientation of their specific tribal group, or even village, clan, or family. (p. 29)

From the conventional usage of the term, as defined by Champagne, there seems to be the *expectation* that all Native-American groups (or First Nations Peoples, which is the term currently being used) are similar. It is, therefore, the *responsibility* of the groups that are labeled under this term to act and behave accordingly (i.e., share the same cultural values, languages, and customs). *Conflict* potentially transpires as specific groups defy these conventional constructions of truth. As an *alternative,* constructed understanding can be broadened by consideration of the diversity that exists within the meaning of the term *American Indian (Native American, First Nations Peoples)*, as well as among individuals, families, groups, and communities being identified by the term.

This case demonstrates that language can reduce understanding by trying to describe many groups with one term; in other words, the term *American Indian* does not seem to capture the diversity that exists among various indigenous groups. Perceiving all the groups that are indigenous to the North American continent as the same minimizes their vast experiences, histories, and cultures. Consequently, diverse groups of First Nations Peoples are represented as being less than they truly are. Zuniga (1997) echoes and broadens this point when she critiques the language used in ethnic studies: "Certainly the jargon and social science research used to analyze minority groups needs to be improved so it is less biased and more reflective of the unique within group differences the author underscores" (p. 35). Clearly, language that fails to seek out the diversity that exists within diverse groups often leads to the formation of stereotypes among and between groups.

Risks that exist in stereotyped understandings of language are exhibited through interactions between groups and families. For instance, after the September 11, 2001, attacks, large numbers of groups and families bearing a "Middle-Eastern appearance" were sometimes perceived as Arab-Muslims and were consequently associated with the religion of Islam. These perceptions and the suggestion of threats on the national level sometimes translated to feelings of insecurity for groups and families, regardless of their actual ethnic identities. The facts that more than three-quarters of the American Arab population are Christian and that the proportion of Arabs in America who practice Islam is approximately one in eight reveal the misconceptions in the conventional understanding (Derbyshire, 2001). Therefore, without a circumspect analysis of the context for such terms as *American Indian (Native American, First Nations Peoples)* and *Arab-Muslim,* families and groups may be placed at varying degrees of risk. On the other hand, the multidimensional contextual perspective employs the critical framework to explore such terminology in order to yield a more complex understanding of and deeper respect for the richness that exists between and among groups and families.

Micro

The critical framework of the multicultural contextual perspective accepts the many and varied levels of individuals as they relate to themselves and others. Language, on the micro level, seems to influence the intrapersonal and interpersonal exchanges for each person; it informs the construction of their notions of truth about themselves and the world around them. Because of its significance in this process, language can be used to either broaden or reduce understanding. Application of the critical framework can facilitate a process that promotes the former over the latter.

As an example, examine the word *lesbian*. One of the *expectations* of this term seems to be that it applies to a woman who is in a relationship with another woman. The *responsibility* stemming from this expectation seems to be to make distinctions between the person labeled by this term and other groups. This expectation also seems to hold those who are so labeled *responsible* for behaving in a way that mirrors beliefs about the term itself. *Conflicts* may occur for those labeled as *lesbian* through violent and oppressive reactions, as the term itself lies outside the realm of acceptability in many social contexts (Shriver, 2001). Thus, from a conventional standpoint, the term connotes a sense of compartmentalization, victimization, and stigma. However, a greater understanding of the term offers the possibility of connection rather than isolation and marginalization. This concept is demonstrated by the writing of Moraga (2001), who discovered a connection with her mother through an evaluation of her own lesbianism:

> When I finally lifted the lid to my lesbianism, a profound connection with my mother reawakened in me. It wasn't until I acknowledged and confronted my own lesbianism in the flesh, that my heartfelt identification with and empathy for my mother's oppression—due to being poor, uneducated, and Chicana—was realized. (p. 30)

The implicit emphasis in this writing appears to be found in the *profound connection* that is achieved with an honest and thorough assessment of the meaning of the term *lesbianism*. This example provides a definition of connection rather than division and, furthermore, appears to describe a notion of commonality within diverse contexts. However, this process requires a strong commitment to openness and integrity:

> When we are not physically starving, we have the luxury to realize physic and emotional starvation. It is from this starvation that other starvations can be recognized—if one is willing to take the risk of making a connection—if one is willing to be responsible to the results of the connection. (Moraga, 2001, p. 30)

Thus, an *alternative* (and expanded) understanding of the term *lesbian* demonstrates that it can be conceived of as a form of oppression by which other forms of oppression also may be identified. In other words, it is a powerful link to and representation of oppression that exists for many people across contexts.

While language can be used to construct truncated understandings through stereotypes, the multidimensional contextual approach holds that it is also possible to use language to promote connection among and between individuals. In other words, language can create notions of truth that may facilitate (rather than abridge) an understanding of commonalities within and across diverse experiences and contexts. This is not to suggest that such language should focus exclusively on commonalities while neglecting the importance and richness of our differences. Instead, language may be used to construct a sense of "truth" that reveals integral threads among and between people while respecting their diverse contexts and inherent differences. Words that yield connection without sacrificing the significance of difference may require a certain level of precision in a social environment with so much divisive rhetoric. The key is to use language impeccably, to capture ideas that promote connection within the context of diverse circumstances.

Framing discourse in a way that seeks commonalities and also recognizes diverse contexts may begin with a series of questions:

- When do I feel the least comfortable around others?
- What are some experiences that have led to these feelings?
- How do these feelings influence my behavior?

- What kind of language is used to describe this behavior when I do it?
- How about when others do it?
- Do I observe examples of my behaviors in the media? How are they portrayed?
- What did I learn about my behavior in school? How did this education affect my beliefs about myself? How did this education affect my beliefs about others?

The purpose of asking such questions is to begin to engage in a process akin to that described by Moraga (2001)—mainly, stimulating a critical awareness of self. The more we begin to understand ourselves from a larger array of contexts, the more we may understand others in a similar way. And the more opportunities we have to describe ourselves in terms of diverse contexts, the more we are able to do the same for others. In this way, conceptualizations conveyed through language create notions of "truth" that resist stereotypes by moving beyond myopic perceptions and descriptions.

MULTIDIMENSIONAL CONTEXTUAL PRACTICE AND LANGUAGE

Social/health/human service practitioners interact with a wide variety of clients in diverse capacities. For some practitioners, transactions with clients take place on an individual basis in a clinical setting; other practitioners are involved with clients in the form of groups, families, or communities. Understanding the context of a client's environment allows practitioners to tune into their personal use of language, acknowledging its limitations, attributes, and tendencies to include and exclude. These particular areas are covered and expanded throughout this section, and exercises demonstrating application of these concepts are provided.

Limitations of Language

The multidimensional contextual approach recognizes that language contains an inherent power to include and exclude specific subject matter, depending largely on the context. For this reason, awareness of language is vital to active and effective relationships with clients. *Awareness,* in this case, does not suggest that practitioners need to be ultravigilant, but only that they recognize the need for a fitness between their choice of language and the context of their environments and clients.

Practitioners may benefit from the realization that whatever language they use has limitations that may be inclusive in one context and exclusive in another. For example, while engaging a client, the use of jargon that is specific to the academic context of the profession (e.g., *empowerment, assessment, biopsychosocial,* etc.) may have adverse repercussions: Although the use of these words may be appropriate when practitioners are speaking with other practitioners, using such words with clients may place common understanding at risk. This example demonstrates how the use of a particular kind of language (in this case, professional jargon) can have limitations in one context (i.e., with a client) but be effective in another context (i.e., with other practitioners).

Language often contains assumptions or takes for granted certain notions about what is true. This tendency may have consequences for work with clients in some unexpected ways. For instance, practitioners may characterize the behavior of clients who bite themselves as being self-destructive, while the clients, on the other hand, may understand the same behavior as a self-defense strategy, given the context of their environments. Such a scenario frequently occurs in cases involving child abuse. By using language that frames clients' behavior with connotations of deficiencies and dangers, rather than language that recognizes the behavior in the way clients do, practitioners create a weak fitness between their language and the context of the client. As a result, the language appears to impose limitations on the relationship between the practitioner and the client.

Alternatively, practitioners may choose to ask clients about how they understand their behaviors within their environments. This kind of investigation can help practitioners discover a context for the language and, thus, establish a strong fitness between the language they employ and the relationships they have with clients. The key is the use of context to guide the language, instead of the other way around. When practitioners too quickly engage clients with language that does not fit the context, relationships with clients may become strained, and the level of rapport and trust between the practitioner and client may become endangered.

Finally, human service practitioners can challenge themselves to look at meaning from a dynamic rather than a static perspective. That is, although language attempts to define meaning in absolute terms, it cannot capture the ephemeral nature of life. Take, for example, the term *spirituality*. There are as many (or more) understandings of this term as there are people who use it. As a result, this one specific word fails to capture the exact reality represented by the word. Instead, language provides only signs and directions that scaffold each subjective notion of its meaning. There is no standard by which to measure each and every individual notion of the term *spirituality*. The multidimensional contextual perspective honors the flexibility of language and, in turn, recognizes that language can be used to expand the meaning of a term and, thus, influence notions of truth.

Attributive Language

Since language frames content in varied contexts, practitioners must be aware of the way that language identifies attributes, especially when discussing concerns that clients have brought to their attention. It is not uncommon for clients to understand their issues in terms of cause and effect. That is, they often describe a particular issue as being the product of an internal flaw. For example, clients with eating disorders may indicate, while visiting practitioners, that they attribute their eating disorders to a personal deficit. In doing so, the clients employ language that frames their concerns in exclusively internalized terms. The language that a practitioner uses to respond to the client in such a case may affirm, challenge, or offer alternatives to the attributes the client applies to the issue. In deciding on what language to use in such instances, practitioners may do well to acknowledge that any language they choose to use in framing the issue will have limitations and consequences.

From the perspective of multidimensional contextual practice, rather than searching for the "right" words by which to respond to clients, it is more appropriate for practitioners to employ language that considers the environmental contexts of clients and that refrains from perpetuating stereotypes or blaming the clients for their concerns. Moreover, using language that undermines the client's standpoint or sense of reality may be equally debilitating to the relationship. Examples of this kind of language include biased ascriptions about a client's culture, socioeconomic experience, status of mental health, and physical abilities. In following these principles, the context of the client-practitioner relationship should ultimately guide the response.

When clients approach practitioners with concerns that bear internally oppressive attributes, they provide the practitioners with opportunities to hone in on the specific language that clients use to frame their concerns. Multidimensional contextual practice recognizes that language builds and frames perceptions of each person's notions of truth. For this reason, practitioners and clients enter into a relationship whereby a new vocabulary is often needed and formed. This new vocabulary consists of language that helps clients reframe or reconstruct notions about themselves that generate novel perspectives in dealing with their concerns. The following questions can serve as a baseline for practitioners as they begin the process of exploring and understanding clients' meanings and interpretations:

- How would you describe your current circumstances and challenges?
- How do your current circumstances and challenges affect your day-to-day performance and functioning?
- What do you perceive as some of your strengths and abilities in confronting and dealing with your current circumstances and challenges?
- What type of support could you or do you receive from family members and friends?

The point is not to ignore the validity of the client's concerns by using rosier language or euphemisms, but to explore new language that, in turn, constructs alternative ideas that ideally will lead to a recognition of greater options for the client.

Framing Exercise

Picture yourself holding an empty frame. Allow this frame to be quite large so that it can display a fairly big scene. Now, use your imagination and picture yourself holding that frame while looking through it, down a street in an urban environment. Capture a scene within the frame of a woman walking with two small children. The children appear to be happy, but the mother appears to be tired and stressed out. Shift the position of the frame, and notice a group of people walking down the street in a procession, mourning the death of an aged man. Again move the frame so that now you can see a young man with a large bruise on his face and ragged clothing. He does not appear to be altogether aware of where he is at the moment.

Each "frame" in this exercise contains a specific context, and as such, certain language might commonly correspond to each context. For instance, a person speaking to an observer of the funeral procession would likely use a different choice of words in that context than in speaking to the woman with the children. Similarly, this same observer would probably choose an altogether different way of speaking to the young man. The meaning of words would likely vary for the subjects of these frames; for instance, the words *happiness, future,* and *work* might all be comprehended in different ways, according to the context of each situation.

- If you were speaking with the group in the funeral procession, how would you use the term *closure?*
- Would your use of that term change if you were speaking to the young man?

- And what about your use of the term *responsibility* if you were talking to the woman and children?
- Would that same term be constructed in a different way if you were to address the people in the funeral procession?

Practicing this brief exercise opens some new ways to consider the issue of context and language. Practitioners may be able to expand their own notions of language by focusing on context.

Language: A Gateway to New Paths

Despite its limitations and ability to exclude, language may be used to help practitioners bridge gaps with their clients. One of the first steps in this process is exploration, since the language that constructs the thoughts of a practitioner is not usually the same language that composes the "realities" of the practitioner's clients. Thus, engaging a client may be greatly enhanced through the practice of learning about the client's use of language. How are the ways the client uses language different from or similar to the ways in which the practitioner uses it? Furthermore, how can the practitioner use these similarities and differences to find common ground with the client? For the former, practitioners can point out commonalities; for the latter, they may be able to begin to expand their own understanding of words and terms. In this way, the practitioner can join together with the client in ways that promote change for both parties.

Perhaps the most important term for this section is *awareness,* since it is through awareness that understanding of meaning is possible. The point of this section is not to show language as a border between practitioners and their clients, but rather to reveal language as a medium for change that can profoundly influence clients and practitioners alike. Through mindful exchanges between clients and practitioners, language can provide a powerful tool to enhance communication, clarify intent, and promote client well-being, as well as create collective meaning for an effective ongoing relationship.

PRINCIPLES FOR PRACTICE

The purpose of this section is to provide the reader with activities through which to practice the principles outlined in the section of this chapter entitled "A Critical Framework: The Dynamics of Language and Change on the Magna, Macro, Meso, and Micro Levels."

Activity 1

Use the four areas of inquiry from the critical framework (*expectations, responsibilities, conflicts,* and *alternatives*) to analyze the following terms:

Resilience   Oppression   Diversity   Privilege   Minority   Equality   Spirit

For each of these terms, take a moment to consider the levels of interaction (magna, macro, meso, micro) on which each term seems to exist. Does your understanding of each term seem to change when it is considered on different levels? If so, what seem to be some of the underlying causes for the change?

Activity 2

For this activity, read the following scenario and answer the questions that follow.

A practitioner arrives at the home of a family that has been self-referred for help with a drug abuse issue. When the practitioner arrives, she immediately notices that the home is cluttered with clothes and toys, and bits of food have been ground into the rug. The mother of the family invites the practitioner to have a seat, and they begin to discuss the issue. The mother reveals that she and her husband frequently use alcohol and marijuana. She is concerned because her husband has been becoming increasingly aggressive after use of the drugs and, lately, has become harsher with their two children. The mother does not want the children to be hurt or taken away. She appears scared, confused, and desperate.

The practitioner reflects the mother's concern and tells her they can do a number of things that may help the situation. In fact, the practitioner indicates there may be services available to assist the family in improving their interactions, and other services available to help them with appropriate housing. Upon hearing these suggestions, the mother quickly becomes quiet and more reserved. She seems to be in a hurry to end their meeting and does not call the practitioner back the following day as she agreed she would.

- In reading this scenario, what ethnic group did you envision for the family requesting aid?
- What ethnicity did you envision for the practitioner?
- What context clues influenced your construction of the characters' backgrounds?

Now, list three key terms that you noticed while reading the scenario. Analyze each of these key terms, using the critical framework (i.e., *expectations, responsibilities, conflicts,* and *alternatives*). How did the characters understand and respond to the terms you have chosen? Consider how different understandings of the terms could alternatively affect the outcome.

Activity 3

Read three articles from different newspapers and magazines. Choose three terms from each source that are used to describe individuals, families, groups, and communities or the interactions among them. Record each term on a sheet of paper, and apply the critical framework (i.e., *expectations, responsibilities, conflicts,* and *alternatives*) to each term. Consider ways in which a broader understanding of each term you have chosen might change the meaning of the article in which it appeared.

Activity 4

Identify and reflect on some of the expressions and terms you use most frequently in professional conversations. How might these expressions and terms be received by culturally and ethnically diverse clients? That is, would differences in gender, sexual orientation, socioeconomic background, age, mental and physical abilities/

disabilities, and so on affect the meaning, understanding, and interpretation of these expressions and terms? What might be some of the possible consequences if what you are trying to communicate is misunderstood, as reflected by a client's interpretation? What steps would you take to make your communication more successful?

References

Champagne, D. (1997). Does the focus on multiculturalism emphasize differences and foster racial/ethnic stereotypes? In D. de Anda (Ed.), *Controversial issues in multiculturalism* (pp. 27–40). Boston: Allyn & Bacon.

Derbyshire, J. (2001). At first glance—Racial profiling, burning hotter. *National Review, 53,* 1.

Elrich, M. (1994, May). The stereotype within. *Educational Leadership, 51*(8), 12–16.

Hartman, A. (1991). Words create worlds. *Social Work, 36*(4), 275–276.

Miller, J. (2001). Border lines—What to do about immigration after 9/11. *National Review, 53*(20), 1.

Moore, M. (2002). How to be un-American. *Hip Mama, 27,* 8.

Moore, R. B. (2001). Racist stereotyping in the English language. In M. L. Anderson & P. H. Collins (Eds.), *Race, class, and gender: An anthology* (4th ed., pp. 322–332). Belmont, CA: Wadsworth/Thompson Learning.

Moraga, C. (2001). La guera. In M. L. Anderson & P. H. Collins (Eds.), *Race, class, and gender: An anthology* (4th ed., pp. 28–34). Belmont, CA: Wadsworth/Thompson Learning.

Pinderhughes, E. (1994). Diversity and populations at risk: Ethnic minorities and people of color. In F. G. Reamer (Ed.), *The foundations of social work knowledge* (pp. 264–308). New York: Columbia University Press.

Robbins, S. P., Chatterjee, P., & Canda, E. R. (2001). *Contemporary human behavior theory: A critical perspective for social work* (pp. 267–269). Boston: Allyn & Bacon.

Saleebey, D. (1994). Culture, narrative, and theory: The intersection of meaning in practice. *Social Work, 39*(4), 351–361.

Shriver, J. M. (2001). *Human behavior and the social environment: Shifting paradigm in essential knowledge for social work practice* (3rd ed.). Needham Heights, MA: Allyn & Bacon.

Webster's universal collegiate dictionary. (1997). New York: Random House.

Zuniga, M. (1997). Does the focus on multiculturalism emphasize differences and foster racial/ethnic stereotypes? In D. de Anda (Ed.), *Controversial issues in multiculturalism* (pp. 27–40). Boston: Allyn & Bacon.

O' Great Spirit, help me always to speak the truth quietly, to listen with an open mind when others speak, and to remember the peace that may be found in silence. —**Cherokee Prayer**

6 | Spirituality and Multidimensional Contextual Practice

JUDY A. GUADALUPE

Several texts have been written regarding the rich and diverse religious and spiritual practices among human beings that may influence practitioners and potential clients (Frame, 2003). It may be beneficial to become familiar with some of the various traditions and practices if we intend to work with and be of service to the diverse body of humankind. This chapter, however, is not a reference of that kind; it does not explore diverse religions and spiritual practices. Rather, the purpose of this chapter is to explore multidimensional contextual experiences of human beings (i.e., client and practitioner) in the realm of what has been termed the magna-spiritual. In this author's perception, spirituality or transcendent realities/consciousness is not separate from us or conventional realities/consciousness. Therefore, to explore the realm of the magna (transcendent realities/consciousness), we do not have to go anywhere, or investigate something that exists outside of ourselves. It is this author's intention to investigate spirituality as something that is here now—the very fabric within which we have our existence.

Over the last century, people-centered employment, be it teaching, researching, counseling, community organizing, or some other activity, has been influenced by the work of various teachers, scholars, and writers of psychology, education, philosophy, spirituality, sociology, social work, science, metaphysics, and more. We are rich with information regarding scientific and social theories about people, families, groups, communities, and nations, and with theories about how best to work with diverse populations and communities. *A theory means what?* The first definition that comes to mind is: "Maybe we could look at it this way (for a moment)." *Webster's II New College Dictionary* (1999) defines theory as: "1. a. Systematically organized knowledge applicable in a relatively wide variety of circumstances, esp. a system of assumptions, accepted principles, and rules of procedure devised to analyze, predict, or otherwise explain the nature of behavior of a specified set of phenomena. . . . 3. An assumption or guess based on limited knowledge or information: Hypothesis" (p. 1144).

When the "specified set of phenomena" is human beings, can we truly rely on our assumptions to create "accepted principles, and rules of procedure to . . . predict, or . . . explain?" In certain contexts and areas regarding the human experience, theories may be beneficial and valuable in assisting us to verbalize through language and understand glimpses of the human condition. With that said, in the area of human diversity and spirituality, can it be that theories contribute to stereotyping and placing limitations on the diverse body of humankind? Can acknowledging the great mystery inherent in all life assist us in releasing limitations and stereotypes while we allow the spirit within all life to present itself through all our interactions? The intention of this chapter is not to create or discuss theories regarding human diversity and spirituality of human beings, but rather to touch briefly on the possibility of having no theory, no preconceptions, no idea of who someone or some group is or are or should be, and instead relating to each other from the place of limitless possibilities and potential.

Multidimensional contextual practice is presented as a framework from which readers can gain insight as they allow the open-mindedness and possible expansion of consciousness that assists us in fathoming the vast diverseness of each individual, family, group, and community—a diverseness that shares its very essence with the unfathomable whole. This chapter will touch on the perception of a connected whole—a oneness of consciousness, of spirit (life force energy, the soul) having the opportunity to find physical expression in innumerable and unlimited ways. As Guadalupe and Lum have stressed in this book, the intention is not to define what is but to serve as a possible "plan from which something not yet constructed can be produced." Through discussion and examples, let us take a swim together in the vast possibilities of perception, consciousness, and connectedness that can affect our assessments, interventions, styles, and work with both our clients and ourselves.

SPIRITUALITY AND HUMAN DIVERSITY

Spirituality, like the experience of human diversity, means different things to different people. The term *spirituality* can and often does evoke mixed reactions. While some reactions embrace concepts and experiences associated with the term *spirituality,* others do not. Perhaps, as readers, it may be beneficial for you to initially explore some of your own perceptions and experiences prior to continuing with the exploration in this chapter. Remember that perceptions are not right or wrong; they simply are. "Truth" within one context may be irrelevant in another.

- How would you define spirituality?
- Would your definition of spirituality differ from your definition of religiosity? How?

- How have your upbringing, schooling, individual experiences, and religious influences affected the meaning that you apply to the concept and experience of spirituality?
- How would you address situations with a client whose religious identification or spiritual rituals conflict with your own religious or spiritual associations and practices (or nonpractice)?

Exploring language and the various meanings, and thus attitudes, that diverse people hold toward specific words and concepts can be interesting and mind-expanding. One can see that words and language are often related to personal perceptions, preferences, and experiences. Both *spirituality* and *human diversity* have become buzzwords, and people in many professional fields and arenas are being encouraged not to ignore these aspects or parts of the human experience. At times it may appear that lip service is being offered to these concepts more because it is "the popular thing to do" than because of any conscious engagement in creating substantial understanding or effecting changes in orientations and approaches used with diverse clients. This author's perception is that usually there is intention to create and affect changes in paradigms and practice modalities that have been exclusive and neglectful. Nevertheless, even in such explorations, experiences affiliated with spirituality and human diversity often continue to be reduced to concepts that are compartmentalized and fragmented.

In other words, human diversity is often associated with certain aspects of clients, be they micro or macro (e.g., culture or ethnicity), while spirituality is often considered as something "separate from," a belief or dogma rather than an essence or spirit that is pervasive in all of life. By playing with language, we can explore the restrictions that may stem from separation and compartmentalization. Is it possible to truly separate spirituality or human diversity from anyone, any group, or any concept? From religion to science, mathematics to history, politics to social services, and in just about any other area we can speak about (e.g., food, children, parenting, art, exercise), can you and I not have a conversation about diverse aspects of these subjects? As for *spirituality*, there may be as many definitions of this term and unique experiences in this area as there are people breathing. Let us generally investigate various definitions and perceptions.

Each person has words and beliefs that reflect that person's ideas about spirituality. Some people are uncomfortable with the word *God*; others have a strong sense or definition of who or what *God* is. Furthermore, some people allow the words *God, Allah, Yahweh, Great Spirit, Divine Imagination,* and *Dios* to encompass an ever-changing and expanding energy that others might rather call *Source, the Creator, life* or *life force, the mystical, spirit, the divine, divine imagination,* or by any other of the myriad words used in the multitude of languages and traditions that exist on this planet. *Webster's II New College Dictionary* (1999) defines *spirituality* as "the state, quality, or fact of being spiritual" (p. 1065). The same source characterizes *spiritual* as "1. The vital principle or animating force, traditionally believed to be within living beings. 2. The soul, considered as departing from the body of a person at death. 3. *Spirit.* The Holy Ghost. 4. *Spirit.* Christian science. God. . . . 5. A supernatural being. 6.a. The part of a human being associated with the mind and feelings as distinguished from the physical body. b. A person's essential nature . . ." (p. 1065).

Faiver, Ingersoll, O'Brien, and McNally (2001) note:

> Spirituality may be described as a deep sense of wholeness, connectedness, and openness to the infinite. . . . We believe spirituality is an innate human quality. Not only is it our vital life force, but at the same time it is also our experience of the vital life force. Although this life force is deeply part of us, it also transcends us. It is what connects us to other people, nature and the source of life. The experience of spirituality is greater than ourselves. (p. 2)

In her book *Traits of a Healthy Spirituality,* Svoboda (1996) quotes three definitions of *spirituality:* "Spirituality is meeting God [source, the divine] in all that life is (by Patricia Livingston); Spirituality is the experience of integrating self transcendence within the horizon of ultimacy (by Sandra Schneiders); [and] Spirituality is how I cope with life (by Gerard Broccolo)" (p. 4). Kilpatrick (1999) stresses that:

> A definition of spirituality would need to encompass the person's understanding of and response to meaning in life. . . . It would include faith and values as spiritual dimensions . . ., and also include the process of conceptualizing the individual's connection with others, the world, and the Creator. . . . Spiritual expression could also be defined as the individual's response to the events in life over which they have no control. (p. 58)

Kilpatrick (1999) uses Canda's (1988) definition of *spirituality* as an example of "an encompassing" description. Canda views spirituality as:

> The gestalt of the total process of human life and development relates to the person's search for a sense of meaning and totally fulfilling relationships between oneself, other people and the encompassing universe and ontological ground of existence, whether a person understands this in terms that are theistic, atheistic, nontheistic, or any combination of these. (Kilpatrick, 1999, p. 58)

Spirituality also can be described as an experience that is "beyond or before belief. Belief does not enter into it when one has direct experience. To believe is to convince one's mind about something and to hold a mental position about that belief" (Sananda, 2002). Yet beliefs offer a structure to existence, and as one grows and evolves, beliefs are let go of, expanded, and changed. There is not one way to experience truth or spirit, not even for one person; over a lifetime, spiritual truths and experiences evolve. Those who know or experience spirit would never denigrate any other person's way of doing the same. However, such a person might speak clearly about those spiritual practices or religious dogmas that do put down others or treat others as though each person is not a unique manifestation of the one spirit (Lerner, 2000). *To incorporate a spiritual perspective in your work as a social/health/human service practitioner may simply mean that you expand your concepts and beliefs, and hold them very loosely, since the next client you see may be the one who offers you the next key to the evolution of your soul, your beliefs, and your experiences of relationship, spirit, and life.*

Acknowledgment of the importance of human diversity, as it relates to multiple meanings, interpretations, and experiences affiliated with spirituality, has encouraged practitioners and researchers to develop spiritually based practices. Robbins, Chatterjee, and Canda (1998) speak of "spiritually sensitive practice." They write, "Spiritually sensitive practice respects the diverse religious and nonreligious forms of spirituality that are working within the clients' systems of meaning and supporting and helping them to achieve their highest potential for development" (p. 361). Based on the aforementioned definitions as well as Robbins and associates' call for a degree of understanding of spiritually sensitive practice, multidimensional contextual practice offers an avenue to allow respect for human diversity within multiple contexts and dimensions. Addressing both practitioner and client and how dimensions of being overlap and intertwine, allows for an environment conducive to the achievement of "their highest potential for development." The gift that often comes is that both client and practitioner can grow toward their highest potential, as clients become teachers and vice versa. Imagine the professional as well as personal learning and development likely to emerge as practitioners allow themselves to be taught about the diverse spiritual interpretations and experiences of communities of clients being served. Imagine the potential that exists for healing and transcending human pain and suffering if client-practitioner relations are fundamentally built upon a sense of connectedness that underlines the importance of growing through differences and connecting through commonalities.

The definitions examined here generally explain spirituality as something that encompasses life, is pervasive within our experience, and is an inherent quality or life force (or the force of life). As briefly illustrated through these definitions and our discussion, spirituality is not one thing. Although inclusive, its nature is also not restrained to any particular experience. Words that describe spirituality are vast and varied. The meanings and interpretations of those words and concepts are as vast and varied as the number of humans who are alive. *It is really awesome, and may actually be quite freeing, for people to realize that their experience and understanding of spirit is unique and unduplicated, regardless of the similarities they share.* This realization can assist practitioners to recognize the importance of beginning where the client is, while remaining open to the limitless spiritual and diverse potential in the beings before them.

Languaging (verbalizing) spirit has been the domain of all world religions, as well as various religious dogmas. To language spiritual concepts with no intention to create dogma is often a challenge. This point is illustrated by Lerner (2000) in his book *Spirit Matters*. He states:

> The deepest spiritual thinkers warn us that the realm of Spirit is the realm of the ineffable. It simply can't be adequately expressed in language. The best we can get is poetry and song, not prepositional knowledge. Again Abraham Joshua Heschel: "The heart of being confronts me as enigmatic, incompatible with my categories, sheer mystery. All we have is a sense of awe and radical amazement in the face of a mystery that staggers our ability to sense" (p. 32)

We may derive that spirituality does not actually mean anything, because spirituality simply is. People who experience the delight of spiritual life attempt to language it, yet words fall short, and the need to prove anything disappears with this understanding.

A Moment of Reflection

Take a moment to briefly reflect on the definitions and conceptions regarding spirituality that have been presented so far:

- What are your perceptions of spirituality?
- How different or similar are your perspectives from those discussed?
- Do you believe that spirituality can be compartmentalized, separated fully from other aspects and qualities of life?
- To what degree are your perceptions similar to or different from the notion that language and definitions of terms cannot convey all that is inherent in the experience of spirituality?
- What would you add to the content you have already read?

SPIRITUALITY: RELATING FROM A PLACE OF ENDLESS POSSIBILITIES

Allowing ourselves to be touched by the spirit in all life may be made easier when we think of children and their ability to gaze at and be fully present in the wonder of the moment. Not long ago, while waiting for help in a broken-down car with two of my children, I watched my son start playing and laughing as he jumped from the front to the back seat. For him, the external situation had nothing to do with the enjoyment of the present. After all, that is all there is. He teaches me.

Lerner (2000) speaks about how some claim or offer evidence to show that seeing life through the lens of the awe and wonder of a child is immature and unrealistic at best; they think that looking at life challenges and world issues through an optimistic lens is naïve. Some adults today seem to be caught in a double bind where, in their personal lives they strive for meaning, loving relationships, and to offer spiritual values to their children and loved ones; but at the same time, they are influenced by the belief that in the public arena, these abstract ideals have no place, and are not compatible with "making it" in the "real world." The deep skepticism and cynicism about society, economics, and our world that results from this and other similar beliefs are devastating, and often become self-fulfilling prophecies. Lerner writes, "I call these pathogenic beliefs (adopting a usage from psychologists Hal Sampson and Joseph Weiss), because when we hold these ideas, we tend to create a world that has the very pathologies or self-defeating ways of thinking and feeling we feared" (p. 17). The ability to see beyond, to experience this world without being attached to it, to hold a sense of peace in the face of suffering and pain, is not to be confused with being irresponsible or lacking commitment to take necessary actions to promote needed change. This position does not involve feeling sorry for the client, but instead holding a space of compassion. When allowed, spirit reminds us that crises are also opportunities. One can react to human pain from a place of helplessness or a sense of needing to control, or one can respond from a place of compassion, often strengthened through spiritual practices. Spirituality is about honoring the present of endless possibilities; it is about recognizing and transcending constructed senses of conventional realities/consciousness.

Take a moment and pretend you are putting on a pair of glasses. Yet, these are not regular glasses. These glasses allow you to see through the eyes of wonder and awe like a young child. These glasses allow you to see without any influence of the past or worry about the future. How does your life look through this lens? Focus particularly on your decision to work as a practitioner, knowing that everything you need is accessible to you in the present moment. What are your dreams and aspirations for your career and for what you can bring to your clients, be they individuals, families, groups, or communities? How does it feel to see through the spirit of wonder and the newness of the moment? Can we allow wonder to influence our perceptions about others and ourselves in order to have room for acceptance and surprise? Imagine what it might be like to let your clients surprise you, and to surprise them as well.

I am not suggesting using "rose-colored glasses" (although rose is a great color) to deny the challenges, and sometimes the horror and devastation, of the experiences of those with whom you will work. I am not suggesting that, as a practitioner, you be naïve and pretend that those you serve have had no experiences of pain or injustice. Rather, the suggestion here is to simply allow yourself to be present with clients while acknowledging human pain, and to see clients in a way that goes beyond the reflections of human despair and dissolution resulting from natural or constructed adversities. A sense of spiritual guidance and connectedness can remind us that the glass is not only half empty, but also half full. Try it: Allow spirit to guide your steps beyond the restrictions of the human mind.

Encouraging empowerment in clients requires listening to their experiences beyond preconceived ideas and judgments. The knowledge that in an energetic sense, we are composed of energy, of light, can assist us in opening to an expanded consciousness. The realization that thought is vibration and attracts to itself other similar vibrations is beneficial. The energy of worry and fear attracts (as Lerner mentioned) the exact things one fears or worries about. One does not have to wear blinders and pretend that nothing is in need of change and that no one is in pain. Rather, one can take in the whole situation and send out thoughts and energy of the knowing that there is space for limitless potential and possibility. For instance, the lives of people such as Martin Luther King, Jr., and Mahatma Gandhi have reflected the power of the human spirit in the face of human adversities. Both of these social leaders advocated for societal and cultural changes based not on skepticism and cynicism, but rather on an ability to see and sense a transcendent reality/consciousness that ignites hope and belief in possibility. Martin Luther King's "I Have a Dream" speech supports this observation.

Being a "yes" person in clients' lives—someone who, like a child, allows grace and possibility to flow—may be one of the greatest gifts you can give to clients. *Webster's II New College Dictionary* (1999) describes *grace* as "[a]pparently effortless charm or beauty of movement, form or proportion. . . . A disposition to be generous or helpful: Good Will. . . . A favor rendered voluntarily. . . . Divine love and protection bestowed freely on human beings" (p. 482). Perhaps grace, as this "divine love," this favor, this "beauty of movement" is the inexplicable life force energy that supports the overcoming of obstacles and strengthens resilience. Clients' empowerment is not simply encouraged through changes in their external life demands and circumstances, but through the process of opening themselves to the internal nudges and guidance of spirit as well.

There is a distinction between denial of the internal and external situations facing clients and the ability to hold a space of acceptance for clients that allows for change and healing. As readers, you may be able to reflect on stories of people who, individually or as part of communities, have overcome adversity against all odds.

When encouraged, most people could share turning points in their lives that have proven to be life-changing for the better. Often these turning points are initially instigated by crisis, hardship, or loss of some kind. Through multidimensional contextual practice, one can expand views and suspend knowledge while allowing the silver lining to present itself. Lerner (2000) speaks of creating the society that we fear through the individual and collective fears that we entertain. That same premise can be used here. Recognizing and transcending personal and societal-cultural fears can allow one to open to the limitless potential of the present moment.

Vibrationally, like attracts like (i.e., fear attracts fear, clarity attracts clarity, love attracts love, etc.). If one holds thoughts of, and believes in, the resilience and potential of all beings, an energy or atmosphere of possibility and potential can be created. Physicists and scientists tell us that we are made of energy; and in the science of energy, there is an experience called entrainment: Energy is compelled to match the vibration of the energies with which it comes in contact. If we can hold the lighter vibrations of acceptance, possibility, compassion, and love, then we can assist our clients in moving from the sometimes-debilitating cycles of vibrations of fear, anger, self-doubt, and so on. As Mahatma Gandhi emphasized, if we want to see change, we must be that change.

MULTIDIMENSIONAL CONTEXTUAL PRACTICE AND SPIRITUAL SENSITIVITY

Multidimensional contextual practice, as stressed in previous chapters, is derived from the strengths observed in a number of practice orientations, including principles drawn from the ethnographic perspective. Ethnographic perspectives and approaches support the notion that both the client and the social/health/human services practitioner can benefit from the practitioner's reliance on a commitment to learn from clients and their experiences and perceptions (Bein, 2003). Two major principles honored by the ethnographic perspective, and embraced by multidimensional contextual practice, are to begin where the client is, and to support client attainment and maintenance of well-being. Rather than putting clients into a box based on assumptions and preconceived ideas, the practitioner is encouraged to trust the client's understanding, capability, resources, and resilience. Through the formation of a partnership in which clients are perceived as the *experts* within the context of their experiences and the practitioner as a *skillful supportive system,* client and practitioner are encouraged to develop a plan of action that considers the contextual experiences within the multidimensions of micro, meso, macro, and magna influential factors.

Spiritually sensitive practice is comparable to ethnographic perspectives and intervention methods. Similar to ethnographic approaches, spiritually sensitive practice honors the roles that contexts as well as multidimensionality play in people's life experiences. For instance, spiritually sensitive practice provides the place for examining how spiritual orientations, meanings, interpretations, rituals, and so on may differ from one context to another or change from time to time. By the same token, spiritually sensitive practice recognizes that principles such as the idea of *unconditional love* (expressions of innate affection, tenderness, devotion, and caring that are not confined to constructed restrictions) seem to be principles embraced by multiple spiritual practices.

Spiritually sensitive practice recognizes that change is constant and that, yes, family, culture, social demands, ethnicity, gender, sexual orientation, and degrees of abilities all influence human beings. Spiritually sensitive practice calls practitioners to sharpen their ability to hold this information without placing on it either value judgments or judgments about how the practitioner believes one must have been affected by one's biological and biographical history. In other words, practitioners working within the context of human diversity are encouraged to explore and engage in necessary change regarding preconceived ideas that are likely to limit their interactions and exchanges with clients. How often do we, as practitioners, label (and thus limit) our clients? Statements like "Omar always acts out with violence because he was abused as a child," "Tammy cannot do that—she is too shy," and "Shannon is a recovering alcoholic, and that is why she . . ." reflect limited perceptions of the human spirit and potential. Spiritually sensitive practice advocates for recognition that although people are influenced by contextual and multidimensional factors, the uniqueness of each experience is filled with endless possibilities.

A gift to clients and fellow human beings is to allow them to let you know how they perceive themselves as well as to share their interpretations of experiences at any given moment. Examining possible effects of biological and biographical histories is valuable while assessing and working with diverse client systems. Identification of possible effects generated through biological and biographical histories can assist the human service practitioner in recognizing the roles that these histories may play in enhancing or injuring clients' ability to live a comfortable life, access necessary or valuable resources, maintain harmonious relationships, and so on. From a social/health/human service practitioner's perspective, a state of neutrality (nonjudgment, unconditional acceptance) can be helpful while supporting clients in a process of healing and letting go, allowing clients to be more than their past may dictate. As practitioners, we can look upon clients and give them a clean slate; we can judge nothing about them. This same gift can be given to our children, our loved ones, and ourselves. Through nonjudgment, the opportunity is presented for necessary changes to be influenced from a state of compassion.

As practitioners, we can honor clients with open minds and hearts, allowing them to be before us with unlimited potential and possibilities, no matter what external situations are present. This is one of the major principles of spiritually sensitive practice—the embracing of context (Rose, 1990) and the multidimensions of life experiences. Much of our job can be as simple as creating a space, an atmosphere, in which one can be and feel completely safe, respected, and honored. As is suggested in many spiritual traditions, being fully in the present, in unconditional acceptance, can create a space in which those involved can embrace needed healing, clarity, inner peace, and strength (Hawkins, 1995).

Hawkins (1995) has worked as a psychiatrist with people diagnosed with a variety of mental illnesses. In his writing, he speaks about having a number of remarkable "spiritual experiences" as a child and as an adult that changed his life and perceptions. Hawkins stresses that his perception has gone from what has been termed "ordinary consciousness," or conventional reality/consciousness, to what has been called "nonordinary" or transcendent reality/consciousness. Hawkins states:

The person I had been no longer existed. There was no personal self or ego left, just an Infinite Presence of such unlimited power that it was all that was. This Presence had replaced what had been "me," and the body and its actions were controlled solely by the Presence's infinite will. The world was illuminated by the clarity of an Infinite Oneness, which expressed itself as all things revealed in their immeasurable beauty and perfection. (p. 12)

According to Hawkins, he began to experience life from a consciousness of oneness and peace that allowed for powerful effects in relation to his work with clients (referred to by Hawkins as patients). Hawkins states:

This, in essence, happened with countless patients. Some recovered in the eyes of the world, and some did not, but whether or not a clinical recovery had occurred no longer mattered to the patients. Their inner agony was over; as they felt loved and at peace within, their pain stopped. This phenomenon can only be explained by saying that the compassion of the Presence recontextualized each patient's reality so that he or she experienced healing on a level that transcended the world and its appearances. The inner peace in which I existed encompassed us both, beyond time and identity. (p. 17)

Hawkins's (1995) experience reflects the power associated with a *sacred space of healing* (i.e., a space of inner peace that may or may not be accompanied by a cure in the eyes of the world). People such as Mother Theresa, Mahatma Gandhi, sages and saints from all religions, as well as other inspirational people have also demonstrated a capability to promote healing simply by their presence or being in the Presence. Each of us has the potential of being in the Presence or creating this healing environment. Some report that this experience happens when it is uninvited, for example, during an extraordinary event such as an accident in which a person feels a great sense of peace and well-being ensues. On the other hand, in daily interactions, people can and do consciously intend to be fully in the present, which can allow for the manifestation of sacred healing space.

Most practitioners do not consider themselves to be sages or saints; however, the point is, it is the Presence in the present moment that allows for the sacred healing space. Have you known someone in your life with whom you have felt completely loved and at peace to be yourself even without a spoken word? Or have you known someone in whose presence you felt more alive, more capable, and more motivated? Would an intention to be that kind of presence in clients' lives be unreasonable or unattainable? Would it not be beneficial to investigate what keeps us from being fully in the present moment, with compassion and nonjudgment? Spiritually sensitive practice encourages exploration of prejudices, perceptions, and willingness to heal or release whatever wounds and belief systems do not enhance our professional interactions and exchanges with clients.

Spiritually sensitive practice recognizes that transcendent realities/consciousness and conventional realities/consciousness are constantly in relationship with one another. These relationships reflect the importance of watching belief, thought, and value systems that affect professional behaviors and practices. Spiritually sensitive practice embraces the five principles put forward by the multidimensional contextual practice framework introduced in Chapter 2:

1. *Client well-being needs to be prioritized.*
2. *Clients are multidimensional contextual entities who are constantly changing.*

3. *Client well-being is affected by multidimensional contextual micro-intrapersonal, meso-interpersonal, macro-environmental, and magna-spiritual interactions and exchanges.*
4. *The human service practitioner's professional competence is vital during the helping process.*
5. *Individual and collective well-being can be promoted, strengthened, and reinforced through a multidimensional contextual perspective of services.* (Refer to Chapter 2 of this text for more details.)

The ultimate purpose of these principles is to strengthen professional practice within the context of human commonalities and differences. In this way, one can honor the uniqueness of the person, family, group, and community, and also avoid the pitfalls of stereotypical perceptions.

Spiritually sensitive practice enriches client-practitioner relationships by encouraging practitioners to acknowledge and embrace the potential that exists in the human spirit to transcend human adversities (Andrews, Guadalupe, & Bolden, 2003). There is no secret. Human pain exists within the realm of human experiences. Human pain is generated through natural events (e.g., the death of a loved one) and through constructed means (e.g., oppressive forces). Human pain and challenges are perpetuated through intrapersonal, interpersonal, institutional, environmental, cultural, as well as social patterns and dynamics. Thus, when exploring human pain, one must be eclectic, as proposed by multidimensional contextual practice. Ultimately, practitioners are employed to be of assistance in the alleviation or elimination of diverse forms of human pain and challenges. Spiritually sensitive practice reminds practitioners to be present within the face of human pain and resilience. As stressed by Mahatma Gandhi, "action without contemplation is blind."

It is important to recognize that human pain as well as resilience has individual and collective components. The literature on constructivist and social constructionist thoughts supports the notion that perceptions are subjective, and therefore, there is no one true reality for all. When looking at constructivism and social constructionism in relation to human diversity, Burris and Guadalupe (2003) stated, "The constructivist lens emphasizes the importance of taking into account individual narratives in order to reduce misunderstanding of individual experiences" (p. 203). Individual narratives affect individual consciousness. It is important to recognize that through interactions and exchanges, human beings co-create their reality, resulting in collective consciousness. Therefore, both individual and collective narratives can be explored within context with the awareness that both practitioner and client are affected by the consciousness of the individuals and communities by which they are influenced (Andrews, Guadalupe, & Bolden, 2003).

A Moment of Reflection

Take a moment to investigate diversity through your personal perceptions, influenced by your own personal narrative, history, and belief systems. Then step further into your heart space and investigate that which exists beyond the senses—your intuition, and your ability to love, honor, and be compassionate with yourself and others.

Knowledge and understanding of self in these areas allows enhancement of the practitioner's professional competence as well as *our primary goals: client well-being and social justice.*

- When reflecting on personal past experiences that you have encountered, what have been the effects of such experiences on your current belief and value systems? (Suggestion: Choose and reflect on two to three major experiences; for example, you might select a childhood experience, an experience that occurred during your adolescence, and another that you have encountered as an adult.)
- What role, if any, have your spiritual beliefs and values played when you confronted adversities?
- Is it possible that by exploring the realm of the magna-spiritual, the micro, mezzo, and macro goals (i.e., *client well-being* and *social justice*) can be effected and actualized? In other words, can an investigation of spirituality (transcendent realities/consciousness), of our connection to all beings, assist us in our work with clients and communities, and ultimately help us reach the critical mass needed to truly allow for world peace and an end to wars, food for every hungry person, a world community of human beings?

Practitioners intend to be of *service* to clients at the micro, mezzo, and macro capacities. Sometimes the greatest service may be simply accepting and honoring each other first. This often requires taking a deep and clear look within ourselves and exploring the wisdom and wonder that exist beyond the senses—the greater "truth" that gives meaning and purpose to our work with others and ourselves.

Information about the client that is gathered by practitioners is to be used for the client's benefit. It can allow for sensitivity in the client-practitioner relationship and awareness of the client as a whole being who is influenced by contextual and multiple factors (i.e., ethnic identification, culture, abilities, sexual orientation, gender, religious and spiritual orientation, family history, socioeconomic and political dynamics, transcendent realities/consciousness, etc.). Sensitivity building is important, as it influences the practitioner's ongoing engagement with the client during the process of mutual planning, advocacy, and action.

WOUNDS AS CATALYSTS/MUTUAL OPPORTUNITIES FOR GROWTH

Most people who choose service work with other human beings know and understand, or at the very least have heard about, the importance of self-discovery and self-knowledge in relation to becoming and being a skillful practitioner, educator, researcher, and so on. The wounds and challenges that our clients and we encounter, or have experienced, due to harmful patterns of interacting, culturally suppressive forces, social dynamics, and discrimination, among other factors, often serve as catalysts in the process of self-discovery, healing, and spiritual growth. Many times wounds and challenges promote the opportunity to experience a greater depth and meaning in life. In other words, crises are often opportunities, and opportunities do not always come without challenges.

Spiritual growth is often orchestrated by life experiences, conditions, and choices. When we speak of resilience within people, we may be talking about people who have experienced levels of discrimination and painful life experiences that some of us, as practitioners, cannot even imagine. Or, in some cases, practitioners may have experienced personally what appears to be similar oppression, discrimination, or abuse. As practitioners, it is never our job to deny or minimize hardships, oppression, and experiences encountered by clients. From a spiritual perspective, we are all interconnected, and what affects one affects the whole. At the same time, the practitioner's job is not to pretend to "know exactly" what clients feel, need, or experience in their presenting circumstances. Although an experience encountered by two or more individuals may seem similar in appearance, the effects of and responses to the experience are shaped by the individual's beliefs, values, and previous encounters.

Trusting the "wisdom of uncertainty" is, therefore, essential. Within the trust of not knowing lies the wisdom that allows each person, moment, and experience to present itself, along with limitless possibilities for response, intervention, and results. Briefly reflect on the following questions:

- Is it part of our life purpose, and the work of the souls experiencing discrimination or life challenges, to experience the depth of the inhumane treatment that is often part of our society?
- How often have we heard that people could get out of a situation if they were not "lazy," "drug addicts," or any number of conditions that we blame on individuals and populations?
- Can we dare to see the strength and resilience of these souls that manifest such difficult circumstances?
- Is part of the journey of these souls to be catalysts for change by bringing awareness and clarity to the imbalances that permeate our society?
- Can we see that the life conditions for many are based on belief systems, politics, and national policies that are not working?
- Can we, without judgment or blame, assist clients to honor themselves simply for their willingness to exist, and from that place of acceptance look at making beneficial changes in the micro, mezzo and macro experience?
- How can practitioners truly be of service to their clients?

While working with clients we are provided with an opportunity to reflect on our personal points of reference and how those points of reference are likely to change as we expand the knowledge base from which we view the world. Exploration of our personal narratives can allow us to embrace and utilize the lessons that life offers us. Willingness and commitment to a process of self-discovery and change can assist practitioners' ability to hold a space within themselves of honor and respect that is conducive to client well-being and growth. As practitioners, we may or may not come from cultures, life influences, and conditions that are similar to those of our clients. If we are willing, we are always learning.

CASE STUDY

Jane, a Caucasian woman, was raised in New York. Jane's grandparents had certain prejudices toward African Americans and Latino/a Americans. However, while Jane was growing up, her parents felt that there was something unjust and harmful in their parents' perceptions. Therefore, they raised Jane with the idea that it is important to treat other people equally, regardless of ethnic differences. At the same time, she had limited contact with people outside of her ethnicity, culture, and religious influence.

As an adult, Jane began working as a practitioner for a social service agency that served a large African-American population. During her initial professional interactions with African-American clients, Jane began to recognize that although her parents' intention was honorable, the notion that equality was about treating others the same left her with the idea that she knew what her clients needed and wanted. "Well, of course they want the same things and have the same dreams and expectations that I have," Jane thought. Through client encounters, supervision, and self-discovery, Jane began to observe that her sheltered reality, limited perceptions and belief systems, and lack of contact and connection with other ethnic groups and cultures (within this context, with African Americans) had left her unprepared to accurately be of service. Of course, Jane, or any other human service practitioner, cannot fully become part of a culture or reality experienced by someone else. Yet, self-evaluation allowed Jane to realize that each person's reality is different, and that her job was not so much to know what her clients needed as it was to treat her clients with respect, love, and honor so that a safe space could be established for her clients to create or obtain what would most benefit them from their perception. Jane soon learned how to enter into relationships with her clients from a place of "not knowing," and remain receptive to learning from her clients' unique life encounters, meanings, and interpretations.

Another growth experience presented itself to Jane with the uncovering of a hidden prejudice after an unexpected move to the Southeast. There she came face to face with her own insidious belief that somehow being from New York made her more intelligent than the people with whom she worked. This realization shocked her. The belief was not based on gender, class, or ethnicity; it was an insidious belief that permeated the belief systems of those who were influential in her growing years. During times of reflection and self-evaluation, Jane remembered hearing her father say that most of the "gray matter" (intelligent people) of all "Americans," or possibly the world, lived within a 100-mile radius of New York City. This experience exposed Jane's belief systems about the intelligence of people from "down south." Jane's opportunities to have these thought processes uncovered and challenged allowed her to consciously engage in necessary changes, move beyond such limiting beliefs, and enter into relationships with her clients and new friends.

Over the years, Jane has committed herself to ongoing professional self-evaluation. She has learned that working with the vastness of human diversity continuously allows for the raising of consciousness and expansion of one's present view of reality. Each realization and subsequent growth can be seen as the great gift of the spirit through diversity in relationships.

Reflection on Case
Take a moment to briefly reflect on the diverse relationships in your life—familial relationships, personal friendships, and professional associations. Use the following questions as guidelines:

- What have been some of the most significant relationships in my life? What types of influences have each of these relationships had in the development of my perceptions toward self and others? What roles have such perceptions played in my interactions with self and others?
- What experiences have triggered the major turning points of my life? What challenges and wounds from my past have taught me beneficial life lessons? How has my self-identification, as well as the ways that I perceive other people considered different from me, changed over time?
- Who is the other? What seems to separate me from and connect me with this other?

- Are there examples in my life where interactions with another allowed me to experience an unexpected lesson or growth opportunity?
- How might I use my interactions with clients as opportunities for growth for myself as well as my clients? Do I trust my intuition? How may I strengthen my trust in it?

BEING AND BECOMING: JOURNEYING IN LOVE AND COMPASSION

As mentioned earlier, change is the one constant in life—the one thing of which we can be sure. Whether it is called evolution, progression, regression, revolution, life, fruition, advancement, transformation, enlightenment, alteration, or movement, change carries with it a degree of uncertainty. Trust of this uncertainty has been explored in previous chapters as a vital component in recognizing and experiencing the "wisdom of uncertainty." The notion of "wisdom of uncertainty" reminds us to embrace change from a place of nonattachment, from a place in which we may experience an encounter without becoming it, since we know that this experience, too, will pass.

Change is inevitable. Being present in it is optional. Within the present moment exists the wisdom that allows for the uncertain to be, in a sense, certain. If one can realize that an outcome instigated by change may be uncertain to the mind, then from this state of presence, one has the opportunity to move from reliance on sensory perceptions (conventional realities/consciousness) to the perceptions of nonordinary consciousness (transcendent realities/consciousness). Inherent in this wisdom is an opportunity for an expansion of consciousness that allows us to expand our abilities to perceive, to feel, and to know. This awareness can assist people to acknowledge changes that have occurred in their lives. However, nonordinary consciousness does not necessarily rely on observable understanding. It is an invitation to the often invisible, intuitive wisdom. Multidimensional contextual practice holds an open door to expanding our perceptions of human diversity and spirituality. It encourages an expansion of consciousness.

Multidimensional contextual practice, as stressed in this text, has at its center client well-being, whether the client is an individual, family, group, or community. Practitioners' willingness to continue to expand their consciousness and broaden their perceptions will have an impact on their relationships with clients, self, and others. Multidimensional contextual practice affects the multidimensions of individual clients, groups, and communities, both local and global, allowing for use of the multidimensions of consciousness in both conventional and transcendent consciousness. Ritberger (2001) stresses that a shift in perception creates expansion of consciousness, which in turn affects different domains (micro, mezzo, macro, and magna). Ritberger writes:

> Approaching consciousness from a multidimensional perspective suggests that it is possible to connect the physical realm of ordinary consciousness with the subtle realms of nonordinary consciousness. However, this is not possible if our perceptions of consciousness are entrenched in the belief that only the physical sensory system can be trusted for the collection of data, or if we view reality only from the dimensions of ordinary consciousness. (p. 4-2) . . . [Ritberger continues,] The non-ordinary dimensions [i.e., transcendent realities/consciousness] rely more on the extended sensory system and intuition for their input, feedback and direction. . . . Accessing the wisdom found in non-ordinary consciousness requires that we bypass the interference created by the conscious mind, so it

cleverly uses daydreaming, dreams and deep states of relaxation to facilitate accessing new inner images and heighten our sensitivity to the perspectives of reality they offer. (p. 4-10)

Within each moment, one is presented with choices. Do I choose to experience this moment and my interactions based on input from my physical senses, or might I intend to shift my perception and see in a new and expanded way? Investigating and verifying the results of following "gut feelings" and intuition can be inspiring. Perhaps taking a few moments to move into a deeper state of relaxation or meditation before we make decisions or take actions affecting our clients may prove to be valuable. In the stillness of the moment may lie a wisdom that presents itself when the mind is on snooze or simply resting. Nourishing your own ability to let go and relax may allow you to respond calmly and with clarity, even in a crisis situation. Interaction with our clients in the conventional and transcendent realities is happening all the time, whether consciously or unconsciously. Learning to trust more than our physical senses can hone our skills and sharpen our trust of the inner and universal wisdom of life. As practitioners, we can expand our storehouse of resources from which we assist our clients.

As evolution continues, the human species is experiencing the mystery in both new and ancient ways. The mystery (the unknown, transcendent realities/consciousness) is one place from which human service practitioners can meet and honor clients. The abstractness of the mystery (transcendent realities/consciousness) can be explored within everyday life (conventional realities/consciousness) by moving beyond the senses into the experience and demonstration of the forces of love and compassion. An exploration of spirit as the fabric within which we exist is an investigation of that which cannot be seen (transcendent realities/consciousness). *If seeing is believing, then we already omit any truth or validity in the qualities and experiences of love, compassion, wisdom, courage, resilience, and spirit* (Hawkins, 1995). Perhaps it is simply that there is a need to redefine love. *Can we imagine love to be not an emotion or an attraction but instead a vibration of energy (light) that is inherent in all life—an energy that carries within it subtle and powerful qualities that can heal, restore, and revitalize? Compassion* can be viewed as a state of acceptance, an empathetic (not sympathetic, or sorry-for) loving, nonjudgmental embracing of what is before you. Compassion is a natural result of self-evaluation and the realization that we are in fact all one—we are all connected to and affected by each other.

Bein (2003) explores love and compassion within the ethnographic perspective as he utilizes expanded dimensions of "spiritual connectedness, suspension of knowledge, and practitioner love and mindfulness. [Bein goes further to stress that] . . . after deep understanding and love, compassion is the final ingredient of a spiritual ethnographic approach" (p. 142). Through the use of a case example regarding a young 16-year-old Latino man with a history of gang involvement, child abuse, and juvenile detention, Bein explores love and compassion as powerful forces for healing, change, and relationship. Love and compassion can be seen as inherent elements in the fabric of spirit and essential in effective and enriched relationships between clients and practitioners.

Compassion and love are foundations of spirituality. Could it be part of our life's work to explore what it is that keeps us from being fully in the present moment, in love, with compassion, and with nonjudgment? At the base of the teachings of many ancient spiritual traditions, there are two appealing guiding principles: Do no harm, and love others as yourself. Some spiritual practices and traditions understand these principles as a basic tenet: We are one with each other; or, in other words, we share a "fundamental sense of mutual connectedness (or a common source of divinity, for some traditions)" (Bein, 2003, p. 142). Imagine, if you will, an entire human race living from this premise—this knowing of connectedness; the awareness that every thought, word, and action touches and affects each of us and humanity as a whole.

Twyman (2002) interviewed a group of remarkable children who pose a question and a challenge to humanity. The question is, "What would you do if you knew right now that you were an emissary of love?" The challenge they offer is for each of us to view one another and ourselves as emissaries of love. From their perception, this is true: You are an emissary of love. They ask us, as adults, to take some time to contemplate this, and then to simply pretend that it is true. Take a moment to reflect on yourself and your life: What would you and your life be like if you heeded this call and began to act as if you and others are emissaries of love? Do you think this would influence you to be in relationships differently? How might knowing or believing that your sole (or soul) purpose here is to be an emissary of love change the way you are with your clients, your family, and your colleagues? The children are offering us an opportunity to, in a sense, return to the innocence of childhood—to let go of our attachment to (not our knowledge of) our history and future in order to be in the present moment as an expression of the energy of love and compassion. We can also see our clients as emissaries and their actions and circumstances as acts of love, or perhaps a need for love. This may be a way for the human service practitioner to give practical life to their already professed or written codes of ethics and to be a guiding force.

SUMMARY

This chapter has touched on spirituality and human diversity. It has also addressed a possibility of seeing oneness, connectedness, separation, differences, and multidimensionality as kind of synonyms for one another. Connectedness and oneness are often of the spirit. Human beings may be connected in ways that are less tangible than the physical senses, originating in spirit, in the essence that is pervasive in all life, in the very force that we are and that we come from. On the other hand, differences, separation, and multidimensionality can be seen as that which constitutes the diversity in all life. Multidimensional contextual practice offers guidelines to dance within both the individual and the whole, within both the spiritual and human dimensions of relationships with clients and ourselves. Using this framework with awareness of our own and our clients' spiritual natures, as well as diverse influences, may bring us joy in our work, and bring us closer to our primary goal of well-being for our clients in the micro, mezzo, macro, and magna capacities.

This chapter has attempted to touch on the vast and multidimensional world of human beings in the realms of human diversity and spirituality. As Guadalupe and Lum have emphasized, each chapter is simply the perceptions or ideas of the particular author and those who influence the author. *As the reader, hopefully you have been inspired in some way to investigate your own beliefs, attitudes, feelings, and behaviors around spirituality and human diversity.* The two terms themselves, *spirituality* and *human diversity,* are loaded with influences from history, culture, education, family, and so on. You are encouraged to move beyond your conditioned and learned responses to these arenas and explore them on the inner and outer planes of existence. In other words, on the inner planes, check in with yourself, your heart space, your intuition; quiet the mind to allow a deeper knowing to emerge. On the outer planes, explore the possibilities of holding a safe and compassionate space for the diverse spiritual beings who will come into your life as clients, and of exploring with clients their worlds, their inner and outer experiences, and their influences.

Multidimensional contextual practice can assist us in expanding perceptions, learning from (and changing, when appropriate) our conditioning, and limiting or eliminating interventions that are based on false assumptions and stereotypes. This framework may simply serve as a reference, guideline, or springboard from which one might dive into the multidimensions of relationships with clients. The perception of spirit as being pervasive in and connecting all life and spirituality, and our experience of and response to this spirit, may open doors for us to new and expanded ways of relating to and acting on behalf of clients. Finally, seeing our clients as our teachers—diverse and with infinite potential—may catapult us into self-discovery and awareness that will serve to enrich our lives, both professionally and personally. "May the [life] force be with you!"

References

Andrews, A. B., Guadalupe, J. L., & Bolden, E. (2003). Faith, hope, and mutual support: Paths to empowerment as perceived by women in poverty. *Journal of Social Work Research and Evaluation, 4*(1), 5–18.

Bein, A. (2003). The ethnographic perspective: A new look. In J. Anderson & R. W. Carter (Eds.), *Diversity perspectives for social work practice.* Boston: Allyn & Bacon.

Burris, J., & Guadalupe, K. L. (2003). Constructivism and the constructivist framework. In J. Anderson & R. W. Carter (Eds.), *Diversity perspectives for social work practice.* Boston: Allyn & Bacon.

Faiver, C., Ingersoll, R. E., O'Brien, E., & McNally, C. (2001). *Explorations in counseling and spirituality: Philosophical, practical, and personal reflections.* Belmont, CA: Wadsworth/Thomson Learning.

Frame, M. W. (2003). *Integrating religion and spirituality: A comprehensive approach.* Pacific Grove, CA: Brooks/Cole.

Hawkins, D. R. (1995). *Power vs. force: The hidden determinants of human behavior.* Carlsbad, CA: Hay House.

Kilpatrick, A. C. (1999). Ethical issues and spiritual dimensions. In A. C. Kilpatrick & T. P. Holland (Eds.), *Working with families: An integrative model by level of need.* Boston: Allyn & Bacon.

Lerner, M. (2000). *Spirit matters.* Charlottesville, VA: Hampton Roads.

Ritberger, C. (2001). *Consciousness and the human psyche: Module two.* Pollock Pines, CA: BCR Enterprises.

Robbins, S. P., Chatterjee, P., & Canda, E. R. (1998). *Contemporary human behavior theory: A critical perspective for social work.* Boston: Allyn & Bacon.

Rose, S. M. (1990). Advocacy/empowerment: An approach to clinical practice for social work. *Journal of Sociology and Social Welfare, 17*(2), 41–52.

Sananda, S. (2002, December). *Revealing God.* Living Spirit Eletter, Living Spirit Foundation, Sacramento, CA, http://www.livingspiritfoundation.org.

Svoboda, M. (1996). *Traits of a healthy spirituality.* Mystic, CT: Twenty-Third Publications.

Twyman, J. F. (2002). *Emissary of love: The psychic children speak to the world.* Charlottesville, VA: Hampton Roads.

Webster's II New College Dictionary. (1999). Boston: Houghton Mifflin.

Multidimensional Contextual Practice with Diverse Groups

*General Population Groups
and Ethnic-Specific Communities
of People*

Now that the reader has an understanding of the multidimensional contextual practice framework, the authors turn to an application of this framework to a range of diverse groups. We have asked a talented group of contributors to write about a number of general and ethnic-specific population groups to illustrate how multidimensional contextual practice principles can be applied. The general population groups cover gender, sexual orientation, abilities/disabilities, and aging, while the ethnic-specific communities of people consist of the broadly recognized census groups in the United States.

We hope that as you read about these diverse groups of people, you will understand them as interconnecting entities. Suppose, for example, that you are working with a client who is an elderly African-American working-class lesbian woman. She has recently suffered a major disability, and the experience has been life-altering for her. How can you understand the multidimensional nature of your client and the particular contextual situation that she is facing as you try to work with her in the helping process? Which of the major elements of her multidimensional identity are important sources of identity strength? Is one of them her African-American ethnic identification? Is she supported by a partner or, perhaps, part of a support network within the lesbian community? Does she have medical and emotional services as an aging person? Which elements may be sources of assistance? These are the kinds of multidimensional and contextual questions and issues that rise to the surface as the multidimensional contextual practice framework is applied to working with diverse clients in this part of the book.

Do what you can with what you have
from where you are. —**Anonymous**

7 | Women

General Population Groups

ARLENE BOWERS ANDREWS

Women, who comprise over half of all humanity, express gloriously diverse characteristics, some associated with the groups with which they identify (e.g., ethnicity, sexual identity, spiritual community, ability, age, socioeconomic class, geographic location, political affiliation), and others stemming from their uniquely individual beliefs, preferences, traits, and capacities. Traditionally, women's diversity has often been overlooked in most cultures because of stereotypes about women based in patriarchal, oppressively sexist political-economic systems. As women around the world have increasingly asserted their voices, they have celebrated the rich variations among people of their gender while addressing the similar oppression many have confronted because of their gender. Multidimensional contextual practice, which is partially grounded in feminist principles, promises to respond to women's assets and needs in ways that are considerably more relevant than traditional helping methods.

I begin and end this chapter with illustrations of typical contexts in which women live. The first addresses their challenges; the last, their hope. The vast variations among women cannot be addressed in a single writing, so I have chosen to illustrate multidimensional contextual practice with women by focusing on the prevention of violence against women. This focus is appropriate for several reasons. Violence illustrates the ultimate harmful consequence of failure to attend to diversity and context: death to the body or crippling of the body, heart, mind, and spirit. Women are targets of violence because of stereotypes and rigid expectations related to their status *as women*. As I write this, the world is at war, many nations are torn by civil conflict, and millions of homes survive under a shroud of domestic and external terror. Yet, in the midst of this, the glorious life-giving and community-building efforts of women persist. Even in the face of imminent destruction, they preserve the homes and communities, keep the economy alive, tend the sick and wounded, teach the children, grow and serve the food, and, increasingly, push for a place at the post-conflict political table so that lasting peace and community substance can be built. Therein we find hope for the future.

This chapter will emphasize the strengths of women as they work to build civil and safe societies and promote the well-being of all people, male and female. First, we will review the context in which they enact their healing.

THE CHALLENGE

In the early years of the global fight to end violence against women, we would talk about "breaking the silence"—shattering the secrecy that shrouded violence behind closed doors of the home and protected the perpetrators. Yes, there are still those who deny that violence against women is a problem; but you would have to be cut off from the entire human race, physically or emotionally, to remain unaware of it at this point in history. In the context of the public world (e.g., the mass media and political-economic decision-making circles), the silence persists, but in the context of women's worlds, the voices are heard. Women, rendered invisible by the oppressive context of the threat of violence, use silence in the public world as a method of self-preservation. They suffer "unspeakable" acts of torture and oppression against their bodies, hearts, minds, and spirits. Their silence is often their language.

Silence born of fear . . .

- *fear of retaliation; the beatings and threats to life will get worse if the silence is broken;*
- *fear of humiliation, the shame and blame that others put on you when they know you are a victim of violence;*
- *fear of being misunderstood; anyone who has worked with the media knows this one, because if you speak out about violence against women, you will be seen as anti-men or anti-family;*
- *fear of political repercussions; in a polarized environment, opponents of violence against women are seen as too liberal, too feminist, too racist.*

Silence born of despair . . .

- *despair of hopelessness and helplessness, believing that because all attempts to stop the violence have failed, there are no others worth trying;*
- *despair of depression, the lost dreams, and the gloom that comes with frustrated coping.*

Silence of the children . . .

- *who watch and listen as the adults in their house argue and fight and threaten to kill one another;*
- *the silence of the parent who doesn't know what to say.*

Silence of vigilance . . .

- *watching, waiting to detect the next sign that violence is imminent.*

Silence of self-defense . . .

- *during the violent episodes, the silence of the victim, trying hard not to do anything to aggravate the perpetrator, trying to reduce the damage, trying not to assert any communication into the situation that might make it worse;*
- *the self-defensive silent dissociation that occurs during the rape or beating to numb the agony;*
- *the secret planning for escape.*

Silence of confusion . . .

- *being stumped—what to do???*

Silence of pretending to be normal . . .

- *the pretense of happiness in the midst of despair;*
- *the denial and minimization of danger;*
- *the make-up and full garments to cover the injuries.*

Silence of pathology . . .

- *those with repressed memories, dissociation, eating disorders, mental illnesses;*
- *those who are drugged into oblivion;*
- *those who use alcohol and drugs to silence their own anxiety.*

Silence of revenge . . .

- *secretly plotting retaliation.*

Silence of the dead . . .

- *those who have been murdered;*
- *those who have resorted to suicide.*

Silence born of fatigue . . .

- *being just too darned tired to say anything.*

Silence of the people you turn to for help . . .

- *people who say they care and act like they're listening, but do nothing after you speak out;*
- *family members who defend the perpetrator and blame the victim.*

Silence of solitude . . .

- *the victim who feels all alone in the world, like no one will understand.*

Silence while we are waiting . . .

- *waiting for the police to come;*
- *waiting for the lawyer to call back;*

- *waiting for a space to open in the shelter;*
- *waiting for the judge or jury to decide;*
- *waiting to know if the grant was funded;*
- *waiting in the emergency room for someone to sew the stitches;*
- *waiting for the bus, or the call-back about the job.*

In the United States, women are up to six times more likely than men to suffer violence at the hands of a partner or ex-partner (Bachman & Saltzman, 1995; Koss et al., 1994). The results of a National Crime Victimization Survey conducted by the Bureau of Justice Statistics (Bachman, 1994) found that women were 10 times more likely to be victims of male intimates than vice versa. The National Violence Against Women Survey (NVAWS) (Tjaden & Thoennes, 2000b), was a nationally representative telephone survey of 8,000 women and 8,000 men that asked about their experiences with rape, physical assault, and stalking. It included questions on the victim-perpetrator relationship and, for victims of a current or former spouse or opposite-sex cohabiting partner, it gathered information on frequency, duration, and consequences of victimization. Findings indicated that women experienced significantly more violence by intimate partners than men, whether the time period was their lifetime or the preceding 12 months, and whether the victimization involved rape, physical assault, or stalking. Of those participating in the survey, lifetime rates indicted that 20.4% of the women and 7% of the men reported having been physically assaulted by an intimate partner; 4.5% of the women and 0.2% of the men reported having been raped by an intimate partner; and 4.1% of the women and 0.5% of the men reported having been stalked by an intimate partner. American-Indian/Alaskan-Native women are significantly more likely than white women, African-American women, and mixed-race women to report they were raped (Tjaden & Thoennes, 2000a).

Violence against women is a global problem. One cross-cultural comparison of physical aggression and battering behavior in 14 countries revealed that physical aggression between romantic partners occurs in most of the cultures sampled and is perpetrated by both men and women, while battering (the more severe acts of violence that are not condoned by society) occurs in several cultures and is perpetrated primarily by men (Campbell, 1992). Among women aged 15–44 worldwide, gender-based violence accounts for more death and illness than cancer, traffic injuries, and malaria put together; and each year, two million new girls between ages 5 and 15 are inducted into the commercial sex industry (Spindel, Levy, & Conner, 2000). The World Health Organization estimates that one out of five women in the world will be a victim of rape or attempted rape in her lifetime. Between 20% and 50% of women will experience domestic violence. The range of gender-based acts of violence occurs from birth through old age. Violence against women includes: prenatal sex selection in favor of male babies, female infanticide and abandonment, sexual abuse, female genital mutilation, sexual harassment in schools and the workplace, trafficking, forced prostitution, dowry-related violence, domestic violence, battering, and marital rape. Violence against women and girls occurs in every segment of society—regardless of class, ethnicity, culture, or country.

Across the world, women and girls live in areas where war is raging, such as Iraq, Afghanistan, Israel/Palestine, Rwanda, Somalia, Zimbabwe, and Cambodia. These are wars they did not start and cannot stop. Yet the majority of war victims are women and children—they suffer rape, torture, loss of their male kin, loss of homes and provisions for subsistence, and loss of everything except their spirits. Armed conflict and displacement bring their own distinct forms of violence against women with them. Some forms of violence resulting from conflict/refugee situations include:

- Mass rape, gang rape, military sexual slavery, forced prostitution, forced "marriages," and forced pregnancies
- Sexual assault associated with violent physical assault; often women are seen as territory to be claimed by their male family members' enemies in the conflict
- Resurgence of female genital mutilation, within the community under attack, as a way to reinforce cultural identity
- Women forced to offer sex for survival, or in exchange for food, shelter, or "protection"
- Increased incidence of domestic violence against women, related to male perceptions of powerlessness and loss of traditional male roles associated with displacement and increased polarization of gender roles during periods of armed conflict (United Nations High Commission for Refugees, 1995)

In the aftermath of war and civil conflict, girls and women tend to be the primary victims of human trafficking as they are lured or forced into sexual slavery, domestic servitude, or agricultural or manufacturing sweat camps.

Across many cultures and political boundaries, women work their healing ways against what seem to be overwhelming odds, in a context of threat and challenge. Together, women and men of reason and compassion are working to change this context, locally and globally.

THE HOPE

Over the past 20 years, recognition of the problem of gender-based violence has changed dramatically. The voices of women have explained, argued, cried, sang, and otherwise exposed the systemic processes at work. By joining together, women have broken their isolation and exercised their collective power to influence the economic, political, and social infrastructures of various societies. The international community has come to acknowledge the range and frequency of gender-based violence, and has redefined how these acts of violence are dealt with in international policies. The Trust Fund in Support of Actions to Eliminate Violence against Women, established at UNIFEM (United Nations Development Fund for Women), was created by the UN General Assembly in response to the urgent call for action on these issues that emanated from the women's summit in Beijing. To mark the 50th anniversary of the UN Declaration on Human Rights, in 1998 UNIFEM organized a photo exhibit at the United Nations that contrasted the "wall of shame," depicting women's plight and suffering, with the "wall of hope" that illustrated women's initiatives to end violence across the globe (Spindel, Levy, & Conner, 2000).

Across the world, from the halls of the United Nations to the villages of Pakistan and towns of the U.S. Midwest, grassroots groups have organized to shed light on the harm caused by traditional constructions of male-female relations and to reconstruct new ways of understanding gender relations and gender roles. Violence is the way women are forced into subordination to men and compliance with stereotypical social constructions of femininity and masculinity. Historically, the stereotypical construction regarding women was that they are passive, silent victims in the broader political-economic context. They had been perceived by many, particularly those with political power, as unable to protect themselves or others and were categorized, along with children, as dependent people who need special assistance. Certainly, female humans who are young, very old or frail, or coping with illness or disability may have special needs. Yet the vast majority of women are, when portrayed through their own voices and reflections of reality, proactive and competent protectors of themselves and others. When faced with threats of domestic or external violence, they devise elaborate systems of coping that minimize physical and psychological harm. In the movement to stop violence against women, participants have cast aside the term *victim* and claimed their *survivor* status. Not only have they survived, but they also have sustained life and quality of life in the face of horrific threats.

Cultural stereotypes promoted tolerance, if not approval, of domestic violence for so long that women's advocates and criminal prosecutors, including the U.S. Attorney General, took to opening their educational messages about violence against women with facts to debunk stereotypical myths. Consider this example from the Web site of the Clark County, Indiana, Office of the Prosecutor:

- **Myth:** *Domestic violence occurs mostly in heterosexual, low-income, and ethnic minority families.*
- **Fact:** Battering and abuse are issues that cross all boundaries, including those of race, class, and sexual orientation.
- **Myth:** *There is no way to break out of a battering relationship.*
- **Fact:** Women can free themselves when they discover their own strengths and take advantage of community resources that offer safe and secure environments.
- **Myth:** *Domestic violence is rare and affects only a small percentage of the population.*
- **Fact:** National studies estimate that 3 to 4 million women are beaten each year in the United States; about 31% of all women have been beaten in their lifetimes.
- **Myth:** *Women are just as violent as men in domestic situations.*
- **Fact:** Women use violent means to resolve conflict in relationships as often as men, but when context and consequences of an assault are measured, the majority of victims are women. In 95% of cases, the injured party is the woman.
- **Myth:** *Men who batter women are often good fathers and should have joint custody.*
- **Fact:** Men who batter their wives also abuse their children in 70% of cases.
- **Myth:** *Domestic violence results from a dynamic involving all members of the family, so they all must change for it to stop.*
- **Fact:** Only the batterer has the ability to stop the violence. Battering is a behavioral choice for which the batterer must be held accountable. (Clark County, Indiana, Office of the Prosecutor, 2002).

Such myths keep women "in their place" even while they are fighting for justice. Bringing forth the truth, which has been bolstered by substantial social scientific research, has helped people to reconstruct their regard for women. Community education, activism by law enforcement officials, and provision of services for safety, support, and healing are happening all over the world as part of the global effort to end violence against women.

Prevention of violence against women, and violence in general, evolves from economic and political reforms that support women's power in society. Women increasingly claim their places in business, government, and all public arenas of life. We hear their voices:

- *Speaking as political leaders, prime ministers, governors, senators, members of parliament*
- *Negotiating business deals at stock exchanges, street markets, board rooms, bank offices*
- *Singing stories, broadcast across vast spaces, of their victories and defeats*
- *Preaching from pulpits*
- *Directing surgical teams, astronaut research, biological laboratories, teaching faculty, and law firms*
- *Asserting their needs at nursing homes, physicians' offices, welfare departments, schools where their children are taught*
- *Barking orders to construction crews, employees of their own businesses, military units, athletic teams, staff at fast-food restaurants*
- *Writing novels and poems, policy briefs, court opinions, documentaries, parenting skills booklets, nightly news*
- *Guiding policy deliberations and decisions, adventure tours, meetings of Alcoholics Anonymous, orientations for new prison inmates*

In positions of formal leadership and everyday cooperative endeavors, women are expressing themselves in growing numbers, and with increasing influence. Whereas they once tended to be confined to domestic arenas, where violence can be most subversive, they now lead more public lives, where the silence is broken and light is cast on the threats. Their new status helps to change the historic context.

DIVERSITY OF WOMANKIND IN A WORLD TORN BY VIOLENCE

Women, constituting slightly over half of humankind,[1] express the entire range of human characteristics. They are young and old, rich and poor, strong and weak, gay and straight, aggressive and passive, solitary and interdependent, healthy and sick, adventuresome and hesitant, promiscuous and celibate, nurturing and rejecting, faithful and unfaithful, clean and dirty. They come from any of the 140 nations of the world, in all shapes, sizes, and colors, speaking all the languages of the world, embracing all the cultural practices. They live and work as corporate executives, slaves, physicians, child care providers, athletes, beggars, ministers, engineers, teachers, maids, artists, prostitutes, merchants, and farmers. They live in houses they own, refugee camps, structures they have built with their own hands, tenant dwellings, prisons, and under the stars. They are daughters, sisters, mothers (birth-, foster-, step-, adoptive, surrogate moms), aunts, wives, in-laws, ex-wives, intimate partners, widows, grandmothers, and increasingly, great- or great-great grandmothers. They follow the teachings of Meher Baba, Buddha, Hinduism, Taoism, Islam, Sappho,

Christ, Judaism, and hundreds of other faiths. Women suffer violence, but some among them also perpetuate it. Women assume roles as soldiers, perpetrators of domestic violence, sex offenders, battering parents, and exploiters of others.

Violence against women is not randomly distributed. Certain groups are more vulnerable. In conflict and displacement situations, these include targeted ethnic groups, where there is an official or unofficial policy of using rape as a weapon of genocide. Unaccompanied women or children, children in foster care arrangements, and lone female heads of households are all frequent targets. Elderly women and those with physical or mental disabilities are also vulnerable, as are those women who are held in detention and in detention-like situations including concentration camps. Women express their pain and healing in diverse ways, often influenced by the cultures with which they affiliate. For example, women of fundamentalist faith are likely to suffer within their homes, sharing only with a few other women, acting subtly within the role constraints of their social systems. Lesbians may have trouble getting heterosexuals to understand their situations, and are likely to seek help for themselves and their violent partners through mutual support. Resources for prevention and healing must be culturally relevant to the various cultures with which women affiliate. In developed geographic areas, specialized resources have emerged to respond to the unique needs of various women.[2]

In the 21st century, human societies across the globe are persistently changing more rapidly than at any other time in human history (Zeitlin et al., 1995). Evolving technology has fostered myriad short-term relationships and exchanges based on instant communication and easy transportation. People generally have fewer stable, long-term, close relationships. A century ago, community change could be described in periods of human generations, whereas now communities grow and shrink dramatically in periods of months or just a few years. Women, individually and collectively with their families and social networks, who have adequate resources manage, with relative ease, to garner not only what they need but also what they desire from their communities. Their lives may be troubled, but they generally can overcome access barriers and benefit from high-quality health care and education, fair access to justice, and other such privileges. Women who have been historically denied adequate resources or have become marginalized fare less well. They suffer the burden of disparities. Many feel politically impotent, economically oppressed, and psychologically helpless in community arenas outside the comforting circle of their own family and friends. They struggle with unemployment or poor job conditions, racial and ethnic discrimination, inferior schools, lack of child and elder care, and insufficient health and mental health care. Even when marginal groups gather strength, their more endowed neighbors tend to gather even greater strength, and the relative disparities persist. This dynamic makes for fragile and fragmented communities rather than strong, sustainable communities.

In the United States, women have experienced dramatic change in the past three decades (U.S. Bureau of the Census, 2002). Women are more likely to delay marriage and childbearing, taking time to attend college or establish a career instead. Most women are in the labor force and carry a load of household and family responsibilities as well. When compared to men, women perform more home responsibilities and earn less in the workforce. Increasingly, a large number of women are raising their children alone. Women who maintain families with no husband present are more likely to be poor than married-couple families; the poverty rate of female-headed households has not changed in 30 years. Similar changes are occurring worldwide, although in developing countries, women are still struggling to attain parity with men on basic rights such as access to education and literacy.

Given the splendid diversity of women and their historic resilience as survivors and protectors in the face of adversity, professional interventions with women promises to be always interesting and often fruitful.

APPLICATION OF MULTIDIMENSIONAL CONTEXTUAL PRACTICE FRAMEWORK

Applying the multidimensional contextual practice framework to the issue of violence against women starts with the three standard goals of intervention: (1) to provide for the safety of the victim while recognizing her right to self-determination; (2) to hold the offender accountable and create a specific deterrent to his repeated use of violence; and (3) to change the climate in the community, creating a general deterrence to the use of violence as an acceptable practice in the home. In addition, the following factors can guide practice.

Multidimensional Contextual Services

Leadership is the *sine qua non* for a context that promotes effective enhancement of individual and group well-being. At the contextual level, in many communities, a group, typically a nongovernmental organization (NGO) (in the United States, most often, a grassroots nonprofit), has assumed this leadership role. Such groups have, in coalition with other similar NGOs, advocated for political and economic leaders to support the cause. Practitioner support of these leading NGOs is absolutely critical to the sustainability of contextual resources that address violence against women. The NGOs are generally driven by women of passion and conviction.

Major roles of the leadership group, which may include the NGO in partnership with other community leaders, include:

- *Coordination with inclusive participation.* The entire community must be mobilized to address a threat that affects over half its population. This requires skilled collaboration across various groups who represent diverse income levels, racial and ethnic backgrounds, ages, organizational cultures (e.g., government, nonprofit, and business organizations tend to have different cultures), faiths, gender, sexual orientation, and others. The key skill required is facilitation of collaboration, an art in itself. A risk to avoid is excluding people or groups because this process is easier if it occurs among people who are familiar with one another.
- *Planning and evaluation.* From community needs and resources assessments to strategic plans to continuous evaluation of how the system works, the group has to call the shots. The key skills required are production of information for and facilitation of decision-making processes. Key issues to consider are: What are the effective practices for ending violence against women? Will they work in this community, in this context, for each woman?

- *Resource development and equitable allocation.* People, materials, place, and money make up the resources that allow the action. These resources must be continually replenished and distributed in ways that are fair and just. For example, allocations for programs often must be divided among survivor services, offender services, law enforcement, and others. Exceptional skill and wisdom are required to devise a process to achieve equity and maximum benefit without causing alienation or tension among the recipients.
- *Culturally competent public awareness and education.* A foundation of social change lies in the reconstruction of social norms, which can be done through interpersonal and mass communication that is targeted to unique communities. Consistent messages to debunk myths and promote truth, understanding, and action help sustain the vitality of the system of care. People need to know about and understand the positive alternatives to violence.
- *Policy reform and accountability.* The context for community action is heavily influenced by laws, enforcement of laws, policies, and procedures that promote effective prevention, crisis intervention, support, and recovery. These policies require continual monitoring—just because laws exist does not mean they are applied or interpreted properly. And as society and communities change, the needs for policy frameworks change.
- *System components:*
    - *Housing: A continuum of emergency, transitional, and affordable, safe long-term housing*
    - *Faith-based services:* Religious and spiritual communities with understanding of violence against women and competent skills to address it
    - *Education:* Access to resources to enhance level of education
    - *Economic resources:* Jobs, job training, employment assistance, income maintenance
    - *Workplace support:* Protection from batterer while in the work environment; job security
    - *Health/mental health resources:* Skilled practitioners who can provide relevant care for the short and long term for issues related to physical health, injuries, illnesses, mental illnesses, emotional problems, and alcohol and other drug abuse
    - *Civil law:* Nonthreatening, easy-to-access support for protection, child support and care, property concerns, divorce, immigration, and other issues
    - *Criminal law:* Prompt intervention with the perpetrator and supportive assistance to the victim/survivor
    - *Perpetrator services:* Skilled assistance to ensure the perpetrator is unlikely to reoffend
    - *Family and children's care:* Safety resources for family members who are cared for by the survivor (e.g., child care, elder care, care for family members with disabilities)
- *Training and professional competence.* Practitioners in each of the systems, as well as those who facilitate the processes of the system, must be trained in understanding violence against women and skilled in practicing their roles with regard to intervention. This can be accomplished in part by training but also by enactment of agreements among various professionals, procedures to hold practition-

ers accountable for practice standards, and ongoing peer support and mentoring to promote continuous quality improvement. For example, many physicians fail to screen for violence when they do a medical history, or they may keep poor records of injuries they treat. Such neglect exposes a woman to risk; concerted efforts to make violence screening, treatment, and record keeping part of routine medical practice are now underway. Similarly, uninformed religious traditions have placed women in harm's way, such as Christian women who feel compelled to stay in abusive relationships by scripture mandating them to "submit to their husbands" or "turn the other cheek" and Jewish women who may feel pressure to not bring shame to their community by revealing the abuse in their marriage, or that it is their responsibility to maintain *shalom bayit,* or peace in the home. Programs to educate ministers, rabbis, imams, and other religious leaders have begun to change these practices.

Taken as a whole, these resources comprise the context in which multidimensional contextual practice occurs.

Practitioner's Professional Competence

In many ways, the practitioner's art in this system can be characterized as brokering, that is, facilitating open, trusting communication and resource exchange between the client and other people in the micro, meso, macro, and magna environments.

With regard to the micro environment, practice is likely to focus on identifying and mobilizing the family and social support network resources of the client. This often requires direct personal communication within the practitioner's own micro environment, such as contact with another practitioner (e.g., the client's child's protective services worker). Meso-system facilitation may require enabling trust-building between the client and her micro system with elements of the macro system. A classic example of this is when an interpreter is found to facilitate mobilization of resources for a person who is deaf or speaks English as a second language. In battered women's programs, human service practitioners often, with clients' permission, speak to the clients' lawyers, so that they can help the clients better understand what the lawyers have said and thus make appropriate decisions. Macro-system interventions include a whole range of advocacy options related to accessing the system described previously and ensuring its accountability. Magna-environmental issues can be addressed by attending carefully to the client's spiritual needs and resources and by linking her to additional resources in the community.

Interactions/Exchanges and Effects

The key to competent practice lies in the quality of relationships that the practitioner maintains with other diverse members of the community and, of course, with the client and her support system. Beyond knowledge and understanding of the client and her culture, the practitioner must know and understand the community and its various cultures. Maintaining effective relationships is hard work.

For example, in an effort to develop a model intervention protocol for children whose mothers have experienced domestic assault, a team involving law enforcement, child protection services (CPS), and a survivor services program (an NGO) was formed. Representatives of other groups such as the children's emergency shelter, alcohol and drug treatment program, and legal services were also present, but the three primary groups were those listed first. Each had a vastly different perspective on the problem. The NGO was concerned that women were unjustly having their children taken into state custody for supposed failure to protect. The law enforcement officers wanted the women survivors to take the lead in pressing charges against their assailants, who often were a major source of financial support for the children and who became even more dangerous when they were released from custody (and so the women were hesitant to take such a lead). The CPS workers perceived that they had to protect the children regardless of immediate disruption to the family; if the batterer could not be detained, the children must be removed from the situation. Facilitating such an interaction by moving through the conflict and arriving at a win-win solution that provides safety while maintaining the dignity and integrity of the individuals in the family requires exceptional skill. Model protocols have been developed, and examples can be found on the Internet (see, e.g., Spears, 2000). What the models cannot tell you, however, is the art and processes of arriving at the model and the skill required to enact the model according to plan.

Effective practice requires practitioners to conceive of their role as a critical partner not only with the client but also with the many other players in the community. Being known and understood through familiarity and trust can enable sustained change to occur. Being ignorant of who the key players are or what resources are available can hinder effective practice, or create a situation where another person (e.g., someone in the client's support network or another organization) can undermine (intentionally or not) the interests and plans of the client as developed with the practitioner. Violence prevention and intervention is a conflict-ridden process. Practitioners must be prepared to manage the conflict and move beyond it. They must establish supportive, collegial relationships based on trust and honesty while acting according to networking agreements and procedures. Community partners enhance the system by training together, mentoring one another, and providing peer support to constantly enrich each other's understanding of the diverse aspects of women who experience violence.

Well-Being and the Multidimensional Contextual Client

"Keep your eyes on the prize" was a slogan of the 1960's civil rights era. The physical, social, emotional, mental, and spiritual well-being of the woman and group of women are the overarching goals of practice. Continual communication between the client and practitioner must occur as the practitioner, in equal partnership with the woman, maneuvers with her through the context of her situation, mobilizing relationships and resources. The focus of the communication is on understanding her personal culture and choices and helping her to construct, deconstruct, and reconstruct perceptions of her experience and her own identity.

For example, women often arrive at survivor services programs feeling exhausted and weak. They may perceive their batterers as all-powerful and feel stuck about how to respond. They are sometimes willing to place themselves in the hands of police officers, lawyers, physicians, or criminal victim assistants who provide much information about their options and basically tell them what to do. The individual woman sees them as powerful, too. By engaging the client in reflections about these relationships, the practitioner can coach her to re-examine her role and claim the survival actions she has taken thus far to preserve herself and her children. The woman can acknowledge her power and strengths and learn to communicate with other people she perceives as powerful by asserting her interests and asking for specific assistance. She can deconstruct her perceptions of the others as guiding or manipulating her to fit their systems and reconstruct a perception of herself as her own agent, with support from the practitioner. At the doctor's office, with her family and friends, in the classroom, with her therapist or lawyer, and with her minister or spiritual guide, she can assert herself in ways that lead to her holistic well-being, which is her human right. In this sense, she will feel her essence, look beyond the way others have rejected or trivialized her, and assert direction for her own life.

SKILLS FOR ADDRESSING CHALLENGES AND STRENGTHS PRESENTED BY TARGET POPULATION

Feminist theory and practice rely on a core set of principles, rather than techniques, to guide practice with all people. Five principles suggested by Van Den Bergh and Cooper (1986) include:

1. Eliminating false dichotomies and artificial separations
2. Reconceptualizing power
3. Valuing process equally with product
4. Validity of renaming
5. The personal is political

When the focus is on women, a key place to start is with the last point, which would suggest the practitioner should assess the effects of systemic oppression on the individual woman or group of women. Using violence against women as the illustrative topic, the practitioner can assume that all women face the threat of gender-based violence, imminently or distantly, consciously or unconsciously, and adapt their lives accordingly. This is a contextual reality. As Spindel, Levy, and Conner (2000) observe in their report on international model programs, "Finally, it is clear that no issue unites women more across the many lines that can divide us than violence against women" (p. 19).

Thus, when practitioners work with individual women, they should be aware of their own history and perspectives about violence against women, and should explore the women's history and perspectives as well. Practitioners are likely to discover a wide range of individual differences, such as denial, revenge, perceived helplessness, or accommodation. They should work to overcome any preconceived notions about what "battered women" feel or think, and should be open to individual, diverse expressions.

Returning to the first principle, dichotomies such as victim-offender, man-woman, husband-wife, and powerful-powerless pervade this field. The practitioner can work with clients to explore the meanings of such terms in their lives so that the unique attributes of the individuals who possess these traits can be recognized and can be unifying, rather than polarizing, ideas that are explored. This is a core issue in practice with men who batter, for they often have a tendency to frame their emotions in polarized terms (e.g., "I'm mad" and "I'm glad"). The "mad" state is generally when they feel overwhelmed and tempted to assault. A common tactic is to offer them a list of a hundred words that can be used to describe feelings so that they can get in touch with the breadth of human emotional experience within themselves, and then to coach them to express themselves verbally using the terms, to avert frustrated communication.

With regard to the second principle, the idea that power is an entity that a person has or does not have can still be heard, unfortunately, in conversations among human service practitioners. Skilled practitioners will have closely examined their own understanding of power, and be open to the idea that everyone who lives has power. One way to regard power is that it simply *is*. Power exists in each person, in his or her social network, in the broader environment, and through spiritual influence. How people understand their own power and learn to use it for well-being should be a core focus of practice. For example, when working with a woman who has suffered battery, the practitioner may discover she has lost touch with the power outside herself and is using her personal power to be hypervigilant, anticipating the next attack so that she can minimize damage to herself or others. She has turned her power inward, and feels the weight of it as an excessive burden. Most likely, she has done this in defensive response to her batterer's use of his own power, which he believes he has lost, and thus he attacks in a futile effort to regain it. He may also mobilize resources in the social network and broader environment to attempt to enhance his own sense of perceived power, which exacerbates her sense of isolation. The practitioner who works with the woman can help her reconceptualize and claim the power from her environment, which is her human right. The practitioner who works with the man can help him to claim his own internal power and better understand how to get his needs met in healthy ways.

The matter of valuing process rather than product assumes that life is a journey, and that what is done now builds on what was done yesterday and affects tomorrow. For example, the story between a husband and wife who have experienced domestic violence is not over when the legal divorce is "final." Their relationship does not end; it simply takes on new form and meaning. This milestone also does not mean the domestic violence has stopped; in fact, much knowledge suggests that, without ongoing support or treatment, it will happen again, through repeated battering or victimization by the husband, wife, their children, or future partners. Thus, treatment goals such as "get a separate, stable place to live," "finalize the divorce," and "get a stable job," while important, are not as critical to stopping the violence as goals such as "use social supports when safety feels threatened," "manage household budget within means," and "communicate with children about how they are feeling about their father." The latter processes indicate life skills that can promote future safety and well-being.

Renaming becomes an important process whether a woman has suffered an "unspeakable" act that has no name or one of the many acts that fall onto lists of assaultive behaviors (e.g., hitting, slapping, punching). The term *violence against women (VAW)* took years to evolve; it started with "rape and wife abuse" and then evolved through terms such as "sexual assault," "domestic violence," and "violence between intimate partners." The term *VAW* places responsibility for the action on the offender, and this nonlegal term captures the breadth of intimidating and harmful acts that are targeted against women primarily because of their gender. Using person-first language (e.g., "woman assaulted by a batterer" rather than "battered woman") removes the suggestion that being assaulted creates a category of people. Over time, the field has changed its terminology (e.g., from "victim" to *survivor,* "my partner" to *my batterer,* and "treatment plan" to *safety plan*) to avoid placing blame on the person who experienced assault and to acknowledge personal power. The National Coalition Against Domestic Violence (U.S.) has a campaign, "Remember My Name," to maintain a national registry of all women killed by domestic violence, so that victims are recognized as human beings, not statistical data.

The points discussed here are not comprehensive, but they do illustrate the application of feminist principles in direct practice by people involved with violence against women. They also embody the ethics of multidimensional contextual practice by emphasizing respect for the person who has experienced the indignity and injury of any form of violence and for the person's right to self-determination about the future. Practitioners must be truthful and open, disclosing their own perceptions of meaning while being open to hearing clients' perceptions. A case in point: The author directed the establishment of one of the first battered women's programs in the South in the early 1980s. When the doors opened, the staff was sorely disappointed that the program participants were less than willing to listen to feminist ideas. At that time, feminism was just taking hold and was, especially in the U.S. South, regarded as radical and subversive by many people. The program participants' experience was different, and the staff learned to listen actively for the power the participants felt within their own realms. Models of professional competence evolved that helped the staff to maintain ongoing self-awareness while promoting the participants' resilience. To try to convert them to feminism would have been exploitive, although use of feminist principles could certainly promote their well-being. We had to balance our personal values and professional ethics by behaving as feminists while respecting the chosen values of women whose lives had led them to places where they embraced principles other than feminism.

Significantly, violence against women is not and cannot be addressed by working to promote individual well-being alone. As multidimensional contextual practice suggests, the pursuit of *social justice* (i.e., social-political activism to promote and sustain equality of access to resources, equal treatment, and elimination of discriminatory/oppressive forces) has always been part of the international movement to end violence against women. Through this individual advocacy activity, the institutional obstacles faced by battered women in the religious, welfare, medical, mental health, educational (if they have children), and civil and criminal justice systems were exposed, and the practice of *systems advocacy* emerged. Sometimes called class advocacy, systems advocacy is an effort to reform institutional responses to battered women, collectively, so that the totality of their experience is taken into account, leading to greater safety for victims and greater accountability for batterers.

The global community recognizes gender-based violence as a human rights issue, challenging the almost universal tendency to condone, deny, or minimize the problem. The most comprehensive international policy statements about gender-based violence have been the Declaration on the Elimination of Violence against Women, adopted by the UN General Assembly in 1993, and the Platform for Action from the UN Fourth World Conference on Women in Beijing in 1995. Both documents define gender-based violence as a violation of women's human rights and a form of discrimination that prevents women from participating fully in society and fulfilling their potential as human beings. In the United States, where each of the 50 states has separate responsibility for civil and criminal justice frameworks to address violence against women, model codes have been developed and federal laws created to encourage state practices that aim to detain perpetrators, support people affected by gender-based violence, and prevent violence against women.

Bringing the global to the local level, all practitioners should be involved in efforts to enhance the local context in which violence against women is prevented and addressed. A core goal, based on self-determination, is that a woman should be able to enhance her well-being within her own natural support system, which includes the people within her immediate family, social support system, and culture, as well as her broader community and sociopolitical and economic environment. Many models exist for how to do this and end violence against women (see, e.g., "Toolkit to End Violence against Women," 2002; VAWnet, 2002). These resources include information about the prevention of and response to violence against women in sectors of society that deal with international issues, the military, faith-based communities, health and mental health systems, economic security, civil and criminal justice, children and youth, Native women, sports, media, and the workplace. Lack of information can be no excuse in this millennium. Where lack of action affects a community, the problem is one of moral will, not lack of knowledge.

CASE STUDIES

MS. JONES

As a specialist in family violence, you have been asked to consult with a child protection agency (CPA) following the death of an infant who was receiving home-based family services. The infant's mother, Sara Jones, says she heard voices telling her to smother the baby (her only child), so she did, then called the police herself and admitted her guilt. The CPA staff feels guilty and concerned that they did not detect any warning signs that such an action was imminent. The state office of the local CPA has responded to angry calls from politicians who want to know why the agency performed so poorly in this case. The baby's noncustodial father and paternal grandmother appeared on the evening news and in the newspapers, obviously torn by grief.

For four months, since the baby was treated for nonorganic failure to thrive at age one month, the mother and baby had received a full range of services that were court-approved. The treatment plan included weekly home visits by a CPA worker (who had been to the house just two days before the baby's death), weekly sessions at the mental health center (diagnosis was post-partum depression, attendance at counseling was good), legal services (she had a restraining order against her boyfriend, who had not bothered her in over six weeks), weekly visits by an early childhood home visitor, and participation in a support group, which she did through a Bible study at the fundamentalist church she has attended since childhood. The CPA worker had presented the case at the agency's peer supervision meeting just two weeks before this event, reporting that the mother seemed to be providing good care to the infant and was complying with all opportunities through the treatment plan, but she seemed to have little energy. The CPA worker was allowed to visit the mother in jail after her arrest. The mother was highly agitated and in despair, insisting that she had heard commanding voices from God and bemoaning the fact that she had done the best she could—all she wanted to do was to be a good mother.

Your job is to review the case and its treatment plan, counsel the CPA team (which includes the CPA worker, mental health therapist, and home visitor), and make any recommendations for policy or practice changes that seem to emerge from the case.

Reflection on Case

Before you read the "Consider This" section that follows, reflect on these questions as if you were the consultant:

1. *What is the goal of your intervention?*
2. *The plan for Ms. Jones and her baby seemed to be working perfectly. What might have gone wrong?*
3. *What could have been done differently?*

Consider This

1. *What is the goal of this intervention?* As intervention goals, consider that prevention of future harm, healthy recovery from this situation, and policy or procedural reform to prevent replication of a negative outcome in other cases are in order. Many people are traumatized: the mother, the baby's other kin, and the various workers (CPA, therapist, home visitor, support group members, fellow church members). For the mother, you might suggest that the mental health therapist do a linked referral, with the mother's permission, to the program that provides psychiatric care at the jail and prison. The linked referral would allow case consultation, during which time the mental health therapist could share her perceptions of the mother's situation, including her tendency to mask severe symptoms of psychopathology and hesitance to reach out for help. Her stoic faith may have exacerbated her isolation, so all these issues could be considered in therapy. The therapist is in a position to shed light that may help the mother in the long run. In many cases, the therapist would just drop contact after the arrest, but the compassionate action is to follow the mother until she is in appropriate care.

   A restorative justice approach to the extended kin would promote a healing and restitution action rather than vengeance. This is difficult to achieve in a system that is polarized, such as the criminal justice system. In this case, the CPA worker may be able to identify a neutral person, perhaps the mother's pastor, or a male family member, or her attorney, who could approach the baby's father or grandmother to open a dialogue. The goal is to promote their understanding of the mother's severely deteriorated mental health condition.

   Your principal direct intervention will be to help the CPA team re-examine their intervention and manage their grief and sorrow.

2. *What might have gone wrong?* The mother was apparently compliant. Conforming behavior that reflects her desire to please and thereby avoid trouble is one way that many women mask their serious problems (which, in this case, seems to have been a psychotic depression). Women also may try to fit the stereotype of the caregiver, even when their mental health status leaves them so drained that they have no care to give, because they are unwilling to ask for help or because being a care recipient is out of role for them. While Sara was acting according to a stereotype, no one noticed her despair. The problem was not with the plan itself, but how the plan was carried out. At least one trusting, open relationship through which Sara could express her true feelings might have allowed

her to send a clue about how desperate she was becoming. You will, of course, want to work with the various workers to hear their perceptions of the situation and to help them understand, from their perspectives, what might have happened.

3. *What could have been done differently?* Continual monitoring among the CPA team members to ascertain whether they felt they were engaged in truly open and trusting communications with Sara would have helped. Role-playing with her on how to reach out and ask for help when she felt confused or unusual would have prepared her for a crisis point, such as hearing voices. At the outset, it is unclear why the father and paternal grandmother had not been involved in the original care plan, whether Sara felt safe from him, and whether she had received adequate recovery services subsequent to being threatened by him. Working with family systems is difficult and often avoided by various workers, even though promoting family connections can create a much more solid foundation for child and mother care over the long term. A visit by the CPA worker with the minister or support group leader might have helped them to understand Sara's situation so that they could have helped to relieve her perceived isolated caregiving burden. Sometimes, workers avoid contact with faith-based groups because they have preconceived notions about what those groups believe. Such workers thus create an artificial barrier; more often than not, someone in the faith group is willing to act compassionately and is open to information and guidance. The key here is in building strong relationships that would have made Sara's context warm, open, and connected. From a policy perspective, across the globe, it is considered rather unnatural for a mother to live alone with a baby, with no other resource people at hand except for weekly contacts. For a mentally disturbed mother to live alone with a baby raises policy concerns. Advocacy to promote daily in-home care, companionship services, or group care is in order.

MS. SALINA

Antonia Salina, who migrated from Guatemala to the United States with her husband and two children, a daughter age 12 and a son age 7, came to a battered women's shelter after a severe beating by her husband while he was drunk. Throughout their marriage, Antonia had suffered occasional beatings, but they accelerated after they moved away from her family system two years ago. Antonia's children were quite happy in the United States. Their English was excellent, and they often served as interpreters for their parents. Antonia was a part-time maid at a local motel, and her husband was a partner in a profitable landscaping company. Antonia knew that her husband had a mistress and that he often stayed at her apartment rather than at their home. When she came to the shelter, she had resolved that she would get a divorce.

During the time that Antonia was at the shelter and in the transitional housing program, she developed a relationship with a primary social worker and received counseling that focused on her sense of self and psychological stress. She also was linked to medical treatment for her physical injuries and civil legal help for divorce, child support, immigration matters, and assistance in the criminal legal system for an order of protection and for court-ordered treatment for her husband. The social worker helped her enhance her social support by connecting her to a club for women of Central America, a support group for survivors of domestic violence, and a faith-based group that made a long-distance phone call available to her each week so that she could talk to kin back in Guatemala. Antonia started right away to advance her education, enrolling in ESL (English as a second language) classes and job training to become a chef. She obtained a steady, well-paying job (with benefits) at a country club. Her children participated in after-school and summer enrichment programs.

Three years later, when Antonia's divorce had been final for a year, she had stable employment as a chef. She also had been accepted to become a homeowner through Habitat for Humanity. Her children were in honors programs and on soccer teams, and she had become a volunteer interpreter at the survivor services program. Her husband returned to Guatemala. She regards herself as a woman of faith and confidence. She exercised her own personal power, and with support from the social worker and community programs, she was able to protect herself and her children from violence.

Reflection on Case

Before you read the "Consider This" section that follows, reflect on these questions:

What went right with this case?
What stereotypes did Antonia overcome?
What are the contextual factors that facilitated this case?

Consider This

The agency that served as the base for Antonia's transformation was obviously well connected with community resources. The worker took a professional stance that honored Antonia's self-direction with regard to solving her own problems. She connected her to culturally appropriate resources and let Antonia do her own case management. Meanwhile, the agency was behind the scenes not at the case level, but at the policy and procedures level, ensuring that lawyers were trained to handle requests like Antonia's, physicians were skilled at treatment, church groups knew how to provide appropriate support, and few barriers were thrown into the paths of women like Antonia.

SUMMARY

Are You or Is Anyone You Know a Battered Woman?
Para Mujeres ¿Es Tu Vida Complicada?
You are not alone.
You can get help.
You can take legal action.
Be prepared. —**Pennsylvania Coalition Against Domestic Violence**

The days of mass silence are long gone, even though many women still suffer quietly. The needs of such women are expressed through the voices of others. Any visit to the Internet for a search of resources about violence against women will yield volumes of information on an array of topics for local, national, and international users. The topics covered are diverse: special networks for groups focus on communities of color, people with disabilities, immigrants, gay/lesbian/bisexual/transsexual/two-spirited people, survivors, victims fighting back, aging women, teens, Asian Americans, African Americans, Hispanics/Latinas, Native women, and what men can do. Topics include sexual assault and exploitation, domestic violence, stalking, children exposed to violence against women, emotional abuse, self-defense, and batterers' treatment. You can join networks for researchers, lawyers, law enforcement personnel, psychologists, physicians, social workers, nurses, and educators allied to stop domestic violence. There is a global alliance against trafficking in women. And much more can be done. The resources are extraordinary.

Survivors have long observed that perpetrators use the secrecy of their physical and sexual assaults as a weapon. Breaking the secrecy disturbs their power and restores the survivor's integrity and ownership of her own story.

Knowing is not enough to produce effective action for the well-being of survivors and their social support networks. *Understanding* and *acting* through trusting, open relationships among representatives of all segments of the community create the context in which true healing and recovery can occur. The competent practitioner will realize how to navigate the complex multiple dimensions of a woman's life and intervene in ways that elicit the resources and hinder the barriers for her well-being. The most critical factor is that the practitioner will partner with her, not serve her or direct her. The woman will claim her own voice amidst the cacophony of sounds within her context, express her needs and desires, and act on her own behalf, if only the practitioner will relate to her, understand her, inform her, and at times, accompany her for support. In this process, she will realize the positive, life-giving power within her and around her.

Notes

1. Rates vary from one country to another and by age. For example, in 2000, the female population of the United States (140 million) was 6 million higher than the male population (134 million) (*Population Profile, 2000*). Yet among the group under age 20, there were 105 boys for every 100 girls. This male-female ratio declined as age increased. For men and women aged 20 to 44, the ratio was 98 men to every 100 women. Among the group aged 85 and older, there were only 50 men for every 100 women. Of the total U.S. female population in 2000, 71% were white; 13% were African American; 11% were Hispanic; 4% were Asian or Pacific Islander; and 1% were Native American or Alaskan.

2. Note, for example, the following selection of Web sites in the United States; many other specialized groups also exist:

- AABL/The Northwest Network of Bisexual, Trans and Lesbian Survivors of Abuse, http://www.nwnetwork.org/

- Ayuda, *Resources and Information about the Rights of Battered Immigrant Women,* http://www.buscapique.com/latinusa/buscafile/wash/ayuda.htm

- Asian Task Force Against Domestic Violence, http://www.atask.org/

- Native American Women's Health Education Resource Center, http://www.nativeshop.org/nawherc.html

- Abuse of Women with Disabilities, The National Women's Health Information Center, http://www.4woman.gov/wwd/wwd.cfm?page=24

- Institute on Domestic Violence in the African American Community, http://www.dvinstitute.org/

References

American Bar Association, Commission on Domestic Violence. (1994). *Model code on domestic and family violence.* http://www.abanet.org/domviol/code.html.

Bachman, R. (1994). *National crime victimization report: Violence against women.* Washington, DC: U.S. Department of Justice, Office of Justice Programs, Bureau of Justice Statistics.

Bachman, R., & Saltzman, L. (1995). *Violence against women: Estimates from the redesigned survey.* Bureau of Justice Statistics special report (Publication No. NCJ-154348) Washington, DC: U.S. Department of Justice, Office of Justice Programs, Bureau of Justice Statistics.

Campbell, J. C. (1992). Nursing Network on Violence Against Women. Prevention of wife battering: Insights from cultural analysis. *Response to the Victimization of Women and Children, 14,* 18–24.

Clark County, Indiana, Office of the Prosecutor. (2002, August 15). http://www.clarkprosecutor.org/html/overview/office.htm.

Koss, M. P., Goodman, L. A., Browne, A., Fitzgerald, L. F., Keita, G. P., & Russo, N. F. (1994). *No safe haven: Male violence against women at home, at work, and in the community.* Washington, DC: American Psychological Association.

Population profile of the United States, 2000. (2002, August 15). Internet release. Chapter 20: His and Her Demographics. Washington, DC: U.S. Bureau of the Census.

Spears, L. (2000, February). *Building bridges between domestic violence organizations and child protective services.* National Resource Center on Domestic Violence, http://www.vaw.umn.edu/FinalDocuments/dvcps.asp.

Spindel, C., Levy, E., & Conner, M. (2000). *With an end in sight: Strategies from the UNIFEM Trust Fund to Eliminate Violence Against Women.* New York: United Nations Development Fund for Women.

Tjaden, P., & Thoennes, N. (2000a). *Full report of the prevalence, incidence, and consequences of violence against women* (Publication No. NCJ83781). Washington, DC: U.S. Department of Justice, Bureau of Justice Statistics. Available from http://www.ojp.usdoj.gov/bjs.

Tjaden, P., & Thoennes, N. (2000b). Prevalence and consequences of male-to-female and female-to-male intimate partner violence as measured by the National Violence Against Women Survey. *Violence Against Women, 6,* 142–161.

Toolkit to end violence against women. (2002). From the National Advisory Council on Violence Against Women and the Violence Against Women Office, http://toolkit.ncjrs.org/.

United Nations High Commission for Refugees. (1995). *Sexual violence against refugees: Guidelines on prevention and response.* Geneva: United Nations High Commission for Refugees.

U.S. Bureau of the Census. (2002). *We, the American women.* Washington, DC: U.S. Bureau of the Census, Population Division, Age and Sex Statistics Branch.

Van Den Bergh, N. (Ed.). (1995). *Feminist practice in the 21st century.* Washington, DC: NASW Press.

Van Den Bergh, N., & Cooper, L. (1986). *Feminist visions for social work.* Silver Spring, MD: National Association of Social Workers.

VAWnet, the National Electronic Network on Violence Against Women Library. (2002, August 16). http://www.vawnet.org/.

Zeitlin, M. F., Megawangi, R., Kramer, E. M., Colletta, N. D., Babatunde, E. D., & Garman, D. (1995). *Strengthening the family: Implications for international development.* New York: United Nations University Press.

We constantly travel outwards
toward the vastness of outer space
'til we once again find ourselves
never having lost our place. —**Santos Torres, Jr.**

Men

General Population
Groups

SANTOS TORRES, JR.

8

The opening poem was written sometime in the early 1970s, and this author thought it a good springboard for a discussion on the topic of men. The author, when writing those words, believed in the notion (not really a new idea at all) that one's search for meaning, at its core, is an inward journey of self-discovery and exploration that, nevertheless, always begins with an outward sojourn into the incredibly complex outer world of human existence. "That is the exploration that awaits you. Not mapping stars and studying nebulae, but charting the unknown possibilities of existence" (Q to Captain Jean-Luc Picard, in the episode "All Good Things . . .," as cited in Hanley, 1997, p. xiii). The stories of these journeys all represent important contributions to the narrative of the collective experience and the development of a collective identity, whether one is considering race, ethnicity, or—as is the case of the present chapter—part of the gender equation (in this case, men).

Interestingly, when the author's son was a preschooler, the author would tell him bedtime stories made up on the spot, and for a good practical reason: Children are more likely to succumb to sleep in a darkened room versus one flooded with the light a parent might need to read from a book. The real pleasure and treasure of these stories were in witnessing the effects they had on the fertile imagination of a young child. Immediately after telling a story, the author would be treated to a new rendition of the story just told to his son. The experience was marvelous. The story would always be clearly recognizable, since it was only slightly modified from the original, but, oh, how much better it was for the hearing, for it was told in a voice yearning to find its own way. In his words, the story's characters and themes were hewn from the stuff of his father's imagination but remade and recast as characters and storylines that made more sense to him and taught the older listener more than could be recounted in words. It is quite an experience to tell one's story into the darkness and hear it echoed back in a voice that is not one's own, but is nonetheless strangely familiar.

Over time, these stories became "ours" in more ways than one. We gradually moved from simply telling the story again to telling the story for the author to learn and echo back to his son. The reader may have noted that at no time has the author ever claimed that the original story was "his" own to begin with; it was just a story told to his son. Perhaps so it is with men in general. That is, we tell our stories into the darkness and hear other voices reasoning them out, and then our stories echo back for us to consider anew. This chapter is an attempt to tell such a story, one designed to be told and echoed and heard and retold and echoed and heard and so on. This chapter then is an attempt to share the narrative of men as a collective. It is through this strangely familiar process of hearing and telling a story that is not quite one's own that the author has set out to answer the question of what one person can write about the collective experience of an entire gender.

CORPORATE VERSUS TRIBAL MAN

It might be best to begin this narrative on *the male collectivity* by considering what many view as the inherent duality in man's nature. The dual nature of man's inner-most self appears to be an oft-used starting point that can be neither easily ignored nor dismissed. Recording artist Nick Lowe performed a song called "The Beast in Me" that sums up nicely this dual nature of maleness:

THE BEAST IN ME

by Nick Lowe

The beast in me is caged by frail and fragile bonds restless by day and by night rants and rages at the stars. God help the beast in me.

The beast in me has had to learn to live with pain and how to shelter from the rain and in the twinkling of an eye might have to be restrained. Gold help the beast in me.

Sometimes, it tries to kid me that it's just a teddy bear or even somehow managed to van-ish in the air then that is when I must beware of the beast in me that everybody knows, they've seen him out dressed in my clothes patently unclear if it's New York or New Year.

God help the beast in me, the beast in me.

"The Beast In Me" written by Nick Lowe. Copyright 1994, Plangent Visions Music Ltd. Reprinted with permission.

This thematic is played out in many ways, especially in both popular writing and classical literature, such as in the infamous case of Dr. Jekyll and Mr. Hyde. One finds other well-known examples in science fiction, such as superheroes with their dual identities, who are supposedly employed to protect the innocent but who always act out the dualistic nature of the heroic identity.

In this chapter, the author presents this theme of man's dual nature as the *corporate* versus *tribal* man in order to stir thoughts and feelings that are deeply embedded in the sociologic mind of the reader. For some, these terms may conjure up imagery that pits domesticated against wild, conformity against independence, or perhaps the mechanical against the organic. Robert Bly, in his 1990 book *Iron John: A Book about Men,* chronicles the journey from boyhood to manhood (evolving from the tribal to the corporate) with the active involvement of older men (mentors) in the lives of younger ones. Although not entirely "bloodless," Bly's vision appears a little less "bloody" than the journey proposed by other writers (e.g., Shakespeare in *Othello* and *Hamlet*).

Perhaps the epitome of this duality can be found in Shelley's *Frankenstein: The Modern Prometheus.* In this story, *self* is found in the creation of life but paid for at a premium. Like the mythological Prometheus, Shelley's Victor Frankenstein either neglects or forgets to be cautious in his pursuit of the *perfected self.* His creation, the monster, comprised of disparate parts that are mysteriously reanimated through the essential life force (symbolically shown as lightning or the fire stolen from the gods), later destroys his creator because he is rejected by the townspeople (society) for being too tribal and not quite corporate enough.

In two classic works from the 1970s that examine a wide range of philosophical perspectives on the essential nature of mankind, readers are treated to the thought-provoking polemics of two philosophers, LeFevre (1977) and Stevenson (1974). LeFevre, in *Understandings of Man,* provides a comparative treatise on the question of the meaning of man's existence, which considers the matter from such diverse perspectives as Huxley's humanism, Marx's economics, Freud's psychology, and Kierkegaard's existentialism. Stevenson, in *Seven Theories of Human Nature,* examines theoretical and paradigmatic arguments on the nature of man that range from Plato's mind-body dualism to Skinner's conditioning of human behavior. It may be possible that this duality is not a dichotomized either-or issue at all but, rather, closer to an analog from biology, such as the paired strands of the DNA double helix with interconnecting bits that work in unison acting as the fundamental building block of life itself. That is, perhaps what we share, and not how we differ, is what speaks most directly to our real nature. Or, as Franck (1993) wrote:

> Going back a mere five hundred years: you and I each have a pedigree including some 100,000 forebears. A thousand years ago, it numbered some hundred million humans! The proud male-transmitted "family name," adorned perhaps 0.01% of our "legitimate" ancestors. Related to every single being that lives on earth, our identity is: to be Human . . . no more, no less, and even that only potentially! All self-labeling, ethnic, religious, national is pitifully ludicrous. (p. 21)

STEREOTYPES, PROTOTYPES, AND ARCHETYPES

Stereotypes, prototypes, and archetypes might readily be placed on a continuum and presented through dimensions on which they are related to and different from one another (see Figure 8.1).

Figure 8.1 | The Stereotype, Prototype, and Archetype Continuum

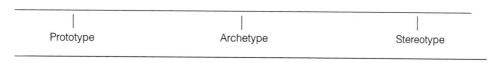

| Prototype | Archetype | Stereotype |

To begin the discussion, consider the following list of grossly overgeneralized and assumptive descriptions of what modern men are supposed to be like. This list has made its way around so many office bulletin boards as well as the World Wide Web in so many iterations that it is now impossible to attribute authorship of it to anyone but anonymous. Stereotypes appear to engender an ineffable quality that contributes to their compelling nature. There is something in the way that stereotypes are generally constructed from a kernel of truth or reasonably accurate facts, but then mixed with gross overexaggerations, that makes this list simultaneously humorous and hurtful, preposterous and still a bit truthful.

Men Are Like . . .

- Men are like . . . Laxatives. They irritate the crap out of you.
- Men are like . . . Bananas. The older they get, the less firm they are.
- Men are like . . . Vacations. They never seem to be long enough.
- Men are like . . . Bank Machines. Once they withdraw, they lose interest.
- Men are like . . . Weather. Nothing can be done to change either one of them.
- Men are like . . . Blenders. You need one, but you're not quite sure why.
- Men are like . . . Cement. After getting laid, they take a long time to get hard.
- Men are like . . . Chocolate Bars. Sweet, smooth, and they usually head right for your hips.
- Men are like . . . Coffee. The best ones are rich, warm, and can keep you up all night long.
- Men are like . . . Commercials. You can't believe a word they say.
- Men are like . . . Department Stores. Their clothes should always be half off.
- Men are like . . . Government Bonds. They take so long to mature.
- Men are like . . . Horoscopes. They always tell you what to do and are usually wrong.
- Men are like . . . Lawn Mowers. If you're not pushing one around, then you're riding it.
- Men are like . . . Mascara. They usually run at the first sign of emotion.
- Men are like . . . Popcorn. They satisfy you, but only for a little while.
- Men are like . . . Snowstorms. You never know when he's coming, how many inches you'll get, or how long he will last.

Next the author offers a functional working definition of *archetype* for the reader to consider: *an original or standard or models upon which subsequent forms of a thing are to be based.* Similar to stereotypes, there is something fundamentally attractive and yet repugnant about how this concept is played out in the real world. Researching and writing about archetypes, Jung wrote, "They are part of the collective unconscious and they emerge in the individual psyche through dreams and visions" (Berry, 2000, p. 23). Although the term *prototype* is often used interchangeably with *archetype,* in this discussion, the author approaches the former as the *not quite finished* or *less evolved version* when compared to an archetype, or the model upon which subsequent others are made.

Now we move one step further to the final construct to be introduced and blended into the present discussion on stereotypes, prototypes, and archetypes. Borrowing from the name of the first letter of the Greek alphabet *alpha,* this particular type of male ranks first in the group and functions as the leader. Sometimes through brawn, sometimes through brain, but most often through a balanced proportioning of both, alpha males (and alpha females) lead the group and may contribute greatly to the group's survival, or at least the alpha male may contribute significantly to reduction in the degree of vulnerability a group might experience. Enhancement of a group's survival and reduction of a group's vulnerability seem to be highly associated with the presence or lack of an alpha male. The archetype of the alpha male has many different manifestations, so the author has constructed a quick typology of the archetypical alpha-like male. In constructing the typology, the author intended to be arbitrary, not exhaustive nor mutually exclusive, in his categorizations. The typology is really meant to be a simple schema that others can use as a conceptual springboard for further exploration or elaboration in the future.

- *Servant/leader:* Jesus, Gandhi, Moses, Muhammed, Martin Luther King, Jr.
- *Hero/lone wolf:* James Bond, Superman, Lone Ranger
- *Genius/eccentric:* Albert Einstein, Howard Hughes, Leonardo da Vinci, Socrates, Don Quixote
- *Warrior chief/über (super) father:* Hannibal, Genghis Khan, Alexander the Great, George Washington
- *Ultimate lover/androgynous:* Don Juan, Valentino, Fred Rogers (of *Mister Rogers' Neighborhood* fame)

What can one do with the idea of a stereotype-to-archetype continuum and a typology of archetypal alpha males? Essentially, one may want to consider the ways in which prototypes, archetypes, and stereotypes have permeated (and currently do permeate) the thoughts and expectations society holds about any group and its members, in this case about men. When taken to the outermost extremes of applicability, one encounters stereotypes and gross overgeneralizations that far outstrip existing evidence about men, and there one arrives at the place, and the process, of stereotypic thinking. To think stereotypically is to use elements or fragments to describe a whole that usually yield only a slight (sometimes insightful) glimpse into the true nature of the thing. Sometimes archetypes can be just as problematic as stereotypes, since they may be so firmly entrenched in the human psyche that any man perceived as not working hard at becoming more like the model is seen as a failure and viewed with suspicion, socially marginalized and isolated, or worse.

What may be important to consider is the extent to which stereotypes derive from "seeds of truth" and how they assist or impede our understanding of the perpetuation of archetypes that expect more than what could be delivered by anyone, including men. Stereotypes as well as archetypes are actually symbols, and not real flesh-and-blood beings. They are symbols used in replacing real analysis and understanding with streamlined thinking. When applying a stereotype in lieu of real knowledge, the "thing" being stereotyped does not have to be appreciated nor respected for its real attributes, or for that matter, its truer nature. Likewise, an archetype is another kind of symbol that appears to be an idealized form of a thing. Men who are striving to attain archetypal status or who are compared to an archetypal original can, at best, achieve only successive approximations toward becoming the symbol used for comparison. That is, one cannot be both the original and the so-called "evolved" version of the original simultaneously. Thus, the situation contains a temporal as well as conceptual paradox. More specifically, even Albert Einstein was not "Einstein."

ON THE MATTER OF MEN AND POWER AND PRIVILEGE

"Because male dominance is so universal, many people believe that it is an innate male personality trait" (Franklin, 1988, p. 30). Dominance by a patriarchal system of social stratification seems alive and well even after the advent of women's liberation. Table 8.1 is based on a 1982 study of university students designed to examine gender stereotypes. Although a bit dated, the results of this study remain relevant today. According to this study, with only slight variation when compared to other countries, adult sex stereotypes tend to favor males and stem from the interaction of biological factors, social functions, and ascribed sex-role expectations and justifications. "The establishment of these beliefs has been tantamount to the development of an international value system which favors men" (Franklin, 1988, p. 45). This value system apparently favors men driven by ascribed versus achieved qualities.

Perhaps it is this latter point where it seems that those with greater power often acquire it (or at least are able to maintain it) via no real or special achievement of their own, but more often their power appears to be the result of what others are willing to ascribe to them. Indeed, making this type of assertion involves walking a slippery slope. One must be careful not to go too far in this "achieved versus ascribed power" argument so as to avoid committing the error of "blaming the victim," as Ryan (1976) expounded upon in his book of the same name—specifically, to avoid taking the position that the oppressed are in their situation because they invited the oppressor to sit at the head of the table. That society would ascribe power and influence to those who do not merit it appears to be antithetical, and yet generally true. Herein may lay the basis of great social, political, and economic inequity experienced by humankind. However, the issue of ascription versus achievement may also hold promise for changing the power arrangement between those with privilege and those at whose expense such privilege is obtained.

A very useful example from history might assist those who are interested in striking a balance between achieved versus ascribed power and influence. The following quotation is from an account of an exchange between two groups whose worldviews differed greatly. The groups were the leadership of the Indians of the Six Nations at Lancaster, Pennsylvania, and the Commissioners from Maryland and Virginia in the 1700s. What appears here is from a letter the Indian leadership sent to the Commissioners:

> We know that you highly esteem the kind of learning taught in those Colleges, and that the Maintenance of our young Men, while with you, would be very expensive to you. We are convinced, that you mean to do us Good by your Proposal; and we thank you heartily. But you, who are wise must know that different Nations have different Conceptions of things and you will therefore not take it amiss, if our ideas of this kind of Education happen not to be the same as yours. We have had some Experience of it. Several of our young People were formerly brought up at the Colleges of the Northern Provinces: they were instructed in all your Sciences; but, when they came back to us, they were bad Runners,

Table 8.1 | Core Values Underlying the Beliefs and Behaviors of Men and Women in America

Values Associated with Men	Values Associated with Women
Active	Affected
Adventurous	Affectionate
Aggressive	Anxious
Autocratic	Attractive
Coarse	Complaining
Courageous	Curious
Daring	Dependent
Dominant	Dreamy
Enterprising	Emotional
Forceful	Fearful
Independent	Feminine
Inventive	Gentle
Masculine	Mild
Progressive	Prudish
Robust	Self-pitying
Rude	Sensitive
Severe	Sentimental
Stern	Sexy
Strong	Soft-hearted
Tough	Submissive
	Superstitious
	Weak
	Whiny

Source: Adapted from J. E. Williams, *Adult Sex Stereotypes.*

ignorant of every means of living in the woods . . . neither fit for Hunters, Warriors, nor Counsellors, they were totally good for nothing. We are, however, not the less oblig'd by your kind Offer, tho' we decline accepting it; and to show our grateful Sense of it, if the Gentlemen of Virginia will send us a Dozen of their Sons, we will take Care of their Education, instruct them in all we know, and make Men of them. (McLuhan, 1971, p. 57)

This historical communication reveals much about the nature of language as a mechanism that can be used to promote or thwart socially approved arrangements regarding privilege and oppression. Notice the not-so-subtle ethnocentric posturing in the excerpt.

Taken together, values, language, symbols, and norms contribute much to our understanding of the construction and maintenance of a male-dominated culture. Based on a fairly practical definition of the term *values,* Franklin (1988) wrote, "Values are defined generally as shared assumptions about what is right and wrong in society. They do not tell us explicitly what behaviors are appropriate and which ones are not appropriate. Values do, however, provide us with criteria and conceptions by which we evaluate people, objects, and events as to their relative worth, merit, beauty, or morality"(p. 44). Additionally, Franklin suggests "a rather common classification scheme for understanding norms: folkways, mores, and laws" (1988, p. 45). These elements can be used to increase our understanding of the ways in which male dominance works and is perpetuated.

Driven by elements from the preceding discussion on values, folkways are the customary ways of doing things that govern day-to-day behavior and are passed on from one generation to the next. Men ask women out on dates, since women who ask men out might be viewed as too independent, too strong-willed, and too forward. Boys play with action figures while girls play with dolls, but both products are made by the same toy companies, on the same assembly lines. The Marines are "looking for a few good men"; that branch of the military does not look for qualified persons. The Marine slogan has a certain ring to it, but what this author hears in the expression is linguistic imperialism for one.

Legal and moral injunctions, such as those against committing adultery and murder, are examples of mores. Mores (norms) are thought to be essential for society's survival, or at least for the survival of groups (such as men) in society. These types of norms are more strictly enforced, as compared to folkways, and violation of them can bring the full force of the community's sanction down on the heads of those who violate them.

Finally, laws that are norms have been enacted by the various levels of government (national, state, local, and municipality) that are designed to regulate human behavior. Laws governing peaceful assembly and acceptable forms of protest are quite often rooted in the very constitutions of many democratic societies. Interestingly, also embedded in the history of many democratic nations is a legacy of behaviors in direct violation of such laws. In times of civil and military insurrection, the factions that successfully sue for independence then get to redefine the nature of the conflict to assuage what were clearly their side's legal misdeeds. Thoreau (1996), in his short essay on civil disobedience, wrote, "Law never made men a whit more just, and, by means of their respect for it, even the well-disposed are daily made the agents of injustice" (p. 7). Many times, too, either from not learning history's lessons or learning from them all too well, these self-same patriots of independence then blithely go about creating their own legacy of repressive actions and social institutions of oppression and violence toward some faction within their "bold new world." C. S. Lewis (2001), in *Abolition of Man,* wrote, "There are two kinds of injustice: the first is found in those who do an injury, the second in those who fail to protect another from injury when they can" (p. 98).

Lum (2003) believes that there are various types of oppression, including exploitation, marginalization, powerlessness, cultural imperialism, and violence. Further, he argues:

Oppression occurs when a segment of the population, systematically and over a period of time, prevents another segment from attaining access to scarce and valued resources. Oppression is a process whereby specific acts are designed to place others in the lower ranks of society and is also a structure that creates a bottom rank in a hierarchical system of ranks. (p. 55)

Exploitation and marginalization are outward manifestations of oppression, but it is their ability to create, maintain, and strengthen boundaries between in-group members and outsiders that may be the foundation of the power and privilege enjoyed by most men in modern society. Some of the more familiar boundary maintenance mechanisms are prejudice, isolation, discrimination, incarceration, and ultimately genocide. The Reverend Dr. Martin Luther King, Jr., clearly articulated his understanding of the nature of boundary maintenance when he wrote:

Racism is a philosophy based on contempt for life. It is the arrogant assertion that one race is the center of value and object of devotion, before which other races must kneel in submission. It is the absurd dogma that one race is responsible for all the progress of history and alone can assure that progress of the future. Racism is total estrangement. It separates not only bodies, but minds and spirits. Inevitably it descends to inflicting spiritual or physical homicide upon the out-group. (King, 1968, p. 70)

Many other forms of power and privilege are enjoyed by most men in these modern times. Only a few of these, those that this author thought to be particularly relevant but which are not always discussed in the literature, have been presented here for the reader's consideration.

ON THE MATTER OF MEN AND PAIN

In the dark night we call to one another and cry for help, while the ghost of Death stands in our midst stretching his black wings over us and with his iron hands, pushes our souls into the abyss. —**Ferris (1960, p. 44), citing the work of Kahlil Gibran regarding the famine in Lebanon during WWI**

What is the current *dark night* for men as a group? Perhaps it is as Berger (1963) writes, "[M]odern man, and especially modern educated man, is in a perpetual state of doubt about the nature of himself and of the universe in which he lives" (p. 50). But what would the dominant group, in this, the modern era, have to be doubtful of, and why not simply avoid it and thus avoid needless suffering altogether? "According to Buddhism, it is our fear at experiencing ourselves directly that creates suffering" (Epstein, 1995, p. 17). One cannot avoid self; or, as one of the editors of this book is so fond of saying, "We take ourselves everywhere we go." And so we revisit a central theme of this chapter, the search for the *perfected self*.

To better focus attention on the matter of men and pain, consider what King (1989) wrote: "'What is a man?' is one of the most important questions confronting any generation" (p. 9). Shakespeare, in one of Hamlet's speeches, tells us, "What a piece of work is a man! how noble in reason! how infinite in faculty; in form and moving how express and admirable! in action how like an angel! in apprehension how like a god! the beauty of the world! the paragon of animals!" From the lowly to the lofty is a man, and what hurts him and binds him is not so much from the outside as it is from the inside, gone unrecognized. Gibran (1975) wrote, "Much of your pain is self-chosen. It is the bitter potion by which the physician within you heals your sick self. Therefore trust the physician, and drink his remedy in silence and tranquility . . ." (p. 52). Millman (2000) tells a story, through the words of a character named Socrates, that brings home the point of how men may be responsible (albeit as unwitting culprits on occasion) for their own pain:

> I once knew a guy like you: I met him on a construction site in the Midwest. When the lunch whistle blew, all the workers would sit down together to eat. And every day, Sam would open his lunch pail and start to complain. Son of a gun! He'd cry, peanut butter and jelly sandwiches day after day after day until one of the guys on the work crew finally said, Fer crissakes, Sam, if you hate peanut butter and jelly so much, why don't you just tell yer ol' lady to make you something different? What do you mean, my ol' lady? Sam replied. I'm not married. I make my own sandwiches. Socrates paused, then added, We all make our own sandwiches. He handed me a brown bag with two sandwiches in it. Do you want the cheese and tomato or tomato and cheese? He asked, grinning. (p. 28)

It is the opinion of this writer that man's unfulfilled quest to be both his own progenitor and progeny is at the center of his greatest pain and suffering. Ironically, nothing more than a shift in perspective may be required to resolve this conundrum. "[T]he individual's choice of viewpoint will determine the way in which he looks back upon his biography. . . . [W]e would prefer to use the more neutral term of 'alternation' to describe this phenomenon . . . the possibility that an individual may alternate back and forth between logically contradictory meaning systems" (Berger, 1963, pp. 51–52). May (1953) wrote the following to express a similar sentiment:

> We have seen that one of the unique characteristics of man is that he can stand outside his present time and imagine himself ahead in the future or back in the past. . . . This power to "look before and after" is part of man's ability to be conscious of himself. . . . Psychologically and spiritually, man does not live by the clock alone. His time, rather, depends on the significance of the event. . . . Memory is not just the imprint of the past time upon us; it is the keeper of what is meaningful for our deepest hopes and fears. As such, memory is another evidence that we have a flexible and creative relation to time, the guiding principle being not the clock but the qualitative significance of our experiences. (pp. 256, 257, 258)

APPLYING THE MULTIDIMENSIONAL CONTEXTUAL PRACTICE FRAMEWORK

No matter how men are conceptualized, as a group they are complex, multifaceted, and multidimensional, to say the least. When applying the multidimensional contextual practice framework, it is important to look beyond the prototypes, archetypes, and stereotypes that have existed throughout history and still pervade society's psyche. All too often men are characterized as single-dimensional beings who are aggressive and prone to act as victimizers, are in constant pursuit of power, and are interested only in being in control (versus being controlled). Professional helpers must cultivate realistic views of men, and their interventions must be informed by understanding men from where they are, how they truly function, and how they see themselves. Practitioners can operate from a more sensitive and understanding point of departure if they open themselves to being willing to abandon generally accepted notions of who men are, especially when those notions do not fit how men, as clients, see themselves. Whether helping an individual, family, group, or community, the practitioner needs to assist the client in understanding his well-being and in maximizing his own essence and understanding of self.

Principle One: Client Well-Being

The central sphere of the framework, client well-being, asks practitioners to recognize human diversity, client's adversities and client's resilience, clients' essence, and the variations in the definition of time among different peoples. One cannot pigeonhole all men as being a certain way or having a certain set of main characteristics. All groups of people have variance between and within them, and men are no exception. The diversity among men is what makes them rich and complex, and it functions as a chief mechanism in leading men to make such incredibly interesting contributions to the human mosaic of society. The author wants to encourage practitioners to recognize this diversity, and yet also seek to find what meaning being a "man" has for clients, and especially what they see as their differences from other men.

A strength found among men is that through much adversity, much resilience is expected and quite often demonstrated. Society expects that men will demonstrate endurance. In fact, many turn to men in times of adversity due to this expectation. Society expects men to be problem solvers and rescuers, and to remain pragmatic in the face of adversity. The danger here is that a man's vulnerability may be overlooked, not accepted, not recognized, or just plain denied as being real. Therefore, practitioners must seek the client's story and understand what affects him and what he views as an issue or problem. They must acknowledge that not all men have the previously mentioned skills, and clients may not possess them in their current presenting situations.

Another important aspect of the client-centered principle is to both allow and, when possible, facilitate the client's essence to surface, to become known, and to be fully acknowledged by both client and helper. A man's essence (spiritual core and being) is greatly affected and shaped by his past experiences, as well as by other societal groups to which he might belong (e.g., biological as well as psychological age cohort, racial identity, ethnic identification, sexual orientation). Essence functions as part of who we are; it contributes to our individuality as well as our identity within groups. Essence, like the biological system, evolves and grows, and as such needs to be recognized and affirmed by helpers. Berger (1963) stated:

> The same relationship between society and identity can be seen in cases where, for one reason or another, an individual's identity is drastically changed. The transformation of identity, just as its genesis and its maintenance, is a social process. We have already indicated the way in which any reinterpretation of the past, any "alternation" from one self-image to another, requires the presence of a group that conspires to bring about the

metamorphosis. What anthropologists call a rite of passage involves the repudiation of an old identity, (say, that of being a child) and the initiation into a new one (that of being an adult). (p. 103)

Principle Two: The Multidimensional Contextual Client

The multidimensional contextual client is the second framework principle. This principle addresses the reality that an individual's sense of self is shaped by others (e.g., groups one belongs to, family systems, etc.), and a man is also part of the community at large within which he finds himself embedded (and, occasionally, at odds with). As mentioned previously, one's identity is not static but is dynamic and continuously involved in complex social interactions and transactions within a complex, but subtle, context and between multiple dimensions. Throughout a man's developmental process, his needs change, including what he requires for personal fulfillment, as well as what may be demanded by or at least expected by others in his social system. In fact, what he defines as a need versus a want evolves as well. A man needs to belong to family and to both primary and secondary social groups, and he needs to be accepted by multilayered, multidimensional, multifaceted systems such as family (whether his family of origin or other identified familial group). Similar to the how the nature and function of membership in groups change, so too does a man's need to belong and to be accepted by these systems change over time.

Although it may appear to be a statement of the obvious, professional helpers need to work specifically at recognizing that no two individual men (or clients in general, for that matter) are likely to develop and perceive their needs in precisely the same way. This is true despite the general way in which clients present with issues. For example, on the surface, it may seem that many men are using a shared set of coping strategies (i.e., adaptive methods for coping), but most likely different men apply these strategies differentially. In addition, helpers can provide a great deal of support to their male clients by focusing early work on discovering what perceptions these men have of the different influences (multiple dimensions) in their lives and what they need from them, if anything. The subtle differences in adaptive strategies—once brought to surface, acknowledged, and more fully recognized—can serve as a very useful storehouse of information about behaviors, thoughts, and feelings to be tapped during the course of the helping process.

This discovery, exploration, and construction of a storehouse of information may not only prove to be enlightening but may also prove to be pivotal in determining the client's strengths and resilience as a man. Despite modern culture's willingness to place others' opinions at the top of the list of things that influence how we interact with our social environment, practitioners should not assume that how others see a man is quite that all important to him, nor should they assume any unimportance to him in terms of how he sees himself and what is relevant and important to him according to his own standards and expectations. Our society expects men to be breadwinners, strong, pragmatic, and stable. As such stereotypes are deconstructed and dismantled, practitioners have a responsibility to help their male clients not be bound by these perceptions.

Principle Three: Influences of Micro, Meso, Macro, and Magna Contexts

Client well-being is affected by the micro, meso, macro, and magna dimensions of the client's life, thus making the context truly multidimensional. Although often represented in diagrams as concentric circles overlaying the individual, the social (organizational/institutional) dimensions of this framework are complex structures that interweave, interact, and are highly interdependent compared to the static circles of diagrams. Additionally, the magna dimension appears to operate somewhere between the material, corporeal, and social systems. In some ways, this approach is similar to understanding the client within his social environment in that it explores the intrapersonal (micro), interpersonal (meso), and environmental (macro) contexts, but it also strives to examine and understand the spiritual (magna) context as being important to understanding a client's contextual process and experience. Practitioners who employ this framework will indeed want to explore with the male client how his individuality is both influenced by and interacts with others (e.g., groups he belongs to, his neighborhood and community) and in what ways he experiences himself on a level of spiritual being. Understanding the importance of the interplay of these different contexts (to both client and helper) can lead to the development of new and innovative interventions informed by complex insights and perceptions that are of critical importance to the client, and not just the helper.

Utilizing this framework in one's work with men can provide support to male clients when they are faced with times of change, challenge, and crisis. Professional helpers who are only able to address, or are overly reliant on, the more traditional types of intervention and support will be likely to overlook something very significant to the helping relationship. How the different contextual facets interact with the male's experience and how his spiritual or religious experiences affect him will be likely to have a profound shaping influence on his resulting worldview. It is important for practitioners to recognize the influences and transactions within and between these very dynamic micro, meso, macro, and magna contexts while exploring issues of change and growth with their male clients.

Principle Four: Practitioner Professional Competence

Practitioners who seek to grow and further assist their clients have a responsibility to become self-aware, that is, more in tune with who they are in the helping context and how their own behaviors, attitudes, motivation, assumptions, and system of beliefs function. As others have argued, being and becoming self-aware is not so much an outcome or destination as it is an ongoing, dynamic process. Professional helping may be informed by many things in general, not the least of which includes empirical research that has been validated and disseminated, practitioner wisdom informed by practice over time and experience, and theoretical assumptions based on sound and current ethical practice. In general, professional helping may be guided by all of these, but one characteristic that makes multidimensional contextual practice distinctive should be clearly identified as well: In this kind of practice, an ongoing effort by helpers to become more multidimensionally and contextually oriented in their own self-awareness is essential.

This type of practitioner self-awareness is characterized by a demonstrated integration of nonstereotypical thinking, knowledge, skills, and values regarding the various client groups the practitioner serves. Of necessity, the elimination of all stereotypes may be impossible or even undesirable, but nonetheless, professional helpers can endeavor to limit the assumptive qualities and destructive impact of their stereotypical as well as archetypal thinking and behaviors. Removal of these from practice begins with practitioners' regular assessment of their own approaches to look for telltale signs of such thinking and behaviors. Stereotypes, as discussed earlier, are often made manifest as judgments that exceed existing evidence. Regardless of the presenting client issue or problem, it is important to keep in mind that the main goal is to identify, understand, and honor the client's multidimensional characteristics and contextual factors. How the individual sees himself and how he connects to men as a group may need to be brought to the surface, and then the client must be respected for whatever strengths and resources might be derived from an examination of those perceptions. Dispelling societal stereotypes that all men are insensitive, enjoy sports and participating in sporting activities, yearn for power and control, and oppress women and other disadvantaged groups in society, is important for the practitioner not only on an individual level relative to conducting practice, but also on a larger professional level in order to perpetuate social justice.

Practitioners may also carry stereotypes about adolescent males, for instance, that they are generally conflicted and at odds with the people and the world around them, perhaps due to raging hormones, untested bravado, or the lack of adult-recognized social symbols that clearly tell the world they are simply "manly men, doing manly things, in a manly sort of way." Such stereotypes might lead an otherwise wisdom-prone helper to assume that any useful assessment and intervention will invariably be directed at the assumed emotional tempest, and that the adolescent male client will need to be educated about that along with associated alternative socially acceptable behaviors. As discussed earlier, the other end of the assumptive continuum, archetypes, might also be embraced by practitioners, resulting in assessments, interventions, and evaluations of male clients that are framed by the societal model for men instead of by the real men to whom practitioners are providing help.

Ultimately, when practitioners embark upon a helping relationship with a male client, regardless of the practitioner's gender or the client's presenting issues, they may find it very useful to engage in ongoing assessment of their own expectations and standards relative to who men are and are not, and relative to how professional helping services should be planned and implemented for male clients. Practitioners also need to approach the helping relationship utilizing the four practice guidelines: mutual discovery, mutual exploration and planning, mutually arrived at intervention, and mutual evaluation. (See Chapter 2, pp. 52–53).

Principle Five: Multidimensional Contextual Service

The final sphere of the framework focuses on helping services that place a special emphasis on the development and promotion of individual and collective well-being through the helping relationship. "Healing is a matter of time, but it is sometimes also a matter of opportunity" (Millman, 1991, p. 32, quoting Hippocrates). Service to men (as a client system) should consider the needs of multilayered, multifaceted, multidimensional, and multicontextual systems such as individuals, families, groups, neighborhoods, and communities, and especially the readiness of these various systems to change. Practitioners should not attempt to fit the client into their understanding of maleness, familial and group arrangements, or even their view of what constitutes community, in terms of what role men should play within it. Helpers must be willing to cultivate openness to how the client system defines the types of and interactions with systems the clients view as relevant or having an impact on them. Which stands as a reminder that in one's work with men, a great deal of importance must be placed on how the client system defines what is important. How do individual clients define the community and its needs and strengths?

Being positively predisposed to viewing one's clients as viable resources in assisting the helper with *what* is important and *how* systems are viewed is an important starting point in improving one's approach to multidimensional contextual service. Helpers then are able to more usefully examine what resources are available in the community to promote growth and well-being for men. Since so many services are rendered via organizational structures like the traditional social service agency, it is helpful for practitioners to explore how organizations and programs within their own contexts go about the business of doing some of their most basic activities, including what and how important information about services is packaged and disseminated. For example, in an agency providing counseling services that is staffed by female practitioners, it is conceivable that the organization and the helpers hold to certain political or social perspectives such as feminism. Though obviously this is not automatically true, some might assume that such an agency would be insensitive to men and their unique issues. Even in agencies composed primarily or entirely of male practitioners, however, there may be a perceived failure of the agency and helpers to serve men well, because the organization may be viewed as not understanding the "renaissance male," or what the author referred to earlier as man's struggle to achieve the *perfected self*. Instead, the agency might be seen as only being capable of serving the traditional idea of who men are, what men do, and what men need. It does not necessarily matter whether these perceptions are accurate, since they occur as a result of how those outside the agency view the organization's composition.

Many organizations might be best described as being *in* the community but not *of* the community. That is, agencies have realities and contexts that arise from concerns such as funding, staffing, service delivery, and so on—concerns that appear to be only peripherally related to the clients the agency serves. Such contextual realities may make it difficult for the organization to place any but the most superficial emphasis on the development and promotion of individual and collective well-being of a specific client base, such as men. Nevertheless, although some organizations are affected by regulatory and legal mandates that restrict how the agencies may operate relative to their clients, nothing prohibits an organization from committing time and resources toward the development of client-sensitive services that reflect the organization's commitment to be *of* as well *in* the community it serves.

CASE STUDY

Application of Multidimensional Contextual Practice

During his first session with his therapist, a 45-year-old Puerto Rican male named Robert indicated that he was having difficulty sorting out his emotions regarding a recent medical diagnosis he had been given. Four months prior, Robert had experienced some chest discomfort and heart palpitations. He drove himself to the emergency room as a preventive strategy for a possible heart attack. After an examination and being monitored while hooked to an EKG for more than an hour, the attending physician informed Robert that there were no indications of a heart attack, but ordered blood to be drawn for testing as a precaution before sending him home with a prescription for an antianxiety medication. The blood tests included thyroid function tests among others.

Just prior to his emergency room visit, Robert had quit a long-standing smoking habit; he had been dealing with an addiction to tobacco for approximately 30 years. He had also begun a regular daily exercise regimen of walking four to six miles. After a few more tests, and within few weeks of his emergency room visit, Robert was informed that he had Graves' disease (i.e., a hyperactive thyroid) and that this disease was more than likely responsible for the various symptoms and health-related issues he had been experiencing, including chest palpitations that would disturb his sleep.

Robert is now required to take both an antithyroid medication and antianxiety medication to reduce the overactivity of his thyroid and to relieve palpitations and mild anxiety, respectively. He is required to have thyroid function blood tests on a monthly basis. He is now faced with the reality of taking medication two or three times a day in order deal with his disease, but reports that overall he really does not feel significantly different. Robert explained to his therapist, however, that he had come to the stark realization that an unexpected side effect of having a condition that must be treated for an indefinite period of time is that having to take medication regularly keeps his *not being well* at the forefront of his thinking.

Robert grew up in Chicago and had a successful early career in educational institutions in the Midwest and on the East Coast prior to his current career as a professor at a large West Coast university. Robert is married and has a son in his mid-teens. As he confronts this diagnosis, he also is dealing with the possibility of a career advancement change, as he is being courted by educational institutions for possible placement in an administrative role. Actively pursuing any of these career opportunities would mean uprooting his family, and especially his son, a freshman in high school. He has sought counseling, even though he is a nonpracticing counselor himself, to help him deal with his health-related issues.

Reflection on Case

When applying the multidimensional contextual practice framework, the therapist must remember to keep the client well-being as the focus of the work. The practitioner would want to explore with Robert the importance of time in the contexts of health, family, and work. How this coincides with the medical prognosis might help provide a context for his anxiety. The helping professional also would want to explore the impact of having ceased his smoking habit of over 30 years. Areas to explore in this regard might include the relatedness of changing such a complex habitual pattern of behavior like smoking and his preventive visit to the emergency room. What prompted Robert to quit smoking? What has he noticed in terms of physical, behavioral, social, and emotional changes since he has stopped smoking? It would also be important to acknowledge that this is not a small feat, and to recognize that it is a battle Robert continues to encounter every day.

Seeking to understand Robert's sense of self is very important. As Berger (1963) wrote:

The same relationship between society and identity can be seen in cases where, for one reason or another, an individual's identity is drastically changed. The transformation of identity, just as its genesis and its maintenance, is a social process. . . . [A]ny "alternation" from one self-image to another, requires the presence of a group that conspires to bring about the metamorphosis. What anthropologists call a rite of passage involves the repudiation of an old identity, (say, that of being a child) and the initiation into a new one (that of being an adult). (p. 103)

Exploration of Robert's identity development relative to his Puerto Rican heritage would provide insight into how he may see himself in the context of greater society as well as how that affects the struggles and successes he encounters in academe. Additional exploration of how he has adjusted to the various moves he has made would identify his views on adaptability and resilience. Discussing his family of origin and his relationship with family might provide insights to the helper interested in understanding more about the client's resilience and essence in the face of achievement as well as adversity. This also may reveal strengths that the practitioner can highlight to help Robert deal with this current adversity. The helper also would want to identify how being male and 45 years of age affects how Robert sees himself. Does he see himself differently than he did 10 years ago? Why or why not? How has being a man who is Puerto Rican influenced how he sees himself?

Robert's identity is subject to change, as are his relationships with family individuals, friends, colleagues, and other small groups, as well as the communities he participates in both professionally and personally. The practitioner may want to explore the significance of different people and groups and whether Robert maintains many relationships from past contexts or communities in which he has operated or lived. This will provide more insight into his view of the meaning and importance of time as related to the past, present, and future. It will also help to identify what kind of external support system he has and considers important. Some insight also could be gathered by exploring why he drove himself to the emergency room and how he feels about that.

The fact that Robert has practiced as a professional helper himself is important to keep in mind. The practitioner will want to explore how he feels about seeking help from a professional in the field. Does he feel awkward, or is he comfortable with the relationship? The practitioner may want to help Robert identify what he sees as his needs in the *here and now,* to what degree those needs are being met, and to what degree he has control over getting those needs met. Control relative to the different groups and people he interacts with as well as the current medical diagnosis may demonstrate importance.

Another aspect to be explored is Robert's sense or meaning of the spiritual, including whether he identifies with a religious organization, and what importance religion or being spiritual has in his life. Many times this understanding changes when an individual encounters a medical crisis; therefore, the practitioner will want to find out whether Robert has experienced a change in his spiritual identity since his emergency room visit. If he participates in organized religion of some type, this might provide an opportunity for the helper to further explore Robert's support systems and how they meet his needs for help with his depression and anxiety.

The practitioner will want to find out as much as possible about the medical condition known as Graves' disease. This process of inquiry and discovery should include Robert as a partner. The practitioner may do some research, as well as facilitate Robert's sharing of the information he has received from medical professionals. At the same time, the helper can supplement this knowledge with reading materials and networking in order to demonstrate to Robert that the helper, too, is interested and wants to understand more about how the presenting issue affects him. It would be very important to not take the information and use it to try to minimize his feelings and/or perceptions of what is happening to him. The information should be used to provide more insight and background for the practitioner as Robert discusses what has impact and meaning to him.

In this element of the multidimensional contextual framework, the helping professional would want to be mindful of stereotypes as well as traditional expectations that both the helper and Robert might have regarding how men deal with medical or health-related concerns. It would be important to not assume that Robert "should" be able to handle this confronting issue. The practitioner should not make the assumptions that this issue is outside of what Robert is able to handle because men are not used to dealing with medical issues; that there must be a deficit on Robert's part that he is having difficulty with this issue and the possibility of career advancement, because men are naturally problem solvers (an expectation of men that was discussed earlier); or that because myriad issues are happening at once, Robert is unable to assimilate these issues and move on, since men have difficulty multitasking. The practitioner needs to put such notions aside and really focus upon what Robert is experiencing. What other potential stereotypes might practitioners have toward a client such as Robert because of his being Puerto Rican and male? Many believe that all Latino men have machismo as part of their identity. This may or may not be the case, regardless of Robert's ethnicity and gender. Some might assume that since Robert is 45, he is simply dealing with elements of a mid-life crisis and has not yet had time to grapple with the fact that he is getting older and, therefore, needs to focus some energy on coming to terms with his own mortality. All of these issues, as well as others not mentioned here, are elements of the rich narrative that Robert brings to the helping relationship. An important dimension of cultivating a strong work relationship will depend on the helper's skill at making the client's story fully discovered and clearly understood.

By using the various dimensions of the multidimensional contextual framework, the practitioner remains open to learning and hearing *from* the client *about* the client. This provides an important means to enhance the client's individual well-being and to assist him in understanding more about himself. Such an approach empowers both the client and the practitioner, while assisting Robert to understand more about himself and what he can do to address his own needs, vulnerabilities, and successes.

SUMMARY

While we may argue and rail against the outward manifestation of what the basic nature of man is, we cannot argue that we are possessed of an essence. This essence is different for everyone, not just men. The duality of the male identity embodies the male's struggle to find balance between his corporate and tribal essence while attempting to perfect the self. Society attempts to cast men into all-encompassing, overgeneralized, and idealized categories, with the expectation that they will provide stability and strength for themselves and for all those around them. Often men are vilified as oppressors. They are seen as those who prevent all others from achieving and accessing the resources to make it in society. This not only neglects the attendant pain and suffering experienced by men but also reinforces the damage done by stereotyping and measuring men against idealized archetypes. An important challenge for helpers is to recognize how their assumptive approaches to clients as members of groups, including men, are usually an admixture of misconceptions and fact that impinges on upon the real nature of the males encountered in both professional and personal life. The author hopes that this chapter has generated a willingness to try out new lenses in viewing men and in providing professional helping services to them.

Discussion Questions

1. List the males in your life whom you consider to be of importance. What expectations do you have of each of these men? What types of emotions, attitudes, and behaviors do you expect them to engage in? Do you see any patterns among your answers?
2. How do the corporate and tribal male identities compare and contrast with, and complement, each other?
3. In what ways have your expectations and stereotypes of men been oppressing or uplifting to men? In what ways have men oppressed or uplifted you as an individual?
4. What meaning do you take away from the discussion regarding the experience of telling one's story into the darkness and hearing it echoed back?

References

Abbot, F. (Ed.). (1993). *Boyhood, growing up male: A multicultural anthology.* New York: The Crossing Press.

Berger, P. L. (1963). *Invitation to sociology: A humanistic perspective.* New York: Anchor Books.

Berry, R. (2000). *Jung: A beginner's guide.* London: Hodder & Stoughton.

Bly, R. (1990). *Iron John: A book about men.* New York: Addison-Wesley.

Calaprice, Alice. (Ed.). (1996). *The quotable Einstein.* Princeton, NJ: Princeton University Press.

Castaneda, Carlos. (1968). *The teachings of Don Juan: A Yaqui way of knowledge.* New York: Pocket Books.

Castaneda, Carlos. (1987). *The power of silence: Further lessons of Don Juan.* New York: Pocket Books.

Castaneda, Carlos. (1998). *The active side of infinity.* New York: Harper Collins.

Clayton (Ed.). (1968). *Martin Luther King: The peaceful warrior.* New York: Pocket Books.

Einstein, Albert. (1954). *Ideas and opinions.* New York: Crown.

Epstein, Mark. (1995). *Thoughts without a thinker: Psychotherapy from a Buddist perspective.* New York: Basic Books.

Ferris, A. R. (Ed.). (1960). Kahlil Gibran, *Thoughts and meditations.* New York: The Citadel Press.

Franck, F. (1993). *A little compendium on that which matters.* New York: St. Martin's Press.

Franklin, C. W. (1988). *Men and society.* Chicago: Nelson-Hall.

Gandhi, M. K. (1993). *Gandhi, an autobiography: The story of my experiments with truth.* Beacon Press.

Gibran, Kahlil. (1960). *Thoughts and meditations.* New York: The Citadel Press.

Gibran, Kahlil. (1975). *The prophet.* New York: Knopf.

Green, J. W. (1999). *Cultural awareness in the human services: A multi-ethnic approach.* Boston: Allyn & Bacon.

Hanley, Richard. (1997). *Is Data human? The metaphysics of Star Trek.* New York: Basic Books.

Hawking, Stephen. (1994). *Black holes and baby universes, and other essays.* New York: Bantam Books.

Hearn, J. (1987). *The gender of oppression: Men, masculinity, and the critique of Marxism.* New York: St. Martin's Press.

King, Martin Luther, Jr. (1964). *Why we can't wait.* New York: Penguin Books.

King, Martin Luther, Jr. (1968). *Where do we go from here: Chaos or community?* Boston: Beacon Press.

King, Martin Luther, Jr. (1989). *The measure of a man.* London: Fount Paperbacks.

LeFevre, P. (1977). *Understandings of man.* Philadelphia: Westminister Press.

Lewis, C. S. (2001). *The abolition of man.* San Francisco: Harper Collins.

Lowe, N. (1999). "The beast in me." On *The Sopranos: Music from the HBO original series.* [CD]. New York: Columbia Records.

Lum, Doman. (Ed.). (2003). *Culturally competent practice: A framework for understanding diverse groups and justice issues.* Pacific Grove, CA: Brooks/Cole, Thomson Learning.

May, R. (1953). *Man's search for himself.* New York: Dell.

McDonough, C. J. (1997). *Staging masculinity: Male identity in contemporary American drama.* North Carolina: McFarland.

McLuhan, T. C. (1971). *Touch the earth: A self-portrait of Indian existence.* New York: Simon & Schuster.

Messner, M. A. (1997). *Politics of masculinity: Men in movements.* Thousand Oaks, CA: Sage.

Millman, Dan. (1984). *Way of the peaceful warrior: A book that changes lives.* Tiburon, CA: H. J. Kramer.

Millman, Dan. (1991). *Sacred journey of the peaceful warrior.* Tiburon, CA: H. J. Kramer.

Millman, Dan. (1995). *The laws of spirit: Simple, powerful truths for making life work.* Tiburon, CA: H. J. Kramer.

Millman, Dan. (2000). *Way of the peaceful warrior: A book that changes lives.* Tiburon, CA: H. J. Kramer.

Rantisi, Audeh. (1990). *Blessed are the peacemakers.* Grand Rapids, MI: Zondervan Books.

Rosenthal, Ted. (1973). *How could I not be among you?* New York: Persea Books.

Ryan, W. (1976). *Blaming the victim.* New York: Vintage Books.

Stevenson, L. (1974). *Seven theories of human nature* (2nd ed.). New York: Oxford.

Thoreau, H. D. (1996). *Civil disobedience.* New York: Book-of-the-Month Club. (Originally published in 1849 as *Resistance to civil government.*)

Tolson, A. (1977). *The limits of masculinity: Male identity and women's liberation.* New York: Harper & Row.

Tzu, Lao. (1990). *Tao te ching: The classic book of integrity and the way.* New York: Bantam Books.

Wolpert, Stanley. (2001). *Gandhi's passion: The life and legacy of Mahatma Gandhi.* New York: Oxford University Press.

When I dare to be powerful—to use my strength in the service of my vision, then it becomes less and less important whether I am afraid. —**Audre Lorde**

Transgender, Bisexual, Lesbians, and Gays | 9

General Population Groups

SUSAN L. KIRK*

This chapter on transgender, bisexual, lesbian, and gay (TBLG) general populations addresses uniqueness, commonalities, and multidimensionality and explores challenges and strengths. It further evaluates comprehensive ways that can be used by the human service practitioner during the process of servicing these communities.

Diversity factors can be defined as those things that unify a group, as well as those things that separate the group members from non–group members. Often these are the same factors seen from differing perspectives of group inclusion or exclusion. The TBLG "community" is inclusive of groups of people who are primarily defined by their differences in relation to heterosexual people. This definition as "other than" reflects the heterosexist bias that exists in society. In mainstream society, either one is heterosexual, or one is not. Being heterosexual is often perceived as the norm; it is assumed that all people are heterosexual unless they are specifically identified as not. If one is not heterosexual, then one becomes the "other" (and is usually considered to be lesbian or gay). But, what does it mean to be lesbian or gay? What does it mean to be heterosexual? How do you name or label peoples' gender or sexual orientation

*The author would like to acknowledge and thank Mary Ellen Chaney for her invaluable editing and research assistance; without her generous support and aid in the writing, this chapter would not have been possible.

in a way that is thorough, and yet does not discount parts of who they are? Consider these examples and questions:

- A woman is legally married to a man for twenty-five years, and they have three children together. She then divorces him and "comes out" as a lesbian, taking another woman as her sexual and life partner. Was her relationship with her ex-husband simply a mistake in some way? Is she or was she heterosexual? Is she or was she lesbian?
- A child is born female, and then as an adult has a sex change operation, becoming physiologically male. This person had a female lover before the gender reassignment surgery was completed, and the couple remains together after the surgery. Is the transgender person's female lover a lesbian or not? Is the transgender person a lesbian? Who decides?
- A self-identified bisexual man has had sexual relationships only with other men. How is he not gay?

Furthermore, consider people who are open to intimacy and sexual relationships with either same- or opposite-sex partners and who choose or have chosen both men and women as partners. What about individuals who choose or feel compelled to identify with a gender that was not their gender biologically at birth? These people probably would not be labeled lesbian or gay. Are they heterosexual? What would one call them?

The purpose of this chapter is to raise issues, survey areas of concern, and apply these themes to multidimensional contextual practice as they pertain to transgender, bisexual, lesbian, and gay people. The author begins with a historical perspective to prepare readers for the discussion of current issues.

HISTORICAL OVERVIEW

There have been nonexclusively heterosexual people all throughout human history. As early as 1924, "homosexual" organizations began forming, with the founding of support groups and publications dedicated to the gay community (National Museum and Archive of Lesbian and Gay History, 1996). However, the transgender, bisexual, lesbian, and gay (TBLG) movement in the United States often references its beginnings as occurring around the 1950s and 1960s. The movement initially focused almost exclusively on lesbian and gay issues, largely ignoring bisexual issues and almost completely ignoring transgender/transsexual issues.

Both the Mattachine Society and the Daughters of Bilitis were formed in the early 1950s and represent some of the earliest homophile groups preceding the present gay rights movement (Kirsch, 2000). These organizations, formed in New York and Los Angeles, advocated for acceptance and assimilation into mainstream (heterosexual) society. Their work was directed largely toward white-collar lesbian and gay individuals. The expansion of sexual mores in the 1960s and 1970s, however, brought about more openness regarding most sexual issues, including discussions of sexual orientation. The groundbreaking work of Dr. Evelyn Hooker, in 1957 and 1967, furthered the increasing openness toward lesbian and gay people. Dr. Hooker's research provided indisputable evidence that homosexuality is not a mental illness (Mallon,

1998b). Despite this, it was not until 1973 that the American Psychiatric Association removed "homosexuality" from the *Diagnostic and Statistical Manual of Mental Disorders* as a mental disorder (Mallon, 1998b).

As these events were occurring in the 1960s and 1970s, the gay rights movement was becoming less focused on assimilation and becoming more a movement of resistance to oppression and of challenge to current social conditions that promoted discrimination and prejudice (Kirsch, 2000). During the 1960s, several notable protests and demonstrations in support of gay and lesbian rights were held. Some demonstrations, like the Jannus Sit-In and The Village "Sip-In" (Romesburg, 1995), were not as well known as others, such as the Stonewall Riots, which demonstrated the increasing militancy of the growing gay liberation movement.

During this period, there was ongoing harassment, violence, and repeated raids and arrests made by law enforcement in bars where gay, lesbian, and cross-dressing individuals met and socialized. One such bar was the Stonewall Bar in New York. On June 28, 1969, after years of harassment and discrimination, the patrons (cross-dressers, gay men, and lesbian women) resisted the harassment and intimidation of the police by resorting to throwing bottles and committing other violent acts. Rioting ensued (Johansson, 1990). Many consider this the key turning point in the change of the gay rights movement from one of suggested assimilation to one of resistance and insistence on civil rights and fair treatment.

The advent of the AIDS epidemic in the early 1980s and the initial lack of strong or compassionate response by medical and governmental leaders, along with a growing understanding of the interconnected nature of various oppressions, led to a more militant resistance and organization of lesbian and gay people. The movement also began to include bisexual and transgender people. Organizations such as Act Up and Queer Nation insisted that civil rights be afforded to nonexclusively heterosexual and transgender people. Part of this grassroots, political, and militant organizing included, and occurred simultaneously with, others' efforts to move legal and statutory discrimination off the books.

The development of "Queer" politics, or a self-defined "Queer" culture, started out (and continues) to challenge the external defining of people who do not feel they fit into heterosexist norms. "Queer politics" or "Queer theory" is the attempt of people to point out that they do not feel they fit precisely or completely into the categories that have already been defined (Turner, 2000). Turner tells us that "queer theory begins with a suspicion: that the predominant modes of intellectual and political activity in western culture during the late twentieth century do not serve the needs and interests of queers . . . queer theory is oppositional" (Turner, 2000, pp. 9–10). In other words, some people were beginning to question the heterosexist assumptions of limits on sexual/relational and gender expression. Many of these people, especially young people, found that the wide definitions associated with the label *queer* met their needs—which were, specifically, to both define themselves outside the expected heterosexist norm and to unify themselves with others who also did not or chose not to fit into this limiting norm, including others who might not be exactly like them.

With this historical understanding in mind, we now turn to an analysis of the use and meaning of language as it pertains to TBLG people.

USE AND MEANING OF LANGUAGE

Language and the categories that language offers us may seem to reflect an "objective reality." However, often what language and categories really offer us are reflections of the dominant cultural values and understandings, that is, what mainstream culture defines as possible and acceptable (Bohan & Russell, 1999). Said another way, "in language lie the assumptions of a culture, its rules of conduct, what it will acknowledge as possible and permissible . . . language marks out the limits of the possible" (Pellegrini, 1992, p. 43). To define all nonexclusively heterosexual and transgender people as "other than" is to limit the definitions and imaginations of what is possible in terms of affectional, sexual, and gender expression. And to use language that does not acknowledge the existence of TBLG people is to continue the oppression of these people.

Inclusive language is very important. It is a major way in which TBLG people may decide whether a human service practitioner is "safe" or not (i.e., homonegative or heterosexist). One never knows when a coworker, client, or acquaintance one is dealing with is, or has a close emotional bond to, a TBLG person. But beyond demonstrating to TBLG people that one is sensitive to and inclusive of their existence, inclusive language presents possibilities to all of society. Language not only communicates one's experiences, but it also reflects one's attitudes, thinking, beliefs, values, and norms. Language shapes "realities" and possibilities—it sets the definitions of who and how one can be in the world. To never hear one's "reality" reflected in the world can, and often does, send a clear exclusionary message to one, implying a seemingly intrinsic wrongness. For example, inquiries into whether someone is "married or single" completely excludes not only same-sex couples, who are not able to legally marry (although the state of Massachusetts began to issue same-sex marriage licenses on May 17, 2004, based on a ruling by the Massachusetts State Supreme Court), but also anyone who is in any type of relationship that is not defined by marriage. Or, as another example, the term *partner* is often used to refer to a spouse or significant other, rather than "wife" or "husband." The use of the word *partner* by heterosexuals is a way to show gay and lesbian couples that they are respectful and sensitive to this term. Even if one is married to someone of the opposite gender, use of non–gender-specific language is a way to supportively, proactively include TBLG people. Not only does it validate those TBLG people who hear one speak, but it also gives shape to the reality of TBLG lives, which often are invisible and therefore easily ignored, devalued, and oppressed. It is a form of heterosexism to never acknowledge by our language that people other than stereotypical heterosexual people exist in the world.

Consider the implications of fully incorporating nonheterosexist and non–gender-specific language into our speech. Often we say to children, "When you grow up and get married. . . ." This propagates just the types of limitations on possible lifestyle choices that feminism and TBLG people have challenged, and continue to challenge. Why is it assumed that people will marry? But, beyond that, since marriage to a same-sex partner is generally illegal in the United States and in most parts of the world, presenting to children the inevitability of marriage also presents to them the exclusion of the possibility that they or other children may grow up to not be heterosexual. The identity, experience, and, indeed, the world of such children are limited from an early age by the perimeters language has placed on them.

It is disconcerting that significant numbers of people who seem to have positive attitudes toward the TBLG population will still laugh at antigay jokes and use derogatory terms, thereby "trivializing the stifling effect of such jokes and remarks on LGB[T] people" (Schope & Eliason, 2000). While such overt oppression by language and words is clearly harmful, it is also destructive to covertly oppress the reality of an entire population of people by never making visible their lives or realities. One might begin to counter this by acknowledging the possibility that a particular person may have a boyfriend or girlfriend, or both. If people seem surprised or even upset by such inclusiveness, one can ask them how they would feel if they did have a same-sex partner or multiple partners of differing genders and the possibility of that was never even acknowledged. Another way to counter oppression is to, for example, not assume that a young child wearing blue jeans and a plain t-shirt, and sporting a short haircut, must be a boy. One can avoid referring to a child as "him" or "her" until one knows the child's gender or gender preference/orientation.

Consider, even, the language of pronouns. In English, pronouns referring to people all reflect gender. What does this mean to a transgender person who either does not identify with the biological sex that s/he was born with, or who identifies as neither exclusively "male" nor "female"? What if an individual is in the process of altering her/his gender surgically and/or medically? At what point does the pronoun selection change?

Part of the solution may be to have each person specify to others her/his gender preference; however, this does nothing to address the deeper gender bias of this culture. There is no intermediate zone where one who questions what it is to be a "real" man can explore masculinity or where a young woman, for example, might explore what being a very "butch" lesbian might mean to her gender identity. While the suggestions of transgender liberationist and activist/writer Leslie Feinberg may seem radical, maybe it is time to look for non–gender-specific pronouns, such as Feinberg's *sie* and *hir* (pronounced like *see* and *here,* respectively), to refer to people without needing to publicly identify gender before we can even speak of them (Feinberg, 1998).

Heterosexism and oppressive gender expression sometimes can be seen most clearly in language and in the invisibility of TBLG people's lives. It is present in simple and thoughtless speech and actions, such as in talking about attracting "the opposite sex" or in gently ridiculing a little boy for playing with a doll. It is also present when we, for example, assume that a woman who has short hair, wears no makeup, and typically does not wear dresses is a lesbian. Each of us must allow the expression of gender and affectional/sexual orientation to be broader if it is to be truly reflective of our individual lives. Human service practitioners can learn to use the power of language to alleviate constructed human pain, rather than creating more pain by carelessly excluding individuals in their speech.

TOWARD A WORKING DEFINITION AND UNDERSTANDING

In speaking of the TBLG communities, it can become difficult to be sure of terms and meaning. It is assumed that most individuals have at least a working definition of lesbian and gay at this point in history, but we will include elements in our definition of not only being sexually attracted to members of the same sex, but also of choosing affectional and life partners who are of the same sex. While this may be fairly common knowledge, exact definitions of transgender and bisexual remain somewhat more elusive. This may not present the problems that such a lack of clarity may imply, however, since the ultimate factor in defining a person's affectional, sexual, or gender orientation is, and must remain, self-identification rather than social classification.

In one of the examples presented earlier, we asked the question of whether a woman married to a man for 25 years is a lesbian or not. This is really a non-question for a human service practitioner, or for any person other than the woman herself. The woman is "who" she is; the "what" of who she is (heterosexual turned lesbian, lesbian who came out late in life, etc.) is part of her own self-definition. Self-determination applies not just to the encouragement of people's empowerment to decide for themselves which behaviors and actions they will engage in, but it also applies to the labeling or naming of their experiences and identities. It is crucial that human service practitioners allow nonexclusively heterosexual and transgender people the opportunity to define themselves and their experiences. Having said that, at least working definitions are necessary in order for people to communicate. Language, as already discussed, is limited; however, it also is the primary way by which we communicate. So, for the purposes of this chapter, we will use the following definitions of transgender and bisexual:

- *Transgender:* Individuals who feel their gender is not adequately defined by the categories rigidly specified by the culture; people whose gender expression cross or transcend traditional definitions of gender
- *Bisexual:* Individuals who have "the capacity to feel sexual attraction toward, and to consummate sexual performance with, members of the opposite and one's own sex" (Dynes, 1990, p. 143)

It has been estimated that 10% to 20% of any given population is lesbian or gay (Gallup, 1977; Gebhard & Johnson, 1979; Kinsey, Pomeroy, & Martin, 1948; Kinsey, Pomeroy, Martin, & Gebhard, 1953). There is significantly less documentation and reliable information about how many people would identify as transgender or bisexual. At the height of the civil rights movement in the 1960s, the U.S. census estimates placed the number of African Americans/Blacks at about 11% to 15% of the U.S. population. This number of individuals was sufficient to warrant changes in both society and in the law to begin to create more equality for this group (Kirk, 1989). By analogy, then, numbers alone might be argued to be significant enough to warrant the needed changes to promote justice and freedom from oppression for the TBLG community. But more importantly than the numbers of individuals affected are the ethical considerations. Human service practitioners are called upon to promote social justice, to help individuals reach their highest potential and well-being, as well as to promote growth and freedom from oppression, discrimination, and violence.

The inclusion of the bisexual and transgender populations in the fictionally unified entity known as *the* lesbian and gay community is problematic in some ways. While all the special concerns discussed in the preceding sections potentially refer in some ways to all TBLG people, there are special issues that apply to people who claim a bisexual or transgender identity. These two subgroups of the TBLG community are not always acknowledged or offered support, even within the TBLG (or, in some cases, the lesbian and gay) community. They consist of groups of people who often find their identities subsumed by the lesbian and gay community, or they are lumped into the nonexclusively heterosexual, nontransgender community, with no consideration for the individual needs and gifts they bring. Additional research is desperately needed to determine the needs of these two groups of people as unique and diverse communities within the larger TBLG grouping. Acknowledgment of the rigidity of gender roles that limit human expression cannot be delegated only to feminists, but must be considered to be a great challenge and opportunity presented to society by transgender individuals. Lesbians and gays must seek coalitions and links with bisexual and transgender individuals.

Heterosexism and homophobia present many obstacles to TBLG individuals. The term *homophobia* is often used to discuss societal fear, dislike, and hatred of lesbians and gays; it is also associated with the efforts to try and exert societal control over nonexclusively heterosexual individuals through propagation of discrimination and prejudice. The use of the root *phobia* implies that there is an irrational and fear-based element to this prejudice (Appleby & Anastas, 1998; Weinberg, 1972). *Heterosexism* is defined as "an ideological system that denies, denigrates, and stigmatizes any nonheterosexual form of behavior, identity, relationship, or community" (Herek, 1992, p. 89). It is present in institutional, individual, and societal customs and beliefs (Appleby & Anastas, 1998; Herek, 1992). Heterosexism is understood not only to be a root of homophobia, but also to embody broader and more deeply held beliefs about sexuality and gender. Although both of these concepts can have individualized use and meaning, more and more often the literature is tending to move away from the specificity of these individualized terms toward the use of more general terms such as *homonegativity* (Appleby & Anastas, 1998; Halpert & Pfaller, 2001), which can be more generically and universally applied. At times, in this chapter, *homonegativity* will be used; however, *heterosexism* often will be the preferred term, as it is more precise because it includes discrimination against transgender individuals, which is often based in heterosexist prejudice. Likewise, since homosexuality is not always a consideration or issue for transgender individuals, *homonegativity* and similar words may leave transgender people out of the discussion.

SOCIAL ISSUES AND CONCERNS: A MULTIDIMENSIONAL CONTEXTUAL CALL

How do homonegativity and heterosexism impact nonheterosexual or nontraditionally gendered people? Most of the literature in the field of human diversity discusses, in some form or another, the effects of oppression on individuals, families, groups, and communities. The effects of homonegativity and heterosexism, however, can produce stressors that are specific to the TBLG community. Although much of the available research specifically addresses the stresses and life problems that lesbians and gay men face, many of these problems are assumed to also affect transgender and bisexual people. These stressors include visibility issues (e.g., how "out" one can safely be), family conflict, work and economic discrimination, generalized discrimination in areas such as housing and receipt of needed services, violence and harassment, HIV/AIDS, conflicts over sexual orientation and gender identity, and misunderstanding or lack of acceptance (Lewis, Derlega, Berndt, Morris, & Rose, 2001).

In addition, heterosexism and oppression have resulted in higher rates of risk for isolation, suicide, substance abuse, HIV exposure, violence, and homelessness, especially for youth, in the TBLG community (AIDS Office, 1991; Gibson, 1989; Hetrick & Martin, 1987; Hunter, 1990; National Gay and Lesbian Task Force, 1984; Remafedi, 1987; Rosario, Hunter, & Rotheram-Borus, 1992). A number of researchers have indicated that as early as age 4 or 5, many lesbians and gays sensed that something was different about them; and before the age of 20, 28% of boys and 17% of girls have had same-sex sexual experiences (Kinsey, Pomeroy, & Martin, 1948; Kinsey, Pomeroy, Martin, & Gebhard, 1953; Saghir & Robins, 1973). It has been estimated that about 80% of bisexual, lesbian, and gay youth express severe feelings of isolation (Hetrick & Martin, 1987). Being different from their peers in any way is traumatic for adolescents. Belonging to a sexual or gender-expressive minority that is ridiculed and oppressed in the wider society obviously can create almost unbearable pressure for youth; this presumably helps to explain why the rate of suicide attempts for lesbian and gay youth is two to three times higher than that for heterosexually identified youth (Gibson, 1989). In addition, alcohol and drug use among lesbian and gay youth is increased relative to heterosexual youth (Rosario, Hunter, & Rotheram-Borus, 1992).

Transgender and bisexual people—both adults and youth—generally face all of the same issues that lesbians and gay men often encounter. In addition, these groups of individuals face some unique issues as well. Bisexual people have an added burden of being able to "pass" as heterosexual, or to claim heterosexual privilege, when they are in relationships with opposite-sex people. This can create a more complex "coming out" process for them, both internally and externally. If there is little general visibility of lesbians and gays in society, there is even less visibility of bisexual individuals. What few resources may be available to assist lesbian women and gay men in understanding and forming their affectional and sexual identities may actually further confuse bisexual people who both find themselves and do not find themselves reflected in these resources. In addition, revealing one's sexual/affectional orientation as being nonexclusively heterosexual, and yet not exclusively lesbian or gay either, is an ongoing process that often requires continual explanation to members of both gay/lesbian and heterosexual communities. Any assumption made about a bisexual person's sexual orientation on the basis of that person's current partner's sex is likely to be incorrect.

The feminist and womanist movements, especially the second wave of feminism that began in the 1970s, did much to challenge the roles and expectations of what it is to be a woman and, consequently, a man (Feinberg, 1998). To be female in Western culture, especially in the United States, does not necessarily mean that one is required to cook and sew. Likewise, a woman can work outside the home, be educated, choose whether or not to live life with a partner, and choose whether or not to have and raise children. People did not always assume that women had these options. At one time, the gender roles and expectations of society dictated much more narrow definitions of appropriate behavior and expression for women.

Transgender individuals present the same types of challenges to gender roles and expectations today that feminism presented in the recent past. Suppose a person is born with female genitalia and is raised as a girl; but as an adult, this person chooses to dress in male clothes, to not wear makeup, to wear a "man's" short haircut, and to be in an intimate relationship with a woman. Depending upon this individual's bodily appearance, strangers who are not familiar with this person will probably call this person "sir" or "he." If this person decides that being addressed as "he" or "sir" is preferable to being called "she" or "ma'am," does this person have the right to so decide? Would the human service practitioner and the health and human service professional disciplines accept this form of self-determination?

Now let us expand this example. What does such an individual put on the driver's license issued by the state? Our culture is a binary-gendered, or bi-gendered, society. Does our "female" who is self-defined as "he" check the M box (for male) or the F box (for female)? Consider the nightmare that could ensue during a simple traffic stop if the person in our example has checked the F box because biologically or physiologically the gender of female applies. In appearance and dress, this individual looks male. How might the interaction between the officer and the driver go? What are the possible ramifications—in terms of discrimination, harassment, and possibly even verbal or physical violence—of this seemingly "simple" decision? Or, for another example, consider what happens when this person applies for a passport. It is a felony for this person to check "male" on the passport application (Feinberg, 1998), but if "female" is checked, how many difficulties, and in how many countries, might this person who looks "male" face? But what other options does our bigendered culture offer to such people?

Generally, *transgender* is not synonymous with *transsexual*. For our purposes, we will define *transsexual* as someone who experiences an intense conflict between her/his gender identity, and who either desires to undergo, or has undergone, medical treatment to address this issue through hormone therapy and/or gender reassignment surgery. As the reader will recall, *transgender* individuals fall into a broader category of people who cross (or transcend) the culturally defined categories of gender. Transgender people do not necessarily alter their anatomy, although sometimes alterations (surgically or otherwise) may occur, with or without complete sex/gender reassignment. In the transgender/transsexual community, there exists a continuum of expression and a variety of ways in which gender traits are blended. Since the definition of *transgender* is broader (and, for self-chosen reasons, the preferred term of most people in this group), it will be the term we use in this chapter. But the challenge presented by transgender folks is broader than one of definition—or even of finding ways for such individuals to fit into the binarily limited gender options of society. The challenge presented by transgender folks is one of questioning the limiting expressions of gender that our culture forces on people by assuming that an individual is either male or female. Traits, behaviors, likes and dislikes, attitudes, careers, and general endeavors are no longer seen to be linked inexorably to gender or sex, but the transgender person often leads us even further in challenging our cultural assumptions: If we are open to a larger expression of what being a "real" man or woman means, then why do we allow exclusive identification of individuals as being of either one or the other gender?

Oftentimes, transgender people face, in their assumption-challenging expressions of gender, many obstacles formed by ignorance and prejudice. As demonstrated in our previous example, the simple use of pronouns and simple actions of self-identification in terms of gender can present challenges. Consider how many times a day we use sex-assigned pronouns to refer to a person. Each use of a pronoun presents an invitation or demand of the transgender person: Will this person (and how will this person) disclose or reveal her/his chosen gender expression? "Coming out" issues are compounded for these individuals. In addition, issues regarding sexual orientation are often overlooked. If some people do not consider themselves to be exclusively male or female, then how do they determine if they are "heterosexual," "lesbian," "gay," or "bisexual"? Heterosexist bias compounds things not just in light of choosing sexual, affectional, or life partners, but also in terms of expressing gender that is not traditionally binary as well.

Whether a person is viewed as male or female by strangers affects that person's functioning in society. A perceived "woman" in pants will not be harassed as often as a perceived "man" in a dress even though the level of exposure to harassment and violence experienced by women is greater than that experienced by men in general. Acceptance and creation of support systems for transgender individuals are other challenges. Although many segments of the population may not easily or willingly accept gay men and lesbian women, more and more cultural and legal sanctions promote at least curbing homonegative actions and words. But, acceptance of transgender individuals is even less than that afforded to lesbians and gays. In fact, many lesbians and gay men themselves fail to see the connection between the need for expansion in gender expression and the need for expansion in sexual/relational expression. Many transgender folks, therefore, end up in a double bind of rejection from both heterosexually identified, bigenderist communities and lesbian/gay communities. Gay and lesbian communities that seek acceptance into heterosexual culture by arguing that they are just like heterosexual folks except for the gender of their life/sexual partners may be especially threatened by and unwelcoming toward transgender individuals. The use of multidimensional contextual practice is vital when servicing TBLG communities. Differences, commonalities, and controversies are reflected within the lives of these uniquely and multifaceted groups of people. The human service practitioner is encouraged to rely on such understanding while honoring individual and collective experiences encountered by the general TBLG population.

At this point, we turn to a discussion of a number of common concerns that confront the various TBLG individuals, families, groups, and communities.

Identity Formation and Coming Out

Some transgender, bisexual, lesbian, and gay (TBLG) people have a sense, from as early as they can remember, that they are somehow different from others or that something about them does not quite fit. Others feel that all is fine until they meet a certain person or have a certain experience that brings issues of gender expression and affectional/sexual orientation into question. Some TBLG people realize when they are young teens (or even earlier) that they are attracted to people of the same sex, or that they are attracted to people of both the same and opposite sex, while others are much older when they realize that the gender the world assigned to them might not represent who they really are or be a full enough expression of who they are.

How people come to be transgender, bisexual, lesbian, or gay is largely an issue that many feel should be left alone, if only because often people's motives in trying to determine how one became TBLG is in reality an attempt to figure out how to cure what is seen as an anomaly. While there is little research in general, and very little at all that includes transgender and bisexual people, the weight of the research indicates that there is in fact no identifiable factor or set of factors that "cause" a lesbian or gay identity to form (Hitchens, 1979; Hitchens & Price, 1979; Martin & Lyon, 1972; Pollack, 1987). For our purposes, it is more helpful to look not at etiology, but rather at the coming-out processes that a large number of TBLG people engage in and how those processes affect them. Understanding this coming-out process, however, is not simple. Some developmental theories discuss the forming of (particularly) gay and lesbian identities. They tend to indicate that once one starts to become aware of how one does not fit into the heterosexist paradigms, then the process is really one of continuing on a linear path of self-discovery, incorporating and accepting more and more of the new identity. But, some alternatives to this developmental view posits that desire, behavior, and identity are three separate constructs that influence a fluidity of sexual identity (Horowitz & Newcomb, 2001). It is unclear whether a coming-out process is primarily a linear process of self-discovery and acceptance or whether there is continual interplay between the person and the person's environment and how the person chooses to define him/herself.

How then does a human service practitioner effectively support or assist a client who presents with coming-out issues when the process of coming out can be ambiguous? Furthermore, the process of coming out in a heterosexist society is a continual one. Transgender, bisexual, lesbian, and gay people are consistently assumed to be that which they are not—that is, people who fit into the heterosexist norms. Every day in many, if not all, life arenas, TBLG people must make decisions about whether or not to disclose their gender or sexual orientations, or whether to let assumptions go by unchallenged. The weight of dealing with this need to constantly make such decisions clearly can be overwhelming. For a human service practitioner to know how to help with this issue is also very challenging, yet assisting TBLG clients with coming-out issues is often key in assisting those who are seeking social services.

The first person one comes out to is oneself (Chaney, 2002). In many instances, the social service practitioner will be called upon to assist TBLG clients to explore the possibility that their identities are not ones that fit comfortably into the heterosexist norms. The next step, if the determination is that their identities do not fit the norm, is to help the clients accept and celebrate, understand and incorporate, their identities into their self-concepts. The National Association of Social Workers (NASW, 1997) states that it takes the position, which human service practitioners should also take, that "same-gender sexual orientation should be afforded the same respect and rights as opposite-gender orientation" (p. 202). This position should also be extended to apply to those with a bisexual orientation and to gender expressions that are not necessarily within either a heterosexist norm or gay/lesbian/bisexual definitions.

Human services practitioners need to be mindful of and to help create ways to affirm the emerging identities of TBLG clients. Furthermore, they may be called upon to communicate this affirmation to clients and to help them determine their own ways of affirming their identities. Part of this work incorporates the need for both the client and the human services practitioner to educate themselves about TBLG issues and to affirm that homophobia and heterosexism are not reflections of any real inferiority in regard to sexual/gender orientations and expressions. Transgender, bisexual, lesbian, and gay sexual and gender expressions are normal variations on human sexual/gender expressions, while homophobia and heterosexism within individuals and society are a reflection of the biases and oppression of the culture, and not of any intrinsic flaws in the individuals (Appleby & Anastas, 1998).

Once a client has a firmly established sense of identity, however, the issues related to, and the process of, coming out are far from over. Many questions remain: Should one come out to one's family of origin, and if so, how? What about telling a new employer? Is an individual's gender presentation an issue in regard to a new romantic/sexual partner? Do we owe our partners full life histories, and if so, at what point in the relationship should we present them? How visibly identifiable as TBLG does one want to be? How safe is it to hold a same-sex partner's hand while walking down the street at night? Can a TBLG partner of a parent attend a PTA meeting? What effect might such attendance (or lack of it) have on the child?

All of these questions involve coming-out issues, and all of them reflect the ongoing process that the TBLG client confronts daily, and will continue to confront until heterosexist assumptions no longer underline all our interactions in society. Although there are no solid answers to any of these sorts of questions, a few factors need to be taken into consideration when exploring such issues with a client.

First, one has to always consider safety, both physical and psychological. Is one likely to be fired from one's job if one comes out? Being fired will definitely undermine one's psychological safety and security, at least in a financial way. And yet, does not coming out take a larger toll in terms of the effort required to keep key parts of one's life secret or in terms of losing integrity? If one walks down the street holding the hand of a same-sex person, there is always, unfortunately, the possibility of being assaulted with verbal or physical violence. In some countries, states, towns, and neighborhoods, this is more likely than in others. Weighing all the factors involved with coming out against the psychological costs of inhibiting spontaneous affection and denying one's identity is not easy.

Second, one has to consider comfort levels and psychological integrity. Different people have different comfort levels in displaying affection in front of others. Some people are more demonstrative than others. Some people share personal information easily and find self-disclosure to be a good means of bonding with others, while other people find self-disclosure to be something they engage in only after more time has passed. All these factors influence how comfortable one is in coming out, and in which circumstances. In addition, psychological integrity comes into play. If an individual feels it takes great effort to not share important information with her/his family of origin, but is fearful of the reaction to coming out, the stress will weigh more heavily on that person than it would on a more naturally private or reticent person. In addition, some people feel an obligation to reveal their gender or affectional/sexual orientation out of a sense of self-esteem, or an unwillingness to accept the assumed sense of shame they may feel at hiding. The cost to such people of *not* coming out may be much higher than it might be for others. Also, by not coming out, one may have to hide a significant relationship. Take, for example, the gay man who cannot take his life partner to his birth family's Chanukah celebration because he feels he cannot come out to his family. He may feel an overwhelming conflict between not denying his relationship with his partner and not wanting to risk losing the love and acceptance of his family (and possibly even his larger extended family, friends, and religious community).

Third, does one feel a responsibility to the larger TBLG community and to working toward reducing homonegativity and heterosexism in society at large, both now and in the future? Studies (such as those cited earlier, as well as Herek, 1988) have shown that exposure to TBLG people increases acceptance of this population and decreases homonegativity. Therefore, the argument is sometimes made that the more "out" and visible TBLG people are, the easier it will be for others to come out in the future, and the easier life will be for all TBLG people. The visibility of TBLG lives makes the invisibility harder to maintain, which in turn makes efforts (both passive and active) to limit options for affectional/sexual and gender expression harder to achieve. Visibility gives faces to those in the TBLG group, and provides expression of what it means to oppress "those" people. The specific reality of denying your friend from work the right to raise her children, or denying your neighbor his right to dress as he chooses, or denying your mother her right to "marry" the love of her life is much more potent and clear in its oppressive nature than denying such rights to strangers in some distant place.

An overall theme that in some ways affects all of these areas is the theme of belonging. If a TBLG person comes out to her/his family of origin and is disowned, what will that cost be? If one is active in one's church, in a homonegative tradition, and comes out as a lesbian, thereby losing one's religious community, what will that cost be? But on the other side of these losses are the potential losses of honesty, of self, and of self-worth. And there is also a larger loss to the individuals or communities that one chooses *not* to come out to, since those individuals and groups lose the opportunity to see one of the faces of the TBLG community and, as a result, be challenged to arrive at a fuller definition of community and a less oppressive and discriminatory way of dealing with people. Society loses the opportunity to further the work of lessening the blindness toward the TBLG population and of promoting the view of this population as existent, worthwhile, and productive members of society. How TBLG people choose to belong, or risk not belonging, to society and communities is one of the ultimate coming-out questions.

Social Stress Concerns

Stress caused by being part of a so-called minority group is defined as resulting from "culturally sanctioned, categorically ascribed inferior status, social prejudice and discrimination, the impact of these environmental forces on psychological well-being, and consequent readjustment or adaptation" (Brooks, 1981, p. 107). The assumptions and paradigms that support oppression of TBLG people support a belief, both by self and others, in the inferior status of nonheterosexual, transgender people and support the prejudice and discrimination to which Brooks refers. The reactions of the person experiencing the stress affect the person's psychological well-being, and the reactions of the helping professional to the stressors that brought to the person to the professional will either help or hinder in the adaptation or readjustment needed to overcome these stressors.

The stresses experienced by people who either do not identify themselves as exclusively heterosexual or who identify as transgender are numerous. Given that there is oppression of this population, and that this oppression causes stress, three factors in particular may help with the successful navigation of these stressful life challenges: self-affirming reactions by the person experiencing the stressors; positive and competent reactions by helping professionals to people experiencing these stressors; and understanding and informed assumptions and paradigms about the stressors, and the levels of oppression inherent in them.

Health Care Concerns

Heterosexism and homophobia is rampant in the medical field (Peterson, 1996). Both lesbians and gays are more likely than their heterosexual counterparts to not seek needed or routine medical care or to withhold pertinent information from medical providers due to their sexual orientation and prior negative experiences with these providers (Peterson & Bricker-Jenkins, 1996; Robertson & Schachter, 1981; Schwartz, 1996). This can be a concern especially for TBLG youth, who may not get needed physicals, immunizations, and laboratory screenings that other youth their age (at least those of the higher socioeconomic classes) are routinely able to access. There may be fewer opportunities for TBLG people to engage in conversations about safe sex habits if medical care is not available and screenings for sexually transmitted diseases, including HIV infection, are delayed or completely missed.

Mental health issues are also clearly of concern to the TBLG population. Almost 30% of gay men (Remafedi, Farrow, & Deisher, 1991) and 29% to 42% of lesbian/gay youth are said to have attempted suicide (Hammelman, 1993; Herdt & Boxer, 1993; Hershberger, Pilkington, & D'Augelli, 1996). Erwin (1993) notes that studies continue to document not only higher rates of suicide among TBLG populations, but also higher rates of depression, substance abuse, and other factors associated with psychological distress, at least in lesbian women and gay men, when compared to heterosexuals. However, complete, adequate, and reliable statistics are not available for the mental health needs of the TBLG community, let alone adequate services provided by expert providers.

In addition, although it has been well documented in the literature and is common Western cultural knowledge that HIV/AIDS infections may be of crucial concern to the population of men who have sex with men, there are also other, possibly less known or less obvious, issues relating to health care of which human service practitioners should be aware. One of these issues concerns body image and eating disorders, an issue that is underreported, yet documented, in the literature (Herzog, Norman, Gordon, & Pepose, 1984; Pope, Hudson, & Jonas, 1986; Siever, 1996; Yager, Kurtzman, Landsverk, & Wiesmeier, 1988). Eating disorders among men who have sex with men are often not recognized due to a lack of knowledge of the existence of (and possibly, according to sources noted earlier, an increase in) these disorders. Due to a strong emphasis within the gay and male-identified bisexual communities on youth and attractiveness as defined by the cultural norm of low body weight, eating disorders can present a significant health risk to men who have sex with men. This risk can go undetected by uninformed medical personnel.

The chronic stress that oppressed people live under can be (and undoubtedly, will be shown to be) a source of increased incidents of stress-related diseases and mental health challenges. The burden of living under the weight of oppression, especially for those with inadequate support systems or those suffering from internalized homophobia, can create an ongoing and chronic state of stress—and one that is not, from the author's own anecdotal research, routinely acknowledged or addressed by medical providers.

There are also systemic concerns regarding health care for TBLG people. This population has concerns that go beyond those faced by many regarding adequate health insurance. Although domestic partner benefits are becoming more available for some, partners of TBLG people usually still are not offered health insurance benefits. The children of working TBLG parents, who may not be biological or adoptive parents, may not be eligible for insurance. And, although all people may benefit from having a living will or durable power of attorney, should a TBLG person not have such legal documentation giving her/his partner the right to make medical decisions, such decisions and input frequently will be denied to that partner. Even visitation in many hospitals, nursing homes, and health care facilities often is denied to life partners of TBLG people.

Transgender people also face special health concerns. Insurance often excludes medical procedures needed by transgender individuals, especially gender reassignment surgery (GRS). This happens despite court rulings that have tended to point to excluding GRS simply because it is GRS as being insupportable (Israel & Tarver, 1997). Mental health professionals who are adequately trained in transgender needs are few. Although this population has been seriously understudied, anecdotal comments seem to indicate (and common sense supports) that the lack of compassion and understanding that many transgender people encounter in medical professionals creates a resistance to seeking needed treatment. Feinberg (1998) relates an incident of being told to leave a hospital emergency room without treatment for a serious infection, and with a temperature of 104 degrees, because of a doctor's intolerance of (and malpractice toward!) Feinberg, who is a transgender person. This kind of blatant risking of human life is intolerably antithetical to the professional codes of ethics of the helping professions and must be addressed immediately if ill individuals and their families are to get the care to which they are entitled.

Substance Abuse

Many studies have reported higher incidences of alcohol and drug abuse and alcohol dependency among bisexual, lesbian, and gay people than among heterosexuals (Paul, Stall, & Bloomfield, 1991). While there is criticism that these studies may focus on a disproportionately clinical population (Sell & Petrulio, 1996), there nevertheless seems to be, according to research by Orenstein (2001), a higher alcohol and other drug use rate among at least the BLG (if not the TBLG) population. This seems to hold true for TBLG youth as well, and there is also an indication that such youth tend to use harder drugs, such as cocaine, more often than their heterosexual counterparts (Faulkner & Cranston, 1988). There seems to be several reasons for this, some of which involve issues that may affect treatment and lower the success rate of TBLG people getting clean and sober if they are not addressed.

Finnegan and McNally (1996) note that internalized homophobia may lead to substance abuse or to depression, which may then lead to substance abuse. Addressing the symptoms of a problem like chemical dependency without also addressing the root usually results in being less successful at eradicating the problem. Therefore, where internalized homophobia is a root of substance abuse, this issue needs to be addressed, along with the addiction issues, if there is to be lasting change. Self-medicating over issues of shame, low self-esteem, and even self-hatred can be hard to remedy in TBLG people who correctly perceive widespread social condemnation of their sexual, affectional, and gender orientations.

Other factors may increase substance abuse in the TBLG communities, or at least be factors in lessening resistance to substance abuse and decreasing the chances of success at staying clean and sober. Often TBLG communities have few visible sources of contact, especially for vulnerable youths and others who are just coming out, and therefore TBLG individuals can be more prone to anxiety and possibly decreased coping skills. Two of the most common points of contact with the TBLG community are bars and parties (Orenstein, 2001). When these meeting grounds routinely combine alcohol, and possibly drugs, with sexuality (being possibly the only readily accessible way to meet potential dating, sexual, or life partners), the exposure can create a decreased resistance to and increased opportunities for addictions to form or manifest themselves. In addition, reports have indicated that tobacco, alcohol, and pharmaceutical companies are increasingly targeting advertising to TBLG populations whose publications, services, and events are routinely resource-poor and in need of available advertising dollars (Drabble, 2000).

Certain drugs, specifically methamphetamines, are seen as having aphrodisiaclike qualities that are thought to enhance or prolong sexual stimulation (Frosch, Shoptaw, Huber, Lawson, & Ling, 1996; Gawin, 1978). These drugs seem to have a growing popularity among men who have sex with men (Halkitis, Parsons, & Stirratt, 2001) and may increase HIV exposure by decreasing the use of safety precautions by intoxicated individuals. In fact, any sexual activity while under the influence of drugs or alcohol is less likely to involve safe sex precautions. Gay men who are intravenous drug users are often at higher risk for HIV infection (Pohl, 1995), and the dually diagnosed person with HIV and a substance abuse problem may well be dealing with an increased number of issues, such as shame, stigma, concerns about disclosure, and a feeling of uniqueness that results in a sense of isolation from both treatment communities (Pohl, 1995).

Treatment providers who address issues of chemical dependency and abuse with TBLG people need to examine many issues. They need to understand that internalized homophobia may be one of the root problems, and this problem will have to be understood if recovery is to be maintained. Coping with externalized homophobia or stigma from society, family, friends, and/or church may become a focus of the recovering person's treatment as well. Increasing the addicted person's social supports and decreasing the person's sense of being alone or unique are also crucial. Many find it beneficial to make use of TBLG Alcoholics Anonymous (AA) or Narcotics Anonymous (NA) meetings for TBLG people. Kus and Latcovich (1995) note that engagement with such groups can provide the TBLG person with an increased sense of trust in the group, a feeling of sharing similar life experiences with others, an opportunity to develop clean and sober TBLG networks, help in decreasing internalized homophobia, and possibly an increase in the person's exposure to positive views of spirituality (which may provide increased supports), among other positive considerations. While honoring a multidimensional contextual practice approach, human service practitioners can network with such organizations as the National Association of Lesbian and Gay Alcoholism Professionals (NALGAP) whose goals include advocating for competent and effective nonhomophobic recovery services, educating lesbian and gay providers about alcoholism and addiction, and providing support and communications for and among lesbian/gay and other interested providers (Finnegan & McNally, 1995).

Addressing issues of sexuality and relationships may be slightly different for TBLG people than for other clients as well. Sexuality may have always been associated with chemicals for TBLG clients, especially for those people whose only source of social contact has been in bars or at parties. While exclusively heterosexual people in recovery often have initial issues about having sober sexual relationships, too, if the meeting places for finding sexual partners are eliminated by the dictates of maintaining sobriety, there may be additional pressures for TBLG addicts to relapse. Relationship issues that may be common to all addicts, such as partners rescuing the addict or boundary issues with the partners (commonly thought of as codependency issues), may be exacerbated in TBLG people. These issues may be magnified by differences in partners' personal coming-out stages and by their different levels of internalized homophobia (Kus & Smith, 1995). In addition, differing dependencies on bars and other social spots wherein chemicals are present and available may present problems. Addressing these issues with couples may be vital if the recovering person is to succeed in maintaining sobriety.

Multidimensional contextual practice encourages exploration of the multiple factors that increase a TBLG person's or community's ability to remain in recovery from chemical dependency/alcoholism and to avoid relapse. Some of the factors have been briefly identified in this section. The human service practitioner is reminded to individualize client assessments and to honor clients' individual narratives while supporting clients' construction, deconstruction, and reconstruction of perceptions of self during the process of strengthening well-being.

Domestic Violence

Despite an almost conspiratorial silence, it is important for human service practitioners to recognize that violence between partners (domestic violence) exists within TBLG communities. For numerous reasons, this type of violence is often severely underreported or not taken seriously when reported, and survivors are underserved when they are identified. Tigert (2001) notes that lesbian intimate partner battering is underrecognized and misunderstood. One study conducted in New York with Latin men who have sex with men indicated that 51% of them had experienced some type of domestic violence at the hands of partners (Nieves-Rosa, Carballo-Dieguez, & Dolezal, 2000).

Violence can include not only physical or emotional abuse, but also forced sexual contact. In the case of men who are forced to be receptive to anal intercourse, the increase risk of HIV infection is no small concern in addition to the trauma inflicted and other possible physical injury (Nieves-Rosa, Carballo-Dieguez, & Dolezal, 2000). Another study conducted by Merrill and Wolfe (2000) indicates that the abuse experienced by men who have sex with men and who are battered by them tends to be similar in form to the abuse experienced by heterosexual and lesbian women who are abused by intimate partners. The main reasons that these men stay in the relationship (in the hope that the abuser will change and in the hope for love) are very similar to the reasons cited by women who encounter domestic violence, although men tend not to cite reasons of financial dependency. In addition, HIV status may lead some men to stay in abusive relationships (Merrill & Wolfe, 2000).

Often same-sex intimate partner violence is minimized. Sometimes assumptions are made that two women are not capable of truly inflicting harm on one another. This can create a minimization of the harm of such battering and other forms of abuse (Hammond, 1989). Sometimes a cultural assumption of women as more nonviolent or loving can keep human service practitioners and others from validating reports of woman-on-woman violence. With men it is sometimes assumed that they will fight back and be more capable of resisting physical or sexual assault than will female partners of men. All of this minimizes what is known of the emotional and power differentials that often exist in domestically violent situations.

In addition to external denials, often the people involved and the TBLG community at large is reluctant to discuss such abuse. There can be many reasons for this, and some of them are no different than those exclusively heterosexual people may have for not reporting abuse (shame, reflections on personal judgment, etc.). Those in the TBLG community, however, may also fear that acknowledging the existence of intimate partner abuse may reinforce homophobia and therefore cause greater impediments to social acceptance (Morrow & Hawxhurst, 1989). Or there may be concerns about perceived or actual homophobic responses from law enforcement officers or from medical providers. In addition, some may be concerned about being forced to reveal their sexual or gender orientation to strangers or that their orientation may inadvertently be revealed in the process of pressing charges or gaining access to services. Another major factor that influences the needs of this population on many levels can be internalized homophobia. The internalized hatred of one's sexual orientation can lead to shame or a feeling of deserving to be treated poorly or even violently. It can be assumed that this possibility of shame or a lack of self-acceptance could be present for transgender people as well, despite the literal exclusion of this population from the phrase "internalized homophobia."

Perceived or actual homophobic responses to battered TBLG people (Merrill & Wolfe, 2000; Turell, 1999) and inadequate supportive responses (Tigert, 2001) often keep people from reporting or seeking needed services for intimate partner violence in the TBLG community. Male survivors may be further shamed or may experience a "blaming of the victim" mentality for not leaving abusive situations sooner. A man may not be allowed into a battered "women's" shelter even if he has no other safe place to escape to. Human service practitioners may be more likely to employ a couples theory model of treatment with two female partners, thus ignoring the safety precaution of seeing individuals separately that is usually taken when a male–female battering couple is seen. Sexual abuse of female partners by other females may be minimized or ignored completely. Thus, the human service practitioner may be relied upon to have knowledge of and sensitivity to an issue that even the domestic violence survivors may not feel safe in approaching.

Legal and Policy Limitations

Changing language and heterosexist/homonegative assumptions is a basic, human, pervasive intervention strategy for resisting oppression and assisting clients and others who are TBLG. But it is only a beginning. The ways in which legal and policy limitations often oppress TBLG people are many and varied. Discrimination in housing; in the workplace; in the ability to wed and indulge in the economic benefits that brings, in raising, adopting, and keeping custody of children; in the very acts of being intimate with a same-sex partner—all of these, and others, are ways in which TBLG people can, and often do, experience legalized discrimination.

Appleby and Anastas (1998) have identified nine areas in which they feel much of the public policy agenda of people working toward equalizing the rights of TBLG people should focus. These are:

1. *Civil rights* (e.g., the repeal of state sodomy laws, passage of antidiscrimination statutes, and legal recognition of relationships, i.e., marriage or domestic partnership)
2. *Violence/hate crimes* (e.g., protection against gay-bashing, harassment, and abuse)
3. *Substance abuse* (e.g., increased awareness of, access to, and the development of drug and alcohol services that are sensitive to the needs of gay, lesbian, and bisexual [and transgender] clients)
4. *Health care* (e.g., ensuring access to as well as the quality of gay-sensitive services in regard to sexually transmitted diseases, AIDS care, reproductive rights, equity for women's health issues, and new reproductive technologies such as alternative insemination)
5. *Mental health services based on affirming models*
6. *Community, family, and social life* (e.g., custody, child and foster care rights)
7. *Youth services* (e.g., expansions of services to reflect the increase in numbers and the different life histories and expectations of the gay and lesbian elders of the future)
8. *Elder care* (e.g., expansion of services to reflect the increase in numbers and the different life histories and expectations of the gay and lesbian elders of the future)
9. *Equity in tax, insurance, and retirement benefits* (Appleby & Anastas, 1998, p. 407)

These issues, strictly speaking, go beyond legislation and possibly in some areas, such as sensitivity in social services, beyond a narrowly focused definition of public policy. However, when the basic laws, which are supposed to provide protection and a basic level of privacy, are actively reflective of discriminatory beliefs and oppressions, it is likely that any other changes will either result from opposition to these laws and policies, or will call them into question in a relatively short period of time.

Therefore, as they are encouraged to do by multidimensional contextual practice, human service practitioners must include a focus on the larger social issues that are legislated, adjudicated, and determined by social policy. Any other work toward alleviating homonegativity and heterosexism, or any other individual work with TBLG individuals, will ring hollow if the practitioner remains inactive in attempting to address the legalized and socially condoned forms of homonegative and heterosexual violence and oppression. There is a need to actively campaign for antidiscrimination laws and candidates (including openly TBLG candidates) and against any limiting of the civil, equal rights of TBLG people. Limiting custody, inheritance, insurance options, same-sex marriages, and other legal rights afforded to presumably exclusively heterosexual people is discriminatory.

Children and the Transgender, Bisexual, Lesbian, and Gay Communities

Possibly nowhere else is it so obvious that problems will be eradicated once oppression is eliminated as it is when addressing issues of children and the TBLG communities. TBLG people were children, they interact with children, and some will have children. This seems obvious, but it creates concerns for many people and causes problems for many others.

Most TBLG people have (or had) heterosexual parents (regarding lesbians specifically, Pollack, 1987). Family dynamics and background have repeatedly been shown not to cause a person's sexual orientation (Hitchens, 1979; Hitchens & Price, 1979; Martin & Lyon, 1972). Even asking what causes a nonexclusive heterosexual sexual orientation or a transgender orientation is often viewed suspiciously. Efforts to identify causes have been precursors to attempts to "cure" TBLG people of their identities, a mind-set that clearly implies a problem with being TBLG. But it is this very mind-set that leads to multiple problems for children and for TBLG people who interact with or parent children.

An immediate and incredibly painful issue for TBLG people is child custody. "In the eyes of most heterosexual people, the nonbiological or nonadoptive [TBLG] parent is simply not a parent at all" (Slater, 1995, p. 10). In a survey of studies done between 1985 and 1995, there were no developmental or emotional deficits found in children raised by gay or lesbian parents, and there has been at least one other study indicating that children of lesbians may have better-than-average self-confidence, independence, and self-acceptance (McDaniel, 1995). Despite these findings and others, custody of children by biological parents who are TBLG is still sometimes effectively contested by the other biological parent or by grandparents. Laws vary from state to state, and judgments have been inconsistent. But when biological parents can (and sometimes do) lose custody due solely to their sexual or gender orientation, can it be any surprise that the partners of TBLG biological or adoptive parents are not acknowledged as parents?

The same-sex partners of biological parents cannot be placed on the birth certificates of children, even when those children are conceived through *alternative insemination* (a term preferred to *artificial insemination*). The partner, who may have been involved in the process of the conception and birthing of the child, and who may support the child emotionally and financially, cannot be legally acknowledged without a formal adoption process that is not in any way automatic. Should a judge rule or a human service practitioner advocate against such an adoption, even if only on the grounds of the sexual/gender orientation of the parent, the adoption may be permanently blocked, and the child may be denied the safety and emotional satisfaction of having two legally recognized parents. Inheritance, insurance, rights to stay with a second parent should one parent die—all of these will be denied the child whose parents are not both legally recognized.

Beyond the risks to the immediate family, there are other concerns for TBLG people and their children that originate in the prejudice and discrimination levied against this population. "Although intergenerational interdependence was obvious in the past, it is now more hidden" (Lehr, 1999, p. 142), and interaction between elders and children is becoming more and more intermittent and infrequent. When TBLG parents are concerned about acceptance from their extended families, or from the larger community, such intergenerational interactions are likely to continue to decrease, thus limiting the sense of community, continuity, and history that children of TBLG people and, indeed, the whole community, may experience. There are also other ways that children are affected. Partners sometimes bring children into TBLG relationships. The partners of these parents often act as any stepparent would, providing emotional and financial support to the children and parenting them. However, the societal or even extended familial recognition of this role may be denied to these stepparents, and the existence and legitimacy of this family structure may be invalidated by schools, social services agencies, hospitals, and other institutions that deal with children and their parents.

Children with TBLG parents are often the victims of heterosexism; it is assumed that they have two opposite-sex parents. Although there may be an increasing allowance for a single-parent structure to families, what about the children who live with dual parents who are of the same sex? There is a burden placed on these children to "come out" as children of same-sex parents or to allow heterosexist misconceptions and assumptions to stand. And what about children whose friends are not allowed to come to their home because of their TBLG parents, or those who are teased or subjected to violence by peers for having parents who are different, or those who are denied the opportunity to have their parents as room-parents because of the legitimate fear of teasing or violence against the children if the parents are seen and known? The human services practitioner who works with these children may need to be aware of resources for networking like PFLAG (Parents and Friends of Lesbians and Gays) or COLAGE (Children of Lesbians and Gays Everywhere) in order to provide some community and referrals to resources for these children and their families.

TBLG people who are parents sometimes feel they must hide their true sexual/gender orientation or risk creating stress for their children. They may fear losing custody of their children, even when some research indicates that the more open and honest one is about one's sexual orientation, the fewer problems will be created in the relationship with the child (Kirk, 1989). TBLG teachers, therapists, daycare providers, girl/boy scout leaders, church ministers, and even human service practitioners who work with children often feel, accurately, that they will not be accepted or allowed to continue working with children if their sexual/gender orientation is known, so they hide. This not only creates stress for the individual hiding and perpetuates oppression, but it also robs society of the opportunity to see the competency and commitment that many TBLG professionals exhibit daily. This exposure would help ease the discomfort and the unfamiliarity of those who mistakenly assume that they have little or no contact with TBLG people.

Transgender, Bisexual, Lesbian, and Gay Youth

Many human services practitioners have difficulty believing that teenagers, or even younger children, can know that they are transgender, bisexual, lesbian or gay. Other members of society, including parents, also may have such difficulties. As has been noted previously, sexual orientation issues may indeed be first known or suspected in early adolescence, and sexual orientation itself is often determined well before that. The continued denial of adults who do not want to be confronted with TBLG identities in youth contributes to ongoing difficulties for these young people that can include health problems, chronic stress, poor self-esteem, homelessness, abuse, and even suicide.

One of the greatest problems for TBLG youth can be the loss of support of the family. All youth, to some degree or another, have a desire to please their parental figures, and they have a fear of rejection—from parents, from peers, and from society at large. In addition, adolescence is a time of discovering identity and exploring sexuality. Often, when young people start to learn of a TBLG identity within themselves, they have a fear that they will both displease and be rejected by those they care about and who care for them. Overlaid on top of all this is the need for TBLG youth to come to grips with an identity that society tells them is despised and hated (Mallon, 1998a). Youth may therefore feel they need to hide or to change themselves. Denying the gender/sexual orientation, they often discover, is one approach that can be taken, especially initially. But as the identity becomes more undeniable, the young person may decide to hide out of fear of both exposure and its consequences. If the young people do not have a sound knowledge base about the normalcy of TBLG orientations, or do not find supportive figures, they may determine that their best option is to try and change or "fix" themselves by refusing their identity. This might include blatant homophobia directed at others, or dating or sexual activity that feels forced and is not actually desired.

Parents, too, when confronted with the TBLG identity of a child, may deny it or refuse to deal with it, creating a familial silence or culture of avoidance. Parents may also try to hide the truth from themselves or may deny their child's ability to know or claim such an identity. Sometimes parents insist it is just a phase and will pass as the child/youth gets older and has more life experience. Parents may feel embarrassment or even a sense of personal failure that their child is TBLG. There may be a sense of fear or shame about how extended family members might react. Ultimately, some parents reject their TBLG children/youth, excluding them from family life and even possibly putting them out of the home (Mallon, 1998b). If parents do accept their youth's TBLG identity, they may well require some assistance from supportive resources in the TBLG community or from professional support (like that which social workers, counselors, or psychologists may be able to provide).

In addition to family rejection, TBLG youth also face other risks. Lesbian and gay youth are often targeted for violence because of their sexual orientation (Comstock, 1991; Garnets et al., 1992; Herek & Berrill, 1992). In fact, the more gender-nonconforming the youth, the higher the risk of violence or abuse (Mallon, 1998b). Sexual assault, including rape, of nonexclusively heterosexual youth is not uncommon as well (Comstock, 1991). Gibson (1989) notes that there is an increased risk of suicide attempts among lesbian and gay youth (rates are two to three times higher than among heterosexual youth), and that an estimated 30% of completed teen suicides are committed by lesbian and gay youth. Escapism into alcohol or other drugs may increase. Youth who are evicted from family homes may become homeless or live on the streets, with all the accompanying dangers of exposure to survival sex, substance abuse, violence, and health concerns.

Youth who are marginalized or abused may not complete school, may not have regular health care or immunizations, and may not have any reliable sex education or information on safe sex precautions. This increases the risk to adolescents who are already at high risk for HIV infection. Worldwide, one out of every two people who are HIV positive became infected between the ages of 15 and 24 (Ryan & Futterman, 1998). With unstable or unsupportive living environments, these young people will be even less likely to receive adequate health care or information on how to decrease the spread of the infection.

Gay youth also face ostracization by friends, schoolmates, and even educators. In addition, as mentioned previously, they may be kicked out of their homes by parents who are unaccepting, forcing them to live on the streets or in shelters, sometimes having to participate in survival sex in order to support themselves. Youth who are placed in out-of-home care are often there as a result of family violence or abuse. Out-of-home placements are often not warm and friendly, and minors tend to experience multiple placements. It is rare to find group or foster homes that are openly accepting and supportive of TBLG youth. Staff may have all the reactions of disbelief or rejection that a family of origin may have for a TBLG youth. Youth may find that staff, in some extreme cases, may try to sexually abuse them in the name of "curing" them of their same-sex attractions (Mallon, 1998b); or the other youth in these facilities may be verbally or physically abusive, and staff may or may not be willing or know how to decrease this abuse.

School environments are increasingly finding themselves at risk of lawsuits when they fail to protect TBLG youth from harassment or abuse from other students (or from teachers). One risk for harassed and abused youth is that they may drop out of school when they do not receive adequate protection from school staff. Additionally, not addressing this type of harassment or violence only perpetuates more violence. It allows this type of environment to continue in the schools, and does nothing to stop or challenge the socialization of these abusive youth into abusive adults.

Clearly, then, TBLG youth not only face incredible stresses that place them at risk, but they also face these stresses during a developmental period in their lives that is full of challenges and difficulties in and of itself. The sense of worthlessness and isolation that many of these youth feel, on top of dealing with the adolescent tasks of identity formation, while also dealing with issues of sexual/gender orientation, can be overpowering. The task of the human services practitioner is to help the youth incorporate the TBLG identity as a positive part of the self. By engaging in multidimensional contextual practice, the human service practitioner may be able to help TBLG youth see that the poor fit is from an intrinsic wrongness not in them, but rather in the society that does not accept TBLG expressions of gender and sexuality (Mallon, 1998a).

Human services practitioners should also provide a safe place for all teens, TBLG or not, to express concerns and questions about identity issues and sexuality. The human services practitioner needs to worry less about identifying TBLG youth and more about creating a safe, open space that will communicate to TBLG youth that this is a place/agency that is accepting of TBLG people. Human services practitioners need to:

- Develop resources in the community that specialize in TBLG issues and be able to refer teens to them.
- Be aware of nonsexualized safe referrals and community resources.
- Never pretend to have all the answers or to pretend a comfort level that they do not have. An all-or-nothing approach to competency or comfort should be avoided. When it is appropriate or needed, practitioners can ask questions about the youth's sexual/affectional orientation and gender presentation, but they must be clear about why they are asking. If it is idle curiosity, it is probably not appropriate. If practitioners need to ask, they should tell the client/youth why they are asking and what they want to know.
- Seek out training specific to TBLG youth and ask for consultation.

Mallon (1999) also suggests some guidelines for working with TBLG youth who are coming out to family members. How generally closed or open is the family system? How has the family dealt with new situations in the past? How flexible is the family? Are there other "out" TBLG family members? If so, how have they been treated? If the youth feels closer to, safer with, or more accepted by certain family members than by others, these may be the people the youth should first come out to. However, the spread of information within the family must also be considered. Will the people in whom the youth confides keep the information to themselves? Human services practitioners should help youth role-play and should be available to moderate or to provide crisis intervention to the family and the youth if needed. The human services practitioner may need to educate the youth that coming out is an ongoing process, even within the family. An initial disclosure may be a hurdle in and of itself, but the process the family begins of becoming accustomed to and integrating the information is probably not a quick one, and TBLG youth may not know or may forget that. Families may go into denial or ignore the disclosure in the future, and they may not be comfortable with or welcoming of friends and significant others who may be TBLG.

As with any resistance to oppression, macro-level interventions must also be undertaken. Training and education of school staff must be implemented, and staff at both schools and out-of-home care facilities must be made accountable for keeping minors safe from harassment or violence. Ongoing efforts to organize and support community centers are needed. Centers like the Minnesota Youth and AIDS Projects and District 202 (Yoakam, 1999), and Project 10 in Los Angeles, which is described as a place dedicated to "education, reduction of verbal and physical abuse, suicide prevention, and accurate AIDS information" (Friends of Project 10, Inc., 1989, p. 1), must be afforded funding and staff support as well as referrals. Advocacy for safer out-of-home placements must occur, and continuing education training is needed for workers involved in such placements. There is also a need for more social services agencies like the Gay and Lesbian Adolescent Social Services (GLASS), which both advises child welfare agencies and serves as a licensed care home for TBLG youth (Mallon, 1998b).

One last consideration involves the possible presentation of TBLG youth and their understanding of oppression and belonging. The designation of a "Queer" identity is appearing more and more frequently in the literature about TBLG issues (Atkins, 1998; Kirsch, 2000; Lehr, 1999; Turner, 2000). There is a call for community and coalition building between TBLG people and an understanding of the underlying "otherness" from the heterosexual paradigm. Sometimes this becomes so pronounced that people who identify as "Queer" refuse to further classify themselves. This may come from a desire to claim community with a larger group (than simply bisexuals or gay men, for example), or it may be the expression of exclusively heterosexual youth who support TBLG friends. It might also be an expression of the fluidity that some feel can make up some people's experience of gender and affectional/sexual orientations. Whatever the reason, more and more youth are presenting with a self-named "Queer" identity. Human services practitioners may not know or be comfortable with this nomenclature, and sometimes even other members of the TBLG community are uncomfortable with it, especially some older, more conservative, or assimilationist members. It is important that human services practitioners increase their familiarity and relative comfort with this term, and also that they consider the possible implications for choosing it.

In addition to the aforementioned factors, human service practitioners have a responsibility to identify and honor the resilience and powerful spirits of the youth they encounter. Often TBLG youth, regardless of adversities encountered, continue to strive for attainment and/or maintenance of well-being. The human spirit cannot be underestimated.

Couple Issues

Research on issues that couples face when one or both partners are bisexual or transgender is very sparse. There is a great need for research in this area, not just for the people who are directly affected and service providers to these groups, but also for the sake of the information about human experience and relationship issues in general. Most of the information available about issues with couples in the TBLG community has to do with lesbians and gay men. As with all couples, many areas need to be examined if healthy relationships are to be created. These areas at least include personal, family of origin, and legal and societal issues, as well as issues that may be particular to the couple.

Discordant levels of outness have been shown to be a factor in relationship failure for lesbian and gay couples (Keeler, 1999). The stress of hiding such a basic tenet of one's identity, such as one's gender or sexual orientation, is inordinate. In a couple, this stress level is increased simply because both people bring this stress to the relationship. If one partner is more open than the other, the level of stress of both will increase. The less open partner will have to deal with concerns of disclosure by the other partner, either direct or accidental disclosure. Even being associated with a more out person, especially if the couple chooses to live together or socialize in public, will present a higher possibility of disclosure. The more out partner will, in turn, have to deal with an increased level of secretness. Both partners will also have the added stress, and possible guilt, of creating this stress in the other partner. The less out partner may have very tangible repercussions if that partner's identity is disclosed (losses of job, housing, etc.). Fear of disclosure can lead a couple who lives together to hide the true nature of the relationship when relatives come to visit or stay. The added threat of loss, whether of family affection, job, or loss in other significant areas, *makes* discordant levels of outness an even more pressing issue for some.

It is relatively self-evident that prior relationship issues and prior childhood abuse issues may be stressors for a couple. A woman who was sexually abused may have sexual intimacy issues, or a man whose prior partner had multiple affairs may find himself less trusting and willing to commit to another partner. Prior history influences all people's current and future relationships. Such issues may need to be distinguished by therapists as issues that really are more about the past history of a person and less about issues intrinsic to the person's gender or sexual orientation.

Family of origin issues may affect a couple as well. How out each partner is to that partner's family may be an issue. Some people choose not to reveal a primary relationship to their family, which may contribute to their partners' feeling rejected or disrespected by their partner. The partner of someone who chooses not to reveal the primary relationship may feel that their relationship is not as valued by that partner or that the partner is ashamed of the relationship. While these issues are admitted to be part of the general consensus of possible issues lesbian and gay couples encounter, at least one survey indicates that the level of outness to families of origin is not indicative of the level of satisfaction in relationships (Green, Bettinger, & Zacks, 1996), although this study did not indicate if differing levels of outness between partners were significant.

Some families are more accepting of and inviting to lesbian and gay couples than others. Some continue contact with the family member only and ignore or directly exclude the partner from family activities and invitations. The level of acceptance in the families of origins of partners can contribute to the social supports available to a couple. Exclusion and nonacceptance, or partial acceptance, can lead to feelings of anger, rejection, and loss in either or both partners. These factors can create stress for the couple's functioning.

Legal and societal issues of discrimination also create stressors for lesbian and gay couples. Such issues may include the lack of societal recognition of such relationships (e.g., in the form of rejection of same-sex marriage), and the inability of same-sex partners to take sick leave to tend to their ill partners or family death leave to grieve their passing. Raising children together as couples is still a legal and social challenge for most same-sex couples (see the previous section on children). These issues not only require the human services practitioner to help individual or both members of a couple to cope, but they also present a reminder of the already-stated need for human services practitioners to work toward eradicating these legal and social prohibitions that contribute to the oppression of same-sex couples.

When dealing individually with people with relationship issues, or when dealing with a couple together, human services practitioners need not only the same skill set that any counselor, social worker, psychologist, or psychiatrist would need, but they also need to be acquainted with some of the issues particular to same-sex couples. It is important to remember that lesbian and gay couples may present for human or health services for a multitude of reasons. Presupposing that the issues are specific to sexual or gender orientation is a stereotyping danger that social services practitioners need to avoid. There are, however, some issues that McVinney (1998) has identified as being common issues that bring, at least, gay male couples into supportive social services. These include conflicts associated with

- Different levels of being "out" about their gay identities
- HIV health status concerns
- Internalized homophobia
- Differences in extended family involvement
- Differences in constructions and expectations of coupling
- Differences in age
- Differences in expectations of sexual exclusivity/nonexclusivity
- Perceived inequalities of power and difficulty in negotiating
- Chemical use, chemical dependency, and recovery
- Finances and financial disparity

Other issues that sometimes are presumed to be common in lesbian and gay relationships center on the amount of fusion/enmeshment and disengagement in these relationships. Lesbians are sometimes presumed to easily fall into fusion or enmeshment, while gay men are sometimes presumed to be too disengaged. Research by Green, Bettinger, and Zacks (1996) seems to contradict the assumption that gay male couples are more disengaged than heterosexual couples. Their research indicates that couples with the highest degree of cohesion are first lesbian couples, then gay male couples, and then heterosexual couples, and that such cohesion leads to greater flexibility in couples and greater levels of satisfaction. Barranti (1998) posits that high emotional closeness in lesbian couples can be an adaptive response to hostile or non-nutritive environments to which they may be subjected.

As noted previously in McVinney's (1998) list, couples may also have issues around sexuality, including frequency of sexual contact and exclusivity that limits a partner's sexual expression within the couple. Lesbians, in particular, have complaints about differing levels of desire between partners; these may have to do with genital sexual contact or complaints about the infrequency of such contact (Roth, 1989). However, lesbians experience higher levels of nongenital contact that is experienced as sexual (such as hugging, kissing, touching, etc.) than do gay or heterosexual couples (Blumstein & Schwartz, 1983: Loulan, 1984). This does not negate some lesbian couples' concerns about lessening of sexual genital contact between partners.

This issue has been tied to internalized homophobia, differences in partners' abilities to vocalize sexual desires, women's acculturation to being sexually responsive to another and not initiating sexual activity, and to having fewer opportunities than heterosexual women to speak to confidants (e.g., sisters) about sexual issues (Gair, 1995; Kirkpatrick, 1991; Loulan, 1984).

Gay male couples may be sexually exclusive or not; gay men may form couples out of sexual interests and needs primarily, out of affectional needs primarily, or out of a combination of these needs or other needs completely. The assumption that gay males couple only out of sexual needs/desires is a presumption made by practitioners who rarely work with gay couples (McVinney, 1998). Gay male couples also may experience stressors around sexual dysfunction, but because of stereotypes of gay men being very sexually active or focused, or because of providers' discomfort levels, service providers may ignore or minimize these issues (George & Behrendt, 1988). For the same reasons, a man himself may feel ashamed of or inhibited from identifying such issues.

Loss of any significant relationship, through dissolution of the relationship or through death of one of the people in the relationship, is difficult. Loss of partnered TBLG relationships can be exacerbated by the lack of acknowledgment of these relationships when they were intact, and by the lack of resources for dealing with the loss of these relationships when they dissolve or are severed by death. People who are not "out" about their sexual orientation or relationships can have layers added to the grief process by their inability to openly acknowledge their loss or seek support (Seabold, 1997). Western societal prohibitions against openly expressing grief, especially for men, make it hard for anyone to grieve, but they can create even more of a homophobic environment for gay men who choose to express grief (Dane & Miller, 1992). The lack of acknowledgment of the longevity of some TBLG relationships and the additional weight of grief experienced by someone who had a long-term established relationship also can diminish the support given to TBLG widowers. Recognition of the added complications that may exist for this population in relationship dissolutions or deaths is important for any human service practitioner doing grief work with a TBLG person.

All of the issues discussed here can complicate the myriad issues that all couples, same-sex or opposite-sex, may bring to human service practitioners. In addition, some researchers posit that both lesbian and gay couples have specific couple formation and life stages (McWhirter & Matteson, 1984, 1985, 1988; Slater, 1995) with which practitioners may be wise to be familiar. Some authors accentuate the effects of one set of stressors over another on the possible success rate of particular couplings (Green, Bettinger, & Zacks, 1996). Knowledge of all these and other factors is important for practitioners dealing with same-sex couples.

Aging People

Apuzzo (2001) says that aging TBLG people are doubly or triply discriminated against due to sexual orientation and ageism, as well as possible prejudice based on race, gender, and socioeconomic status. Other sources state that most aging gay men have experienced discrimination based on sexual orientation, and many experience discrimination based on age (Brown, Alley, Sarosy, Quarto, & Cook, 2001).

Some authors say that TBLG people have no more special needs or considerations than their exclusively heterosexual counterparts, but many others say that aging TBLG people have at least special needs, if not advantages (Ehrenberg, 1996). Ehrenberg points out that many of the studies that have been done about aging in the TBLG community have been limited to unrepresentative samples of predominantly white, well-educated, affluent, and physically healthy older adults. These samples tend to be psychologically healthy and to have good social and coping skills. But, what about the less affluent, less physically healthy, and less mobile seniors? Jones (2001) says there are issues of depression, alcoholism, and other substance abuse, as well as decreasing social systems due to age-related and AIDS-related deaths in the aging TBLG population. In addition, ageism and loneliness are compounded for many older people depending on the societal views that were prevalent when they were younger (Mitchell, 2000). Those who grew up in times when there was little support in the form of strong and visible TBLG communities, or who felt unsafe in coming out to friends and family, may have more trouble with social isolation, although some research indicates that there is no correlation between increased mental health and increased supports from TBLG communities (Grossman, D'Augelli, & O'Connell, 2001). An extensive study of 416 adults who were 60 to 91 years old in North America (Grossman, D'Augelli, & O'Connell, 2001) showed that while most reported fairly high self-esteem, many experienced loneliness, and those who were victimized in some way had decreased mental health. An incredible number of those in the study (93%) knew someone infected with HIV/AIDS. The emotional losses suffered by gay men due to the devastation of the gay community by AIDS have had a significant impact on the normal aging process of this group (Brown, Alley, Sarosy, Quarto, & Cook, 2001).

What seems to complicate aging in the TBLG community is the homophobia often encountered in other aging communities and resources for the aging, and the ageism that is experienced in the TBLG communities (Apuzzo, 2001). What is needed, says Apuzzo, is the education of politicians and service providers of the needs of TBLG elders and the education of the TBLG community as to the existence of as well as the needs of this population.

The aging TBLG population faces risks that do not exist for exclusively heterosexual people. For example, transgender elders may be at higher risk of poverty and financial insecurity due to lifelong exposure to discrimination in employment (Donovan, 2001). Transgender elders also may be less able to keep their transgender identities hidden from medical providers who may treat them in a discriminatory manner. Age-related health deterioration may then present increased risk to this population. As discussed in the section on legal and social concerns, elders in the TBLG community also may face concerns regarding their relationships. Even more than other people, they may need to have clear wills covering property, pets, and burial plans, so that partners are not barred from inheritance and planning roles. Durable powers of attorney (including for health care), living wills, and provisions for the conservatorship of jointly owned property may be necessary for the protection of partners of aging TBLG people (Ettelbrick, 1991). Lifelong partners of TBLG people may be excluded from decisions about placement in nursing homes, from visitation in hospitals (especially in intensive care units) and nursing homes, and from access to medical information unless extraordinary legal measures are taken, given that marriage and its privileges are legally barred for these individuals. As discussed previously, there are typically no resources available for the partner of a TBLG elder who has died. Bereavement support groups do not usually acknowledge grieving life partners in such relationships. Hospice services often do not validate the relationships of TBLG people (Connolly, 1996), and caregiver supports and respite services are not readily available for same-sex partners who are caregivers.

Despite all these concerns for TBLG elders, at least one study (Berger & Kelly, 2001) says that gay men, and presumably other TBL people, have advantages that exclusively heterosexual people do not have in aging. A lifetime of fighting discrimination and stigma may make some people more adept at handling ageism and the loss of respect that this entails. Some TBLG people may find themselves more independent, having felt less able to rely on community, government, and family support, and thus having formed support systems outside the norms that may assist and support in old age.

While it remains to be seen if these strengths (which Berger and Kelly themselves admit are anecdotal rather than research-based) will bear out, it is important that the concerns faced by TBLG elders are not ignored and that they do not go unaddressed by human services practitioners who deal with the aging population. As in other arenas, social evolution away from discrimination and oppression will lessen the effects of homonegativity on the aging TBLG population, and human services practitioners need to work on further establishing the needs of aging TBLG communities and exploring services such as senior centers, senior social services, and assisted living for TBLG people.

IMPLICATIONS FOR MULTIDIMENSIONAL CONTEXTUAL PRACTICE

Multidimensional contextual practice, with its emphasis on multiple identities and person and environment contexts, seems ideally suited for working with and addressing the needs of TBLG people (Appleby & Anastas, 1998). The supports of diversity and multiple levels of intervention are essential to eradicating homonegativity and heterosexism and to increasing the functioning and opportunities for all TBLG people.

Social and Professional Attitudes

I start by identifying dimensional and contextual concerns confronting the various groups discussed in this chapter. Ample research has documented the dislike, disapproval, and fear of many presumably exclusively heterosexual people toward (specifically) lesbian and gay people (for reviews, see Herek, 1994, 1998). Recent research, however, has shown that a substantial minority of heterosexuals seem to have positive attitudes toward (specifically) bisexual, lesbian, and gay people (Devine, Evett, & Vasquez-Suson, 1996; Devine, Monteith, Zuwerink, & Elliot, 1991). Research also has indicated that human services practitioners, such as social workers, are less likely than the general population to hold homophobic views (Berkman & Zinberg, 1997).

This does not mean, though, that human services practitioners in general are completely immune to homonegativity. Some research has differentiated between heterosexism and homophobia, and found heterosexism to be more common and pervasive, and more likely to be found in human services practitioners as well as in other groups. One study found that while 90% of the human services practitioners interviewed were not homophobic, the majority of them did hold heterosexist attitudes (Berkman & Zinberg, 1997).

Specifically, people who have less contact with bisexual, lesbian, gay (and presumably transgender) individuals tend to be more homophobic and heterosexist (Berkman & Zinberg, 1997; Sakalli, & Ugurlu, 2001). Human services practitioners with higher levels of religiosity have an increase in these negative views, while those with a history of having been in psychotherapy tend to have lower rates of homonegativity and heterosexism. Other factors also may influence the level of homonegativity and heterosexism among human services practitioners, including gender of the human services practitioner (men being slightly more homophobic and significantly more heterosexist), gender of the nonheterosexual person (gay men seem to be targeted for more homonegativity than are lesbian women), and age (younger people tend to be less homophobic and heterosexist than older practitioners) (Berkman & Zinberg, 1997).

Age seems to influence human services practitioners' level of acceptance of nonexclusively heterosexual clients in more than one way. As mentioned, the age of the human services practitioner can be influential, but the age of the client is a factor as well. Human service practitioners seem to have a strong bias, when confronted with TBLG youth, toward discounting their sexual orientations as a phase, or as something not to be held as firm due to their young age (Mallon, 1998a). There is an overwhelming, heterosexist assumption that all youth are heterosexual. When people tell youth that they should wait until they are older to determine if they are really transgender, bisexual, lesbian, or gay, or when they indicate to them that it is possibly "just a phase," they send a clear message that to be other than exclusively heterosexual (i.e., to be transgender, bisexual, lesbian, or gay) is undesirable. Such statements may even imply that TBLG people have inferior sexual/gender orientations (Malyon, 1982), or these assertions, in rare cases, may be seen as a tenet of the older belief that homosexuality can be "cured." Although currently little belief is left in this curative social services approach (Bieber, et al., 1962; Cautela, 1967; Feldman, 1966; Feldman & MacCullough, 1965; Mayerson & Lief, 1965), the history of such approaches has tainted professional services in the eyes of many members of the TBLG community.

Human services practitioners need to be aware that some TBLG clients may see them as oppressive agents of social control. Many TBLG clients, over the course of their histories, have had negative experiences with practitioners—whether it was a psychologist, psychiatrist, or social worker who tried to "cure" them, or whether they were forced into psychotherapy or even medicated, hospitalized, or otherwise "treated" against their will (and better sense). Human services practitioners need to actively work to overcome the effects of such histories of oppression as well as the generalized fear and suspicion of homonegativity and heterosexism that many TBLG people will bring to services.

Professional Education

"Research on gay and lesbian people provides new and enhanced paradigms and ways of thinking about the whole of human behavior" (Strickland, 1995, p. 139). This is especially true in the study of the diversity of human experience, but also true in the education of students and human services practitioners about the range of human adaptation and resiliency (Appleby & Anastas, 1998). Education about and research on the TBLG populations, therefore, are important for many reasons. The primary reason remains the need to understand this population so as to end discrimination and oppression of these people as well as to adequately provide needed social services.

Pertaining to the curriculum of human services practitioners, especially about TBLG people, the Council on Social Work Education (CSWE) has set an outstanding example by requiring teaching content in these areas. This council requires schools of social work to include curriculum about the needs of and service provision to lesbian and gay people (CSWE, 1992). (They do need to update their inclusiveness of language to include transgender and bisexual people.) But, are inclusive texts and language in the curriculum adequate? Perhaps there are field placement opportunities that can be actively procured to allow further education on these populations. Such further efforts need to be made in several arenas. Nondiscrimination policies to ensure protection for both educators and students need to be in place. How can an institution logically teach against the oppression of TBLG people, and yet allow unequal or discriminatory practices to exist in its own practices? Even if there are no active inequities, a failure to vocalize support of TBLG people or to state that oppression toward TBLG people will not be tolerated is complicity with the shroud of silence and invisibility placed around this population.

As discussed previously, homonegative and heterosexist language is unacceptable and oppressive. Curricula and policies need to be reviewed periodically for such language, which can be pervasive and insidious in this culture. There also must be support for and encouragement of TBLG scholarship and research. It must be afforded the same respect and support that such work is afforded in any other field of interest or in regard to any other cultural group (Morrow, 1996). Attention also must be paid to recruiting and retaining not only openly TBLG faculty, but also students (Mackelprang, Ray, & Hernandez-Peck, 1996). Diversity of staff, faculty, and the student body shows a commitment level that is more integrated into the daily functioning of the institution than simply adding one textbook or one class lecture on the needs of the TBLG community.

MULTIDIMENSIONAL CONTEXTUAL PRACTICE PRINCIPLES

Any effort to effectively counter well-organized or deeply ingrained oppression and discriminatory behavior will require both micro-level and macro-level interventions (Kirsch, 2000), as well as trust in the "wisdom of uncertainty." The view of this text is that other levels and contexts also have to be addressed if oppression is truly to be challenged and if individuals from oppressed backgrounds and cultures are to become fully functioning members of the greater society. Addressing these specific issues will offer social services students the opportunity to increase their general knowledge of the issues of this population and to develop micro skills with these clients. But, it is not enough to know that, for example, TBLG people have to continually navigate a coming-out process, or that spirituality remains simultaneously a source of resilience and oppression for nonexclusively heterosexual and transgender people. Knowing about specific issues is only the beginning of the educative process for gaining competency in dealing with issues affecting TBLG people.

Human services practitioners are taught to put people at ease and to form positive relationships with clients. In our desire to demonstrate that we are not discriminatory or prejudiced, we sometimes may make overreaching efforts to demonstrate our nonjudgmental attitudes. Conley, Calhoun, Evett, and Devine (2001) identified the major or most common mistakes that lesbians and gays attributed to some heterosexuals. Pointing out that one knows a gay person and continuing to emphasize one's lack of prejudice seem to be common mistakes of well-meaning but anxious heterosexuals. In addition, relying on stereotypes or making assumptions from them, ignoring TBLG issues, using subtle prejudicial language, and not owning up to one's discomfort with TBLG people were all found to be common mistakes that communicate homonegativity and heterosexism to TBLG people (Conley, Calhoun, Evett, & Devine, 2001).

Most people would probably think it obvious that blatantly oppressive behaviors and language are inappropriate and unacceptable. Schope and Eliason (2000), who identified such blatantly discriminatory and counterhelpful behaviors, indicated that people who may not be actively homophobic can still fall very short of engaging in behaviors that are considered helpful to and supportive of TBLG people.

The following fifteen points provide a useful guide for beginning to incorporate positive and affirming attitudes and behaviors toward nonexclusive heterosexuals and transgender people. This list is offered as a beginning threshold for becoming competent or increasing competency while working with TBLG people.

1. Be aware of the generalizations you make. Assume there are TBLG people where you go to school, where you work, in your family, and so on.
2. Notice the times you disclose your heterosexuality.
3. For sensitization, hold hands with someone of the same sex in a *safe* public place.
4. Wear pro-TBLG buttons and t-shirts.
5. Read positive TBLG books and periodicals, and include them in your school or workplace libraries and offices.
6. Attend TBLG cultural and community events.
7. Challenge homophobic jokes and epithets.
8. Use inclusive, affirming, and gender-neutral language when referring to sexuality and human relationships in everyday speech, on written forms, and so on. Say the words *lesbian, gay, bisexual,* and *transgender* each day in a positive way.
9. Include "sexual orientation" as a protected category in your antidiscrimination policies.
10. Extend "domestic partnership" benefits to TBLG employees on a par with those extended to heterosexual employees.
11. Develop support groups and heterosexual allies for TBLG people.

12. Monitor politicians, the media, and organizations to ensure accurate coverage of TBLG issues.
13. Work and vote for candidates who take pro-TBLG stands.
14. Coordinate discussions and workshops, and include material in educational curricula on the topics of homophobia and TBLG experiences.
15. Implement and participate in a "safe space" program in your school or workplace. (Blumenfeld, 1998)

MULTIDIMENSIONAL CONTEXTUAL AGENCY CONCERNS

Like educational institutions, social service institutions that wish to meet ethical expectations and to provide competent, compassionate, and equitable services to TBLG clients must also provide safe and fair work environments. Antidiscrimination policies and equity in benefits (e.g., sick leave for domestic partners, domestic partner benefits, parental leave for same-sex partners) constitute the basic minimum that social services agencies should offer. Agencies also need to modify their workplace cultures to incorporate ongoing trainings for staff, encourage the use of inclusive language in the workplace as well as in all policies and procedures, and demonstrate sensitivity to the diverse expressions of gender and affectional/sexual orientation of both staff and clients.

Sexual orientation can become an issue in social service agencies. Agencies must recognize and deal with their own internal issues, and reevaluate means of addressing these periodically, or it will be evident to both staff and clients that the particular agency is not supportive or safe for TBLG people. It has been shown that not dealing with sexual orientation issues related to lesbian and gay people can interfere with supervision if the issues are not addressed and if people in agencies do not receive needed education about these issues (Halpert & Pfaller, 2001). Agencies should consider the impressions that they create for someone coming into the place for the first time. Is there a solely heterosexist impression in the art decorating the waiting room walls? Do the intake forms provide "married or single" as the only relationship choice? Are the forms worded so that transgender people will know how to identify their chosen gender expressions on the forms? Do staff members react visibly if someone's appearance is different from what is expected? For example, if a "masculine-looking" person came into the agency wearing a dress and makeup, would the staff display an attitude of acceptance and welcome the person, or would the individual be judged?

Appleby and Anastas (1998) offer some affirmative practice guidelines for working with TBLG people. In this model, human services practitioners:

Do not automatically assume that a client is heterosexual.
Assume it is likely that homophobia within the client and/or in society is the problem, rather than the client's sexual orientation, and view same-gender sexual desires and behaviors as a normal variation in human sexuality.
Accept the adoption of a transgender, bisexual, lesbian, or gay identity as a positive outcome of the process in which individuals question or work on developing their gender or sexual identity.

Accept the development of a transgender, bisexual, lesbian, or identity as positive, meaning that a goal of affirmative practice is to reduce any internalized homophobia that the client may experience.

Are knowledgeable about the coming-out process and its stages, as well as about the typical differences in the process for men and women.

Deal with their own homophobic and heterosexual biases, whatever their own sexual orientations are (p. 402)

Frost (1998) provides some resources that human services practitioners can return to again and again as guides or basic references, but more importantly, he points out the need to remain current with the research and knowledge base about TBLG populations. He offers some points about how practitioners can do this. In addition to identifying and referring back to key books and articles in their own field, practitioners need to be aware of and review professional journals and journals in other fields that relate to this population. Continuing education in the form of conferences and workshops is also vital, as is continuing to initiate and engage in conversation and professional consultation with colleagues. Perhaps, however, one of the most important ways for practitioners to remain sensitive to issues of homonegativity and heterosexism is to continue to observe their own values, beliefs, behaviors, and language and to continue in the ongoing process of creating a safe and less oppressive self while also working for justice in the external world.

BUILDING SOCIAL SUPPORT SYSTEMS

A basic tenet of good social/health/human services is to assess and to help people build solid and healthy support systems. "At least in some parts of the United States [and throughout parts of the industrialized world], there is a vital and well-developed gay and lesbian community that is an important source of strength to its members. Even those who do not participate directly in it benefit from it and may feel supported simply by knowing it is there" (Appleby & Anastas, 1998, p. 120). Helping TBLG people access not only the TBLG community, but also other communities that are open and accepting, can be a powerful social service intervention. In order to be aware of these connections, human services practitioners must sometimes actively search out the ways that people can connect with the visible TBLG community and other supportive communities. One way to do this is to look in telephone and social services directories for community centers, services, bookstores, and bars with the TBLG words in the title or that advertise themselves as TBLG places or "TBLG-friendly." Remember, however, that *lesbian* and *gay* may be the only words used if the local community does not yet actively accept and incorporate transgender and bisexual individuals. Once practitioners have located such bars, bookstores, social clubs, and community centers, they often can obtain further information through newspapers, flyers, and group announcements that can be found at these locations.

People who in rural communities rather than large cities may find connecting with other people to be particularly challenging. Gay and lesbian people (and I would add, transgender and bisexual people) who reside in rural areas tend to remain

socially isolated as well as geographically confined in terms of social and health services and outreach organizations (Foster, 1997; Mancoske, 1997; Smith, 1997). One
possible link to a larger TBLG community may be through literature, magazine sub-
scriptions (e.g., to national magazines such as *The Advocate*), and the Internet (Haag
& Chang, 1997). Links to clean and sober communities, supportive spiritual communities, and TBLG-positive parenting supports also will be necessary for many
TBLG people. Not only looking for, but also creating such groups when needed, is a
key factor in effective practice with these populations.

ESTABLISHING MAGNA-SPIRITUAL CONNECTIONS

If a TBLG person's "ultimate concern" is God/Great Creator/High Power/Divine
Source/etc. (as theologian Paul Tillich says all people's ultimate concern is; Tillich,
1957), then that person will face challenges above and beyond those of the ordinary
spiritual seeker. While spirituality and belonging to a spiritual community can be a
source of resilience and strength for many (Hines, 1998; Walsh, 1998), for the TBLG
person, they can be a source of deep shame and learned self-hatred. It is hard to find
self-acceptance and self-esteem when one is told that God/the Divine hates one simply due to whom one loves (Booth, 1995). Some TBLG people dive deeply into religiosity as a means of denying their sexual, affectional, and/or gender orientations,
and some move completely away from spirituality and religious institutions (Booth,
1995).

The general antibody, antisexual attitude of the Bible (Comstock, 1993;
Countryman, 2001) and the use of biblical references as justification for homophobia
or outright violence against TBLG people have had a profoundly negative effect on
many TBLG people who might otherwise find community, solace, and strength in religious or spiritual communities. Such attitudes and references may also be sources of
internalized self-hatred, self-violence, and/or denial of identity. People who are more
reliant on such communities will feel the threat of loss of these communities much
more intensely when they are coming out or contemplating sharing their identities
(Baez, 1996).

Some religious institutions, in some countries, encourage open hostility,
homonegativity, and even violence against TBLG people (Baez, 1996). Other traditions, such as Mormons and Orthodox Jews, assert that either the person who is
TBLG, or at least the practice of this identity, is sinful and/or to be avoided and that
this is just the individual's burden to bear. Many who hear such messages, such as
many Mormons (Goodwill, 2000), leave their churches, and some never return to a
spiritual community or practice.

Perlstein (1996) delineates five categories of TBLG spiritual seekers: (1) people
who attend mainstream denominational churches or temples, whether closeted or
openly out; (2) those who belong to mainstream denominations but attend TBLG
subgroups of the denominations; (3) those who attend TBLG (mainly lesbian or gay)
churches; (4) those who form personal relationships and practices through their own
understanding of the Divine; and (5) those who form and work to evolve spiritual

practices and possibly rituals in newly formed groups. Human services practitioners who encounter TBLG spiritual seekers or those who have been wounded by religious rejection may need to be able to offer options to these people. In addition to the possibilities already mentioned, human services practitioners who are addressing these needs may need to be aware of welcoming congregations that openly accept TBLG members (e.g., the Metropolitan Community Church, the United Church of Christ, and the Unitarian Universalists). Some mainstream Christian churches also have communities that welcome TBLG members, and some traditionally less-welcoming traditions, such as the Roman Catholic Church, have groups such as Dignity (a subgroup mentioned by Perlstein) for TBLG members. Other traditions (e.g., Reformed Judaism and some Eastern traditions such as Buddhism) generally are welcoming of TBLG people. Some TBLG people turn to less traditional spiritual communities, such as New Age and Spiritualist groups, as sources of support.

Whether a human services practitioner is working with a client who is looking for an affirming and welcoming spiritual/religious community, or is helping a TBLG person heal from the homonegativity experienced at the hands of a church/temple community, understanding that the oppression of TBLG people has long been perpetuated by religious communities is vital in offering needed assistance. Also, understanding one's own religious beliefs as they pertain to TBLG people will better help the human services practitioner to offer nonjudgmental, affirming, and ethically appropriate services to this population.

SUMMARY

We have identified some of the issues and challenges that are faced by both TBLG and non-TBLG people. For example, we have examined how coming out is navigated on a day-by-day basis, and is an ongoing issue and topic of focus for TBLG people. Areas that present challenges and potential problems for all people, like having and raising children or dealing with issues in the workplace, often have additional layers of difficulties for TBLG people due to homonegativity and heterosexism. It is important to recognize that the TBLG "community" really represents incredibly diverse populations within this one group. This group (transgender, bisexual, lesbian, and gay) has one thing in common—the members of this group have affectional/sexual orientations and gender expressions that are outside the heterosexual norm. In terms of other areas of diversity and life experiences, however, they may have incredibly different life mosaics. Between the categories themselves (lesbian and transgender, for example), there are differences. Sometimes the TBLG population lacks the sense of unity that could benefit the members of this group. Some issues cross the boundaries between the different groups within the TBLG population (e.g., coming-out issues), while other issues are more particular, although maybe not exclusive, to one or another group (e.g., how a bisexual woman maintains ties to the lesbian community when she is in a relationship with a man). Thus, multidimensional contextual practice is crucial when servicing TBLG communities.

References

AIDS Office, Bureau of Epidemiology and Disease Control, San Francisco City Clinic Special Programs for Youth and San Francisco Department of Welfare (1991). *The young men's survey: Principal findings and results.* San Francisco, CA.

Appleby, G. A., & Anastas, J. W. (1998). *Not just a passing phase: Social work with gay, lesbian and bisexual people.* New York: Columbia University Press.

Apuzzo, V. M. (2001). A call to action. *Journal of Gay and Lesbian Social Services, 13*(4), 1–11.

Atkins, D. (1998). *Looking queer: Body image and identity in lesbian, bisexual, gay and transgender communities.* Binghamton, NY: Haworth.

Baez, E. J. (1996). Spirituality and the gay Latino client. In M. Shernoff (Ed.), *Human services for gay people: Clinical and community practice* (pp. 69–81). Binghamton, NY: Harrington Park Press.

Barranti, C. C. R. (1998). Social work practice with lesbian couples. In G. P. Mallon (Ed.), *Foundations of social work practice with lesbian and gay persons* (pp. 183–207). Binghamton, NY: Harrington Park Press.

Berger, R. M., & Kelly, J. J. (2001). What are older gay men like? An impossible question? *Journal of Gay and Lesbian Social Services, 13*(4), 55–65.

Berkman, C. S., & Zinberg, G. (1997). Homophobia and heterosexism in social workers. *Social Work, 42,* 319–332.

Bieber, I., Dain, H. J., Dince, P. R., Drellich, M. G., Grand, H. G., Gundlach, R. H., Kremer, M. W., Rifkin, A. H., Wilbur, C. B., & Bieber, T. B. (1962). *Homosexuality: A psychoanalytic study.* New York: Basic Books.

Blumenfeld, W. J. (1998). "Homowork": Ways to increase LGBT visibility and reduce homophobia (Appendix 2). In G. A. Appleby & J. W. Anastas (Eds.), *Not just a passing phase: Social work with gay, lesbian and bisexual people.* New York: Columbia University Press.

Blumstein, P. W., & Schwartz, P. (1983). *American couples: Money, work, sex.* New York: William Morrow.

Bohan, J. S., & Russell, G. M. (1999). Conceptual frameworks. In J. S. Bohan & G. M. Russell (Eds.), *Conversations about psychology and sexual orientation* (pp. 11–30). New York: New York University Press.

Booth, L. (1995). Spirituality and the gay community. In R. J. Kus (Ed.), *Addiction and recovery in gay and lesbian persons* (pp. 57–65). Binghamton, NY: Harrington Park Press.

Brooks, V. R. (1981). *Minority stress and lesbian women.* Lexington, MA: D.C. Heath.

Brown, L. B., Alley, G. R., Sarosy, S., Quarto, G., & Cook, T. (2001). Gay men: Aging well! *Journal of Gay and Lesbian Social Services, 13*(4), 41–54.

Cautela, J. (1967). Covert sensitization. *Psychological Reports, 20*(2), 459–468.

Chaney, M. E. (2002, September). My personal statement. In J. Terra (Chair), *Peer helper diversity training.* Training conducted at 3rd & B, Emerson Jr. High, Davis, CA.

Comstock, G. D. (1991). *Violence against lesbians and gay men.* New York: Columbia University Press.

Comstock, G. D. (1993). *Gay theology without apology.* Cleveland, OH: Pilgrim Press.

Conley, T. D., Calhoun, C., Evett, S. R., & Devine, P. G. (2001). Mistakes that heterosexual people make when trying to appear non-prejudiced: The view from LGB people. *Journal of Homosexuality, 42*(2), 21–43.

Connolly, L. (1996). Long-term care and hospice: The special needs of older gay men and lesbians. In K. J. Peterson (Ed.), *Health care for lesbians and gay men* (pp. 77–91). Binghamton, NY: Harrington Park Press.

Council on Social Work Education (CSWE). (1992). *Curriculum policy statement.* Alexandria, VA: Author.

Countryman, L. W. (2001). The church and sex—A checkered history. In L. W. Countryman & M. R. Ritley, *Gifted by otherness: Gay and lesbian Christians in the church* (pp. 31–41). Harrisburg, PA: Morehouse.

Dane, B., & Miller, S. (1992). *AIDS: Intervening with hidden grievers.* Westport, CT: Auburn House.

Devine, P. G., Evett, S. R., & Vasquez-Suson, K. (1996). Exploring the interpersonal dynamics of intergroup contact. In R. Sorrentino & E. T. Higgins (Eds.), *Handbook of motivation and cognition: The interpersonal context* (3rd ed., pp. 423–464). New York: Guilford.

Devine, P. G., Monteith, M. J., Zuwerink, J., & Elliot, A. J. (1991). Prejudice with and without compunction. *Journal of Personality and Social Psychology, 60,* 817–830.

Donovan, T. (2001). Being transgender and older: A first person account. *Journal of Gay and Lesbian Social Services, 13*(4), 19–22.

Drabble, L. (2000). Alcohol, tobacco, and pharmaceutical industry funding: Considerations for organizations serving lesbian, gay, bisexual, and transgender communities. *Journal of Gay and Lesbian Social Services, 11*(1), 1–26.

Dynes, W. (1990). Bisexuality. In W. Dynes (Ed.), *Encyclopedia of homosexuality* (pp. 143–147). New York: Garland.

Ehrenberg, M. (1996). Aging and mental health: Issues in the gay and lesbian community. In C. J. Alexander (Ed.), *Gay and lesbian mental health: A sourcebook for practitioners* (pp. 189–210). Binghamton, NY: Harrington Park Press.

Erwin, K. (1993). Interpreting the evidence: Competing paradigms and the emergence of lesbian and gay suicide as a social fact. *International Journal of Health Services, 23,* 437–453.

Ettelbrick, P. (1991). Legal protection for lesbians. In B. Sang, J. Warshow, & A. J. Smith (Eds.), *Lesbians at midlife* (pp. 258–264). Minneapolis, MN: Spinsters Ink.

Faulkner, A. H., & Cranston, K. (1988). Correlates of same-sex sexual behavior in a random sample of Massachusetts high school students. *American Journal of Public Health, 88*(2), 262–266.

Feinberg, L. (1998). *Transliberation: Beyond pink or blue.* Boston: Beacon.

Feldman, M. (1966). Aversion therapy for sexual deviation: A critical review. *Psychological Bulletin, 65,* 65–69.

Feldman, M., & MacCullough, M. J. (1965). The application of anticipatory avoidance learning to the treatment of homosexuality: Theory, technique and preliminary results. *Behavior Research and Therapy, 2,* 165–183.

Finnegan, D. G., & McNally, E. B. (1995). The National Association of Lesbian and Gay Alcoholism Professionals (NALGAP): A retrospective. In R. J. Kus (Ed.), *Addiction and recovery in gay and lesbian persons* (pp. 83–90). Binghamton, NY: Harrington Park Press.

Finnegan, D. G., & McNally, E. B. (1996). Chemical dependency and depression in lesbians and gay men: What helps? In M. Shernoff (Ed.), *Human services for gay people* (pp. 115–130). Binghamton, NY: Harrington Park Press.

Foster, S. J. (1997). Rural lesbians and gays: Public perceptions, worker perceptions and service delivery. In J. D. Smith & R. J. Mancoske (Eds.), *Rural gays and lesbians* (pp. 23–36). Binghamton, NY: Haworth.

Friends of Project 10, Inc. (1989). *Project 10 handbook.* Los Angeles: Author.

Frosch, D., Shoptaw, S., Huber, A., Lawson, R. A., & Ling, W. (1996). Sexual HIV risk and gay and bisexual methamphetamine abusers. *Journal of Substance Abuse Treatment, 13*(6), 483–486.

Frost, J. C. (1998). Staying current with gay and lesbian research and practice knowledge. *Journal of Gay and Lesbian Social Services, 8*(4) 5–27.

Gair, S. R. (1995). The false self, shame and the challenge of self-cohesion. In J. M. Glassgold & S. Iasenza (Eds.), *Lesbians and psychoanalysis: Revolutions in theory and practice* (pp. 107–123). New York: Free Press.

Gallup, G. (1977, July 18). *Homosexuals in U.S. society.* Gallup Poll.

Garnets, L., Herek, G. M., & Levy, B. (1992). Violence and victimization of lesbians and gay men: Mental health consequences. In G. M. Herek & K. T. Berrill (Eds.), *Hate crimes: Confronting violence against lesbians and gay men* (pp. 207–226). Newbury Park, CA: Sage.

Gawin, F. H. (1978). Drugs and eros: Reflections on eros. *Journal of Psychedelic Drugs, 10*(3), 227–235.

Gebhard, P. H. & Johnson, A. B. (1979). *The Kinsey data: Marginal tabulations of the 1938–1963 interviews conducted by the Institute for Sex Research.* Philadelphia: W. B. Saunders.

George, K. D., & Behrendt, A. E. (1988). Therapy for male couples experiencing relationship problems and sexual problems. In E. Coleman (Ed.), *Integrated identity for gay men and lesbians: Psychotherapeutic approaches for emotional well-being* (pp. 77–88). Binghamton, NY: Harrington Park Press.

Gibson, P. (1989). Gay male and lesbian youth suicide. *Report of the Secretary's task force on youth suicide.* Washington, DC: U.S. Department of Health and Human Services.

Goodwill, K. A. (2000). Religion and the spiritual needs of gay Mormon men. *Journal of Gay and Lesbian Social Services, 11*(4), 23–38.

Green, R. J., Bettinger, M., & Zacks, E. (1996). Are lesbian couples fused and gay male couples disengaged? Questioning gender straightjackets. In J. Laird & R. J.

Green (Eds.), *Lesbians and gays in couples and families: A handbook for therapists* (pp. 185–230). San Francisco: Jossey-Bass.

Grossman, A. H., D'Augelli, A. R., & O'Connell, T. S. (2001). Being lesbian, gay, bisexual and sixty or older in North America. *Journal of Gay and Lesbian Social Services, 13*(4), 23–40.

Haag, A., & Chang, F. (1997). The impact of electronic networking on the lesbian and gay community. In J. D. Smith & R. J. Mancoske (Eds.), *Rural gays and lesbians* (pp. 83–94). Binghamton, NY: Haworth.

Halkitis, P. N., Parsons, J. T., & Stirratt, M. J. (2001). A double epidemic: Crystal methamphetamine drug use in relation to HIV transmission among gay men. *Journal of Homosexuality, 41*(2), 17–35.

Halpert, S. C., & Pfaller, J. (2001). Sexual orientation and supervision: Theory and practice. *Journal of Gay and Lesbian Social Services, 13*(3), 23–40.

Hammelman, T. L. (1993). Gay and lesbian youth: Contributing factors to serious attempts or considerations of suicide. *Journal of Gay and Lesbian Psychotherapy, 2*, 77–89.

Hammond, N. (1989). Lesbian victims of relationship violence. *Women in Therapy, 8*, 89–105.

Herdt, G., & Boxer, A. M. (1993). *Children of horizons: How gay and lesbian teens are leading a new way out of the closet.* Boston: Beacon.

Herek, G. M. (1988). Heterosexuals' attitudes toward lesbians and gay men: Correlates and gender differences. *Journal of Sex Research, 25*(4), 451–477.

Herek, G. M. (1992). The social context of hate crimes: Notes on cultural heterosexism. In G. M. Herek & K. T. Berrill (Eds.), *Hate crimes: Confronting violence against lesbians and gay men.* (pp. 89–104). Newbury Park, CA: Sage.

Herek, G. M. (1994). Assessing attitudes toward lesbians and gay men: A review of empirical research with the ATLG scale. In B. Greene & G. M. Herek (Eds.), *Lesbian and gay psychology: Theory, research, and clinical applications* (pp. 206–228). Thousand Oaks, CA: Sage.

Herek, G. M. (1998). *Stigma and sexual orientation: Understanding prejudice against lesbians, gay men, and bisexuals.* Thousand Oaks, CA: Sage.

Herek, G. M., & Berrill, K. T. (Eds.). (1992). *Hate crimes: Confronting violence against lesbians and gay men.* Newbury Park, CA: Sage.

Hershberger, S. L., Pilkington, N. W., & D'Augelli, A. R. (1996). Categorization of lesbian, gay, and bisexual suicide attempts. In C. J. Alexander (Ed.), *Gay and lesbian mental health: A sourcebook for practitioners* (pp. 39–59). Binghamton, NY: Harrington Park Press.

Herzog, D., Norman, D., Gordon, C., & Pepose, M. (1984). Sexual conflict and eating disorders in twenty-seven males. *American Journal of Psychiatry, 141*, 989–990.

Hetrick, E. S., & Martin, A. D. (1987). Developmental issues and their resolution for gay and lesbian adolescents. *Journal of Homosexuality, 14*(1/2), 25–43.

Hines, P. M. (1998). Climbing up the rough side of the mountain: Hope, culture, and therapy. In M. McGoldrick (Ed.), *Re-visioning family therapy: Race, culture, and gender in clinical practice* (pp. 78–89). New York: Guilford.

Hitchens, D. (1979). Social attitudes, legal standards and personal trauma in child custody cases. *Journal of Homosexuality, 5*(1/2), 89–95.

Hitchens, D., & Price, B. (1979). Trial strategy in lesbian mother custody cases: The use of expert testimony. *Golden Gate University Law Review, 9*, 453.

Horowitz, J. L., & Newcomb, M. D. (2001). A multidimensional approach to homosexual identity. *Journal of Homosexuality, 42*(2), 1–19.

Hunter, J. (1990). Violence against lesbian and gay male youths. *Journal of Interpersonal Violence, 5*(3), 295–300.

Israel, G., & Tarver, D., II. (1997). *Transgender care: Recommended guidelines, practical information and personal accounts.* Philadelphia: Temple University Press.

Johansson, W. (1990). Stonewall rebellion. In W. Dynes (Ed.), *Encyclopedia of homosexuality* (pp. 1251–1254). New York: Garland.

Jones, B. E. (2001). Is having the luck of growing old in the gay, lesbian, bisexual, transgender community good or bad luck? *Journal of Gay and Lesbian Social Services, 13*(4), 13–14.

Keeler, W. (1999). Growth inducing conflict resolution strategies as a means of reducing the impact of discordant outness on relationship satisfaction. *Journal of Gay and Lesbian Social Services, 10*(2), 1–33.

Kinsey, A. C., Pomeroy, W. B., & Martin, C. E. (1948). *Sexual behavior in the human male.* Philadelphia: W. B. Saunders.

Kinsey, A. C., Pomeroy, W. B., Martin, C. E., & Gebhard, P. H. (1953). *Sexual behavior in the human female.* Philadelphia: W. B. Saunders.

Kirk, S. (1989). *Lesbian parents.* Unpublished master's thesis, California State University, Sacramento.

Kirkpatrick, M. (1991). Lesbian couples in therapy. *Psychiatric Annals, 8,* 491–496.

Kirsch, M. (2000). *Queer theory and social change.* London: Routledge.

Kus, R. J., & Latcovich, M. A. (1995). Special interest groups in Alcoholics Anonymous: A focus on gay men's groups. In R. J. Kus (Ed.), *Addiction and recovery in gay and lesbian persons* (pp. 67–82). Binghamton, NY: Harrington Park Press.

Kus, R. J., & Smith, G. B. (1995). Referrals and resources for chemically dependent gay and lesbian clients. In R. J. Kus (Ed.), *Addiction and recovery in gay and lesbian persons* (pp. 91–107). Binghamton, NY: Harrington Park Press.

Lehr, V. (1999). *Queer family values: Debunking the myth of the nuclear family.* Philadelphia: Temple University Press.

Lewis, R., Derlega, V., Berndt, A., Morris, L., & Rose, S. (2001). An empirical analyses of stressors for gay men and lesbians. *Journal of Homosexuality, 42*(1), 63–88.

Loulan, J. (1984). *Lesbian sex.* San Francisco: Spinster/Aunt Lute.

Mackelprang, R. W., Ray, J. A., & Hernandez-Peck, M. (1996). Social work education and sexual orientation: Faculty, students and curriculum issues. *Journal of Gay and Lesbian Social Services, 5*(4), 17–32.

Mallon, G. (1998a). Lesbian, gay and bisexual orientation in childhood and adolescence. In G. A. Appleby & J. W. Anastas, *Not just a passing phase: Social work with gay, lesbian and bisexual people* (pp. 123–144). New York: Columbia University Press.

Mallon, G. P. (1998b). *We don't exactly get the welcome wagon: The experiences of gay and lesbian adolescents in child welfare systems.* New York: Columbia University Press.

Mallon, G. P. (1999). Gay and lesbian adolescents and their families. *Journal of Gay and Lesbian Social Services, 10*(2), 69–87.

Malyon, A. K. (1982). Biphasic aspects of homosexual identity formation. *Psychotherapy: Theory, Research, and Practice, 19*(3), 335–340.

Mancoske, R. J. (1997). Rural HIV/AIDS social services for gays and lesbians. In J. D. Smith & R. J. Mancoske (Eds.), *Rural gays and lesbians* (pp. 37–52). Binghamton, NY: Haworth.

Martin, D., & Lyon, P. (1972). *Lesbian/woman.* New York: Bantam.

Mayerson, P., & Lief, H. (1965). Psychotherapy of homosexuals: A follow-up study of 19 cases. In J. Marmor (Ed.), *Sexual inversion* (pp. 302–344). New York: Basic Books.

McDaniel, J. (1995). *The lesbian couples' guide.* New York: HarperCollins.

McVinney, L. D. (1998). Social work practice with gay male couples. In G. P. Mallon (Ed.), *Foundations of social work practice with lesbian and gay persons* (pp. 208–227). Binghamton, NY: Harrington Park Press.

McWhirter, D. P., & Matteson, A. M. (1984). *The male couple: How relationships develop.* Englewood Cliffs, NJ: Prentice-Hall.

McWhirter, D. P., & Matteson, A. M. (1985). Psychotherapy for gay male couples. In J. C. Gonsiorek (Ed.), *A guide to psychotherapy with gay and lesbian clients* (pp. 79–91). Binghamton, NY: Harrington Park Press.

McWhirter, D. P., & Matteson, A. M. (1988). Stage discrepancy in male couples. In E. Coleman (Ed.), *Integrated identity for gay men and lesbians: Psychotherapeutic approaches for emotional well-being* (pp. 89–99). Binghamton, NY: Harrington Park Press.

Merrill, G. S., & Wolfe, V. A. (2000). Battered gay men: An exploration of abuse, help seeking and why they stay. *Journal of Homosexuality, 39*(2), 1–30.

Mitchell, V. (2000). The bloom is on the rose: The impact of midlife on the lesbian couple. *Journal of Gay and Lesbian Social Services, 11*(2/3), 33–48.

Morrow, D. F. (1996). Heterosexism: Hidden discrimination in social work education. *Journal of Gay and Lesbian Social Services, 5*(4), 1–16.

Morrow, S. L., & Hawxhurst, D. M. (1989). Lesbian partner abuse: Implications for therapists. *Journal of Counseling and Development, 68,* 58–62.

National Association of Social Workers (NASW). (1997). Lesbian, gay and bisexual issues. In *Social work speaks: NASW policy statements* (pp. 198–209). Washington, DC: NASW Press.

National Gay and Lesbian Task Force. (1984). *Anti-gay/lesbian victimization.* New York: Author.

National Museum and Archive of Lesbian and Gay History. (1996). *The gay almanac.* New York: Berkley Books.

Nieves-Rosa, L., Carballo-Dieguez, A., & Dolezal, C. (2000). Domestic abuse and HIV risk behavior in Latin American men who have sex with men in New York City. *Journal of Gay and Lesbian Social Services, 11*(1), 77–90.

Orenstein, A. (2001). Substance use among gay and lesbian adolescents. *Journal of Homosexuality, 41*(2), 1–15.

Paul, J. P., Stall, R., & Bloomfield, K. A. (1991). Gay and alcoholic: Epidemiologic and clinical issues. *Alcohol Health and Research World, 15*(2), 151–160.

Pellegrini, A. (1992). S(h)ifting the terms of hetero/sexism: Gender, power, homophobias. In W. Blumenfeld (Ed.), *Homophobia: How we all pay the price* (pp. 39–56). Boston: Beacon.

Perlstein, M. (1996). Integrating a gay, lesbian, or bisexual person's religious and spiritual needs and choices into psychotherapy. In C. J. Alexander (Ed.), *Gay and lesbian mental health: A sourcebook for practitioners* (pp. 173–188). Binghamton, NY: Harrington Park Press.

Peterson, K. J. (1996). Developing the context: The impact of homophobia and heterosexism on the health care of gay and lesbian people. In K. J. Peterson (Ed.), *Health care for lesbians and gay men* (pp. xvii–xx). Binghamton, NY: Harrington Park Press.

Peterson, K. J., & Bricker-Jenkins, M. (1996). Lesbians and the health care system. In K. J. Peterson (Ed.), *Health care for lesbians and gay men* (pp. 33–48). Binghamton, NY: Harrington Park Press.

Pohl, M. I. (1995). Chemical dependency and HIV infection. In R. J. Kus (Ed.), *Addiction and recovery in gay and lesbian persons* (pp. 15–28). Binghamton, NY: Harrington Park Press.

Pollack, S. (1987). Lesbian mothers: A lesbian-feminist perspective on research. In S. Pollack & J. Vaughn (Eds.), *Politics of the heart: A lesbian parenting anthology* (pp. 316–324). New York: Firebrand Books.

Pope, H., Hudson, J., & Jonas, J. (1986). Bulimia in men: A series of fifteen cases. *Journal of Nervous and Mental Disease, 174*(2), 117–119.

Remafedi, G. (1987). Male homosexuality: The adolescent perspective. *Pediatrics, 79,* 326–330.

Remafedi, G., Farrow, J. A., & Deisher, R. W. (1991). Risk factors for attempted suicide in gay and bisexual youth. *Pediatrics, 87*(6), 869–875.

Robertson, P., & Schachter, J. (1981). Failure to identify venereal disease in the lesbian population. *Sexually Transmitted Diseases, 8*(2), 16–17.

Romesburg, D. (1995). Seven demonstrations before Stonewall. In L. Witt, S. Thomas, & E. Marcus (Eds.), *Out in all directions: The almanac of gay and lesbian America* (pp. 208–210). New York: Warner Books.

Rosario, M., Hunter, J., & Rotheram-Borus, M. J. (1992). [Lesbian adolescents]. *HIV Center for Clinical and Behavioral Studies, New York State Psychiatric Institute.* Unpublished data.

Roth, S. (1989). Psychotherapy with lesbian couples: Individual issues, female socialization, and the social context. In M. McGoldrick, C. M. Anderson, & F. Walsh (Eds.), *Women in families: A framework for family therapy* (pp. 286–307). New York: W. W. Norton.

Ryan, C., & Futterman, D. (1998). *Lesbian and gay youth: Care and counseling.* New York: Columbia University Press.

Saghir, M. T., & Robins, E. (1973). *Male and female homosexuality: A comprehensive investigation.* Baltimore, MD: Williams & Wilkins.

Sakalli, N., & Ugurlu, O. (2001). Effects of social contact with homosexuals on heterosexual Turkish university students' attitudes toward homosexuality. *Journal of Homosexuality, 42*(1), 53–62.

Schope, R. D., & Eliason, M. J. (2000). Thinking versus acting: Assessing the relationship between heterosexual attitudes and behaviors toward homosexuals. *Journal of Gay and Lesbian Social Services, 11,* 69–91.

Schwartz, M. (1996). Gay men and the health care system. In K. J. Peterson (Ed.), *Health care for lesbians and gay men* (pp. 19–32). Binghamton, NY: Harrington Park Press.

Seabold, G. (1997). Surviving a partner's death deeply in the closet. *Journal of Gay and Lesbian Social Services, 7*(2), 7–14.

Sell, R. L., & Petrulio, C. (1996). Sampling homosexuals, bisexuals, gays, and lesbians for public health research: A review of the literature from 1990 to 1992. *Journal of Homosexuality, 30*(4), 31–47.

Siever, M. D. (1996). The perils of sexual objectification: Sexual orientation, gender, and socioculturally acquired vulnerability to body dissatisfaction and eating disorders. In C. J. Alexander (Ed.), *Gay and lesbian mental health: A sourcebook for practitioners* (pp. 223–247). Binghamton, NY: Harrington Park Press.

Slater, S. (1995). *The lesbian family life cycle.* New York: Free Press.

Smith, J. D. (1997). Working with larger systems: Rural lesbians and gays. In J. D. Smith & R. J. Mancoske (Eds.), *Rural gays and lesbians* (pp. 13–22). Binghamton, NY: Haworth.

Strickland, B. R. (1995). Research on sexual orientation and human development: A commentary. *Developmental Psychology, 31*(1), 137–140.

Tigert, L. M. (2001). The power of shame: Lesbian battering as a manifestation of homophobia. In E. Kaschak (Ed.), *Intimate betrayal: Domestic violence in lesbian relationships* (pp. 73–86). New York: Haworth.

Tillich, P. (1957). *Dynamics of faith.* New York: Harper Brothers.

Turell, S. (1999). Seeking help for same-sex relationship abuses. *Journal of Gay and Lesbian Social Services, 10*(2), 35–49.

Turner, W. (2000). *A geneology of queer theory.* Philadelphia: Temple University Press.

Walsh, F. (1998). Beliefs, spirituality and transcendence: Keys to family resilience. In M. McGoldrick (Ed.), *Re-visioning family therapy: Race, culture, and gender in clinical practice* (pp. 62–77). New York: Guilford.

Weinberg, G. H. (1972). *Society and the healthy homosexual.* New York: St. Martin's.

Yager, J., Kurtzman, F., Landsverk, J., & Wiesmeier, E. (1988) Behaviors and attitudes related to eating disorders in homosexual male college students. *American Journal of Psychiatry, 145*(4), 495–497.

Yoakam, J. R. (1999). The Youth and AIDS Projects: School and community outreach for gay, lesbian, bisexual, and transgender youth. *Journal of Gay and Lesbian Social Services, 9*(4), 99–113.

The greatest teaching is to live with an open heart. —**Anonymous**

10 | People Living with Disabilities

General Population Groups

KATHRYN S. COLLINS,
DEBORAH P. VALENTINE,
AND DEBRA L. WELKLEY

INTRODUCTION

This chapter establishes the experiential reality of the disability community and deconstructs stereotypes confronting people with disabilities. First, how *disability* is defined will be addressed, for it is only through understanding varying definitions that we can begin to deconstruct our already formed ideas about people who have disabilities. Features of disability identity, social and political construction of the disability community, and the attributes of diversity as they pertain to the disability community are explored. The next section addresses the myths and stereotypes attributed to people with disabilities and how they affect people with and without disabilities. Myths and stereotypes applied to the disability community create greater limitations within society. The focus of the third section is how the experiences, needs, and issues of people with disabilities can be understood in nonstereotypic ways. The topic of women with disabilities is specifically considered. The chapter concludes with a discussion regarding the professional knowledge, skills, and values that are necessary to provide professionally competent practices when serving members of the disability community.

DEFINITION OF PEOPLE WITH DISABILITIES

Conceptually, *disability* is a term that is both frequently used and poorly understood. According to the Americans with Disabilities Act (ADA) of 1990, a person with a disability is defined as one with "a physical or mental impairment that substantially limits one or more of the major life activities of such individual." Section

504 of the Rehabilitation Act of 1973, the legal antecedent of the ADA, defines physical impairments as any physiological disorder or condition, cosmetic disfigurement, or anatomical loss that affects the major body systems. Mental impairments are defined as any mental or psychological disorder, such as mental retardation, organic brain syndrome, emotional or mental illness, and specific learning disabilities. By using the qualifying words *substantial* and *major life activity,* the ADA definition intends to focus on significant limitations in human activities (see Table 10.1).

Historically, disability has been regarded as a problem "of the individual." *Impairment, disability,* and *handicap* are not interchangeable terms. The United Nation's World Program of Action (1995) defines these terms as follows. *Impairment* is any loss of psychological, physiological, or anatomical structure or function. *Disability* is any restriction of ability to perform an activity in the method or within the scope considered relevant for able-bodied individuals. Disabilities are often a consequence of impairment. *Handicap* is a disadvantage that limits or prevents the fulfillment of typical social roles. Handicap is a function of the relationship between people with disabilities and their environment (D'Aubin, 1991). A handicap is a social disadvantage that results from a disability. For example, a woman who uses a wheelchair may have a disability; a building without appropriate wheelchair access is a handicap to the woman with the disability (Solomon, 1993). There are four types of disabilities that encompass the population of people with disabilities. Cognitive/developmental, sensory/neurological, physical, and emotional/behavioral are the typical categories of disabilities.

The Americans with Disabilities Act (ADA) was enacted on July 26, 1990, and as of July 1994, all provisions of the act became effective across the United States. This act prohibits discrimination in employment, discrimination by public entities and in public transportation, and discrimination in public facilities and services oper-

Table 10.1 | Theoretical Frameworks and Practice Orientations

The term "disability" means, with respect to an individual—(A) A physical or mental impairment that substantially limits one or more of the major life activities of such individual; (B) A record of such an impairment; or (C) Being regarded as having such an impairment. Physical or mental impairment means: (1) Any physiological disorder, or condition, cosmetic disfigurement, or anatomical loss affecting one or more of the following body systems: Neurological, musculoskeletal, special sense organs, respiratory (including speech organs), cardiovascular, reproductive, digestive, genitourinary, hemic and lymphatic, skin, and endocrine; or (2) Any mental or psychological disorder, such as mental retardation, organic brain syndrome, emotional or mental illness, and specific learning disabilities. Major life activities means functions such as caring for oneself, performing manual tasks, walking, seeing, hearing, speaking, breathing, learning, and working. Substantially limits . . . means: (i) Unable to perform a major life activity that the average person in the general populations can perform; or (ii) Significantly restricted as to the condition, manner, or duration under which an individual can perform a particular major life activity as compared to the condition, manner, or duration under which the average person in the general population can perform that same major life activity.

ated by private entities (Kopels, 1995). From this discussion, one can see that the ADA's definition is functional and social and includes people who experience substantial impairments, as well as social perceptions of such impairments.

People with disabilities seem to be the single largest minority group in the United States (U.S. Department of Labor, 2003). People who have a disability cut across lines of gender, sexual orientation, class, ethnicity, and age, which can be juxtaposed with what society generally typifies as a person with a disability. Many times, society only thinks of people in certain age groups or social class categories as having disabilities. Many people assume that people with disabilities are asexual. People with disabilities are often assumed to live in poverty or in residential communities. Additionally, people with disabilities are typically defined by their disabilities rather than their humanness. These beliefs and assumptions influence our perspectives and worldviews.

According the 2000 U.S. Census Bureau, nearly 49.7 million, or one in five, Americans age five and over has a disability (U.S. Census Bureau, 2002). This comprises 19% of the U.S. population and is the population covered by the ADA. Although the ADA definition is the legal definition of disability and is frequently used to qualify people for social services, the following discussion will include all people who self-identify as having a disability.

NATURE OF PROBLEMS FACED BY PEOPLE WITH DISABILITIES

People with disabilities contend with discrimination and oppression that may be subtle, and unbiased analysis may be required for discrimination to be identified and addressed. Discrimination can affect all conditions of the lives of people with disabilities across the life span: education, employment, economic status, health, marriage, family, and rehabilitation (Rajah, 1991).

Diversity within the disability community also exists. For example, although people with disabilities have less income and are less educated than the general population (Kopels, 1995), women with disabilities are poorer than men with disabilities (Owen & Topaz, 1995; Pfeiffer, 1991). Employment, for example, is a crucial ingredient in enabling women with disabilities to sustain themselves financially and to achieve self-esteem and social recognition (Swedish Handicapped International Aid Foundation [SHIA], 1995). Collins and Valentine (2003) conclude that among people with disabilities, societal injustice is replicated with regard to employment and income. That is, within the disability community there is a social class structure that is similar to the able-bodied community that enables in particular more white males in the United States to have access to such things as education, jobs, and higher income than able-bodied women (Pfeiffer, 1991). Women with disabilities are more than twice as likely as other women and men to not be paid in the workforce, and they are five times as likely as able-bodied women to leave school at the minimum age. Women with disabilities are also less likely to receive sufficient disability benefits and are served less frequently than men in the vocational rehabilitation system (Quinn, 1994).

DIVERSITY WITHIN DISABILITY CULTURE

Culture is an integration of human behavior that encompasses the "customs, habits, skills, technology, arts, values, ideology, science, and religious and political behavior of a group of people in a specific time period" (Barker, 1999, p. 114). The disability culture, much like how the Deaf culture is defined, has its own history, language, perspectives, priorities, humor, norms, and sense of pride in its identity. One cannot presume to know the complexities of a person with disabilities without first knowing and understanding that person's culture.

People with disabilities also have an internalized culture. Ho (1995) defines internalized culture as:

> the cultural influences operating within the individual that shape (not determine) personality formation and various aspects of psychological functioning. Individual cognition, for instance, is influenced by internalized cultural beliefs. . . . Differences in internalized culture arise from differences in enculturation. The concept of internalized culture explicitly addresses both between-group and within-group variations in cultural processes." (pp. 5–6)

These authors would add that a person's spiritual practice, the experience of magna, also affects the individually internalized culture, as well as a person's interactions and exchanges with others. Ho stresses that a distinction needs to be made between internalized culture (the inner experiences) and cultural group membership (the collective outer experience). We agree with Ho that even when people are members of the same cultural group, no two persons have the same worldviews. Thus, individual narratives cannot be neglected in the name of the collective or vice versa. Social factors such as gender identity, sexual orientation, socioeconomic status, ethnicity, and age, to mention a few, affect the construction, deconstruction, and reconstruction of the internalized culture and its manifestation in the outer world.

SOCIOPOLITICAL MODEL OF DISABILITY

Rather than focusing attention exclusively on smaller systems, such as individuals, families, and groups for assessment and intervention, a biopsychosocial model looks toward all systems, including the macro systems. A "sociopolitical model of disability is based upon the assumption that disability results from the failure of a structured environment to adjust to the needs and aspirations of disabled citizens rather than from inability of a disabled individual to adapt to the demands of the society" (Hahn, 1985, p. 93). The focus of analysis is therefore the interaction between the individual and the physical environment and the attitudes and behaviors within environments that create and foster both risks and opportunities. An individual's functional limitations are viewed within the environments (Fowler, O'Rourke, Wadsworth, & Harper, 1992).

A sociopolitical understanding of disability is an effective alternative to the medical definition. It rejects the notion of pathologizing and categorization, and examines the social and economic barriers to full community participation (Corbett, 1994). Thus, the concept of disability is not given to the individual, but is the result of a "relationship between an individual and specific environments" (p. 26). The disability community is an especially vulnerable group of people who frequently encounter extreme societal discrimination and stigmatization often perpetuated and fueled by internal oppression of the people with disabilities. Gatens-Robinson and Tarvydas (1992) propose that a social and political model of disability leads to the conclusion that disability is socially constructed. Using a social model of disability, Lloyd (1992) states that it is

> not the physical or mental impairments of the individual which disables, but the handicapping effects of a society geared to "ablebodiedness" as the norm. The disablement is therefore socially created and the experience of disability is another form of oppression. Exponents of the social model have arrived at this position via a sharp critique of individual models, which largely see disability as some form of personal tragedy which the individual must learn to accept, and to "cope" with life lived in its shadow. (pp. 208–209)

Thus, just as gender, ethnicity, and sexual orientation can place individuals and groups of individuals at risk for pathologizing, "disabilities" also may place people in a position of vulnerability.

A next step in the process of thinking about the meaning of "disabilities" to people with and without disabilities is to begin identification of salient characteristics or attributes. Two such characteristics are visibility and permanency. These attributes may be viewed along several dimensions, including a continuum of *visibility and invisibility* and a continuum of *permanence and temporariness*. For example, in the United States, in most cases a person's gender is visible; observers recognize cues of maleness or femaleness. Similarly, a person's race is typically visible, although on a visibility-invisibility continuum, race may be less recognizable to observers. Sexual orientation, on the other hand, is typically invisible to observers, even though cues can often be taken from the environment or in interactions with others. Thus, sexual orientation may be considered to fall more on the invisible side of the continuum. Religious affiliations, culture, and political beliefs are similarly observed in context rather than as personal attributes.

Disability can fall anywhere on the visibility-invisibility continuum, however. A disability may be readily apparent, such as it is for a person with cerebral palsy using a puff directed wheelchair, or a disability may be completely invisible, as in the case of a person with a severe math disability. These features may lead to varying assumptions and interactions.

Personal attributes also may be viewed on a continuum of permanency-temporariness. For example, race and gender are generally considered to be permanent (with some exceptions, such as transgendered people who have surgery). Social class, on the other hand, tends to be more toward the "temporary" end of the continuum. Disability, however, can be located anywhere along the permanent-temporary continuum. People without disabilities may consider themselves to be only "temporarily able-bodied," since all of us run the risk of an illness or injury that may change our status to that of a person with a disability. How do expectations, assumptions, and interactions change for individuals with temporary versus permanent disabilities?

Thus, an individual's status of "disability" may be visible or invisible, and it may be permanent or temporary. Many people with and without disabilities are likely to be unaware of the complexity and far-reaching implications of what it means to live with a disability in a society of people who make judgments about the cause and course of disability and injury. (This will be discussed in more detail later in this chapter.)

A third attribute to consider is type of disability. A review of the literature conducted by Wasow and Wikler (1983) suggests that many professionals view families caring for children with developmental disabilities in positive terms (as part of the treatment team). In contrast, professionals view family members caring for children with mental illness in negative terms (as part of the problem).

ISOLATION, SEGREGATION, AND EXCLUSION

What do people seem to often value in this society?
Intelligence, appearance, strength, work roles, and
independence. —**Asch (1984)**

Our societal values seem to enforce the segregation and exclusion of people with disabilities. Civil rights activists have worked to legally eliminate segregation and exclusion based on racial identities; however, even with the implementation of overt legal institutions such as the Civil Rights Act, affirmative action, and nondiscriminatory statements, much more must be done to eliminate the segregation and exclusion that often happens at covert and systemic levels within our society. This type of covert operation also applies to people with disabilities. The Americans with Disabilities Act was swiftly accepted and adopted in the United States, yet there is still covert segregation and exclusion of the disability community within our society. For example, the Civil Rights Project at Harvard University recently released the results of fourteen research studies that investigated educational and legal issues in the special education system of the United States. They found that Black students were nearly three times as likely as White students to receive the diagnosis of "mental retardation" and thereby be in need of special education services. These studies also found that as the wealth of school districts increased, Black male students were at greater risk of being disproportionately labeled as having mental retardation (Civil Rights Project, 2002). Children, especially minority children, are given the status of disability when it is possible that unprepared teachers, uninformed school administrators, fearful parents, lack of funding, and community attitudes utilize the label "disability" to isolate students who are different or difficult regardless of disability. Thus, some children may receive a different educational experience and be subject to different expectations than their similar but nonlabeled peers. Would we tolerate this segregation based on other attributes such as ethnicity or gender?

The attribution of these types of stigma by society (and, in particular, by professionals) on people with disabilities and their families has implications for practice. What determines a person versus a nonperson? Goffman (1963) in Asch (1984) states that people view a person with a stigma as "not quite human" and therefore accept and even justify treatment of the stigmatized people, including people with disabilities, that would not be tolerated for the rest of humanity. Weiss (1994) conducted research on child abandonment of newborns based on differences between infants with internal versus external "defects." Children with external defects are abandoned at a much higher rate. "We can infer from the literature that abnormality in children leads to their being defined as 'non-persons' and licenses violence against them. Defects are culturally defined: a child is deemed abnormal according to a certain concept of normality which differs from one society to another and which determines what achievements the child must attain in order to be called a 'real person' who is 'useful and legitimate' in his or her society" (Weiss, 1994, p. 59). Understanding these occurrences when clients share similar experiences are important in the helping process. Additionally, human service practitioners need to be cognizant of not viewing their clients with disabilities as individuals who are abnormal, as that could negatively affect the helping relationship.

Another dynamic that may influence beliefs and behaviors is the attribution given to the "cause" of a disability. Segregation, exclusion, discrimination, and oppression often happen because of this attribution, or the belief system that people carry about "why" a person or group has a disability. Was the disability "caused by external forces" (e.g., genetics) that are out of the control of the individual person or group, or was the disability "caused" by individual behaviors (e.g., substance abuse) that are considered to be within a person's control? Research indicates that in the United States, if people with disabilities could have prevented their disabilities or illnesses, they are less likely to be treated with sympathy and understanding (e.g., AIDS/HIV; drug exposure; spinal cord injuries; lung cancer versus Down's syndrome; diabetes; breast cancer). Research conducted by Bordieri and Drehmer (1989) suggest that both type of disability and cause of disability are important determinants of personnel decisions made by potential employers about applicants with disabilities. "Regardless of disability type, applicants whose disability was attributed to an external factor were given higher recommendations to be hired and were perceived as having greater productivity potential and greater longevity with the company than the applicant whose disability was attributed to an internal cause" (Bordieri & Drehmer, 1989, p. 205). Parents of children with disabilities frequently report being made to feel guilty and defensive by professionals (Turnbull & Turnbull, 1985). Not long ago, for example, mothers were considered to have been the primary cause of autism. (See the works of Bruno Bettleheim.)

Isolation, segregation, and exclusion also happen at a familial level. Another way in which the culture of disability differs from other cultures is that family members of people with disabilities may not be members of the disability community. Family members without disabilities may not be able to teach their children with disabilities "all the rules and tools for success in the mainstream society. Families cannot give meaning to values they do not share or to experiences that do not exist in their environment" (Norton, 1993, p. 84). Often the support of the "disability community" does not come until adulthood.

What advantages and disadvantages do children with disabilities experience by being isolated from a disability community until they are adults? Children and adults with disabilities who experience only the able-bodied environments of their families and neighborhoods often build their perceptions of the world and construct a reality based on these experiences. This reality may not always be one that values the qualities of people with disabilities. Likewise, when people with disabilities have children, it is likely that their children will not be members of the disability community. People with disabilities may be isolated (e.g., in terms of communication, activity, education) even within their own families. The "dual perspective" suggests that people are embedded in at least two interrelated systems: "(1) that of their immediate socioeconomic, cultural, or racial environment represented by their family and community and (2) that of their economic, political, and educational systems of the wider society" (Norton, 1993, p. 83). Disability culture must include a third perspective that takes into consideration the potential for people with disabilities to experience disenfranchisement from all systems, including family, community, and socioeconomic, cultural, and racial environments.

Women with Disabilities: A Special Case

Women with disabilities experience isolation and segregation both from their "status" of being disabled and because of being women. Dragonsani Renteria (1993) expressed her isolation, exclusion, and discrimination in her poem, "Rejection," when she said:

> SOCIETY REJECTS ME for being Deaf.
> The Deaf community rejects me for being a Lesbian.
> The Lesbian community rejects me for not being able to hear them.
> The Deaf-Lesbian community rejects me for being into S & M.
> The S & M community rejects me for being Deaf.
> Society rejects me for being Chicana.
> The Hispanic community rejects me for being a Lesbian.
> The Gay Hispanic community rejects me for being Deaf.
> Patriarchal society rejects me for being a woman.
> I am rejected and oppressed,
> Even by those who cry out readily
> Against rejection, oppression, and discrimination.
> When will it end? (p. 38)

More than 26 million women who have an ambulatory disability in the United States are noninstitutionalized (Kaye, LaPlante, Carlson, & Wenger, 1996). Data from the U.S. Census Bureau in 2002 indicate that there are also over one million female residents with developmental disabilities living in nursing homes, mental hospitals, or institutions. Collins and Valentine (2003) state that

> standards and guidelines are set and policies implemented as though all people with disabilities are male. Women with disabilities frequently face double, triple, and sometime quadruple oppression and stigmatization and are placed in a position of little power to be seen or heard. Belonging to two disadvantaged groups (women and people with disabilities), women with disabilities often face multiple barriers to achieving important life goals.

According to Healey (1993b), some of the problems facing women with disabilities are gender-related and shared by women without disabilities, and some are disability-related and are shared by men with disabilities. But many problems and needs are simply unique.

Stereotypes, Myths, and Stigma

Stereotypes, myths, stigma, and negative attitudes often devalue the population of people with disabilities. Upon meeting a new person, immediate impressions are often formed and coherence is presumed based on the myriad bits of information received from the interaction. These impressions are oftentimes stereotypes based on central characteristics, attractiveness, and personal cognitive schema from past and present experiences (Olkin, 1999). Social psychologists relate that stereotypes are fixed, rigid, simplified, and "usually fallacious conceptions that people hold about other people" (Lindesmith, Strauss, & Denzin, 1991, p. 47). Stereotypes are manifested through personal visual images and preestablished classifications (Holaday & Wolfson, 1997). They do damage by creating, in the minds of powerful others, enduring images of a person that incorporate widely held beliefs regarding that person's community and deny unique differences that exist among the members of that community, even after evidence is produced that contradicts the established viewpoint. *Stigma* is a term that refers to some characteristic, such as a "disfigurement or limp," which devalues a person (Beuf, 1990; Holaday & Wolfson, 1997; Stafford & Scott, 1986), and the words used to describe the characteristic often carry negative connotations (e.g., "deaf and dumb," "crippled," "deformed"). Attitudes are evaluative judgments and behaviors toward a particular individual or group of people that are comprised of the interactions between personal feelings (affect) and beliefs (cognitions) (Devine & Monteith, 1993; Esses, Haddock, & Zanna, 1993; Holaday & Wolfson, 1997; Mackie & Hamilton, 1993).

The stereotypes that are held of people with disabilities—for instance, those attributes we believe to be true of people who are mentally ill—in turn influence and create our attitudes. Attitudes influence behavior, social relationships, education, employment, and health (Yuker, 1994). When nothing is done to recognize and understand the existence of our stereotypes and their grounding in myth, we are more apt to indeed stigmatize those who have a disability, no matter what type of disability they may have. This then contributes to the cycle of discrimination and oppression. As professionals in the helping professions, it is our responsibility to become aware of these myths and stereotypes so that such stigmas do not compound society's impact on potential client well-being.

Several factors and explanations promote negative stereotypes and attitudes toward the disability community by the general population of able-bodied, helping professionals, as well as those who are within the disability community. Individuals and groups stereotype people by having an image of a person that incorporates widely held beliefs regarding that person's community and denying unique differences that exist among the members of the community. Often, negative stereotypes are held against groups because of fear (Vickers, 1987). For example, able-bodied individuals might fear that they will contract multiple sclerosis or that their children may "catch" cerebral palsy. Others may fear people with developmental disabilities or mental illness, attributing to them unfounded assumptions about violent behavior.

Negative stereotyping not only occurs between groups, but also within groups and communities. There is evidence that people with disabilities share the same beliefs and stereotypes as able-bodied people when it comes to disabilities other than their own (Miller, 1989). Further, stereotypes and myths lead to internalized oppression within the disability community. Internalized oppression is seen by Goffman (1963) to be inherent in how people view themselves. Thus, self-stigma is perpetuated and fueled by the internal oppression. "It needs no external policing; stigmatized individuals police themselves" (Foucault, 1984, in Corbett, 1994). As a result, people with less visible disabilities may attempt to appear "normal" and "pass," and may only disclose their disability in safe situations and among trustworthy people.

According to Vickers (1987), one benefit of using stereotypes "derives from the human attribute of facilitating the speed of decision-making by making generalizations. Short-cuts tend to be reinforced because they avoid the pain of careful thought" (p. 323). Many human service practitioners hold the same types of stereotypes as the general public. Stereotypes trivialize the reality of the experience of people with disabilities. When the reality of one's experience is ignored, it is likely that the human service practitioner will be unable to sufficiently develop understandings that are deep, accurate, and attuned to the transformative potentials of individuals with disabilities. Human service practitioners without this insight may use approaches that fail to help or that even hurt (Blotzer & Ruth, 1995).

Impact of Stereotyping People with Disabilities

Disability is commonly considered a central characteristic of an individual. The feelings and beliefs that one holds about disability (e.g., having a disability involves suffering) constitute the attributions one has regarding individuals with disabilities. These attitudes are an integral variable in the lives of people with disabilities because it is the attitudes of individuals and larger society that lead to the oppression, discrimination, and prejudice against the disability community (Olkin, 1999).

Overall, stereotypes and attitudes toward the disability community are frequently negative. Some disabilities are reported to have fewer stigmas than others, and there is a stable hierarchy of acceptability of various physical disabilities (Olkin, 1981, 1999). "The notion that the body reflects the soul is well entrenched in our society" (Olkin, 1999, p. 57). Yet, Olkin (1999) outlines three ways that this notion snares the disability community. First, a person's value is often judged at least partially on attractiveness. The media as well as general society attributes being thin, beautiful, and vivacious as being healthy and well adjusted. In our society, it helps to be considered attractive (with or without disability). Second, a disability may be judged to be "unattractive" by typical cultural standards of beauty, thereby leading the person with the "unattractive disability" to try to correct or change body appearance to be more acceptable. For example, a growing number of parents of children with Down's syndrome are choosing elective cosmetic surgery to minimize the typical facial features that characterize the syndrome. Third, a visible disability may give misleading cues about the person with the disability. For example, a child with Tourette's syndrome, a disorder that is characterized by motor and vocal tics, may be seen to another person as hyperactive or seriously emotionally disturbed.

Selective attention, a type of information-processing model, refers to the phenomenon of focusing on a single cue that evokes emotionally arousing images. These images cloud judgment and interaction because they limit the ability to integrate other information cues that might eliminate erroneous thinking or faulty processing (Holaday & Wolfson, 1997). For example, an individual may notice the motor tics of a child with Tourette's syndrome. This observer may then focus on the tics as the child's defining feature, thereby devaluing or negating the child's unique qualities and strengths without further investigation of personality, intelligence, or behavior. "In order for society to move beyond current concepts of people with disabilities, we must start by reexamining the origins of 'accepted' definitions of attractiveness and autonomy. We should then ponder why we find it necessary to create social categories and hierarchies based on these definitions" (Asch, 1984, p. 535).

DISABILITY AND THE MULTIDIMENSIONAL CONTEXTUAL PRACTICE FRAMEWORK

Multidimensional contextual practice provides a framework for understanding and working with clients with disabilities. Whether the client is a person who was born with fragile X syndrome or cystic fibrosis, a child who became deaf at the age of 6, an adolescent who has been diagnosed with juvenile diabetes, a young adult who began to hear voices and has been diagnosed with schizophrenia, or a person in middle adulthood who has suffered a spinal cord injury, that person is a unique individual who now shares some commonalities with others with disabilities. Furthermore, people with disabilities continue to grow, evolve, and change in response to biological, psychological, social, and community demands and pressures.

Understanding that a person with a disability is both unique and shares experiences with other people with disabilities is an essential ingredient of applying the multidimensional contextual practice framework. As discussed earlier in this text, cultural influences and choices all contribute to the multidimensional context. Recognizing that a client may share some common experiences relative to feelings of frustration, oppression, disenfranchisement, and stigma with other individuals with disabilities is important; however, it is equally important to focus on the integrity of the whole client. One way in which human service practitioners can do this is to affirm the person as an individual with his or her own experiences, definitions, and needs relative to the specific disability.

The social construct model of disability indicates that communities and cultures define the concept of disability. For example, the personal characteristic of poor eyesight was once considered a disability, but with the invention of corrective lenses and surgery, poor eyesight is no longer considered a disability. Individuals may also self-identify as people with disabilities. One person may define her or his ability or lack of ability as a "disability," and therefore identify with a disability reference group and the common experiences of members of that group, while another individual with a similar ability or lack of ability may not self-identify as having a disability, and therefore may not identify with other individuals who do. For example, one person with a very high activity level and impulsivity may self-identify as a person with attention deficit/hyperactivity disorder and join the local and national organizations, while another person with similar characteristics may embrace her or his high activity level and quick decision-making abilities as gifts and perceive these characteristics as being advantageous in employment (e.g., as a stock broker). The issue of self-identification is important for human service practitioners to explore because the success of linking the client with other services and opportunities in the community can be affected by it. Following an exploration of the ways that a client defines his or her disability and how this relates to a sense of self and sense of belonging or place in the family, community, and other relationships, the practitioner can investigate how these perceptions have changed over time. This can help in acknowledging that there is an ongoing construction of a client's self-identity and her or his relationships with others.

Understanding the client's view of self and how that self relates to family, groups, communities, and society at large is important to maximize the client's growth and healthy functioning. It is also essential for the human service practitioner to gain an understanding of how the client's view of self and the perceptions of others interact. Questions may include: How do family members relate to the family member with the disability? Is that different from how they related to the person prior to the disability? How do family members relate to one another, and how does that affect the client? What does the client's disability mean to the client and family members? Who defines the characteristic as a "disability"? Does the community in which the client lives attach a stigma to people with disabilities? Are invisible disabilities more acceptable? What stereotypes are attached to permanent disabilities? What judgments are made about people with disabilities when their disabilities may have been caused by lifestyle choices? What services does the community offer to groups of people with various disabilities? This is by no means an exhaustive list of questions to explore, but it could be a starting point for the practitioner in helping the client to identify her or his needs and strengths.

Earlier in this chapter, ways that stereotypes may stigmatize those who are living with disabilities were discussed. The beliefs one holds about a disability and about the people who have that particular disability affect how the person living with the disability is treated and the characteristics that are attributed to that person. Many people think that if a person possesses a physical, mental, developmental, emotional, or health limitation, the person is not a "whole" person. The individual is then further stigmatized through selective attention from others, depending on the disability possessed (i.e., visible versus invisible, permanent versus temporary, causation) and the limitations and dependencies that society assigns to the disability. Stigma acts as a barrier for individuals with disabilities, preventing access to goods and services in society, and thereby acting as an agent of discrimination and oppression.

Human service practitioners are challenged to deconstruct stereotypes and stigmatization by listening to clients' stories and learning the meaning and effects of their experiences. Practitioners further this deconstruction and reconstruction by supporting clients in their personal worldviews and assisting them to embrace their essences and self-identities despite the views that society holds relative to their disabilities. Recognizing how age, gender, socioeconomic status, previous experiences, time, resilience, and essence affect self-identity, as well as the views of others, assists the human service practitioner in connecting with the client and identifying strengths at all system levels. Providing opportunities for individuals to talk with and listen to family members about how the disability affects the family system and how the family system affects the person with the disability is also an avenue for deconstruction and reconstruction.

Practitioners need to continually challenge their own views about people living with disabilities both in a general perspective and in regard to specific disabilities. As Guadalupe and Lum state earlier in this book, it is important to "acknowledge and move beyond one's point of reference" when demonstrating practitioner competence. Remembering that client well-being is paramount, and trying to help the individual understand and accept how others view the individual's disability, can help to ensure optimization of client well-being.

Embracing a statement made by Judith Rothman (2003) that people living with disabilities are "people, human beings, who, like all human beings, are attempting to live their lives in a meaningful way" (p. xvii) can assist us in understanding the commonalities, differences, and controversies that people with disabilities face. Becoming knowledgeable of the ADA provisions, services in the community, theories relative to disability, and theories regarding identity development of people with disabilities—and, most importantly, listening to the experiences and stated needs of our clients living with disabilities—will further our application of multidimensional contextual practice.

SKILLS FOR ADDRESSING CHALLENGES AND STRENGTHS PRESENTED BY PEOPLE WITH DISABILITIES

Changing attitudes is a complicated process that must first challenge prejudicial thinking. Bogdan and Taylor (1989) maintain that the "definition of a person is to be found in the relationship between the definer and the defined, not determined either by personal characteristics or the abstract meaning attached to the group of which a person is a part" (p. 136). They identified people without disabilities who formed "accepting relationships." "An accepting relationship is one that is long-standing and characterized by closeness and affection. . . . The difference is not denied but does not bring disgrace" (p. 137). People in "accepting relationships" view people with disabilities as full-fledged human beings, in contrast to the dehumanizing perspectives that view people with severe disabilities as nonpersons. Bogdan and Taylor identify four dimensions of the characteristic of accepting behavior:

1. Attributing thinking to the other (to reason, understand, and remember)
2. Seeing individuality in the other (personality, likes and dislikes, feelings and motives, life histories, managing appearances)
3. Viewing the other as reciprocating (contributing something to the partnership: companionship, sense of accomplishment)
4. Defining social place for the other (defined as being an integral part of a group or social unit)

Deegan (1985) argues:

[T]raditional, institutional power relationships are dehumanizing precisely because they lack the possibility of true mutuality. These are hierarchical relationships in which clinicians have most of the power and patients have little if any power to control their own lives and the resources that affect their lives. These hierarchical and paternalistic relationships not only set the stage for dehumanization to occur, but also prescribe the role of passivity, dependence, and helplessness for the patient. (p. 5)

There is an alternative to this hierarchical and paternalistic relationship. Power need not mean "having power over" but can mean "having power with" or having power together, urging us to enter into relationships that are mutually empowering for both the clinician and the client. Relationships between professionals and clients are empowering when both parties in the relationship are available to be "moved by" the thoughts, perceptions, and feelings of the other. In this case, both are experiencing "themselves as being heard and responded to and are experiencing a fuller sense of being human together" (p. 5).

The stereotypes and attitudes held by human service practitioners can be unintentionally communicated to people living with disabilities; negative consequences can result. Changing attitudes is a complicated process that requires recognizing prejudicial thinking. Positive opinions toward individuals with disabilities are enhanced through verbal persuasion by someone who is credible and powerful; by information that emphasizes similarities, not differences, between individuals with and without disabilities; and through interaction with people who have disabilities and also have good interpersonal skills, enjoy leisure activities, have good academic abilities, are gainfully employed, or display competence in some other area that is valued by others.

Videotaped exposure emphasizing the unique personalities of individuals with disabilities within groups can be as effective as live interaction, especially when the presenter is a person with disabilities who does not reinforce a stereotype. A new member's attitude is also more likely to change when a majority of the respected group, familiar with a certain topic, holds a different opinion (Holaday & Wolfson, 1997, p. 64). For example, if students are convinced that higher-status human service practitioners have positive attitudes toward individuals with disabilities, they will be more willing to adopt positive opinions as well. Attitude changes must be accomplished through direct manipulation of both cognitive beliefs and emotional correlates. Therefore, continual exposure to information about people with disabilities is important when expanding one's skills relative to multidimensional contextual practice with people who have disabilities.

Effective practitioners are competent practitioners. To become an effective human service practitioner working with people living with disabilities, one needs to address prejudicial thinking and acquire clear, accurate, relevant, and practical information about disabilities and the disability community. Helping professionals' efforts to work with and on behalf of people with disabilities should also be based on an understanding of the construction of meaning for people with disabilities, not on external perceptions. Joining with and approaching the client as expert can assist with understanding not only how society has stigmatized, and continues to stigmatize, individuals with disabilities, but also how the client perceives and experiences the stigma, discrimination, and oppression.

The negative consequences of stereotyping by helping professionals may lead to misdiagnoses, improper interventions, and exacerbation of clients' problems. Helping professionals must work to uncover and *reject* stereotypes as they apply to people with disabilities. "When we reject a stereotype, we concentrate on a person as an individual, we see differences in that person from other members of the same group and we see similarities to members of other groups or, what is more important, to ourselves" (Vickers, 1987, p. 323). Although talking about older people, Vickers's

(1987) suggestion applies to many people with disabilities, and it liberates professionals from the functionalist ethic. It is not necessary to judge people by their work roles or their independence. "Assimilation" is no answer. It denies our differences, our needs, and our perspectives. It makes our identities invisible. Yet such is the power of the *status quo* that we are usually socially conditioned to hide our differences.

Helping professionals can also *reject* the "personal tragedy model," and confront the double, triple, and multiple oppressions faced by their clients (Corbett, 1993). By doing so, they will also learn to *reject* the medical model of disability and use the social model of disability. The medical model maintains that difference is an abnormality that should be treated and cured. It carries with it a stigma and is backed by a strong force: Collective Power. The culturally aware and skilled social service practitioner constantly seeks new ways of thinking about people with disabilities.

Deegan (1985), a woman with a PhD in psychology who identifies herself as a person living with a psychiatric disability, describes a professional danger that human service practitioners must avoid: The danger is that we can over identify with the professional roles we play and forget the people we are. The danger is that our minds can become severed from our hearts such that our human hearts no longer guide, inform and shape our work" (p. 1). She states that not only must we understand the experience of dehumanization that people living with disabilities face, but we also must "go to the real experts, the people who have lived the experiences, to understand it more fully" (p. 4). For example, many people with developmental disabilities want to eliminate the term *mental retardation* from the English vocabulary and would prefer to be referred to as having a learning disability. Honoring this wish is an example of listening to the real experts and understanding their experiences. We ask of you: Please respond humanly and with compassion to the cries of a real person.

CASE STUDY

Application of Multidimensional Contextual Practice

At the age of 33, Scott, a White man, survives a car accident. Waking to find his head immobile, unable to move his arms or legs, he is frightened. His wife, mother, and oldest sister immediately left their responsibilities and families to travel to Virginia where the accident occurred. They are there as Scott opens his eyes. Several days later, both of his brothers also join him as he begins his recovery from the accident. Before the accident, Scott was a father of two children, ages 8 and 5; he had a satisfying and promising career. Before the injury, he and his wife, Janet, were estranged and were planning to file for divorce. Before, he and his friend were enjoying a week without work, just hanging out without any particular appointments or meetings.

Scott's injuries were multiple and the pain was excruciating during those first few weeks. Yet everyone in his family comments that Scott's spirits are very positive. Each time his older sister spends time with him, she tears up. His mother has a hard time not becoming depressed, but is encouraged by Scott's jokes and jovial attitude. His wife stays by his bedside, and there is no discussion of divorce. His friend, who drove the car, also survived the accident with a broken leg. He recovers in several weeks, and no physical limitations are expected.

Once Scott is able to return to his home in Indiana, his spirits remain positive, but the reality of his limitations is more apparent. Scott will not be able to walk again and will have extremely limited use of his arms and hands. Doctors state that he is lucky to be alive. Scott went to college on a football scholarship and loved all athletic competitions. He will not be able to enjoy sports in the same ways that he has in the past. Financial stress is mounting, and Scott and his wife deplete their savings.

The church in their community collects donations to help the family. Others throughout the community collect money for the *Scott Fund*. Extended family members pray and visit as much as they can. Scott's mother moves back to the town where Scott lives to help care for him. Janet accepts a job and finds a new home that is wheelchair accessible. They move and set things up so that Scott can do as much as he wants for himself. Physical therapy continues. The children live with Scott's sister for a month so that Janet can focus attention on Scott and her new job. Scott's friend, who drove the car in the accident, helps financially.

As Scott's physical condition improves, he creates mechanisms to facilitate work on the computer again (it had been a major tool in his life). The money that continues to be collected enables them to purchase a motorized wheelchair and a van that is equipped with technology so that Scott can drive and not always rely on other people. His friend decides that he will not help out financially anymore. Scott's daughter, 9, has some difficulties in school and throws tantrums in the home to get her way. The 5-year-old is very fearful of spending time alone with his dad and seems more interested in spending time away from home. Scott watches his children grow up very fast, and feels like his life has been set back. His jovial, upbeat, and optimistic demeanor has waned. Now he feels very distant from his wife; he knows deep down that she stays with him because of the catastrophic accident. They never speak of the divorce that never happened. Scott feels alone, but has no intention of giving up on his life. Despite everything, he is glad he is alive.

Reflection on Case

The multidimensional contextual practice framework can be applied to this case scenario. If Scott were to request services due to his feelings of dissonance after his spinal cord injury, the human service practitioner would first want to understand what meaning the limited use of his legs and arms have for Scott. While listening to Scott's story, the practitioner would want to identify the client's strengths and protective factors. Scott demonstrated his resilience through his humor and his uplifting attitude while his family was dealing with his limitations. Scott found ways to use his intellect by adapting his computer even though that took much effort. His ability to learn to drive via the use of specialized equipment is another area of resiliency and may reflect this culture's emphasis on independence. His essence is shown throughout the scenario. Scott's protective factors include a close relationship with his family of origin and a faith community that is committed to his and his family's well-being.

Questions the human service practitioner may want to pose to Scott while focusing on client well-being might include: What does time mean to him? Was it different before the accident than it is now? How does Scott see himself as being different from and similar to others?

Moving to the second sphere of the framework, the multidimensional contextual client, a practitioner would want to explore the ways that Scott sees himself. It would be important to explore how he perceives himself differently now from how he saw himself before the accident. For example, it may be helpful to explore ways that Scott can continue to enjoy sports through participation, observation, or volunteer efforts. Obviously he has gained much support from family, friends, and the community, but what does this mean to Scott? Does he see this support as helpful, or does he perceive it differently? Scott may appreciate talking about his needs and how he feels about his relationships with his wife, children, and other family members. Does he feel they are stigmatizing him due to his new "status" as a person who has a disability? Or do they not acknowledge it at all for fear of losing the person they knew for so many years? How has Scott's injuries affected his wife? What decisions have been influenced by Scott's disability? Who are the caretakers in Scott's family? Are women expected to play out self-sacrificing behaviors?

Since the exchanges are transactional in nature, they are ever-changing. It is important to acknowledge that Scott's relationships are not static, nor would they have been if the injury did not occur. However, the fact that he is now living with a disability does affect the transactions and relationships he has with others. In addition to exploring his interactions with individuals important in his life and various community groups, analyzing magna-spiritual interaction and exchange factors is also important in applying the multidimensional contextual framework. Listening to Scott's personal beliefs about a Higher Power may be important to his developing concept of self and may guide his transactions with people at the church that is providing material (and possibly emotional) support for him and his family. Delving into religious practices that Scott identifies as important and unimportant and the meanings he ascribes to them would be another aspect in considering the effects of the magna-spiritual.

At the macro level, the exchanges that occur between Scott and his family, the neighborhood they live in, the school the children attend, the area merchants with whom he interfaces, and the community at large are important areas to discuss. How receptive are Scott's children's teachers to his involvement in school activities? Is the school wheelchair-accessible? To what degree does Scott want to be involved? What barriers does Scott identify in the community? Are stores accessible? Do merchants treat him respectfully?

An examination of the ways that Scott is affected by age, gender, ethnicity, self-identity, and physical and mental abilities can provide insights into the micro-intrapersonal interaction and exchange factors. This list is not inclusive, but it provides a good foundation with which to begin.

The fourth part of the multidimensional contextual practice framework is that of practitioner competence. To maximize Scott's well-being and to support him in ways that optimize his sense of self, competent practitioners would realize that no matter how much they might know about people living with disabilities, Scott's story is both similar to those of others with spinal cord injuries and also very unique and unduplicated. Gaining an understanding of Scott and what he identifies as his needs is important for the human service practitioner to keep in mind. The human service practitioner should approach Scott from a place of mutual discovery, mutual exploration and planning, mutual intervention, and mutual evaluation. Challenging one's own stereotypes and previous knowledge demonstrates an awareness that Scott is unique in his own right, and begins the process of deconstructing stereotypes.

One can consider the questions and ideas presented in the discussion about working with Scott in this particular scenario through an empathic and "seeking to understand" approach. This case study application demonstrates areas to be explored and understood when assisting a client such as Scott. Assessment and intervention with each client need to be individualized while applying multidimensional contextual practice.

SUMMARY

This chapter has explored some of the multiple realities encountered by people living with disabilities. Both commonalities and diversity have been addressed. The chapter also has examined possible cognitive, emotional, behavioral, and sociopolitical effects of stereotypes held toward various disability communities. The reader is encouraged to continue an exploration of the content introduced in this chapter and to make a commitment to support disability communities from a multidimensional contextual practice perspective.

Discussion Questions

1. Take a moment, close your eyes, and think about the phrase "people living with disabilities." What images come to mind? Write those down, and once you have exhausted your list, think about what they reveal regarding stereotypes you hold.

2. Do you believe it is important to know about clients' disabilities in order to help them? Why or why not? What is important to know?

3. Do you consider disability a culture? How would you describe the "culture" and "subcultures" of disability? Do you think all disabilities have the same culture?

4. How can human service practitioners help people in the community deconstruct stereotypes relative to people who have disabilities?

5. There are many ways to advocate and raise awareness for people with disabilities. How would you work to deconstruct disability stereotypes, challenge sexism and heterosexism, and find ways to include people with disabilities in community and organizational settings?

6. A study conducted by Van Hook (1992) found that simple contact with people living with disabilities did not result in an increased level of acceptance. She advises that special efforts may be required to facilitate acceptance of children with disabilities, yet she also states that social skills of children with disabilities must be improved. Is this a way to, once again, "blame the victim"?

7. The concept of diagnostic overshadowing refers to the tendency for professionals to be less likely to identify the presence of coexisting psychopathological disorders if there is a concomitant diagnosis of mental retardation (Garner et al., 1994). "When client descriptions included mental retardation, professionals were less likely to note such conditions as schizophrenia, personality disorders, phobias, and thought disorders, than when the client description included an average IQ. This unrecognized bias operating among professionals may lead to a failure to note, and to take into account the presence of a serious psychopathology, which in turn may lead to clients not receiving appropriate services" (p. 33). In what other situations or systems might diagnostic overshadowing occur?

References

Asch, A. (1984). The experience of disability: A challenge for psychology. *American Psychologist, 39*(5), 529–536.

Asch, A., & Fine, M. (1988). Introduction: Beyond pedestals. In A. Asch & M. Fine (Eds.), *Women with disabilities* (pp. 1–37). Philadelphia: Temple University Press.

Barker, R. L. (1999). *The social work dictionary.* Washington, DC: NASW Press.

Beuf, A. H. (1990). *Beauty is the beast: Appearance impaired children in America.* Philadelphia: University of Pennsylvania Press.

Black, R. B. (1994). Diversity and populations at risk: People with disabilities. In Frederic G. Reamer (Ed.),

The foundations of social work knowledge. New York: Columbia University Press.

Blotzer, M., & Ruth, R. (Eds.). (1995). *Sometimes you just want to feel like a human being: Case studies of empowering psychotherapy with people with disabilities.* Baltimore: Paul H. Brookes.

Bogdan, R., & Taylor, S. (1989). Relationships with severely disabled people: The social construction of humanness. *Social Problems, 36*(2), 135–148.

Bordieri, J. E., & Drehmer, D. E. (1989). Hiring decisions for disabled workers: Looking at the course. *Journal of Applied Social Psychology, 16*(3), 197–208.

Civil Rights Project. (2002). *Racial inequity in special education: Executive summary for federal policy makers.* Cambridge, MA: Harvard University.

Collins, K., & Valentine, D. (2003). Discovering women with disabilities: Responsive and relevant practice. *Journal of Social Work and Disability, 2*(4), 29–44.

Corbett, J. (1994). A proud label: Exploring the relationship between disability politics and gay pride. *Disabilities and Society, 9*(3), 343–357.

D'Aubin, A. (1991). The power of the pen: Empowering words. In D. Driedger (Ed.), *Disabled people in international development.* Winnipeg, Canada: Coalition of Provincial Organizations of the Handicapped (COPOH).

Deegan, M. J. (1985). Multiple minority groups: A case study of physically disabled women. In M. J. Deegan & N. A. Brooks (Eds.), *Women and disability: The double handicap* (pp. 37–55). New Brunswick, NJ: Transaction.

Devine, P. G., & Monteith, M. J. (1993). The role of discrepancy-associated affect in prejudice. In D. M. Mackie & D. L. Hamilton (Eds.), *Affect, cognition, and stereotyping: Interactive processes in group perception* (pp. 317–344). New York: Academic Press.

Esses V. M., Haddock, G., & Zanna, M. P. (1993). Values, stereotypes, and emotions as determinants of intergroup attitudes. In D. Mackie & D. Hamilton (Eds.), *Affect, cognition, and stereotyping* (pp. 137–166). San Diego: Academic.

Fowler, C., O'Rourke, B., Wadsworth, J., & Harper, D. (1992). Disability and feminism: Models for counselor exploration of personal values and beliefs. *Journal of Applied Rehabilitation Counseling, 23*(4), 14–19.

Gatens-Robinson, E., & Tarvydas, V. (1992). Ethics of care, women's perspectives and the status of the main-

stream rehabilitation ethical analysis. *Journal of Applied Rehabilitation Counseling, 23*(4), 26–33.

Goffman, I. (1963). *Stigma: Notes on the management of spoiled identity.* Englewood Cliffs, NJ: Prentice-Hall.

Hahn, H. (1985). Towards a politics of disabilities: Definition, discipline, and policies. *Social Science Journal, 22*(4), 87–105.

Healey, S. (1993a). Coming out in voices. *Women in Therapy, 14*(3/4), 9–17.

Healey, S. (1993b). The common agenda between old women and women with disabilities and all women. *Women and Therapy, 14*(3/4), 65–77.

Ho, D. (1995). Internalized culture, culturocentrism, and transcendence. *The Counseling Psychologist, 23,* 4–24.

Holaday, M., &. Wolfson, A. (1997). Attitudes toward children with severe burns. *Rehabilitation Counseling Bulletin, 41,* 54–69.

Kaye, S., LaPlante, M. P., Carlson, D., & Wenger, B. L. (1996). Abstract 17. Disabilities Statistics Center: A Rehabilitation and Training Center, http://dsc.ucsf.edu.

Kopels, S. (1995). The Americans with Disabilities Act: A tool to combat poverty. *Journal of Social Work Education, 31*(3), 337–346.

Lindesmith, A. R., Strauss, A. L., & Denzin, N. K. (1991). *Social psychology.* Englewood Cliffs, NJ: Prentice-Hall.

Lloyd, M. (1992). Does she boil eggs? Towards a feminist model of disability. *Disability, Handicap and Society, 7*(3), 207–221.

Mackie, D. M., & Hamilton, D. L. (Eds.). (1993). *Affect, cognition, and stereotyping: Interactive processes in group perception.* New York: Academic Press.

Miller, C. T., Loboto, D., Fitzgerald, M. D., & Brand, P. (1989). What mentally retarded and nonmentally retarded children expect of one another. *American Journal on Mental Retardation, 13*(4), 396–405.

Norton, D. G. A. (1993). Diversity and early socialization, and temporal development: The dual perspective revisited. *Social Work, 38*(1), 82–90.

Olkin, R. (1999). *What psychotherapists should know about disabilities.* New York: Guilford.

Owen, C., & Topaz, A. (1995). Women's health statewide. [Online] Retrieved on October 3, 2000, from http://www.peg.apc.org:80/whs/disable.htm.

Pfeiffer, D. (1991). The influence of the socio-economic characteristics of disabled people on their employment status and income. *Disability, Handicap and Society,* 6(2), 103–114.

Quinn, P. (1994). America's disability policy: Another double standard? *Affilia: Journal of Women and Social Work,* 9(1), 45–59.

Rajah, Z. (1991). Thoughts on women and disability. In D. Driedger (Ed.), *Disabled people in international development.* Winnipeg, Canada: Coalition of Provincial Organizations of the Handicapped (COPOH).

Reinharz, S. (1992). *Feminist methods in social science research.* New York: Oxford University Press.

Renteria, D. (1993). Rejection. [Online] http://www.deafqueer.org/drago/rejection.html.

Rothman, J. C. (2003). *Social work practice across disability.* Boston: Allyn & Bacon.

Solomon, S. E. (1993). Women and physical distinction: A review of the literature and suggestions for intervention. *Women and Therapy,* 14(3/4), 91–103.

Stafford, M. C., & Scott, R. R. (1986). Stigma, deviance, and social control: Some conceptual issues. In S. C. Ainlay et al. (Eds.), *The dilemma of difference: A multidisciplinary view of stigma.* New York: Plenum.

Swedish Handicapped International Aid Foundation (SHIA). (1995). Women walk on water. *Fourth World Congress on Women,* Bejing, China, September 1995. [Online] http://www.empowermentzone.com/womenkit.txt.

Turnbull, H. R., & Turnbull, A. (1985). *Parents speak out: Now and then.* Columbia: Merrill.

United Nations. (1983). *World program of action concerning disabled persons.* New York: Author.

U.S. Census Bureau. (1990). *Disability characteristics, 1990 census.* U.S. Census Bureau, http://www.census.gov/hhes/www/disable/census.html.

U.S. Census Bureau. (2002). *12th Anniversary of Americans with Disabilities Act.* Retrieved May 24, 2004, from http://www.census.gov/Press-Release/www/2002/demoprofiles.html.

U.S. Department of Labor. (2003). *Disability data resources.* Retrieved May 24, 2004, from http://www.dol.gov/odep/pubs/ek99/resources.htm.

Van Hook, M. (1992). Integrating children with disabilities: An ongoing challenge. *Social Work in Education,* 14(1), 25–35.

Vickers, R. (1987). A psychological approach to attitudes towards blind persons. *Journal of Visual Impairment and Blindness,* 323–325.

Wasow, M., & Wikler, L. (1983). Reflections on professionals' attitudes toward the severely mentally retarded and the chronically mentally ill: Implications for parents. *Family Therapy,* 10(3), 299–308.

Weiss, M. (1994). *Conditional love: Parents' attitudes toward handicapped children.* Westport, CT: Bergins & Garvey.

Wendall, S. (1989). Towards a feminist theory of disability. *Hypatia,* 4(2), 104–124.

Yuker, H. E. (1994). Variables that influence attitudes toward people with disabilities: Conclusions from the data. *Journal of Social Behavior and Personality,* 9(5), 3–22.

Life is always at a turning point. —**Irwin Edman**

11 | Aging Persons

General Population Groups

J O Y C E   B U R R I S

In my town, there is a woman who wins marathon races on a regular basis. She is featured on the front pages of the local newspapers. The news articles are written with a tone of incredulity. Is it an important feature that she is also 80 years old? The fact of her age is stressed by the reporters as an important feature: Why is that so? At every age, some people are outstanding athletes, yet in the United States, such accomplishments are marveled at when the actors are over the age of 65. In some other cultures, good health and physical accomplishment in old age are not considered noteworthy.

A man who is over 100 years old is featured in a documentary about aging in the state of Georgia in the former Soviet Union. His good health and good spirits are not considered unusual by his neighbors, as there are many in his community who also enjoy high levels of activity and equal levels of good health. He is asked if there are things that he cannot do now that he is over 100. He admits that it is a little harder for him to climb trees. My students always laugh upon hearing this story: Why do they laugh?

INTRODUCTION

The purpose of this chapter is to explore the constructs that are used to define an extremely diverse group of people, sometimes euphemistically called "seniors" or "the elderly," and to critically examine the ways in which cultural constructs obscure the diversity among a people that this author will refer to as older people or the aging populations. Human service practitioners who work with the aging populations must be knowledgeable about the diverse ways that older people experience and live their lives and be informed about the diversity of racial and ethnic experiences, social classes, genders, sexual orientations, effects of disabilities, and so on that create varying realities for aging people within this group.

In exploring diversity among the aging, one becomes aware that knowledge is structured around sets of perceptions and preconceptions, images and beliefs, and stereotyping notions. The interpretation of data or "facts" often serves preconceived notions of which people are included in the aging population, and of what their needs are. Further, these perceptions affect the distribution of kind and quantity of resources available to the aging individuals within this population. In this chapter, both social constructs and statistical data about aging will be discussed, along with an application of the multidimensional contextual practice framework to a case example.

AGING AND THE LIFE CYCLE

The years beyond age 65 are a part of one's life that, in the United States, is often culturally defined as old age. The aging portion of the life cycle may vary in duration, but can span upward to twenty or, in many cases, thirty years or more of an individual's life, depending on a variety of factors. Adolescence, in comparison, is assigned one half to one third (ten years) of the length of time in the life span as is aging. Many changes may occur in twenty or thirty years of one's life, such that those at one end of this phase of the life span may have very different realities from those at the other end. Neugarten (1974) proposed that aging be divided into "old-old" (individuals in the aging population who are over 85 years old, and who may be statistically more likely to experience chronic health problems and a possible increase in economic and social problems), "young-old" (those aged 65–75 years, who are usually indistinguishable from middle-aged adults except that individuals are in retirement), and the "middle-young" who are in between (75–85). Neugarten's definition, while resisting trends to lump all older people into a single vision of aging that existed at the time she proposed these distinctions, still assumes an "average" stagelike aging experience that is inevitable, linear, and predictable among members at each phase of the aging process.

Another way to view this group has been recommended, however, for human service practitioners. It involves viewing this group as "clients" who may have a variety of realities and experiences at any age of the aging process and who may require different "levels of intervention," including primary, secondary, and tertiary interventions (Kropf & Hutchison, 2000). Primary interventions are aimed at healthy and active older people at any age and may include preventive measures, that is, educational, social, and recreational opportunities of support that help in the maintenance of optimal health and well-being. Secondary interventions are utilized to provide early detection and intervention of a potential "problem" in order to arrest or act against possible deleterious effects. Tertiary intervention includes responses to chronic, serious, and disabling "problems and dysfunctions" that may include, but are not limited to, end-of-life care in a variety of settings.

DEMOGRAPHICS AND DIVERSITY WITHIN DIVERSITY OF AGING PEOPLE

It has long been recognized that the aging population is expected to grow tremendously in the next ten to fifteen years as baby boomers, who represented a 35% increase in babies born between 1946 and 1964, will begin their 65th year (Burris, 1994). Sixty-five years is often cited in the United States as the beginning of a time in life that has been culturally and socially constructed to be set aside as the start of the last stage of life or aging (Burris & Guadalupe, 2003). By the years 2010–2040, the numbers of people 65 and older are projected to double, from about 38 million in 2010 to about 79 million in 2040 (U.S. Bureau of the Census, 1999). The average life expectancy in the United States has increased from 46 years in the early 1900s, to 72 years by the early 1990s, and is expected to reach 82 years by 2020 (Morales & Sheafor, 2002). Since these statistics represents an average, they belie the truth that many people will outlive the average life expectancy. Further, the fastest-growing proportion of the population is the group of people who are over 85 years of age. The expectation is that there will be a fivefold increase in this group of the old-old (Soldo & Manton, in Burris, 1994, p. 4). As a result of this population trend, an increase in the need for dialogue, planning, resources, and services is expected by human services practitioners and gerontologists (Ginsberg, 2001; Greene, 1989; Kane, Solomon, Beck, Keeler, & Kane, 1980; Morgan & Kunkel, 2001; Peterson, 1990; Poulin & Walter, 1992; Quam & Whitford, 1992; Schneider, Kropf, & Kisor, 2000; Soldo & Manton, 1985; Solomon & Mellor, 1992; Wendt & Peterson, 1992).

While it is a well-known fact that women live longer than men in general, people of color (including the women) and the poor have a shorter-than-average life expectancy from birth than people in other social classes. For example, the American Indian tribal populations have the shortest average life expectancy, with an average of 67 years, and this group also has among the highest poverty rates, of nearly 50% (U.S. Bureau of the Census, 1999). The interactions of social class, race, and sex strongly influence both life expectancies and the distribution of health statuses (Quandagno, 1999). Diverse consequences are created among aging individuals by the stress and hazards of poverty; immigration; discrimination; oppression; racial, gender, and socioeconomic stratification; educational and occupational barriers; environmental racism; and so on. There is an interesting "crossover phenomenon" regarding race and life expectancy. Although African Americans have a shorter life expectancy from birth (65 years for males and 74 years for females) compared with whites (73 years for males and 79 years for females), once African Americans reach the age of 85, their life expectancy (5 more years for males and 6 more years for females of both races) nearly equals that of Whites (Morgan & Kunkel, 2001).

Older people are ethnically and racially diverse, and becoming more so, due to the fact that some racial or ethnic groups of individuals within this population have historically had higher fertility rates and/or have immigrated to the United States from many diverse ethnic regions of the world. For example, the numbers of people who live in the United States with backgrounds such as Asian/Pacific Islander, African

American, Latino/a, and First Nations/Native American are increasing more rapidly than the numbers of people from other racial and ethnic groups (Morales & Sheafor, 2002). In 1990, these groups made up 13% of the aging population in the United States, and they are predicted to jump to 25% by 2025 (American Association of Retired Persons [AARP], 1996).

The poverty rates within the United States are generally very high compared with those of other "developed" nations. The poverty rate for the aging population as a whole is 11%, which is about equal to the national rates of poverty when comparing all age groups. However, African Americans within the aging population experience a poverty rate of 26%, Latino/as have a rate of 21%, and Asians have a 12% poverty rate, compared with Whites who have a poverty rate of 9% (U.S. Bureau of the Census, 1999). Prior to the 1960s, poverty rates among the aging population as a whole reached as high as 35%, and it was only after passage and implementation of Medicare legislation and indexing of Social Security to inflation, among other things, that poverty rates were lowered (Preston, 1984; Schiller, 1984). While there is a general concern regarding the hardships of poverty on the aging, it is important to note that most economic deprivation among this population may be traced to income inequality during the life span before retirement. Generally, those who live in poverty in old age lived in poverty as younger adults (O'Rand, 1996; Schiller, 1984). This is less true for women as a group, while being generally true for the aging population as a whole.

Due to the fact that women as a collective live so much longer than men, the sex ratio of the aging population becomes increasingly skewed with age, resulting in "sixty men for every one hundred women" at the age of 65; and in just the part of the aging population that is over the age of 85, there are "thirty-nine men for every one hundred women" (Morales & Sheafor, 2002, p. 95). Susan Sontag (1972) wrote a classic essay depicting what she called a "double standard of aging," whereby the forces of ageism and sexism make old age more difficult for women than for men. Nearly three quarters of aging people who live below the poverty line are women, and the low income is attributed to reasons that are cumulative and multiple (Administration on Aging, 1999). Among the reasons for the increased poverty rates for aging women compared with men are: (1) lower levels of education, especially in lucrative fields; (2) lower wages for women in the same jobs as men; (3) employment that is often in segregated job sectors with no benefits or lower levels of benefits (i.e., health care, pension, Social Security); (4) the fact that much of the work women do is unpaid (e.g., family caregiving, volunteer work, agricultural work) (Stoller & Gibson, 2000); and (5) longer life expectancy with high rates of widowhood and a consequence that more than half of these women who were not poor before the death of their husbands now live in poverty (AARP, 1998; Okin, 1989).

Sexual orientation is another source of diversity among the aging population. Although the majority of the current aging population is considered heterosexual, it is very difficult to estimate the numbers of gay, lesbian, bisexual, and transgendered (GLBT) members within the population. During the youth of the current aging population, the circumstance of being "out" was an extremely dangerous experience, exposing individuals to harassment (and sometimes brutality and death), unemployment, difficulty finding housing, and discrimination of various other sorts. Only since the Stonewall rebellion in 1969, the liberation movements in the 1970s, the removal of homosexuality from the list of "diseases" in the *Diagnostic and Statistical Manual* in 1973, and the passage of antidiscrimination legislation in some areas, have GLBT people had a modicum of "safety" that makes it comparatively more possible to estimate the size of the GLBT population now in their midlife years (Barranti & Cohen, 2000). Gay and lesbian populations over the age of 65 have been estimated to be as high as 3.5 million (Rogers, 1993); however, the accuracy of that estimate is difficult to evaluate.

Although not universal, the benefits of laws in some states and in some businesses do provide recognition of domestic partnerships that extends to gay and lesbian partners health benefits, leave for illness and bereavement of a partner, access to visit partner who is hospitalized or in intensive care, protection of property and financial benefits acquired together, and so on. As these are not universal, much still must be done to make sure that aging GLBT people receive the same rights as non-GLBT partners. In states that have domestic partnership laws, GLBT people may still have trouble locating housing, acquiring insurance, and locating assisted living or nursing home care, among other important considerations (Stoller & Gibson, 2000).

Having a physical disability is another source of diversity among the aging population. Although there is some difficulty identifying when a health condition becomes a "disability," having a disability has a profound effect on one's life. Many people acquire disabilities as they age, while others have had lifelong experiences with disabilities. According to survey data from the 1990 and 1991 Survey of Income and Program Participation, Bureau of Census, there is a disability prevalence rate of 13.4% among males 65 and older, and this made up of 15.5% of all people with a disability, while 20.4% of females in the same age group lived with a disability, making up 27.7% of all people with a disability (McNeil, 1993, in Gilson, 2000). Aging people with a disability needing personal assistance with "activities of daily living" made up 17.7% (McNeil, 1993, in Gilson, 2000). The unpredictability of the disabling condition, loss of control, changing definitions of self in relation to others, and fears of being alone and of being stereotyped and discriminated against are some of the issues that people with disabilities must deal with on an ongoing basis, as well as stress about systems of services that are disjointed, scarce, difficult to navigate, and difficult to procure payment for (Cohen, 1992).

Diversity within the aging community can be described as endless. The content here provides only glimpses of such diversity. Aging people may also differ in their political orientations, interests, values, beliefs, language spoken, and spiritual practices, among many others areas. Human services practitioners are encouraged to be aware of such diversity while attempting to be of service to this population.

SOCIAL CONSTRUCTION OF AGING

A personal experience regarding how older people are viewed affected this author's life in a profound way. It began with meeting a young man from Zimbabwe who came to the United States to get an education at California State University in Sacramento. He was 18 at the time and had never seen snow, having come from an

African country where the average year-round temperatures are about 70 degrees. Our family then had the great joy and privilege of taking him into the mountains in the winter to see the snow. Having come from a land-locked country, he also had never seen the ocean. We took him to the Pacific Ocean where the beach borders the end of Golden Gate Park. He was so excited to witness both snow and ocean, but was especially thrilled at seeing the ocean. He ran up and down the beach with glee and abandon as he enjoyed the beauty of the waves gently rolling onto the shore. He ran over to us and announced the following, "Now I am old!" He said this with such pride and happiness that I encouraged him to speak further about what he meant by the statement. He said that in his country, when a person gets to see something that others do not in their lifetime witness, that person is granted the status of being "old," which is considered a source of greatness.

The attitude of this man from Zimbabwe, where being considered old is a compliment, represented a stark contrast to the attitude of mainstream culture in the United States, where being old is often so distasteful that euphemisms are created so that, linguistically, individuals may escape the negative association of the word. Being "elderly" or a "senior citizen" or living in the "golden years" is preferable to being "old." Why are these euphemisms created? What do people fear in cultures in which euphemisms are used? Who is it that creates these labels and images and concepts?

When students in this author's social work classes speak about these questions, they suggest that fear of aging exists in the United States, because old age is associated with disease and death, loneliness and loss. Someone invariably reports having visited a nursing home where people sat in wheelchairs and stared blankly at nothing in particular. For many students, this is the face of the objective biological nature of old age. The fact that, at any given time, the older people in long-term care facilities represent only a very small portion (about 4%) of the aging population is not widely known (AARP, 1998). In fact, when students are asked in class to guess what percent of people over the age of 65 currently live in long-term care facilities, their answers usually fall between 50% and 80%. Further, students do not usually question the context in which aging takes place, nor do they usually question the institutions of care that surround the aging individuals and affect well-being in fundamental ways that are not biological imperatives in the aging person.

Ageism, Labeling, and Stereotypes

The term *ageism* was coined in 1969 by Robert Butler and was explored in his Pulitzer Prize–winning book, *Why Survive? Being Old in America* (1975). The term is used to describe negative attitudes and stereotypes of older people and was used by Butler to describe a form of bigotry or prejudice. Kalish (1979) outlined what he called a "new ageism" that obscures individual and group differences among the aging population and defines older people in terms of characteristics of the least healthy, least well-provided-for, and least capable. This view is often promoted by those who profess to care most about the needs and well-being of older people. Ironically, Kalish cites Butler's (1975) book as a source of examples of this type of ageism.

Theoretical explanations are numerous in attempts to account for ageism. Among theoretical factors that have been attributed to the comparatively lowered status of older people are the rapid changes in society that accompanied modernization and that render the contributions of older people obsolete (Cowgill & Holmes, 1972); demographic changes and late development of emphasis on values of equality and liberty in the 19th century (Fischer, 1977); need to scapegoat (Binstock, 1983; Levin & Levin, 1980); overuse of descriptions of aging generated from professionals in policy positions, long-term care institutions, and hospitals (Harding & Palfrey, 1997; Kalish, 1979; Quinn, 1987); stereotypes perpetrated in the media (Harris & Feinberg, 1977; Kubey, 1980); linguistics or use of language that perpetuates stereotypes (Barbato & Fezzel, 1987; Nuessel, 1982); development of an aging subculture in response to marginalization (Rose, 1965); age stratification (Riley, 1971, 1987); and political economy (Estes, 1980; Hazan, 1994; Phillipson, 1982).

This author has chosen the term *aging* to identify the group of people that is sometimes referred to as "elderly." Attempts to use the term *old* have been met with horror and misunderstanding on the part of students and colleagues alike. Perhaps culturally, there is not yet a readiness to face old age and to question the negative cultural view that the word *old* conjures. Another reason for using the term *aging* is that it connotes a process of aging that is continuous and fluid. In truth, aging is not a static objective state. Additionally, all people are aging all the time, and thus the term *aging* has the potential to not split off and segregate all who are arbitrarily assigned, at age 65, to be "senior citizens" by government entities, medical establishments, professionals, and corporations.

One of the myths of the aging population is that it represents a homogenous grouping of people who are alike as they face what is often perceived as the "declining" years. On the contrary, the age of 65 has little to do with a sudden loss of productive capacities, decline in physical or mental abilities, abrupt change in personality, or decreased interests and creative juices that common stereotypes suggest. Culturally, old age is most often portrayed as a time of life that is fraught with problems of illness, disease, dementia, depression, loneliness, and loss.

The descriptive phrase *young at heart* refers to a state of wonder or a lightness of spirit. Occasionally this phrase is used to describe an older person, and it is often accompanied with a tone of surprise, as though wonder, joy, and lightness belong solely to young people. Interestingly enough, a phenomenon has been entering the advertising campaigns of drug companies, vitamin marketers, cruise lines, and financial establishments to portray a "silver" lining in the visual images of older people who are enjoying life; however, these images are being used to sell things to the older people of the burgeoning baby boom. Presumably, if the older person buys the products being sold, that person will not become the declining and decrepit stereotype of aging that is more common in the culture.

Another phrase that is commonly heard is the expression, "I'm having a senior moment." This is used, usually accompanied by laughter, when a temporary lapse in memory occurs. The statement is often made by a person who is younger by far than the age of 65, which is the age that has been culturally assigned the label of "senior citizen." Momentary forgetfulness occurs at every age and is often a symptom of intense emotional states, stress, and strain from the fast-paced, goal-oriented life that is demanded in the dominant culture. Certainly, changes in the functions of the mind and body do occur in the aging process, but aging takes place continually over the life span and does not suddenly occur at age 65. Further, there is much diversity of mental functioning at every age, and the overwhelming majority of older people do not have difficulties in mental functioning that would warrant such universal labeling (Schneider et al., 2000).

Aging as a Problem and Structural Views of Aging

The professional social service literature and "knowledge" about aging often is guilty of inadvertently stereotyping and labeling older people by focusing exclusively on the "problems" of aging. The focus in many textbooks is placed on what is "wrong" with the aging population and the individuals within this population, as defined in an ageist culture. There is little or no focus on the diversity within the aging population or on structural and cultural realities of discrimination in a context of social and political marginalization (Estes, Binney, & Culbertson, 1992; Hazan, 1994; Kalish, 1979). Nor is there a significant attempt to connect structural conditions of the older person's life to structural conditions that existed when that person was younger. If the economic, social, and political arrangements were different for some people during their life span, different aging outcomes may have resulted. In fact, the answer to successful aging often lies in the collective political, economic, and social decisions of an earlier era. For example, nutritional status and healthy conditions in early life contribute to increased health throughout the life cycle.

Kenneth Pelletier (1977), author of *Mind as Healer, Mind as Slayer: A Holistic Approach to Preventing Stress Disorders,* conducted a study of cultures in which a large proportion of the population lived to be 100 years or older (centenarians), and in which those who lived to be over 100 did so in good health. There were no hospitals in these cultures, as herbal and homeopathic remedies were sought for troubles. None of the physical difficulties that are attributed to "aging" in the United States even existed in these cultures; there were no cancers and no heart attacks. These cultures included, among others, the Abkhasians who live in the northern part of the Republic of Georgia, the Vilcabambans who live in the Andes Mountains of Ecuador, and people in other locations, including Paros, Greece, and Yagodina, Bulgaria. The following general structural characteristics were reported:

- The cultures were located in mountainous regions primarily, and were primarily agricultural.
- There was no such thing as retirement; people worked at agricultural tasks throughout their adulthood.
- Diets consisted of organically grown fruits, vegetables, and grains, for the most part. No processed foods, loaded with fats and sugars, were eaten.
- Rather high consumptions of homemade wine were common, but there was no binging. Wine was consumed with family and friends at meals.
- There were no electromagnetic waves in their environments.
- People exercised at a moderate pace regularly; they walked everywhere they went.

- Sexuality was considered a normal adult interest, regardless of age.
- Old people were highly regarded and given an honored place within the close-knit relationships of the culture.
- People expected to live long lives in good health.

Studies such as these have their critics, who suggest that the ages of the members of these cultures were exaggerated. The reported ages of 130 or 140 years may have been overestimated beyond the actual 105 or 110 that might have been closer to the truth (Holmes & Holmes, 1995); however, it cannot be denied that the structural elements just described contribute to good health at any age. Indeed, there are groups within the United States that experience some of what Pelletier describes. For example, the Amish live comparatively long and healthy lives, and the oldest members of Amish communities are not marginalized.

At the same time, many of the experiences and structural supports identified by Pelletier as responsible for the health and longevity of the aging populations he described are absent in the lives of many members of the United States. Environmental hazards, toxic pollution, overuse of fatty and starchy fast food, lack of exercise due to overuse of automobiles, fast-paced lifestyles, binging on chemical substances (i.e., alcohol and drugs), breakdown of community cohesiveness and social support, disrespect, and marginalization all take their toll in the aging process, beginning in childhood. Therefore, what is attributed to a "natural" decline in old age is highly acerbated by the institutionalized unhealthy lifestyles and life chances in the larger culture.

There is a very strong tendency in the United States to place responsibility for whatever a person experiences within the individual, rather than to see how the multidimensional contextual structures limit the range of choices available to the person. In a study conducted by Estes (1980) of staff and members of community planning agencies for the aging, all participants in her research worked for agencies that were accommodative (i.e., placed the "problems" of the aging within the aging individuals themselves and offered services that assist or augment rather than restore or prevent). This, in spite of the fact that a majority (72%) of the professionals, when asked to describe them, conceptualized problems of aging to be structural in origin rather than being located "in the person." This was compared with only half (51%) of the general population who took a structural view. However, the most powerful and expert planning members were more likely to describe the process of growing old in terms of "problems" associated with individual causes or origins. Estes (1979) argues that in the process of defining aging as a problem, "problems" of old age and old age itself are commonly viewed as follows:

1. Aging individuals are viewed as being so different from others in society that they require segregation and special, different, or no treatment.
2. Aging people are characterized by an inevitable physical decline of the individual that justifies the stigmatization and continuing marginality of the aged.
3. The aging population has a divisible set of needs that can be converted into commodities or services for consumption by the aged.
4. The "problems" of the aging are remediable largely through national policies focused on the socialization of the elderly (rather than policies that would

address the disadvantaged status of the aged and thus might improve their social and economic status).

5. Having reached crisis proportions, the growing aging population justifies developing policies and expending funds to expand the service economy. (Estes, 1979, p. 16)

Estes (1979) raised the question of whether there is indeed a need for the academic discipline called gerontology. Her argument is that older people are adults, so why are they separated out for study instead of being included in the study of adulthood? Why not address the political and social needs of all adults as adults, regardless of their ages? She further argues that the segregation of older adults from other adults has led to defining them as having problems primarily, and particularly as having medical problems, which has led to the "medicalization of the aging." This is a process of labeling older people as medical problems and assessing the basis of whatever is happening to older individuals as primarily a health problem that must be treated by medical means.

Medicalization of Aging

Older people are frequently identified with and as health problems in the United States, which contributes to stereotypes at the individual level of older people being defined primarily by their health. The medical model that dominates in the United States has been traditionally used not to define health in a holistic way, but to assess bodies that are seen as having the presence of unhealthy symptoms (Estes, 1979; Estes et al., 1996). Bodily functions are defined in terms of biological mechanics, and the causes of illness or disease are discovered in the cellular and biochemical systems within the body. A sign of distress in the individual calls for some intervention in the individual body, as opposed to a more ecological view that would also include the interaction with structural factors of the economic, social, and political institutions and consequent problematic distribution of needed and uncontaminated resources (Minkler & Estes, 1999; Vincent, 1999).

Thus, rather than viewing the socioeconomic stratification system as the source of health problems, or rather than taking corporations to task for polluting air, water, and soil and selling unhealthy food and other consumables, individuals are given radiation treatment, chemotherapy, triple bypass operations, and many daily prescription medications. Of particular concern in this whole process is the present tendency toward enriching the medical sector with the profits from overmedicalizing the process of aging for the wealthier classes within the aging population, while at the same time neglecting to provide even minimal levels of medical and other kinds of support for members of less advantaged classes of aging (Estes, 1979; Estes, Linkins, & Binney, 1996; Estes, Swan, & Gerard, 1982; Minkler & Estes, 1999; Navarro, 1976; Reynolds, 1987; Vincent, 1999). In fact, according to Vincent, "There is a strong case to be argued that it is not increasing numbers of older people which are placing a strain on medical services. Rather, it is the medically dominated way of thinking about old age and the resulting pattern of service provision that has created the dilemma" (1999, p. 60).

MULTIDIMENSIONAL CONTEXTUAL PRACTICE FRAMEWORK

Multidimensional contextual practice begins with the recognition that individuals have many different influences on their behaviors, identities, beliefs, and choices. An individual, family, or group's relationship to the structure of life chances and opportunities is something that may be totally outside their immediate control, but will greatly influence what happens in their lives. The effects of one's location on continuums of the social structure regarding income, race, gender, sexual orientation, and disability are obscured by the reductionism and stereotypes of aging as a medical problem. The consequence, in addition to the harm caused by stereotyping and mistreating the aging, is that larger social needs for a balanced healthy life and improvements regarding housing, social supports, employment, income security, pensions, and ending discrimination against the aging get little attention by comparison. These structural barriers to well-being are obscured at every age, but such blindness is particularly present in the views about old age. Thus, rather than producing outrage that the structure of opportunities is not adjusted so that people have enhanced chances at well-being in late life, language such as "problems with aging," "frail elderly," or "what can you expect at your age" normalizes the inequities of the distribution system. In fact, the connection between the distribution systems of opportunities disappears with language that implies that old people are beset with problems, particularly health problems, as a natural aspect of getting older (almost as though this were a biological phenomenon).

One impact of the "problems-with-aging" approach on education may be to turn students against wanting to work directly with this population on a micro or meso level, while at the same time eliciting empathy for older people who are disadvantaged, chronically ill, or discriminated against. Certainly, such "problem-focused" education inadvertently reinforces stereotypes that limit professional effectiveness and stunt commitment to and interest in working with the population (Lowy, 1983). One study (Davis-Berman & Robinson, 1989) found, in pretest and posttest designed research, that after taking a single course specializing in content on aging, students had increased their awareness and improved their attitudes toward older people, but they indicated a decreased desire to work with this population. One can only imagine the change for aging populations that might be created if the professional and cultural views of aging were more positive and if there were more recognition of the interaction of structural context and availability of personal resources in the creation of well-being at every age. At the very least, old age would be viewed more from a structural perspective, and this would lessen victim blaming.

Multidimensional Contextual Case Example

Robertson (1991) traced the social history of Alzheimer's disease—a condition that, in the 1980s, was identified by medical professionals as the "fourth or fifth leading cause of adult deaths in the United States." The number of subsequent diagnoses of Alzheimer's disease soared. Individuals over the age of 65 with Alzheimer's were described in greatly varied ways, depending on the source. Epidemiclike scenarios appeared, with estimates of incidence in those over 85 years of age ranging from 15 or 20%, at the low end, to nearly 40% at the high end. Estimates of the prevalence of Alzheimer's disease in individuals over 65 years of age produced figures that ranged from as low as 5% to more than 11% (Robertson, 1991, p. 136).

Alzheimer's disease is difficult to diagnose directly and is usually diagnosed by the elimination of other possible diagnostic categories of diseases. Postmortem identification of the presence of plaques in the brain structure is the only way to ensure the diagnosis of Alzheimer's. Robertson (1991) argues that "the politics of Alzheimer's" in conjunction with social stereotypes of aging have contributed to the expansion of estimates of this disease among the aging. To make her point, she cites the imprecise criteria of diagnosis and the increase in hospital use of people over the age of 65 whose diagnoses fell into a small number of categories (Hertzman, Pulcins, Barer, Evans, Anderson, & Lomas, 1989). An increase of 500,000 patient days occurred between 1969 and June of 1985 among the aging (80% of whom were women) that were attributed to the diagnosis of dementia, which loosely clusters together perceived memory, thought, and emotional and behavioral changes. Robertson (1991) attributed the rise in diagnosis and hospital use to changes in the perceptions of medical staff and to what many authors refer to as the social construction of aging. Others have identified similar patterns of diagnosis of a degenerative disease that has no cure and leads to a slow and terrible decline in functioning (Harding & Palfrey, 1997).

Recently, public radio programming featured a discussion of the problems created by the overmedication of aging individuals, which can produce dementia-like symptoms. Older people under medical care receive an average of twelve medications. Medical care is increasingly being provided by HMOs, with the result that services are fragmented: The oversight that used to be provided by a family doctor and a pharmacist, who could alert a patient to harmful interactive effects of drugs, is weakened. Many of the interactive effects alter the ability to concentrate, affect memory, and create in the patient symptoms (sometimes called "side effects") that are mistaken for dementia. Featured on the program were numerous cases of families whose loved ones had initially accepted the diagnosis of dementia but who, with further questioning and investigation, had discovered the interactive effects of medications. When medications were pared back and simplified, the symptoms of disorientation and memory loss disappeared. The end result included not only restored functioning but also the abandonment of plans for institutionalization in long-term care homes.

Empowerment Perspective

Empowerment begins with the recognition that the personal is also political (Mills, 1959). What happens to the individual is connected to the dynamic interplay of forces taking place in the structures of the larger society. Knowledge is not just a flawed product that scientific experts and professionals produce; it is also part of the process of questioning, experiencing, and challenging the social constructions of power arrangements. The forces of oppression, particularly the oppressive experience of having one's existence defined by others who may have good intentions, but who also have something to gain in the way of power, status, or profits, work against self-knowledge and empowerment. Promoting social and individual change in terms of both process and outcome is a crucial aspect of empowerment. It requires raising the consciousness of aging individuals themselves, as well as among family members and of helping professionals, so as to think critically about the taken-for-granted arrangements in society and to challenge them. Social action is at the heart of the empowerment approach, and it requires the active involvement of individuals, groups, and organizations as they seek solutions that challenge the status quo.

An example of past actions that tried to create change is the Omnibus Budget Reconciliation Act of 1987, L.L. 100-203, which spells out federal requirements for directors of nursing homes with 120 or more aging clients and requires the hiring of social service practitioners to assess the psychosocial functioning of residents. This law went into effect October 1990. The law was passed to require that client functioning in nursing homes be more broadly assessed than how it is typically defined narrowly through a medical examination that focuses primarily on cellular function. Behavioral, emotional, spiritual, and mental states are the result of integrated biopsychosocial interaction in the context in which the individual exists. Requiring a broader assessment was viewed as a first step toward increasing the possibility of a context in which treatment models might include social interaction, empowerment, self-determination, and so on, rather than sole reliance on medical interventions. One would think that this improvement in assessment would result in more positive and more holistic programs within long-term care facilities.

However, many long-term care homes have met these obligations on the cheap. Social service practitioners have been hired part-time to do the assessments only. Locally, this author has received reports that these assessments sometimes take place over the phone. Optimally, human service practitioners should be employed full-time to develop well-rounded programs after the psychosocial assessment to meet the holistic needs identified in the assessment process. The existence of this law on a macro level might have provided a starting point for advocacy for more balance, holism, and individual rights on both a meso and micro level. The passage of L.L. 100-203 illustrates another important principal of the empowerment perspective, which is that the promotion of social action must be ongoing. The passage of a bill, no matter how well intentioned, is only one of many actions that are required to humanize the structures of care. Ongoing vigilance is required for social change to be truly meaningful.

Implications for Health and Human Services

Human service practitioners who are concerned about the aging in all of its diversity must be attuned to the use of power. What Vincent (1999) says about power is important to remember, whether working on a macro, meso, micro, or magna level:

> Power is about powerful people doing things to less powerful people. Power comes before language and interaction, it is the basis for them. Whose definitions of the situation become to be accepted as real, whose language dominates a discourse, are the consequences of power. Ageist language, like sexist language, is an expression of power. It is the relationships of unequal power in domestic and economic structures which become embedded in language use. Thus, it is possible and desirable to give an account of the cultural construction of old age—how images of old age and . . . people are built up in specific contexts. (p. 137)

Human service practitioners must question the definitions of aging by powerful forces, particularly the medical professions, but also the powerful forces within the health and human service professions (including human work, psychology, and counseling itself) and the forces in larger society. They must have the sociological imagination to visualize the impact of social forces on the conditions of aging individuals (Mills, 1959). This will be an ongoing struggle, as human service practitioners are often employed to care for the aging within medical settings and are thus subject to powerful socializing forces that have the potential of silencing the critical voice that is paramount for social change. However, the history of a number of health and human service professions such as social work has been dotted with efforts to challenge the status quo in the interests of social justice. It is a tradition that must be continued at the micro, meso, macro, and magna capacities so as to transform structural conditions.

It is important to explore how human service practitioners often offer services that perpetuate oppressive conditions for individuals who have been defined by powerful others according to ageist stereotypes, whereby older people are seen: as being all the same; as being beset with individual rather than being subject to structural problems; and as being primarily in poor health due to the "natural" biological forces of decline rather than due to environmental forces. The unique strengths and personal lives of older people are often overlooked. By the same token, positive stereotypes of the aging also exist, as reflected in the venerated grandparent image or the image of the wise older person who is the source of stories of the old days. Unfortunately, even the positive images tend to disempower, marginalize, and trap older people in a very small social space that often exploits their strengths by using them as inexpensive caregivers and volunteers (Hummert, 1994).

Overcoming ageism requires constant vigilance and questioning. Effort must be made to make age an interesting, but not the defining, quality of a person. This approach requires careful attention to the entire life of the person in the context of a life course lived with environmental pressures that often are at odds with social justice. It requires that emphasis be placed not on only one moment of a person's life, but on the person's entire life in context.

Discussion Questions

1. What is ageism? Give examples, and explain what interests are served by ageism. What do culture and the structural elements of society have to do with the life chances of all people, including the aging?

2. One of the stereotypes of aging is that older people are all the same. Discuss how this stereotype is not true, and give examples of the diversity among the aging to illustrate its lack of truth.

3. Another stereotype of aging is that older people may be defined primarily by their problems, particularly by their medical problems. This is called the "medicalization of aging." Explain how this occurs, and comment on whose interests are served by this approach.

4. What approaches and actions may social service practitioners take in order to improve both the way older people are viewed and the social conditions that exist?

References

Abramovitz, M. (1986). The privatization of the welfare state. *Social Work, 31*(2), 57–64.

Administration on Aging. (1999). *Older women: A diverse and growing population.* Fact Sheet. [On-line]. Available: http://www.aoa.gov/factsheets/ow.html.

American Association of Retired Persons (AARP). (1996). *A profile of older Americans.* Washington, DC: Author.

American Association of Retired Persons (AARP). (1998). *A profile of older Americans.* Washington, DC: Author.

Barbato, C. A., & Fezzel, J. D. (1987). The language of aging in different age groups. *The Gerontologist, 27*(4), 527–531.

Barranti, C. C. R., & Cohen, H. L. (2000). Lesbian and gay elders: An invisible minority. In R. L. Schneider, N. P. Kropf, & A. J. Kisor (Eds.), *Gerontological social work: Knowledge, service settings, and special populations* (2nd ed., pp. 343–367). Belmont, CA: Brooks/Cole.

Binstock, R. H. (1983). The aged as scapegoat. *The Gerontologist, 23*(2), 136–143.

Burris, J. (1994). *Working with the aging: Factors affecting career choice of social workers.* Unpublished dissertation, School of Social Work, Arizona State University.

Burris, J., & Guadalupe, K. (2003). Constructivism and the constructivist framework. In J. Anderson & R. W. Carter (Eds.), *Diversity perspectives for social work practice* (pp. 199–226). Boston: Allyn & Bacon.

Butler, R. N. (1969). Ageism: Another form of bigotry. *The Gerontologist, 9,* 243–246.

Butler, R. N. (1975). *Why survive? Being old in America.* New York: Harper & Row.

Butler, R. N. (1980). Ageism: A foreword. *Journal of Social Issues, 36*(2), 8–11.

Butler, R. N. (1989). Dispelling ageism: The cross-cutting intervention. *The Annals,* 138–147.

Cohen, E. S. (1992). What is independence? In E. F. Ansello & N. N. Eustis (Eds.), *Aging and disabilities: Seeking common ground* (pp. 91–98). Amityville, NY: Baywood.

Cowgill, D. O., & Holmes, L. D. (Eds.). (1972). *Aging and modernization.* New York: Appleton-Century-Crofts.

Davis-Berman, J., & Robinson, J. D. (1989). Knowledge on aging and preferences to work with the elderly: The impact of a course on aging. *Gerontology and Geriatrics Education, 10*(1), 23–36.

Estes, C. L. (1979). *The ageing enterprise.* San Francisco: Jossey-Bass.

Estes, C. L. (1980). Constructions of reality. *Journal of Social Issues, 35*(2), 117–132.

Estes, C. L. (1986). The ageing enterprise: In whose interests? *International Journal of Health Services, 16*(2), 243–251.

Estes, C. L., Binney, E. A., & Culbertson, R. A. (1992). The gerontological imagination: Social influences of the development of gerontology, 1945–present. *International Journal of Aging and Development, 35*(1), 49–65.

Estes, C. L., Linkins, K., & Binney, E. (1996). The political economy of aging. In R. Binstock & L. George (Eds.), *Handbook of aging and the social sciences* (4th ed.). New York: Academic Press.

Estes, C. L., Swan, J. H., & Gerard, L. W. (1982). Dominant and competing paradigms in gerontology: Toward a political economy of aging. *Aging and Society, 2*(2), 151–164.

Fischer, D. (1977). *Growing old in America.* New York: Oxford University Press.

Gilson, S. F. (2000). Disability and aging. In R. L. Schneider, N. P. Kropf, & A. J. Kisor (Eds.), *Gerontological social work: Knowledge, service settings, and special populations* (2nd ed., pp. 368–395). Belmont, CA: Brooks/Cole.

Ginsberg, L. H. (2001). *Careers in social work* (2nd ed.). Needham Heights, MA: Allyn & Bacon.

Greene, R. (1989). *Curriculum for gerontological careers.* Washington DC: Council on Social Work Education.

Harding, N., & Palfrey, C. (1997). *The social construction of dementia: Confused professionals?* London: Sage.

Harris, A. J., & Feinberg, J. F. (1977). Television and aging: Is what you see what you get? *The Gerontologist, 17*(5), 464–468.

Hazan, H. (1994). *Old age: Constructions and deconstructions.* Cambridge, MA: Cambridge University Press.

Hertzman, C., Pulcins, I., Barer, M. L., Evans, R. G., Anderson, G. M., & Lomas, J. (1989). *Flat on your back to your flat: Sources of increased hospital services utilization among the elderly in British Columbia*. Vancouver: Health Policy Research Unit, University of British Columbia.

Holmes, E. R., & Holmes, L. D. (1995). *Other cultures, elder years* (2nd ed.). Thousand Oaks, CA: Sage.

Hummert, M. L. (1994). Stereotypes of the elderly and patronizing speech. In M. L. Hummert, J. M. Wiemann, & J. F. Nussbaum (Eds.), *Interpersonal communication in older adulthood: Interdisciplinary theory and research*. Thousand Oaks, CA: Sage.

Kalish, R. A. (1979). The new ageism and the failure models: A polemic. *The Gerontologist, 19*(4), 398–402.

Kane, R. L., Solomon, D. H., Beck, J. C., Keeler, E., & Kane, R. A. (1980). *Geriatrics in the United States: Manpower projections and training considerations*. Santa Monica, CA: Rand.

Kropf, N. P. & Hutchison, E. D. (2000). Effective practice with elderly clients. In R. L. Schneider, N. P. Kropf, & A. J. Kisor (Eds.), *Gerontological social work: Knowledge, service settings, and special populations* (2nd ed., pp. 3–25). Belmont, CA: Brooks/Cole.

Kubey, R. W. (1980). Television and aging: Past, present and future. *The Gerontologist, 20*, 6–10.

Levin, J., & Levin, W. C. (1980). *Ageism, prejudice and discrimination against the elderly*. Belmont, CA: Wadsworth.

Lowy, L. (1983). Incorporation and specialization of content on aging in the social work curriculum. *Journal of Gerontological Social Work, 5*(4), 37–55.

McNeil, J. M. (1993). Americans with disabilities, 1991–92. *Bureau of the Census, Current population reports* (pp. 70–33). Washington, DC: U.S. Government Printing Office.

Mills, C. W. (1959). *The sociological imagination*. New York: Oxford Press.

Minkler, M., & Estes, C. L. (Eds.). (1999). *Critical gerontology: Perspectives from political and moral economy*. Amityville, NY: Baywood.

Morales, A. T., & Sheafor, B. W. (2002). *The many faces of social work clients*. Boston: Allyn & Bacon.

Morgan, L., & Kunkel, S. (2001). *Aging: The social context* (2nd ed.). Thousand Oaks, CA: Pine Forge.

Navarro, V. (1976). *Medicine under capitalism*. New York: Prodist.

Neugarten, B. (1974, September). Age groups in American society and the rise of the young-old. *Annals of the American Academy, 187–198.*

Nuessel, F. H. (1982). The language of ageism. *The Gerontologist, 22*(3), 273–276.

Okin, S. M. (1989). *Justice, gender, and the family*. New York: Basic Books.

O'Rand, A. (1996). The cumulative stratification of the lifecourse. In R. Binstock & L. K. George (Eds.), *Handbook of aging and social sciences* (4th ed., pp. 188–207). San Diego: Academic Press.

Pelletier, K. R. (1977). *Mind as healer, mind as slayer: A holistic approach to preventing stress disorders*. New York: Delta Books.

Peterson, D. A. (1990). Personnel to serve the aging in the field of social work: Implications for educating professionals. *Social Work, 35*(10), 5.

Phillipson, C. (1982). *Capitalism and the construction of old age*. London: Macmillan.

Poulin J. E., & Walter, C. A. (1992). Retention plans and job satisfaction of gerontological social workers. *Journal of Gerontological Social Work, 19*(1), 99–114.

Preston, S. (1984). Children and the elderly in the U.S. *Scientific American, 251*, 44–49.

Quam, J. K., & Whitford, G. S. (1992). Educational needs of nursing home social workers at the baccalaureate level. *Geriatric Social Work Education, 2*, 143–156.

Quandagno, J. (1999). *Aging and the life course: An introduction to social gerontology*. Boston: McGraw-Hill.

Quinn, J. (1987). Attitude of professionals toward the aged. In G. Maddox (Ed.), *The encyclopedia of aging*. New York: Springer.

Quinn, J., & Whitford, G. (1992). The present and future economic well-being of the aged. In R. Burkhauser & D. Salisbury (Eds.), *Pensions in a changing economy* (pp. 5–18). Washington, DC: Employee Benefit Research Institute.

Reynolds, J. (1987). Social work, survival and the commercialization of health care. *Health and Social Work, 12*, 231–232.

Riley, M. W. (1971). Social gerontology and the age stratification of society. *The Gerontologist, 11*, 79–87.

Riley, M. W. (1987). Age stratification. In G. Maddox (Ed.), *The encyclopedia of aging*. New York: Springer.

Robertson, A. (1991). The politics of Alzheimer's disease: A case study in apocalyptic demography. In M. Minkler & C. Estes (Eds.), *Critical perspectives on aging: The political and moral economy of growing old.* Amityville, NY: Baywood.

Rogers, P. (1993, February). How many gays are there? *Newsweek,* 46.

Rose, A. (1965). The subculture of the aging: A framework in social gerontology. In A. M. Rose & W. A. Peterson (Eds.), *Older people and their social world.* Philadelphia: R. A. Davis.

Schiller, B. R. (1984). *The economics of poverty and discrimination* (4th ed.). Englewood Cliffs, NJ: Prentice-Hall.

Schneider, R. L., Kropf, N. P., & Kisor, A. J. (Eds.). (2000). *Gerontological social work: Knowledge, service settings, and special populations* (2nd ed.). Belmont, CA: Brooks/Cole.

Soldo, B. J., & Manton, K. G. (1985). Health status and service needs of the oldest old: Current patterns and future trends. *Milbank Memorial Fund Quarterly: Health and Society, 63*(2), 286–319.

Solomon, R., & Mellor, M. J. (1992). Interdisciplinary geriatric education: The new kid on the block. *Geriatric Social Work Education, 2,* 175–185.

Sontag, S. (1972). The double standard of aging. *Saturday Review of the Society, 23*(9), 30.

Stoller, E. P., & Gibson, R. C. (2000). *Worlds of difference: Inequality in the aging experience.* Thousand Oaks, CA: Pine Forge.

U.S. Bureau of the Census. (1999). *Current population reports.* Washington, DC: U.S. Government Printing Office.

Vincent, J. A. (1999). *Rethinking ageing: Politics, power and old age.* Philadelphia: Open University Press.

Wendt, P. R., & Peterson, D. A. (1992). Transition in use of human resources in the field of aging. *Journal of Aging and Social Policy, 4*(1/2), 107–123.

May Your Spirit guide your Way Home. —**Unknown**

First Nations Peoples

| **12**

Ethnic-Specific Communities of People

HILARY N. WEAVER

First Nations Peoples, also known as Native Americans, American Indians, and indigenous people, are the original inhabitants of North America. This population consists of more than 500 distinct nations with different languages, cultures, religions, political structures, and histories. Significant diversity continues to exist among First Nations Peoples, although colonizing practices and U.S. social policies have often treated First Nations Peoples as one group.

DEMOGRAPHIC OVERVIEW

The size of First Nations populations has fluctuated significantly since European contact. While overall the population has declined significantly, some nations that were once large are now small or nonexistent, while others that were once small are now large. Estimates of the size of the North American indigenous population at the time of first European contact vary significantly from 1 million to around 18 million (Stiffarm & Lane, 1992). While many current books still quote figures at the low end of the spectrum, contemporary archeological estimates are significantly higher. In part, low estimates are based on political and moral justifications designed to minimize the significant destruction and depopulation that resulted from European incursions into North America.

As a collective, the First Nations Peoples reached its lowest point around the turn of the 20th century. Indigenous populations had been confined to reservations, and even reservation land was being quickly lost under the Dawes Act that allotted land to nuclear families and then opened "excess" land to White settlement. While the U.S. government, during the first centuries of colonization, did not officially count First Nations Peoples, the 1900 census identified 237,196 First Nations people within the borders of the United States (Stiffarm & Lane, 1992).

The population of First Nations Peoples began to rise after the beginning of the 20th century, and it has grown every decade since 1930 (Stiffarm & Lane, 1992). While the First Nations population is still small when compared with other ethnic groups in the United States, high birth rates have led to continuous growth. The 2000 census identified 4.1 million First Nations Peoples (including Alaska Natives). This accounts for 1.5% of the U.S. population and represents a 110% increase over the 1990 figure (Ogunwole, 2002). In addition to a high birth rate, other possible explanations for this phenomenal growth include more people identifying with their First Nations heritage and changes in how census data is collected that now allow people to identify with more than one ethnic group. In spite of the growing number of documented First Nations Peoples, the U.S. census may still undercount this population. Some First Nations Peoples continue to live in remote areas where streets have no names and houses have no numbers, and thus may not have received census forms. Additionally, some First Nations Peoples do not consider themselves to be Americans and strongly resist being counted by what they view as a foreign government.

Various U.S. policies, economic necessity, and a variety of other factors have led many First Nations Peoples to relocate to areas away from their traditional homelands and contemporary reservations. Indeed, the majority of First Nations Peoples now live in urban areas. The cities with the largest First Nations populations are New York City, New York (87,241), and Los Angeles, California (53,092). Over half of the indigenous population lives in ten states, with the largest populations being in California (627,562) and Oklahoma (391,949) (Ogunwole, 2002). Indigenous people still identify as members of distinct nations (also known as tribes). These nations vary considerably in size. Some have just a few members while others have thousands. The largest First Nations groups are the Cherokee (729,533), Navajo (298,197), Sioux (261,632), and Chippewa (255,576) (Ogunwole, 2002).

TERMINOLOGY

First Nations Peoples are descendants of the original inhabitants of the Americas. These aboriginal people were organized into hundreds of tribal groups and, prior to European contact, never conceived of themselves as belonging to the same group. The labels *American Indian* and *Native American* were applied to these diverse tribal groups initially by outsiders, regardless of tribal distinctions. Each First Nations group had its own name that it used for itself; often the name was something that roughly translated to "The People." Even today, most First Nations Peoples identify primarily with their own nation (e.g., Salish, Wampanoag, Paiute) and secondarily as First Nations.

There is no consensus among First Nations Peoples about preferable terminology when overarching labels are used. *American Indian* is a term that is widely used by the U.S. government and is still used by many indigenous people. In fact, the terms *American Indian* and *Indian* are both derived from Columbus's erroneous belief that he had sailed to India and that, thus, the people he encountered must be Indians. This centuries-old mistake has a lingering legacy, and some indigenous people reject this term because they do not want to be known by a term given by someone who paved the way for colonization. Additionally, some do not see themselves as Americans, but rather as members of sovereign nations that continue to exist within the United States. The term *Native American* poses a similar problem for those who do not see themselves as U.S. citizens. It can also be somewhat confusing, as some U.S.-born Americans who wish to distinguish themselves from immigrants use the terms *Native* and *Native American,* even when they have no indigenous heritage. While no term is perfect, the term *First Nations Peoples* has begun to gain popularity, especially among younger generations. Although still somewhat problematic, given its limited recognizability and the fact that it encompasses so many diverse groups, this term is associated with a strong sense of sovereignty, self-determination, and cultural pride.

HISTORICAL EXPERIENCES

The history of First Nations Peoples after European contact is one of diminishing power and subsequent colonization. In early interactions, European nations and later the United States interacted with First Nations as sovereign entities. As Europeans pushed westward across the continent, First Nations populations became decimated through disease and warfare. Growing American numerical superiority led to increasing power and ability to subjugate the First Nations. Sometimes whole First Nations were wiped out as epidemics spread quickly among indigenous people, who had no immunity to diseases such as smallpox and diphtheria. Some nations were hit harder than others, but few escaped unscathed. Most remaining First Nations Peoples were confined to isolated reservations by the late 1800s.

Once the weakened First Nations were no longer perceived as a threat, policies of eradication and isolation shifted to assimilation. These policies were logical successors to earlier attempts at physical genocide. The remaining First Nations Peoples were seen as capable of fitting into the American mainstream—if they would only give up their indigenous ways of life, including their religious and cultural practices. Various policies were developed to integrate First Nations Peoples into U.S. society, thus effectively ending their existence through incorporation. Assimilationist policies promoted allotment of reservation land, family disruption, paternalism, relocation, termination, and statistical elimination. The 1960s and 1970s ushered in a new era of resistance to assimilation and a push for self-determination, yet new ideas continued to be fettered by old policies.

Allotment of Reservation Land

As part of a program of cultural assimilation, First Nations Peoples were encouraged to give up their communal lifestyle and values and become organized as nuclear families headed by men. In 1887, the Dawes Act, also known as the General Allotment

Act, was passed as a way to break up reservation land held communally into parcels held by nuclear family units. The policy led to the loss of 100 million acres or approximately two thirds of all reservation land prior to its repeal in 1934 (Churchill & Morris, 1992). Allotment affected different First Nations groups in different ways. The policy was never fully implemented; thus, some reservations experienced no loss of lands, while other reservations experienced significant losses and today have up to 90% nonindigenous residents.

Family Disruption

Other significant methods of assimilation involved various forms of family disruption. In particular, boarding schools, foster care, and adoption led to extensive separation of First Nations children from their families and communities, and thus to significant alienation and cultural loss.

After the U.S. Civil War, the federal government initiated a policy of removing First Nations children from their homes and communities and educating them in distant, residential schools. These schools were designed to teach First Nations children to fill certain roles within American society. Girls were taught domestic skills, and boys were taught agricultural skills. Additionally, First Nations children were taught English and Christianity. Children were not allowed to speak indigenous languages or practice their religions. Any rule violation often led to brutal physical punishment (Weaver & White, 1997).

Today, many boarding school survivors and scholars who examine the impact of this policy regard the boarding schools as a tool of cultural genocide. The slogan of the boarding schools, "Kill the Indian, Save the Man," clearly reflects the philosophy of the day, which was that indigenous cultures must be eradicated for First Nations Peoples to have any place in American society. Adults were viewed as being too set in their ways for meaningful cultural change; thus, children were often targeted as being malleable enough to be successfully inculcated with American cultural values (Iglehart & Becerra, 1995).

In spite of the generally negative reputation of boarding schools, some boarding school survivors reflect that their time in the schools enabled them to leave communities filled with starvation and hopelessness. Not all boarding school residents experienced the brutal physical punishment and sexual abuse that are the hallmarks of so many survivors' experiences. While not all First Nations Peoples were taken to boarding schools, the impact of these schools on First Nations Peoples in general is so strong that few families exist in which at least one member was not taken away to school.

One result of so many First Nations children being raised in institutions is the lack of positive parenting role models, leading to generations of family problems (Morrisette, 1994). The boarding schools set in motion a lasting legacy of child abuse and neglect. School survivors did not know positive ways of guiding and disciplining children. This, combined with the extensive governmental oversight in the lives of First Nations Peoples, opened the door to many indigenous youth entering the foster care and adoption systems. In the 1970s, an estimated 25–35% of all First Nations children were being raised outside of First Nations families and communities (Jaimes

& Halsey, 1992; Mannes, 1995). While overall the large numbers of First Nations children in foster care or adopted by nonindigenous families are seen as detrimental to the well-being of First Nations in general as well as the well-being of specific families, some youth were able to successfully adapt to their new lives. Indeed, some First Nations Peoples see fitting into American society as desirable.

Boarding schools, foster care, and adoption have all placed First Nations children in an alien cultural context, which in turn has led to significant cultural erosion, feelings of alienation, and an inability to transmit cultural traditions to future generations. Loss of children is also a major concern in terms of maintaining a strong indigenous population. The large numbers of First Nations children raised in nonindigenous foster care and adoptive placements mean that fewer First Nations Peoples will know their culture and identify as First Nations Peoples (Jaimes & Halsey, 1992; Weaver & White, 1997, 1999). In this way, cultural loss leads to population loss. Additionally, the large numbers of First Nations women of childbearing age who were either coerced or unknowingly sterilized have served to reduce the First Nations populations (Jaimes & Halsey, 1992; Lawrence, 2000; Torpy, 2000).

Paternalism in U.S. Social Policies

The federal government has taken on a protective role as a guardian of First Nations Peoples, whom it often views as being childlike and incapable of protecting their own interests (Churchill & Morris, 1992; Deloria, 1992). For instance, the government often handles arrangements to lease reservation land to ranchers or mining companies, collects the rents, and holds the money in trust for First Nations Peoples. The government, however, has not been a reliable trustee and cannot account for billions of dollars that it supposedly holds in trust for its First Nations wards. First Nations Peoples living in poverty often have difficulty finding out how much, if any, of their money the federal government may have in its possession.

Paternalistic policies have existed and continue to exist in virtually every aspect of First Nations peoples' lives. For example, during some of its earliest interactions, the federal government instituted a policy of prohibition whereby no alcohol could be sold to First Nations Peoples. This, however, had several significant detrimental consequences, such as individuals giving up their legal status as First Nations people in order to purchase alcohol, the smuggling and hiding of alcohol, and other factors encouraging dysfunctional patterns of consumption (Maracle, 1993; Weaver, 2001b).

Being treated as incompetent wards has undermined the self-sufficiency and self-determination of First Nations Peoples. There have been examples, however, of First Nations Peoples attempting to use paternalistic policies to their advantage. For instance, early policies like the Trade and Intercourse Act declared First Nations Peoples incompetent to sell land or participate in similar agreements without the approval of the federal government. Such policies have been used to support arguments in contemporary land claims. In other words, in instances where First Nations Peoples sold land without federal approval, it is argued that the sale should now be declared void and the land returned, because First Nations Peoples were incompetent to sell their land in the first place.

Relocation, Termination, and Statistical Elimination of First Nations Peoples

Economic and employment policies were also used as tools of assimilation. In the 1950s and 1960s, the federal government relocated many First Nations Peoples to cities and offered them job training. This policy was a means of decreasing reservation populations and encouraging indigenous people to enter the economic mainstream through wage labor. The relocation policy took First Nations Peoples away from their traditional communities, support systems, and ways of life. By 1980, over half of all First Nations Peoples resided in urban areas (Robbins, 1992).

Assimilation was designed to incorporate First Nations Peoples into the general American society. If First Nations Peoples ceased to exist as culturally and linguistically distinct people, then treaty obligations and other federal responsibilities could be declared null and void. Indeed, beginning in 1952, the federal government took legal steps to terminate the existence of 109 First Nations groups that it deemed to be adequately assimilated. Through termination, groups like the Menominee and Klamath lost all claims to federal benefits designated for First Nations Peoples. Their land was taken out of reservation status and became subject to taxation and regulation just like any other land (Robbins, 1992).

Blood quantum is another way First Nations Peoples are often subject to statistical extermination. Because of its obligation to provide a variety of services and supports to First Nations Peoples, the federal government has a significant interest in monitoring the number of people identified as members of First Nations and in ensuring that this number is not too large (Jaimes, 1992). One of the primary ways in which someone can prove qualification as a First Nations person is through documenting blood quantum, or the percentage of heritage the person has from a First Nations group. Even though biological ideas about race have long been discredited, many First Nations Peoples are required to prove their identity in this way.

Intermarriage is a common phenomenon among First Nations Peoples. Indeed, more than 50% of First Nations Peoples marry nonindigenous people (Snipp, 2002). Thus, many contemporary First Nations Peoples cannot document the required biological heritage to meet some definitions based on blood quantum. Some activists, social scientists, and other indigenous people strongly reject the application of blood quantum standards in defining identity, particularly when used by nonindigenous entities such as the federal government. Application of blood quantum standards is considered a form of statistical genocide (Jaimes, 1992).

Quest for Self-Determination and Ongoing Barriers

The 1960s and 1970s were the beginning of a new era of First Nations activism. First Nations governments asserted their rights to self-determination; however, such assertions were and continue to be hampered by the effects of 500 years of colonization (Churchill, 1993). Federal programs and policies have created a web of dependency that is hard to escape. Even nations that strongly try to assert their sovereignty are fettered by their dependence on federal funds and services. Generations of colonization have left many First Nations with little infrastructure that is not directly dependent on their relationship with the federal government. Additionally, in spite of rhetoric about self-determination, the federal government has not reduced its paternalistic oversight of First Nations. For example, many economic development projects must receive federal approval through the Bureau of Indian Affairs prior to implementation (Robbins, 1992).

One by-product of colonization is the development of classes in some First Nations communities. Communities are sometimes divided according to who is "traditional" and who is "assimilated." Those who receive higher education grounded in dominant society traditions are often viewed with suspicion by traditional people, while educated First Nations Peoples may view traditional people as backward relics of a bygone age (Weaver, 2001a). Divisions also exist along economic lines. While many First Nations Peoples, particularly in reservation communities, have low incomes, a small elite wealthy class, typically made up of business owners, has developed. The development of an elite class undermines the traditional values of communalism found in First Nations societies. Indeed, initiating economic development along Western models (i.e., tribally owned industries such as fisheries) may ultimately lead to the destruction of indigenous value systems and ways of life (Murray, 1992).

Internalized oppression has developed into a major force for First Nations Peoples. Divisions exist along lines such as educational levels, skin color, language abilities, level of cultural knowledge, blood quantum, enrollment status, and many other factors (Weaver, 2001a). Addressing the divisive issues arising from internalized oppression is a prerequisite to strengthening First Nations communities and making self-determination a reality.

CHANGING, DYNAMIC NATURE OF FIRST NATIONS

Although often associated with history, First Nations Peoples continue to be members of dynamic cultures. Although some First Nations Peoples still live without electricity and indoor plumbing, many have accepted modern technology and use it to their advantage. For example, many First Nations governments have Web pages and make active use of the Internet.

First Nations communities are actively exploring how they fit into the socioeconomic context of the United States. While some reservations are in remote areas with few economic opportunities or chances for interaction with others, other reservations are close to populated areas. In such cases, tribal members may interact with nonmembers in work and social situations. Additionally, reservation communities may actively entice nonmembers through such venues as tourism, cultural events, and gaming designed to produce economic revenues for their nations. Today, the majority of First Nations Peoples do not live on reservations. They typically live their lives in a multicultural social and economic context.

Economic development is an issue that poses challenges and is sometimes controversial in First Nations communities. For some, economic development is perceived as exploiting limited resources (i.e., allowing timber or mining interests on indigenous lands) or harming future generations (i.e., accepting nuclear waste for storage). Economic development may be seen as a betrayal of the trust between generations and the traditional mandate to protect generations that are to come. Others see economic development as a way to provide for needy community members. Revenue can either be distributed per capita to all individuals or invested in bettering the community as a whole (i.e., used to build housing for community members).

One of the most common yet controversial forms of economic development is casino gaming. Some First Nations are concerned that allowing gaming in their communities is likely to foster addiction, vice, and community dysfunction (Peacock, Day, & Peacock, 1999), while others see its potential for economic rewards (Napoli, 2002). Because First Nations have retained some separation and independence from states, reservation territories are legally able to offer casino gaming when this is prohibited in surrounding states. Ironically, however, the federal government now requires any First Nation that wants to establish gaming within its territories to sign a compact with the surrounding state, thus allowing more state regulation and eroding sovereignty.

First Nations Peoples occupy a unique place in the political structure of the United States. These nations continue to exist within the United States and retain some rights of self-governance. Sovereignty, while an important principle, is far from a total reality for First Nations Peoples. The federal government has asserted the right to oversee tribal governments in many cases and has claimed criminal jurisdiction on reservation lands. Additionally, in states that have passed Public Law 280, the state can assert many rights on indigenous land (Churchill & Morris, 1992).

One way in which citizens participate in U.S. political processes is through voting. This activity is illustrative of the ambivalence among First Nations Peoples about their full incorporation into the United States. Some First Nations Peoples are diligent about voting, see it as their civic duty, and even run for political office. For example, Ben Nighthorse Campbell has served in the U.S. Congress for many years, and Winona LaDuke ran for vice president of the Unites States in 2000. On the other hand, for some First Nations Peoples, participation in U.S. political processes conflicts with their sense of sovereignty and membership in their own nations (Weaver, 1997). In 1924, the U.S. federal government declared that all First Nations Peoples within its boundaries were citizens (Churchill & Morris, 1992). This unilateral decision was welcomed by some but scoffed at by others. To this day, some reject the concept of U.S. citizenship, do not vote in U.S. elections, resist being counted by the U.S. Census Bureau, and do not carry a U.S. passport.

Diversity within Diversity

First Nations Peoples are very diverse. Historically, these nations existed as independent entities with no common language, social structure, religion, or culture. Centuries of colonization have treated First Nations Peoples as one group, thus leading to some commonalities. For example, the majority of First Nations Peoples now speaks English and has had common experiences with oppression. Still, even U.S. social policies intended to apply to all First Nations Peoples have been implemented to a greater or lesser extent in various areas, thus leading to different experiences. First Nations groups in the eastern United States had contact with Europeans earlier than those in the central part of the country. Variation also exists according to which European groups colonized the various First Nations territories. The primary colonizers in the East were English, French, and Dutch, while the Spanish had a major impact on the First Nations Peoples of the Southwest and the Russians on the First Nations of Alaska.

Even within one First Nations group, experiences may vary. For example, one person may experience social conditions to be more or less harsh than the group as a whole. Individuals may interpret their experiences or respond to them differently, even when they are in comparable situations.

Culture is one layer in an individual's identity. Yet, in any particular circumstance, other aspects of identity may be of equal or greater importance. For example, knowing someone is a member of the Kickapoo First Nation gives only limited information about that person as a human being. It is also important to examine the influences of other layers of identity such as gender, sexual orientation, socioeconomic status, spiritual practices, and issues of physical and mental abilities/disabilities.

Centuries of colonization have often left First Nations communities feeling oppressed and powerless. A closer examination, however, reveals that dynamics of privilege and power exist. While First Nations are in a submissive position relative to the federal government, tribal governments are capable of exercising considerable power over their own people. Such power is not always wielded fairly. Tribal politics play a major role in who gets jobs and various types of assistance (e.g., educational loans). Most First Nations communities now have an elected government. It is not uncommon for many tribal jobs to change hands in the wake of an election. Even positions that would seem immune to politics like a cashier at the tribal gas station or a human service practitioner are often unstable at election time. This can have a major impact in reservation communities where the nation is the source of 80–90% of all jobs.

Sometimes First Nations governments are accused of neglecting the needs of the people while they satisfy their own or outside interests. Tribal councilors and presidents may wield power in inappropriate or corrupt ways. One of the most prominent examples of First Nations leadership oppressing their own people was found on the Pine Ridge Reservation in the 1970s. Under the leadership of Tribal Chair Dick Wilson and his enforcers known as goons (Guardians of the Oglala Nation), Pine Ridge was known for its violence, oppression, corruption, and the shoot-out between First Nations Peoples and FBI agents that led to deaths on both sides and the lifetime incarceration of American Indian Movement activist Leonard Peltier (Matthiessen, 1991).

Adversity and Resilience

Clearly First Nations Peoples have suffered significant adversities, including starvation, disease, and forced assimilation. What is less visible, however, is the resilience that has led to their survival, even after over 500 years of colonization. Traditions and practices were often forced underground in the wake of detrimental federal policies. Since some cultural practices could no longer continue openly, aspects were lost, but many others were preserved. For example, the Sun Dance, a ceremony of renewal integral to many of the First Nations Peoples of the Great Plains region, was outlawed, and yet this practice continued in secret as a way of maintaining the well-being of the people.

In spite of uncertainties in terms of cultural continuity and physical survival, First Nations Peoples have weathered, and continue to weather, adversities. Although they may emerge with scars, they emerge nonetheless. The turn of the 20th century was the nadir of the First Nations populations and a bleak time during which many felt their cultures were doomed. However, the turn of the 21st century is a time of more optimism and renewal. The First Nations populations are quickly growing, in part because of a high birth rate and in part because some people of mixed heritage now claim an indigenous identity. Even discounting the small number of people who may inaccurately claim an indigenous identity (ethnic fraud), the numbers and strength of First Nations Peoples are growing significantly.

First Nations Peoples are trying to position themselves for true self-determination. For example, First Nations social scientists are capable of doing their own research that benefits rather than exploits indigenous people. As the tide of renewal swells, First Nations Peoples face two significant challenges.

First, indigenous nations are still structurally in a submissive position relative to the United States and are subject to paternalism and policies that may not benefit their communities. This is not likely to change, and in fact, the remnants of sovereignty are currently being eroded. For example, the Supreme Court of the United States is now hostile to First Nations' interests and has not made a ruling favorable to indigenous people in years. Indigenous strategists are reluctant to position cases to go before the Supreme Court in the current climate, for fear that dangerous and lasting precedents will be set that further damage sovereignty.

Secondly, the internalized oppression that permeates First Nations communities poses a significant barrier to indigenous renewal and resilience. Corrupt, politically motivated, dysfunctional leadership is incapable of making decisions in the best interest of the people. Erosion of traditional values that focus on the community instead of the individual has left communities vulnerable. Elected governments that were imposed on First Nations have diminished traditional values and ways of doing things. Now, many First Nations communities find themselves with the desire to return to the best of traditional ways while living within a contemporary society. However, they also find themselves without the skills to discover and achieve this delicate balance.

Different Ways of Knowing

Traditional indigenous thought gives great weight to wisdom that comes with age. Elders and the knowledge and traditions that have been passed down through generations are revered. However, generations of contact with the dominant society have led to a diversity of thought, and now traditional knowledge is held in less esteem by some First Nations Peoples. Some believe that modern ways of knowing and doing things are preferable to traditional wisdom. These different ways of thinking and prioritizing are a major component of the divisions between those who see themselves as "traditional" and those who see themselves as "progressive."

Traditionally, a spiritual aspect of being permeates all aspects of a First Nations person's life. All creation is seen as living and part of an interactive whole. Not all contemporary First Nations Peoples, however, continue to follow traditional beliefs or spiritual practices. Many have become Christian and have accepted values that separate the sacred and the secular. Others who have accepted a Christian belief system continue to hold some traditional beliefs about the sacred as an integral part of daily life. The interconnectedness of all beings necessitates respect and guides behavior.

Multicultural Influences

Most First Nations people live in a world surrounded by multicultural influences. Many live in communities with people from a variety of cultures. Given high rates of intermarriage, many First Nations Peoples are actually multicultural themselves or have relatives from other cultural groups. Many First Nations Peoples can and do identify with more than one culture (Weaver, 1996). For example, First Nations Peoples living in New York City may experience cultural influences from Latino/a and African-American groups, thus shaping their values and behaviors. Indeed, the influences of the dominant society are so prominent that even people in remote First Nations communities are exposed to cultural influences through venues such as television and the Internet.

Each individual experiences his or her culture somewhat differently. It is inappropriate to make assumptions about who someone is as a cultural being based on factors such as skin color and whether a name sounds "ethnic." Indeed, ultimately people have some level of choice in how they respond to the cultural influences in their lives. While environment plays a major role in shaping culture, choices are also made, consciously or unconsciously, about whether to follow traditional values and beliefs.

Effects of Stereotyping

Stereotyping plays a major role in how people see themselves and how others see them. Stereotypes of First Nations Peoples abound, from drunken savages to noble but naive remnants of ecologically and spiritually centered societies. These stereotypes influence how people think, feel, and behave. If they receive the message that they are likely to become drunks to fill the void left by cultural loss, they may feel this fate is inevitable and participate in behavior that leads to this self-fulfilling prophecy. The impact of stereotypes is particularly painful when it limits the ambitions and life possibilities of the young, thus hindering the future of all First Nations Peoples. For example, one 5-year-old Apache became fearful of "Indians" after seeing old movies on television. In particular, he knew about "bad Indians," and this made him not want to be indigenous at all. He plaintively expressed the hope that he would not be a bad Indian. However, since this was the primary image he had been exposed to, it seemed inevitable to him.

Even today, stereotypical images of First Nations Peoples abound. Some of the most prominent images are sports logos. At many sporting events, both nationally and locally, First Nations Peoples are still treated as mascots. Fans and half-time activity leaders participate in "war dances," wear "war paint," threaten to "scalp" people, and chop at people with toy or imaginary tomahawks, thus perpetuating the image of the savage warrior.

APPLYING THE MULTIDIMENSIONAL CONTEXTUAL PRACTICE FRAMEWORK

The multidimensional contextual practice framework recognizes that First Nations Peoples have many different aspects to their identities and are affected by various, interrelated contexts. Recognition of this interactive and interdependent existence helps challenge static and stereotypical notions of First Nations Peoples. The central focus of the multidimensional contextual practice framework is client well-being. Social/health/human service intervention revolves around enhancing client well-being, whether the client is an individual, family, group, or community.

Principle One: Client Well-Being

The client well-being principle recognizes time as a cyclical continuum. This fits well with the sense of connection many First Nations Peoples feel across generations. The concept of Seven Generations is central in many First Nations societies. For some, this means that seven generations ago ancestors made plans that ensured the survival of contemporary First Nations Peoples and those living today have a responsibility to plan for the continuance of the next seven generations. Others interpret the concept as a description of ancestors from three generations ago, contemporary indigenous people in the middle, and the three generations that are to come. This concept is a powerful motivator in prevention programs. For example, First Nations Peoples are reminded of their responsibilities toward future generations in campaigns that encourage the use of condoms to prevent HIV transmission.

The client well-being principle recognizes the dynamics and complexities of human diversity. First Nations Peoples come from distinct societies with different traditions and histories. First Nations Peoples vary considerably in their knowledge of and adherence to traditional ways. Other layers of identity (e.g., gender, age, ability/disability, sexuality) influence their lives, values, and behaviors. Human service practitioners must avoid stereotypical notions of First Nations Peoples and learn about each client through a comprehensive assessment process that includes a cultural dimension.

The client well-being principle recognizes that First Nations Peoples experience adversities and display resilience. This is true for both individuals and nations. The assessment process must include a balanced examination of both, and an exploration of how resilience can be strengthened through the intervention process. This includes a recognition of essence, the life-giving force that supports human endurance.

Principle Two: The Multidimensional Contextual Client

The second principle of the multidimensional contextual practice framework recognizes that clients are constantly influenced by their multidimensional contexts. This dynamic environment is a shaping influence on how individuals view themselves. Indeed, self-perceptions frequently shift according to environmental influences. For example, children raised in First Nations families are likely to see themselves differently once they are taken away to nonindigenous foster care settings. The environment, whether First Nations or nonindigenous, reservation or city, low-income or wealthy, Longhouse or Catholic, is a shaping force on how these children experience their identities as First Nations people.

It is important to recognize that people participate in multiple identities. For example, one person can be a Southern Ute, middle-aged woman, with a hidden disability, who sees herself as an activist and educator. While she is all of these at once, different aspects of her identity may hold more meaning for her at any given time. A comprehensive assessment examines all aspects of a client's identity and gives the client an opportunity to identify which aspects are most pertinent to the current case situation. The assessment must also examine identity within a collective context. For example, with the woman just described: Is she enrolled (i.e., formally a member entitled to various rights and benefits) in her nation? Does she live within a reservation or in a First Nations community context? If so, how do her experiences as a member of this particular First Nations society influence her?

Principle Three: Influences of Micro, Meso, Macro, and Magna Contexts

The third principle of the multidimensional contextual practice framework recognizes the influences of the micro, meso, macro, and magna contexts on the client's life. This builds on and goes beyond examining the client within a social environment. The added magna dimension makes explicit the much-neglected spiritual dimension in clients' lives. This examination of context is critical in working with First Nations Peoples. The colonial context has had a major shaping influence on First Nations societies, including shaping what language most First Nations Peoples speak, the most common forms of governance, and contemporary spirituality. For some, at least in part, First Nations identities are often grounded in resistance to these colonizing influences.

Client well-being is affected by these various contexts. As part of a comprehensive assessment, human service practitioners can explore the impact of these contexts on the client's life in general and on the client's current situation specifically. These contextual influences are likely to be complex and may be a mixture of both positive and negative.

Principle Four: Professional Competence

Human service practitioners are also shaped by the micro, meso, macro, and magna contexts of their lives. As responsible professionals, it is important that they become self-aware and critically evaluate how these contexts shape their beliefs and values. These shaping influences may be either conscious or unconscious, and thus substantial self-examination may be required to identify them. This process of examination is often a major function of professional supervision and is particularly important in working past ethnocentrism in cross-cultural situations.

Professional values, often codified in a code of ethics, are a critical component of professional competence. Social justice is a central value that sometimes becomes obscured when human service practitioners focus heavily on clinical aspects of their work. An oppressive, colonial context, in which federal paternalism is the guiding force behind many social policies, is still the norm for First Nations Peoples. In order to live up to the professional value of social justice, human service professionals need to recognize this macro context and actively use their skills to confront injustice and shape policies and bureaucracies to make social justice a reality for First Nations Peoples.

Respect for individual and collective dignity is also a key professional value. Even though First Nations Peoples may have values, beliefs, and behaviors that differ from those of the human service practitioner, it is imperative that the worker communicates respect for the client. In particular, the value that many First Nations Peoples place on the group or the collective often feels alien to human service practitioners who have been socialized with individualism as a primary value. For example, the Indian Child Welfare Act recognizes that First Nations have a voice in the future of their children. A First Nations government has the right to intercede when one of its children is placed in foster care or for adoption. When a First Nation exercises this power and it conflicts with the wishes of a parent, some human service practitioners view this as a violation of that parent's rights while failing to recognize and respect the value and the rights of the collective.

Integrity and self-determination are also important professional principles. Sometimes human service practitioners see adversity rather than resilience and fail to recognize the integrity of First Nations communities. First Nations communities are viewed as fragmented, victims of colonization who have lost their cultural identity. This deficit perspective only further harms First Nations Peoples. Rather, it is important to look for cultural continuity and integrity in new and changing forms. This strengths perspective is central to any real self-determination. In order for self-determination to become a reality for First Nations Peoples, there must be substantial change in federal laws and policies that continue to regulate First Nations entities. This change can begin only when public officials reflect on the implications of current ways of doing things and begin to alter their own ways of thinking and doing things.

In an age in which empirically based practice is seen as the highest standard, practice wisdom tends to be trivialized or discredited. Multidimensional contextual practice, however, recognizes that knowledge comes from multiple sources, not all of which have been systematically tested or verified. This fits with First Nations values and ways of knowing. Traditional knowledge, like practice wisdom, is based on generations of predecessors who developed tried and true ways of doing things that are both efficient and effective.

Mutuality is emphasized throughout the helping process. This is an important way to balance out the hierarchy inherent in client-professional relationships. It also serves to counteract the paternalistic and condescending ways of interacting with First Nations Peoples that have characterized relationships with representatives of the dominant society.

In the multidimensional contextual practice framework, an understanding of the client develops through multiple sources. First, human service workers bring with them their own background knowledge and understanding of First Nations Peoples. Ideally this knowledge is specific to the particular First Nations society of the client and is grounded in an understanding of the diversity among First Nations Peoples. Secondly, human service practitioners learn about particular clients through interactions. These interactions may challenge or reinforce practitioners' preexisting ideas. Third, an understanding of clients is enhanced by glimpses of understanding and intuition that go beyond what can be explained by conventional realities. These three ways of knowing come together to provide human service practitioners with a well-rounded picture of First Nations clients.

Principle Five: Multidimensional Contextual Service

The fifth principle of the multidimensional contextual practice framework focuses on service. Services must be rendered with consideration for community needs, strengths, and readiness to change. In a First Nations context, this reinforces the importance of community input, rather than having an outside entity such as the federal government determine the nature and extent of services.

Services must be rendered with consideration for the availability of fundamental resources. For example, are funds available to initiate a program in an urban First Nations community, or have funds been designated exclusively for a tribal entity? Resources also include human service professionals who are trusted, culturally competent, and capable of offering appropriate services to First Nations Peoples. A shortage of such professionals requires that professional education become more accessible to First Nations Peoples (i.e., programs in tribal colleges and mainstream universities) and that non–First Nations people receive appropriate content in their professional education to adequately prepare them to work with First Nations populations.

Examining the agency or program within its context also provides important information about services. For example, services housed within a hospital may be avoided if a hospital is perceived as a place where people go to die (Hammerschlag, 1998). Likewise, services offered under the auspices of the Indian Health Service may be avoided because of this federal agency's association with sterilization programs in the 1960s and 1970s (Weaver, in press).

Overall Fit of the Multidimensional Contextual Practice Framework for First Nations Peoples

Generally, the multidimensional contextual practice framework is a good fit with First Nations people. In particular, it offers two strengths. By examining multiple dimensions, both within the client and within the environment, human service practitioners are less likely to stereotype clients. Additionally, the magna or spiritual/transcendent layer of the framework calls explicit attention to these influences in the lives of First Nations clients.

Like other frameworks, however, this one can be limited if not fully implemented. In particular, the macro context, ignored by many clinicians, is key to real change. The federal government continues to play a persistent and intrusive, although sometimes invisible, role in the lives of First Nations Peoples. Defining who is considered to be a First Nations person, requiring federal approval for many economic development enterprises, and holding money and land "in trust" for First Nations Peoples are just a few examples of ways the federal government prevents self-determination and undermines the values of human service professions. Until significant, positive changes take place on the macro level, the multidimensional contextual practice framework cannot fully be implemented.

SKILLS FOR ADDRESSING CHALLENGES AND STRENGTHS

A number of factors may enhance or injure human service practitioners' competencies. These include the ability of a human service worker to recognize the impact of his or her own experiences with privilege and disenfranchisement, the practitioner's own balance and well-being, and issues of transference.

As human beings, human service practitioners bring their own backgrounds, strengths, and challenges to the helping relationship. It is important that they recognize the impact of their own experiences on their work. This requires consciously examining experiences with privilege. Some human service practitioners come from backgrounds where they have had few personal experiences with struggles such as racism, classism, homophobia, and other forms of bigotry and oppression. They have had an opportunity to pursue a professional education that was not available to others. It is important that such human service practitioners recognize and reflect on the advantages they have experienced and continue to experience in their lives and how these may influence their values, beliefs, and behaviors. For example, someone who has had few struggles with oppression is likely to feel that life is fair and that making an effort is likely to have a positive payoff. Someone who has had lasting struggles with oppression may have a significantly different perspective.

Some human service workers, on the other hand, have experienced oppression and disenfranchisement, and this may influence their values, beliefs, and behaviors. For example, a human service worker who has overcome adversity in order to pursue a professional education may emphasize the benefits of hard work and may have some negative feelings, conscious or unconscious, toward a client who has had more opportunities yet has not taken advantage of them. It is important that human service practitioners actively examine how their own experiences with disenfranchisement may influence their work.

Social service work is difficult and stressful. Unless practitioners make conscious efforts to take care of themselves, they will not have use of their full resources to aid others. The balance and well-being that are primary goals for clients must not be neglected for practitioners. This has become a particular concern for human service practitioners working with First Nations clients (Weaver, 1999). Often First Nations Peoples are presumed to have an innate balance, grounded in spirituality and connection to all living beings. Some practitioners consciously or unconsciously envy this balance and seek to enhance their own well-being through contact with indigenous clients. While practitioner well-being is crucial, it is not the function of the helping relationship, and seeking such goals through interactions with clients is exploitive and unethical. Practitioners must find other resources (e.g., supervision, their own spirituality, their own cultural resilience) to help them find and maintain their own balance and well-being.

Issues of transference may come into play for human service practitioners serving First Nations clients. With transference, the professional does not fully see the client but sees a distorted image of the client influenced by stereotypes and the practitioner's experiences with others. Practitioners need to be aware of, and critically examine how, they perceive their First Nations clients. The book *The Dancing Healers* by Carl Hammerschlag (1988) gives explicit examples of recognizing and struggling with transference issues. Hammerschlag, a community psychiatrist of German Jewish heritage, made a choice to focus his life's work on assisting the First Nations Peoples of the Southwest. He made this choice based on his own background and his beliefs about what First Nations Peoples were like. As a Jew whose family experienced the Nazi holocaust, suffering and disenfranchisement were major themes that influenced how he experienced the world. He believed that First Nations Peoples were kindred spirits with similar experiences, and thus he felt called to work with them. His beliefs and motivations were based strictly on his own experiences and perceptions of First Nations Peoples. Upon arrival in the Southwest, he was shocked to find that First Nations Peoples did not live up to his expectations and did not in any way see him as a kindred spirit. Likewise, other human service practitioners need to examine their own experiences with transference and how these may influence their expectations and beliefs about First Nations people.

SKILLS FOR DIFFERENT LEVELS OF PRACTICE

Human service practitioners need skills in assessing within and/or between different levels of practice without perpetuating stereotypes. On a micro level, this involves the ability to conduct an assessment that includes culture and other layers of identity such as gender, age, and sexual orientation. Practitioners must examine the various layers of a client's identity and determine which ones may be particularly relevant to the case situation. It is also important that practitioners explore how multiple cultures may influence the client. The orthogonal model of cultural identity developed by researchers at the Tri Ethnic Center for Prevention Research (Oetting & Beauvais, 1991) moves beyond earlier models of identity to posit that different cultural identities are independent of each other. In other words, someone could identify as both Tewa First Nations and Mexican American. Identification with one in no way lessens identification with the other. This contrasts with linear models of assimilation, which posit that an increasing identification with one culture must lead to decreasing attachment to another. Many standardized assessment tools that examine cultural identity are still grounded in earlier linear models and thus are of questionable use (Weaver, in press).

Culturally competent service provision is not something that a skilled practitioner can do independently with no attention to environment. The meso or agency context of practice enables or hinders the work that human service practitioners can accomplish. As a natural outgrowth of self-reflection and evaluation, it is important to examine how the agency context shapes a practitioner's ability to work with First Nations clients. A few checklists have been developed to examine the cultural competence of agencies (see, e.g., Dana, Behn, & Gonwa, 1992), but so far, this meso context has received minimal attention. Agency administrators have an important role to play in examining and adapting agency policies and procedures to make them hospitable for First Nations clients. It is important for agency leadership to reflect on how cultural competence is integrated in supervision, administration, and board functions.

Skills in intervening at the macro level are crucial in work with First Nations clients. Even practitioners who do primarily clinical work must have an awareness of the macro context and its impact on First Nations Peoples. This includes an understanding of policies and knowledge of the relationship of federal and state governments to First Nations. It is also important to be knowledgeable about the relationship of individuals to their nations. For example, an enrolled member of a First Nation may be entitled to a variety of benefits, including health care, housing, and counseling services. Someone who is not enrolled may have a more tenuous relationship to his or her nation (or multiple nations), thus influencing how that person sees him- or herself as a First Nations person. Human service practitioners need skills for both assessing and intervening in the macro environment. In particular, advocacy is an important skill at this level. Nonindigenous practitioners advocating for positive change for First Nations Peoples need to ensure that they work as allies of First Nations Peoples, not outside crusaders working on their behalf, thus replicating paternalism (Weaver, 2000).

Human service practitioners also need skills in working at the magna level. This is an area often left untouched in professional training programs. It can be important to acknowledge the sacred and transcendent in all levels of work. In order to do this, practitioners must be aware of, and consciously examine their own feelings and beliefs about, the transcendent. Practitioners' own values are likely to influence how this area is or is not addressed in the helping relationship. Practitioners should also be aware of clients' comfort level in exploring these issues and follow their lead. First Nations Peoples have a right to spiritual privacy and nonexploitation. Practitioners must not probe into these areas unilaterally. Mutuality must be present in order to examine spiritual areas. Otherwise, the practitioner is likely to replicate the colonial privilege of disrespecting clients' boundaries.

CASE STUDY

Clyde Little Horse has just been referred to Wilma Hatfield for a mental status evaluation and psychiatric counseling. Clyde, a Sicangu Lakota from the Rosebud reservation, was detained by the police when he was found "ranting" at the Mount Rushmore National Monument. He yelled to the gathering crowd about how this sacred area was stolen and defaced. He stated that while people get angry about the burning of African-American churches in the South, tourists from around the world bring their children to see the defilement of Paha Sapa (the Black Hills). In his first session with Wilma, an African-American practitioner, Clyde sits with his head bowed, barely speaking a word.

Reflection on Case

Client well-being is the focus of the work. Wilma must determine what is in Clyde's best interest. The way that the referral comes about suggests Clyde is already seen as a public nuisance and a problem to be removed. Wilma needs to carefully assess Clyde and examine his perception of the situation. The limited information in this case suggests that Clyde is very angry and feels that violations of his cultural and spiritual beliefs are ignored. This justifiable anger may or may not be compounded by mental health issues that led Clyde to express his concerns in the way that he did.

Wilma will need to explore Clyde's sense of self and how this is influenced by various aspects of his identity (e.g., culture, gender, age) as well as how it is influenced by external contexts. In particular, it is important to explore his sense of self as a cultural and spiritual being, since that seems directly related to this case. These micro issues are key features of Wilma's assessment, along with an exploration of anger and possible mental health issues. As Wilma examines the meso context, she will want to get a history of Clyde's interactions with other agencies (i.e., has he been referred for a mental status evaluation before?) and with various entities in the Lakota community (i.e., is he a member of an activist group concerned about indigenous rights?).

In examining the macro context, Wilma will want to gather information about how sacred First Nations' territory came into the possession of the federal government and what legal and moral claims each side has to this disputed territory. In exploring the magna context, Wilma can learn from Clyde about the spiritual significance of Paha Sapa. She can supplement her growing understanding with reading.

Wilma, a skilled mental health practitioner, is presented with some challenging issues. Her professional values of social justice and respect lead her to strive for a more comprehensive understanding of these complex issues. Even if she determines that Clyde does indeed have some mental health concerns, this does not mean that his concerns about racist disregard for First Nations spirituality should in any way be minimized or ignored. Additionally, Wilma is troubled by Clyde's assertion that she possesses an unrecognized privilege in his comparison of the burning of African-American churches and the destruction of his sacred site. The assertion that the violation of African-American sacred sites is seen as anathema while the violation of First Nations sacred sites goes unmentioned leads Wilma to do some in-depth reflection and processing of her own feelings of privilege, disenfranchisement, and transference in supervision.

Wilma comes to appreciate the complexity and depth of this case that goes far beyond a simple mental status evaluation and possible psychiatric counseling. She sees an important link between clinical intervention and activism. Administration in her agency, however, would prefer that she stay away from advocacy and taking on controversial issues and instead focus on her clinical responsibilities. Somewhat overwhelmed, but not discouraged, Wilma finds herself in a position in which she must struggle for long-range internal change within her agency in order to be truly responsive to the needs of Clyde and her other clients.

SUMMARY

The multidimensional contextual practice framework is a good tool to guide human service practitioners working with First Nations clients. In order to work effectively with this population, the professional needs to bring three types of knowledge to the helping relationship. First, practitioners need knowledge about First Nations Peoples. This includes knowledge of their diversity and of the various contexts that influence them. Secondly, practitioners must learn from clients. Only in this way can generalized background knowledge be refined so that practitioners can move beyond assumptions and stereotypes and interact with clients as complex, multifaceted human beings. Thirdly, practitioners can have glimpses of understanding that go beyond conventional reality. This is the art of the helping professions that surpasses the limitations of conventional empirical knowledge. Throughout these three areas, it is imperative that practitioners use conscious self-awareness and grounding in the values of respect and social justice to make their work with First Nations Peoples effective and culturally appropriate.

References

Churchill, W. (1993). *Struggle for the land: Indigenous resistance to genocide, ecocide, and expropriation in contemporary North America.* Monroe, ME: Common Courage Press.

Churchill, W., & Morris, G. T. (1992). Key Indian laws and cases. In M. A. Jaimes, *The state of Native America: Genocide, colonization, and resistance* (pp. 13–21). Boston: South End Press.

Dana, R. H., Behn, J. D., & Gonwa, T. (1992). A checklist for the examination of cultural competence in social service agencies. *Research on Social Work Practice,* 2(2), 220–223.

Deloria, V., Jr. (1992). Trouble in high places: Erosion of American Indian rights to religious freedom in the United States. In M. A. Jaimes, *The state of Native America: Genocide, colonization, and resistance* (pp. 267–290). Boston: South End Press.

Hammerschlag, C. A. (1988). *The dancing healers: A doctor's journey of healing with Native Americans.* San Francisco: Harper & Row.

Iglehart, A. P., & Becerra, R. M. (1995). *Social services and the ethnic community.* Boston: Allyn & Bacon.

Jaimes, M. A. (1992). Federal Indian identification policy: A usurpation of indigenous sovereignty in North America. In M. A. Jaimes, *The state of Native America: Genocide, colonization, and resistance* (pp. 123–138). Boston: South End Press.

Jaimes, M. A., & Halsey, T. (1992). American Indian women: At the center of indigenous resistance in North America. In M. A. Jaimes, *The state of Native America: Genocide, colonization, and resistance* (pp. 311–344). Boston: South End Press.

Lawrence, J. (2000). The Indian Health Service and the sterilization of Native American women. *American Indian Quarterly,* 24(3), 400–423.

Mannes, M. (1995). Factors and events leading to the passage of the Indian Child Welfare Act. *Child Welfare,* 74(1), 264–282.

Maracle, B. (1993). *Crazywater: Native voices on addiction and recovery.* Toronto: Penguin.

Matthiessen, P. (1991). *In the spirit of Crazy Horse.* New York: Viking.

Morrisette, P. J. (1994). The holocaust of First Nation people: Residual effects on parenting and treatment implications. *Contemporary Family Therapy,* 16(5), 381–392.

Murray, D. W. (1992). Self-sufficiency and the creation of dependency: The case of Chief Isaac, Inc. *American Indian Quarterly,* 16(2), 169–188.

Napoli, M. (2002). Native wellness for the new millennium: The impact of gaming. *Journal of Sociology and Social Welfare,* 29(1), 17–34.

Oetting, E. R., & Beauvais, F. (1991). Orthogonal cultural identification theory: The cultural identification of minority adolescents. *International Journal of the Addictions,* 25(5A & 6A), 655–685.

Ogunwole, S. U. (2002). *The American Indian and Alaska Native population: 2000.* U.S. Bureau of the Census, http://www.census.gov/population/www/cen2000/briefs.html.

Peacock, T. D., Day, P. A., & Peacock, R. B. (1999). At what cost? The social impact of American Indian gaming? *Journal of Health and Social Policy,* 10(4), 23–34.

Robbins, R. L. (1992). Self-determination and subordination: The past, present, and future of American Indian governance. In M. A. Jaimes, *The state of Native America: Genocide, colonization, and resistance* (pp. 87–121). Boston: South End Press.

Snipp, C. M. (2002). American Indian and Alaska Native children in the 2002 census. *A Kids Count/PRB Report on Census 2000.* Annie E. Casey Foundation.

Stiffarm, L. A., & Lane, P., Jr. (1992). The demography of Native North America: A question of American Indian survival. In M. A. Jaimes, *The state of Native America: Genocide, colonization, and resistance* (pp. 23–53). Boston: South End Press.

Torpy, S. J. (2000). Native American women and coerced sterilization: On the trail of tears in the 1970s. *American Indian Culture and Research Journal, 24*(2), 1–22.

Weaver, H. N. (1996). Social work with American Indian youth using the orthogonal model of cultural identification. *Families in Society: The Journal of Contemporary Human Services, 77*(2), 98–107.

Weaver, H. N. (1997). Which canoe are you in? A view from a First Nations person. *Reflections: Narratives of Professional Helping, 4*(3), 12–17.

Weaver, H. N. (1999). Indigenous people and the social work profession: Defining culturally competent services. *Social Work, 44*(3), 217–225.

Weaver, H. N. (2000). Activism and American Indian issues: Opportunities and roles for social workers. *Journal of Progressive Human Services, 11*(1), 3–22.

Weaver, H. N. (2001a). Indigenous identity: What is it and who *really* has it? *American Indian Quarterly, 25*(2), 240–255.

Weaver, H. N. (2001b). Native Americans and substance abuse. In S. L. A. Straussner (Ed.), *Ethnocultural factors in substance abuse treatment* (pp. 77–96). New York: Guilford.

Weaver, H. N. (in press). Evidenced-based social work practice with Native Americans. In D. F. Harrison, J. S. Wodarski, & B. A. Thyer (Eds.), *Human diversity and social work practice: An evidence-based approach.* Springfield, IL: Charles C. Thomas.

Weaver, H. N., & White, B. J. (1997). The Native American family circle: Roots of resiliency. *Journal of Family Social Work, 2*(1), 67–79.

Weaver, H. N., & White, B. J. (1999). Protecting the future of indigenous children and nations: An examination of the Indian Child Welfare Act. *Journal of Health and Social Policy, 10*(4), 35–50.

*I am a human being. Nothing human
can be alien to me.* —**Terrance**

13 | White Ethnics

Ethnic-Specific Communities of People

DEBRA L. WELKLEY

What does it mean to be "White"? This is a question that plagues our society. People who may identify and/or are identified as fitting into the category of White, as well as those who do not, have to grapple with the conceptualization and impact of what it means to be White on a daily basis. For some, this is readily apparent, while for others, it is taken for granted; regardless, it is evidenced in an omnipresent state of privilege. Because of this pervasive impact of the classification of White and "Whiteness," it is an important area of study for all peoples.

Exploration of the demographics and historical conception of "White" will be provided in this chapter. A look at the reality of the impacts of this construct on the individual as well as society at large will be provided, hopefully leaving many questions for the reader to continue to explore and ponder. Features of White identity and how it has been socially, politically, and economically constructed will be another aspect of this discussion. Myths and stereotypes relative to White people will be explored, along with how they affect White people's interactions with each other and with people who have not been classified as White. One premise of the discussion, which is emphasized throughout the chapter, is that Whites need to be responsible for deconstructing the stereotypes that contribute to the definition of "Whiteness." Focus will be given to how people in the helping professions, whether classified as White or not, can understand the experiences, needs, and issues of White people, and how they can approach these multidimensional contextual areas in nonstereotypical ways. Like many of the other chapters in this book, this chapter concludes with a discussion regarding the professional knowledge, skills, and values that are helpful in providing competent practice through a case example approach.

DEMOGRAPHICS AND HISTORICAL CONCEPTUALIZATION

According to the U.S. Census Bureau, in 2000, there were 216,930,975 people classified as White. This number constituted 77.1% of the total U.S. population at that time. In only eight states and the District of Columbia was less than 70% of the population White. Hawaii and the District of Columbia were both below 50% (39.3% and 32.2%, respectively). Recently, it was reported that the state of California currently has a population where less than 50% of the population is White.

In 1565, the Spanish founded St. Augustine, Florida. Then 42 years later, in 1607, the English founded Jamestown, Virginia. By 1790, White Protestants from England comprised 60% of the total White population of the colonies, which at that time was 3 million (Schaefer, 1993). As immigration continued from various European countries, the English were soon outnumbered. Yet they maintained their dominant position in the newly forming country, in part because they were the ones who held the positions of power economically, which then carved out the power for the political and social arenas.

When literature is reviewed throughout many racial and ethnic texts, if attention is given to Whites as a group, it is generally in the context of immigration and how that affected society, laws, and the White English people. Very little is written in this context about who, indeed, belongs in the group of people referred to as White. Many who are not English are identified and identify themselves as White. There are also many groups of people who, due to the country from which they immigrated, were initially seen as non-White or as ethnic White, but who today are seen as White (i.e., the Irish, Italians, French, and Polish). This distinction was primarily made based on economics and religious differences. "White" people and communities had a more difficult time when the nations from which they immigrated were primarily Catholic and/or seen as poorer countries economically. However, because their ancestry, ability to speak English (at least in some cases), and skin color were close to characteristics of the White English, assimilation was much more attainable for people coming from parts of Europe than for those coming from Asia, Southeast Asia, and Mexico, as well as those who were taken from their homeland of Africa.

Initially the United States had open immigration to all groups, and people were allowed, just by coming here, to become natural citizens. In 1790, all that changed when Congress decided to restrict naturalization to "White persons" (Lopez, 1996). It was not until 1952 (just over 50 years ago) that racial restrictions were removed from the requirements for becoming a citizen of this country if the person was born somewhere else. Until then, decisions about who was to be classified as White, and therefore able to become naturalized, were made on a case-by-case basis (see Table 13.1). Even the basic law of citizenship for those born in this country did not include all racial groups (minorities were not all included) until 1940 (Lopez, 1996).

The term *White* has been assigned to describe people who are traditionally of northwestern European descent and who migrated to this country to form what we know today as the United States. What is interesting to note is that even at that point and time in history, although people noticed differences in the skin color of people, skin color was not something that was used to distinguish people or to identify peo-

Table 13.1 | Racial Prerequisite Cases

Year	Case	Decision
1878	*In re Ah Yup*	Chinese are not White
1880	*In re Camille*	Persons half White and Native American are not White
1889	*In re Kanaka Nian*	Hawaiians are not White
1890	*In re Hong Yen Chang*	Chinese are not White
1894	*In re Po*	Burmese are not White
1894	*In re Saito*	Japanese are not White
1900	*In re Burton*	Native Americans are not White
1909	*In re Knight*	Persons half White, one-quarter Japanese, and one-quarter Chinese are not White
1909	*In re Balsara*	Asian Indians are not White
1909	*In re Majour*	Syrians are White
1909	*In re Halladjian*	Armenians are White
1910	*Bessho v. United States*	Japanese are not White
1912	*In re Alverto*	Persons three-quarters Filipino and one-quarter White are not White
1912	*In re Young*	Persons half German and half Japanese are not White
1913	*In re Akhay Kumar Mozumdar*	Asian Indians are White
1914	*Ex parte Dow*	Syrians are not White
1921	*Petition of Easurk Emsen Charr*	Koreans are not White
1922	*Ozawa v. United States*	Japanese are not White
1923	*United States v. Thind*	Asian Indians are not White
1925	*United States v. Ali*	Punjabis are not White
1928	*In re Feroz Din*	Afghanis are not White
1928	*United States v. Gokhale*	Asian Indians are not White
1935	*De La Ysla v. United States*	Filipinos are not White
1941	*De Cano v. State*	Filipinos are not White
1942	*Khariti Ram Samras v. United States*	Asian Indians are not White
1942	*In re Ahmed Hassan*	Arabians are not White
1944	*Ex parte Mohriez*	Arabians are White

ple as being superior or inferior to one another, nor did people identify themselves as White. That ascription seemed to materialize once the social, economic, and political development of this country got underway. As is evidenced in the many court cases delineated in Table 13.1, laws shaped the social context of the White "racial" identity. Generally speaking, the courts defined who was "not White" more often than they were able to provide a definition for who was "White." Initially the courts relied on what they considered scientific evidence to justify the racial assignments made. This implied that race existed as a physical fact. However, as the courts continued to review cases, they came to rely more on common knowledge demonstrating "that racial taxonomies devolve upon social demarcations" (Lopez, 1996, p. 9).

This is an important point to understand, not only when attempting to understand what it means to be White, but also when coming to understand the concepts of race and ethnicity. Lopez (1996) states, in his book *White by Law,* that the law not only shapes the social context of racial identity, but it also "creates the racial meanings that attach to features in a much more subtle and fundamental way: laws and legal decisions define which physical and ancestral traits code as Black or White, and so on" (p. 16). Therefore, the concept of White is more a figure of speech than it is anything else—a social convention that we have come to understand by examining someone's looks. This observation extends to the terms we use to categorize people we think are non-White as well.

Even recently, it has been demonstrated that race is not biologically based but, rather, is a social construction. The need for this social construction came out of the need of early settlers in this country to find some easily identifiable feature and/or explanation to demonstrate that slaves were inferior. Skin color was an easy way to mark the differences that they constructed between themselves and slaves to ensure that the people they removed from the homeland of Africa indeed remained their servants and assisted them in creating a better economic situation for themselves. This is not to say that early settlers were not ethnocentric and xenophobic. Their interactions with First Nations Peoples also demonstrate their ideology that their group was "better" and had the "right" values and norms. Such historical facts, however, do not mean that all people socially identified as White shared (or share) these sentiments. However, those who maintained power economically and politically often used the construction of race and racial inferiority to foster the many systems of oppression that exist in our society today.

Prior to the slave trade and during its early development, there were White indentured servants; but indentured servants used their work to pay a "debt" of some sort, and they were usually allowed their freedom once that was paid. Generally, indentured servants in this country offered their servitude to pay for their passage to this country. Africans paid dearly for their passage to this country without volunteering to provide servitude, let alone making a voluntary decision to come to this country. Many paid with their lives before arriving here to provide services to a people who believed they were superior to others. The construction of Whiteness was, and still is, a social fact created to maintain privileges of resources, power, and opportunity that otherwise would translate into a greater distribution of wealth and prestige (Lipsitz, 1998). This social construction helps to maintain the profits often shared by Whites due to racial and ethnic discrimination and assists with the preservation of oppression.

Although ethnic Whites are classified by society as being White, many have faced discrimination based on their ethnic origin when coming to this country. Yet, as a collective, they also have profited from being able to identify themselves as White, in that they have been chosen for employment opportunities, provided with the ability to secure housing, and have benefited from educational opportunities, over peoples who did not physically appear White. Initially, people from White ethnic groups may not have been classified as White and were seen as inferior to those who identified themselves as White. Generally, individuals from such White ethnic groups combated oppression and discrimination through lack of jobs, poor living conditions, and barriers to educational opportunities and many other resources afforded to the already established "Whites" in this country. Many ethnic Whites from Irish and the Italian communities (as well as others) have historically harbored hostilities and ill feelings toward non-White groups (e.g., African Americans, Puerto Ricans, Mexicans) due to a fear of having to compete with them for resources that those holding power dole out sparingly. This occurred, for example, following the Emancipation Proclamation as African Americans emigrated north and west to obtain better job opportunities, to gain the ability to own land, and to escape the suffocating Jim Crow laws of the South. Due to animosity from a large number of Whites in the North, they ended up facing racism and discrimination in the North and the West, although it was less overt and more covert than in the South.

As people in the United States moved around, the construct of Whiteness certainly demonstrated that there was a privilege associated with being able to identify as White no matter where one went. White privilege was not limited to the South, as so many had attempted to indicate. Judy Helfand (2003) writes that most studies on Whiteness agree that "racial oppression is a key element in whiteness and that, as a group, white people do benefit disproportionally from the race and class hierarchy maintained by whiteness" (p. 2). Because this prevailing oppression has been interwoven into the fabric of our society, there is no possible way that we (whether White or non-White) can escape the reality of being shaped to some degree by the knowledge, ideas, norms, and practices of "Whiteness." This seems to be true whether one self-identifies as White or is so defined by society. Either way, privileges are bestowed on those with paler skin pigmentation.

WHITE PRIVILEGE AND OPPRESSION

Whether the term *Anglo, Caucasian, WASP, Waspito, Anglacito, honky,* or *White* is used, we tend to know what peoples are being referenced. As a White person myself, I know that these terms apply to me, and yet a piece of who I am feels that they do not fit with who I am, that I cannot be defined by the lack of pigment in my skin. The "White" aspect of who I am has felt uncomfortable to me because the realization that I have had privileges others have not had, and I have not always understood why. These privileges have included being able to go into a store without being carefully followed, to write a check without being scrutinized, to go just about anywhere whenever I choose without having to wonder whether I will be accepted, and so on—the list could go on and on.

Peggy McIntosh (2001) wrote a paper on White privilege in which she delineated a list of forty-six privileges that those who are White experience just because they are White. Her statement, "Whites are carefully taught not to recognize white privilege" (p. 95), is one that I think most Whites want to overlook even when they do become aware of the privileges they have. To accept that one has privilege is sometimes difficult enough, but to then go a step further and accept that one has been "taught" to not see the privileges one has because one is White means one has to distrust those who were responsible for teaching this paradigm. That can be difficult to internalize. Abby Ferber (1999) states that due to not having to think about "Whiteness" when Whites think about race, "white people like myself have failed to recognize the ways in which our own lives are shaped by race" (p. 121).

The truth is, from the time we are born and/or become a citizen in the United States, we all learn about White privilege. Either we benefit from it and attempt to disregard its existence, or we do not benefit from it and know all too well about its existence. Judith Katz (1978) writes, "[T]his country is based on and operates under a doctrine of white racism" (p. 4), and "racism escapes no one. It is a part of us all and has deeply infiltrated the lives and psyches of both the oppressed and the oppressors" (p. 5). A White person learns early on how to benefit from the system, especially if that person maintains contacts and networks with Whites. The fear of many Whites about accepting that many privileges are granted to them just because they are White is that what they believe to be "their" individual accomplishments might not be "their" achievements (won through hard work and dedication) but rather due to White privilege. Unfortunately, "white privilege is not something [we] get to decide whether or not [we] want to keep" (Jensen, 1998, p. 3). The question, therefore, might be: How do we remove White privilege so that everyone is indeed treated justly, and not according to social constructions of race and a system of hierarchy based on social constructions of racial superiority? Is this system not something that everyone, whether White or non-White, should take part in deconstructing? Removing tools of oppression that have been created and maintained for more than five centuries is certainly something that needs the attention and intention of all people.

Oppression is defined in many different ways by researchers and laypeople. Lum (2003) defines it as a process in which "a segment of the population, systematically and over a period of time, prevents another segment from attaining access to scarce and valued resources" (p. 55). This process helps to develop and establish the hierarchical structure in society, supports the efforts of those in the higher ranks to maintain their membership there, and blocks those who are placed in the lower ranks from moving out of those social strata. This phenomenon coexists with "White privilege" and helps to sustain it. It is difficult to say which might have created the other, as they work to mutually reinforce one another. Yamato (2001) states that those who are the oppressors seem to have an "innate ability to access economic resources, information, respect" (p. 90). We can see the emulation of this in the "White privilege" that is interwoven into our society in the United States.

White supremacy is evidence of oppression. White supremacists believe in racial purity and racial superiority; in their view, Whites are superior to all others. Any individual or group that threatens their ideas of how to maintain and generate racial purity becomes a hated enemy. Therefore, the White supremacist identity is rooted in "the maintenance of secure boundaries" (Ferber, in Andersen & Collins, 2004, p. 117). The verbal and physical acts of hate, the rallies, the socialization of young children, the dissemination of White supremacist literature, and other behavior that supports their beliefs are all indicative of boundary maintenance, which is a vehicle for oppression. White supremacists' behavior is directed toward not only "non-White" individuals, but also toward any individual or group perceived to threaten the maintenance of White racial purity (e.g., homosexuals and Jews).

As Guadalupe and Lum state in Chapter 1 of this text, oppression is not merely a "White" and "Black" issue, nor does it exist only between diverse racial and ethnic groups. Therefore, it is important to explore oppression that exists between groups of people as well as within group membership. This is especially important if we hope to eliminate the oppressive forces that exist in society.

One aspect to investigate is that an individual may be oppressed in one context and then be privileged (and possibly an agent of oppression) in another. For instance, some White immigrant groups, such as the Italians, Irish, Greeks, and Jews from various European countries, were looked down upon and seen as outcasts in our society, were allowed limited access to economic opportunities through meager employment, and were segregated into what were considered low-income neighborhoods. In applying the definition of oppression to an Italian immigrant 100 years ago, or even to immigrants from Slavic and Russian countries today, it would be very easy to discern how White immigrants have been oppressed by the social structure created by White Anglo-Saxon Protestants. Yet, when compared to non-White immigrants, or non-White peoples who did not immigrate, one can see that opportunities have been bestowed on the ethnic White that could not even be entertained by the non-White immigrant. Does this erase or dismiss the pain and strife that the White immigrant may have endured? Certainly not, but it does provide a different perspective and indicates that oppression is not merely a class issue, as some indicate, but interacts with society's construct of race and what that means in our society. Class differences within the population classified as White, however, do demonstrate systems of oppression that affect those individuals as well as the groups they identify with.

Yamato (2001) briefly discusses what she considers to be the flipside of oppression: "internalized oppression." This occurs when "Members of the target group are emotionally, physically, and spiritually battered to the point that they begin to actually believe that their oppression is deserved, is their lot in life, is natural and right, and that it doesn't even exist" (p. 91). Generally, people suppose that this is applicable only to non-White oppressed groups. This author proposes that it can be applied to within-group oppression as well. Struggle arises when the oppressed group feels a need to protect and fight for, or feels at risk of losing, the few scarce resources they indeed have (e.g., employment, housing, autonomy). When White ethnic groups begin to realize that although they were oppressed, they also experienced privilege, they are sometimes unwilling to accept that one can encounter such pain and persecution and yet still be privileged. Pain, guilt, anger, and many other emotions can result from the experience of being both oppressed and privileged. The experiences of privilege, like internalized oppression, may become an internalized view that this privilege is natural and right, or even that such privilege does not really exist—that those aspects are there because the people deserve them. This outlook can lead to varying degrees of ethnocentrism in an attempt to hold onto what one believes is true about oneself and the group to which one belongs.

Some White people experience conflicted feelings and pain through the experience of oppression when they also have membership in a group with characteristics that are not deemed acceptable by those in charge of the structural hierarchy in this country. Until the women's suffrage movement in the early 1900s, for example, both White and non-White women in the United States had very few rights and privileges recognized by the dominant White male population. The historical oppression of women is not erased because a woman is White. There are still painful struggles and barriers that are encountered. The same holds true for people with disabilities, for those who are poor, and for homosexuals and any other group that has been and/or is ostracized in our society. Further, the experience of individuals who identify individually or are identified by society as belonging to these other groups is, in many ways, similar to that which White ethnics once encountered. Boundaries are built around resources (social and material) to which Whites who are *not* identified as part of these other groups have more complete access and are allowed fuller utilization.

DEVELOPING A WHITE IDENTITY

White Americans have suffered from a deeper inner
uncertainty as to who they really are. —**Ralph Ellison**

As Guadalupe and Lum state earlier in this text, the term *ethnicity* reflects a collective individualism and indicates a constructed social identity based on an individual and collective sense of connectedness and/or perpetuated by combination of factors such as a unique set of cultural or biological ties and a degree of solidarity that ascribes membership. Generally, people think of ethnicity as referring to a common set of customs, values, traditions, and shared heritage of a group of people. It does not always pertain to what is considered the biological features of an individual or group, which is usually referred to as race. Just as *race* is a socially constructed term, so is *ethnicity*. Many White Americans of European ancestry do not feel they have an ethnicity, or much of one. Those groups that are identified as White ethnics (e.g., Italian Americans, Irish Americans, Polish Americans, and Russian Americans) do not per se share this "lack" of ethnic identity, but depending on the degree of acculturation, they may not identify with their country of origin as much as they do with being an "American." This speaks to the dilemma of individuals identifying themselves as part of a group, White or non-White, and also to the experience of stigma due to society assigning a label to them. This is true not only for Whites but for all people, due to the social construction of race and how it is used to identify and "maintain boundaries" throughout the course of societal interactions and development.

Additionally, how one identifies oneself or is labeled by society reaches beyond race, creating an intersection and interaction that cannot be overlooked. The experi-

ences of being female and White, of being a White male with physical or mental disabilities, and of being a homosexual who is White and part of the working class are
all part of the human experience and, therefore, part of any identified racial/ethnic
experience (i.e., being White). There are aspects of membership in and identification
with these groups that make the experience of "being White" complex and intriguing. This further delineates the notion that people are not static but ever-changing,
and that there is no specific formula per se to ascribe to any group of people. Many
times in discussions such as this, there is a tendency to single out and focus on a more
finite area of exploration in order to demonstrate concepts and ideas being presented.
Hopefully, the reader will utilize the expanded discussions in this chapter to further
investigate and illuminate the experiences of those facets not fully discussed in this
chapter.

Being White affords one the opportunity to choose among different ethnicities.
Whites who, due to intermarriage, have various "White" ethnicities to choose from,
will generally select the one that has suffered the least amount of discrimination and
is seen as the least outcast. Herbert Gans (1979) coined the term *symbolic ethnicities*
to indicate that Whites are often able to choose an ethnicity that is individualistic and
does not have much social cost associated with it. This selection is voluntary and
rooted in the traditions of their nuclear family. This is juxtaposed to non-White ethnicities (e.g., African American, Mexican American, Native American, Japanese
American) where members of those groups generally do not have the opportunity to
choose a symbolic ethnicity.

Symbolic ethnics tend to select an identity that they feel good about being able to
say out loud, and then generalize their identification and experience of this chosen
ethnic group to how all people relate to their ethnicities. The presumption becomes
that all identities are equal and, to some extent, are interchangeable. As an example,
suppose that I indicate to people that I am Swiss and, in speaking about the experiences of Japanese Americans in our country and the difficulties they have faced, I state
that their struggle has been similar to that of my ancestors when they came here from
Switzerland. The truth is that the two experiences are *not* similar; they are distinct
experiences, as these two groups have had very separate paths to pave while carving
out their places in this country. I have no traditions, food preferences, customs, or
even physical distinctions that might indicate that I am Swiss, and even though initially my ancestors did not speak English, they learned the language and were able to
assimilate very easily. Japanese Americans, on the other hand, may have many traditions, food preferences, customs, and physical characteristics that people in our society might use to identify them as Japanese, and their language might also indicate that
identification. Although these experiences are not "similar," the two groups may still
share aspects of the struggles in their heritage and, therefore, can connect together as
people coming to this land from a different one and/or as people who want to have
the freedom that empowers all people in their progress and development. The differences between experiences should not be minimized, but neither should the points of
interconnection that the two groups can share.

The differences between group identities affect our individual identities differently. No one besides myself, and possibly my family, imposes the Swiss ethnic identity upon me, which is what makes it a symbolic ethnic identity. However, if I were

Japanese American, society would impose many expectations, assumptions, and obstacles on me because of my ascribed "Japanese identity." By and large, Whites seem to have a difficult time grasping this reality. This is an area where we do not seem to want to be different from others, or have others be different from us. Often enough, we do not want to accept the fact that because of our Whiteness, not only do we reap benefits, but others also reap barriers and blockades. The unwillingness to really see and understand this very basic difference acts as an obstacle for many Whites in their own identity development.

For non-White groups, identity development is complex and more complicated than it is for Whites. This is due to the element of racial discrimination and how being the recipient of such discrimination on a daily basis affects one's identity, as well as to the imposition of racial identity on such groups from the outside. White people, by contrast, have the option each day of whether or not to think of themselves in racial terms. Barbara Flagg states that there "exists a tendency among Whites not to see themselves in racial terms" (in Lopez, 1996, p. 22). She identifies this tendency as one of the defining characteristics of being White and labels it the "transparency phenomenon." It is easier to not see one's self as White than to deal with the reality of how Whiteness has constructed a hierarchy of privilege and has served as the source of society's injustices. Lopez (1996) posits that Whites need to develop a consciousness of race that sees how Whiteness, and one's own Whiteness, has contributed to the systems of racial superiority and inferiority. He further states, "a self-deconstructive white race-consciousness is key to racial justice" (p. 156).

White identity development models have been constructed to help us look at how Whites undergo a process of understanding who they are as White people in the larger society and the degree to which they accept the social implications of membership in their racial group. Leading theories in the area of White identity development indicate that more attention should be given to helping students explore their White identity and that continued focus in this area would assist in understanding increasing racial tensions in our country (Pedersen, 1994; Ponterotto & Pederson, 1993). Four primary theories of White identity development will be explored here.

Rita Hardiman developed a model of social identity in 1982, prior to developing her White Identity Development (WID) model that same year, that examined social constructs of racial identity and sex-role identity (Pedersen, 1994; Ponterotto & Pederson, 1993). She defined social identity as "all the various social groups that an individual consciously or unconsciously has membership in and the conscious or unconscious use of that social frame of reference in self-perception, in social perception or in social interaction" (Ponterotto & Pedersen, 1993, p. 64). Her model consisted of five stages: (1) no social consciousness; (2) acceptance; (3) resistance; (4) redefinition; and (5) internalization. The first stage deals with spontaneous and natural behavior. As one moves into the second stage, one identifies with role models. In the third stage, the individual questions previously held beliefs. Introspection about social groups and defining one's specific needs separate from those groups occurs in the fourth stage, redefinition. The final stage is where integration of aspects of identity from the previous stages is achieved as they are absorbed into the individual's overall identity.

Hardiman's WID model also has five stages. She developed this model in the context of her social identity model and by studying six autobiographies written by White authors. A brief summary of the WID model follows:

1. *Lack of social consciousness:* In this stage, Whites are unaware of the complex codes of appropriate behavior for White people.
2. *Acceptance:* This comes as a result of socialization. Shared opinions are learned. The person is socialized in the acceptance of behavior and beliefs that support social codes.
3. *Resistance:* Whites acknowledge the reality of the Black experience in America; personal experiences raise conflict between their own values and the values deemed appropriate by their own racial group. The transition to this stage is frequently stimulated by interaction with people, social events, or information presented in the media or books. Many times, this stage elicits feelings of guilt and embarrassment.
4. *Redefinition:* As White people begin, in this stage, to search for a new White identity, they acknowledge the reality and pervasiveness of racism and act to change undesirable situations. They begin to search out aspects of White identity not linked to racism and may develop a sense of pride in their own group.
5. *Internalization:* Whites incorporate their new racial identity with their overall social identity. A positive White identity is now a healthy part of the individual. Whites in this stage direct energy at liberating other Whites from racism and at educating themselves about other forms of oppression and their relationship to race.

The only White identity model that has been operationalized in the form of an assessment that can be administered by paper-and-pencil is one developed by Janet Helms (1990). She started developing her model in 1984 and further refined and elaborated upon it in 1990 (Ponterotto & Pedersen, 1993). Her model consists of six stages, which fall into two phases.

Phase one is referred to as the *abandonment of racism* phase, and it encompasses three of the six stages: contact, disintegration, and reintegration. The contact stage begins as soon as the White person begins to have contact and/or an awareness that African Americans exist. The second stage of disintegration is where the individual begins to acknowledge Whiteness and understands the benefits or privileges associated with being White. During the second stage, individuals go through internal conflict in that they want to be accepted by the larger group to which they belong (White), but at the same time, they have difficulty with treating people of other racial groups as inferior, since this does not mesh with their internalized idea that "all people are created equal." In coming to terms with this inner turmoil, the White individual will at some point conform to the pressure of racism and progress to the third stage of reintegration. During this stage, people accept the belief in White racial superiority and believe that the negative conditions and/or lack of opportunities experienced by African Americans are due to their own inadequacies, which furthers the cycle of racism and feelings of White superiority. As individuals begin to question the premises and existence of this racist identity, they enter the second phase and stage four.

The second phase of the model is *defining a nonracist White identity*. Whites begin to acknowledge the responsibilities that Whites have for racism. During this pseudo-independent stage, the individual is no longer content with a racist identity and searches for a new one. This may be evidenced by an "intellectual acceptance and curiosity about Blacks" (Ponterotto & Pedersen, 1993, p. 73). Next, White people may immerse themselves in readings (e.g., autobiographies of "enlightened Whites," readings about the African-American experience, etc.). This is coined the immersion/emersion stage and is the fifth stage of the model. In this stage, White people attempt to establish a positive identity for themselves and try to reeducate and change other Whites. They become more aware of the myths and stereotypes that have been interwoven into history and are conscious of such erroneous beliefs. The final stage is autonomy; the person is flexible and open to opportunities to learn about other cultures, not just African Americans. The White person now consistently acknowledges and works to eliminate oppression in society at all levels and of all types (e.g, individual and institutional; sexism, ageism, etc.).

A third model for understanding racial consciousness and White identity development has been presented by Ponterotto (1988). He constructed this model initially for White counselor trainees. The previous two models discussed focus on interactions between Whites and African Americans; Ponterotto's four-stage model is different in that his model extends to all White-minority interactions. During the first stage of *preexposure*, Whites give little attention to multicultural issues. According to Ponterotto, during this phase, Whites do not understand the notion of subtle or covert racism. Instead, they think of only overt displays and see racism as being primarily a thing of the past. It is during the second stage of *exposure* that Whites are first confronted with multicultural issues. They are exposed to the realities of continuing racism in this country and begin to develop an understanding of the nature of racism and of how non-Whites are treated differently.

Zealot-defensive Whites are in the third stage of Ponterotto's model. After the recognition and exposure accomplished in the second stage, Whites either become very zealous about multicultural issues/topics and immerse themselves in minority issues, or they become very defensive due to their anger and guilt. If they become defensive, they tend to take criticisms of the system developed by Whites and benefiting Whites very personally. They may withdraw from discussions about multicultural issues and may see professors who confront these issues as "anti-White." The final stage of White identity development, according to Ponterotto (1988), is integration. This is when Whites begin to demonstrate a rekindled interest in and openness to exploring and discussing multicultural issues. They acknowledge and accept the realities associated with racism in today's society. They recognize their own acts and thoughts of subtle racism, and feel empowered in terms of eliminating racism in themselves and in society (Ponterotto & Pedersen, 1993).

As the reader may have noted, there is some overlap among the three models presented so far. In 1991, Sabnani, Ponterotto, and Borodovsky integrated these three models into a five-stage model of White racial identity development. The five stages are as follows:

1. *Preexposure/precontact:* At this stage, the individual lacks awareness of self as a racial entity and has an unquestioned acceptance of stereotypes.
2. *Conflict:* There is a conflict as individuals expand their knowledge of race relations. Through more interaction with people from different racial groups and through books such as this one, as well as hands-on knowledge, White people are challenged to acknowledge their Whiteness and to examine their own cultural values.
3. *Pro-minority/Americanism:* Two reactions to the struggle experienced during the conflict stage may occur: a strong pro-minority stance or self-focused feelings of anger and guilt.
4. *Retreat into White culture:* This stage is marked by the second of the two reactions in the previous stage. The White person retreats from situations that will stimulate further conflict. Behaviorally and attitudinally, the person retreats into the comfort, security, and familiarity of same-race contacts. The sentiment is that it is easier to just stay in the "White world."
5. *Redefinition and integration:* Whites acknowledge their responsibility for maintaining White privilege and racism, while also identifying with a new White identity that is nonracist and healthy. They see the good and bad in their own group as well as in groups throughout society. People in this stage focus their energy on issues beyond race and display an interest in fighting all forms of oppression and injustice.

A common emphasis throughout these four models of White identity development is that, as part of the journey to creating a society with inequality between races (as socially constructed), Whites need to take responsibility for the part their "Whiteness" has played in society's structure of oppression and come to a point where they can embrace that responsibility and use it to dismantle the racist system that has operated for centuries in this country. Ponterotto and Pedersen (1993) suggest that "facilitating the development of a healthy and positive racial/ethnic identity among all Americans is a prerequisite to a tolerant, racially harmonious society" (p. 37). Many Whites may not think this is important in the grand scheme; however, Ian Lopez (1996) states, "Reflecting on one's own Whiteness, on one's construction as a person at the center, as the privileged source of society's injustices, is the only way to span the racial divide created in the name of Whiteness" (p. 186). Support for the development of a White racial identity is not so that White people will create feelings of guilt, pity, and anger and operate out of those feelings, but to indeed reflect on the impact of their Whiteness, embrace that which has been bad and that which has been good, and then move to a new plane of respect for all people and for everyone's journey of identity. "We must feel good about who we are before we can respect and feel good about others" (Ponterotto & Pedersen, 1993, p. 39).

A strength presented by these models is that they provide a way of discussing and analyzing how a White person develops what others might consider a higher sense of "White personhood." All of these models, however, appear to typify a person's "Whiteness" as a master status and the characteristic that defines him or her as a person. This negates the reality that people are human and that we all go through a developmental process to become who we are and how we see ourselves. Also, some of the same criticisms that apply to other developmental theories apply here. All four

WID models seem to progress in a linear fashion, which may not be how a person's sense of self develops, especially if we accept a symbolic interactionist perspective and believe that our realities as well as understanding of self are constantly being created through our interactions with others and our environment. Additionally, these models do not provide a path for those who do not self-identify as White and yet deal with the stigma and stereotypes cast upon them because society labels them as "White."

These models might be developed into a fully integrated identity model for Whites that would be more helpful to individuals as they strive to advance their own journey of self-awareness by including such issues as: how we become aware of our Whiteness; how some may move through the stages delineated in grappling with the realities of how being White affects others in society, while others may not; and a discussion of how people, whether White or non-White, can join together and work toward peace and tranquility regardless of the social constructs imposed by society.

STEREOTYPES AND MYTHS

Walter Lippmann (1922), who brought the term *stereotype* to the attention of social scientists, referred to stereotypes as pictures in our heads that "provide a connection between the individual and his/her world" (Welkley, 1993). The concept stereotype has been defined and elaborated upon in many different ways. Feagin (1989) defined a stereotype as "an overgeneralization associated with a racial or ethnic category that goes beyond existing evidence" (p. 11). Earlier in this text, Guadalupe and Lum note that stereotypes perpetuate images that are frequently exclusive of individual and collective uniqueness, are based on a monolithic lens or one-dimensional approaches that often promote invisibility and underrepresentation of variables affecting groups of people, encourage imbalance when presenting interpretations of experiences, and portray unrealistic expectations. Generally, theorists and scholars agree that a stereotype involves an overgeneralization not based on fact that affects individuals and groups unrealistically.

Stereotypes play an integral role in how society views dominant and subordinate groups, as well as in how individuals view themselves as members or nonmembers of those groups. This author has referred to stereotypes as the "language of prejudice" because of the role they play in developing attitudes about people who may seem different. This impact can be very subtle because many people know the stereotypes society has of groups of people, even if they do not believe them and/or know that it is inappropriate to use them.

Stereotypes are not restricted to subordinate or non-White groups of people. Generally, we are most familiar with stereotypes about non-White groups and disadvantaged populations; however, studies have surveyed Whites about the generalizations they think other groups hold about them, as well as non-Whites regarding the general attributes they think are ascribed to them by Whites. Welkley (1993) indicated, in a study conducted about stereotypes on a college campus, that although Whites are aware that generalizations about their group exist, they do not seem "to know particularly how others perceive[] their racial group" (p. 58). However, the data indicated that there were more similarities than dissimilarities relative to non-

White groups' perception of specific traits other groups would use to describe them and how those other groups indeed typified them. This gives support to the notion that Whites are not subject to the perceptions of other groups due to their dominant position in society.

Whether the stereotypes one holds are about Whites, non-Whites, or other groups of people, they can be detrimental due to their generalizing nature. For example, if one meets people who are Irish American believing that the Irish are known for drinking and partying, one will most likely disregard the Irish people one meets who do not drink at all or who drink minimally. One may also believe that all Irish people are Catholic and therefore overlook the possibility that another religious orientation is important to some Irish peoples' lives. Stereotypes are wrought with assumptions, whether they are about "privileged Whites" or White and non-White people who do not have those same privileges ascribed to them.

In drawing attention to the myths about White people: Wouldn't it be nice to develop a list of such myths and then go through the list and debunk each one? The problem is that any possible myth that comes to mind has an element of truth in it. Unfortunately, many times that is the case not only with myths, but with stereotypes as well. When comparing the results of Welkley's 1991 study to those of earlier similar studies (Gilbert, 1951; Gordon, 1986; Karlins, Coffman, & Walters, 1969; Katz & Braly, 1933), three consistent and constant stereotypes relative to Whites have emerged: materialistic, ambitious, and progressive (Welkley, 1993). Are those myths? They probably are if we say that "all Whites" are materialistic, ambitious, and progressive. There are, however, some Whites who exhibit those traits. What is important to remember about the nature of stereotypes is how they contribute to myths about a group of people—and that we then attach the stigma of particular character types, personality traits, and behaviors to the whole group—when, in reality, people are individuals. We do individuals from all groups a disservice when we accept such generalizations.

W. I. Thomas stated in his renowned "Thomas theorem" that perceptions are real in their consequences (Thomas & Thomas, 1928). In other words, beliefs and characteristics we assume to be true of people have influence and affect what actually happens. Our relationships with others are constructed out of the meanings we attach to symbols, whether material or nonmaterial ones. These symbols and their meanings influence our behaviors, interactions, aspirations, lifestyles, employment, and all aspects of our social existence. Therefore, it is important as practitioners to be careful of accepting statements such as, "White people are ____." Anyone can fill in that blank and find a White person who will fit the bill, and yet we can also find a White person who will not fit the bill, if we look. If we do not search for those who do not fit the stereotypes, we will not know if the characteristics do, indeed, fit the person, or whether we have made our perceptions of a group fit the person. Challenging what we believe to be true and realizing that "things are not always what they seem" is an important step in the deconstruction of stereotypes.

Although Whites seem to be immune to the impact of stereotypes other groups may hold about them, many certainly have an ethnocentric view in which what they experience and come to believe as true and proper is what all Whites either do believe or should believe. When one finds oneself taking this point of view, caution should be taken, and further introspection is encouraged. All people have different experiences that create who they are and what constitutes their belief system. White people who are racist and hold superior attitudes need to understand that although they may feel they have reasons to hold those beliefs, not all White people do hold such beliefs, even when they have had similar life experiences. Additionally, Whites who have developed to stage five or six of one of the White racial identity models should be careful not to expect that everyone else in that stage will hold onto the same "truths" they do, or that Whites who are at different levels of development will progress to where they are, or even want to do so. In fact, Whites should be careful about assuming that all White people need to indeed develop a "White identity."

In order to truly embrace who we are and work at understanding others, we must actively work at debunking all stereotypes. As has been stated previously, one imperative for Whites is to take responsibility for the role "Whiteness" has played in the construction of stereotypes, prejudice, and racism. One way to put this responsibility into action is to consistently raise questions about the assumptions that are held about White peoples' individual and group experiences, as well as the assumptions held about other individuals and groups. Another way is to constantly look for the ways in which an individual distinct in his or her own right, even though the individual might share characteristics with others in a group. Yet another way to put responsibility into action is to recognize that the characteristics that individuals of one group do share with others in their group most likely are shared by individuals in other groups as well. It is not characteristics and experiences, but the meaning they have for individuals, that is most intriguing and important.

MULTIDIMENSIONAL CONTEXTUAL PRACTICE FRAMEWORK

Earlier in this text, Guadalupe and Lum explained how the multidimensional contextual practice framework acknowledges and embraces human complexity while creating avenues for addressing human adversity. This practice framework entails exploring commonalities, differences, and points of conflict. In applying the framework, it is important to keep in mind that "people are more than what they seem." This encourages human service practitioners to look beyond stereotypes, to explore more than what the client initially presents, and to assist individuals in their journeys of growth and empowerment.

How can one apply this framework to working with Whites? When working with any client, regardless of the client's presenting issue, practitioners should keep in mind the principle of meeting clients where they are. Keeping client well-being as a focal point is instrumental in applying the framework.

Life cycles, cultural influences, and cultural choices all contribute to the client's multidimensional contexts. When working with White people, it is important to recognize that clients may share some common experiences (e.g., feelings of and/or experiences with frustration, superiority, privilege, guilt, always being around others who look like them, power, and the stigma of all that others may associate with what it means to be White and with other individuals who are White); however, it is also essential to focus on the wholeness and healthy functioning of the client. Some differences in how White people experience their "Whiteness" will be present because of such influences as gender, propinquity to other Whites, geographic and cultural norms, family system, sexual orientation, age and/or historical period, socioeconomic class, level of education, and other characteristics that one finds across other groups of people as well. A way in which human service practitioners can focus on the healthy functioning of the individual is to affirm each client as a human with unique experiences, definitions, and needs in terms of how that person's being White uplifts, obstructs, and/or impedes that person's growth.

When discovering the client's story, it is important for the human service practitioner to identify the individual definitions, peak moments, and other influences on the client's current level of development and worldview. Listening to the person's story and assisting the White person in further exploring that story can promote success in linking the client with other services, opportunities, knowledge, and experiences in the community. Helping individuals ascertain at what stage they might identify themselves in terms of White identity development may be useful if that is an issue with which clients are grappling. Exploring and embracing how the client views his or her self and how that "self" relates to family, the groups with which the client is involved, and the community at large is important to maximize the client's growth and healthy functioning. Additionally, investigating the constitution of the client's family, neighborhood, and primary and secondary groups relative to race and ethnicity, and what meaning those concepts have for the client, can be a useful tool. It is also essential for the human service practitioner to gain an understanding of how these entities interact and view the client. Major questions to explore might include: What expectations and norms do these different groups have for the client? How does the client respond to these expectations and norms? Such questions may help in identifying the strengths and weaknesses of the client.

Once the practitioner has identified how the client views his or her Whiteness, as well as the views of other racial/ethnic groups, and how this relates to his or her sense of self and sense of belonging or place in the family, community, and other relationships the client holds important, the practitioner can explore how these perceptions might have changed over time. This can help in the acknowledgment that a client's self-identity and relationships with others involve ongoing construction.

A stigma that may have been either consciously or unconsciously attached to a White client is that White people do not have problems except for those caused by members of the "out-group." This may be a result of privilege and the "transparency phenomenon." However, practitioners can help to deconstruct this stigma and stereotypes by listening and learning about the impact of the client's experiences and how they have helped to create resiliency for the client. We further this deconstruction and reconstruction by supporting clients in exploring their White identities and by supporting them in their worldviews while assisting them to take responsibility for their role in perpetuating stereotypes and stigma. Providing opportunities for them to see how they have contributed to the cycle and have benefited from it can also help them to embrace their essence and self-identity. Recognizing how their age, gender, socioeconomic status, previous experiences, time, resilience, and essence affect their self-identity and view of society assists the practitioner in connecting with the client and in identifying strengths of the client.

Practitioners, White and non-White alike, need to continually challenge their own views about people: those who are White, those who are at differing levels of White racial identity development, and those who are non-White. As Guadalupe and Lum state earlier in this book, it is important to "acknowledge and move beyond one's point of reference" when demonstrating practitioner competence. Remembering that client well-being is paramount can help ensure growth and development of a client's well-being.

CHALLENGES AND STRENGTHS

Practitioners can unintentionally communicate stereotypes and attitudes to clients. Whether practitioners providing assistance to White people are White or non-White, it is important for them to be aware of their own views and perceptions about Whites. If practitioners are not aware of not only what these views and attitudes are, but also how they are transmitted both verbally and nonverbally, negative consequences may result.

Changing attitudes does not happen quickly and requires recognizing prejudicial thinking. Contact with people of differing personalities who are White and have different views relative to "Whiteness" can be helpful. For Whites exploring their own White identity development, such contact can increase their understanding of others' journeys. Realizing that although Whites are overrepresented in the top tiers, they do occupy all social strata—and that they can be male or female, heterosexual or homosexual, and may have been raised in any segment of the world—can assist with both the deconstruction of stereotypes and helping the client identify his or her strengths. Ongoing exposure to information about White people and theories of White identity development is important when expanding one's skills relative to multidimensional contextual practice.

Challenges that may face a helping professional when assisting White clients include: the "transparency phenomenon," which is the tendency of Whites to not see themselves in racial or ethnic terms; an ignorance of privileged status and what that entails; racism; guilt; denial; educational myths individuals have about their race, other races, and contributions made to society; a socialized superior self/group identity; as well as others, to be sure. A competent practitioner will explore these areas if they exist and attempt to help clients identify what meaning and/or purpose these aspects provide in their own lives. Such a practitioner will investigate with the client questions such as the following: Do these areas help the client to be a healthy functioning individual? Do the client's beliefs that have been constructed due to these different things contribute to the client's essence?

Some may have difficulty in identifying strengths that are presented by a White client, especially after digesting the concepts of White privilege, oppression, and the overarching ideology that "White is right." However, the competent professional will search for what strengths the individual possesses not only as an individual but also because of the person's "Whiteness." One strength may be that, due to having experienced privilege regardless of one's merit, the client has a sense of entitlement—a feeling that whatever problems exist are manageable. If individuals are accustomed to situations generally working out in their favor, then there is a resiliency in their belief that their current situation will also work out. Another strength can be found in the practitioner's helping clients to reveal their own stories, and where and how the client wants that story to continue. Demonstrating an understanding that not all Whites have extreme attitudes and/or behaviors of racism and that many Whites do seek to arrive at a better understanding of race/ethnic relations, and exploring how White privilege has detrimentally affected others, can assist practitioners to deconstruct and construct new beliefs and attitudes about Whites.

Practitioners need to recognize that although a client is White, the client may also be a member of another group that historically has been discriminated against and oppressed (e.g., homosexual, woman, lower-class, disabled); therefore, the client may have experienced oppression while also being a member of the "oppressor" group. Assisting the client to deal with any pain and possible confusion that exists as a result of this is very important. Finally, as is important with all groups of people, recognizing this particular individual's unique essence and how it can contribute to his or her own continued growth and potential will surely bring to light other strengths of the client.

CASE STUDY

Application of Multidimensional Contextual Practice

This is Jennifer's first time away from the small town of Winslow, Maine, except for a two-week vacation with her family on the coast and the one time she went to Boston for a long weekend last spring with her cousins. Her parents helped her move into her college dorm room a day ago. Her roommate is scheduled to arrive today and classes start tomorrow. In addition to all the anxiety Jennifer has regarding being in college now and living 1,200 miles away from home and everything that she has been familiar with for the past 19 years, she is excited and yet nervous about meeting her roommate. All she knows about her so far is that her name is Kerri, that she too is a freshman, and that she is from Chicago, Illinois. Jennifer hopes they will become friends and will be able to help each other adjust to this new experience, especially since they are both a long way from home. Since she was very involved in things at her high school, Jennifer hopes to become involved in many things here as well, but she is not as outgoing as she would like to be.

Kerri arrived at their dorm room while Jennifer was out for a walk around the campus. When Jennifer walked into the room on her return, she discovered suitcases and boxes everywhere, along with a television, stereo system, and more things than what her eyes could take in. She looked around the small room searching for a person she could introduce herself to, feeling shocked by all the stuff she saw in "her" room. Suddenly, she felt a tap on her shoulder and, as she turned around, she heard a voice saying, "Hi, you must be Jennifer. I am Kerri."

Jennifer and Kerri sat down and began to talk about how they would like to decorate the room together so that it would be appealing to both of them. They shared their different high school experiences. Jennifer graduated from a high school class of less than 200 people, and from a school with about 1,000 students in all, whereas Kerri graduated from a high school class of 463 and a total high school student body of about 2,400. Kerri proudly shared how she was the first African-American valedictorian of her high school. The two young women discovered they had quite a few interests in common and easily got their room situated before the orientation session the next day.

Several weeks passed and Jennifer and Kerri found themselves in one class together among the four each of them were taking that semester, an honors history class. Jennifer was having difficulty adjusting to life away from home and to the rigorous study schedule. Initially, she and Kerri ate all their meals together, but now they were eating together only once or twice a week. Kerri had already become very involved in several campus activities and was making many different friends through those experiences, and so she was gone from the room quite a bit. Jennifer had not found any activity or club that particularly interested her, so she spent a lot of time in her room studying, writing letters to friends back home, and phoning home to her mom. Kerri invited her to do things with her and the friends she had made, but Jennifer declined, saying she needed to study.

One afternoon Jennifer was on the phone with her mother, talking about how much she missed being at home, how she really wished some of her friends had come to this college, and how miserable she was. Her mother asked about her roommate and how they were getting along. Jennifer stated that she really liked Kerri and wished she would spend more time with her, but that Kerri seemed to be more comfortable hanging out with her Black friends. As she continued talking about how she did not understand why Black people always have to hang out together (saying, "They sit together in the cafeteria, they have an area in the quad where they hang out, and they go to a lot of the same activities together . . ."), Kerri walked through the door. Kerri had heard most of what Jennifer had said and just looked at her with disbelief in her eyes.

From that afternoon forward, the two roommates did not converse much with one another, except when it was necessary. They did not eat any meals together, and Kerri stopped asking Jennifer to do things with her, alone or with her friends. Jennifer became depressed and isolated.

Reflection on Case

If Jennifer initiated a visit to the campus counseling center, the counselor would first want to explore with her what expectations she had about coming to this college and making friends. Exploration of what Jennifer envisioned as good adjustment would be important. The practitioner would attempt to encourage her to tell her story regarding her life in Winslow and what things were meaningful and important to her that she did not feel were a part of her life now. By listening and seeking to understand Jennifer's story, the practitioner would gain insight into Jennifer's background and would learn there were no non-White people in her hometown. The town was comprised of various ethnic Whites. Jennifer might identify herself as being French (her grandfather was French), and so she might feel she could understand Kerri's feelings relative to discrimination. This would provide a window for the practitioner to explore Jennifer's "symbolic ethnicity" and might provide an opportunity to help Jennifer see how, although aspects of the effects of discrimination might be similar, the path of African Americans in this country has been a very different phenomenon from the journey of French immigrants in New England.

Jennifer's desire to belong is a strength that can be developed and explored. Her intellectual abilities indicate that she has an aptitude for understanding. Exploration of how much she knows about the histories of different cultures might be a stepping-stone for helping her further explore the history of non-White groups and the contributions such groups have made in the United States. Her essence of wanting to connect with Kerri, but feeling hurt or rejected because she was not receiving as much attention as she was used to having or would have liked, is demonstrated in the scenario. Questions the helper might want to pose to Jennifer while focusing on her individual well-being could include: What does friendship mean to her? Did it have a different meaning for her before coming to college and meeting Kerri from what it means now? How does she see herself as being different from and similar to others (Whites as well as non-Whites)? Does she think Kerri might have a different understanding or definition of friendship than she does? Encouraging Jennifer to talk with Kerri about her definition and understanding of friendship, and then to inquire about Kerri's experiences, might help them begin communicating again and demonstrate a willingness, on Jennifer's part, to understand Kerri's point of view.

The multidimensional contextual client is the second sphere of the framework. Here one would want to look at how Jennifer sees herself. How does she understand her Whiteness, and does she see ways in which that affects her interactions with others? It would be important to explore with her what differences and similarities in how she perceived herself before coming to college and meeting Kerri and how she perceives herself now. Her understanding of herself may have been different when she interacted only with other Whites from what it is now that she is interacting with some people who are non-White as well as other White people.

Her family is obviously a source of support for Jennifer. The practitioner should explore with her what her family means to her. Additionally, determining in what ways her family helped her learn about being White, about White privilege, and about how to relate to others who are not White might help Jennifer identify beliefs, values, and attitudes she has been socialized to hold. Another issue to explore with Jennifer would be what she identifies as her needs and what role her Whiteness plays in getting those needs met and/or not getting them met if she continues to embrace being White in the same way she has in the past. It would also be important to discuss the connections she has with other individuals and groups and what not belonging to any groups yet on campus means to her. Understanding more about how she feels about her relationships with Kerri, her family, and her friends at home, as well as peers in college, would provide a deeper understanding of her desires. Does she feel they encourage her to dispel stereotypes that she holds? Or do they help her perpetuate them?

Since these exchanges are transactional in nature, they are ever-changing. Jennifer's relationships are not only nonstatic now, but they will continue to be so whether she is in Winslow, at college, in Chicago, or elsewhere. Helping Jennifer recognize this social fact will help her in identifying her responsibility relative to the expectations she has of herself and others. Helping her understand, regardless of her level of White racial identity development, the role that being White and possessing White privilege plays in her transactions and relationships will help her establish where she wants to develop from the point she is at currently.

In addition to exploring her interactions with individuals in her life, looking at the magna-spiritual interaction and exchange factors is also important in applying this multi-dimensional contextual framework. Finding out what Jennifer identifies as her personal beliefs about a Higher Power (God) would be important not only in supporting her concept of self, but also relative to how that affects her understanding of race relations and what effect her being White has on others. Exploring religious practices that Jennifer may see as important or unimportant and what that means to her may help her establish her individual identity, as she is probably dealing not only with her White racial identity development but also with her own social identity away from home and her family. This is very important in considering the impact of the magna-spiritual and may be a source of strength for the client.

At the macro level, looking at the exchange that occurs between Jennifer, her family, the college she selected to attend, peers who are also attending that college, and the community in which the college is located would be important areas of discussion. What is the makeup of the college's student body? What does the college do, if anything, to foster healthy interactions between students of different races? To what degree did "sameness" (being White) affect Jennifer's decision, and the decisions of other students, to attend this college? How does the college respond to students who are non-White versus those who are White? How does the community at large respond to students who are non-White versus those who are White? Exploring with Jennifer how she feels about the answers to these various questions and how these things affect her view of self as well as her interactions with others may prove beneficial.

Insights into the micro-intrapersonal interaction and exchange factors would be provided through examination of Jennifer's age, gender, self-identity, geographical location, and "symbolic ethnicity." This list is not inclusive but provides an initial set of areas to explore. In what ways she may have seen these areas as affecting her life prior to college and how they affect her now, as well as how her being White contributes to the meaning she attributes to each of these factors, would provide additional insight into her well-being.

The fourth part of the multidimensional contextual practice framework is that of practitioner competence. The helping professional would need to realize that regardless of how much the practitioner knows about White people (and regardless of whether this knowledge has been gained from being White or, if the helper is non-White, through experience and literature that has helped the practitioner develop an understanding), the real tool the practitioner can use to help Jennifer optimize her sense of self would be acknowledging that the source and amount of information are only useful to the extent that Jennifer's story is recognized as being unique to her as an individual. It would be important for the practitioner to seek knowledge about events that are important to Jennifer and about what Jennifer identifies as being important to meeting her needs. The helper should approach Jennifer from a place of mutual discovery, mutual exploration and planning, mutual intervention, and mutual evaluation (see Chapter 2, pp. 52–53) if the practitioner is focused on demonstrating practice wisdom. Challenging one's own stereotypes and previous knowledge also would display an awareness that Jennifer is unique and that she needs and wants to explore and develop her White racial identity in her own way. This approach would work toward deconstructing stereotypes.

As readers, you can utilize the questions, dialogue, and ideas in this chapter to think about how to explore issues of Whiteness and White identity while empowering clients to recognize their uniqueness. An empathic and "seeking to understand" approach is of paramount importance in using this model, regardless of the client profile. This case study application demonstrates areas to be explored and understood when assisting a client such as Jennifer, as well as the skills that will assist any practitioner in applying the multidimensional contextual practice model.

SUMMARY

This chapter by no means contains all there is to know, understand, and keep in mind relative to White people. The author's hope is that it has provided some new insights and areas to further explore in seeking to understand White privilege and White identity development and how these affect our relationships, work environments, families, politics, education, economy, and life choices. If we are to debunk and ultimately deconstruct stereotypes, it is vital that we question what has been taken for granted as being part of the way people are or the way organizations operate, explore what is acceptable in society, and challenge generalizations that we, as people, tend to make on a daily basis. Many times stereotypes are used to make sense of the world around us so that we can feel secure in knowing "how things operate." The problem with this is that it has led to many destructive and oppressive operations—ones that need to be dismantled.

How can we as White people use the privilege that has been socially constructed to promote social justice and change is a remaining question that has not been fully addressed in this chapter. This author believes that the answer is different for each White person, and is influenced by a myriad of experiences, processes, and perceptions of knowledge. To generate social change that promotes social justice, it is important for us to challenge how things operate; to look beyond how things are and have been, and push to dismantle barriers that restrict others' access to resources because they are non-White; to analyze our own actions, words, life choices, and opportunities and how those came to be; and to investigate current political and social issues. Most importantly, however, we must explore ways to connect with others and join with others in this struggle, which is not merely a White or a non-White struggle, but one that should be embraced as a human struggle. This struggle is vital to generating a society that promotes social justice for all people.

Although the author herself is White, many times she has found herself thinking, "There is something about being White I just do not understand." It is through challenging the norm and attempting to learn as much about others as possible, while exploring one's own taken-for-granted beliefs, that one (whether White or non-White) comes to understand one's own definition and identity of what it means to be White in today's society. In addition to furthering one's own development and identity and moving beyond stereotypes, it is also important to learn as much as possible about the benefits that Whites, as an identified group, have incurred due to the social construction of racial differences. As discussed in this chapter, a complex economic, political, and social system was created and is supported by interrelated systems through which the social construction of race intertwines. The reader, therefore, is challenged to explore and learn more about this system of oppression and to develop innovative ways for dismantling it.

Discussion Questions

1. What privileges have you encountered in the past 48 hours that either you experienced because of being White or you were blocked from experiencing because of being non-White?

2. Make a list of all the adjectives and nouns you can think of that use the word *White* or refer to being White. Then do the same for Black. Examine your lists. Do you see any patterns in thinking and assignments that society has internalized?

3. How might the concept of "symbolic ethnicity" be applied to Whites who are disabled, homosexual, women, poverty stricken, and so on? Are there social costs involved? How is this identification different from what Gans conceptualized?

4. How can practitioners help people deconstruct stereotypes relative to White people?

5. Considering the various White identity development models, how could you use these models to assess your own development (if you are White) or to assist someone else in assessing his or her development? What utility do you think they would provide?

6. In what ways have you internalized feelings of superiority over people who belong to a different group than you do? How are these feelings evidenced? How do you know they exist? What purpose do they serve for you?

7. How often do you go to movies or films, read books, attend lectures, or visit museums that focus on a racial group different from your own and/or that deal with racial issues?

References

Feagin, J. R. (1989). *Racial and ethnic relations* (3rd ed.). Englewood Cliffs, NJ: Prentice-Hall.

Ferber, A. L. (2004). What white supremacists taught a jewish scholar about identity. In M. L. Andersen & P. H. Collins (Eds.), *Race, class and gender* (pp. 117–121). Belmont, CA: Wadsworth.

Gans, H. (1979). Symbolic ethnicity: The future of ethnic groups and cultures in America. *Ethnic and Racial Studies, 2,* 1–20.

Gilbert, G. M. (1951). Stereotype persistence and change among college students. *Journal of Abnormal and Social Psychology, 46,* 245–254.

Gordon, L. (1986). College student stereotypes of Blacks and Jews on two campuses: Four studies spanning 50 years. *Sociology and Social Research, 70,* 200–201.

Helfand, J. (2003). Constructing Whiteness. [On-line]. Available: http://academic.udayton.edu/race/01race/white11.htm.

Helms, J. E. (Ed.). (1990). *Black and White racial identity: Theory, research, and practice.* Westport, CT: Greenwood.

Jensen, R. (1998). White privilege shapes the U.S. [On-line]. Available: http://uts.cc.utexas.edu/~rjensen/freelance/whiteprivilege.htm.

Karlins, M., Coffman, T. I., & Walters, G. (1969). On the fading of social stereotypes: Studies in three generations of college students. *Journal of Personality and Social Psychology, 13,* 1–16.

Katz, D., & Braly, K. (1933). Racial stereotypes of one hundred college students. *Journal of Abnormal and Social Psychology, 28,* 280–290.

Katz, J. H. (1978). *White awareness: Handbook for antiracism training.* Norman, OK: University of Oklahoma Press.

Lipsitz, G. (1998). *The possession investment in whiteness: How White people profit from identity politics.* Philadelphia: Temple University Press.

Lippman, W. (1922). *Public opinion.* New York: Macmillan.

Lopez, I. F. H. (1996). *White by law.* New York: New York University Press.

Lum, D. (Ed.). (2003). *Culturally competent practice: A framework for understanding diverse groups and justice issues* (2nd ed.). Pacific Grove, CA: Brooks/Cole.

McIntosh, P. (2001). White privilege and male privilege. In M. L. Andersen & P. H. Collins (Eds.), *An anthology: Race, class, and gender* (4th ed., pp. 95–105). Belmont, CA: Wadsworth.

Pedersen, P. (1994). *A handbook for developing multicultural awareness* (2nd ed.). Alexandria, VA: American Counseling Association.

Ponterotto, J. G. (1988). Racial consciousness development among white counselor trainees: A stage model. *Journal of Multicultural Counseling and Development, 16,* 146–156.

Ponterotto, J. G., & Pedersen, P. (1993). *Preventing prejudice: A guide for counselors and educators.* Newbury Park, CA: Sage.

Sabnani, J. B., Ponterotto, J. G., & Borodovsky, L. G. (1991). White racial identity development and cross-cultural counselor training: A stage model. *Counseling Psychologist, 19,* 76–102.

Schaefer, R. T. (1993). *Racial and ethnic groups* (5th ed.). New York: HarperCollins.

Thomas, W. I., & Thomas, D. S. (1928). *The child in America: Behavior problems and programs.* New York: Knopf.

Welkley, D. (1993). *The language of prejudice.* Unpublished master's thesis, Baylor University, Waco, Texas.

Yamato, G. (2001). Something about the subject makes it hard to name. In M. L. Andersen & P. H. Collins (Eds.), *An anthology: Race, class, and gender* (4th ed., pp. 90–94). Belmont, CA: Wadsworth.

Resources for Further Exploration

Alba, R. (1990). *Ethnic identity: The transformation of White America.* New Haven, CT: Yale University Press.

Delgado, R., & Stefancic, J. (Eds.). (1997). *Critical white studies: Looking behind the mirror.* Philadelphia: Temple University Press.

Flagg, B. (1994). Enduring principle: On race, process, and constitutional law. *California Law Review, 82, 935.*

Frye, M. (2001). Oppression. In M. L. Andersen & P. H. Collins (Eds.), *An anthology: Race, class, and gender* (4th ed., pp. 48–52). Belmont, CA: Wadsworth.

Gallagher, C. (1995). White reconstruction in the university. *Socialist Review, 24*(1–2), 165–187.

Guzzetta, C. (1995). White ethnic groups. In R. L. Edwards (Editor in Chief), *Encyclopedia of social work* (19th ed., pp. 2508–2517). Washington, DC: NASW Press.

Helms, J. E. (1994). *A race is a nice thing to have: A guide to being a white person or understanding the white persons in your life.* Topeka, KS: Content Communications.

Moore, R. (2001). Racist stereotyping in the English language. In M. L. Andersen & P. H. Collins (Eds.), *An anthology: Race, class, and gender* (4th ed., pp. 322–333). Belmont, CA: Wadsworth.

Nakayama, T. K., & Martin, J. (Eds.). (1999). *Whiteness: The communication of social identity.* Thousand Oaks, CA: Sage.

Rubin, L. (2001). Is this a white country or what? In M. L. Andersen & P. H. Collins (Eds.), *An anthology: Race, class, and gender* (4th ed., pp. 419–427). Belmont, CA: Wadsworth.

Takaki, R. T. (2001). A different mirror. In M. L. Andersen & P. H. Collins (Eds.), *An anthology: Race, class, and gender* (4th ed., pp. 52–65). Belmont, CA: Wadsworth.

Thomas, R. R. (1996). *Redefining diversity.* New York: AMACOM.

Vargas, S. R. L. (2003). The homogeneity assumption: The white ethnic narrative as cultural ideology. [Online]. Available: http://academic.udayton.edu/race/01race/white06.htm.

Ware, V., & Back, L. (2002). *Out of Whiteness: Color, politics, and culture.* Chicago: University of Chicago Press.

Waters, M. (2001). Optional ethnicities for whites only? In M. L. Andersen & P. H. Collins (Eds.), *An anthology: Race, class, and gender* (4th ed., pp. 430–439). Belmont, CA: Wadsworth.

West, C. (2001). Race matters. In M. L. Andersen & P. H. Collins (Eds.), *An anthology: Race, class, and gender* (4th ed., pp. 119–124). Belmont, CA: Wadsworth.

> *To engage in a serious discussion of race in America, we must begin not with the problems of black people but with the flaws of American society—flaws rooted in historic inequalities and longstanding cultural stereotypes.* —**Cornel West**

African Americans

Ethnic-Specific Communities of People

ROBIN WIGGINS CARTER

DEMOGRAPHIC OVERVIEW

An overview of the current demographics of African Americans as reported by the latest census report provides a national snapshot of the African-American population. According to the U.S. Census data (2002), African Americans represent 12.3% of the U.S. population. Individuals who identified themselves as African American and at least one other race count for 1.8 million or 0.6% of the population and, if added to the total African-American count, would increase the total to 12.9%. Individuals of African descent, such as those from the Caribbean or from Africa, are counted as African American as well (U.S. Census Bureau, 2002).

Census data also indicate that the African-American population increased by 15.9% between 1990 and 2000. If the group of individuals who identified as African American and one other race is included, this number rises to 21.5%. The total population grew at a rate of 13.2% during the same period, indicating that the number of African Americans grew at a slightly higher rate than the total (U.S. Census Bureau, 2002).

Who Are African Americans?

African Americans are a group of individuals who have African descendants and who identify themselves as such. The terms *Black* and *African American* are often used interchangeably in the literature and in the U.S. census reports. Blacks are identified as anyone having African descent, and may include other Blacks living in the United

States—Cubans, Haitians, Jamaicans and those from other Caribbean islands, and Black Africans—while African Americans are actually a large subgroup of Blacks (those with African heritage) that reside in the United States and are associated with native-born Blacks. African Americans are a very heterogeneous group, yet they share a cultural legacy that contains many themes that have arisen from their unique historical experience of forced migration and enslavement followed by systematic discrimination and victimization (Boyd-Franklin, 1989).

Geographic Distribution

In terms of geographical distribution, 54% of African Americans live in the South, while 19% live in the Midwest and 18% live in the Northwest. The western states have the lowest concentration of African Americans with 9% (U.S. Census Bureau, 2002).

The Great Migration marked the massive movement of African Americans from the southern to the northern states beginning in 1910 and continuing until about 1970. Between 1910 and 1920, about one half of the African Americans left the South for the Northeast and Central states. In spite of this, the current data suggest that the southern states are home to more than half of the African-American population. This is likely due to the more recent migration of African Americans from the northern and western states back to the South beginning in the 1980s. As many African Americans became disillusioned with the promises of better living conditions and job opportunities when they discovered they were relegated to living in overcrowded slums and forced to take menial jobs, they began to migrate back to the South. Additionally, many found it difficult to try to establish themselves in northern industrial cities after leaving the familiarity of the rural south. The more recent movement indicates that African Americans with southern roots are "going home" in large numbers, leaving behind large city life for the attraction of the slower pace and the lower cost of living of the South (Glazer, 2001).

The 2000 census findings report that the average White person lives in a tract that is 80% White, down from 85% in 1990; the average Black person lives in a tract that is 51% Black, down from 56% in 1990; the average Hispanic lives in a tract that is 45% Hispanic, an increase from 43% in 1990; and the average Asian lives in a tract that is 18% Asian, up from 15% in 1990. This report shows that most Blacks are still "segregated" in predominantly Black communities, yet 49% of Blacks live in communities that are not Black dominated (Glazer, 2001). Although there is greater integration in housing, the majority of Blacks still live in predominantly Black communities. Is it because they prefer to be around those who share a similar history and cultural attributes—or is it because systematic historical discrimination has limited their options in deciding where they want to live? We know that the greatest majority of Blacks migrating from the South during the Great Migration landed in large urban ghettos, mainly because Whites did not want to live around them.

Some researchers suggest that when African-American families move out of predominantly African-American communities, increased interactions with Whites and other non-Blacks contributes to greater social distance from Blacks as a group (Demo

& Hughes, 1990; Glazer, 2001). An alternative hypothesis contends that movement into predominantly White communities decreases the time spent interacting with social groups and organizations within the Black community, and it is this decline in interaction with other Blacks that leads to greater social distance from Blacks (Harris, 1995).

Consistent with the latter hypothesis, Dawson (1994) argues that racial group identity depends a great deal on the extent to which individuals have access to information relevant to that identity and believe that a particular identity is consistent with their own reality. Racial identification becomes less salient to individuals when information about the political, economic, and social worlds of Blacks is not accessible. This inaccessibility is more likely to occur when individuals do not reside in Black communities, lack social networks to inform them of the happenings within Black communities, or when they have become upwardly mobile, all of which may lessen the saliency of race in their lives (Dawson, 1994, p. 11).

Socioeconomic Status

The income of African Americans is significantly lower than the national mean. Mean annual earnings for all workers 18 years old and over in 2001 was $35,805. For African Americans during the same time period, it was $27,031 (U.S. Census Bureau, 2002). This disparity in income is evident across all levels of educational attainment and indicates that, although African Americans have made gains in both educational achievement and income levels in the past ten years, the effects of decades of institutional discrimination and social stratification are still evident (Hill, 2001).

Even when educational levels are the same, African Americans earn less than their White counterparts in most occupations. African Americans are less likely to land the higher-paying white-collar jobs. In addition, African Americans earn only 84% of the median earnings of White men in comparable positions. The only category where African Americans earn more than Whites is in lower-paying, lower-skilled jobs for which they are overqualified. One reason this occurs is because African Americans are more likely to work for the government, education, or health and human services, which are industries in which the pay is lower than in corporate positions (Dortch, 1994).

Even though disparities in income and educational attainment indicate a large and growing group gap between African Americans and their White counterparts, attacks on affirmative action in recent years spring in part from the widespread perception that African Americans are no longer in need of protective policies designed to make them more competitive in educational and career achievement. Proponents of these policies ignore the growing underclass of African Americans left behind. Many African-American families were able to benefit from the policies and programs developed from the civil rights movement and the more recent economic boom of the late 1990s. Though there is considerable evidence of the advancements made by Blacks in the areas of educational achievement, income, and occupational diversity, what is also evident is that there is a lot to be done to level the playing field for the 31% of African Americans who live in poverty.

Black suburban households have incomes 44% higher than urban-dwelling Blacks (Koretz, 2001). Large numbers of more prosperous Blacks are moving to the suburbs; thus, they are no longer in the inner city where they can help the community. Glazer (2001) points to the presence of "what appears to be an almost permanent lower caste composed of the black race" (p. 4).

According to a study by the Children's Defense Fund, the poverty line for a family of three was a disposable income of about $14,100; extreme poverty is considered half that amount, or $7,060. In 2001, nearly one million Black children under the age of 18 were living in extreme poverty, which was a sharp increase from 2000. It is also evident that there has been a general decline in poverty among Black children since the vast overhaul of the U.S. welfare system in 1996. In 1995, 41.5% of Black children lived below the poverty line, but by 2001, only 30% were living in poverty. Even as overall poverty has declined, however, record numbers of Black children are now living in extreme poverty. The conclusion drawn from these statistics is that the disappearance of what has long been regarded as safety net programs has driven some of the nation's poorest families deeper into poverty even as some families' status has improved (Dillon, 2003). The impact of this disparity, according to Hill (2001), is: "In the current political discourse, it is increasingly common to ignore the impact of racism and socioeconomic inequality on family problems and, under the rubric of individual responsibility, attribute poor socialization outcomes to family instability, personal lifestyles, and cultural values" (p. 1).

Diversity Within

Although there are important intragroup differences among African Americans, it is equally important to note that the literature validates the presence of central tendencies among African Americans. Much has been written about the commonalities among African Americans. The identification of traditional practices or the common cultural attributes of African-American families began appearing in the revisionist literature published during the 1960s and through the 1980s. Coinciding and in some cases responding to the proliferation of publications about Black families portraying them as deficient, these writings sought to paint a more accurate picture of African-American family life.

Much of the earlier research and writings about African-American families was influenced by the larger sociopolitical context of the time. Fueled in part by the writings of Frazier (1966) and Moynihan (1965), asserting that much of African-American culture brought over from Africa had been destroyed during slavery, the racial comparative model contrasting what were seen as "healthy" White families with "dysfunctional" African-American families became the most common tool for inquiry into Black family life. This discourse promoted the idea that there was a single homogenous American culture that was the normative standard by which all families should be viewed. White-American, two-parent, middle-class families were viewed as the ideal and then contrasted with African-American single-parent households with limited income, resulting in a dearth of literature that denigrated African-American family values and held them up as deficient in comparison. Little attention was paid, during this period, to the positive cultural attributes and unique contributions of Blacks (Kane, 2000).

In the past three decades, a more balanced depiction of Black family life has emerged as researchers have identified the adaptive and resilient aspects of African Americans and employed additional methods of inquiry that allow for recognition of the strengths and diversity among African Americans. The benefit of this research on Black families is that it challenges practitioners not to accept unquestioningly what is defined as "adaptive," "healthy," or "normal." Billingsley's (1968) significant contribution to this effort was his identification of the "strengths of black families," therefore effectively identifying and naming the characteristics common to African-American families that are both adaptive and functional. Afrocentric writers (Carter, 2003; Robinson & Howard-Hamilton, 1994; Schiele, 1998) have identified five major characteristics as common to African-American family functioning: (1) extended family kinship networks, (2) egalitarian and adaptable family roles, (3) strong religious orientation, (4) strong education and work ethic, and (5) flexible and strong coping skills (Boyd-Franklin, 1989; Nobles, 1985).

English (1991) refers to these attributes as worldviews and acknowledges that not all African Americans adhere to these values. He stresses that, "Variations occur based on a range of complex factors, including social mobility, urban experiences, the impact of racism and discrimination on life experiences, and childhood socialization" (p. 23). The widespread acceptance of these cultural attributes as definitive descriptors of African-American culture and the tendency among some to use them as intractable has raised questions about whether culturally specific behaviors or patterns can be studied without promoting stereotypes. Concern is that they can lead to unnecessarily simplistic recommendations for intervention and policy by inexperienced practitioners and uninformed policy makers. Carter (2003) referred to these culturally specific behaviors as "central tendencies" and not universal descriptions, urging practitioners to recognize the many factors that mediate one's adherence to these tendencies.

Alongside the literature and research suggesting similarities among African Americans, there is also an acknowledgment that tremendous in-group diversity exists among African Americans as well. Culturally sensitive researchers recognize that there is no such thing as the African-American family. There is variation among African-American families, just as there is variation among families in any culture. According to English (1991):

> Theoretically, it is assumed that the more African American culture is an essential core of the individual's life-style, the more these traditional kinship and community values are reflected in the individual's family life. The less African American culture is a component of the individual's life, the more likely "assimilated" family values are an essential part. When one has a deeply felt commitment neither to one's own culture nor to the mainstream culture, the result is a "marginal" world view. A "bicultural" world view occurs when the individual deals effectively with mainstream culture without sacrificing African American culture. (p. 23)

The theoretical framework supporting the assumption of similarities among Blacks asserts that individuals who share similar interests, values, social norms, and attitudes with a particular reference group will identify more strongly with them. Similarly, the shared history of oppression and current experiences of felt discrimination and racism draws these individuals to their reference group.

The use of culturally specific patterns assumes a common culture among African Americans, yet these patterns can be used effectively only when used along with consideration of such important conceptual issues as the fact that racial identity is dynamic across situations; that race is not important to all African Americans; that the individual's assessment of what is African American is most important; and that racial identity cannot be understood without examining the social context.

Biracial Individuals

With the recent discourse about racial identity brought on by the 2000 census, the meaning and usefulness of racial categories have been widened. For the first time since the inception of the U.S. census, individuals were allowed to check multiple categories when describing their racial identity. Individuals could select fifty-seven combinations of two or more races with the six stand-alone race categories of White, Black/African American, Asian, Hispanic, Indian/Alaskan Native, Asian, and Native American/Other Pacific Islander. According to the U.S. Census Bureau, the new categories reflect the changing face of the country's ethnic composition (U.S. Census Bureau, 2002).

The Census Bureau's statistical data is used determine how more than $100 billion in U.S. federal monies are channeled annually by decision makers for funding public services such as schools, housing, community development projects, health care programs, and libraries. In addition, companies use the data gathered in the survey to decide where to locate factories, shopping centers, and other businesses. In past census reports, Blacks were customarily undercounted due to slight Black participation in the survey. The mixed race choices complicate the issue of choosing a base on which to measure the progress of, or possible discrimination against, minorities, an important step in affirmative action programs. If the base becomes smaller, the degree of discrimination that one may claim in noting how many members of a group have attained this or that position is reduced (Rodriguez, 2003).

For the reasons stated previously, many African-American leaders and organizations were pushing for all Blacks to categorize themselves in a single racial category (Black or African American), but some people of mixed race and some members of Black immigrant communities see more value in identifying themselves under different labels. The 2000 census has become the event that changed how race is conceptualized in the United States.

According to Glazer (2001), "five percent of blacks, 6 percent of Hispanics, 14 percent of Asians and 2.5 percent of whites identified themselves as multi-racial" (p. 8). The Office of Management and Budget oversees the race and ethnic statistics compiled by federal agencies, and it has determined that for its purposes, all multirace choosers who chose White and a minority race are to be counted as being part of the minority. The increase in interracial contact among Blacks can be evidenced in two ways: first, through the increase in integration of Blacks into the larger society; and second, through the increase in the number of interracial marriages that are reported. There has been considerable rise in interracial marriages since 1990 (Glazer, 2001). According to census reports (U.S. Census, 2002) Black interracial couples made up 24 out of 1,000 couples in 1998. According to Rodriguez (2003), the rate of intermarriage among African Americans is climbing, and the prediction is that 37% of African Americans will claim mixed ancestry by 2100.

The social science literature on biracial persons consistently identifies two areas of conflict for biracial people: racial identity and social marginality (Gibbs, 1998; Williams, 1999). While the process of racial identification poses some difficulty for monoracial individuals, it can be extremely challenging for biracials. Although born with dual or multiple racial and cultural identities, children of different-race parents are often expected to identify with one race, usually the one of the minority parent. In the United States, children born of Black-White interracial unions have historically been defined as Black, a practice that has strongly been supported by Black and White communities, laypersons, and clinicians alike (Daniel, 1996). However, as the trend toward biracial identification grows, so too does interracial tension among Blacks, as some within the community ostracize self-identified biracials whom they perceive as downplaying their Black identity in favor of their Whiteness to gain special treatment from Whites.

Intimately tied to the issue of racial identity is social marginality. Researchers and clinicians (Deters, 1997; Gibbs, 1998; Glazer, 2001) have found that biracial individuals often have a difficult time answering the question, where do I fit? Rejected by both majority and minority peers because of their exotic features, biracial adolescents can experience difficulty with identifying peers who will accept and validate their racial and cultural uniqueness. The extent to which biracial individuals are accepted depends on the extent to which their physical characteristics, style of dress, speech patterns, and general mannerisms match those in the Black community, as well as the extent to which biracials accept a Black racial identity and show commitment to the mores of the Black community. The odds of social acceptance are high for biracial individuals who are easily identified as Black given certain physical features, cultural style, and commitment to the Black community, but the odds of acceptance are low for biracial individuals who are racially and culturally difficult to categorize.

Foreign-Born Blacks

Consistent throughout many studies that have examined the process of assimilation and acculturation among foreign-born Blacks is the finding that intraracial tensions and social distance pervade relations between communities of foreign-born and native-born Blacks (Mann, 1996; Waters, 2000). The reasons for these tensions are not mutually exclusive. According to Waters, instead of attempting to fully integrate into the larger Black community, many foreign-born Blacks have instead distinguished themselves from native Blacks by choosing to identify primarily in terms of ethnicity and nationality instead of race, and by maintaining the cultural norms of their homelands, such as style of dress and manner of speech.

In addition, the foreign-born are accused of taking jobs that would otherwise go to natives or of taking jobs that natives shun due to low wages (Waters, 2000). Moreover, given the many social and economic obstacles native-born Blacks have had to overcome in order to obtain their piece of the American pie, they are often confused and frustrated by the ability of the foreign-born to reach economic goals soon after immigrating. Feelings of antagonism between these two groups have led to mutual stereotyping. According to Waters, the foreign-born brand native-born Blacks as lazy and lacking commitment to education, upward mobility, and family; they also perceive native-born Blacks as being overly sensitive to issues surrounding race. Meanwhile, natives criticize the foreign-born for what they perceive as their arrogance and their ignorance of the race and class issues that divide this country.

Thus, work in this area establishes that, although race is an important identifying group marker, other components of individuals' identities may more strongly determine with whom they feel bonds. That some foreign-born Blacks may choose their ethnic identification over their racial identification indicates that they may perceive themselves differently from other Blacks. They may eat different foods, speak with foreign accents, listen to different music, and dress and act differently. In addition, they may have values, attitudes, interests, and issues that identify them as distinct from the native-born Black community. Their decision to identify ethnically suggests that they perceive themselves differently from their non–ethnic-identified counterparts and signals their social distance from Blacks as a racial group.

The emigration of Africans has increased radically since the 1980s coinciding with the end of European colonial rule of Africa. Although there is no single reason Africans report for having left their country of origin, in general it is their desire for a better life in better socioeconomic and political conditions. The United States is also seen as a major center for advancing education and therefore is the major recipient of foreign students. Most of the Black Africans come from the North African countries and from countries with political and cultural ties to the United States. Many came as students during the 1970s and 1980s and then stayed on after college. Nearly all Black Africans live in the South Atlantic states, with some settling in the Pacific Coast states as well (Takyi, 2002). They are, as a group, young, upwardly mobile, and well educated. They are distinguished from native-born African Americans by their unusually high educational attainment and their ability to make significant career advances after having been in the United States for a relatively short period of time.

Native-born Blacks have a higher poverty rate than any other Black immigrant group except for those from the Dominican Republic. African-born Blacks and Jamaicans have the highest median family income of all Black groups; and in New York City, where most of the Caribbean population resides, they have higher incomes than Whites. Immigrant Blacks are less likely to get into trouble with the law. To some degree the explanation lies in the immigrants themselves. According to Kalmijn (1996), they tend to be a self-selected group of highly educated individuals who migrated for economic reasons, thus giving them more impetus to succeed. African immigrants, who account for roughly 16% of the foreign-born Black population, are the most highly educated ethnic group in the United States. They also tend to be more likely to marry, thus they have more people in their households working. There is also speculation that foreign-born Blacks suffer less from racial discrimination than native-born Blacks. White employers find Black immigrants more desirable employees, although those from English- and French-speaking countries tend to be looked on more favorably than those from Spanish-speaking countries. An additional theory explains Caribbean achievement by tying it to the people having had more positive examples of Black achievement in their native countries.

Integration and assimilation reduce the differences between groups with each generation. Ethnic distinctions become less and less meaningful after two or three generations. This is so even with Caribbean and African immigrants who identify strongly with their ethnic origins in the first generation, yet their native-born children consider themselves African American. This does not, however, allow them "full inclusion" into American society, as that, according to Glazer (2001), is reserved for White immigrants only.

Racial Identity Development and Socialization

How African Americans identify themselves to the rest of the world is a topic of much debate among African-American racial identity scholars. The concept of self-identity is explored through the issue of "Blackness" and its meaning for African Americans. The reason why the definition of Blackness is so confusing is because the rules that govern inclusion in the "Black race" are different from those for any other group. According to Brunsma and Roquemore (2002), this is "because black group membership has been defined by a strict application of the one drop rule that deems any individuals with any black ancestry whatsoever (regardless of their physical appearance) as members of the black race" (p. 106). This means that mixed raced persons who are removed from their Black ancestry, which may be one individual four generations ago, are identified as Black. This system, with its roots in the institution of slavery and grounded in White-supremacist logic, has defined the existence of African Americans in the United States.

The current discourse about the "social construction" of race has very real meaning for African Americans in light of the continued use of the "one drop" rule. Gould (2000) argues that, for the most part, people's racial categorizations occur through ascription. The ascriptive identity is one that is assigned to someone by others, usually the dominant group, and typically on the basis of physical characteristics. This type of categorization by the dominant group has historically determined and reinforced social stratification on the basis of race. Gould argues for a type of social constructivism that encourages self-ascription, meaning that individuals be allowed to interpret for themselves what their embodied characteristics mean. In regard to this, Gould states, "One implication of this notion of embodiment for group identity in political contexts is that it introduces a more open and fluid conception of group in place of the traditional categorical ascription of fixed physical characteristics of defining groups" (p. 5).

Helms (1990) stated that racial identity "actually refers to a sense of group or collective identity based on one's perception that he or she shares a common racial heritage with a particular group" (p. 3). Over the years a number of competing models of racial identity development have been brought forth, theorizing the ways that African Americans come to identify themselves as members of the group. One of the most widely recognized racial identity theories is William E. Cross, Jr.'s Nigrescence theory. Cross's theory (Worrel, 2001) suggests that differences in self-identity in African Americans have their roots in the history of discrimination and oppression in the United States and the resultant response of individuals to this oppression. Cross's Nigrescence theory was first proposed in 1971 and was strongly influenced by the sociopolitical context of the civil rights movement. His was a process stage approach in which he theorized that African Americans come to accept and affirm their Black identity through a series of developmental stages. Cross's theory identified four stages: (1) preencounter, (2) encounter, (3) immersion or emersion, and (4) internalization. In later revisions of the theory (Vandiver, 2001), the stages were identified as distinct worldviews adopted by individuals at different points in their development. Parham and Williams (1993) saw the stage of internalization as the point at which individuals become comfortable and secure in their racial identity. They further theorized that the development of a strong racial identity would assist them in facing the challenges of racism and oppression.

Another widely used racial identity model is the triple quandary theory (Boykin, 1986). In this theory, Boykin suggests that the level of participation and orientation in African-American culture varies across social contexts. He posits that African Americans are simultaneously part of three cultural realms: (1) the mainstream, which reflects White middle-class values, including individualism and competition; (2) the Afro-cultural, which is a reflection of the unique cultural experiences of African Americans in the United States; and (3) the minority realms, which represent the oppression that African Americans have experienced in America.

The multidimensional model of racial identity (MMRI) posits that the definition of what is and is not African American lies within the individual. This model theorizes that the relative importance of being African American varies across settings (Sellers, Smith, Shelton, Rowley, & Chavous, 1998). The MMRI has a racial salience component that measures the extent to which race is important at a particular point in time. A bicultural racial identity may be conceived of as one in which racial salience varies widely across social situations (Sellers et al., 1998). Bicultural individuals adjust the relative importance of race, as well as other identity variables, according to the demand in a particular setting. Specifically, the MMRI focuses on four dimensions of identity: (1) salience, how important being African American is to one's overall self-concept; (2) centrality, the extent to which African Americans use race to define themselves; (3) ideology, personal philosophies on what behaviors are appropriate for African Americans; and (4) regard, the positive or negative evaluations of oneself as a function of being African American. The regard dimension of the MMRI model best reflects the concept of racial self-esteem.

A criticism of some of the current racial identity models is that they tend to assume that the only way to be African American is to focus on the degree to which the individual adheres to behaviors that are deemed either pro–African American or pro-White. The weakness of using these concepts as a focus of analysis in Black identity theories is that they do not recognize the "variability and diversity of blackness" (Cross, 1991). Thompson (1999) believes that "racial ethnic identity is not only related to discrimination and exclusion but also to the characteristics of the group itself" (p. 3). For this reason, Thompson focuses on the importance of racial salience in the development of identity in African Americans.

Racial ideology is often conceptualized in an oversimplified form as a continuum ranging from assimilationists to those who hold a more nationalistic view (Sellers et al., 1998). Thus an individual considered to have a strong racial identity would be nationalistic, and an individual with a weak or nonexistent racial identity would be fully assimilated to White cultural expectations. There is evidence, however, that individuals' racial ideologies are complex and therefore cannot be easily categorized. The same person may be nationalistic regarding social and cultural issues, but more assimilationist when it comes to politics and economics.

Racial socialization involves the transmission of values, norms, and expectations pertinent to group identity. A number of scholars (Boyd-Franklin, 1989; Carter, 2003; Robinson & Howard-Hamilton, 1994; Schiele, 1998) believe that racial socialization that includes messages promoting a strong racial identity provides a buffer against oppression for African Americans. These messages and practices can act as a buffer for ethnic minority group members from the antagonism of a hostile environment (Stevenson, 1994). Similarly, Miller and MacIntosh (1999) have demonstrated that a strong racial identity promotes resilience in African-American youth.

APPLICATION OF MULTIDIMENSIONAL CONTEXTUAL PRACTICE TO AFRICAN AMERICANS

Application of the theory of racial socialization to African Americans presents a challenge in and of itself because of the basic assumptions on which the theory is built. The theory suggesting that race is a defining element of identity is imperfect; therefore, to apply the theory to a category of individuals, we must create and perpetuate the use of the previously established boundaries and definitions. This is especially challenging for African Americans for the reasons noted throughout this chapter. They are a heterogeneous group of native- versus foreign-born; many are of mixed racial heritage; not all who would be assigned to this category might assign themselves to the same category if given their preference; not all Blacks view the salience of race in their lives in the same way; and they are diverse in where they live, in terms of income levels, and in their educational and career achievement.

In light of the diversity African Americans present, the multidimensional contextual practice framework has many advantages over other frameworks, which impose a dominant Eurocentric worldview and intervention strategies. This framework does not replicate existing frameworks or attempt to make the individual fit the framework; instead, it seeks to redefine practice.

The multidimensional contextual practice framework is based on five principles, which include client well-being; the multidimensional contextual client; the micro, meso, macro, and magna principle; the practitioner's professional competency; and multidimensional contextual services. The multidimensional contextual approach supports the use of a multidimensional and client-centered exploration process in which clients are encouraged to express the factors they believe are important in the development of presenting problems. This approach honors clients' belief systems and, in doing so, validates their ways of knowing and experiencing their life challenges. The approach recognizes not only the multiple dimensions that individuals possess, but also the multiple systems that affect the daily lives of individuals and how they must seek to negotiate those systems.

Many African Americans have internalized the negative societal messages about their value in society. Any effective strategy must assist African Americans in defining themselves and resisting attempts by others to define them. Multidimensional contextual practice can avoid the internalization of these negative self-images and externally imposed negative messages through the use of strategies that are culturally congruent.

Client Well-Being

The psychological well-being of African Americans is associated with involvement in extended family and other informal support networks (Boyd-Franklin, 1989). African Americans who report a well-developed system of social support are found to have higher self-esteem and a higher sense of self-efficacy that those who do not. In addition, the use of other informal support networks such as the church is common practice for most African Americans. Even those African Americans seeking formal supports will likely use them in conjunction with informal supports.

CASE STUDY

The Multidimensional Contextual Client

Jill is a 26-year-old African-American female who has just graduated from a prestigious private college and has begun her first corporate job. Jill lives with her twin brother, Jay, who is a student and is also gay and HIV positive. Jill has accompanied Jay to his support group meetings every week since he became involved with a local agency serving HIV/AIDS clients. Since joining the group, she has come to realize that she, too, could use some support in dealing with her brother's diagnosis and her own struggles with "fitting in."

Jill and Jay were raised by their African-American father, Larry, and their paternal grandparents. Their Italian-American mother, Laura, became pregnant with the twins while still a teenager. When Laura's parents strongly encouraged her to put the infants up for adoption, Larry and his family insisted that they be allowed to raise the children instead. Jill and Jay did not have regular contact with their mother and their mother's family for the first ten years of their lives. They lived in a small three-bedroom home, which housed not only them, their father, and their grandparents, but also one of their aunts and her three children. On many occasions other family members or family friends also lived in the home during temporary unemployment or some other social situation. Their father was one of ten children, most of whom lived nearby and visited frequently. Jill's fondest childhood memories are of the tiny house in the neighborhood in which they were allowed to run freely, going to the park, and attending the nearby school. The value placed on family and community was reinforced through the informal as well as the formal institutions to which she belonged. The tight-knit community also included their church, in which a third of the members were extended family members.

Jill's grandfather owned a car repair shop, in which her father worked. Her grandmother was primarily a homemaker who occasionally took jobs as a domestic to supplement the family income. Money was tight, as her grandfather, a very skilled mechanic, was a very generous and kind-hearted individual who provided his services either at a greatly reduced cost or for free.

When Jill was 10, her mother married, and soon after Jill and her brother began to have regular visits with their mother on the weekends. Their mother lived in a home built on the same property as the home of her maternal grandparents, who were well-to-do land developers. Jill's visits to her mother's and grandparents' homes provided a stark contrast to her simple home environment. Her mother and grandparents had large, stately, mansionlike homes on acres of property. They owned horses and drove late-model luxury cars. Her mother took Jill and Jay shopping and bought them nice clothes and toys, and she took them on vacations. She also insisted that they attend a private parochial school, which she and her husband paid for. Laura's family was openly hostile toward Larry's family and often expressed their discomfort about the way the children were being raised. Larry resented the increased interference with the children and began limiting their visits to Laura's home. Laura's family responded by hiring an attorney and suing for custody of the children. By this time, the children were 12 years old. Jill does not remember all of the details, but knows she decided to remain with her father, while her brother Jay, who had often longed to be reunited with his mother since early on, chose to live with her. For the first time in their lives, they were separated.

Jill graduated high school with honors and, because of her academic performance, was admitted to the college of her first choice. Jay, in contrast, struggled in high school due to an undiagnosed learning disability. By then, his mother had two additional children, and there was increased tension between him and his stepfather over his poor academic performance and his refusal to obey the household rules. Jay began using marijuana and skipping school. A suspension from school in his senior year resulted in his stepfather telling him to leave. He moved back in with his father, who by this point was also remarried and had his own place. It was at this time that Jay revealed his sexual orientation to Jill and his father, but to no one else.

Jill encouraged Jay to come live with her during her junior year of college. She encouraged him to enroll in the local community college, and he found a job in the evenings at a bookstore. When Jay was diagnosed with HIV, Jill accompanied him to tell both parents individually. His mother cried at the news. She had suspected he was gay, but stated she hoped he would "grow out of it." Although she vowed to support him through his illness, she begged Jay not to tell her parents, as she stated, "It would kill them." His father insisted that Jay tell his grandparents. They expressed genuine sadness about his illness, yet never addressed the revelation about his sexual orientation.

Reflection on Case

According to Stevens (2002):

> The hypothesis that development is context dependent—a reciprocal and transactional process of engagement within multifarious domains, such as family, neighborhood, peer group, school, and church—is a relatively novel notion. It is an idea well suited to the ecological life span developmental model since it suggests that decisive developmental challenges be calibrated by transactional relationships occurring at pivotal periods and in critical domains throughout the life course. This viewpoint also suggests a preventive perspective that indicates that social work intervention should occur at decisive times throughout the life course. (p. 17)

First, on an individual level, Jill reports having felt most of her life that she did not "fit in." In spite of having spent her early years in a warm nurturing environment, she was often faced with the reality that she was different. Her father often had to explain that she was his daughter, as her physical features were in stark contrast to her father's dark skin. Her cousins all looked liked they belonged, and never had to explain to whom they belonged. She was the only child she had ever known who did not live with her mother. She never got over feeling rejected by her mother, something she attributed to being half African American. In addition, once she had more contact with her mother, the contrast in lifestyles was confusing for her. Although she preferred to be in the presence of her father's family, she loved the comforts her mother could afford. She struggled through adolescence with feelings of shame and guilt about this, especially as she and her brother were often made to choose between the two homes during holidays and birthdays.

It is particularly important to consider the multiple avenues of socialization that have contributed to Jill's identity development. Her family, her community, her school, and her church contributed a great deal to her development. Stevens (2002) agrees that it is "in the familiarity and closeness of communal relations that African-American adolescents learn to rely on established knowledge that will help navigate the situated locations where social inconsistency is met head on" (p. 66). The family, thus, is the primary source for cultural adaptation.

According to Stevens (2002), "African Americans girls must develop strategies of resistance for self-liberation to counteract racial victimization and gender devaluation" (p. 84). These strategies (i.e., assertiveness, willfulness, determination) may appear to outsiders as being defiant and oppositional—characteristics that are not valued in women and not always understood by those who are unfamiliar with the normative behavior of African-American women. Stevens refers to this as healthy resistance for the purpose of countering societal devaluation. According to Stevens:

> Without question, African American families socialized their offspring to cope with the daily hassles of institutionalized racism. Socialization into the ways and means of managing daily racial hassles occurs in families by explicit directives and by subtle cultural conventions. (p. 64)

Spirituality and religion have always played an important role in Jill's life. Fundamental values about how she should relate to others and how she should direct her life choices were reinforced through her church. For Jill, the church played a central role in the community as a strong organizing and mobilizing force. She, along with other family members, had participated in the development of a program to feed the homeless in the community. She was proud to be part of a church that served the community in the way that it did.

Just as spirituality can be a major factor in effective coping, at times the beliefs held by individuals can be authoritarian and repressive. Boyd-Franklin (1989) specifically addressed the adherence to some fundamental religious teachings suggesting that homosexuality is sinful. According to Lewis (2003), "beliefs about homosexuality and support for gay rights vary substantially by religion and by intensity of religious feeling" (p. 66). Blacks are more religious than Whites and are more likely to be fundamentalist Protestants, both factors that are associated with increased homophobia. Education is a factor that leads to greater acceptance of difference in others; thus, Blacks who are more highly educated are more highly committed to democratic values and civil liberties.

As with many African Americans (Hines & Boyd-Franklin, 1982), religion and spirituality had been Jill's most effective tools for coping with adversity, especially in her experiences with racism and societal oppression. Unlike Jill, Jay had stopped attending the family church when he moved in with his mother, and now he refused to go. Although he never experienced covert rejection from his African-American family and friends, he expressed that he felt he could not be who he was in their presence—he likened it to the "don't ask, don't tell" policies adopted by the military.

Jill identifies herself as African American, not biracial, and although she admits her light skin raises questions, she knows she does not look "White," and thus she finds it more comfortable to identify with her Black roots. Recognizing that the socially constructed categories of race to which she is bound are often misconstrued as biological, she finds it easier to opt into a category that does not quite fit than to consider herself biracial, a category for which there is little outside affirmation from family or others. Her self-identification as African American was also Jill's attempt to claim an identity, as opposed to having one imposed on her from the outside. Andersen and Collins (2001) explain:

> [R]ace, class, and gender are interlocking categories of experience that affect all aspects of human life; thus, they simultaneously structure the experiences of all people in this society. . . . [Although at times] race, class, or gender may feel more salient or meaningful in a given person's life, . . . they are overlapping and cumulative in their effect on people's experience. (p. 3)

The Micro, Meso, Macro, and Magna Principle

Spirituality and religion have been documented as an important element in the lives of many African Americans (Daly, 1995). Taylor and Chatters (1996) stress that "African Americans have been found to (a) report higher levels of attendance at religious services than Whites, (b) read more religious materials and monitor religious broadcasts more than Whites, and (c) seek more spiritual comfort through religion more so than Whites" (p. 406).

The centrality of spirituality in the lives of African Americans dates back to slavery when expressions of spirituality were tied to the quest for liberation from injustice. African Americans' spirituality was a source of coping that helped them to endure the harsh realities of slavery as well as provided them with faith that freedom was within their reach. For these reasons, spirituality is deeply rooted in African-American culture. According to Frame and Williams (1996), "much of what is spiritual in the African-American tradition is not named as such by Western standards, and its significance is therefore overlooked" (p. 3).

In many African-American communities, the church is the center of activity not only for workshops, but also for a range of social and charitable activities. For the most part, human services practitioners historically have neglected the spiritual needs of clients. Due to limited education and training for practitioners in the use of integrating spirituality into practice, many are not comfortable with addressing their clients' spiritual needs. Further complicating this issue is the fact that practitioners may have their own struggles with spirituality. According to Constantine, Lewis, Conner, and Sanchez (2000), "Practitioners who dismiss spiritual issues as outside of their professional domain may be greatly limiting their ability to understand the totality of many of their African American clients" (p. 9).

Spirituality is different from religion in that it connotes a personal inner journey that individuals embark on in an attempt to develop a relationship with a Supreme Being; it helps us define where we fit in the world and our relationships with others (Dunn & Dawes, 1999). Religion, on the other hand, provides a system in which to express one's spirituality through symbols, ceremonies, and rites and leads to a systematic set of beliefs that guide one's journey toward spirituality (Frame & Williams, 1996). Spirituality can be pursued and experienced in one's daily life or in personal metaphysical experiences—activities not tied in any way to formalized religion.

Frame and Williams (1996) outline the challenges faced in attempting to integrate spirituality into counseling. They identify Freud's belief that religion is a "neurotic illusion" as contributing significantly to the distancing of psychotherapy and religion. In addition, the field of psychology views itself as having a scientific base and thus validates those interventions that have a logical, quantifiable, and objective base. This view is a great departure from the spiritual realm, which is largely subjective, unquantifiable, and based on faith rather than evidence. Lastly, practitioners' own unresolved religious and spiritual issues can be a barrier when working with clients who have a strong spiritual orientation.

Practitioner's Professional Competency

The practitioner perpetuates cultural definitions of health and wellness, thus defining and labeling clients from a normative standard that is not culturally congruent. Practitioners must recognize that they have the power to name—not only by seeing clients from a unidimensional framework that discounts the diversity within the African-American community, but also by not recognizing the many possible dimensions of individual African-American clients when they present themselves.

Many theoretical approaches to diversity do not recognize the differences within any racial or ethnic group that shape their experiences. It is the same for people who are African American. The pressures one feels from racial discrimination and structural oppression can also be compounded when one is a woman and/or is gay or lesbian. The response to oppression from an African American who is well educated and has attained some career achievement may be radically different from that of the African American who lives in poverty in a crime-ridden neighborhood and whose sense of injustice is shaped by day-to-day experiences.

Practitioners' own exposure to and experiences with those who are culturally different from themselves is a crucial factor in determining both perception of mental and physical capacity and definitions of acceptable social roles for clients (Cayleff, 1996). Practitioners need to know and understand the factors that have contributed to the survival and continued resilience of African-American families. Multidimensional contextual practice encourages the focus of attention to be "client well-being"; it moves away from a deficit model to identifying strengths and successes. Practitioners should understand the traditional values and beliefs associated with African Americans in an attempt to understand the coping skills and capacity for adaptation that have been evident as they have battled oppression and discrimination.

Human service practitioners must resist the temptation to buy into stereotypes that move them to deliver services that are not culturally competent and can be harmful. For example, Daly (1995) suggests that interventions based on the assumption that an African-American male who is absent from the family is not involved with the family can lead to inappropriate interventions that discount the types of nontraditional family arrangements often seen in African-American families. African Americans are more likely to be labeled psychotic than Whites. Likewise, African Americans who are depressed are often misdiagnosed as schizophrenic. Practitioners must recognize the dangers of mislabeling or pathologizing based on a rigid set of criteria that do not allow for cultural differences in the expression of pain and suffering. "[C]ounselors should be aware that their own place within the larger culture—their social status, sex, and race—will probably influence both what they perceive as problems and dilemmas and how they respond to them" (Cayleff, 1996, p. 346).

Multidimensional Contextual Services

In order to provide culturally congruent services, the agency providing services must place the client, the client's family, and the community at the center of its operations. Agencies that most closely mirror the principles of the multidimensional contextual practice are those that have arisen from a need identified by the community they serve. Likewise, in those agencies, the community has been central in developing the mission, designing and delivering the services, and guiding the agency's ongoing existence. The services of these agencies stand in sharp contrast to those that have been conceptualized, developed, and delivered by someone outside of the community who does not understand the unique characteristics and subtle patterns of interaction. Too often, services stem from a poorly constructed policy response that results in a "one-size-fits-all" mentality, in which communities over a large geographical area are given the same mandate. Fully recognizing the multidimensional and contextual nature of individuals means addressing their needs, which can be done effectively only through services that are dynamic in nature and willing to go against the status quo, even if that means less funding. Such services recognize the client as the only true "expert."

SUMMARY

Jill's story exemplifies the principles of the multidimensional contextual practice framework. She brings with her the multiple aspects of her identity, including the dimensions of race/ethnicity, social class, and gender. In keeping with the MMRI model of racial self-identity, the social context dictates which aspects of her identity are salient at any given time. She has found her own place in a society that devalues many aspects of her identity by exercising the protective factors of resilience and adaptability gained through the strong ties with her family, who recognized the need to prepare her for racism, sexism, and classism.

Jill's interaction with her family was significant in her development as a strong and independent African-American woman, not only because of the nurturing and support she received, but also because of the imperfections her family allowed her to witness in their struggles within the multidimensional context. While Jill experienced unconditional regard by some family members, she was also hurt by the perceived rejection by others in her family as well as her family's unwillingness to acknowledge her brother's sexual identity. She gained strength and independence as she came to understand her need to stand up when she encountered social injustice in the contexts of the social institutions to which she belonged or sought membership, as well as in her family.

Jill's case further exemplifies the benefits of the multidimensional contextual practice framework in recognizing the cumulative effects that the multiple dimensions of race/ethnicity, class, gender, and sexual orientation have on people's experience. The framework treats these aspects of identity as different but not separate by recognizing their interrelatedness and symbiotic relationship to each other. Approaching the study of race/ethnicity, class, gender, and sexual orientation from the perspective of the multidimensional contextual practice framework allows the practitioner to view the different aspects of identity, not from an additive perspective, but from one that recognizes their relative salience in people's lives in different contexts.

References

Andersen, M. L., & Collins, P. H. (Eds.). (2001). *Race, class, and gender: An anthology* (4th ed.). Belmont, CA: Wadsworth/Thomson Learning.

Billingsley, A. (1968). *Black families in white America.* Englewood Cliffs, NJ: Prentice-Hall.

Boyd-Franklin, N. (1989). *Black families in therapy: A multisystem approach.* New York: Guilford.

Boykin, A. W. (1986). The triple quandary and the schooling of African American children. In U. Neisser (Ed.), *The school achievement of minority children* (pp. 57–75). New York: Teachers College, Columbia University.

Brunsma, D., & Roquemore, K. A. (2002). What does "black" mean? Exploring the epistemological stranglehold of racial categorization. *Critical Sociology, 28,* 101–121.

Carter, R. (2003). Ethnic-centered (Afrocentric) framework. In J. Anderson & R. Carter (Eds.), *Diversity perspectives for social work practice.* Boston: Allyn & Bacon.

Cayleff, S. E. (1996). Ethical issues in counseling gender, race and culturally distinct groups. *Journal of Counseling and Development, 64,* 345–347.

Constantine, M., Lewis, E., Conner, L., & Sanchez, D. (2000). Addressing spiritual and religious issues in counseling African Americans: Implications for counselor training and practice. *Counseling and Values, 45,* 28–39.

Cross, W. E., Jr. (1991). *Shades of black: Diversity is African-American identity.* Philadelphia: Temple University Press.

Daly, A. (1995). Effective coping strategies of African Americans. *Social Work, 40,* 240–249.

Daniel, G. R. (1996). Black and White identity in the new millennium. In M. Root (Ed.), *The multiracial experience: Racial borders as the new frontier* (pp. 121–139). Thousand Oaks, CA: Sage.

Dawson, M. (1994). *Behind the mule: Race and class in African American politics.* Princeton, NJ: Princeton University Press.

Demo, D. H., & Hughes, M. (1990). Socialization and racial identity among Black Americans. *Social Psychology Quarterly, 53,* 364–374.

Deters, K. (1997). Belonging nowhere and everywhere: Multiracial identity development. *Bulletin of the Menninger Clinic, 61,* 368–385.

Dillon, S. (2003, April 30). Report finds number of Black children in deep poverty rising. *New York Times,* www.nytimes.com.

Dortch, S. (1994). The earnings gap in black and white. *American Demographics, 16,* 18–20.

Dunn, A., & Dawes, S. (1999). Spirituality-focused genograms: Keys to uncovering spiritual resources in African American families. *Journal of Multicultural Counseling and Development, 27,* 240–255.

English, R. (1991). Diversity of worldviews among African American families. In S. Chipungu, J. Everett, & B. Leashore (Eds.), *Child welfare: An Afrocentric perspective* (pp. 1–14). New Brunswick, NJ: Rutgers University Press.

Frame, M. W., & Williams, C. B. (1996). Counseling African Americans: Integrating spirituality in therapy. *Counseling and Values, 41,* 16–29.

Frazier, E. F. (1966). *The Negro family in the United States* (Rev. ed.). Chicago: University of Chicago Press.

Gibbs, J. T. (1998). Biracial adolescents. In J. T. Gibbs & L. N. Huang (Eds.), *Children of color: Psychological interventions with minority youth* (pp. 322–350). San Francisco: Jossey-Bass.

Glazer, N. (2001). American diversity and the 2000 census. *Public Interest, 144,* 3–19.

Gould, C. (2000). Racism and democracy reconsidered. *Social Identities, 6,* 425–440.

Harris, D. (1995). Exploring the determinants of adult black identity: Context and process. *Social Forces, 74,* 227–241.

Helms, J. E. (1990). *Black and White racial identity: Theory, research and practice.* New York: Greenwood Press.

Hill, S. (2001). Class, race, and gender dimensions of child rearing in African American families. *Journal of Black Studies, 31,* 494–509.

Hines, P., & Boyd-Franklin, N. (1982). Black families. In M. McGoldrick, J. K. Pearce, & J. Giordano (Eds.),

Ethnicity and family therapy (pp. 84–107). New York: Guilford.

Kalmijn, M. (1996). The socioeconomic assimilation of Caribbean American Blacks. *Social Forces, 74,* 911–930.

Kane, C. (2000). African American family dynamics as perceived by family. *Journal of Black Studies, 30,* 691–703.

Koretz, G. (2001). Giant strides for U.S. Blacks. *Business Week,* (3747), 28.

Lewis, G. (2003). Black and white differences in attitudes toward homosexuality and gay rights. *Public Opinion Quarterly, 67,* 59–78.

Mann, T. (1996). Profile of African Americans 1970–1995. *Black Collegian, 26,* 64–69.

Miller, D., & MacIntosh, R. (1999). Promoting resilience in urban African American adolescents: Racial socialization and identity as protective factors. *Social Work Research, 23,* 159–170.

Moynihan, D. P. (1965). *The Negro family: The case for national concern.* New York: Bantam.

Nobles, W. W. (1985). *Africanity and the Black family: The development of a theoretical model.* Oakland, CA: Black Family Institute.

Parham, T. A. & Williams, R. (1993). *Psychological storms: The African American struggle for identity.* Chicago: African American Images.

Robinson, T., & Howard-Hamilton, M. (1994). An Afrocentric paradigm: Foundations for a healthy self-image and healthy interpersonal relationships. *Journal of Mental Health Counseling, 16,* 327–340.

Rodriguez, G. (2003, January/February). Mongrel America. *Atlantic Monthly,* 95–97.

Schiele, J. H. (1998). Cultural alignment, African American male youths and violent crime. In L. Lee, *Human behavior in the social environment from an African American perspective* (pp. 165–181). New York: Haworth.

Sellers, R. M., Smith, M. A., Shelton, J. N., Rowley, S. A., & Chavous, T. M. (1998). Multidimensional model of racial identity: A reconceptualization of African American racial identity. *Personality and Social Psychology Review, 2,* 18–39.

Stevens, J. W. (2002). *Smart and sassy: The strengths of inner-city black girls.* New York/Oxford: Oxford University Press.

Stevenson, H. C. (1994). Racial socialization in African-American families: The art of balancing intolerance and survival. *Family Journal: Counseling and Therapy for Couples and Families, 2,* 190–198.

Takyi, B. (2002). The making of the second diaspora: On the recent African immigrant community in the United States of America. *Western Journal of Blacks Studies, 26,* 32–41.

Taylor, R., & Chatters, L. (1996). Black and white differences in religious participation: A multi-sample comparison. *Journal for the Scientific Study of Religion, 35,* 403–414.

Thompson, V. L. (1999). Variables affecting racial-identity salience among African Americans. *Journal of Social Psychology, 139.*

U.S. Census Bureau. (2002). *Race and ethnicity: Terms and definitions.* Retrieved from: http://www.eire.census.gov.

Vandiver, B. (2001). Psychological Nigresence revisited: Introduction and overview. *Journal of Multicultural Counseling and Development, 29,* 165–176.

Waters, M. (2000). Immigrant dreams and Americans realities. *Work and Occupation, 26,* 352–365.

Williams, C. B. (1999). Claiming a biracial identity: Resisting social constructions of race and culture. *Journal of Counseling and Development, 77,* 32–36.

Worrel, F. (2001). Nigrescence theory: Current status and challenges for the future. *Journal of Multicultural Counseling and Development, 29,* 201–214.

In our differences we grow,
In our sameness we connect. —**Virginia Satir**

15 | Latino/a Americans

Ethnic-Specific Communities of People

CHRYSTAL C. RAMIREZ BARRANTI

"Of every hue and caste am I," writes Richard Rodriguez (2002, p. 230) in his exceptionally thought-provoking book, *Brown: The Last Discovery of America*. Powerful words are these. They describe the grandeur of the multidimensionality and great diversity of a distinct people while honoring the many shared commonalties in cultures, languages, attitudes, and experiences that weave them together. These words poignantly identify both the diversity and the commonality shared within the full spectrum of the rich shades and tones of "brown" that color those who make up what the U.S. Census Bureau has so simplistically defined as "Hispanic/Latino/a" (Therrien & Ramirez, 2000).

Who then are the Hispanics or Latinos/as? Are they the Chicanos/as, the Mexican Americans? Might they be Newyoricans or Borinqueños/Boricuas, Cubans or Cubanos, Dominicans, Guatemalans, Salvadorans, and so on (Jimenez-Vazquez, 1995; Longres, 1995; Suarez-Orozco & Paez, 2002)? Are they the many Latin American immigrants who venture far from their homes and families for work in the United States? Are they only those of Latino/a heritage who are native-born? Are they simply those who make up what the 2000 U.S. Census describes as the "two Hispanic origin categories—Hispanic or Latino and Not Hispanic or Latino" (U.S. Census Bureau, 2002)? In fact, this diverse and yet dynamically connected peoples is all of the above and more. They are made up of multiple identities, differences and similarities, all of which may coexist within unique individuals, among particular national origins, as well as between each and all of these.

15.1 Reflection Exercise

Take a moment to reflect on and to write down your thoughts on the following questions:

- What images, descriptors, and ideas come to mind as you begin to ask the question, "Who are the Latinos/as?"

- How would you describe Latino/a culture(s)?
- What has been your personal experience with Latinos/as?

This chapter begins with an introduction to the complexity and multidimensionality of the Hispanic and Latino/a peoples with the goal of providing a base from which to begin multidimensional contextual practice. This foundation of information identifies the commonalties of rich and dynamic cultures while illuminating diversity within diversity. As you take the "journey" through this chapter, you are encouraged to be cognizant of the rich reality of tremendous diversity within each individual, within each group, as well as between individuals and between the various groups of peoples who make up the larger assemblage traditionally referred to as Latino/a or Hispanic. The multidimensional contextual practice skill of using a constructivist approach, in which clients define who they are in terms of chosen cultural traditions, beliefs, and sense of origin, facilitates conscious movement away from the possibility of stereotyping. (See Reflection Exercise 15.1.)

THE TERMS *HISPANIC* AND *LATINO*: IDENTITY AND COMMON CULTURES?

The U.S. government officially created the ethnic group known as "Hispanic" in 1978 (Office of Management and Budget, 1978). The population category of Hispanic has been defined as being made up of anyone of "Mexican, Puerto Rican, Cuban, Central or South American or of other Spanish culture or origin, regardless of race" (pp. 19, 269). In 1997, the Office of Management and Budget directed that new terminology be implemented by January 2000 to include the use of the term *Latino* interchangeably with the term *Hispanic* (Therrien & Ramirez, 2000). Like the definition of the first inception of the category of Hispanic, the Hispanic/Latino category is made up of Mexicans, Puerto Ricans, Cubans, Central or South Americans, and "other" Hispanics and can be of any race (Office of Management and Budget, 1997, pp. 58, 782). "Hispanics" can be either born in the United States (native-born) or in their particular country of origin (foreign-born).

While the term *Hispanic* by definition affords at least a surface recognition of its multiethnic makeup, undoubtedly it has contributed to the deconstruction of the great diversity among those who may or may not share the Spanish language. In fact, some scholars (Gimenez, 1999; Longres, 1995; Martinez, 2001; Pew Hispanic Center/Kaiser Family Foundation [PEW/KFF], 2002; Sanchez, 2002) argue that the heterogeneous nature inherent in the rich diversity of those who make up the politically constructed group of "Hispanics" is essentially deconstructed when compacted into an umbrella label that denies the multidimensionality of diversity within diversity. Gimenez (1999) writes:

> This umbrella term includes colonized people of Spanish, Mexican, and Puerto Rican descent who have been in this country for generations, having been incorporated together with their lands after the 19th century wars between the U.S., Mexico, and Spain. It also includes the waves of legal and undocumented immigrants from Cuba, Mexico, Central and South America; businessmen, professional, and skilled workers "pulled" by better opportunities; and political and economic refugees fleeing from political repression and the chronic unemployment and poverty of their countries of origin. In addition to immigration experience in the U.S., citizenship status and national origin (variables which determine vast cultural differences), this population is divided by class, socioeconomic status, language (not everyone speaks Spanish, and many do not speak English), and race/ethnicity. "Hispanic"/Latinos could be of any "race" and many are multiracial, from Native American, European, Asian, or African ancestry. (Gimenez, 1999, pp. 167–168)

It is critical, then, that in the honoring of the Latino/a individual, the uniqueness of heritage, country of origin, particular culture, immigration experience, social class, educational experiences, language, gender, sexual orientation, spirituality, and so on be of great consideration. In maintaining such recognition of the great diversity among this population, it is helpful to see the benefit of bringing the many diverse national origins together under such an umbrella term. The fact is that the construction of the category of Hispanic/Latino has enabled documentation of this large group as a whole. In fact, as of June 2003, Hispanics have been identified by the U.S. Census Bureau as making up the largest minority group in the nation, numbering 38.8 million or 12.5% of all Americans (cited in Ledger, 2003). This in itself has lent some degree of growing political power to Latinos/as as a whole, and the U.S. Census continues to find increasing numbers among the greater U.S. population.

The caution of stereotyping still remains, however. While the opportunity for applying generalized stereotypical qualities is tempting, the necessity for applying the multidimensional contextual practice framework is paramount if moving beyond stereotypes is to be accomplished. A case in point is the reality that Latinos/as come from as many as twenty-six different countries. This factor encompasses a wide range of differences including ethnic and racial diversity within and between countries, cultural customs, language and dialects, economic resources, educational systems, and sociopolitical structures (Castex, 1994). Family forms, religious affiliations, spiritual practices, sexual orientation, and gender roles are also among the important aspects of identity, which influence diversity both within and between individuals of a group and between the many groupings that come together to create the Latino/a peoples.

Recognition of diversity as well as commonalties within and between the individuals and groups of Latinos/as supports a multidimensional contextual view and moves away from stereotyping. For example, a common thread through the historical experiences of many of the Latin American countries includes a strong presence and influence of the Roman Catholic Church. While Catholicism continues to remain a predominant religious affiliation of many in Latin America, a common but errant assumption held by many is that all Latinos/as are Roman Catholic. Is this a true assumption? The multidimensional contextual perspective would steer us away from such a stereotype. For instance, research by Guadalupe and Torres (2001) on spiritual practices embraced by Puerto Ricans has illustrated the dynamic diversity of religiosity and spirituality, highlighting the importance of moving beyond stereotypes. To illustrate the importance of understanding commonalties while being receptive to the rich possibilities of diversity in religiosity, they write:

> Many sets of spiritual and religious beliefs and values are reflected when exploring Puerto Rican spiritual healing practices. Christianity as illustrated by Catholic and Protestant religious paradigms, various Pentecostal denominations, Mormonism/Church of Jesus Christ of Latter-day Saints, Buddhism, Hinduism, Hari Krishna, Santería/Yoruba Religion, Spiritualism, Shamanism and Curanderismo, are among the multi spiritual and religious perspectives embraced by Puerto Ricans. This observation illustrates a multiplicity of viewpoints embraced within a community often glued by history, traditions, beliefs and value systems, language, biological types, or a combination of these. Thus, the traditional and stereotypical notion that all or most Puerto Ricans are Catholics can no longer be perpetuated. Instead, individualization of our professional interactions, as we simultaneously engage in an exploration and confrontation of our stereotypical perceptions likely to injure rapport building when working with Puerto Ricans, also identified as Boricuas, seems vital. . . . It cannot be overemphasized the amount of diversity that exists among Puerto Ricans as well as the spiritual and religious practices that historically they have embraced. (pp. 61–62)

The discussion thus far has focused on labels imposed upon a diverse people by outside forces such as the U.S. Census Bureau, but what of the people themselves? How do those who make up the diversity of Hispanic or Latino/a wish to be referred to? For the most part, the largest groups of Latinos/as—Mexicans, Puerto Ricans, and Cubans—indicate that they prefer their specific national origin identity rather than the generic term of *Hispanic* (Castex, 1994; PHC/KFF, 2002).

Yet, the multiple identities lending to diversity and uniqueness, along with those similarities that provide a common connection, truly defy a simplistic characterization of Latinos/as. The Pew Hispanic Center and Kaiser Family Foundation (2002) recently conducted a national survey of Latinos/as based on a nationally representative sample of 3,000 individuals who identified themselves as Latino or Hispanic. When exploring the area of "identity," findings indicated that when asked which terms one would use to describe oneself, 54% of the sample indicated that they would identify themselves by their or their parents' country of origin. Twenty-four percent would first use the word *Latino* to identify themselves, while 21% said they would first choose to use the word *American* in defining themselves (PHC/KFF, 2002).

In reflecting on the multidimensionality of the Latino/a population, the 2002 National Survey of Latinos (PHC/KFF, 2002) found that the first choice in identifying terms used by Latinos/as was significantly related to how many generations one's family had been living in the United States. More than two-thirds (68%) of those who had immigrated to the United States stated that they solely used their country of origin to identify themselves. Second-generation Latinos/as (those with immigrant parents) almost equally either identified with their parent's country of origin (38%) or as American (35%). Third-generation Latinos/as and those whose families had been in the United States for many generations self-identified for the most part as American (57%).

Other research has indicated a difference in the self-application of the terms *Hispanic* and *Latino* among those who make up what some scholars have called the pan-ethnic group of Hispanic (PHC/KFF, 2002; Torres-Saillant, 2002). The 2002 National Survey of Latinos (PHC/KFF) found that while 13% of the survey population preferred the use of the term *Latino* over the term *Hispanic,* 34% preferred the use of the term *Hispanic* over *Latino.* Fifty-three percent of the participants indicated that they had no preference between either identifying term.

The national survey findings indicating that slightly over half of those surveyed had no preference between self-application of the two terms are of interest in light of additional research. For example, some of the literature has tied the self-application of the terms *Hispanic* and *Latino* to such variables as social class, degree of acculturation and/or assimilation, regional differences, and political ideology (Gimenez, 1999; Longres, 1995). Those whose focus is on political activism and issues of equality prefer the term *Latino,* as it also links them with their pre-Hispanic heritage (before colonization by Spain), while others who are more intent on cultural advancement and social assimilation espouse the term *Hispanic* (Falicov, 1998; Foley, 2002; Longres, 1995). The potential volatility of the term *Hispanic,* however, may be tied to its strong support and endorsement by "politically conservative groups that regard their Spanish European ancestry as superior to the 'conquered' indigenous groups of the Americas" (Falicov, 1998, p. 34). Similarly, those who find its connection to the colonial exploitation of Spain express some disdain for the term *Hispanic.*

Some scholars have viewed the European roots of *Hispanic* as avenues to access White privilege. For example, Neil Foley (2002) contends that for the 1980 U.S. Census, the Hispanic category solved the Census Bureau's problem of how to count Hispanics without racializing them as "non-Whites." Foley goes so far as to argue that identification as "Hispanic" allows for the acknowledgment of ethnicity while retaining the privilege of "Whiteness" and a distance from the oppression of color.

The discussion thus far is revealing of a complex and multilayered context for considering such deceivingly simple terms as *Hispanic* and *Latino/a.* These are certainly terms that, when properly understood, can tell a history of struggle, adversity, oppression, and resilience. The following section provides a sociohistorical context for understanding this complexity and will hopefully enrich understanding of the multidimensional context of those who make up this grouping called Hispanic and Latino/a.[1]

EXPANDING UNDERSTANDING: A BRIEF HISTORICAL JOURNEY OF COMMONALITY WITHIN DIVERSITY

One cannot begin to understand Latino/a experiences in the United States without first exploring the historical and sociocultural context in which these experiences have unfolded and taken shape. In fact, a sociohistorical perspective can often provide the bridges necessary to move beyond stereotypic and homogeneous views of a people (Zavella, 1994). Likewise, the unraveling of common sociohistorical themes experienced by the diverse Latino/a collective illuminates the broader shared context.

Historian Jose Sanchez (2002) has identified two common themes that almost all the various groups of Latinos/as in the United States share with one another. The first shared theme is that of a history of colonialism in relation not only to the Spaniards but also to the United States. Second, Latinos/as share a history of immigration and migration as the common means of coming to live within the borders of the United States. While these are shared commonalties, it is helpful to realize that the actual experience and processes of both colonizing and immigration are also unique within individuals and between groups.

On Being Colonized

A profoundly significant fact, which is often startling to those educated in the United States, is that the history of North America does not solely originate within a European history but within a Spanish history (Zavella, 1994). Early in the 16th century, Spain began the colonization of the Americas (present-day Mexico, the United States, etc.). The Spanish colonization of present-day Mexico and northern New Mexico in what is now the United States resulted not only in the desecration of many indigenous cultures and peoples, but also in the mixing of Spanish and native peoples. Long before the first English settlers arrived on the North American continent, Spanish soldiers began intermarrying with the indigenous peoples of the area, giving rise to a new people—that of the "mestizo" (Sanchez, 2002; Zavella, 1994).[2] Eventually, the mixing of peoples included not only the Spaniards and indigenous peoples, but also the estimated 200,000 to 300,000 Africans whom Spain had brought to Mexico as slaves (Martinez, 2001). Thus, out of the Spanish colonization of parts of present-day United States and Mexico, as well as other lands in the Americas, came the emergence of the "mestizaje." In the creation of the "mestizaje" were a new people who were considered "less than" their Spaniard ancestors, fathers, or brothers and who were subject to oppression, discrimination, social injustice, and, yes, racism (Klor de Alva, 1999; Martinez, 2001; Suarez-Orozco & Paez, 2002).[3]

Very much like Mexico and what is now northern New Mexico, the present-day Cuba and Puerto Rico were colonized during the same time period by the Spanish-financed expedition led by none other than Christopher Columbus. In these lands, the indigenous peoples were overcome, their lands and cultures taken from them. While many died as a result of fighting off the invasion of their lands, others were killed in the name of Catholicism, and still others died from new diseases brought by the invading people. Those who survived were often subjugated to slavery and eventually joined by thousands of African slaves. A new people was created, often being represented by a mix of indigenous, African, and Spanish blood.

During the 19th century, the then young United States began an expansionist policy with direct impact on Latin American countries. In 1803, the United States purchased Louisiana. In 1819, Spain sold what is now Florida to the United States. However, it was the Monroe Doctrine of 1820 that more fiercely directed a foreign policy aimed at taking colonized Latin American countries from the Europeans (Sanchez, 2002). Several wars, including the Texas Rebellion of 1836, the Mexican American War of 1848–1850, and the Spanish American War of 1898, were instrumental in the western and southwestern expansion of U.S. borders. Significantly, it was the 1848 Treaty of Guadalupe-Hidalgo that delivered about half of Mexico's territory to the United States including what are now Texas, New Mexico, Arizona, Colorado, Utah, Nevada, and California (Moll & Ruiz, 2002). The United States also increased its borders when it took the prize of the Spanish American War of 1898—the island of Puerto Rico, which, even today, continues to remain a colony of the United States.

While land, natural resources, and power were certainly the bounty of the U.S. drive to become the major power of the Western Hemisphere, a great number of Mexicans, through no choice of their own, and without migration, now lived on the U.S. side of the border. In these the newly acquired territories, the principle of "manifest destiny" fueled the removal of Mexicans from their lands and the confiscation of their property by the U.S. government. But perhaps even more significant was the forced "Americanization" of the territories' Mexican population and with that the demolition of the Mexican culture and language in what was now the new American West and Southwest (Moll & Ruiz, 2002; Velez-Ibanez, 1997). This process of "culture-cleansing" was not unlike the processes undertaken by the U.S. government in attempts to Americanize Native Indian Tribes and the newly freed African Americans (Moll & Ruiz, 2002). Similarly, the processes of forced Americanization were later implemented in other countries such as Puerto Rico. Consequently, the oppression of and discrimination against "non-White" populations spread as the United States expanded its borders.

Immigration and Migration: Latino/a Pathways to Life in the United States

Latinos are among the "oldest" Americans—the ancestors of some settled in the Southwest and spoke Spanish, making it their home well before there was a United States. They did not come to the United States; the United States came to them. Latinos are also among the "newest" Americans, for two-thirds of all Latinos in the United States are either immigrants or children of immigrants. —Suarez-Orozco and Paez (2002, p. 4)

The themes of migration and immigration are shared by almost all Latinos/as either as a current life experience or as the experience of parents and grandparents, great-grandparents, and/or great-great-grandparents. As such, Latinos/as are not only among the "oldest" and the "newest" of Americans, but they also constitute one the largest numbers of those immigrating to the United States both legally and otherwise (Rumbaut, 1997). In fact, at least two-thirds of today's U.S. Latino/a populations are recent immigrants (Therrein & Ramirez, 2002).

The 20th century has been one of incredible movements including great numbers of fathers and mothers, brothers and sisters, aunts and uncles, cousins, and friends who have left their homelands to make a "better life" in the United States. Prior to 1965, immigration to the United States was primarily European (Irish, Italian, Polish, etc.) and Canadian, and thus predominantly White (Suarez-Orozco, 1998). However, this picture was drastically changed over the second half of the 20th century. In fact, Latinos/as and other people of color have made up what scholars have called the "new immigration." This "new immigration" refers to the dramatically changing face of immigration that began after 1965 and has continued into the present day (Suarez-Orozco, 1998). In particular, Mexicans account for the largest numbers of the "new immigration" while people from South and Central America, the Caribbean, and Asia join them in making up this historically distinct and large-scale movement (Suarez-Orozco & Paez, 2002).

The decision to leave one's home, one's family, one's culture, and all that is familiar for a new country comes about as the result of a number of complex and intersecting factors. These complex and dynamic factors are much larger and broader than the individual souls who make the arduous journeys of migration. Although it is beyond the scope of this chapter to justly explore the complexity of factors that both push and pull[4] the migration of human lives, it is important that they be identified and briefly addressed, for they are a significant aspect of the larger multidimensional context. To help highlight these dynamically interactive factors, the migration experiences of the three largest Latino/a groups living in the United States—Mexicans, Puerto Ricans, and Cubans—will be briefly explored.

Mexicans   The intersecting factors of globalization, economics, poverty, military interventions, war, immigration policies, and the United States' great labor demand for cheap labor and unskilled workers all dynamically contribute to the "pull" of migration (Suarez-Orozco, 1998; Suarez-Orozco & Paez, 2002). Similarly, these factors, along with the socioeconomic "push" out of a homeland where poverty is persistent, economic and social development is poor, unemployment is high and wages low, all have lent increasing momentum to the ongoing waves of immigration to the United States (Curiel, 1995; Rumbaut, 1997; Suarez-Orozco, 1998; Suarez-Orozco & Paez, 2002). For example, one recent study estimated that in Mexico alone there are 15 million unemployed workers (Dussel, 1998). The impact of political unrest such as that occurring in Mexico's southern states of Chiapas, Guerrero, and Oaxaca is producing large numbers of displaced rural families forced to find new ways of subsistence (Hagan & Rodriguez, 2002). Finally, it is critical to recognize the powerful push of family members left behind in Mexico to reunite with family members who have migrated to the United States.

Although no single factor alone determines migration to the United States, the primary motivation for Mexicans' migration seems to be economic. Clearly, the reality of low wages in Mexico where the GNP per capita was $1,671 in 1995 compared to the possibility of "high" wages in the United States where the GNP per capita was $2,521 contributes tremendous motivation (Dussel, 1998).[5] The passionate drive for work, for a job, provides the courageous drive to go north and across the United States–Mexico border.

> In San Matias and the thousand other Mexican towns where hope sits in a fading light, the young never did consider the idea of danger of going north to the United States. Their destination is the job, not the town or city. And ahead of them, a country fearful and hateful of them has its fences up at the logical crossing points: Tijuana into San Diego on the coast, and through Nogales and Douglas in Arizona, and Laredo in Texas and on into El Paso in the middle of the Southwest, where the Mexicans are pushed into the desert as if they were going through a turnstile. After that, they walk until they make it or die. They walk for the job. It is before all and after all. . . . They come across the riverbanks and the borderlands, these people who want to work. (Breslin, 2002, p. 43)

Braceros   Historically, two of the most startling examples of the complexity of forces influencing Latino/a immigration and migration were the Bracero Program and its antithesis, Operation Wetback (Trumpbour & Bernard, 2002). With the onset of World War II, the need for inexpensive and unskilled labor heightened. The U.S. government sponsored the Bracero Program to meet the need for cheap and abundant labor. Spanning a little over twenty years, the Bracero Program ran from 1942 to 1964 and brought in seasonal farm workers under strict rules that set agriculture as the only employment available to the braceros (Trumpbour & Bernard, 2002). By 1956, more than 445,000 Mexican braceros worked the agricultural business in the United States in an attempt to escape the poverty and the severe economic distress of their home country (Mooney & Majka, 1995). However, despite the braceros' motivation to work and to earn a living, the ugly misuse of the Mexican bracero by the United States was ever present. The following comments of the administrator of the Bracero Program (1959–1964) best sum up the oppressive nature of the program:

> [The program is nothing but] legalized slavery, nothing but a way for big corporate farms to get a cheap labor supply from Mexico under government sponsorship. . . . The braceros were hauled around like cattle in Mexico and treated like prisoners in the United States. (cited in Trumpbour & Bernard, 2002, p. 129)

While braceros were recruited via U.S. government sponsorship, the government initiative called Operation Wetback was implemented in the 1950s and deported more than three million Mexicans within that decade (Trumpbour & Bernard, 2002). Deportations occurred in mass and on the basis of racial profiling, often without verification of documentation or U.S. citizenship. That is, looking Mexican was enough to get one deported. Such programs not only affected Mexicans, but also served to bolster the power of U.S. corporations to break labor unions while encouraging suspicion and division between and among Mexicans and U.S. citizens (Trumpbour & Bernard, 2002). The notion that Mexican immigrants, documented and undocumented, take jobs away from American citizens was born out of large corporate manipulation of both the Bracero Program and Operation Wetback. This anti-immigration sentiment continues today, flaring up especially during hard economic times in the United States.

No contemporary discussion of the socioeconomic issues that drive Mexican immigration can be complete without some mention of the North American Free Trade Agreement (NAFTA) implemented on January 1, 1994 (Baker, Bean, Latapi, & Weintraub, 1998). The intent of the NAFTA was to increase foreign investments in Mexico, generate economic growth, increase employment and wages, and thus decrease Mexican migration to the United States (Suarez-Orozco & Paez, 2002). While some benefit resulted in increased wages, economic growth in Mexico has not been pervasive, and a growing economic inequality continues (Dussel Peters, 2000). Despite the growing inequality and high unemployment, some scholars view the instances of wage increases that have occurred in Mexico as providing increased means to afford the costs of migrating to the United States (Coatsworth, 1998).

Whether or not one has ever risked the migratory trip northward across the border, the impact of globalization encouraged by NAFTA may have resulted in an outcome opposite of that originally intended by its political creators. For instance, the impact of NAFTA and other globalizing strategies has provided opportunities, no matter how small or even meager, for otherwise very poor Mexicans to finally have a taste of social mobility. The natural human drive to better one's situation, to improve the quality of life for one's family, continues to spark a pursuit for improved standards of living, which are to be found in the north, across the border in the United States (Suarez-Orozco & Paez, 2002).

Martinez (2001), in his powerful ethnographic portrait of a southern Mexican migratory family, brings to life the complexity of migration and the economic phenomenon that spurs it forward despite danger and loss. He shares with us the many Mexicans he came to know, and among them are Rosa and Wense, a young Mexican couple from the small town of Cheran in the state of Michoacan.

> Rosa has a junior high school education, which is more than most women or men in Cheran have, but that doesn't make a difference in the local job market. . . . Both Wense and Rosa have been profoundly marked by their journeys north. . . . They'd earned real American dollars and lived in a genuine American apartment with hot and cold running water and an electric stove. They've had their first taste of social mobility and now they want more. They are still by all accounts dirt-poor, but they're also starting to think like the middle class. They have started moving and they don't want to stop. (Martinez, 2001, p. 88)

Puerto Ricans   There is no doubt that economics function as a significant force in the "push-pull" of Latino/a migrations. However, it is also significant that land acquisitions won through 19th-century U.S. expansion made "Americans" not only of the Mexicans living in what was then northern Mexico and is today the southwestern United States, but also of the inhabitants of Puerto Rico (Falicov, 1998; Sanchez, 2002). The impact of U.S. colonization of Puerto Rico has had lasting effects on the people of the island. For example, it was not until 1948 that Puerto Rico was allowed to establish itself as a commonwealth of the United States. Having been continually denied statehood or independence, Puerto Rico remains under U.S. rule in relation to military defense, foreign policy, and U.S. federal policy (Campos, 1995).

Although all Puerto Ricans are considered U.S. citizens and are subject to military service, they do not pay U.S. income taxes, and more significantly, they do not have the right to vote in U.S. elections if living on the Island of Puerto Rico (Falicov, 1998). This pseudo-citizenship status (granted in 1917 under the Jones Act) allows Puerto Ricans to legally move between Puerto Rico and the continental United States without being subject to U.S. immigration laws (Campos, 1995). Despite its intimate connection to the U.S. mainland, Puerto Rico's poverty rate remains nearly twice that of any state in the union (Campos, 1995). Furthermore, as a collective, "when compared to other Latino communities, Puerto Ricans [living in the United States] have encountered the highest rate of poverty, unemployment, and households led by single women" (Guadalupe & Torres, 2001, p. 74).

While U.S. acquisition of Puerto Rico occurred in 1898, Puerto Ricans were already actively involved in commerce with the United States, and with New York in particular (Campos, 1995). However, the first large influx of Puerto Ricans to the

U.S. mainland did not begin until the 1920s (Falicov, 1998). Similar to the push and pull factors experienced by Mexicans, issues of extreme poverty, high unemployment, and low wages to a great extent forced Puerto Rican migration. Like their fellow Mexicans, low-wage and unskilled jobs often were available to them in the United States. It was not until shortly after World War II that the United States saw the largest influx of Puerto Ricans (Moll & Ruiz, 2002). Attracted by the prospects of employment in factories and in the expanding railroad system, Puerto Ricans settled in several of the boroughs of New York City, Philadelphia, Miami, Chicago, and Los Angeles (Falicov, 1998).

Cubans Considered to be political refugees, Cubans immigrated to the United States in approximately six waves (Jimenez-Vazquez, 1995). Several smaller Cuban migrations to the United States occurred before the notable and larger first wave that began in 1959. What all of these migrations held in common was that Cubans were attempting to escape various oppressive political leaders. For example, wave one began in 1959 when Fidel Castro and his communist revolutionaries came into power. Unlike the migrations of Mexicans, Puerto Ricans, and other Latino/a peoples, it was the elite and the upper-class and middle-class professionals who were leaving their homeland (Falicov, 1998; Jimenez-Vazquez, 1995). Often referred to as the "Golden Exiles," this unique group of Latino/a immigrants was able to create a thriving "ethnic enclave economy" and a highly successful Latino/a community within Miami (Stepick & Stepick, 2002, p. 77).

This first wave lasted until 1962 when the U.S. Bay of Pigs invasion failed and all commercial travel between the United States and Cuba was stopped. However, this did not stop some who bravely made up the second wave of Cuban immigrants who escaped to the United States, namely Florida, via boats and rafts. The third wave began in 1965 and lasted through the mid-1970s. Financed through President Kennedy's Cuban Refugee Emergency Program (CREP), thousands of Cubans were airlifted out of Cuba to join family members already in the United States. Almost a billion dollars was allocated for the "Freedom Flights" and also for support of social service programs faced with serving almost 300,000 newly arriving Cuban refugees (Jimenez-Vazquez, 1995; Stepick & Stepick, 2002). The fourth wave that followed included Cubans sponsored by relatives and arriving in the United States via another country (Jimenez-Vazquez, 1995). Cubans who made up the fifth wave were mostly political prisoners and their families, who entered the United States in the late 1970s.

It is probably the last and sixth wave of Cuban refugees that is most well remembered. In 1981, this wave was initiated by Castro himself in an attempt to disgrace the growing and successful Cubans already residing in the United States. Often referred to as the "Marielitos," the almost 125,000 Cubans who were ousted by Castro were made up of those with criminal records, the mentally ill, gay and lesbian people, and those who practiced a form of indigenous religion called "Santería" (Jimenez-Vazquez, 1995). For about five months, this group of Cubans, unwanted by their homeland, were boatlifted from Mariel, Cuba, and brought to Key West, Florida.

Although the Cuban refugees were generally welcomed by the U.S. government and assisted through such programs as CREP, it would be highly erroneous to believe that Cubans were not subject to oppression and discrimination. The first waves of

Cubans came into a United States that not only was fighting the Great War on Poverty, but also was fighting for civil rights and women's rights, and eventually fighting a war in Vietnam. In addition, Cubans were not included in the U.S. Department of Health, Education, and Welfare's definition of Hispanic American, leaving them out of some important social services (Jimenez-Vazquez, 1995). Despite these omissions, Cubans were often viewed as being the recipients of a great deal of federal aid through CREP and, as a result, were often resented by ethnic and racial minorities who were struggling for civil rights as well as badly needed social services (Jimenez-Vazquez, 1995).

Despite the support available through CREP and the growth of a successful Miami "Cuban enclave," Cubans did and do experience oppression and discrimination as members of the Latino/a population living in what has been a White America (Stepick & Stepick, 2002). More recently, however, as more newly arriving immigrants from Nicaragua and other Central and South American countries come to live in and around Miami, hostile tensions have emerged between the established Cuban community and newly arrived Latinos/as (Stepick & Stepick, 2002). For example, recent research has shown that many newly arrived Nicaraguans view Cubans as having greater access to resources and upward mobility in the United States while at the same time experiencing some aspects of discrimination and prejudice from the Cuban community itself (Stepick & Stepick, 2002).

While current U.S. policy now requires that Cubans who wish political asylum in the United States provide evidence of political persecution, a number of policies allow for Cuban entry to the United States as well as citizenship that are not afforded any other immigrant. For instance, although the 1994 Guatanamo Raft crisis gave way to greater regulation of Cuban entry to the United States, the "wet foot–dry foot" policy, which resulted from that crisis, allows any Cuban who makes it to U.S. soil to remain in the country. In addition, through the Cuban Adjustment Act, any Cuban who has lived in the United States for one year is granted permanent residency (Stepick & Stepick, 2002).

The variation in sociohistorical experiences of the three principal groups of the many who make up the Hispanic-Latino/a population provides a critical view of a multidimensional context that has helped to partially shape the present-day experiences of Latinos/as in the United States. Most notable of the experiences that help to create some of the commonality among the diverse groups of Latinos/as are the experiences of immigration and a relationship of colonialism with the U.S. government. The impact of both shared and unique sociohistorical experiences is indeed evident in the daily lives of Latinos/as today. (See Reflection Exercise 15.2.)

The following section helps to provide a view of the present-day contexts of Latinos/as living in the United States.

WE ARE! A DESCRIPTIVE LOOK AT HISPANICS-LATINOS/AS[6] IN THE UNITED STATES

In 2000, the U.S. Census Bureau found that there were 32.8 million Latinos[7] living in the United States, making up over 12% of the total U.S. population (Therrien & Ramirez, 2000). In other words, Latinos/as as a whole now form the largest minor-

15.2 | Reflection Exercise

Take a few moments to reflect on the following exercise. Do your best to put yourself into the full experience of a person who is a Latino immigrant in the United States. You can do this as a small-group exercise. If needed, you can also do this as an individual exercise.

Group Exercise

Break up into small groups of three. Have each member of the group select one of the three principal Latino groups (Mexican, Puerto Rican, or Cuban) discussed in the text.

• Consider the sociohistorical contexts of the group you selected. Imagine what it would be like to have lived in that particular country of origin all of your life. You have tried hard for so long to make a living and to provide for your family, and now you have an opportunity to immigrate to the United States where there are jobs! What are you thinking, feeling, and wondering about as you make this decision? What are your your considerations? What drives you to migrate? What do you expect your experience to be like once in the United States? How might such diversifying characteristics as gender, sexual orientation, education, language, social class, and spirituality affect your decision and thoughts?

• While in your role (as a Mexican, Puerto Rican, or Cuban), share your thoughts on the questions you just answered with others in the group.

• What was your experience of the role-play as a Mexican, Puerto Rican, or Cuban? What was your experience of sharing with other "Latinos/as"?

---

ity group in the United States, having grown by 60% from the previous census survey of 1990 (Therrien & Ramirez, 2000). Another way of thinking about the numbers of Hispanic-Latino/a people living in the United States is to consider the fact that, today, at least one out of every eight people living in the United States is identified as Hispanic-Latino/a (Therrien & Ramirez, 2000). It is projected that by the year 2025, the Latino/a population will grow from 32.8 million to 61 million, representing 18% of the U.S. population (Pew Hispanic Center [PHC], 2002a).

A beginning view of the multidimensionality of this growing multiethnic population reveals that the 32.8 million Latinos/as living in the United States have at least twenty-six different countries of origin. A majority of the Latinos/as, however, are from Mexican origin (66.1% Central and South Americans constitute the second largest category, making up 14.5% of the U.S. Latino populations). The 2000 Census also reported that the U.S. Latino population is comprised of 4% who reported Cuban origin, 9% Puerto Rican origin, and 6.4% reported being of "other" Hispanic origins (Therrien & Ramirez, 2000).

A Geographic View

Of primary consideration when thinking about geography is the place of one's birth. The March 2000 Census Report (Therrien & Ramirez, 2000) found that 12.8 million or 39.1% of the Hispanics-Latinos/as living in the United States had been born in their respective countries of origin. Revealing of the more recent increases in immigration is the finding that 43% entered the United States during the last decade, while 29.7% came in the 1980s and 27.3% reported coming to the United States before 1980 (Therrien & Ramirez, 2000). United States citizenship had been obtained by almost 75% of those who reported entering the country before 1980, while only

23.9% who entered during the 1980s reported having become citizens. Of those who entered the United States between 1990 and 2000, only 6.7% reported obtaining U.S. citizenship (Therrien & Ramirez, 2000).

Further demographic descriptors of the Hispanic-Latino/a population were iden-tified in the data collected by the Census Bureau in March of 2000 (Therrien & Ramirez, 2000). For example, Hispanics-Latinos/as as a whole were found more likely than non-Hispanic Whites to live in the western United States (44.7%), namely California and Texas. They are less likely to live in the northeastern (14.1%) and midwestern (7.9%) areas of the country. Although the 2000 census data indicates a nationwide growth in the Hispanic-Latino/a population, of interest is the significant growth in numbers of Hispanics-Latinos/as now living in the southern United States (33.2%). For example, Georgia and the Carolinas have experienced exponential growth in their Hispanic-Latino/a populations over the last ten years.

A more focused view of geographic location indicates that Mexicans were more likely to live in the West (56.8%) and the South (32.6%), while Puerto Ricans were more likely to live in the Northeast (63.9%), and Cubans gravitated to the South (80.1%). Central and South Americans, on the other hand, were more spread out across three areas of the country: 32.3% in the Northeast, 34.6% in the South, and 28.2% in the West (Therrien & Ramirez, 2000).

Central-city living has often indicated important socioeconomic experiences about residents. Over 90% of all Latinos/as are living in urban areas, and half of these live in the central city (46.4%) within a metropolitan area. This is an important distinction from the lower percentage (21%) of Whites who live in central-city urban areas. Only 8.5% of Latinos/as are found to be living in nonmetropolitan areas. Central-city living within metropolitan areas was made up more by Puerto Ricans (61.2%) and other Hispanics (56.5%), while Cubans (76%) were found to be living outside central cities but within metropolitan areas (Therrien & Ramirez, 2000).

Family, Age, and Marital Status

Generally, Hispanics seem to live in larger family households when compared with non-Hispanic Whites. For example, by year 2000, 30.6% of Hispanic family house-holds were made up of five or more persons (Therrein & Ramirez, 2000). Among the ethnic groups making up the Hispanic population, more Mexican households (35.5%) reported five or more family members than did the other Hispanic house-holds. In contrast, only 21.7% of all Hispanic households were comprised of only two people. Among these smaller households, Cubans (41.3%) were more likely to live in two-person households than those in other Hispanic households.

The Hispanic population in the United States is a young population in relation to non-Hispanic Whites. For example, in 2000, 35.7% of Latinos/as were under 18 years of age, while only 5.3% of this population were age 65 years and older (Therrein & Ramirez, 2000). This is in contrast to 23.5% of non-Hispanic Whites who were under 18 years of age and 14% who were age 65 years and older. Among the Latinos/as, Mexicans had the highest proportion of its population 18 years old or younger (38.4%). Among Latinos/as, 32.4% were ages 25–44 years of age, and 14.5% were among those 45–64 years of age.

While the Latino/a population is youthful, a lower rate of marriage was reported for them than for non-Hispanic Whites (Therrein & Ramirez, 2000). Among those 15 years of age and older, Latinos/as were more likely to never have been married (33.2%) than non-Hispanic Whites (24.5%). Although Cubans were more likely to live in households of two persons than other Hispanic groups, they were also more likely to never have been married (20.4%).

Educational Attainment

To this point, census data have provided fairly neutral descriptors of geographic locations, household sizes, age distribution, and marital status. However, one of the most alarming trends noted in the 2000 census data is the finding that among Hispanics 25 years of age and older, only 57% had at least a high school education in comparison to 88.4% of non-Hispanic Whites 25 years old and older (Therrein & Ramirez, 2000). In fact, Latino/a students across the country are dropping out of school in record numbers. They make up the highest high school dropout rates of any other population group.

A closer look at the Hispanic population reveals that Mexicans have the lowest numbers of those 25 years of age and older who have completed high school (51%), while Cubans report the highest percentage of people 25 years old and older having a high school education (73%). In addition to lower high school completion rates, only 10.6% of Hispanics in 2000 reported completing a bachelor's degree in comparison to 28.1% of non-Hispanic Whites. Even more troubling may be the finding that 27.3% of Hispanics 25 years of age and older report less than a 9th-grade education compared to 4.2% of non-Hispanic Whites.

An Economic View

The alarm sounded by the data on low educational attainment by Hispanics warns of similarly troubling economic trends. For instance, 6.8% of Hispanics 16 years of age and older reported being unemployed in 2000 in contrast to 3.4% of non-Hispanic Whites (Therrien & Ramirez, 2000). A more specific view reveals that 8.1% of Puerto Ricans, 7.1% of Mexicans, 5.8% of Cubans, 5.1% of Central and South Americans, and 7.8% of other Hispanics made up those who were unemployed.

Hispanics were found to be more likely to be employed in service occupations (19.4%) and as operators and laborers (22%) than non-Hispanic Whites (11.8% and 11.6%, respectively [Therrien & Ramirez, 2000]). While only 14% of Hispanics were employed in managerial or professional occupations in contrast to 33.2% of non-Hispanic Whites, Mexicans were least likely of all Hispanics to work in white-collar professions (11.9%).

Given what the 2000 census data revealed about education and occupational distributions, it may not be surprising to find that in 1999, while Hispanics made up over 12% of the total U.S. population, they represented 23.1% of those living in poverty. More specifically, 22.8% of all Hispanics were living in poverty (as compared to 7.7% of non-Hispanic Whites), as were 30.3% of Hispanic children. In fact, although Hispanic children make up only 16.2% of all children in the United States, they constitute 29% of all children living in poverty. When looking more closely at the Hispanic population data, Puerto Ricans (25.8%) were slightly more likely to live in poverty than Mexicans (24.1%). Cubans made up 17.3% of Hispanics living in poverty, while Central and South Americans made up 16.7%.

Although the Hispanic population is disproportionately represented among the poor, 23.3% are among the full-time year-round workers who earned $35,000 a year in 1999 (compared to 49.3% of non-Hispanic Whites [Therrien & Ramirez, 2000]). Among the Hispanic population, Mexicans made up the lowest percentage of Latinos/as whose annual income was $35,000 or more in 1999, and Cubans represented the highest proportion of Hispanics who earned $35,000 a year in 1999 (34.4%). Of those living in the United States who earned $50,000 or more a year in 1999, Hispanics represented only 9.6% in contrast to 27.4% of non-Hispanic Whites. Again, Mexicans made up the lowest proportion of Hispanics at this income level (7.7%)

It is strikingly apparent that despite a high employment rate, overall Latinos/as experience poorer economic conditions than do non-Hispanic Whites. In fact, Latinos/as have been found to experience more severe financial hardships than non-Hispanic Whites who are in the same income level (PHC/KFF, 2002). Likewise, Latinos/as are less likely to own their own homes than their non-Hispanic White counterparts and less likely to make use of traditional financial mechanisms such as credit cards, bank accounts, and loans (PHC/KFF, 2002). In particular, Mexican American families have reported not having enough food to eat at higher rates than non-Hispanic Whites (PHC, 2002b).

Health and Health Care

Health and health care are central issues that clearly affect the well-being of individuals and families. What research has been conducted on Latino/a health has captured a rather troubling contradiction. Despite poverty, immigration status, and lower levels of education, Latinos/as overall have been found to be in better health than their non-Hispanic White peers (Brown & Yu, 2002; Brown, Wyn, Yu, Valenzuela, & Dong, 1998; PHC, 2002b). Adding to the paradox are realities that more than one-third of Latinos/as have no health insurance at all. In fact, the 2002 National Survey of Latinos (PHC/KFF, 2002) found that 35% of those surveyed did not have health insurance in comparison to 14% of Whites and 21% of African Americans. Twenty-two percent indicated that they had trouble paying for health care services, while 15% reported not being able to get needed health care services at all. Twenty percent of those surveyed reported postponing needed health care due to the inability to financially afford treatment. In addition to financial barriers to health care, 29% of respondents reported difficulties in communicating with health care providers due to language, and 18% experienced difficulty in obtaining health care due to their ethnicity.

In light of the lack of health insurance and other barriers to accessing health care, Latinos/as have been found to have death rates equal to or lower than those of non-Hispanic White peers for the top eleven causes of death in the United States (e.g., heart disease, cancer, stroke, chronic obstructive pulmonary disease, motor vehicle accidents [Brown & Yu, 2002]). Diabetes, HIV/AIDS, homicide and death by legal interventions, and chronic liver disease and cirrhosis are the only conditions under which Latinos/as have higher death rates than their non-Hispanic White peers (Brown & Yu, 2002).

Impact of Language Dominance

An important element in the multidimensionality of Latinos/as is the ongoing flow of newly arriving immigrants whose language dominance is other than English. For example, 72% of newly arriving immigrant Latinos/as speak Spanish, while 24% are bilingual in English (PHC/KFF, 2002). The opportunity for stereotyping in regard to language is high, and as such, it is critical to keep in mind diversity within language commonalty. While the majority of Latino/a immigrants speak Spanish, regional differences are apparent within and among the different countries that make up Latin America. For example, there are differences between "Mexican Spanish" and "Colombian Spanish." In addition, many indigenous peoples living in Latin American nations speak indigenous languages. Although some indigenous immigrants may also be fluent in Spanish, many speak their indigenous language alone.

What about native-born Latinos/as and language dominance? The 2002 National Survey of Latinos/as (PHC/KFF) found that 61% of U.S.-born Hispanics speak English predominantly while 35% are bilingual. In considering the native-born children of Latino/a immigrants, 47% were found to speak English predominantly and 7% were Spanish-language dominant. While it is often true that the children of immigrant Latino/a families as well as the first U.S.-born children are more likely to speak English, this ability to speak the dominant language recurrently places them in the role of interpreter for their parents and others in their families who do not speak English.

In considering the multidimensional contextual practice framework, it is important to know that client well-being is considerably intertwined with one's language. Language is the vessel of interaction interpersonally and on the meso and macro levels. The significance of being able to speak the language of the dominant society may go without saying. In fact, the impact of non–English-speaking dominance has been identified as an increase in poorer outcomes for education, financial status, employment, health care, and experiences of discrimination and racism in comparison to Latinos/as who are English dominant or bilingual (PHC/KFF, 2002). It is important to remember that while the ability to speak English is critical when it comes to successful outcomes within the dominant society, it does not, by any means, require the relinquishment of one's primary language.

Religion and Spirituality

Recently, the largest ever bilingual national survey on Latino/a religion and politics was conducted by the Hispanic Churches in American Public Life (HCAPL) research project, a three-year study funded by the Pew Charitable Trusts (Espinoza, Elizondo, & Miranda, 2003). As a result of this groundbreaking study, the most current profile of Latino/a religious affiliations is available. As discussed in an earlier section of this chapter, the historical and present-day influence of the Roman Catholic Church in Latin America and among Latinos/as in the United States has often led to the erroneous stereotype that all Hispanics are Roman Catholic. While there are, today, high numbers of those identifying as Roman Catholic in Cuba (40%), Puerto Rico (85%), and Mexico (89%), there are also a great many other expressions of religion and spirituality (Nationmaster, 2004). The reality is that there are rich diversities of religious and spiritual affiliations that include mainstream Christian denominations (Methodist, Presbyterian, Baptist), evangelical religious groups such as Pentacostal and Neopentacostal, as well as Seventh-Day Adventists, Jehovah's Witnesses, and The Church of Jesus Christ of Latter-Day Saints (Guadalupe & Torres, 2001; Mayer, 2002; Nationmaster, 2004). The Jewish and Muslim faiths are also represented, as are such spiritual traditions as Buddhism and Hinduism. In addition, religious and spiritual practices include indigenous-based faiths such as Santería, Espiritu, Curanderismo, and Shamanism (Bureau of Democracy, Human Rights, and Labor, 2002; Guadalupe & Torres, 2001).

Awareness that Latinos/as in the United States may participate in a number of diverse religious and spiritual practices is fundamental within the multidimensional contextual practice perspective, especially in light of current data indicating that most newly arriving Latino/a immigrants may be Roman Catholic, as are Latinos/as who have been living in the United States. What is the religious profile of Hispanics in the United States? The HCAPL project (Espinosa et al., 2003) found that 93% of Latinos/as self-identify as Christian, 6% embrace other or no religious preference, 1% self-identify as practicing a non-Christian world religion, while less than 0.5% indicate atheism or agnosticism. More specifically, the HCAPL study found that of those 94% indicating a religion, 70% self-identify as Roman Catholic, 23% as Protestant, 1% as other world religions.

Diversity within commonality is beautifully illustrated through a closer look at the HCAPL (Espinosa et al., 2003) survey results. For instance, among the many Latinos/as who self-identify as Roman Catholic, almost half consider themselves part of the Catholic Charisma Mission and/or Catholic charismatic movement. More specifically, 23% regard themselves as born-again Catholics (born again in Jesus Christ), while 26% consider themselves as Catholic charismatics. Likewise, among 23% of Latinos/as who self-identify as Protestant, 85% indicate that they are born-again and evangelical, while 15% self-identify as non–born-again, mainline Protestants. It seems important to emphasize that interpretations and practices of religious doctrines are highly shaped by historical sociopolitical experiences encountered by specific Latino/a groups. As written by Guadalupe and Torres (2001):

> The richness of the Arawak Indian civilization and current influence in spiritual and religious practices observed among Boricuas [an indigenousness way of referring to Puerto Ricans] cannot be ignored. However, current spiritual and religious ways that have also been planted and promoted by other sub-cultures, who through one or another form of migration arrived in Borinquen [an indigenousness way of referring to the Island of Puerto Rico], must not go unrecognized. . . . With the arrival of Santería into Borinquen, Catholic saints were often blended with African mysticism. . . . It may seem elementary to note that one cannot take for granted the fact that within a single Puerto Rican family system various forms of spiritual and religious practices may be manifested. . . . This observation

> supports the need for keeping an open mind when addressing Puerto Rican spiritual heal-
> ing practices. Due to the blend of various sub-cultures that make up the Puerto Rican peo-
> ple, one often sees the richness of each of these sub-cultures reflected in an overlapping of
> influences within spiritual and religious practices. (pp. 64–67)

Again, moving beyond stereotypes is vital if the intention is to reach client well-being.
(See Reflection Exercise 15.3.)

MIGRATION, IMMIGRATION, AND TRANSNATIONALISM

"Latinos are a work in progress; they are a people in the process of becoming as they
settle, in unprecedented numbers, in the United States" (Suarez-Orozco & Paez,
2002, p. 4). In fact, at least two-thirds of all Latinos/as in the United States are themselves immigrants or are the children of immigrants sharing a common immigrant
experience among the diversity of peoples who make up the group Latino/a (Sanchez,
2002; Therrien & Ramirez, 2000). The steady flow of newly arriving Latino/a immigrants sustains a dynamically changing multidimensional context as newcomers join
Latino/a communities of native-born brothers and sisters (e.g., first-, second-, and
third-generation Latinos/as). Likewise, there is a back-and-forth movement between
the homeland and the United States for many Latinos/as, which nurtures connections
across borders and creates transnational lives. It is the experience of immigration and
the uniqueness of transnationalism that provide a critical starting point for understanding both client well-being and the multidimensional contextual client.

> Their lives will be changed—are changing already. . . . Rosa and Wense have strong com-
> mitments that pull at them in opposite directions. Their family pulls them back to Cheran,
> Cheran's economy pushes them away; the economy of the United States beckons, the
> Border Patrol agents stand with their shields at the line. Rosa and Wense live smack on
> the line between the old world and the new, between Cheran and St. Louis, Missouri.
> (Martinez, 2001, p. 90)

Suarez-Orozco and Paez (2002) define *transnationalism* as an "analytical concept
that is often used to refer to the economic, political, and cultural strategies articulated
by a diasphoric peoples across national spaces" (p. 6). Mexicans, for example, historically have lived transnational lives, whereby seasonal and circular migration of mostly
men has meant living "dual" lives—at once in the United States and in Mexico.
However, as migration has become more inclusive of women and children, whole families have become part of this transnational lifestyle. Sending money home, remaining
involved in Mexican political issues, and nurturing family and social relationships on
both sides of the border are significant elements of a transnational life (Falicov, 1998).
The significance of transnationalism to the home countries of Latinos/as is also striking when considering that the monetary remittances to family remaining in the homeland have been estimated to top $18 billion a year (Iglesias, 2002).

Although transnational migration is still the experience of a great number of
Mexicans, there has been a growing trend over the last two decades toward more permanent settlement in the United States. Despite this trend, a new transnational family form has been taking shape in the face of the United States's growing demand for
live-in domestic workers in private homes (Hondagneu-Sotelo, 2002). Hondagneu-

15.3 | Reflection Exercise

Thinking about the view of Latinos/as described in the text, reflect on the following questions as they relate to the multidimensional contextual client, interactions/exchanges and effects, and multidimensional contextual services.

- What client strengths permeate the many challenges described in the demographic view of Latinos/as?

- How might these strengths and challenges affect the identities of Latinos/as?
- What kind of meso and macro multidimensional context is depicted by the demographic view discussed in the text?
- What do these data say about multidimensional contextual services?

Sotelo has done groundbreaking research on what she calls "braceras in the home" (p. 259). In an attempt to provide a better life for their children and families, Mexican and Central American women have been leaving their own children behind for work in the United States. It can take many years, sometimes from ten to fifteen years, for these women to have enough money to send for their children. When it is finally possible to reunite the family, the migratory journey is, at best, risky. While some children enter legally, others enter the United States illegally with the help of coyotes[8] or as a result of running away from caretakers, all of which may mean that children are making the trip unaccompanied (Hondagneu-Sotelo, 2002). Clearly, the impact on mothers and children, extended family, and the transnational family itself must be considered in relation to client well-being and the multidimensional contextual client.

Along with their bracera sisters, Puerto Rican and other Caribbean Latino/a immigrants also experience transnational lives (Falicov, 1998; Suarez-Orozco & Paez, 2002). The transnational migratory life of Puerto Ricans has been described as "a culture of commuting, of constant back and forth (¿alla? ¿aca?), a border culture of transfer and doubt between two intertwined zones" (Falicov, 1998, p. 41). What can this mean for individual family members and for families as a whole to be neither here nor there? How might this ambivalence affect the psychoemotional well-being of a person or family, especially if the individual and/or family has embraced a cultural value and social orientation of family inclusiveness? Some discussion of general cultural traits and the processes of acculturation, assimilation, and other models of adaptation may help respond to such questions while providing some context for multidimensional contextual practice.

CULTURAL INFLUENCES: COMMONALITIES WITHIN DIVERSITY

The uniqueness of a culture can be found in the cultural values or traits that are held in common by a culture's members. These cultural values and traits, which provide a kind of embrace for the members, are often internalized and adhered to in diverse ways by individual and family members of a particular culture. Identifying the general cultural traits and characteristics of a particular culture may be viewed as stereotyping, and it can be just that if individuals and subgroups are forced to fit into these without recognition of unique diverse expression. However, general cultural traits are in themselves unique, as they differentiate, in general ways, one group from another. General cultural traits do provide a necessary common weave of traits that help shape individual identities of the members of a culture and the social identity of the society as a whole. In this manner, general cultural traits and characteristics are to be recognized and celebrated, but not used stereotypically.

In discussing the diversity among Latinos/as, the commonalties of culture are explored to provide a framework from which multidimensional diversity of individual members of each group, the within-group diversity, and the diversity between individuals and groups can be fully appreciated. A brief look to the sharing of commonalties in the midst of rich diversity of Puerto Ricans helps to illustrate this critical approach.

> Although often connected by the experience of language (i.e., Spanish) and/or by an ethnic identity (Boricuas), Puerto Ricans are a mixture of various sub-cultures including native indigenous Arawak Indian, African, and Spanish/European civilizations. (*Boricua* is a term derived from the word *Borinquen,* further translated as "Land of Brave Lord," used by indigenous Arawak Indians, before [they were] conquered by the Spanish crown in 1493, to define what is currently and globally known as Puerto Rico.) (Guadalupe & Torres, 2001, p. 62)

Traditional Cultural Values

When considering culture, it is helpful to be reminded that, generally speaking, culture is thought of as a system of shared beliefs, values, customs, behaviors, and artifacts used by particular groups and/or societies to interact with the world and with one another. The culture of a group is often formed, changed, maintained, permeated, and/or passed from one generation to the next through a socialization process. As emphasized earlier, much diversity exists among and between Latino/a groups. A variety of cultures can be observed simultaneously when exploring the general Latino/a population. Yet common cultural characteristics (cultural commonalties) also seem to exist among and between Latino/a communities, shaping their unique diversity from other major cultural/ethnic groups. The following observed cultural values are not uncommon (though they are by no means universal) among and within Latino/a groups: *familismo, personalismo, respeto, simpatia, confianza,* and *traditional gender roles* (Falicov, 1998, 2002; Sawer, 2000).

Familismo The practice of *familismo* is found in Latino/a communities where the family is highly valued and is held as the primary social unit and source of social support. Cohesion of the family is highly important to family members. The well-being of family is regularly considered primary to that of the individual. One's family is often inclusive of the extended family and honored friends (e.g., godparents—padrinos and madrinas). Elders are important and honored family members. In multidimensional contextual practice, it is important to know that family members are often involved in decision-making processes and may also accompany individual family members to appointments.

Personalismo   *Personalismo* is generally reflected within and between Latino/a groups who value personal contact. Warmth and familiarity in relationships are highly treasured. Establishment of relationship (i.e., rapport building) is considered very important before any formal interaction (i.e., previous to conducting an assessment by a human service practitioner). It is the person who is significant before the agency or even the particular services being sought.

Respeto   Respect is an important part of relationships, as perceived by a large segment of Latino/a communities. A value is placed on the importance of being respected and cherished in relationships. This is not only what is wanted but also what is given in relationships. Elders, human service practitioners, teachers, health care professionals, and others are often held in high regard and respect. A perception of being disrespected may interfere with a Latino/a family's willingness to follow guidance or treatment plans.

Simpatia   Sociability is significantly important among and between many Latinos/as. Smooth human relationships are often highly valued, and conflict, especially direct conflict, is avoided. This seems to be the case especially in relationships with elders and others of authority. Simpatia is reflected in politeness and respect.

Confianza   The building of trust takes time in a culture that highly values the significance of relationships. While respeto and simpatia are highly valued among and between many Latinos/as, the significance of confianza in multidimensional contextual practice is paramount.

Traditional Gender Roles   While many Latino/a family systems do not engage in traditional socially prescribed gender roles (i.e., the man being considered the head of the household while the woman is viewed as being submissive to her husband), others do. Latino/a individuals and families who continue to engage in traditional socially prescribed gender roles reflect a cultural influence of paternalism. The concept of machismo is helpful in summarizing the dominance of the traditional male gender role reflected in the lives of a number of Latino/a individuals. Latinos who ascribe to machismo may incorporate a view of manhood as domineering, controlling, virile, and inexpressive. However, it is important to note that not all Latinos view their definitions of self through a machismo cultural influence.

Through the cultural influence of machismo, a man's worth is often intricately tied to providing for his family, being in control of his family, and being strong and independent. Through processes of cultural choice, some Latinos accept the positive aspects of this influence while rejecting other aspects that they find limiting in self-growth and/or in their relationships with others. For instance, machismo for some men involves keeping a dominant image in public while being more open and mutual with their spouses at home. Others who strictly uphold machismo within the context of U.S. society, however, have a possible risk for a great deal of tension, conflict, and possibly assault to their self-esteem when the women in their lives begin to take on new roles through working, generating income, and so on (Itman, 2004).

Large numbers of Latinas have stepped out of the traditional gender roles of sub-servience and humility. This has been the case within Latin American countries, and it also has been observed among Latino/a families living in the United States (Itman, 2004). Perhaps immigrant Latino/a families experience the challenges to and changes in female gender roles most significantly. When a family comes to the United States, both spouses often find themselves working long hours. The woman in the family, within the cultural influence of traditional roles, is considered responsible for the household and caretaking of her husband and children. However, with long, demanding work hours (and perhaps holding down more than one job), she may physically be unable to fulfill her traditional role. In addition, she may be earning more money than her husband, or may even be the only one able to find employment. At the same time, she may find herself engaging in the process of cultural choice as her own view of herself and gender roles changes. For the male of this family who himself is embraced within traditional cultural influences, the changes he sees in his wife and his home may challenge his sense of manhood. He may feel threatened, disempowered, and confused. Consequently, the opportunity for processes of cultural choice is present for him as well. For some, cultural choice may result in changing gender roles and views about what it means to be a man. For others who choose to adhere to traditional roles, the experience of tension and stress may remain. In fact, for some of these men and their families, domestic violence and substance abuse have been outcomes of this stressful transition (Itman, 2004).

CULTURAL CHOICES THROUGH ACCULTURATION AND ASSIMILATION

Cultural influences and processes of cultural choice are key elements in individual and family well-being for Latinos/as, as well as for all immigrants who have come or are presently migrating to the United States. The concept of acculturation refers to the process of taking on cultural values and traits of the new culture(s) while not totally giving up one's own cultural influences. With each new generation in the United States, for instance, the predominance of traditional cultural influences in the lives of family members tends to diminish. In fact, each member of a Latino/a family may be at different levels of acculturation, and sometimes this causes great tension within family members and the family as a whole. This is often evident in families of immigrant parents and their children as the children become more "Americanized" as they go through school and move through important developmental stages of maturation while living in the United States.

Assimilation is a different concept that was used in earlier thinking about cultural adaptation of immigrants. Unlike acculturation, assimilation assumes a total relinquishment of traditional cultural values, beliefs, and practices and basically assumes an absorption in the cultural traditions of the dominant culture. In earlier periods of U.S. history, assimilation was expected and was often used as a measure of successful adaptation by immigrants and their families.

Moving to a new country, entering a new culture or multicultural society, and perhaps not speaking the dominant language present great challenges. The effects of being "here" and "there," of attempting to adjust to new cultures and subcultures that are welcoming on the one hand (cheap labor for low-paying jobs) and rejecting on the other (discriminating, racist, and oppressive), are astoundingly significant. They provide powerful views of the often deep psychosocial wounding that can occur through the migration journey and the resulting status of an immigrant identity. Critical areas of loss in multiple dimensions of one's internal and external life space and, with that loss the accompanying grief and mourning, are often a shared phenomenon among immigrants (Ainslie, 1998; Falicov, 1998). Whether or not migration was a choice and how much trauma was experienced in the actual process of crossing the border are differentiating factors (Falicov, 1998, 2002). Likewise, gender, age, family form, proximity and accessibility of one's home country, availability and quality of social networks in the new environment, the status of language dominance, and the level of social acceptance/rejection in the new environment dynamically interact to create individual experiences of migration journeys, loss, and grief (Falicov, 1998, 2002). Similarly, these dynamics interact to help form the foundations for resiliency and coping.

While there is the collective level of profound loss in Latino/a migration journeys, there is simultaneously the unique and individual experiencing of that loss and its mourning. Awareness of the diversity and complexity of unique individual experiences of migration journeys is imperative.

> When an immigrant leaves loved ones at home, he or she also leaves the cultural enclosures that have organized and sustained experience. The immigrant simultaneously must come to terms with the loss of family and friends on the one hand, and cultural forms . . . that have given the immigrant's world a distinct and highly personal character on the other hand. It is not only people who are mourned, but culture itself, which is inseparable from the loved ones whom it holds. While the motives for migration (voluntary or involuntary) and the conditions left behind (economic, political) vary from person to person, all immigrants lose something essential to their lives in leaving their native homes. (Ainslie, 1998, p. 287)

Some of the contours of this loss, of cultural mourning, have been aptly described as a great uprooting of physical, social, and cultural multidimensional contexts—the major spheres of life's landscape (Falicov, 1998).

THE ALTERNATION MODEL: A "BOTH/AND" PERSPECTIVE

Despite the complex challenges of immigration and socioeconomic political experiences, the resiliency of Latino/a individuals and families provides a tremendous resource for adjusting to a new life in a very different society (Falicov, 2002). Earlier models of immigration and adaptation have described successful adaptation to the new culture occurring through a process of assimilation into the mainstream of the new dominant society. The assimilation model, based in "either/or" logic, posited that successful integration into the new society required nearly complete relinquishment of one's culture and language of origin. Essentially such a model supported a process of deconstruction, taking with it essential platforms for resilient adaptation (Falicov, 2002). Such a perspective is overtly visible in some of the more recent campaigns against bilingual education and affirmative action.

A newer model rooted in "both/and" logic offers an adaptive perspective, which makes room through cultural choice for both the retention of one's home culture and language and the acquisition of a new language and cultural traditions. The alternation model affirms the reality of multidimensional contexts and multiple identities while ensuring the platforms for resiliency (Falicov, 2002).

> The alternation model assumes that it is possible for an individual to know and understand two [or more] different cultures—old cultural meanings persist while new cultural models are acquired . . . cultural themes meet and mix, with no need or desire to choose between old and new. Rather one can know two perspectives, languages, and cultures, be traditional and modern, conservative and liberal, depending on the context or topic . . . an individual can have a sense of belonging in two cultures without compromising his or her sense of cultural identity [or identities]. (Falicov, 1998, p. 72)

Cultural differences and similarities are defining characteristics of each individual who makes up the larger group of Latinos/as. In reality, individuals and families are uniquely defined by multiple cultural identities shaped through nationality, race, gender, sexual orientation, ethnicity, social class, religion, education, occupation, individual life stories, and spiritual orientations and practices, among many other multidimensional and contextual diverse factors (Falicov, 1998, 2002). The Latino/a identity is at once a collective and uniquely individual one that brings with it memberships in multidimensional contexts. (See Reflection Exercise 15.4.)

DISCRIMINATION? SI! OPPRESSION? SI! SOCIAL INJUSTICE? SI! PERO, RACISM? ABSOLUTEMENTE!

Brown bleeds through the straight line, unstaunchable—the line separating black from white, for example. Brown confuses. . . . Brown is the color most people in the United States associate with Latin America. . . . [W]hat makes me brown is that I am made of the conquistador and the Indian. My brown is the reminder of conflict. And of reconciliation. —Rodriguez (2002, pp. xi–xii)

The concept of "race" traditionally has been used in the United States as an "either/or" category based on physical characteristics in an attempt to place human persons into one of two skin color groups, namely, White or Black (Martinez, 2001; Torres & Ngin, 1997). Despite the empirically based scientific fact that there is no evidence for grouping human beings into phenotypic categories, the social construction of race has undeniably resulted in creating social groupings of those who are generally powerful socioeconomically and politically and those who are not. Those who are not among the powerful do indeed experience oppression, discrimination, social injustice, hatred, and definitely racism (Andersen & Collins, 2001; Torres & Ngin, 1997). Do Latinos/as experience "racism"? To which group do they belong along the color line that is so steadfastly held to by U.S. mainstream culture? Are Latinos/as White? Are they Black? They are neither, and they are both, as they are among a full spectrum of brown!

There has been a long-standing debate on just where Latinos/as fit in relation to the social construction of race. Being of every hue along the White to Black color line

15.4 | Reflection Exercise

Reflecting on the discussion in the text, think through the following small-group exercise. You can also do this on your own if you are not working in small groups.

Group Exercise

Place yourself in the role of an immigrating Latino/a. Open your imagination as you put yourself in this person's place. You are a young adult who has traveled illegally from El Salvador, Central America. It was not an easy experience: Several in your group were caught by the INS Border Patrol (la migra), and you narrowly escaped yourself. When you arrived, you were robbed of what little money you had by the "coyote" who lead you across the border. You speak very little English. You are hoping to make it to your cousin's home. In the role of this person, get in touch with your feelings, thoughts, worries, and so on.

- What are they?
- Introduce your role to your group and share your experiences, feelings, thoughts, worries, and so on.
- What would help you in terms of supporting and enhancing your well-being as this person? What recommendations would you make for multidimensional contextual practice?

---

with predominance among the many shades of brown, Latinos/as have not been spared "racialization" and along with it a status of being "less than":

> Speaking only of Latinos, we have seen in California and the Southwest, especially along the border, almost 150 years of relentless repression which today includes Central Americans among its targets. That history reveals hundreds of lynchings between 1847 and 1935, the use of counter-insurgency armed forces beginning with the Texas Rangers, random torture and murder by Anglo ranchers, forced labor, rape by border lawmen, and the prevailing Anglo belief that a Mexican life doesn't equal a dog's in value. (Martinez, 2001, p. 113)

A very brief look at history reveals blatant examples of early institutional racism. For example, the Civil Practice Act of 1850 that excluded Native Americans and Chinese from testifying against Whites was amended to include Mexicans (Trueba, 1998). Further social construction of racialization of Mexicans was evidenced at the turn of the 20th century and well into the 1920s and 1930s as residential segregation was implemented. In addition, Mexicans were often barred from attending activities in public spaces (swimming pools, theaters, etc. [Trueba, 1998]).

Suarez-Orozco and Paez (2002) have identified three themes they find to be of significance in the racialization process of Latinos/as. These themes include the long-held negative stereotypes of Latinos/as, the predominantly low levels of education and skills of recently arrived and newly arriving Latin American immigrants that result in poverty, and the segregation of Latinos/as in schools, communities, and employment with consequences of marginalization and exclusionary barriers to opportunity.

The issue of skin color is not solely a North American racist phenomenon. Internalization of societal racism is not uncommon for some Latinos/as of varying national origins. For example, in Mexico, lighter skin color is considered more "handsome" or "beautiful" than darker skin tones. In fact, when one reviews the "Novelas" (Spanish-speaking television soap operas), a majority of the actresses are lighter in skin color and often sport blonde hair color. Historically, darker shades of brown have been identified with the indigenous peoples while the lighter skin colors are associated with the more socially valued presence of Spanish and European bloodlines. Latinos/as can, and more frequently than what we would like to acknowledge do, experience discrimination and oppression based on darker skin color from others within the Latino/a assemblage itself. (See Reflection Exercise 15.5.)

SUSTAINING OPPRESSION: STEREOTYPES

Stereotypes, especially negative and demeaning views, of Latin American peoples have been held within the United States since its early formation as a country. Suarez-Orozco and Paez (2002) discuss the work of Lars Schoultz who traced the U.S. public policy toward Latin America over the past two hundred years. A clear and consistent finding was the fundamental and long-standing political belief that Latin Americans have been considered inferior.

Likewise, a study of public opinion polls administered by twenty organizations over the last thirty years has consistently shown that Latinos/as are the least favored of all immigrants, with Mexicans viewed with the greatest anti-immigrant sentiment (Cornelius, 2002). Cornelius suggests that the present-day anti-immigrant sentiment especially toward Latin Americans is based on both economic factors (jobs and wages) as well as noneconomic factors such as ethnicity, language, and culture. For example, drawn by jobs in such industries as carpet, apparel, poultry, and construction, Latinos/as have more recently been immigrating to several areas of the United States that traditionally have not been the receiving points for large numbers of Latino/a immigrants (e.g., Dalton, Georgia). These communities have experienced startling transformations in their social space such as the emergence of Spanish-language newspapers, radio, and television stations along with Latino grocery stores, record shops, restaurants, religious groups, and community celebrations. Other noticeable impacts experienced by these communities in responding to a rapidly growing population have included inadequacies in housing supply, education, and medical services. It is this kind of ethnocultural impact of social space and services that may be driving what Cornelius (2002) describes as a primarily ethnocultural objection to Latino/a immigration—that is, the majority society's fear of losing a "national identity."

Although the anti-immigrant sentiments regarding Latinos/as have been present during the last thirty years, a drop in this sentiment since the mid-1990s has been noted. For instance, findings of late 1990 California public opinion polls revealed that a majority of Californians surveyed viewed Latino/a immigrants, and Mexican immigrants in particular, as being of benefit "because of their hard work and job skills" (Cornelius, 2002, p. 170). Further analysis of public opinion polls administered since the early 1980s supports the notion that economic factors are influential in American's anti-immigrant sentiment. The more secure and optimistic the economy, the more positive the view of immigrants as reflected in the polls (Cornelius, 2002; Jones-Correa, 1998).

Despite views of Latin American immigrants as contributors to the U.S. economy, stereotypical beliefs that Latino/a immigrants come to the United States to take

15.5 | Reflection Exercise

Take a moment to reflect on the following guide questions:

- When you first hear the words Hispanic and Latino/a, what images, words, and thoughts come to mind?
- What stereotypes of Latinos/as do you recognize in your consciousness?

- How might these stereotypes affect your perception of the multidimensional contextual identities of a Latino/a client?
- How might these stereotypes affect Latino/a client well-being?

---

advantage of welfare programs and other public services persist even though they are unsubstantiated. Further disparaging stereotypes depict Latinos/as as lazy, unclean, devaluing of education, academically weak, simple-minded, and having poor family values (Jones-Correa, 1998; Suarez-Orozco & Paez, 2002). In addition, stereotypes that depict Latino/a as criminally minded and responsible for higher crime rates, although unfounded, remain active (Jones-Correa, 1998). Clearly, as Guadalupe and Lum point out in this text, a nonnutritive environment is certainly maintained by such demeaning and disparaging stereotypes, providing fertile ground for the individual and collective internalization of oppression and a sense of rejection.

Insidious Effects of Internalized Oppression

Internalized oppression and discrimination are painful and destructive processes from which Latinos/as are not immune. Those who have been economically successful and/or are educationally accomplished and who may have risen up the social class ladder can be at risk for the tensions and pain of internalized oppression. So, too, can the status of citizenship differentiate one Latino/a from another who is undocumented and in the United States illegally. The insidiousness of internalized oppression can operate as a great distancing mechanism from one's less fortunate brothers and sisters, causing people to cut themselves off from their own, leaving those who are disenfranchised without validation or support.

WORKING HARD AND GETTING WHERE? POVERTY

"To get ahead, hijos. That is why we go a los trabajos" (Hart, 1999, p. 33). And to work Latinos/as do go, with one of the highest percentages of participation in the workforce (Suarez-Orozco & Paez, 2002). Although not every Latino/a has lived in and/or encountered poverty, poverty remains a critical experience for these communities as a collective. Poverty remains the experience for over 22% of the Latino/a population in the United States and affects 34.4% of all Latino/a children who, in turn, are living in poverty (Suarez-Orozco & Paez, 2002; Therrien & Ramirez, 2000). How is it that hard work and an almost total dedication to the "job" are not resulting in larger numbers of Latinos/as moving out of poverty?

A number of dynamically interacting factors in the experience of Latinos/as contribute to high rates of poverty. The "push" and "pull" aspects of economic factors have landed many in this population—who have moved from a homeland where wages are extremely low, unemployment high, and education and training extremely limited to the United States where the economy is insatiable in its need for laborers willing to work for very low pay—in the least desirable of jobs: agriculture, food processing, slaughterhouses, meat packing, poultry processing, construction, domestic services, apparel sweatshops, and so on.

While not all Latino/a immigrants are poorly educated and unskilled, a large number of new arrivals are. Of those who are educated and/or have professions, it is not uncommon for them to be unable to obtain professional work in the United States. Given the poor socioeconomic conditions from which they come, even the United States's minimum wage and wages that are not much higher than the minimum seem like large increases in relation to what is possible in Latin America. For instance, some estimates indicate that Mexicans who immigrate to the United States can potentially increase their incomes by as much as 300% (Coatsworth, 1998).

> Gustavo, who . . . had gone to America earlier had called several times from Brooklyn and said he had a construction job. . . . The pay was immense: Gustavo said he was making $7 an hour. Seven dollars in one hour! Eduardo carried bricks all day for the equivalent of $5 a day. . . . (Breslin, 2002, p. 57)

In comparison to the average earnings of $31,486 by non-Hispanic White men, Latinos on the average are earning $18,430 a year. Latinas earn an average of $12,910 in comparison to the $18,987 earned by non-Hispanic White women (Suarez-Orozco & Paez, 2002). Of course, the kinds of employment open to Latinos/as dictate salaries. Latinos/as are more likely to find employment in the service sector of the economy and twice as likely as non-Hispanic Whites to work as operators and laborers (Therrien & Ramirez, 2000). Similarly, only 14% of Latinos/as are employed in managerial and professional occupations as compared to 33.2% of non-Hispanic Whites, with Mexicans found to be the least likely to work in these higher-paying positions (Therrien & Ramirez, 2000).

Economic factors in the United States have contributed to an entrenchment in poverty. For example, over the last decade, the value of real wages in the United States has continuously lost ground for those workers without college degrees, many of whom are Latinos/as (Suaraz-Orozco & Paez, 2002). Education as a source of human capital is one of the scarce resources available to those living in Latin American economically stressed countries. Hence, it is not surprising to find that newly arriving Mexican immigrants on the average come to the United States with 7.6 years of education (Suarez-Orozco & Paez, 2002). And they come for work, for the job, with the hopes and dreams that they can afford for their own children to complete an education and to earn a higher wage (PHC, 2002a & b; PHC/KFF, 2002).

Finally, the United States itself is not immune from the impact of economic globalization. Global economic structures and knowledge-based economies have inherent divides between the higher-paying skilled and professional positions and the lower- and lowest-paying unskilled positions. Unskilled immigrants, many of whom are Latino/a, while finding work in lower-paying positions, are having a much more difficult time moving up into higher-paying jobs (PHC/KFF, 2002; Suarez-Orozco &

Paez, 2002). This struggle is compounded by the fact that 27.3% of Latinos/as report having less than a 9th-grade education, and only 10.6% have bachelor degrees or higher (Therrien & Ramirez, 2000). These are alarming figures, and it appears they are being sustained by the reality that Latino/a students are currently experiencing the highest rate of high school dropouts.

THE GREAT DIVIDE: SEGREGATION

Segregation is a painful and loaded term in light of U.S. history. The painful realities that this term conjures up are most often tied to a sadly false belief that segregation no longer exists in the United States. Unfortunately, segregation has not been eliminated by either federal mandate or social policy. There is growing and undeniable evidence that segregation of Latinos/as is increasing (Suarez-Orozco & Paez, 2002). The walls of segregation are all too easily built and sustained by the overpowering outcomes of poverty, low-wage employment, poor education, and lack of knowledge-based job skills. There is no doubt that discrimination, oppression, and racism are often the mortar that cements these walls in place. Given such factors as high levels of poverty, high participation and representation in low-wage jobs, often language barriers, large numbers of school dropout rates, and concentrated central-city living, Latinos/as are experiencing increasing rates of segregated living, employment opportunities, and schooling experiences. Of greatest concern is the current finding that Latino/a children and youth are experiencing very high levels of segregation by poverty and race when compared to other minority groups (Orfield, 1998; Trueba, 1998). Undoubtedly, this horrific reality has direct effects on the future of the Latino/a communities and the United States as a whole.

A formidable force perpetuating segregation and the consequent nonnutritive social contexts is found in the unfortunate antibilingual education movement begun in California with the passing of Proposition 227 in 1998 and followed by Arizona in 2000 with the passing of its own proposition eliminating bilingual education (Moll & Ruiz, 2002). Latino/a children whose dominant language is Spanish are particularly at risk for school dropout, increased marginalization, and the development of low self-esteem.

> Mrs. Morales said Jasmine's first-grade teacher had her cleaning tables as punishment for not learning to recite the classroom rules in English. Mrs. Morales clenches her fist as she recalls how cafeteria staff had also denied her daughter lunch for a week because she did not know how to ask for food in English. . . . "She didn't learn nothing. . . . I mean, it was real bad for us because she didn't want to go to school no more." (Sanchez, 2002)

The experience of this little 6-year-old girl will no doubt color her experiences of school, learning, and the educational process. Even more significantly, this child has been wounded at the very core of who she is: a Latina, a little brown girl, with a rich culture who speaks the Spanish language. It is possible that she has learned to be ashamed of these multidimensional contextual identities that make up her self. It is possible that the learning of English, which was once, perhaps, seen as an exciting opportunity for learning, may now be related to fear, punishment, and humiliation.

SI, SE PUEDE![9] (YES, WE CAN!)

The history of the Latino/a people in the United States has been one of great struggle, and yet, this difficult history has not dampened the inherent dedication to family and social connectedness, the strong commitment to work, and the undying striving for an improved quality of life for children and future generations. Negative stereotypes, unending poverty, and community and educational segregation have, no doubt, dynamically interacted to create challenging barriers and decreased access to fundamental resources for Latinos/as and their families. Despite these formidable barriers, however, large numbers of Latinos/as, like many peoples, continue to strive forward with hope and with dreams for a better life.

Skills for working with Latino/a peoples include intervention at all levels of the multidimensional contexts. National and state public policies most certainly need to be addressed, challenged, and changed. Empowering advocacy and community development practice at the family, neighborhood, school, and individual level is essential. A strengths-based approach is critical for working at the micro level with individuals, families, and groups; at the meso level within health and human service organizations, neighborhoods, and local communities; at the macro level within the socioeconomic and political systems; and at the magna level through faith-based organizations as well as individual and collective spiritual orientations and practices.

Building on the strengths identified previously can provide foundations for healing, for overcoming oppression, for breaking through walls of segregation, and for moving out of poverty. In the face of the tremendous adversities experienced by Latinos/as, empowering multidimensional contextual practice most definitely includes partnering with the Latino/a client and family to identify strengths and to build on their relational foundations. Walsh (1998) and Falicov (1998, 2002) have written extensively on relational resiliency. The relational resiliency model, formidably grounded in research, is a strengths-based approach that views individuals and families as being challenged by adversity rather than as being irreversibly harmed by crisis. In this model, individuals, families, and communities have the inherent potential to grow through and emerge from distress and challenge for the better. Resiliency is woven in the relational context of individual and/or collective beliefs and in how individuals, families, and communities make meaning out of adversity and their fit with the challenge at hand (Walsh, 1998). Building on these keys to individual and collective resiliency, the "both/and" perspective of the alternation model (see earlier discussion) brings added significance to the relational strengths of Latinos/as in the face of adversities.

Celia Falicov's (1998, 2002) work with Latino/a peoples and relational resiliency stresses the "both/and" perspective in the simultaneous maintenance of multidimensional cultural identities and the effective and selective incorporation of changing new identities, cultural practices, language, and so on. Both continuity and change can dynamically coexist in a resilient approach to meaningful movement through adversity, transition, and crisis. For Latinos/as, what can be at the heart of relational resiliency and a "both/and" alternation approach is the cultural significance of "la familia" as well as community and the inherent connectedness, inclusiveness, and interdependence that these entities often entail (Falicov, 1998, 2002; Walsh, 1998).

The hope, comfort, support, and faith rendered by spiritual beliefs and practices also can provide significant foundations for resilient outcomes. The participation in and building of church communities can indeed bolster relational resiliency. Through the provision of both the continuity of spirituality and practice that is universal across borders, and the selective incorporation of changes involved in the new and local church community, an individual and collective balance of continuity and change can be supported (Falicov, 1998, 2002).

Relational resiliency (Falicov, 1998, 2002; Walsh, 1998) can provide a guide for empowering practice with Latino/a clients. Identifying and building on strengths that include "la familia," the community, cultural traditions, and spiritual beliefs and practices can provide fundamental foundations for empowering and strengths-based multidimensional contextual practice that addresses micro-intrapersonal, meso-interpersonal, macro-environmental, and magna-spiritual contexts.

SUMMARY

This chapter has provided a brief introduction to some of the multidimensional contextual factors experienced by Latinos/as. Although it might be tempting to say that the information discussed here describes all Latinos/as, it is critical to remember that the reality is otherwise. Cultural similarities and differences are defining characteristics of each unique individual who is a member of the larger group of Latinos/as. Whether one is a newly arrived immigrant or not, there are simultaneously shared similarities and differences within and between Latinos/as that provide a resilient platform for each Latino/a individual. Latinos/as today are often "both/and" in culture, language, gender, family form, migration history, transnationalism, sexual orientation, employment, education, skin tone, religious affiliation, and spiritual practices. They are at once unique multiple identities intimately connected with "la gente grande" (the larger people). "Si, se puede?" "Si! Se puede!" (See Reflection Exercise 15.6.)

Notes

1. Note that the terms Hispanic and Latino/a are used interchangeably throughout the chapter. The author wishes to reinforce, however, the multidimensionality of nationality, ethnicity, sexual orientation, language, and culture embraced in these general terms.

2. The term mestizo evolved over the 16th, 17th, and 18th centuries to define the mixture of Spaniard and indigenous peoples. In fact, scholars have described the essence of Latinos/as, and especially Mexicans, as mestizo (Klor de Alva, 1999).

3. Most contemporary Mexicans and Mexican Americans define mestizaje as a dissolving of distinct cultures into "a Mexican way of being Spanish" (Klor de Alva, 1999, p. 176).

4. The author wishes to remind the readers of the many other countries of origin and their peoples who are included in the larger group of the Latino/a population (e.g., the Caribbean Latinos/as and the Central and South American Latinos/as, to name only a couple).

5. A majority of those emigrating from Mexico have low educational levels and are unskilled. Yet, a fertile job market exists for such workers in agriculture, food processing, service industry, construction, manufacturing, and landscaping. A 1998 study indicated that the mean hourly wage paid was $5.62 (Cornelius, 2002).

6. Census data discussed in this chapter are taken from M. Therrien & R. Ramirez, "The Hispanic Population in the United States: March 2000," Current Population

15.6 | **Reflection Exercise**

You are invited to explore the following case example as an exercise to help you integrate the information presented in this chapter. The guide questions are provided to help you apply the multidimensional contextual practice framework introduced in Chapter 2 of this text. You may use the multidimensional contextual practice framework (see figure 2.1) template as a visual aid in your thinking about these clients and in applying the framework.

Case Example

You are a human service practitioner who works with students and families at three elementary schools in your school district. Over the last three years, you have noticed that at one of your schools, which is located in the central city, the student body has become increasingly Latino/a, both native-born and newly arrived immigrants who are Spanish dominant. Fewer and fewer non-Hispanic white students have been enrolling while more seem to be moving out of the surrounding neighborhood. One afternoon, a young Latino couple comes to the school office politely saying your name. You are called to the office and meet a mother, father, toddler, a 4-year-old, and a first grader whom you recognize. You quickly become aware that the family is Spanish dominant and speaks very little English. You are left to rely on what you know of Spanish and perhaps some help from the oldest child in order to try and work with them. As you invite them into an office, you notice that there is another couple who has come with them. What you learn is that the father had come to Unites States first and was able to send for his wife and three children after three years. He had left his young family and pregnant wife to seek work in the Unites

States and hopefully a better life for his children. You can see that the 4-year-old walks with a limp and seems to have limited use of her left hand. You are wondering if it is the first grader they are concerned about, or whether it is the other children, or perhaps even the adults.

Guide Questions

- How would you apply the multidimensional contextual practice framework practice guidelines of mutual discovery, mutual exploration and planning, mutual intervention, and mutual evaluation to assist in promoting the family's well-being?
- How would you apply these same practice guidelines in your work to promote the collective well-being of the larger school community?
- If you were this human service practitioner, what personal dynamics of cultural influence and cultural choice would you become aware of?
- When you think about working with this family, are you aware of any primary/superficial assumptions you may have? Discuss.
- How might you go about nurturing your awareness of these assumptions? What processes can you use to enrich your awareness? Discuss and describe.
- What competencies do you realize you have in working with this family? What competencies do you want to develop or strengthen?
- How would you go about developing a relationship with the family, understanding what issues or needs they may have come to you with, and determining what kinds of guidance, resources, and interventions you might possibly provide?

Reports (P20-535), U.S. Census Bureau, Washington, DC.

7. Latino and Hispanic are used interchangeably in this section, which discusses the March 2000 census data.

8. Coyotes are persons who illegally take people across the Mexico–United States border. They typically charge a significant fee per person.

9. The empowering phrase Si, se puede! was a rallying call of Cesar Chavez, the inspiring leader of the United Farm Workers.

References

Ainslie, R. C. (1998). Cultural mourning, immigration, and engagement: Vignettes from the Mexican experience. In M. M. Suarez-Orazco (Ed.), *Crossings: Mexican immigration in interdisciplinary perspectives* (pp. 285–305). Cambridge, MA: Harvard University Press.

Allen, K. (2002). *An ethnographic interview: A Mexican-American male.* Unpublished manuscript.

Andersen, M. L., & Collins, P. H. (2001). *Race, class, and gender: An anthology* (4th ed.). Belmont, CA: Wadsworth.

Baker, S. G., Bean, F. D., Latapi, A. E., & Weintraub, S. (1998). U.S. immigration policies and trends: The growing importance of migration from Mexico. In M. M. Suarez-Orozco (Ed.), *Crossings: Mexican immigration in interdisciplinary perspectives* (pp. 79–105). Cambridge, MA: Harvard University Press.

Breslin, J. (2002). *The short sweet dream of Eduardo Gutierrez.* New York: Crown.

Brown, E. R., Wyn, R., Yu, H., Valenzuela, A., & Dong, L. (1998). Access to health insurance and health care for Mexican American children in immigrant families. In M. M. Suarez-Orozco (Ed.), *Crossings: Mexican immigration in interdisciplinary perspectives* (pp. 225–247). Cambridge, MA: Harvard University Press.

Brown, E. R., & Yu, H. (2002). Latinos' access to employment based health insurance. In M. M. Suarez-Orozco & M. M. Paez (Eds.), *Latinos remaking America* (pp. 236–253). Berkeley, CA: University of California Press.

Bureau of Democracy, Human Rights, and Labor. (2002). *International religious freedom Report 2002.* Retrieved from the Internet January 7, 2004, at http://www.state.gov/drl/rls/irf/2002/14051.

Campos, A. P. (1995). Hispanics: Puerto Ricans. In R. L. Edwards (Editor-in-Chief), *Encyclopedia of social work* (19th ed., pp. 1245–1252). Washington, DC: NASW Press.

Castex, G. M. (1994). Providing services to Hispanic/Latino populations: Profiles in diversity. *Social Work, 39*(2), 288–296.

Coatsworth, J. H. (1998). Commentary: Recent structural changes in Mexico's economy: A preliminary analysis of some sources of Mexican migration to the United States. In M. M. Suarez-Orozco (Ed.), *Crossings:* *Mexican immigration in interdisciplinary perspectives* (pp. 75–78). Cambridge, MA: Harvard University Press.

Cornelius, W. A. (2002). Ambivalent reception: Mass public responses to the "new" Latino immigration to the United States. In M. M. Suarez-Orozco & M. M. Paez (Eds.), *Latinos remaking America* (pp. 165–189). Berkeley, CA: University of California Press.

Curiel, H. (1995). Hispanics: Mexican Americans. In R. L. Edwards (Editor-in-Chief), *Encyclopedia of social work* (19th ed., pp. 1233–1244). Washington, DC: NASW Press.

de la Garza, R. O., Falcon, A., Garcia, F. C., & Garcia, J. A. (1992). *Latino national political survey: Summary and findings.* Boulder, CO: Westview Press.

Dussel, P. E. (1998). Recent structural changes in Mexico's economy: A preliminary analysis of some sources of Mexican migration to the United States. In M. M. Suarez-Orozco (Ed.), *Crossings: Mexican immigration in interdisciplinary perspectives* (pp. 53–74). Cambridge, MA: Harvard University Press.

Dussel P. E. (2000). *Polarizing Mexico: The impact of liberation strategies.* Covent Garden, London: Lynne Rienner.

Espinosa, E., Elizondo, V., & Miranda, J. (2003). *Hispanic churches in American public life.* Notre Dame, IN: Institute for Latino Studies at the University of Notre Dame.

Falicov, C. J. (1998). *Latino families in therapy: A guide to multicultural practice.* New York: Guilford.

Falicov, C. J. (2002). Ambiguous loss: Risk and resilience in Latino immigrant families. In M. M. Suarez-Orozco & M. M. Paez (Eds.), *Latinos remaking America* (pp. 274–288). Berkeley, CA: University of California Press.

Foley, N. (2002). Becoming Hispanic: Mexican Americans and whiteness. In P. S. Rothenberg (Ed.), *White privilege: Essential readings on the other side of racism* (pp. 49–59). New York: Worth.

Gimenez, M. E. (1999). Latino politics—Class struggles: Reflections on the future of Latino politics. In R. D. Torres & G. Katsiaficas (Eds.), *Latino social movements: Historical and theoretical perspectives* (pp. 165–180). New York: Routledge.

Guadalupe, J. L., & Torres, S., Jr. (2001). Puerto Rican healing practices: The spiritual, the religious, the human. In W. DuBray (Ed.), *Spirituality and healing: A multicultural perspective*. San Jose, CA: Writers Club Press.

Hagan, J., & Rodriguez, N. (2002). Resurrecting exclusion: The effects of the 1996 immigration reform on communities and families in Texas, El Salvadore, and Mexico. In M. M. Suarez-Orozco & M. M. Paez (Eds.), *Latinos remaking America* (pp. 190–201). Berkeley: University of California Press.

Hart, E. T. (1999). *Barefoot heart: Stories of a migrant child*. Tempe, AZ: Bilingual Press.

Hondagneu-Sotelo, P. (2002). Families on the frontier: From braceros in the fields to braceras in the home. In M. M. Suarez-Orozco & M. M. Paez (Eds.), *Latinos remaking America* (pp. 259–273). Berkeley: University of California Press.

Iglesias, E. V. (2002, November 22). *Remarks: Multilateral investment fund conference on "Remittances and the U.S. financial system."* Retrieved December 28, 2002, from http://www.pewhispanic.org.

Itman, I. (2004, January 8). *Finding help not easy for Latino victims of domestic abuse*. Retrieved January 8, 2004, from http://www.theaxcess.net/health.

Jiminez-Vazquez, R. (1995). Hispanics: Cubans. In R. L. Edwards (Editor-in-Chief), *Encyclopedia of social work* (19th ed., pp. 1223–1232). Washington, DC: NASW Press.

Jones-Correa, M. (1998). Commentary: Immigration and public opinion. In M. M. Suarez-Orozco (Ed.), *Crossings: Mexican immigration in interdisciplinary perspectives* (pp. 404–412). Cambridge, MA: Harvard University Press.

Klor de Alva, J. J. (1999). Cipherspace: Latino identity past and present. In R. D. Torres, L. F. Miron, & J. X. Inda (Eds.), *Race, identity, and citizenship* (pp. 169–180). Malden, MA: Blackwell.

Ledger, M. (2003, November). *New immigrants. The transformers*. Pew Charitable Trusts. Retrieved January 9, 2004, from http://www.pewtrusts.com.

Longres, J. F. (1995). Hispanics: Overview. In R. L. Edwards (Editor-in-Chief), *Encyclopedia of social work* (19th ed., pp. 1214–1222). Washington, DC: NASW Press.

Martinez, E. (2001). Seeing more than black and white: Latinos, racism, and the cultural divides. In M. L. Andersen & P. H. Collins (Eds.), *Race, class, and gender: An anthology* (4th ed., pp. 108–114). Belmont, CA: Wadsworth.

Martinez, R. (2001). *Crossing over: A Mexican family on the migrant trail*. New York: Metropolitan Books.

Mayer, J. (2002, October 4). *Religious changes in Mexico. Geography in the news* (Article 644). Retrieved from the Internet on January 8, 2004, at http://www.nationmaster.com.

Moll, L. C., & Ruiz, R. (2002). The schooling of Latino children. In M. M. Suarez-Orozco & M. M. Paez (Eds.), *Latinos remaking America*. Berkeley: University of California Press.

Mooney, P. H., & Majka, T. J. (1995). *Farmers' and farm workers' movements: Social protests in American agriculture*. New York: Twayne.

Nationmaster. (2004, January). *Demographics*. Retrieved from the Internet on January 7, 2004, at http://www.nationmaster.com/encyclopedia/demographics.

Office of Management and Budget. (1978, May 4). Directive 15: Race and ethnic standards for federal statistics and administrative reporting. *Federal Register, 43*, 19269.

Office of Management and Budget. (1997, October 30). Revisions and standards for the classification of federal data on race and ethnicity. *Federal Register, 62*(280), 58782–58790.

Orfield, G. (1998). Commentary: The education of Mexican immigrant children. In M. M. Suarez-Orozco (Ed.), *Crossings: Mexican immigration in interdisciplinary perspectives* (pp. 276–280). Cambridge, MA: Harvard University Press.

Pew Hispanic Center (PHC). (2002a). *U.S. born Hispanics increasingly drive population developments*. (Fact sheet). Washington, DC: Author.

Pew Hispanic Center (PHC). (2002b). *Hispanic health: Divergent and changing*. (Fact sheet). Washington, DC: Author.

Pew Hispanic Center/Kaiser Family Foundation (PHC/KFF). (2002). *The 2002 national survey of Latinos*. Washington, DC: Pew Hispanic Center.

Rodriguez, R. (2002). *Brown: The last discovery of America*. New York: Viking.

Rumbaut, R. R. (1997). Immigration to the United States since World War II. In Y. Hamamoto & R. D. Torres (Eds.), *New American destinies: A reader in con-*

temporary Asian and Latino immigration (pp. 15–46). New York: Routledge.

Sanchez, C. (2002, December 2). *Debate over how to best bring Latino students up to speed in English as tied to the large issues of politics and culture.* Retrieved December 28, 2002, from http://www.npr.org.

Sanchez, G. J. (2002). Y tu Que? (Y2K). In M. M. Suarez-Orozco & M. M. Paez (Eds.), *Latinos remaking America* (pp. 45–58). Berkeley: University of California Press.

Sawer, F. (2000). *Cultural values: Increasing the participation of Latino/a youth and families in the Oregon 4-H program.* Oregon State 4-H Program, Cooperative Extension Service, Oregon State University. Retrieved January 7, 2004, from http://oregon4h.oregonstate.edu/oregonoutreach/successful_practices/cultural_values.html.

Stepick, A., & Stepick, C. D. (2002). Power and identity: Miami Cubans. In M. M. Suarez-Orozco & M. M. Paez (Eds.), *Latinos remaking America* (pp. 75–96). Berkeley: University of California Press.

Suarez-Orozco, M. M. (1998). *Crossings: Mexican immigration in interdisciplinary perspectives.* Cambridge, MA: Harvard University Press.

Suarez-Orozco, M. M., & Paez, M. M. (2002). *Latinos remaking America.* Berkeley: University of California Press.

Therrien, M., & Ramirez, R. R. (2000). The Hispanic population in the United States: March 2000. *Current Population Reports* (P20–535). Washington, DC: U.S. Census Bureau.

Torres, R. D., & Ngin, C. (1997). Racialized boundaries, class relations, and cultural politics. In Y. Hamamoto & R. D. Torres (Eds.), *New American destinies: A reader in contemporary Asian and Latino immigration* (pp. 269–282). New York: Routledge.

Torres-Saillant, S. (2002). Epilogue: Problematic paradigms: Racial diversity and corporate identity in the Latino community. In M. M. Suarez-Orozco & M. M. Paez (Eds.), *Latinos remaking America* (pp. 435–455). Berkeley: University of California Press.

Trueba, E. (1998). The education of Mexican immigrant children. In M. M. Suarez-Orozco (Ed.), *Crossings: Mexican immigration in interdisciplinary perspectives* (pp. 251–275). Cambridge, MA: Harvard University Press.

Trumpbour, J., & Bernard, E. (2002). Unions and Latinos: Mutual transformation. In M. M. Suarez-Orozco & M. M. Paez (Eds.), *Latinos remaking America* (pp. 126–145). Berkeley: University of California Press.

U.S. Census Bureau. (2002, September 13). *Race and ethnicity: Terms and definitions.* Retrieved October 11, 2002, from http://www.eire.census.gov.

Velez-Ibanez, C. (1997). *Border visions.* Tucson: University of Arizona Press.

Walsh, F. (1998). *Strengthening family resilience.* New York: Guilford.

Zavella, P. (1994). Reflections on diversity among Chicanas. In S. Gregory & R. Sanjek (Eds.), *Race* (pp. 199–212). New Brunswick, NJ: Rutgers University Press.

There is one Light, but many lamps. —**Proverb**

16 | Asian Pacific Islanders

Ethnic-Specific Communities of People

JANLEE WONG

Asian Pacific Islanders are a very diverse collection of dissimilar groups. Asian Pacific Islanders are not alike racially, historically, or linguistically. Are Pacific Islanders lumped together with Asian Americans just because they share a common ocean?

A number of explanations have been offered as to why Asian Pacific Islanders are lumped together in one group. The reasons given are both negative and positive. The failure to acknowledge the diversity of people could be interpreted as acknowledging and reinforcing the hegemony of the dominant culture. Those lumped together may have nothing in common except what the categorizer has in mind for them (Lee, 1996). According to Lee, the dominant culture uses hegemony as a device to keep Whites in power by justifying, erasing, or ignoring social and racial injustices. Asians are often called a model minority given their economic and academic achievements. A minority group unable to achieve success has only themselves to blame, not the dominant culture. Another criticism of separating and identifying groups by their ethnic identity is that it "facilitates the displacement of inter-community difference—between men and women, or between workers and managers into a false opposition of nationalism and assimilation" (Lee, 1996). Some groups, such as Native Hawaiians and Chamorros (native Guamanians) involved with sovereignty issues, reject the Asian Pacific Islander category (Chen et al., 1997).

On the positive side of lumping groups together, it helps increase their numbers collectively for funding and political purposes. As individual groups, most of those who are of Asian Pacific Island heritage would be too small to count for effective political purposes, but grouping them into a single Asian Pacific Islander category allows for strength in numbers.

DEMOGRAPHICS

In the 2000 U.S. Census, about 4.2% or 11.9 million U.S. residents reported their race as Asian or Asian in combination with one or more other races (Barnes & Bennett, 2002). The 2000 census was the first time that the question on race was changed and respondents could identify as one race alone or a combination of races. Approximately 10.2 million reported their race as Asian alone and 1.7 million as Asian in combination with one or more races (Barnes & Bennett, 2002). With a new definition of how race can be reported, the 2000 census data are not statistically comparable to previous census data. This complicates looking at groups racially and ethnically. If comparing 2000 Asian alone statistics, there would be a 48% population increase for Asians from 1990 figures. If using Asian alone or in combination with other races, the increase would be 72% (Barnes & Bennett, 2002). Except where noted, Asian Pacific Islander information will be using the larger figures of those reporting as one race or in combination with other races. For reasons of simplicity, some historical data will be compared to 2000 census data to provide gross indicators of ethnic population growth. See Table 16.1 for data on Asian populations.

Asian Population Distribution

According to Barnes and Bennett (2002), 51% of Asians lived in three states—49% in the western part of the United States, and 49% in major metropolitan areas (Los Angeles, San Francisco Bay area, New York). See Table 16.2 for more information on distribution of Asian populations.

Table 16.1 | Largest Asian Groups by Population

Group	Population (millions)
Chinese	2.7
Pilipino	2.4
Asian Indian	1.9
Korean	1.2
Vietnamese	1.2
Japanese	1.2
Other	1.3
Total	11.9

Source: J. S. Barnes & C. E. Bennett (2002), *The Asian Population: Census 2000 Brief* (Washington, DC: U.S. Government Printing Office, C2KBR/01-16), p. 9. Eighty-six percent reported as Asian alone, and 14% reported as two or more races.

Native Hawaiians and Other Pacific Islanders

Grieco (2001) reported 874,414 U.S. residents as Native Hawaiian and other Pacific Islanders (see Table 16.3); 398,835 (46%) reported as Native Hawaiian or other Pacific Islander alone, and 475,579 (54%) reported as two or more races. Sixty-five percent of Native Hawaiians reported the highest in combination with one or more races, and Tongans (25%) and Fijians (28%) reported the lowest (Grieco, 2001). The U.S. Census data on Native Hawaiians and other Pacific Islanders does not include Pacific Islanders residing in the U.S. Island Areas of Guam, American Samoa, the

Table 16.2 | Asian Population Distribution

State	Population (millions)	Percent of All Asians	Percent of All Population in State
California	4.2	35%	11%
New York	1.2	10%	11%
Hawaii	0.7	6%	28%
Texas	0.6	5%	18%
New Jersey	0.5	4%	8%
Illinois	0.5	4%	11%
Washington	0.4	3%	19%
Florida	0.3	3%	20%
Virginia	0.3	3%	14%
Massachusetts	0.3	3%	10%
Other	2.9	24%	
Total	11.9		

City	Population (thousands)	Percent of All Asians	Percent of All Population in City
New York	873	7%	11%
Los Angeles	407	3%	11%
San Jose	258	2%	29%
San Francisco	253	2%	33%
Honolulu	251	2%	68%
San Diego	189	2%	16%
Other	9,668	81%	
Total	11,899		

Source: J. S. Barnes & C. E. Bennett (2002), *The Asian Population: 2000 Census Brief* Washington, DC: U.S. Government Printing Office, C2KBR/01-16), pp. 5–7.

Table 16.3 | Native Hawaiians and Other Pacific Islanders

Native Hawaiian	401,162
Samoan	133,281
Guamanian/Chamorro	92,611
Other Pacific Islanders	174,912

Commonwealth of the Northern Mariana Islands, and the U.S. Virgin Islands (Grieco, 2001).

The minimum (alone) and maximum (in combination with other races) for Pacific Islander population increases since 1990 are 9.3% and 140%. Three-fourths of Pacific Islanders lived in the West and over half in two states, Hawaii (282,667) and California (221,458) (Grieco, 2001). The places with the largest populations were Honolulu (58,130), New York (19,203), Los Angeles (13,144), and San Diego (10,613) (Grieco, 2001).

Immigration

Immigration is a major source of the growth of the Asian population in the United States. According to the U.S. Census Bureau (2001a), 7.2 million U.S. residents in 2000 (26% of the nation's total foreign-born population) were born in Asia. Reflecting major immigration law reforms in the 1960s and 1980s, the Asian-born share of the foreign-born population increased substantially from 5.1% in 1960 (U.S. Census Bureau, 2001a). The 2000 census (U.S. Census Bureau, 2001a) report indicated the following:

- The five largest contributors to the nation's Asian-born population were China, India, Korea, the Philippines, and Vietnam.
- All five were among the ten leading countries of birth of the foreign-born.
- As recently as 1970, no Asian country was on this list.
- 47% of the foreign-born population from Asia were naturalized U.S. citizens in 2000, compared to 52% of those born in Europe.
- 88% of Asians were foreign-born or had at least one foreign-born parent.

Age and Gender

The median age for Native Hawaiians and other Pacific Islanders is 25.4 years, for Asians 31.1 years, and for Whites 37.3 years (U.S. Census Bureau, 2001b). In regard to language, 6.9 million (62%) reported speaking an Asian or Pacific Islander language at home in 2000 (U.S. Census Bureau, 2001b). Females outnumbered males for Asians, at 51.4% female to 48.6% male, while it was the other way around for

Native Hawaiian and other Pacific Islanders, at 50.3% male to 49.7% female (U.S. Census Bureau, 2001b).

Family Size and Status

According to the U.S. Census Bureau (2001b), Asians and Native Hawaiian and other Pacific Islanders were more likely than other groups to be in intact families, have a higher number of persons per family, and not have as high of a homeownership rate as Whites:

- 74.9% of Native Hawaiian/other Pacific Islander and 73.8% of Asian households were family households (Whites 67.1%; Blacks 67.9%).
- 45% of Native Hawaiian/other Pacific Islander and 40.1% of Asian households were family households with children (Whites 30.5%; Blacks 38.3%).
- 30.6% of Native Hawaiian/other Pacific Islander and 33.9% of Asian households were married family households with children (Whites 23.5%; Blacks 16.1%).
- 4.7% of Asian households were single female-headed households with children (Whites 5.2%; Blacks 19.3%; Native Hawaiian/other Pacific Islanders 10.7%).
- 17% of Native Hawaiian/other Pacific Islander and 18.9% of Asian households were households where the householder lived alone (Whites 26.6%; Blacks 27%).
- 3.2% of Native Hawaiian/other Pacific Islander and 3.3% of Asian households were households with persons 65 years or older living alone (Whites 10.2%; Blacks 6.8%).
- Average number of persons per family:

  Native Hawaiian and other Pacific Islanders 3.84
  Asians 3.09
  Blacks 3.34
  Whites 3.03

- Households with individuals 65 years and older:

  Whites 25.1%
  Native Hawaiian and other Pacific Islanders 18.9%
  Blacks 17.9%
  Asians 17.4%

- Owner-occupied housing:

  Whites 70.9%
  Asians 52.8%
  Native Hawaiian and other Pacific Islanders 46.6%
  Blacks 46%

ASIAN PACIFIC ISLANDER HISTORICAL THREADS

Economic, social, and political pressures pushed the first wave of Asian Pacific Islander immigrants in the 19th and early 20th centuries. In most cases, immigration was encouraged, aided and abetted by American capitalists seeking cheap, docile labor. Those arriving were mostly young and impoverished men. Upon arrival, Asian Pacific Islanders encountered substantial racism, much of it generated by anti-Asian labor elements. Political movements gained power by espousing racist political platforms and led the way for continuous anti–Asian Pacific Islander legislation as well as anti–Asian Pacific Islander court decisions.

As each new Asian Pacific Islander group arrived, legislation was introduced to exclude their immigration, to bar them from owing land, and to prevent them from marrying White women. As these laws were put into place for each Asian Pacific Islander group, their numbers would stop growing and start to decline. Even U.S. nationals such as Pilipinos were discriminated against because of their race.

After World War II, immigration laws began to change partially due to political alliances formed in Asia and the Pacific Rim as well as Americans becoming more exposed to Asian Pacific Islander peoples and cultures. The 1965 Immigration Act reformed U.S. immigration policies and permitted a quota of 20,000 immigrants per country regardless of race and unlimited entry of direct family members. After years of exclusion, Asian Pacific Islander immigration surged and the population became the fastest-growing group in the United States. In this new wave of Asian Pacific Islander immigrants, many were better educated and more professional than their predecessors, although some who came to the United States as refugees following the Vietnam War were not well educated and were considered unskilled.

Vast Diversity

Not only are Asian Pacific Islander groups different by country or national origin, they are different ethnically and sometimes racially within single national groups. Nearly all of the Asian Pacific groups have visible subgroups whose languages and cultures sometimes differ dramatically. To best understand a people or group, multiple dimensions should be examined, including basic historical, cultural, and spiritual information about the countries from which Asian Pacific Islanders have come. The following is a brief glimpse into these national roots.

China   Chinese people are from an ancient civilization that was considered more advanced than Europe for most of world history. The length and age of the Chinese civilization led the Chinese to develop a sense of superiority and domination in East Asia. Significant influences from Chinese culture can be found throughout Asia and especially in Southeast Asia, Mongolia, Manchuria, Japan, and Korea.

With this superiority came an inward sense that nothing outside of China was of interest to the Chinese. The one exception was Buddhism, which came from India around 25 AD. Other outside influences such as the foreign invasions and subsequent subjugation by the Mongols (Yuan Dynasty, 1271–1368 AD) and the Manchurians (Qing Dynasty, 1644–1912 AD) resulted in the conquerors adopting the Chinese language, culture, and imperial system.

By the 19th century, as China was nearing the end of one of its dynastic cycles (Qing Dynasty), conditions in China deteriorated and Western imperial powers were seizing territory and opening ports. This permitted an outward flow of Chinese that was related both to poverty and to the decline of this last dynasty. Internal strife resulted in the Taiping Rebellion in the mid-19th century that engulfed half of China and cost an estimated 30 million lives. This disruptive period allowed large numbers of Chinese from the southern Guangdong (Canton) province to leave China via the British colony of Hong Kong.

Attracted by the demand for cheap labor during the California gold rush period and the construction of the transcontinental railroad (1846–1870), Chinese began to immigrate to the United States in large numbers. By 1870, there were 63,000 Chinese in the United States, mostly in California (Takaki, 1989). The Chinese immigrants, impoverished and without much capital, used an age-old family (extended and clan) quasi-banking system to borrow money for the passage, lodging, and jobs. This system continues today as Chinese borrow and lend large sums of money through informal family and community systems.

By 1882, full-scale racism against the Chinese reached a zenith in the form of the Chinese Exclusion Act, legislation prohibiting further Chinese immigration to the United States. For the next sixty years, Chinese immigration was severely restricted, and only U.S. citizens and their dependents could enter the United States. It was only after America and China formed a strategic wartime alliance during World War II that the United States repealed the Chinese Exclusion Act and enacted immigration reforms that led to increased Chinese immigration to the United States. From a multidimensional contextual practice perspective, important considerations include: the long history of anti-Chinese sentiment in the United States; the evolution of the Chinese from sojourner to immigrant; the regional, ethnic, and linguistic diversity of the Chinese; and the large visible concentrations of Chinese populations in the United States.

Japan   The Japanese, like the Chinese, have a long history and come from an ancient civilization with significant external exchanges of culture and technology. Japan's first imperial era borrowed much from the Chinese, including language, philosophy, architecture, and art. The Japanese imported Buddhism via China and became devout followers. Being an island culture and at risk of becoming isolated and stagnant, Japan borrowed from outside cultures and improved on imported technology. This included metallurgy and the use of gunpowder as a weapon. Japanese art was also significantly influenced by Korean art, and throughout history, the Japanese have had significant cultural and technological exchanges with Korea.

Around 894 AD, Japan turned inward and cut off contacts with the outside, confident that theirs was a superior culture. Until the Meiji restoration in 1868, Japan struggled internally with shogunate and imperial systems competing to gain power. Japan entered its modern period after the Meiji Emperor was restored to power. This was fifteen years after American Commodore Matthew C. Perry opened Japan by force and impressed upon its rulers that it again needed to look outward, to learn and improve.

By the late 19th and early 20th centuries, Japan learned the lesson of modernization well and demonstrated its ability to improve upon imported military technology by defeating China and Russia in two short wars. Fueled by these victories, Japanese imperialism conquered most of Asia and the Pacific Rim by the mid-20th century, culminating in the attack on the United States at Pearl Harbor.

Reflecting long-established anti-Asian sentiments in the United States, over 100,000 Japanese Americans were rounded up at the beginning of World War II and interned in concentration camps without a trial and without charges being filed against them. Rising from an utterly defeated and destroyed country after World War II, the Japanese used their adaptive abilities established over the centuries to develop Japan into a first-world country with a top economy second only to the United States.

Early Japanese immigration to Hawaii and the mainland United States was fueled by the same need for cheap and docile labor that brought the Chinese as well as poverty conditions at home. After the Chinese Exclusion Act shut off Chinese labor, Japanese immigration increased substantially, reaching over 72,000 in 1902 and almost doubling twenty years later (Takaki, 1989). Like the Chinese, the early Japanese were sojourners, hoping to earn a small fortune and return home. Unlike the Chinese, the Japanese brought women and children, hoping to avoid the ill fame the Chinese garnered with houses of prostitution and gambling in the many Chinatowns. More accustomed to Western culture as a result of their country's modernization efforts and able to bring families, the Japanese soon became settlers. Many leased or bought farms, improved the soil, and developed highly productive farming methods. Again, as with the Chinese, the Japanese used their internal banking and support system (kenjinkai) to help each other develop a successful Japanese-American agricultural economy (Takaki, 1989). Also like the Chinese, Japanese were subjected to extreme racism and eventually also found themselves facing racist exclusionary pressures. In 1908, a "Gentlemen's Agreement" was negotiated with Japan to limit the emigration of Japanese laborers, and in 1924 a formal law was passed restricting Japanese immigration (Takaki, 1989).

Important considerations using a multidimensional contextual practice perspective include: the racist and discriminatory experience of the Japanese in the United States; the cultural homogeneity of the Japanese; the mixed heritage of Japanese in the United States (reported the highest percentage of two or more races in the census for Asians); the ability of the Japanese to adapt, adopt, and improve on culture and technology; and the rise of Japan as a first-world economic power and its effect on Japanese in the United States.

Korea   Korea, an ancient civilization on a strategic peninsula, was influenced by exchanges and invasions from the north (China) and south (Japan). Korea borrowed from Chinese culture, adopting Confucianism and Chinese characters into the language. Korea also adopted Buddhism, which came to Korea via China. In the 20th century, many Koreans would adopt Christianity. By the 19th century, like other Asian countries, Korea rejected outside and Western influences. Japanese imperialists annexed Korea in the first half of the 20th century, and by the end of World War II, Korea was divided with a communist government in the north and a U.S.-allied government in the south. The United States fought an inconclusive war against Chinese and Korean communists in the 1950s. The United States–South Korea strategic alliance substantially aided increased Korean immigration to the United States.

Korean immigration to the United States began in the 19th century with Koreans going to Hawaii as plantation workers. As efforts to exclude Chinese and Japanese immigration began, Korean re-migration to California and other western states helped fill farm labor needs. However, unlike the Chinese and Japanese, early Korean immigration never attained large numbers. In 1920, there were less than 2,000 Koreans on the mainland (Takaki, 1989).

Koreans used their internal community credit rotation system (kae) to develop their economic interests in the United States (Takaki, 1989). As with the Chinese and Japanese, Koreans encountered intense discrimination and eventually discriminatory legislation restricting their immigration and ownership of land. Immigration reform in 1965 led to a wave of new Korean immigrants that dramatically increased the Korean-American population from 10,000 in 1960 to 1.2 million in 2000. Many of the new Koreans have been businesspeople and professionals. They have established a very visible community in Los Angeles known as Koreatown. This new visibility has strained relations with other ethnic communities, particularly with African Americans. The killing of a young black female customer by a Korean store clerk in 1991 highlighted the animosity between Blacks and Koreans (Aubry, 1993).

Using a multidimensional contextual practice viewpoint, important considerations include: the historical cultural/technological exchanges and political struggles with China and Japan; the homogeneity of the Korean community; the Korean war experience; the influence of Christianity; the high visibility and economic strength of Korean Americans; and ethnic intergroup relations.

South Asia (India, Pakistan, Afghanistan, Bangladesh, Sri Lanka)   South Asia, with a long and ancient civilization, experienced substantial exchanges of cultures and peoples with its proximity to the Middle East and central Asia. Already home to the world's great religions of Hinduism and Buddhism, south Asia also developed large Muslim populations due to the spread of Islam in 1200 AD. South Asia's influence in the Far East and Southeast Asia has been significant as Hinduism, Buddhism, and Islam spread their respective spiritual and cultural influences eastward.

European colonization of south Asia began in the 17th and 18th centuries and was completed by the 19th century, with most of south Asia becoming part of the British Empire. The British successfully used techniques such as exploiting and pitting one group against another to assume control of one area after another. Under the British Empire, the many different and distinct peoples of South Asia became a single political entity, a British colony. India consists of fifteen major regional languages that are for the most part mutually unintelligible (Bacon, 1996). South Asia's religious and spiritual communities are diverse, consisting of Hindu, Muslim, Sikh, Buddhist, Christian, Jain, and Parsi communities (Bacon, 1996). South Asia gained independence after World War II, and the South Asian colonial block was divided into several countries along religious lines (Muslim Pakistan, Afghanistan, and Bangladesh; Hindu India; and Buddhist/Hindu Sri Lanka).

South Asians came to the United States through Hawaii and then directly to the mainland. As British subjects, South Asians could travel to Canada and the Caribbean, and then on to the United States. South Asians came initially as laborers and farm workers. Despite their facility with English and their familiarity with Western customs, South Asians, with their dark skin and non-Christian religions, encountered significant racism. Initially, their Aryan origins caused controversy as to the definition of their race. Court rulings that finally restricted the definition of White race to northern and western Europe opened the way for anti–Asian Indian laws (Takaki, 1989).

With few South Asian women allowed to enter the United States and South Asian men barred from marrying White women, many South Asian men married Mexican women. The estimates of South Asians with Mexican spouses ranged as high as 76% in California in the early 20th century (Takaki, 1989). As with other Asian Pacific Islander groups, South Asian immigration skyrocketed after the 1965 immigration reform, increasing from 1,500 in 1946 to 1.9 million in 2000 (Takaki, 1989). Also as with the other Asian Pacific Islander groups, many of the new wave of South Asian immigrants were professionals and businesspeople (Takaki, 1989). The post-9/11 experience has been quite negative for the South Asians, as racial profiling and hate crimes against them have increased. From a multidimensional contextual practice perspective, important considerations include: the colonial, racist, and discriminatory experience of South Asian people; their great diversity (including religion and caste); and post-9/11 racial profiling and hate crimes.

Philippines   To an archipelago country of over 7,000 islands, the people of the Philippines migrated from Southeast Asia, China, and other Pacific islands, and by 400 AD they had developed a distinct island and trading culture (Williams, 1976). Europeans (Spanish and Portuguese) began their exploration of the islands in the 1500s, and in 1542, the Spanish claimed the archipelago, naming it "Islas Filipinas" in honor of King Felipe II (Phillip II). Pilipinos resisted the Spanish colonizers, and in the late 19th century, Pilipinos felt they were close to independence (Morales, 1998). However, the Spanish were to be replaced by the Americans when the United States defeated Spain in the Spanish-American War and Spain ceded the Philippines to the United States in 1898 for $20 million. Pilipinos resisted American rule and appealed to American democratic principles. In 1934, the U.S. Congress granted the Philippines independence, effective in 1946. But the Pilipinos had to wait for full independence when they suffered another imperialistic power in the form of the Japanese invasion in 1941.

As with the political impetus that led to the use of *Asian* in place of *oriental* (a term with negative connotations), the civil rights political movement of the 1960s and 1970s led some Pilipino activists to reject the use of the letter *F* in the spelling of Pilipino (i.e., Filipino). The letter *F*, it was argued, was associated with the Spanish colonizers who seized the islands in the name of Spanish King Felipe of Asturias (Morales, 1998). The letter *F* is also associated with a slang and derogatory term used for Pilipinos, "Flip" (Morales, 1998).

Like other Asian Pacific Islander groups, Pilipino immigration to the United States came in several waves. Unlike other Asian Pacific Islander groups, Pilipinos were American nationals, largely Christian, English-speaking, and were familiar with Western culture, having attended American-style schools (Takaki, 1989). The first recorded arrivals of Pilipinos were farm laborers in Louisiana circa 1865 (Hart, n.d.). Between 1900 and 1935, over 100,000 Pilipinos were imported as farm laborers to Hawaii and California under the Secada system, a form of indentured servitude (Morales, 1998). In 1930, there were 110,000 Pilipinos in Hawaii and 40,000 on the mainland; in the 2000 census, the number had grown to 2.4 million (Takaki, 1989). Although a diverse country with many different ethnic groups, the majority of the immigrants to the United States are from the Visayas and Illocos region (Morales, 1998). The Pilipinos filled a significant cheap labor need, since earlier legislation cut off Chinese and Japanese immigration. Racial animosity eventually led to another exclusionary act, the Filipino Exclusion Act of 1934, which limited Pilipino immigration to fifty persons a year (Morales, 1998).

The first Pilipinos to the United States were mostly men, following the similar sojourner path of previous Asian groups. Unlike previous groups, Pilipinos were U.S. nationals and could enter the United States through alternate channels such as serving in the U.S. military. Pilipinos were recruited into the U.S. Navy through the naval bases in the Phillippines. After the 1965 immigration reform, a second wave of Pilipino immigration to the United States included many professionals and businesspeople. From a multidimensional contextual practice view, important considerations include: the island nature and history of the Phillippines; the colonial experience of Pilipinos and the fight for Philippine independence; the diversity of Pilipinos; the influence of Christianity; their military experience; and the effects of racism and discrimination.

Hawaii   Hawaii deserves special mention in that not only did its native people suffer from American imperialism, but Hawaii also has served as a major entry point for Asian Pacific Islander groups.

Prior to the arrival of the first Europeans in 1778, the Native Hawaiian people generally lived in a highly organized, self-sufficient, subsistent social system based on communal land tenure with a sophisticated language, culture, and religion. A unified monarchical government of the Hawaiian Islands was established in 1810 under Kamehameha I, the first unifying King of Hawaii in several centuries. From 1826 until 1893, the Kingdom of Hawaii was recognized as a sovereign and independent nation among the world community of nations, with full diplomatic protocols (*Overview Independent Nation-State of Hawai'i*, n.d.).

American imperialists seized Hawaii in 1893 so American capitalists could exploit the plantation economy further. As a remote island with a shortage of cheap labor, the importation of labor, particularly from Asia, was especially important to the island economy. Since Hawaii was a U.S. territory, the importation of foreign labor was not met with the same racism and xenophobia as it was on the mainland.

In 1853, the native Hawaiians constituted 97% of a population of over 73,000 persons (Takaki, 1989). By 1920, impacted by the arrival of over 300,000 Asian immigrants, the native Hawaiian population declined to just 16.3% of the population (Takaki, 1989). According to the 2000 census, Native Hawaiians reporting alone make up 6.6% (80,137) of Hawaii's population and 19.8% (239,655) reporting in combination with other races (Grieco, 2001). Asians (reporting alone or in combination with other races) make up 58% (703,232) of Hawaii's population (Barnes & Bennett, 2002). Hawaiians became a minority in their own land, but Hawaii became a home to many Asians and other Pacific Islanders, as well as a jumping-off point to the mainland for many immigrants. Long gone is the plantation economy of Hawaii, replaced by one based on tourism and the large U.S. military presence. In the 1990s, Hawaiians began advocating for sovereignty as a native people (Gregory, 2001).

From a multidimensional contextual practice viewpoint, important considerations include: the island nature of Hawaiian culture; the loss of the Hawaii homeland; current island economics; Native Hawaiians of mixed heritage; and Hawaiian nationalist efforts.

Other Pacific Islands Overview   The term *Native Hawaiian and Other Pacific Islander* refers to people having origins in any of the original peoples of Hawaii, Guam, Samoa, or other Pacific Islands. Pacific Islanders include diverse populations that differ in language and culture. Westerners have traditionally divided the insular Pacific into three main cultural areas: Melanesia, Micronesia, and Polynesia (Bunge & Cooke, 1984).

- Melanesia

  Fiji
  New Caledonia
  Papua New Guinea
  Solomon Islands
  Vanuatu

- Micronesia

  Guam
  Kiribati
  Nauru
  Trust Territory of the Pacific Islands

- Polynesia

  American and Western Samoa
  Cook Islands
  Easter Island
  French Polynesia
  Niue
  Pitcairn Islands
  Tokelau
  Tonga
  Tuvalu
  Wallis and Futuna

Pacific Islanders have a long history of ocean migration sailing from mainland to peninsula, from peninsula to island, from island to island. Legendary Pacific Islander voyagers include Kupe, Hotu Matu'a, and Mo'ikeha who sailed around 1000 AD to New Zealand, Easter Island, and Hawaii (Bunge & Cooke, 1984). Long before Europeans discovered sailing technology that allowed them to sail the Pacific, Pacific Islanders had reached most of the Pacific islands and established communities there. In addition to a highly developed sailing and navigational technology, the Pacific Islander culture included a uniquely oceanic worldview and a social structure well adapted to voyaging and colonization (Bunge & Cooke, 1984). Polynesian societies combined a strong authority structure based on genealogical ranking that was useful for mounting long expeditions and founding island colonies (Bunge & Cooke, 1984).

The complex cultures of ancient Polynesia are largely gone (Bunge & Cooke, 1984). The incursions of modern technology, the demands of the world economy and the invasion of foreign cultural, religious, and political ideologies have radically altered the once integrated and largely self-sufficient societies. In some parts of Polynesia, the transformation from the old order is more complete, particularly in Hawaii and New Zealand, where Polynesians are minorities in their own land (Bunge & Cooke, 1984). The next two sections focus on two major contributors of immigrants to the United States, American Samoa and Guam.

American Samoa   Like all the Pacific Islands, little is known about American Samoa prior to European contact in 1722. Europeans competed for domination of the area, and in 1900, U.S. interests in American Samoa were recognized by other European powers (Bunge & Cooke, 1984). American Samoa served as an important military base during World War II, and many Samoans served in the U.S. military. In 1960, Samoa approved its first constitution. As U.S. nationals, Samoans resettled throughout the United States and Hawaii. By the 1980s, there were about twice as many Samoans on the west coast of the United States as there were in American Samoa, and another 20,000 were living in Hawaii (Bunge & Cooke, 1984).

Samoans are predominately Christian, having been converted by American missionaries and English-speaking peoples. One of the key elements in Samoan culture is the role of the chief. The high chief or ali'I (ceremonial functions) and the tutafale (orator), new leader and authority, perform a number of ceremonial and community service duties (Bunge & Cooke, 1984). From a multidimensional contextual practice viewpoint, important considerations include: the role of the Samoan churches; the traditional family and leadership structure; and the military experience of the Samoans.

Guam   The natives of Guam (Chamorros) first encountered the Spanish when Magellan arrived in 1521, and this encounter led to Guam eventually becoming a Spanish colony. A revolt in 1672 after early attempts at Christianization led to warfare over the next twenty years. Combined with disease, the Chamorro population declined by 90% to about 5,000 by 1700 (Bunge & Cooke, 1984). Guam became a U.S. territory in 1898 after the United States defeated Spain in the Spanish-American War. With a U.S. naval presence and territorial status, Guamanians became nationals of the United States, and many resettled in the United States and Hawaii.

After 400 years of colonization, there are no persons of pure Chamorro stock on Guam, and much of the culture is western Spanish and American, but there is revived interest in Chamorro culture and traditions (Bunge & Cooke, 1984). From a multidimensional contextual practice view, important considerations include: the colonial and Christian influence; political and military relationships; and nationalist and current economic issues.

Southeast Asia   Also known as Indochina, the Southeast Asian countries of Vietnam, Laos, Cambodia, Malaysia, Myanmar, and Thailand are located in a geographic crossroads of peoples and cultures from India and China. As with other Asian countries, the peoples of Southeast Asia adopted some Chinese culture and philosophy and fought against Chinese domination and imperialism. Unlike East Asian countries, Southeast Asia was significantly influenced by exchanges with South Asian culture, religion, and spirituality. A new outside influence, European colonial and Japanese imperialistic powers, would subjugate this area by the mid-20th century. With the defeat of the Japanese during the World War II era, the Cold War era ushered in communist and nationalist movements and governments in the area. The United States fought a ten-year war in Southeast Asia before losing to the communists in 1975. After the fall of the Soviet Union in the 1990s, the communist governments in Laos and Vietnam began a transition to a "market" economy, abandoning the socialist and communist economic systems.

Vietnam   Long before the Chinese solidified their nation and empire, a number of distinct peoples lived in what is now known as southern China (Williams, 1976). As the Chinese expanded south, these peoples migrated ahead of them, preserving their own language and culture and refusing to be sinicized. One of the great struggles against Chinese domination militarily and culturally were by the Viet people. As the Viet peoples moved south, they encountered the Cham people whom they eventually defeated and absorbed. Vietnam fought with its neighbors and invaded their areas, leading to a history of distrust in the area. The French who colonized all of Indochina by the mid-19th century in turn exploited Vietnam. The French introduced Christianity (Catholicism) to Vietnam and fostered its existence in a predominately Buddhist country. Vietnam was divided into the communist and noncommunist North and South at the end of the French colonial period (1950s).

Later, the communist victory over the United States reunified Vietnam under a communist regime. The U.S. defeat in the Vietnam War led to two great waves of refugee (Vietnamese, Laotian, Hmong, Mien, Cambodian) resettlement in the United States in 1975. This exodus continued into the early 1980s, with many refugees taking to boats to escape the communist regimes in Southeast Asia ("boat people"). The Vietnamese have established visible and viable economic communities in a number of U.S. cities, established churches and temples, and carried on a tradition of revering education that has resulted in numerous Vietnamese becoming top students in high schools and colleges. From a multidimensional contextual practice perspective, important considerations include: Vietnamese nationalism and the legacy of the Vietnam War; homogeneity of the community; the visibility of U.S. Vietnamese communities; and the changing economic and political situation in Vietnam.

Laos   Migratory people first settled the Laotian area and then came under domination of peoples from Cambodia. Laos struggled to be independent of its neighbors including Myanmar, Thailand, Vietnam, and Cambodia and, in the 19th century, came under French imperialism. After the Japanese invasion and occupation during World War II, Laos gained its independence from France in 1954 and struggled to form a coalition government of its own that included communist Pathet Lao who was allied with the Viet Minh fighting the French in Vietnam. During the Vietnam War period, Laos came under a communist government in 1974. With the fall of Vietnam to the communists, many Laotians affiliated with the United States became refugees and resettled in the United States.

Hmong and Mien   A special group of Southeast Asians are the Hmong, Mien, and other hill or tribal people who lived in the mountainous areas of Laos, Vietnam, and southern China. These peoples were engaged by the CIA and American military forces to fight a secret war against the communists. With the fall of Vietnam, these people also resettled in the United States as refugees. Unlike the Vietnamese and the Laotians, many Hmong and Mien refugees were uneducated and illiterate in their own language, making their resettlement especially difficult. From a multidimensional contextual practice standpoint, Hmong and Mien have been of special interest to the health and human service community because of their high dependence on government aid and the challenges to successful economic and cultural adaptation in the United States.

Cambodia   Khmers were thought to have migrated from the Sino Tibetan borderlands, settling in the Angkor area and establishing one of the great civilizations of Southeast Asia (Williams, 1976). Located in one of the great conflict areas of Southeast Asia, Cambodia would rise and fall, eventually allying with one neighbor against another for a modicum of protection. In the 20th century, the French controlled Cambodia through their colonial bridgehead in Vietnam. However, just as in Laos and Vietnam, the post–World War II period led to the defeat of the French and Americans and the establishment of a communist government in Cambodia under the Khmer Rouge. After a murderous genocidal period, during which an estimated 1 to 3 million persons out of a total population of around 7 million perished, Vietnam invaded and ousted the communist Khmer Rouge. Subsequently, an international effort led to the establishment of a multiparty democracy in the framework of a constitutional monarchy (*Background Note: Cambodia, 1996*). From a multidimensional contextual practice view, the great challenge is the continuing posttraumatic stress of the Cambodian genocide.

Myanmar (Burma)   Burmans are thought to have come from the Tibetan highlands and adapted their culture to the native Mon peoples, a people whose culture was significantly influenced by India (Williams, 1976). Burmans historically struggled with their neighbors for domination in Southeast Asia and, in the 19th century, were defeated and colonized by the British. The Japanese ousted the British during World War II, and Myanmar eventually gained independence. Presently, Myanmar is governed by an authoritarian military regime, which has been condemned for human rights abuses.

Thailand   Thai peoples originated in western China and, during a decline in one of the dynastic periods in China, established a southern dynasty of their own (Williams, 1976). This would eventually lead the Thai south to the geographic base for modern Thailand. The Thai fought both the Khmer and Burmans to gain their independence and fended off French and British colonial designs. Thailand emerged as the only independent country in Southeast Asia during the European colonial 19th- and 20th-century periods.

Malaysia Ancestral Malay peoples were maritime people and established seaports and trade routes along the peninsular and island chain of Malaysia, Indonesia, and the Philippines. These trade routes and ports along the Malay Peninsula would eventually attract colonial powers such as Britain and Holland who influenced, seized, and colonized these ports. The British used their power through the trading bases they established at Singapore, Penang, and Malacca to overcome the small sultanate states on the Malay Peninsula and establish the modern base for the Malaysian state (Williams, 1976). The British were ousted by the Japanese, and after World War II, Malaysia would gain independence. Malaysia and Singapore later agreed to separate and form their own respective countries.

Indonesia Indonesia, an island archipelago of over 13,000 islands (about half of which are inhabited), was settled by people from the Malay Peninsula and influenced by the cultures of India and Islam. Two empires on Java and Sumatra dominated most of precolonial Indonesia (Williams, 1976). European powers struggled to control the islands and the maritime routes. The Dutch eventually colonized what would later be known as Indonesia.

CHARACTERISTICS OF ASIAN PACIFIC ISLANDERS

The risk of stereotyping is high when using a broad overview of general characteristics to describe a particular diverse population such as Asian Pacific Islanders. Applying general characteristics can lead human service practitioners to try and make the "client fit the mold," thereby missing other possibilities. The human service practitioner should consider using a "constructivist" approach, allowing clients to inform the practitioner about their culture, beliefs, and environment. However, because of the human service practitioner's own culture, beliefs, and experience, using commonly found general characteristics can serve a useful purpose. Human service practitioners can contrast those characteristics with their own cultural beliefs, thus permitting a greater sensitivity toward clients and their cultures.

Passiveness and Limited Emotional Expression

One of the most common characteristics (or stereotypes) of Asian Pacific Islander populations is the perception that Asian Pacific Islanders are passive and emotionless (Dhooper & Moore, 2001; Jung, 1998; McLaughlin & Braun, 1999). In Western theories, limited expression of emotion can affect the success of some intervention approaches, such as person-centered therapy (Hong & Domokos-Cheng Ham, 2001). Before assuming that limited expression is dysfunctional, human service practitioners should examine their own cultural beliefs regarding expression of emotion. They may find that their own cultures provide a range of cultural behaviors and situations that limit expression of emotion. Human service practitioners can then reflect on whether their clients' amount of expression is a cultural norm, a culturally appropriate response to an unfamiliar situation, or an indication of a problem.

Family-Centeredness

All cultures have this characteristic, yet it is frequently listed as a uniquely important characteristic of Asian Pacific Islanders (Dhooper & Moore, 2001; Jung, 1998; McLaughlin & Braun, 1999). "Family obligations versus individuality" can be a major conflict issue for Asian Pacific Islanders in the acculturation process. Accordingly, this could become a major focus for intervention for human service practitioners. However, if human service practitioners examine their own cultures and family-centeredness, they may be able to put this characteristic in its proper perspective. For example, a pitfall to avoid is to assume that the client's needs for individuality outweigh the client's needs for family-centeredness and then work on helping the client become more of an individual. A multidimensional contextual approach would be especially useful, as it guides the human service practitioner to view a number of dimensions simultaneously. For example, is family-centeredness reinforced within the client's meso, macro, and magna systems? What elements in these systems reinforce individuality? Are they family-related or work-related, philosophical or spiritual? Can they be integrated or harmonized? The multidimensional contextual practice approach suggests consideration of multiple factors, not just a focus on helping the client become more of an individual person.

Filial Piety

Westerners interpret filial piety to mean obedience to and care for parents above all else, and it is often cited as a major characteristic of Asian Pacific Islanders (Hong & Domokos-Cheng Ham, 2001; Jung, 1998; McLaughlin & Braun, 1999). In Western thought, it may be considered a major sacrifice to care for parents over the individual's needs. Although filial piety is an important concept in Asian Pacific Islander cultures, it may not be as extreme as Westerners have come to believe.

Confucius, the epitome of filial pietists, understood there would be tensions between what the children and parents want. Confucius said,

> In serving his parents, a son may gently remonstrate with them. If he sees that they are not inclined to follow his suggestion, he should resume his reverential attitude but not abandon his purpose. If he is belabored, he will not complain. (DuBarry, Chan, & Watson, 1970, p. 27)

From a Western view, if filial piety causes one to suppress or submerge one's self and desires in relation to the wishes of the parent, then that could lead to significant problems for the individual.

In most cultures, there are conflicts when reconciling what individuals want with what parents want. A multidimensional contextual practice approach considers multiple factors, including communications and expectations (micro-meso) along with environmental and community issues (macro) and the philosophical construct of filial piety (magna). For example, is filial piety part of the collective consciousness of the family, community, and philosophical/spiritual thought system of the client? What elements in these systems support individualism? What is normal and what is extreme? Are these pressures not found in all cultures? What are the many ways in which they are addressed? Using a multidimensional contextual practice approach, one might find that respect and care for parents (filial piety) is quite normal in most if not all cultures.

Fatalism

Fatalism is another concept that may appear to Western eyes to be a potential source of conflict. Fatalism is identified in Asian Pacific Islander cultures as a major belief, and sometimes it is tied to Asian Pacific Islander religions and philosophies (Dhooper & Moore, 2001). A client's resignation to a problem because of fatalistic beliefs can be viewed as incapacitation or passivity leading to inaction, yet fatalism also can be seen as tempering distress over misfortune or the failure to achieve good fortune. From a 3rd-century AD text comes the following:

> Fate said: Since I am called fate, how can I have any control? If a thing is straight, I push it on. If it is crooked, I leave it alone. Longevity, brevity of life, obscurity, prominence, honor, humble station, wealth and poverty—all these come naturally and of themselves. How should I know anything about them? (DuBarry, Chan, & Watson, 1970, p. 250)

While the view of life's events and situations may be a fatalistic one at any one given time, this does not necessarily lead to inaction, nor does it mean dysfunction. The Asian Pacific Islanders who immigrated to the United States were people who shared a culture that held fatalistic beliefs, yet that fatalism did not keep them from searching for a better life. Fatalism may mean more as a source of comfort and inner strength when facing life's challenges. From a multidimensional contextual practice viewpoint, fatalism can be a philosophical/spiritual means of conserving energy and spirit in the face of hardship until circumstances change and the conserved energy and spirit can be applied to other efforts.

Individual/Personal versus Collective

Confucianist Asian Pacific Islanders generally think in terms of a structural philosophical framework that governs the family, and the same construct applies to governing in the community and ultimately governing a nation. This frame of reference to a commonly held philosophy and spirituality might be construed as "collective" thinking. Another interpretation might be that the "family" makes the decision for the individuals, since the individuals subordinate their wishes to those of the "family." After centuries of teaching and adherence to this "family values" of Confucianism, many decisions are made in the context of the family, and much of the thinking is family role and structure oriented. Individuals may be pondering such questions as: What is my role? Am I in concert with the family role and structure? What do I do with conflicts with this system of thinking (e.g., in the acculturation process)?

Much of the collectivist behavior can be seen through role modeling. The son may see his father deferring to elders and acting authoritative with his mother and siblings. The son may see his mother deferring to his father or his mother deferring to his grandmother. By modeling the same behavior, the son can be viewed as exhibiting collectivist behavior.

The Japanese have a strong sense of group and can also be stereotyped as having group thinking and group behavior. In Japanese history, the samurai or warrior class held its members to a group code, known as the code of the "bushido." This code held all members responsible to the clan or group and to the group leader. If something were to befall the group leader, the group would continue to honor the leader by expressing continued loyalty and continuing to behave as a group. Group (including family) identity and behavior are not necessarily unique to Asian Pacific Islanders, as all immigrant and ethnic groups display strong elements of group identity and behavior.

American history and culture contain numerous examples of collectivist or group behavior. Some of these groups are religious, such as the Mormons, and some are ethnic, such as the Irish and the Italians. Individual Native American tribes might also be called collectivist groups. It is not clear if the struggle between individualism and adherence to the group is any more difficult for Asian Pacific Islanders than it is for any group in the United States.

SUBCULTURAL EXPERIENCES WITHIN GROUP MEMBERSHIP

How can one write about the multiplicity and immense diversity of Asian Americans and Pacific Islanders? It may be perceived that the Asian Pacific Islander ethnic group is a single ethnic group, given historic racist and xenophobic attitudes and polemic, and yet Asian Pacific Islanders are just as diverse, if not more so, as Europeans and Latin Americans.

Gender

Historically, the treatment, role, and position of women are linked to the society, the culture, and the religion or philosophy of the times. Confucianism explicitly holds the role of the male and father above all. Christianity, Judaism, and Islam have male-dominant interpretations. The all-male nature of many early Asian Pacific Islander immigrant communities promoted and perpetuated male-dominated cultures.

Hong and Domokos-Cheng Ham (2001) believe that Asians have a high cultural norm regarding social distance and proper behavior between men and women. They believe it is more difficult for clients and human service practitioners of different genders to disclose intimate personal matters to each other. They also hold the same as being true for older clients and younger human service practitioners.

Lee (as cited in Lum, 1996) believes Korean women have developed an ability to absorb insults and injuries without protest and to assume responsibilities for other' faults; in contrast, Korean men have been incapable of bearing responsibility for their own actions, always seeking to blame others. The deposed Taliban of Afghanistan forbid women to be educated and hold jobs using an extreme interpretation of Islam. Female infanticide is practiced in China, as are bride burnings in India. Women accused of adultery, but not males, are stoned in some Islamic cultures.

Gender beliefs in a culture, like philosophy and religion, are much more complex than simply drawing all the connections in a sexist culture. Shih (n.d.) states that while Buddhist doctrines assume equality between males and females, in the "mundane" world, the position of Buddhist women is lower than that of Buddhist men. Taoism does not value males any higher than females. While religion and philosophy may provide some insight into the background of gender relations, societies and cultures may have a stronger influence.

An Afghan refugee in the United States, Qudsia Bekeran, in helping her family understand that Islam does not condone oppression of women, stated that treatment of women "has more to do with custom and culture than religion. If I didn't know about Islam, I wouldn't have known my rights" (Kay, 2002, p. 1). Bekeran is an example of how one can reconcile one's own culture, religion, and society.

This dynamism in society, culture, religion/philosophy, and gender can be seen in Lee's (1996) study of Asian-American high school students. In the category of Asian/Korean identified students, there was sexism, possibly based on old world culture. The so-called "new wavers" students, those who rejected traditional Asian values and opted to embrace the antiestablishment elements of American culture, also held sexist views and had double standards that allowed males to be sexually active but looked down on sexually active females. Asian-American students, whom Lee defined as those who had a combination of traditional Asian education and work ethic values and American political ideas, were more sympathetic to feminist ideas. One of the Asian-American identified students stated: "If I were Asian, I wouldn't support feminist things, but as an Asian American I can" (Lee, 1996).

Lee (1996) describes Harvard Professor Cornell West's theory of "racial authenticity" as playing a factor in how gender roles are viewed in ethnic communities. West concluded that sexism can be perpetuated when men criticize the behavior of women as not being true to their culture and ethnicity. This element should be considered when addressing the sexism that Asian Pacific Islander females face in their communities. Expressions of sexism may involve a power and role issue more than adherence to sexist interpretations of culture, philosophy, or religion.

Role Reversal

In many Asian Pacific Islander communities, a discomforting role reversal sometimes occurs when women assume a more powerful role than men. For example, in refugee communities in the United States, refugee women often obtain employment and become the family breadwinners while their husbands are unable to find work befitting their station or education. Just as Guendelman (as cited in Balls Organista, Organista, & Soloff, 1999) found that migration to the United States helped expand Mexican women's roles beyond the traditional ones, the same is true for Asian Pacific Islander women. Although it may appear that arriving in the United States might improve women's status in male-dominated cultures, Dhooper and Moore (2001) suggest that the results are contradictory, with cultural and gender clashes offsetting gains in status.

Sexual Orientation

According to Liu and Chan (1996), East Asian (Chinese, Japanese, Korean) philosophies and religions do not address the issue of sexual orientation. Sexuality and romanticism have no place where individual desires must be denied or overcome

(Buddhism) or in social and familial hierarchical schemes that stress filial relationships (Confucianism). In a study of Asian Americans, about half the sample denied there was even existence of lesbian, gay, and bisexual Asian Americans (LGBAA) (Liu & Chan, 1996). Gay Asian invisibility is cited with an example of an Asian-American lesbian, when expressing outrage at an incident of homophobia, being asked by another Asian American, "Why are you so upset? This isn't your issue" (Lowe & Mascher, 2001). Yet, despite the lack of official recognition of sexuality, homosexuality existed in the early histories of Asian cultures with reports that it was practiced by Buddhist monks and their novices and that it was first popularized by Chinese Buddhist missionaries in Japan and Korea (Lim & Johnson, 2001).

Lesbian, gay, bisexual, and transgender Asian-American Pacific Islanders have multiple identities to address in their communities and many resort to social invisibility or remaining in the closet (Liu & Chan, 1996). For example, a gay Korean immigrant might face rejection on more than one front: from his community because of his being gay, from the gay community due to his race, and from the dominant American community on both counts. Using the stereotype that families have a higher importance for Asian Pacific Islanders, Lim and Johnson (2001) speculate that the risk of family rejection may be greater for lesbian, gay, and bisexual Asian Pacific Islanders than in it is for such Euro Americans. Liu and Chan (1996) speculate that lesbian, gay, and bisexual Asian Pacific Islanders may find positives in the silence about sexual orientation in Buddhism and Confucianism. If sexual orientation is nonexistent in Buddhist and Confucian thought systems, then Buddhism and Confucianism cannot be used to provoke homophobic attacks as Christianity and Islam are used to attack homosexuality.

Ridge (as cited in Lowe & Mascher, 2001) concluded that certain Asian characteristics such as acting out of respect, collective responsibility, investment in maintaining harmony, and the emphasis on saving face of higher-status partners can be interpreted as "passivity" or "consent" leading to risky and vulnerable situations with Whites. Liu and Chan (1996) note that queer Asian Americans may replicate a Confucian-like hierarchical structure in their relationships. A multidimensional contextual practice approach would thoroughly consider a number of dimensions simultaneously in this context, such as religion, philosophy, spirituality, sexual orientation, family and community environment, self-perception and self-awareness, and so on.

Socioeconomic Status

The Asian Pacific Islander population presents a paradox in that they have income rates higher than all groups and pockets of poverty among certain Asian Pacific Islander subgroups. For a decade and more, Asian Pacific Islanders have had the highest median income of all groups. According to the U.S. Census Bureau (2002), Asian and Pacific Islander households reported a median income of $55,525 in 2000, the highest median income of any racial/ethnic group reporting (Whites $44,232; Blacks $30,436; Hispanic $33,455). Asians Pacific Islanders reported a 10.8% poverty rate in 2000 (Whites 9.4%; Blacks 22.1%; Hispanic 21.2%) (U.S. Census Bureau, 2001c).

Dhooper and Moore (2001) proffer that Asian Pacific Islanders have a higher number of wage earners per household than other ethnic groups and therefore inflate the average household income higher than that of those ethnic groups that have a lower number of wage earners per household. Asian and Pacific Islander households were, on average, larger than White households:

- Native Hawaiians and other Pacific Islanders—3.37 persons per household
- Asians—3.09 persons per household
- Blacks—2.74 persons per household (U.S. Census Bureau, 2001b)
- Whites—2.49 persons per household

Another factor may be that Asian Pacific Islanders might have larger numbers of intact families with two or more income earners. Asian Pacific Islanders reported the highest rate of family households maintained by married couples at 59.3% (Whites 54.2%; Blacks 31.4%), and Asian Pacific Islanders had a low rate of households maintained by women with no spouse present at 9.6% (Whites 9.3%; Blacks 30.7%) (U.S. Census Bureau, 2001b). Takaki (1989) speculates that Asian Pacific Islanders have higher median incomes due to the high-cost and high-wage areas in which they are concentrated (New York, San Francisco, Los Angeles, Orange County, San Diego, etc.). The high participation of Asian Pacific Islanders in business and their success at generating revenues also may be factors contributing to high median income.

Business

Business has been an important avenue of economic advancement for Asian Pacific Islanders since their early arrival in the United States more than a century ago. Chinese identified niche businesses such as food service and laundries that allowed them to maintain economic viability long after contract labor jobs ended. Japanese proved adept at turning land considered to be agriculturally unviable into productive and profitable farms and used the "contract, share, lease, and ownership" method to acquire land to farm (Takaki, 1989). Business continues to be a main economic route for advancement for today's Asian Pacific Islander populations.

The 1997 Economic Census for Minority and Women-Owned Businesses in the United States reported the information shown in Table 16.4. Chinese owned over a quarter of the Asian Pacific Islander–owned businesses; and Asian Pacific Islander businesses employed over 2.2 million people, had $306.9 billion in revenues, and generated 52% of all minority-owned business revenues (U.S. Census Bureau, 2001d).

Education

Newberger and Curry (2000) reported in the March 2000 Current Population Survey high levels of education for Asian Pacific Islanders. Asian Pacific Islanders reported that 86% of the population over age 25 were high school graduates. Living up to one stereotype, Asian Pacific Islanders reported the highest percentage of persons over age 25 with a bachelor's degree or higher (44% versus 26% for all U.S. adults). One million Asian Pacific Islanders had advanced degrees (master's, PhD, MD, or JD). Well-educated, professional, and business-oriented, Asian Pacific Islanders have the

Table 16.4 | Asian Pacific Islander Business Ownership—1997

Total Businesses	20,821,935	Percent
Hispanic	1,199,896	6%
Asian Pacific Islander	912,960	4%
Black	823,499	4%
Total Businesses	912,960	Percent
Chinese	252,577	28%
Asian Indian	166,737	18%
Korean	135,571	15%
Vietnamese	97,764	11%
Japanese	85,538	9%
Pilipino	84,534	9%
Other	90,239	10%

socioeconomic characteristics of the new wave of immigrants to the United States after the 1965 immigration reform.

Exceptions to the Stereotypes

Although the statistics and census data paint a glowing picture of Asian Pacific Islanders, significant exceptions exist that make it important to treat clients individually and to avoid generalizations and stereotypes. Wu (2002) disparages the "myth" of high incomes among Asian Pacific Islanders by detailing how, on an individual and family-by-family basis, Asian Pacific Islander income is not higher than that of other minorities. He points to high rates of poverty among Southeast Asian refugees, and the glass ceiling under which highly educated Asian Pacific Islanders are underpaid when compared to comparably educated non-Asians. He also cites the multitude of Asian Pacific Islanders in low-paid, low-skilled manufacturing and service jobs. A multidimensional contextual practice approach suggests examining multiple factors to derive subtleties that would be normally overlooked if simple stereotypes were used with such groups as Asian Pacific Islanders who have low education or income levels.

RELIGIOUS/SPIRITUAL PRACTICES

Asian Pacific Islanders come from a long and ancient history of religion, spirituality, and philosophy that is not well understood by Westerners and is often confused with Christian concepts of theology. Human service practitioners must have a basic understanding of religion, spirituality, and philosophy and how these relate to culture.

Table 16.5 | Thought Systems of Westerners and Asian Pacific Islanders

	Western (Christianity, Judaism, Islam)	Asian (Hinduism, Buddhism, Confucianism, Taoism)
Individuality	Individualistic	Collective
Thought	Things are separate and many	Monistic; everything is one
Construct	Linear; a beginning, middle, and end (last judgment)	Nonlinear; no last judgment, no judgment
Time	Linear	Cyclic (Hindu), illusion (Buddhist)
Achievement of spiritual, religious, philosophical goals	Individual action oriented	Contemplative; change may happen without action
Social and economic justice	People can be and must be helped	One's status is predetermined, fixed, and not related to achievement of spiritual, religious, or philosophical goals

Source: S. LaFave (n.d.).

Asian thought may be viewed not as a religion in a Western sense, but as a combination of religion, spirituality, and philosophy. As always, it is also important to understand that generalizations and comparisons are a way of beginning an examination but that further research and study are needed to achieve more than a basic understanding. The chart shown in Table 16.5 is a simplification of the complex thought systems of both Westerners and Asian Pacific Islanders. It is intended to provoke additional study and research, not to provide a stereotypical guide to religion, spirituality, and philosophy.

Hinduism

LaFave (n.d.) writes that Hinduism's vision of the world is that all is part of God (Brahman), that everyone has god in them, and that everyone is at one stage or another in their spiritual development. She states that in Hinduism, since everyone is on a different path and all paths are accepted, there is a complete acceptance of unity in diversity. In other words, there is no single right path and thus no dogma. According to LaFave (n.d.), given the general Hindu concept that all of life is in various stages of development, the issue surrounding caste, role, and position in life is not one of oppression by others; rather, the inequalities are due to "karma" and one's stage in spiritual development.

Buddhism

LaFave (n.d.) writes that Buddhism does not have a god in the Western sense, and that the word *Buddhism* is derived from the Sanscrit word *budh*, which means "to awaken" or "to know." According to LaFave (n.d.), the first Buddha, Siddhartha

Gautama, was a Hindu who gave up his noble position and wealth; left his wife, children, and family; and reached the "enlightened" state (being able to end individual suffering and step out of the cycle of rebirth). She states that Buddhism is the way through which an individual can attain an enlightened state (Nirvana) and end individual suffering (suffering based on cravings). LaFave (n.d.) describes the two main schools of Buddhist thought: Hinayana, in which Nirvana is the highest goal and can be reached through detachment and asceticism, and Mahayana, in which the goal is to live the compassionate life of a Buddha-like person to enlighten others.

Although Buddhism began in Hindu India, it is more popular as a separate thought and spiritual system in East Asia (Tibet, China, Japan, Korea, and Southeast Asia) than in India where it simply was absorbed within Hinduism (LaFave, n.d.). Buddhism fit well in East Asia because it explained how one could be linked to all living in the world through reincarnation and how one could be reincarnated into a better life. Buddhism gave an explanation of an individual's path to a higher life, and it helps to explain the high tolerance of some Asians to hardship and struggle, since self-sacrifice and self-denial are all part of that path.

Confucianism

Named after the 5th-century BC Chinese philosopher Confucius, the central belief is that people must practice a righteous lifestyle, with the key ideals being loyalty, filial piety, chastity, heroism, selfless friendship, and one's duty to use one's talents to serve one's family and country (Jung, 1998). Individuals must follow a rigid structure of relationships that are hierarchical in nature and include father–son, husband–wife, elder brother–younger brother, and friend–friend (Jung, 1998).

Living in an era of constant warfare, intrigue, and betrayal, Confucius thought that if people could live moral lives, there would be peace and harmony. Confucianism underpins the cultural imperatives in many Asian cultures of duty and respect (almost reverence) for parents, and of obedience and unequal relationships whereby man is over woman, parents over children. By following these relationships, one can have peace and harmony in the family and therefore in the world.

Taoism (Daoism or Dao—The Way)

Taoism is a philosophy that holds that all is one with nature and that nature is one with all. There is a duality of all things in nature, and this duality must be kept in harmonious balance, as represented by the yin-yang (De Mente, 1996). Another basic concept in Taoism is *wu wei,* action without action, as in not forcing something unnaturally and the belief that things happen for a reason (LaFave, n.d.). Taoism gave the people a way to see the entire natural world in a single system and to explain its conflicts and contradictions as the harmony of complementary parts of a single whole (LaFave, n.d.).

Westerners may see behavior influenced by Taoism as too slow, nonlinear, passive, and not clear-cut (ambiguous). For example, if something unfortunate happens, we often want to praise the good and condemn the bad; but in Taoism, good and bad are integral parts of the whole (the one), and one cannot be both praised and condemned. Interestingly, Confucius was a student of the Tao and later developed his own rigid set of rules that set forth distinctions and absolutes, and dictated specific actions that he thought could change the world.

Shinto

Rarick (as cited in Dhooper & Moore, 2001) describes Shinto as the animistic worship of natural phenomena—the sun, mountains, trees, water, and rocks. Practiced mainly in Japan, Shinto means "way of god" and has a pantheistic orientation that includes elements of nature and ancestor worship (Dhooper & Moore, 2001). In modern-day Japan, thousands of Shinto shrines are present in everyday places—on the street, next to skyscrapers, in parks and homes. Though a thoroughly modern people in a first-world country, many Japanese pay attention to the natural spirit world when they choose sites for buildings and roads or exorcise bad spirits from skyscrapers in Tokyo.

Feng Shui

Feng shui (literally wind water) is the practice of divining sources of energy (chi) within nature and mapping or plotting their most auspicious flow or channels. Popularized in Western culture as a mystical Asian practice that optimizes design, architecture, opportunity, health, and wealth, feng shui is part of the belief system of many Asians and should be recognized as such. In cities such as Hong Kong and Singapore, feng shui plays an important role in choosing sites for buildings so that the optimal flow of energy is enhanced. Some Asians believe "bad feng shui" can be responsible for physical ailments and misfortune.

Imported Religions

The natural philosophies and religions of Asia such as Tao (Dao) and Shinto have been viewed in modern times as animism and superstition, as something mystical and metaphysical. They also translate in modern times to beliefs in natural food, natural health, and healing. But the natural can lead to chaos. As the drive toward civilization progressed, a philosophy of order developed, helping to set structures that could support civilization and government. Confucianism set the order for one's family and cited its application to all of life from the individual person to the government of a country. Confucianism spread to many countries whose peoples were on their own drive toward order in civilization and government. Today, Confucianism demonstrates its influence in ancestor worship, filial piety, and virtues such as honesty, hard work, generosity, and obedience—all found in the underlying beliefs of many Asian Pacific Islanders.

In India, Hinduism and later Buddhism collectively organized and institutionalized the many spirits and supreme beings into a pantheon of gods and goddesses that flowed from within and without. Hinduism's concepts of fate and rebirth, of the god spirit within, formed the basis for Asian fatalism.

Christianity and Islam brought individuality, self-sacrifice, and a trip to heaven for those who accept and fully embrace the monotheistic god. These values and approaches embody the part of Asians that do not want to be collectivist or pressured by the group. Western religions also were used geopolitically, as nations found it advantageous to ally with Western countries and their missionaries against rivals both internally and externally. Many immigrants also have found that by accepting Western religions, they can speed up their resettlement and acculturation goals.

Lum (1996) found that given the philosophical and sometimes radically different concepts behind Asian religions, spirituality, and philosophies, it was not unusual to find many Asian Pacific Islanders without religious affiliations in the United States. He speculated that Asian Pacific Islander families may have Buddhist, Taoist, and Confucianist backgrounds, but may not go to "church" and may consider spirituality to be a personal philosophy of existence that provides meaning and purpose.

POWER

From a human service practitioner standpoint, analysis and understanding of power issues within a society or civilization are essential in determining helping modalities and intervention strategies. Asian Pacific Islanders brought with them the concepts, issues, and structures of power from their homelands to the United States. They encountered new concepts, issues, and structures, losing some of the old ones along the road to acculturation. They also created new concepts, issues, and structures in response to their own situations. Given the depth and breadth of the Asian Pacific Islander communities, only generalities can be discussed here; the reader is advised to explore these topics in greater depth.

What Did They Bring with Them?

As discussed in the religion and spirituality section, some beliefs were by their nature oppressive, including the male chauvinistic beliefs of Confucianism. Some beliefs were structured as such to accommodate, perhaps even rationalize, class structures and exploitation (Hindu caste system). And some thought systems allowed for acceptance of all situations, oppressive or not, exploitive or not (Hinduism, Buddhism, Taoism). Asian Pacific Islanders also brought traditional concepts of power including wealth and privilege. In the 20th century, Asian Pacific Islander refugees were fleeing authoritarian and communist governments and the various power issues associated with political systems.

In the first wave of immigration to the United States, many of the Asian Pacific Islanders were the poor and unprivileged in their own countries. Oppressed at home by the powerful (wealthy and class structure), they sought their fortunes in a new world. Those who attained positions of power within immigrant groups in the United States included the educated; the senior members in terms of class, family/clan, or caste; and those who were first to accumulate wealth or power in America. Those who came first exploited those who came later. But, White capitalists who needed their cheap labor exploited most who came.

Those coming to America had to learn the social, economic, and political systems here and decide how they wanted to participate. In the early wave of immigration,

Asian Pacific Islanders were oppressed by racism and exploited for their labor. Their only recourse to escape the exploitation was to develop their own economic endeavors including small businesses. The existing White power structure tried to suppress their businesses by zoning laws, taxes, and prohibitions against land ownership.

As Asian Pacific Islanders became more acculturated, they began to get involved with and participate in the political system as a means to fight against racism and to protect their rights. Some of these early efforts included labor organizing among the early Chinese railroad workers and cooperative efforts among the Japanese-American farmers. Today's power, oppression, and exploitation scheme is more complex, and the actions within more subtle. Many Asian Pacific Islanders feel there is a glass ceiling that prevents them from advancement and promotion, but this glass ceiling cannot be shown as overtly racist and discriminatory. Politically, Asian Pacific Islanders have enjoyed substantial gains, with a number of Asian Pacific Islanders in elected positions throughout the country, but still not in numbers proportional to their population. Some of this lack of political representation may be attributed to the noncitizen status of immigrant populations.

Oppression and exploitation within Asian Pacific Islander communities continues to exist as wealthier immigrants exploit poor immigrants for their labor in sweatshops, restaurants, and other businesses. Gender exploitation was discussed earlier. Within Asian Pacific Islander families, those holding onto traditional cultures and the power associated with those beliefs are struggling against those who are acculturating or have acculturated.

Resiliency

Asian Pacific Islander cultural beliefs may have a substantial impact on the ability of Asian Pacific Islanders to withstand overt racism and discrimination. According to Greene (2002):

> Culture is a potential protective mechanism and may contribute to resilience, binding a group together and offering a set of norms and values that assist people in facing stress, how to raise resilient children in an oppressive society. Cultural clashes can also detract from resiliency. Western, particularly American, culture promotes individualistic and material, consumerist values that sometimes clash with Asian Pacific Islander culture and values. (p. 246)

Educating children to have a positive racial, ethnic, and personal identity can promote resiliency to racism and discrimination. Asian Pacific Islander cultural beliefs include a long history of advanced civilization, which challenged Western concepts of superiority based on technology. This allowed some Asian Pacific Islanders to withstand significant racism. In many cases, Asian Pacific Islander groups stood up for their rights, not accepting the racist belief that theirs was an inferior race. Asian Pacific Islander spiritual beliefs allowed for accommodation and integration rather than exclusiveness and superiority (Hinduism, Buddhism). Some Asian Pacific Islander groups found acceptance and resiliency by adopting Christianity and allying with Christian groups for protection.

Many Asian Pacific Islander families, placing high values on education, economic success, and community/ethnic cohesion, have been able to use the family values and role models of philosophies such as Confucianism to focus on goals and achieve them. The greater the ability of the family to maintain its positive cultural traits, the more it was likely that the family would achieve successes.

Knowing

Since the Asian Pacific Islander group is so diverse, it would be difficult to singularize how Asian Pacific Islander peoples perceive knowing, believing, thinking, feeling, and behaving. Those Asian Pacific Islanders who subscribe to Buddhist and Hindu thought might be taught that the world is illusory and transcendental, but they continue to live and work in a concrete manner. Some Asian Pacific Islanders may have an amalgamation of different thought and spiritual systems, using elements from many sources to explain or justify various life events. Asian Pacific Islanders also have been influenced by imported religions such as Christianity and Islam, and sometimes they have accepted Western ideas, such as the belief that individuals can determine their own future. As acculturation increases, Asian Pacific Islander ideas become more influenced by the culture and communities in which they reside, but there may not be a wholesale abandonment of old ways of thinking and a wholesale adoption of new ways of thinking. Again, it is important to learn as much as possible from the client while at the same time keeping fully aware of one's own beliefs and ways of knowing, thinking, feeling, and behaving. The basic challenge to the human service practitioner is to discover these aspects of clients without stereotyping or categorizing the clients.

CULTURAL INFLUENCES AND CULTURAL CHOICES

A key factor in the cultural influences and choices for Asian Pacific Islanders is level of acculturation. Each wave of immigration brings an acculturation level that in time and by generation changes and increases. It is important to note that the terms *assimilation* and *acculturation,* though often used interchangeably, are different politically. Assimilation from a political perspective implies that a racial or ethnic group will be completely absorbed into another group. Acculturation means learning about and adopting elements of cultures from other groups. Early usage of the term *assimilation* seemed to imply that eventually the minority group would disappear culturally, ethnically, and racially. *Acculturation* can mean retaining one's own culture while learning the culture of another. For purposes of this chapter, acculturation is used, and we assume that individuals can have multiple cultures.

In the 1970s, Stanley and Derald Sue (1973) developed a conceptual scheme that divided Chinese Americans into three typological characters: the "traditionalist," the "marginal man," and the "Asian American." The Sues' scheme was to follow the response of Chinese Americans to pressures to conform to parental values or rebel against parental values. Those who conformed and adopted Chinese values were typecast as "traditionalist." Those who rebelled and adopted Western values were "marginal." And those who rebelled and developed "Asian-American" values were typed as "Asian American."

In Lee's (1996) study of Asian-American high school students, she found that Asian-American students categorized themselves into three subgroups: Asian, Asian American, and new wave. The Asian groups were foreign-born or newly arrived students. Within the Asian group, some identified ethnically (Korean), and not as the generic Asian. Koreans in the study held their ethnicity as Koreans as their chief identity above any acculturation categories such as Asian, Asian American, and new wave.

Asian students were immigrants who held their parents' cultural values but did not identify racism as a problem. Asian Americans (immigrants who had been in the United States since childhood or for five years or more) were like the Asian-identified students in cultural values but expressed a political consciousness including the need to fight racism. New wavers were Asian immigrant students who were the antithesis of the "Asian model minority"; they did not see education as key to success in the United States. For the Asian new wavers, the most important thing was social acceptance from their new wave peers.

Bankston and Zhou (2000) studied Vietnamese and Laotian high school students at two high schools and found that acculturation levels were a factor in academic achievement. Students who maintained their parents' Asian culture did better in school than those who embraced American youth music and gang-member or rock-star fashions.

Lee (1997) typed five categories of Asian-American families as follows:

1. Traditional family—all members born and raised in Asian countries
2. Cultural conflict family—parents and grandparents holding traditional beliefs, with children and grandchildren having more Western perspectives
3. Bicultural family—acculturated parents born in Asia or America
4. Americanized family—parents and children born in the United States and having little understanding of Asian culture
5. Interracial family—Asian American intermarried with another Asian American or with someone outside the Asian-American group

With global telecommunications shrinking the world through television, movies, and the Internet, people all over the world are learning about other cultures and integrating what they learn within their own cultures. Today's immigrants to the United States are far more acculturated to Western ways than the first 19th-century immigrants. While these characterizations may help develop insight into the dynamics of cultures, cultural influences, and cultural choices, they also can be a tempting shortcut to stereotyping and can cause the human service practitioner to miss important aspects of acculturation and family dynamics and interactions both within the culture and external to the culture. Human service practitioners do need to build a construct of a family from scratch, using as much information that is available directly from clients as possible. Acculturation is so complex that a simple tool such as a matrix might be helpful to provoke thought (but not to use for categorizing or prejudging individuals or groups). (See Table 16.6.)

Table 16.6 | The Acculturation Matrix

	Place of Birth	Education Place and Level	Economic Status and Place of Residence	Experiences with Other Groups
Mostly monocultural	Old country	Old country and low or moderate education	Old country and low or moderate income	Little or none
Bicultural	Old country with early age immigration	Old country with early age immigration and moderate to high education	Old country with early age immigration and moderate to high income	Moderate to high
Multicultural	New country	New country and moderate to high education	New country and moderate to high income	High

EFFECTS OF STEREOTYPES AND ONGOING STEREOTYPING

Stereotyping helps people explain things in a manner that fits in with their general understanding of the world, society, and differences between people. Its allure is that it explains things that are foreign and different, and it resonates with limited observations of and experiences with people from other cultures. There are both positive and negative stereotypes, but both are equally misleading and sometimes harmful. Gonzales (as cited in Lum, 1996) listed the following five major characteristics of stereotyping that can create problems for the person who is stereotyping and the person who is stereotyped:

1. Self-fulfilling
2. Selective perception
3. Negative and supports prejudice
4. Result in rejection and social isolation
5. Based on isolated characteristics of a group that may or may not be true

Positive and Negative Stereotypes

During the anti-Chinese fervor of the 19th century, Chinese were continually described as heathen (non-Christian), morally inferior, savage, childlike, depraved and lustful, as well as excellent docile and compliant workers. The positive stereotypes were used to justify the recruitment and immigration of large numbers of workers, while the negative stereotypes were used to press for their eventual exclusion. The current positive stereotype of Chinese and other Asians includes smart, well-mannered, respectful, industrious, well-educated, and of a monied class. The negative stereotype includes unfair economic competitors (business or labor), primitive or feudal behaviors, and unrestrained population growth. Asian Pacific Islander groups have been labeled with classist stereotypes such as having large numbers live under the same roof, having too many children, and being too cheap. Other negative stereotypes include consumption of pets (dogs and cats) and unsophisticated behavior (cooking over open fires or in fireplaces). Some stereotypes mirror ones directed toward other racial groups, such as welfare dependence (refugees) and youth gang activity. Wu (2002) described the continual negative stereotyping of Asian Pacific Islanders as maintaining them as "perpetual foreigners."

With the fall of the Soviet Union in the early 1990s, communist China became the number one external threat, and Chinese Americans came under increasing suspicion of espionage and sabotage. An American nuclear lab scientist, Wen Ho Lee, was detained for a year, accused of but not charged with giving nuclear weapon secrets to the Chinese. He was finally released after a plea bargain that amounted to an admission of improper handling of classified materials and a sentence of time served. Assaults and murders against Asian Pacific Islanders continue, and hate crimes are common. Vincent Chin was beaten to death by two White Detroit autoworkers in the 1980s who blamed him for the decline of the American automobile industry. The perpetrators received a sentence of two months' probation and $3,780 in fines (Wu, 2002).

These two cases illustrate a continuation of the long history of racism against Asian Pacific Islanders. Since 9/11, several South Asians have been murdered, and racial profiling and hate crimes against South Asians are on the rise.

APPLICATION OF MULTIDIMENSIONAL CONTEXTUAL PRACTICE FRAMEWORK

Client Well-Being and the Multidimensional Contextual Client

The multidimensional contextual practice framework guides the human service practitioner to investigate the concept of "client well-being" from a physical, mental, social, spiritual, and emotional/cognitive perspective. For Asian Pacific Islander populations, the concept of "client well-being" may involve the integration of physical well-being, socioeconomic well-being, emotional/cognitive well-being, and spiritual/philosophical well-being.

For those Asian Pacific Islanders who have Confucianist values, the well-being of the family is directly related to the adherence of the individuals to filial responsibilities. If individuals have any physical, mental, or emotional problems, they can be related to their failure to fully honor their family responsibilities (Jung, 1998). From a spiritual standpoint (which is often coexistent with the philosophical), any disturbance or imbalance in nature (Tao or Dao) or the energy of life can result in health or emotional problems. Other spiritual perspectives view problems in life as fate, karma, suffering from craving, and so on (Hinduism, Buddhism).

Acculturation plays a large role in how all of these systems integrate. The more acculturated individuals, their families, and their communities are, the more some conflicts disappear and others appear. These conflicts may be internal to individuals and families or external in community systems. The classic conflicts include youth versus older generations, American-born versus immigrant, educated versus uneducated, feudal thinking versus modern thinking, and so on. These conflicts may appear as adherence to or distancing from the philosophical (Confucianism) and disturbance in nature (humans over nature).

Identities are formed and reformed through the acculturation process and links with the ethnic cultures and homelands. Immigration is the lifeblood of the ethnic identity forming process. While acculturation and immigration may speed up the construction, deconstruction, and reconstruction process, world globalization and today's modern telecommunications allow the process to occur in any country.

Micro, Meso, Macro, and Magna

Basic social theories introduce the "systems" approach and the "person in the environment" client assessment. The micro, meso, macro, and magna interaction and exchange factors fully utilize this approach and seem to have a natural fit when applied to Asian Pacific Islanders. However, when viewing the client and the client's systems for Asian Pacific Islanders, it may be useful to start with the magna-spiritual interaction and exchange factors rather than taking the usual approach of starting with the micro-interpersonal.

Traditional Asian Pacific Islander thought can be applied to how it influences people as they develop, starting with childhood. What are clients' magna-spiritual and philosophical connections that influenced their upbringing, their future outlook on themselves and life? How does the acculturation factor influence clients' connection to the traditional Asian Pacific Islander thought and value systems? How recent is the past as compared to the present? For a people with a long history of both migration and internal/external influences, Asian Pacific Islanders have an eclecticism about their spiritual world. In the Asian Pacific Islander world, it is possible to have Christian and Buddhist beliefs, Confucian and Taoist philosophies, and fatalistic and self-deterministic views. With the numerous combinations possible, it is very important to learn as much as possible about an Asian Pacific Islander's magna world (about the person's amalgamated philosophy and spirituality) directly from the client.

From a long view of Asian Pacific Islander history, the picture is not much different from that in Europe or the Middle East: There are similar elements of social, civil, and political unrest, as well as wars and economic pressures. The histories of all these areas influence today's current events and conflicts. Koreans and Vietnamese in the United States today fiercely maintain their ethnic identities. Their cultures have had a history of maintaining identity given their long struggles with Chinese and Japanese dominance. But social, economic, and political struggles are far more compressed in today's world of high speed and instant communication, with the vast amounts of knowledge and learning that people absorb. For example, U.S. history is about 300 years old from the colonial period to world superpower. That is equivalent to a single average dynasty in a number of Asian countries, or approximately the time it took for Pacific Islander people to sail and settle the entire Pacific. Now Asian Pacific Islanders in the United States acculturate almost within a single generation. Young Chinese village men immigrating to the United States in the early 20th century were driving cars and wearing Western clothing within a few short years, even though in their entire lives in their villages, they had never seen a car or a Westerner. Today's refugee youth may graduate as valedictorians when only a few years earlier they were in a squalid camp in some border area. American foreign and immigration policy, immigrant and refugee health and social services programs, civil rights and education programs all contribute to the macro-environmental factors. The practitioner should be ready to engage with the client the macro policy issues that influence and define the client's world.

Other macro-environmental factors for the Asian Pacific Islander include physical cultural communities. These communities are the Koreatowns, Chinatowns, Little Indias, Japantowns, Little Vietnams and Saigons, Manilatowns, Little Samoas, and other ethnic communities. People gather in these communities because they provide commerce and culture. In the past, Asian Pacific Islanders were forced to live in these communities because they were not allowed to live elsewhere or because these communities provided protection against the blatant racism of the day.

Social, business, religious, political, cultural, and community organizations are important systems for Asian Pacific Islanders. Clanlike and regionally oriented, Cantonese immigrants formed their first family, social, and fraternal organizations in the 19th century when they first arrived in the United States. These organizations provided traveler's aid services, mechanisms for accumulating capital, and forums for settling disputes. The strongest of these organizations later formed an umbrella coalition known as the "Six Companies," or the Chinese Consolidated Benevolent Association, that continues its existence today. Japanese in the United States formed the Japanese American Citizens League (JACL) after World War I to fight for the civil rights of Asians in the United States. During the Great Depression, the Filipino Social Relief Service in Los Angeles handed out free meals to destitute Pilipinos (Takaki, 1989). Refugees formed Indochinese Mutual Assistance Associations to write and obtain grants to provide resettlement services. The Korean American Coalition and the Korean American Grocers' Association organized boycotts against anti-Asian rap music in early 1990s (Chang, 1994). South Asians in the Hindu Temple of Chicago formed the youth organization In the Wings to provide for youth activities and programs (Bacon, 1996). This is not an extensive list; there are many more organizations for an even wider variety of purposes than can be listed here. The practitioner, using the client as a guide, can assess if the client is involved or needs to be involved with any such organizations, and to what extent and for what purpose.

On the meso-interpersonal level, not only is the communication between and among individuals and groups important, but so also is the structure and hierarchy of relationships. The Confucian construct of obedience to the male and to the elders, as ancient and feudal as it is, continues to have an important influence on many Asian Pacific Islanders today. While a third- or fourth-generation Asian Pacific Islander may not subscribe to such beliefs, they may respect and honor them if their parents or grandparents hold them. It is possible that many Asian Pacific Islanders have a duality of thought that rejects chauvinist elements but maintains some of Confucianism.

Relationships with religious/spiritual leadership may vary among Asian Pacific Islanders. Those who have Western religious beliefs (Christianity, Judaism, Islam) may view their religious leaders as "activists" who may espouse efforts toward the community good. Those with Eastern beliefs (Hinduism, Buddhism, Taoism) may see their religious leaders as moral exemplars to emulate (LaFave, n.d.).

Asian Pacific Islander concepts of relationships with employers are complex and have multiple factors. Many Asian Pacific Islanders own small businesses, and family members (nuclear and extended) work in these businesses. In such businesses, a Confucian-like hierarchy of family relationships may govern the employee-employer relationships. Japanese corporate (Zaibatsu) culture takes paternalistic care of employees from date of hire until mandatory retirement (lifetime employment). Major cultural differences among employees and management styles were found in a study of Japanese and American autoworkers at Japanese automobile plants in the United States (Rhody, 1995). Cultural stereotypes such as Asians being "quiet" and "passive" were cited in a study of South Asian engineers and the lack career advancement ("glass ceiling barrier") in the San Francisco Bay area (Fernandez, 1998). An Asian Pacific Islander may expect to be automatically promoted by demonstrating hard work and outstanding performance rather than being aggressive and requesting a promotion. Asian Pacific Islanders may carry cultural traits and beliefs into the workplace that, depending on the workplace, may be harmonious with it or not.

In considering how to define someone who has an Asian Pacific Islander world-view, the person may be better understood if defined as part of a family, a group, and a community. In that context, is the person in harmony or in conflict with these systems? A traditional Western view may suggest analyzing individuals and how they feel in regard to their world, community, family and nuclear relationships, and themselves. The Western view may be that if the people are in conflict with their systems, then they may be in conflict with themselves. This inward look can lead to typecasting individuals as dysfunctional and pathological instead of considering their multiple systems as being out of balance and out of sync.

The micro-intrapersonal focus for many Asian Pacific Islanders may be their connection to the meso, macro, and magna worlds. In one sense, the circular nature of all these interaction and exchange factors fits in with Asian Pacific Islander philosophical and spiritual thinking. The closer Asian Pacific Islanders are to these thought systems, the more influenced they are in their thinking about themselves, their families, and their friends. Acculturation factors and rates determine how close or distant individual and collective thinking are to the traditional systems.

Professional Competence

According to the NASW *Standards for Cultural Competence in Social Work Practice* (2001), the practitioner should function according to the ethics and values of the profession, develop self-awareness, attain cross-cultural knowledge and skills, and acquire knowledge of community resources and services. These standards also prescribe other requirements that are advocacy- and environment-oriented, including advocacy for social policies and programs for diverse clients, a diverse workforce, professional education that advances cultural competence, language diversity, and cross-cultural leadership.

Meeting the NASW standards requires a major and continuing commitment from human service practitioners. Confronting one's own prejudices and biases requires personal insight and courage. A referral of a client is appropriate when human service practitioners find that their own limitations may be detrimental to client well being. Learning another's culture and the skills needed to work with culture requires direct experience with that culture and cultural informants/experts. When Southeast Asian refugees arrived in the United States, few practitioners knew about their culture and how to work with them. Some of the most successful training experiences included the teaming or pairing of practitioners with refugees for mutual education and support.

Multidimensional Contextual Service

Asian Pacific Islanders have a history of adopting new thought and integrating it into a new perception of reality or worldview. The inclusion of Hindu and Buddhist thought in Southeast Asia, the absorption of Buddhism into Hinduism, the acceptance of Tao and Confucianism—conflicting thoughts, but coexisting in the same world—all demonstrate the Asian Pacific Islander's ability and willingness to receive, share, and integrate multiple thought and spiritual systems. Coupled with the migratory and immigrant nature of many of the peoples, the Asian Pacific Islander lives in a multidimensional and contextual world that makes multidimensional contextual services particularly appropriate. Human services agencies and professionally competent (often bilingual and bicultural or multilingual and multicultural) staff form the bridge and act as translators in a service scheme that may be unlike those to which Asian Pacific Islanders are accustomed.

Agency or organization-based services may be appropriate for some Asian Pacific Islander populations and are often represented as health-related or benefits-related services. Aside from advocating for additional funding for culturally competent, community-based services, another issue of concern is whether a multiethnic agency or a single-ethnic–based agency would be more appropriate to serve the community (Lum, 1999). Although the decision about whether to institute multi- or single-ethnic programs or services is usually a financial and political one, practice issues revolve around adequacy of staff to serve a multiethnic and multigenerational population, as well as people with multiple levels of acculturation.

Skills for Addressing Challenges and Strengths

Self-awareness of ethnicity and diverse cultures has been mentioned as a key skill in working with diverse populations (Jung, 1998; Lum, 1999; NASW, 2001). This may be a challenge for Asian Pacific Islander practitioners brought up in cultures that emphasize the family, the collective, and the community first and who may start by focusing on the Asian Pacific Islander client or family instead of focusing on one's self.

During the helping process, practitioners need to take into consideration cultural influences reflected in clients' values and behaviors as well as clients' perceptions and beliefs regarding their living conditions, support systems, resources, strengths, and challenges. Human service practitioners, however, need prior knowledge, education, and training to make these identifications and assessments. The challenge is to attain this information before starting work with clients. Some (Greene, Jensen, & Harper Jones, 1999; Lum, 1996) suggest that this identification of cultural values, acculturation, and other factors could come from the clients themselves. However, human service practitioners need to be able to evaluate this client-provided information within the context of cross-cultural or transcultural frameworks to allow for a proper assessment.

Integration of cultural values in a problem-solving approach has been identified as being important in working with Asian Pacific Islanders (Jung, 1998; Lum, 1999). Lee (as cited in Jung, 1998) believes this includes supporting the hierarchical structure of the family or community, accepting the roles of authority figures, and acting the role of expert and educator. The challenge to this approach is accepting cultural values that may be in conflict with one's own values. For example, Confucianism is a male chauvinist feudal philosophy, which many practitioners would have difficulty supporting, yet these values may be integral to the client and the client's family.

Jung's (1998) keys to a successful start in working with Chinese-American families include giving a good first impression by "socializing" with clients. He suggests meeting in nontraditional places in which clients feel comfortable, such as restaurants and public places. It requires substantial skill to carefully guard practitioner-client boundaries when utilizing this technique. In conducting helping sessions not in Western-style private offices but instead in family homes, restaurants, and parks, the practitioner needs a substantial ability to focus and to keep the client focused.

Jung (1998) suggests that Chinese-American families expect therapy to be brief. This would require the human service practitioner to quickly become accepted, to identify problems jointly, and to work on resolutions that are feasible in the short term. This challenges the practitioner to identify work that will be helpful and somewhat long-lasting that can be undertaken in a brief period of time.

Another challenge to human service practitioners is to learn about indigenous beliefs and healing practices as another means to help clients. Understanding how clients respond to native or indigenous healing techniques and Western methods is extremely complicated. An Asian Pacific Islander client who is adaptive might accept both traditional and new healing techniques, depending on what works. If neither works, then the client might fall back on philosophical thoughts (fatalism, suffering, etc.). For example, one practice of some Asian Pacific Islanders is "feng shui" or geomancy. A human service practitioner cannot expect to become an expert in feng shui, but it would be important to find out if the client has some belief in it and whether the client relates any problems to bad feng shui. If this were the case, the social service practitioner would need a consultation from a feng shui expert to determine if its application would be useful or not.

An example of native healing practices is "ho'oponopono," a native Hawaiian family-based conflict resolution process. This process uses existing hierarchical roles, shared culture, role expectations, authority figures, sanctions, and consensual agreement (Hurdle, 2002). The challenge for the practitioner is not only in learning about this practice and whether the client believes in this practice, but also in addressing issues such as confidentiality and any negative aspects such as male chauvinism.

One dimension in which Asian Pacific Islanders are building their strength is political power. Historically, Asian Pacific Islander immigrant generations have been severely discriminated against, and often this discrimination was organized, political, and institutional. Consequently, help-seeking behaviors have been internalized to their own communities and influenced by a basic mistrust of government. Increasing political power is a proven means to developing more culturally appropriate services. Asian Pacific Islanders, like many immigrants, do not vote in numbers that represent their populations, largely due to citizenship issues and unfamiliarity with the American political system. A human service practitioner advocating for more funding for Asian Pacific Islander services may find involving the client to be helpful both to the client and to the effort. However, the practitioner must determine if the client is comfortable with and able to take on such a role.

CASE STUDY

A family of Japanese ancestry is having difficulty with the care of the 88-year-old grandmother. The extended family consists of and has experienced the following:

- The grandmother, a widow for twenty-five years, was born in the United States but educated in Japan as a child (Kibei).
- There are four adult children, all baby boomers who were born in the United States. The oldest is male, retired, and married with three adult children (two females and one male) and one grandchild. The next eldest is a sister, married with two adult children (two males), who is taking care of her elderly mother-in-law. The next sister is divorced, with two adult children (male and female). The youngest sister (ten years younger than the second sister) is married with two teenage children. The three sisters work, but only the youngest sister has a dual-income household with her husband working.
- The grandmother and her three oldest children (male and two females) all suffered through the World War II internment camp experience, having been forcibly relocated for five years. After the camp experience, the family relocated to another state instead of returning to California.
- The grandfather, deceased for twenty-five years, had a rocky and difficult relationship with the grandmother toward the end of his life, and the conflict alienated the children from their parents.
- The grandmother, although educated (high school) and a fluent English speaker, does not drive and depends substantially on her children to take care of her.

For the past twenty-five years, the youngest sister has arranged for the care of the grandmother, moving the grandmother every time her family moved. The relationship is not one of love, but of obligation. As the grandmother has aged and become more debilitated, the stress of care has increased, and outside in-home care workers have been brought in to maintain the grandmother's independent living. All the places that the grandmother has lived have had senior services, including meals-on-wheels, transportation, socialization, and adult day care programs (some culturally competent), but the grandmother has refused to participate in these programs, preferring to have her family prepare her meals and to watch television as her principal pastime activity. The grandmother has been eligible for many public benefit programs, but has not applied, preferring family care. The grandmother is resistant to and critical of the in-home care by strangers and really wants her daughter to care for her full-time. The daughter resents the increased demands on her time, as well as her grandmother's attitude and criticisms. This daughter finally has concluded she can no longer care for the grandmother, but she has found her siblings to be incapable or unwilling to assume the care.

Reflection on Case

In this case, the multidimensional contextual practice goal is the well-being of all the persons in the family, including grandchildren and great-grandchildren. Although the family is on its fourth generation in the United States, its cultural values include remainders of Japanese filial piety, fatalism (shikata genai), and perseverance under hardship (gaman suru). Despite what seems to be a large extended family (twenty-two people), only the youngest adult daughter has been willing (to this point) to assume responsibility for full care of the grandmother. In a traditional Japanese family with Confucian values, the oldest adult son would have assumed the role of patriarch when the grandfather passed away. However, the grandmother broke with those values a decade earlier when she chose not to ask her son to assume care for her. The grandmother also has personality characteristics that annoy or bother others, including obsessiveness (with small details, noise, privacy) and an inability to express gratitude and love.

The multidimensional contextual practice perspective would consider the following factors:

- Magna—What are the religious, philosophical, and spiritual beliefs of the family, and how are they supportive or not supportive? In this case, Confucianist values are conflicted, and some family members have a high tolerance for suffering.
- Macro—If adequate support services and programs are available, why haven't they been accepted?
- Meso—What are communications like within and among the family? Could any outside, culturally appropriate counselors or advisers be brought in to help?
- Micro—What factors have influenced the grandmother and her adult children's thinking? Was there an acculturation process prior to the camp experience? And what happened postcamp in terms of help for this family that was so traumatized? Was any help accepted, given the tolerance for suffering and privacy cultural factors? Given the conflicts and breaks with old world values and beliefs, would a culturally competent professional be helpful? Given the availability of culturally appropriate and competent services, why haven't they been called into service? What would be the ideal multidimensional contextual service for this family, and how would the family be engaged to utilize it?

Multidimensional contextual practice does not provide answers but rather a broad framework from which to examine the multiple issues and levels of issues surrounding a client and the client's family and community. There are no canned or rote solutions. Each case must be considered on its own, based in large portion on information provided by the client. Not all solutions are complete and multifaceted. In this case study, the second daughter eventually relocated the grandmother and assumed care responsibilities (in the home, with no outside help). This was the grandmother's second choice and left a broken relationship with the youngest daughter who, until then, had been providing all the care.

The multidimensional contextual practice framework should be strongly considered for many Asian Pacific Islander clients because of its whole view, its integrative approach. The multidimensional contextual practice framework reminds and guides human service practitioners as to the many elements that are crucial to understanding Asian Pacific Islanders.

Discussion Questions

1. How does one learn about so many groups (and become culturally competent)?
2. Spiritual concepts of Asian Pacific Islanders are integrative and adaptive, and in many cases depend on the spiritual level or stage of the individual. Can the human service practitioner apply any of the standard knowledge of Asian Pacific Islander philosophy, spirituality, or religion when it may vary greatly from one individual to the next?
3. A constructivist approach could be helpful when dealing with great diversity and a lack of foreknowledge about a client's culture. Can this approach work when it requires the client to provide substantial information and the client views the human service practitioner as the expert?
4. Multidimensional contextual practice is already complex. How can a human service practitioner consider all of these factors including an acculturation factor for each member of the family?
5. A multidimensional contextual practice framework suggests that the human service practitioner review old world religious, spiritual, and philosophical beliefs, yet a client may be many generations removed from these beliefs or the beliefs may have been forgotten or completely adulterated by outside cultures. Can a review of these beliefs still be useful?
6. Who is and where does one find the best cultural informant outside of the client system?

References

Aubry, L. (1993). Black-Korean American relations: An insider's viewpoint. In E. T. Chang & R. C. Leong (Eds.), *Los Angeles—Struggles toward multiethnic community: Asian American, African American, and Latino perspectives* (pp. 149–160). Seattle: University of Washington Press.

Background note: Cambodia. (1996). Retrieved July 14, 2002, from the U.S. Department of State Web site at: http://www.state.gov/r/pa/ei/bgn/2732.htm.

Bacon, J. (1996). *Lifelines: Community, family, and assimilation among Asian Indian immigrants.* New York: Oxford University Press.

Balls Organista, P., Organista, K. C., & Soloff, P. R. (1999). Exploring AIDS-related knowledge, attitudes, and behaviors of female Mexican migrant workers. In P. L. Ewalt, E. M. Freeman, A. E. Fortune, D. L. Poole, & S. L. Witkin (Eds.), *Multicultural issues in social work* (pp. 519–529). Washington, DC: NASW Press.

Bankston, C. L., & Zhou, M. (2000). De facto congregationalism and socioeconomic mobility in Laotian and Vietnamese immigrant communities: A study of religious institutions and economic change. *Review of Religious Research, 41*(4): 454–471.

Barnes, J. S., & Bennett, C. E. (2002). *The Asian population: 2000, census 2000 brief.* Washington, DC: U.S. Government Printing Office.

Bunge, F. M., & Cooke, M. W. (1984). *Oceania, a regional study.* Washington, DC: U.S. Government Printing Office.

Bush, C. T. (2000). Cultural competence: Implications of the surgeon general's report on mental health. *Journal of Child and Adolescent Psychiatric Nursing.* Retrieved July 17, 2002, from the Yahoo Premium Document Search database.

Chang, J. (1994). Race, class, conflict and empowerment: On Ice Cube's "black Korea." In E. T. Chang & R. C. Leong (Eds.), *Los Angeles—Struggles toward multiethnic community: Asian American, African American, and Latino perspectives* (pp. 87–107). Seattle: University of Washington Press.

Chen, A., Meng, Y. Y., Kunwar, P., Suh, D., Bau, I., Tom, H., et al. (1997). *The health status of Asian and Pacific Islander Americans in California.* Woodland Hills: The California Endowment and the California Healthcare Foundation.

DuBarry, W. T., Chan, W. T., & Watson, B. (1970). *Sources of Chinese tradition* (Vol. 1). New York: Columbia University Press.

De Mente, B. L. (1996). *NTC's dictionary of China's cultural code words*. Lincolnwood: NTC Publishing Group.

Dhooper, S. S., & Moore, S. E. (2001). *Social work with culturally diverse people*. Thousand Oaks, CA: Sage.

Fernandez, M. (1998). Asian Indian Americans in the Bay Area and the glass ceiling. *Sociological Perspectives*. Retrieved July 20, 2002, from the Yahoo Premium Document Search database.

Greene, G. J., Jensen, C., & Harper Jones, D. (1999). A constructivist perspective on clinical social work practice with ethnically diverse clients. In P. L. Ewalt, E. M. Freeman, A. E. Fortune, D. L. Poole, & S. L. Witkin (Eds.), *Multicultural issues in social work* (pp. 3–16). Washington, DC: NASW Press.

Greene, R. R. (2002). *Resiliency, an integrated approach to policy and practice*. Washington, DC: NASW Press.

Gregory, R. (2001). *Dreaming the economics of an independent Hawai'i*. Retrieved July 14, 2002, from Institute for Advancement of Hawaiian Affairs Web site: http://www.opihi.com/sovereignty/r_gregory.htm.

Grieco, E. M. (2001). *The native Hawaiian and other Pacific Islander population: 2000, Census 2000 brief*. Washington, DC: U.S. Government Printing Office.

Hart, J. M. (n.d.). *Roots in the sand*. Retrieved July 16, 2002, from the Public Broadcasting Service Web site at http://www.pbs.org/rootsinthesand/.

Hong, G. K., & Domokos-Cheng Ham, M. (2001). *Psychotherapy and counseling with Asian American clients: A practical guide*. Thousand Oaks, CA: Sage.

Huer, M. B., Saenz, T. I., & Doan, J. H. D. (2001). Understanding the Vietnamese American community: Implications for training educational personnel providing services to children with disabilities. *Communications Disorders Quarterly*. Retrieved July 16, 2002, from the Yahoo Premium Document Search database.

Hurdle, D. E. (2002). Native Hawaiian traditional healing: Cultural based interventions for social work practice. *Social Work, 47*, 183–192.

Jang, M. H., Lee, E., & Woo, K. (1999). Income, language and citizenship status: Factors affecting the health care access and utilization of Chinese Americans. In P. L. Ewalt, E. M. Freeman, A. E. Fortune, D. L. Poole,

& S. L. Witkin (Eds.), *Multicultural issues in social work* (pp. 654–668). Washington, DC: NASW Press.

Jung, M. (1998). *Chinese American family therapy: A new model for clinicians*. San Francisco: Jossey-Bass.

Kay, L. F. (2002). Graduation another step in Afghan's trek. Retrieved June 15, 2002, from *Los Angeles Times* Web site at: http://www.latimes.com/templates/misc/printstory.jsp?slug=la%2D000041732jun14.

LaFave, S. (n.d.). *Asian (non-Islamic) thought*. Retrieved June 15, 2002, from the West Valley College Web site at: http://www.wvmccd.cc.ca.us/wvc/ph/asian_thought.html.

Lee, E. (1997). Overview: The assessment and treatment of Asian American families. In E. Lee (Ed.), *Working with Asian Americans: A guide for clinicians*. New York: Guilford.

Lee, S. J. (1996). *Unraveling the "model minority" stereotype: Listening to Asian American youth*. New York: Teachers College Press.

Lim, H. S., & Johnson, M. M. (2001). Korean social work students' attitudes towards homosexuals. *Journal of Social Work Education, 37*, 547–552.

Liu, P., & Chan, C. S. (1996). Lesbian, gay, and bisexual Asian Americans and their families. In J. Laird & R. Greene (Eds.), *Lesbians and gays in couples and families* (pp. 137–145). San Francisco: Jossey-Bass.

Lowe, S. M., & Mascher, J. (2001). The role of sexual orientation in multicultural counseling: integrating bodies of knowledge. In J. G. Ponterotto, J. M. Casas, L. A. Suzuki, & C. M. Alexander (Eds.), *Handbook of multicultural counseling* (pp. 755–778). Thousand Oaks, CA: Sage.

Lum, D. (1996). *Social work practice and people of color* (3rd ed.). Pacific Grove, CA: Brooks/Cole.

Lum, D. (1999). *Culturally competent practice: A framework for growth and action*. Pacific Grove, CA: Brooks/Cole.

Lum, D. (2002). Social work practice with Asian Americans. In A. T. Morales & B. W. Sheafor (Eds.), *The many faces of social work clients* (pp. 213–237). Boston: Allyn & Bacon.

McLaughlin, L. A., & Braun, K. L. (1999). Asian and Pacific Islander cultural values: Considerations for health care decision making. In P. L. Ewalt, E. M. Freeman, A. E. Fortune, D. L. Poole, & S. L. Witkin (Eds.), *Multicultural issues in social work: Practice and research* (pp. 321–336). Washington, DC: NASW Press.

McNeil, J. (1997). *Americans with disabilities: Household economic studies*. Washington, DC: U.S. Census Bureau.

Milazzo-Sayre, L. J., Henderson, M. J., Manderscheid, R. W., Bokossa, M. C., Evans, C., & Male, A. A. (2000). Chapter 15, Persons treated in specialty mental health care programs, United States, 1997, in R. W. Manderscheid & M. J. Henderson (Eds.), *Mental health, United States, 2000*. Retrieved July 12, 2002, from the U.S. Substance Abuse and Mental Health Services Administration Web site at: http://www.mentalhealth.org/publications/allpubs/SMA01-3537/chp15table2.asp.

Morales, R. F. (1998). *Makibaka 2: The Pilipino American struggle*. Los Angeles: Mountainview.

National Association of Social Workers (NASW). (2001). *NASW standards for cultural competence in social work practice*. Washington, DC: NASW Press.

Newberger, E. C., & Curry, A. E. (2000). *Educational attainment in the United States (update) March 2000: Population characteristics* (Current Population Reports P-20-536). Washington, DC: U.S. Government Printing Office.

Newman, B. S., Dannenfelser, P. L., & Benishek, L. (2002). Assessing beginning social work and counseling students' acceptance of lesbians and gay men. *Journal of Social Work Education, 38,* 273–288.

Overview independent nation-state of Hawai'i. (n.d.) Retrieved July 14, 2002, from the Hawai'i—Independent and Sovereign Web site at: http://www.Hawaii-nation.org/overview.html.

Rhody, J. D. (1995). Learning from Japanese transplants and American corporations. *Public Personnel Management*. Retrieved July 20, 2002, from the Yahoo Premium Document Search database.

Shih, H. C. (n.d.). *Chinese Bhiksunis in the Ch'an tradition*. Retrieved July 17, 2002, from Web site: http://www.geocities.com/zennun12_8/chanwomen.html.

Sue, S., & Morshima, J. K. (1982). *The mental health of Asian Americans*. San Francisco: Jossey-Bass.

Sue, S., & Sue, D. W. (1973). Chinese-American personality and mental health. In S. Sue & N. N. Wagner (Eds.), *Asian Americans psychological perspectives* (pp. 111–124). Palo Alto: Science and Behavior Books.

Takaki, R. (1989). *Strangers from a different shore: A history of Asian Americans*. Boston: Little, Brown.

Tom, S., & Lin, J. (2001). Asian and Pacific Islanders with disabilities: Where do we fit in and where do we go from here? Unpublished paper presented at Asian and Pacific Islanders with Disabilities of California Facing Forward: Creating Disability Pride in Our API Communities Conference.

U.S. Census Bureau. (1998). *The Asian and Pacific Islander population in the United States: March 1997 current population survey (update)* (P20-512). Internet Release Date: June 28, 2001. Retrieved July 13, 2002, from http://www.census.gov/Press-Release/cb98-180.html.

U.S. Census Bureau. (2001a). *Profile of the foreign-born population in the United States: 2000. Current population report, special studies* (P23-206). Washington, DC: U.S. Government Printing Office.

U.S. Census Bureau. (2001b). *General demographics characteristics by race for the United States: 2000* (PHC-T-15). Internet Release Date: October 10, 2001. Retrieved July 13, 2002, from http://www.census.gov/population/www/cen2000/phc-t15.html.

U.S. Census Bureau. (2001c). *Poverty: 2000 highlights*. Retrieved June 18, 2002, from http://www.census.gov/hhes/poverty/poverty00/pov00hi.html.

U.S. Census Bureau. (2001d). *1997 economic census minority- and women-owned businesses, United States*. Retrieved June 18, 2002, from http://www.census.gov/epcd/mwb97/us/us.html.

U.S. Census Bureau. (2002). *Table H-5. Race and Hispanic origin of householder—households by median and mean income: 1967 to 2000*. Retrieved June 18, 2002, from http://www.census.gov/hhes/income/histinc/h05.html.

Williams, L. E. (1976). *Southeast Asia, a history*. New York: Oxford University Press.

Wu, F. H. (2002). *Yellow: Race in America beyond black and white*. New York: Basic Books.

Conclusion

We leave the reader with some thoughts and reflections on the fundamentals of multidimensional contextual practice. In this last part, we summarize the essentials of this book. We hope that we have caught your attention and introduced you to another way of viewing the helping field. Hopefully this text has given you many ideas for constructing a systematic way to understand and work with people in an inclusive way.

Beginnings are filled with endings.
Endings are filled with beginnings.
Possibilities are infinite.
Where can we start? —**Krishna L. Guadalupe**

17 | Conclusion

This book on multidimensional contextual practice has introduced the reader to new perspectives on learning, understanding, and working with diverse communities of people on multiple levels. In Part 1, we began by defining *multidimensional* and *contextual* and then moved toward reinterpreting human diversity themes. We shared A Framework for Human Diversity and Transcendence and offered five principles: client well-being; the multidimensional contextual client; interactions/exchanges and effects (micro, meso, macro, and magna); professional competence; and multidimensional contextual services. We also offered a perspective on the well-being of the multidimensional contextual client in terms of living in harmonious relationships and living with oppressive forces; these dynamics reinforce as well as injure the well-being of people. We focused on the practitioner's professional competence in multidimensional contextual services, emphasizing self-awareness, multiple dimensions (micro, meso, macro, and magna) affecting professional competence, ethical issues and concerns, and practices to strengthen professional competence.

In Part 2, we elaborated on issues of language and spirituality. We discussed the importance of nonstereotypical language as well as the role of spirituality within the context of human diversity. Part 3 addressed multidimensional contextual practice in terms of both general population groups—gender groups, groups with special concerns (people living with disabilities, the elderly), and sexual orientation groups (gay, lesbian, bisexual, and transgender people)—and ethnic-specific communities of people (First Nations Peoples, White Ethnic Groups, African Americans, Latinos/as, and Asian Americans, and Pacific Islanders). Finally, Part 4 concludes with this chapter, which summarizes the essential themes in the previous chapters and raises thoughts for the future of multidimensional contextual practice.

MULTIDIMENSIONAL CONTEXTUAL PRACTICE: SUMMARIES OF THEMES AND ISSUES

We started with the premise that multidimensional contextual practice honors the multiple identities of a person, family, group, and community, which reflect various facets of these entities. At the same time, the intrapersonal, interpersonal, environmental, and spiritual dimensions influence and are influenced by clients' lives and well-being. Thus, multiple identities, experiences, and multidimensional contextual exchanges are parts of the whole of a person, family, group, or community. This perspective honors the multiple ways of knowing, thinking, feeling, behaving, and being while reminding the reader that change is constant and people are not static.

In the midst of this perspective, we are aware of the need to move beyond stereotypical language, and so we have sought to redefine and reinterpret the meaning of major concepts that have been used in the multicultural/human diversity literature. Hence, we have revisited the meaning of human diversity, transcendence, ethnicity and race, culture, human commonalities, ethnocentrism, acculturation and assimilation, and oppression and its expressions of racism, sexism, homophobia, and privilege. Likewise, we have joined together various practice concepts such as client and client well-being, stereotypes and stereotyping, environment, human adversity and resilience, professional competence and the wisdom of uncertainty, mystical experiences, and language. In both instances, our goal was to move the reader toward recognizing the need for conscious change beyond what is usual and accepted, and toward a new dimension of understanding human diversities, commonalities, and complexities while honoring the wisdom of uncertainty.

We have offered the multidimensional contextual practice framework as a means of conceptualizing an approach that can be useful in helping us transcend our stereotypic thinking. To this end, we discussed the meaning of honoring, yet moving beyond, conventional realities/consciousness and toward transcendent realities/consciousness, even esoteric/mystical spiritual experiences. Moving beyond our senses helps us humbly acknowledge that knowledge is not always certain and that understanding involves ambiguity and respect for life, people, and experiences. The framework is spherical, circular, and interactive and involves five principles:

- **Client well-being** is the primary integrative theme. It focuses on the positive, healthy functioning of the person, family, group, or community.
- Individuals, families, groups, and communities are **multidimensional contextual entities** that are constantly changing and interacting with each other. We must reconstruct our understanding of situations in order to determine which entities influence a helping situation at any given time.
- Client well-being affects and is affected by **micro-intrapersonal, meso-interpersonal, macro-environmental, and magna-spiritual interactions and exchanges,** which must be identified and mobilized in order to address interrelated issues.
- **The social/health/human services practitioner's professional competence** is strengthened through ongoing self-awareness and self-evaluation, assessment, a continuum of contact and intervention, as well as primary, secondary, and tertiary interconnections.

- **Multidimensional contextual services** promote, strengthen, and reinforce both individual and collective well-being. Such services rely on community and resource understanding, relevant agency programs, professional expertise, and client-professional as well as interprofessional relationships.

Multidimensional Contextual Client Well-Being

We made the case that people have basic needs and commonalities—such as meaningful relationships, individual and collective identities, community and societal changes, search for the meaning of self, cultural interactions, coping skills for interpersonal and spiritual concerns, and other potentials and strengths—and that honoring these multiple identities and diverse experiences can assist the practitioner in enhancing the well-being of individuals, families, groups, and communities. We discussed variables affecting the multiple self: individual-collective and social-cultural influences and choices, constructed meanings, historical times and contexts, socioeconomic-political experiences, biopsychosocial strengths and challenges, interpretations of internalized experiences, and the magna-spiritual. At the same time, we addressed the oppressive forces that affect individual and collective well-being, including sexism, racism, homophobia, ageism, classism, discrimination based on physical and mental disabilities, geographical colonialism, cultural imperialism, linguistic imperialism, and empirical imperialism. We stressed that these oppressive forces are multifaceted.

Furthermore, we recognized human resilience as strengthening endurance and being integrally related to client well-being. We defined resilience as an innate essence and as the ability to maintain, recover, or regain after adversity. We pointed to examples of individual and relational resilience in terms of historical figures, kinship networks, spiritual practices, and grassroots movements.

Practitioner Competence and Multidimensional Contextual Services

We made the case for practitioner competence and used the metaphor of the interplay of lights and shadows of services to help the reader rethink the concepts of competence and services. Lights and shadows refer to personal and professional patterns of interactions that can assist or injure clients in the name of professionalism. We started by observing that the cultivation and maintenance of a degree of self-awareness is critical for the development of practitioner competence, and then focused on the micro, meso, macro, and magna effects on professional competence. These levels of transactions between client and human service practitioner reflect how lights and shadows coming from the helping professional affect the client.

Another way to support professional competence is to explore personal, interpersonal, and professional codes of ethics, which govern the behavioral performance of the practitioner. We suggested that professional competence can be strengthened by recognizing and exploring the lights and shadows of services, theories of the self, and values as well as reflecting on communication patterns and cultivating an eclectic practice approach.

Regarding multidimensional contextual services, we suggested starting with the contextual nature of services and then designing services to respond to the multiple needs and concerns of clients and client cohort groups. Our task as practitioners is to advocate for agency and program competence without perpetuating stereotypes and prioritizing self-interest over the needs of clients. Thus, in terms of needs assessment, one must take into consideration the strengths and resources of the community, particularly the multiple factors relating to the socioeconomic and political dynamics of the geographical location. A number of guiding principles were given related to the structure of the plan of action, the compatibility between the needs assessment and agency objectives, benefit-risk assessment, and content, context, and process. It is important to keep in mind the agency's mission, vision, objectives, and methods of delivery and evaluation. A number of guidelines were given for effective program evaluation and for strengthening nonstereotypically based services.

Special Issues: Language and Spirituality

Language is generally perceived as socially constructed agreements of use of symbols creating the foundation for written, spoken, and symbolic interactions/exchanges, which convey meaning, values, beliefs, feelings, attitudes, norms, and resolutions. Spirituality generally focuses on the meaning of existence and purpose in life, which are often expressed in personal and institutional settings for renewal and strength.

In his chapter on language and multidimensional contextual practice, Myles Montgomery explained the power of language and the need to demythologize stereotypes in terms of deconstruction and reconstruction. He examined the ways that constructed notions of truth through language affects the construction of human identities and experiences; the use of stereotypes in education and social medias; a critical framework for human service practitioners in the use of language, particularly language as a vehicle of change at the micro, meso, macro, and magna levels; and language perspectives pertaining to multidimensional contextual practice.

Starting with symbolic interaction and the social symbolism of language, identities, and experiences, Montgomery dealt with language as it pertains to diversity issues and its carryover effects in education and the media. Employing a critical framework consisting of four areas of inquiry (expectations, responsibilities, conflicts, and alternatives), he helped us in the reconstruction of language and linked these principles to magna, macro, meso, and micro levels of working with clients. Finally, he discussed the limitations of language and attributive language pertaining to multidimensional contextual practice and offered practical exercise applications on how language is critical in the helping process.

Judy A. Guadalupe, in her chapter, joined spirituality and diversity wonderfully together in a multidimensional context. She offered a broad understanding of spirituality that encompasses life, our experiences, and a relationship to the Great Unknown—the force of life. This spiritual perspective opens us to endless possibilities and is believed to be a source of internal and external empowerment in the client. Guadalupe encourages practitioners to honor the unlimited potentials and possibilities of people in a spiritual way. She discussed the essential characteristics of spiritually sensitive practice and centered us on client well-being, social justice, and world peace as spiritual goals. From the wounds in our relationships, Judy A. Guadalupe stresses, spiritual healing can be cultivated through a journey into love and compassion.

Diverse Groups: General Population Groups and Ethnic-Specific Communities of People

Having presented the multidimensional contextual practice framework, we asked a number of other contributors to apply the framework principles to **general population groups** (women, men, transgender/bisexual/lesbian/gay individuals, people living with disabilities, and the aging) and a number of **ethnic-specific communities of people** (First Nations Peoples, White ethnics, African Americans, Latino/a Americans, and Asian Americans).

Our **general population groups** covered gender, sexual orientation, physical/mental abilities, and persons who are part of the aging process, all of which represent multiple identities covering whole and unique population groups and individuals. Thus, for example, we can draw on the various population identities seen in these chapters when we discuss a lesbian woman who is elderly and living with a physical disability such as a stroke. Grouping these chapters in one section of the text helps us to make these interconnections.

Arlene Bowers Andrews pointed out that large numbers of **women** are survivors of domestic violence, which has become a major defining issue for women in terms of their diversity. In terms of applying the multidimensional contextual practice framework to this concern, it is paramount to provide for the safety of the survivor, to hold the offender accountable as a deterrent, and to change the community's climate. Andrews suggests a community effort against domestic violence, which includes coordination with inclusive participation, planning and evaluation, resource development and equitable allocation, public awareness and education, policy reform and accountability, and system components. All of these together provide a safety net of services and care. Training and professional competence are vital to understand how to deal with domestic violence situations. Feminist theory and practice are applied to fostering skills such as eliminating false dichotomies and artificial separations, reconceptualizing power, valuing process equally with product, renaming, and remembering that the personal is the political.

Andrews focused on nongovernmental organizations, which assume a leadership role in terms of coordinating inclusive participation, planning and evaluation, resource development and equitable allocation, public awareness and education, policy reform and accountability, a range of system components, and training and professional competence. The practitioner's professional competence is brokering communication and resources between the client and other key resources in the environment. It is crucial to maintain interactions/exchanges and effects with the client and the client's support system. Maintaining the well-being of women and related supportive groups and applying feminist theory and practice are important practice skill principles. Along with a concern for domestic violence and mobilizing resources, however, one is reminded that as a collective, women have been proactive agents as well as retrospective responders.

In his chapter on **men,** Santos Torres, Jr., encouraged us to tell our stories to each other as men, in person-to-person exchanges, and to listen to each other in close quarters. Starting with the dualism of the male collectivity (the corporate versus the tribal man), he showed us how stereotypes, prototypes, and archetypes shape our societal perceptions of men. Moreover, he explained how men, power, and privilege (male dominance) color our value system. In turn, these values, language, symbols, and norms create a male-dominated culture. As a result, gender oppression is manifested in exploitation, marginalization, powerlessness, cultural imperialism, and violence. Men are victims of these burdens and experience pain and suffering. They face the dark night of their souls and cry out for help.

The multidimensional contextual practitioner must be aware of these intricacies and must implement the following principles: the diversity and uniqueness of the individual, focusing on the adversity and the resiliency as well as the essence of the person; the dynamic changes and interconnected interactions; the need to understand individual perceptions from one's own storehouse; the need to connect the individual-micro, the group-meso, the community-macro, and the spiritual-magna levels of being; and the need to assist with the deconstruction of stereotypes and the construction of mutual ways of helping and changing. From a gender perspective, men have many barriers and hurdles to overcome if they are to move beyond stereotypes.

In her chapter regarding **transgender, bisexual, lesbian, and gay (TBLG) individuals,** Susan L. Kirk stressed that due to historical oppression and discrimination, these diverse communities have responded with political and radical organizing. Kirk emphasized that, more and more, TBLG individuals are redefining themselves outside of heterosexual norms. She cited the need for judgment-free language for these communities of people and encouraged the reader toward a working definition and understanding of TBLG individuals. Kirk surveyed societal issues and concerns, identity formation and the coming-out process, social stress concerns, health care, substance abuse, domestic violence, and legal and policy limitations, all of which may be common denominators faced by TBLG people. She then touched on issues related to children, youth, couples, and aging persons, giving the reader a life development perspective.

Kirk's thrust for multidimensional contextual practice calls for practitioners to reexamine professional attitudes and education, to implement macro-systemic and cultural change interventions, and to make changes in social service agencies pertaining to policies and procedures. She appeals to support systems and spiritual development that build a respect for human dignity and diversity as well as safe and healthy environments.

Kathryn S. Collins, Deborah P. Valentine, and Debra L. Welkley, in their discussion of **people living with disabilities,** utilized as their reference the American with Disabilities Act of 1990. These authors made the case for deconstructing existing myths and stereotypes about people living with disabilities, moving us toward an understanding that is nonstereotypic. People living with disabilities contend with discrimination and oppression, and so the authors present a sociopolitical understanding of disability that is related to the interactions between individuals and their physical environment as well as related attitudes and behaviors that create and foster disabling conditions.

Individuals, families, groups, and communities living with a disability or multiple disabilities often find themselves coping with segregation and exclusion as well as stereotypes, myths, and stigma; therefore, Collins, Valentine, and Welkley recommended that the practitioner help to deconstruct stereotypes and stigmas through listening and learning, as well as help to reconstruct by support and affirmation. These authors are emphatic about rejecting the stereotype of the personal tragedy model and the medical model of disability and responding humanly and compassionately.

In her chapter on **aging persons,** Joyce Burris pointed out that she prefers the term *aging* over the terms *elderly* and *senior.* She steers the reader away from aging as a problem and advocates the empowerment perspective for aging persons. This proactive stance for aging persons mobilizes individual and social change and requires social action where individuals, groups, families, and communities can come together. In this scenario, Burris envisions aging persons as active participants. Burris bids us to move beyond our traditional stereotypes of aging to a dynamic view of what this age group is able to accomplish together.

In the discussion of **ethnic-specific population groups,** Hilary N. Weaver led first with her chapter on **First Nations Peoples,** in which she portrayed a series of historical experiences, focusing on the allotment of reservation land, family disruption (particularly boarding schools, foster care, and adoption), paternalism in U.S. social policies, and the relocation, termination, and statistical elimination of First Nations Peoples. What is amazing about this chapter is the strengths that Weaver identifies: the quest for self-determination and coping with ongoing barriers, the richness of diversity within diversity of First Nations Peoples, resilience in the face of adversity, the wisdom of the elders, knowledge and traditions that are passed on as different ways of knowing, multicultural influences impinging on First Nations Peoples in a variety of community settings, and the effects of stereotyping.

In her application of the multidimensional contextual practice framework, Weaver pointed out that by examining the environmental context of clients, practitioners are less likely to stereotype clients who are First Nations Peoples, and that by acknowledging the magna or spiritual/transcendent layer, one finds a natural fit with the spirituality of these communities of people. Changing the macro context is key to social change in terms of federal government control of economic development and the holding of money and land "in trust." Thus, Weaver stresses intervention at the macro level and working with clients on the magna/transcendent level.

Debra L. Welkley then discussed **White ethnics,** pointing out that this term is a social construct that historically connoted White privilege and oppression. The question becomes how one moves away from the social effects of "Whiteness" and toward just treatment for all. Welkley carefully covers White identity development models, exploring how White identity has been played out in both negative and positive terms. Major tasks she identifies include finding ways to be inclusive and respectful of everyone's identity journey and dealing with stereotypes and myths about White and non-White ethnics.

According to Welkley, from a multidimensional contextual practice standpoint, it is important when working with White ethnics to affirm the person, family, group, or community and to understand the unique characteristics of each life story. She emphasized that it is critical to assist in the deconstruction and reconstruction of aspects related to White issues and concerns. Although Welkley stresses a strengths perspective, she encourages readers to explore Whiteness in terms of race and ethnicity, privilege status, racism, guilt, denial, educational myths, superiority identity of individuals and groups, and related areas of concern.

African Americans, according to Robin Wiggins Carter, must be understood in terms of their geographic migration, which had socioeconomic motivations; their income levels, which have institutional discrimination and social stratification implications; a more accurate accounting of Americans who have African descendants; and the diversity of Black Americans within various groups. Carter stressed the importance of understanding that even though they share common historical experiences of forced migration and enslavement, African-American people are a heterogeneous group. She pointed out that the terms *African American* and *Black,* while used interchangeably in the literature as well as in U.S. census reports, are not synonymous; African Americans are a subgroup of the total population identified as Black. She further differentiated between native-born Blacks and Black immigrant groups.

Carter moves us away from a deficit model and points us toward a strengths and cultural base. In addition, she provides background on current issues facing African Americans: socioeconomic status and social distance; interracial contact in terms of marriage, housing, and geographic location; foreign-born and multiracial within and between the diversity of groups comprising African Americans; and racial identity and social marginality. The practitioner must have an understanding of these dynamics and how they influence and interplay with each other.

Carter suggested that the multidimensional model of racial identity (MMRI) is quite helpful when working with African Americans and fits with the multidimensional contextual practice approach. The MMRI sensitizes the helping person to the client's self-concept, definition of race, behavioral philosophy, and positive or negative evaluations. Carter generously explained the importance of each theme, and then focused on the magna spirituality and religion level. She cautioned us against stereotyping and urged us to move beyond stereotypes and toward dynamic services in which the client is seen as the expert and teacher. Carter's discussion of commonalities, differences, and controversies with African-American/Black communities reminds the reader of the importance of nonstereotypically based practices.

In her chapter on **Latinos/as,** Chrystal C. Ramirez Barranti stressed the importance of understanding historical encounters with colonization, immigration, and migration as pathways to life in the United States. Focusing primarily on Mexicans, Puerto Ricans, and Cubans, Barranti generally described the historical and present conditions of each group and related demographic profiles. In her section on multidimensional contextual practice, she stressed that we must understand the migration, immigration, and transnational flow of Latinos/as if we are to work effectively with these groups of people.

Barranti proposes models of adaptation in terms of assimilation and alternation. Concerning the latter, Barranti argues for a "both/and" inclusive model that involves the retention of home culture and language and the acquisition of a new language and cultural traditions, which is perceived as a separate and integrated cultural duality. She also tackles discrimination, oppression, social injustice, racism, poverty in the midst of working hard, and segregation. Barranti concludes by pointing out that in the midst of all these contextual realities, Latinos/as have the resiliency and strength to cope, withstand, and press forward: *Si! Se puede! (Yes! We can!).*

Janlee Wong, in discussing **Asian Pacific Islanders,** provided a comprehensive treatment of the various groups that comprise the Asians Pacific Islander populations. His demographics are extensive in terms of population, immigration, age and gender, and family size and status. Wong described etic or universal characteristics of these entities: passiveness, limited emotional expression, family-centeredness, filial piety, fatalism, collective behavior, gender, role reversal, sexual orientation, socioeconomic status, business, education, religious/spiritual practices, physical and mental disabilities, power, immigration, resiliency, knowing, cultural influences and cultural choices, and stereotyping. The complex dynamics of the interaction of these factors are expressed in numerous ways and might be termed *diversity beyond diversity.* That is, given the widespread populations, behaviors, traditions, values, practices, and interactions, the Asian Pacific Islander population comprises one of the most complex of the ethnic population groups.

Wong is aware of the fit between these groups of people and multidimensional contextual practice, and he draws parallels between the two. Concerning client well-being, he applies filial responsibilities to the family in the midst of the reality of societal acculturation. He starts with magna and macro influences of the spiritual and the societal, and then moves to meso-interpersonal and micro-intrapersonal relationships. Wong values the importance of professional competence and multidimensional contextual services that are open to multiple thoughts and spiritual systems, bilingual and bicultural staff, and multiethnic or single-ethnic agencies. The human service practitioner is encouraged to develop awareness of diverse ethnic groups and cultural values, beliefs, and expectations, as well as healing practices honored by Asians and Pacific Islanders. There also must be a concern for political power, which involves advocating for funding, services, and other resources for these groups of people.

THE FUTURE OF MULTIDIMENSIONAL CONTEXTUAL PRACTICE: VISIONS AND HOPES

As we look toward the future of multidimensional contextual practice, we remind ourselves of the antecedents shaping this theme. The concept of **human diversity** in the 1990s helped us to become inclusive of various ethnic, cultural, gender, sexual orientation, social class, religious, and related components of people. The **multiple identities of a person** became a descriptor for the concept of **intersectionality,** which describes "those multiple intersections and crossroads in our lives that are replete with multiple social group memberships that are interconnected and interrelated" (Lum, 2003, p. 42). Spencer, Lewis, and Gutierrez (2000) identify three factors of intersectionality: multiple group memberships and identities, the integrative nature of these factors on our daily lives, and the uniqueness of each social group membership.

We would add that intersectionality can also be viewed as a place or space in which experiences are constructed, deconstructed, and reconstructed—providing ongoing opportunities for newness and endless possibility. Through recognition of intersectionality, practitioners honor changes in group memberships, identities, and experiences. People are not static, and change is constant. Intersectionality reminds us that the personal is not necessarily separate from the political, nor are conventional realities/consciousness separate from transcendent realities/consciousness, certainty from uncertainty, the physical realm from the spiritual realm, and so on. The interdependence between and among these forces is reflected through the exploration of intersectionality. Just as human diversity can be defined as "the points at which people differ," such points can also be seen as the ones "at which people connect." Intersectionalities, which are consciously and/or unconsciously experienced throughout our lives, can also be called *"points of references marking memories of human experiences."*

Through multidimensional and contextual experiences of intersectionality, change can emerge. Take, for example, the situation in which interactions with a particular client or community of clients generate awareness in a practitioner of a set of held racist, sexist, homophobic, and classist attitudes. In this case, intersectionality has played a role in the process of professional awareness through an event or series of events. Although such events are contextual by nature, they also have a multidimensional component. For instance, the specific events that help to generate personal/professional awareness also might be key factors in other transactions that would unfold if and when the practitioner decides to explore the origin of these attitudes and take action to promote necessary change. Thus, awareness of intersectionality is essential when attempting to influence social change, especially in the area of oppressive forces, social justice, and human resilience/empowerment.

If one reads between the lines of this text, these themes emerge in subtle as well as obvious ways. In one sense, we have been concerned with systematizing multiple identities and have used the theme of multidimensionality to secure our discussion on the constructed realities of human diversity and multiple identities and experiences. We also, however, have encouraged exploration of these identities and experiences within context. The theme of **context** has emerged in our discussion of how to work with people. Part of the answer to the question of how to help clients is to *observe and understand the settings or situations of the person, family, group, community, or a combination of these entities.*

Significant others and significant environments go hand-in-hand in the discussion of context. In context, we are concerned about the interaction between the important characteristics of the person, family, group, or community and the environment. Rose (1990) speaks about **contextualization,** or an understanding of self based on the client's reality, which is a reaching inward (into the client) and a reaching outward (toward the setting and situation facing the client). Ragg (2001) furthered the discussion on context when he identified a number of **contextual family and environment issues** such as family rules, family conflict resolutions, emotional expression, family roles, relating to others, neighborhood, culture, and institutions.

Recently, context has taken on a systematic format. Kemp, Whittaker, and Tracy (2002) discuss **contextual practice** in terms of person-environment. They point out that *empowerment is contextualized in the sense that it emphasizes the importance of external circumstances and conditions in client concerns, whereas changes in personal and interpersonal resources and aspirations must be supported and reinforced in external contexts.* Fong (2004) also has pursued contextual practice and has applied this understanding to immigrants and refugees. Regarding the importance of context, she states that social/health/human services are "no longer a straight line journey but one of concurrently switching from one context to another . . . [and] social environments play a key role in the contextuality and intersectionality of people's social group membership, internal and external variables, and social service delivery system" (pp. 310, 312). The **contextual perspective** will be with us for years to come.

The editors and contributors of this book have joined **multiple identities (intersectionality)** and **context (contextual practice)** into **a new synthesis for working with people:** We have called it **multidimensional contextual practice.** Taking into account the literature in both areas, we have sought to integrate these concepts into a helping framework. How well we have succeeded in doing this is left to the readers and reviewers of this text to decide.

Fertile soil for multidimensional contextual practice application has emerged. For example, Root (2003) discussed *five identities for mixed-race people* that have multidimensional and contextual implications: accept the identity society assigns (the hypodescent or "one drop rule"), choose a single identity that builds solidarity with national and community ethnic and racial groups, choose a mixed identity that truly and accurately describes the person, choose a new race identity that declares a blended identity, or choose a White identity, which resolves the issue and moves the person into mainstream America. Whether or not one agrees with Root's conceptualizations and suggestions, by carefully looking at each choice, one can recognize the multidimensional and contextual issues related to such a decision-making process.

In her multidimensional approach to *human consciousness,* Ritberger (2001) stressed: "The concept that consciousness as a whole encompasses multiple dimensions, and that each dimension [which can be perceived as being multidimensional and contextual by nature] superimposes the other, suggests that when one dimension changes its perception of reality, then that change [due to interdependence] will affect all of the other dimensions" (p. 4–3). Ritberger stressed that models of consciousness often rely on "three ways of knowing to suggest that there are only four dimensions of consciousness: (1) mental consciousness, (2) emotional consciousness, (3) higher self-consciousness, and (4) cosmic consciousness" (p. 4-3). In discussing the "ordinary state of reality" associated with personality awareness and the "non-ordinary state of reality" related to the nature of metaphysical light consciousness, Ritberger adds these dimensions into the multidimensionality of consciousness.

Mishne (2002) started her book, *Multiculturalism and the Therapeutic Process,* with **every theme of this text.** Mishne wrote:

> We all have multiple cultural identities. As individuals, we live in a context of family, group, and community; in fact, we may have affiliations or memberships in a number of groups and communities related to our work, education, economics, special interests, and friendship circles. Each of us has varying levels of consciousness of our cultural identities, ranging from naiveté or lack of understanding to a sophisticated, multiperspective integration. Multicultural issues include language, gender, ethnicity/race, religion/spirituality, sexual orientation, age, physical issues, trauma, and socioeconomic realities. These variables commonly have a profound impact on a treatment relationship." (p. ix)

It seems almost prophetic that Mishne penned these opening words of her text while we were spending two years thinking, planning, and writing our book on the very same themes that she identified as being important to the helping professions.

Multidimensional contextual practice is a way to reduce stereotypes and perhaps eliminate stereotyping while strengthening human interactions and exchanges through the valuing of human diversities, commonalities, and complexities. Multidimensional contextual practice provides a strong foundation for reducing marginalization of people's experiences while honoring the interplay between certainty and uncertainty. As practitioners, we have the responsibility to individually and/or collectively initiate and sustain an educational and sociopolitical movement that advocates for transcendence of stereotypes at the micro, meso, macro, and magna capacities while acknowledging and honoring the interplay between **multidimensionality** and **contextualization** in people's experiences. The task is at hand!

The 21st century is filled with endless opportunities, possibilities, and choices. Our encounters with intersectionality can enhance our recognition of our interdependence regardless of differences. Through such encounters, we can move forward into a higher level of consciousness and fulfillment of basic human needs. The human spirit and resilience can guide our experiences. However, as a human race, we can also make the choice to continue perpetuating and sustaining unhealthy patterns of thinking, being, communicating, and relating, thus maintaining the cycle of unnecessary human pain. We, individually and collectively, have a choice.

Social/health/human service practitioners, as well as so-called clients, may relate to the hunger for meaning, authentic intimacy, and love and compassion that Judy A. Guadalupe speaks about in her chapter on spirituality and multidimensional contextual practice. It seems imperative to recognize the interplay between being proactive while addressing micro, meso, macro, and magna historical and current concerns, and committing to acting locally while also thinking globally. Practitioners can join in the process of creating a world that is more inclusive than exclusive by addressing human diversity, commonalities, and complexities through multidimensional contextual practice. The following guidelines can be of initial assistance:

- Identify and explore to what degree your beliefs, values, and behaviors may promote personal as well as others' well-being.
- Commit and follow through with daily spiritual/consciousness-raising practices, rituals, and exercises that enhance your potentiality to assist others from a place of nonattachment to outcomes.
- Remember to listen to people's life experiences without judgment, but rather with a compassionate heart.
- Find humor during encounters with life adversities and challenges. Rather than minimizing difficulties, humor can serve as a reminder of how we can experience challenges without persistently becoming them.
- Avoid participating in and perpetuating racist, sexist, homophobic, and discriminative jokes. These upset intrapersonal processes.
- Become involved in political actions, activities, and movements aimed at strengthening social justice and fulfilling basic human needs.

- Explore ways of learning, living, and working within diversified communities without perpetuating stereotypes.
- Honor and implement multidimensional contextual practice in your personal and professional encounters.

Postscript

We hope that as you read this text, you enjoyed and interacted with the concepts, case studies, and exercises contained in it. The editors of this text would appreciate hearing from you and interacting with you about your ideas, experiences, questions, and thoughts. Please e-mail us at krishnag@csus.edu and lumd@csus.edu. We want to learn from you, and we hope that as you increase and/or strengthen your knowledge about and skills in multidimensional contextual practice, you will add your contributions to this unfolding synthesis and perspective.

References

Fong, R. (Ed.). (2004). *Culturally competent practice with immigrant and refugee children and families.* New York: Guilford.

Kemp, S. P., Whittaker, J. K., & Tracy, E. M. (2002). Contextual social work practice. In M. O'Melia & K. K. Miley (Eds.), *Pathways to power: Readings in contextual social work practice* (pp. 15–34). Boston: Allyn & Bacon.

Lum, D. (Ed.). (2003). *Culturally competent practice: A framework for understanding diverse groups and justice issues* (2nd ed.). Pacific Grove, CA: Brooks/Cole–Thomson Learning.

Mishne, J. (2002). *Multiculturalism and the therapeutic process.* New York: Guilford.

Ragg, D. M. (2001). *Building effective helping skills: The foundation of generalist practice.* Boston: Allyn & Bacon.

Ritberger, C. (2001). *Consciousness and the human psyche: Module two.* Pollock Pines, CA: BCR Enterprises.

Root, M. P. P. (2003). Five mixed-race identities: From relic to revolution. In L. I. Winters & H. L. DeBose (Eds.), *New faces in a changing America: Multiracial identity in the 21st century* (pp. 3–20). Thousand Oaks, CA: Sage.

Rose, S. M. (1990). Advocacy/empowerment: An approach to clinical practice for social work. *Journal of Sociology and Social Welfare, 17*(2), 41–52.

Spencer, M., Lewis, E., & Gutierrez, L. (2000). Multicultural perspectives on direct practice in social work. In P. Allen-Meares & C. Garwin (Eds.), *The handbook of social work direct practice* (pp. 131–149). Thousand Oaks, CA: Sage.

Index